Getting started with Spring Framework
Second Edition

Getting started with Spring Framework is a hands-on guide to begin developing applications using Spring Framework. This book is meant for Java developers with little or no knowledge of Spring Framework. Getting started with Spring Framework, Second Edition includes new chapters on **Spring Web MVC**, **RESTful Web Services** and **Spring Security**.

The examples that accompany this book are based on **Spring 4.0**. You can download the examples (consisting of **60 sample projects**) described in this book from the following Google Code project: **http://code.google.com/p/getting-started-with-spring-framework-2edition/**

Chapter 1 – Introduction to Spring Framework

Chapter 2 – Spring Framework basics

Chapter 3 - Configuring beans

Chapter 4 - Dependency injection

Chapter 5 - Customizing beans and bean definitions

Chapter 6 - Annotation-driven development with Spring

Chapter 7 - Database interaction using Spring

Chapter 8 - Messaging, emailing, asynchronous method execution, and caching using Spring

Chapter 9 - Aspect-oriented programming

Chapter 10 – Spring Web MVC basics

Chapter 11 – Validation and data binding in Spring Web MVC

Chapter 12 – Developing RESTful web services using Spring Web MVC

Chapter 13 – More Spring Web MVC – internationalization, file upload and asynchronous request processing

Chapter 14 – Securing applications using Spring Security

Ashish Sarin
J Sharma

Table of contents

Preface

How to use this book

Download sample projects

This book comes with many sample projects that you can download from the following Google Code project: http://code.google.com/p/getting-started-with-spring-framework-2edition/. You can download the sample projects as a single ZIP file or you can checkout the sample projects using SVN. For more details, refer to the above URL.

Import sample projects into your Eclipse or IntelliJ IDEA IDE

If you see **IMPORT** **chapter<chapter-number>/<project name>** at any point while reading the book, you should import the specified project into your Eclipse or IntelliJ IDEA IDE (or any other IDE that you are using). The sample projects use Maven 3.x build tool for building the project; therefore, you'll find a pom.xml file inside each of the projects. A pom.xml file is also provided at the root of the source code distribution, which builds all the projects.

Refer appendix A to see the steps required for importing and running the sample projects.

Refer to code examples

Each example listing specifies the sample project name (using **Project** label) and the location of the source file (using **Source location** label). If the **Project** and **Source location** labels are not specified, you can assume that the code shown in the example listing is not being used anywhere in the sample projects, and it has been shown purely to simplify understanding.

Conventions used in this book

Italics has been used for emphasizing terms

Comic Sans MS has been used for example listings, Java code, configuration details in XML and properties files

Comic Sans MS has been used in example listings to highlight important parts of the code or configuration

> A callout like this highlights an important point or concept

Feedback and questions

You can post your feedback and questions to the authors in the following Google Groups forum: https://groups.google.com/forum/#!forum/getting-started-with-spring-framework

About the authors

Ashish Sarin is a Sun Certified Enterprise Architect with more than 14 years of experience in architecting applications. He is the author of *Spring Roo 1.1 Cookbook* (by Packt Publishing) and *Portlets in Action* (by Manning Publications)

J Sharma is a freelance Java developer with extensive experience in developing Spring applications.

Chapter 1 – Introduction to Spring Framework

1-1 Introduction

In the traditional Java enterprise application development efforts, it was a developer's responsibility to create well-structured, maintainable and easily testable applications. The developers used myriad design patterns to address these non-business requirements of an application. This not only led to low developer productivity, but also adversely affected the quality of developed applications.

Spring Framework (or 'Spring' in short) is an open source application framework from SpringSource (http://www.springsource.org) that simplifies developing Java enterprise applications. It provides the infrastructure for developing well-structured, maintainable and easily testable applications. When using Spring Framework, a developer only needs to focus on writing the business logic of the application, resulting in improved developer productivity. You can use Spring Framework to develop standalone Java applications, web applications, applets, or any other type of Java application.

This chapter starts off with an introduction to Spring Framework modules and its benefits. At the heart of Spring Framework is its Inversion of Control (IoC) container, which provides dependency injection (DI) feature. This chapter introduces Spring's DI feature and IoC container, and shows how to develop a standalone Java application using Spring. Towards the end of this chapter, we'll look at some of the SpringSource's projects that use Spring Framework as their foundation. This chapter will set the stage for the remaining chapters that delve deeper into the Spring Framework.

In this book, we'll use an example Internet Banking application, *MyBank*, to introduce Spring Framework features.

1-2 Spring Framework modules

Spring Framework consists of multiple modules that are grouped based on the application development features they address. The following table describes the different module groups in Spring Framework:

Module group	Description
Core container	Contains modules that form the foundation of Spring Framework. The modules in this group provide Spring's DI feature and IoC container implementation.

AOP and instrumentation	Contains modules that support AOP (Aspect-oriented Programming) and class instrumentation.
Data Access/Integration	Contains modules that simplify interaction with databases and messaging providers. This module group also contains modules that support programmatic and declarative transaction management, and object/XML mapping implementations, like JAXB and Castor.
Web	Contains modules that simplify developing web and portlet applications.
Test	Contains a single module that simplifies creating unit and integration tests.

The above table shows that Spring covers every aspect of enterprise application development; you can use Spring for developing web applications, accessing databases, managing transactions, creating unit and integration tests, and so on. The Spring Framework modules are designed in such a way that you *only* need to include the modules that your application needs. For instance, to use Spring's DI feature in your application, you only need to include the modules grouped under *Core container*. As you progress through this book, you'll find details of some of the modules that are part of Spring, and examples that show how they are used in developing applications.

The following figure shows the inter-dependencies of different modules of Spring:

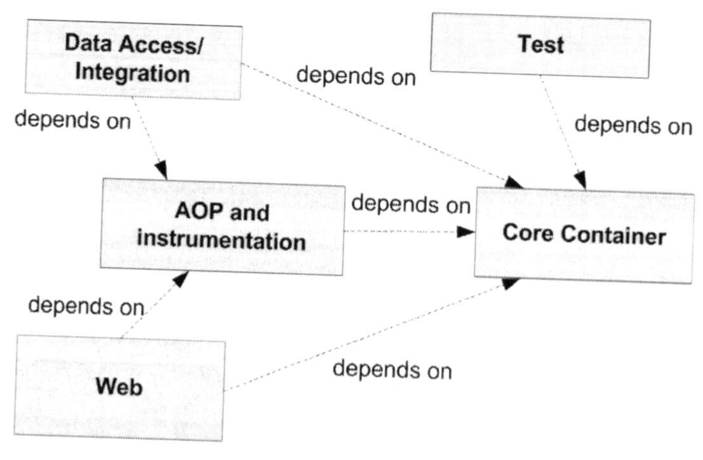

Figure 1-1 Spring modules inter-dependencies

You can infer from the above figure that the modules contained in the *Core container* group are central to the Spring Framework, and other modules depend on it. Equally important are the modules contained in the *AOP and instrumentation* group because they provide AOP features to other modules in the Spring Framework.

Now, that you have some basic idea about the areas of application development covered by Spring, let's look at the Spring IoC container.

1-3 Spring IoC container

A Java application consists of objects that interact with each other to provide application behavior. The objects with which an object interacts are referred to as its *dependencies*. For instance, if an object X interacts with objects Y and Z, then Y and Z are dependencies of object X. DI is a design pattern in which the dependencies of an object are typically specified as arguments to its constructor and setter methods. And, these dependencies are injected into the object when it's created.

In a Spring application, Spring IoC container (also referred to as Spring container) is responsible for creating application objects and injecting their dependencies. The application objects that the Spring container creates and manages are referred as *beans*. As the Spring container is responsible for putting together application objects, you don't need to implement design patterns, like Factory, Service Locator, and so on, to compose your application. DI is also referred to as Inversion of Control (IoC) because the responsibility of creating and injecting dependencies is *not* with the application object but with the Spring container.

Let's say that the MyBank application (which is the name of our sample application) contains two objects, FixedDepositController and FixedDepositService. The following example listing shows that the FixedDepositController object depends on FixedDepositService object:

Example listing 1-1: FixedDepositController class

```
public class FixedDepositController {
  private FixedDepositService fixedDepositService;

  public FixedDepositController() {
    fixedDepositService = new FixedDepositService();
  }

  public boolean submit() {
    //-- save the fixed deposit details
    fixedDepositService.save(.....);
  }
}
```

In the above example listing, FixedDepositController's constructor creates an instance of FixedDepositService which is later used in FixedDepositController's submit method. As FixedDepositController interacts with FixedDepositService, FixedDepositService represents a dependency of FixedDepositController.

To configure FixedDepositController as a Spring bean, you first need to modify the FixedDepositController class of example listing 1-1 such that it accepts FixedDepositService dependency as a constructor argument or as a setter method argument. The following example listing shows the modified FixedDepositController class:

Example listing 1-2: FixedDepositController class – FixedDepositService is passed as a constructor argument

```
public class FixedDepositController {
  private FixedDepositService fixedDepositService;

  public FixedDepositController(FixedDepositService fixedDepositService) {
    this.fixedDepositService = fixedDepositService;
  }

  public boolean submit() {
    //-- save the fixed deposit details
    fixedDepositService.save(.....);
  }
}
```

The above example listing shows that the FixedDepositService instance is now passed as a constructor argument to the FixedDepositController instance. Now, the FixedDepositService class can be configured as a Spring bean. Notice that the FixedDepositController class doesn't implement or extend from any Spring interface or class.

For a given application, information about application objects and their dependencies is specified using *configuration metadata*. Spring IoC container reads application's configuration metadata to instantiate application objects and inject their dependencies. The following example listing shows the configuration metadata (in XML format) for an application that consists of MyController and MyService classes:

Example listing 1-3: Configuration metadata

```
<beans .....>
  <bean id="myController" class="sample.spring.controller.MyController">
    <constructor-arg index="0" ref="myService" />
  </bean>
```

```
    <bean id="myService" class="sample.spring.service.MyService"/>
</beans>
```

In the above example listing, each <bean> element defines an application object that is managed by the Spring container, and the <constructor-arg> element specifies that an instance of MyService is passed as an argument to MyController's constructor. The <bean> element is discussed in detail later in this chapter, and the <constructor-arg> element is discussed in chapter 2.

Spring container reads the configuration metadata (like the one shown in example listing 1-3) of an application and creates the application objects defined by <bean> elements and injects their dependencies. Spring container makes use of *Java Reflection API* (http://docs.oracle.com/javase/tutorial/reflect/index.html) to create application objects and inject their dependencies. The following figure summarizes how the Spring container works:

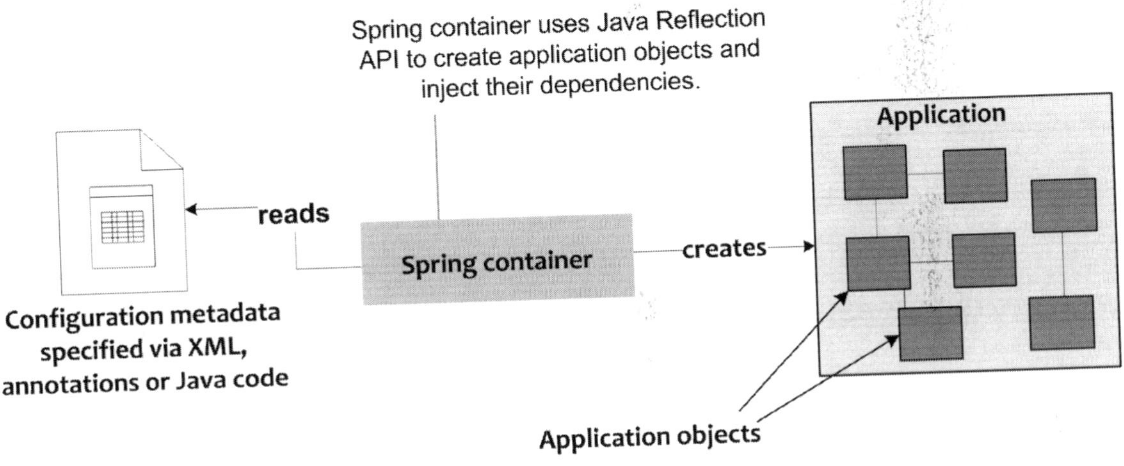

Figure 1-2 Spring container reads application's configuration metadata and creates a fully-configured application

The configuration metadata can be supplied to the Spring container via XML (as shown in example listing 1-3), Java annotations (refer chapter 6) and also through the Java code (refer chapter 6).

As the Spring container is responsible for creating and managing application objects, enterprise services (like transaction management, security, remote access, and so on) can be transparently applied to the objects by the Spring container. The ability of the Spring container to enhance the application objects with additional functionality makes it possible for you to model your application objects as simple Java objects (also referred to as *POJOs* or *Plain Old Java Objects*). Java classes corresponding to POJOs are referred to as *POJO classes*, which are nothing but Java classes that don't implement or extend framework-specific interfaces or classes. The enterprise services, like transaction management, security, remote access, and so on, required by these POJOs are transparently provided by the Spring container.

Now, that we know how Spring container works, let's look at some examples that demonstrate benefits of developing applications using Spring.

1-4 Benefits of using Spring Framework

In the previous section, we discussed the following benefits of using Spring:

- Spring simplifies composing Java applications by taking care of creating application objects and injecting their dependencies
- Spring promotes developing applications as POJOs

Spring also simplifies interaction with JMS providers, JNDI, MBean servers, email servers, databases, and so on, by providing a layer of abstraction that takes care of the boilerplate code.

Let's take a quick look at a few examples to better understand the benefits of developing applications using Spring.

Consistent approach to managing local and global transactions

If you are using Spring for developing *transactional* applications, you can use Spring's *declarative transaction management* support to manage transactions.

The following example listing shows the FixedDepositService class of MyBank application:

Example listing 1-4 – FixedDepositService class

```
public class FixedDepositService {
   public FixedDepositDetails getFixedDepositDetails( ..... ) { ..... }
   public boolean createFixedDeposit(FixedDepositDetails fixedDepositDetails) { ..... }
}
```

The FixedDepositService class is a POJO class that defines methods to create and retrieve details of fixed deposits. The following figure shows the form for creating a new fixed deposit:

Deposit Amount :

Tenure :

Email :

SAVE

Figure 1-3 HTML form for creating a new fixed deposit

A customer enters the fixed deposit amount, tenure and email id information in the above form and clicks the *Save* button to create a new fixed deposit. The FixedDepositService's createFixedDeposit method (refer example listing 1-1) is invoked to create the fixed deposit. The createFixedDeposit method debits the amount entered by the customer from his bank account, and creates a fixed deposit of the same amount.

Let's say that information about the bank balance of customers is stored in BANK_ACCOUNT_DETAILS database table, and the fixed deposit details are stored in FIXED_DEPOSIT_DETAILS database table. If a customer creates a fixed deposit of amount x, amount x is subtracted from the BANK_ACCOUNT_DETAILS table, and a new record is inserted in FIXED_DEPOSIT_DETAILS table to reflect the newly created fixed deposit. If BANK_ACCOUNT_DETAILS table is *not* updated or a new record is *not* inserted in FIXED_DEPOSIT_DETAILS table, it'll leave the system in an inconsistent state. This means the createFixedDeposit method *must* be executed within a transaction.

The database used by the MyBank application represents a *transactional resource*. In the traditional approach to perform a set of database modifications as a single unit of work, you'll first disable auto-commit mode of JDBC connection, then execute SQL statements, and finally commit (or rollback) the transaction. The following example listing shows how to manage database transactions in the createFixedDeposit method using the traditional approach:

Example listing 1-5 – Programmatically managing database transaction using JDBC Connection object

```
import java.sql.Connection;
import java.sql.SQLException;

public class FixedDepositService {
    public FixedDepositDetails getFixedDepositDetails( ..... ) { ..... }

    public boolean createFixedDeposit(FixedDepositDetails fixedDepositDetails) {
        Connection con = ..... ;
        try {
            con.setAutoCommit(false);
```

```
            //-- execute SQL statements that modify database tables
            con.commit();
        } catch(SQLException sqle) {
            if(con != null) {
                con.rollback();
            }
        }
        .....
    }
}
```

The above example listing shows that the createFixedDeposit method programmatically manages database transaction using JDBC Connection object. This approach is suitable for application scenarios in which a single database is involved. Transactions that are resource-specific, like the transaction associated with a JDBC Connection, are referred to as *local transactions*.

When multiple transactional resources are involved, JTA (Java Transaction API) is used for managing transactions. For instance, if you want to send a JMS message to a messaging middleware (a transactional resource) and update a database (another transactional resource) in the same transaction, you must use a JTA transaction manager to manage transactions. JTA transactions are also referred to as *global* (or *distributed*) *transactions*. To use JTA, you fetch UserTransaction object (which is part of JTA API) from JNDI and programmatically start and commit (or rollback) transactions.

As you can see, you can either use JDBC Connection (for local transactions) or UserTransaction (for global transactions) object to programmatically manage transactions. It is important to note that a local transaction *cannot* run within a global transaction. This means that if you want database updates in createFixedDeposit method (refer example listing 1-5) to be part of a JTA transaction, you need to modify the createFixedDeposit method to use the UserTransaction object for transaction management.

Spring simplifies transaction management by providing a layer of abstraction that gives a *consistent* approach to managing both local and global transactions. This means that if you write the createFixedDeposit method (refer example listing 1-5) using Spring's transaction abstraction, you don't need to modify the method when you switch from local to global transaction management, or vice versa. Spring's transaction abstraction is explained in chapter 7.

Declarative transaction management

Spring gives you the option to use *declarative transaction management*. You can annotate a method with Spring's @Transactional annotation and let Spring handle transactions, as shown here:

Example listing 1-6 – @Transactional annotation usage

```
import org.springframework.transaction.annotation.Transactional;

public class FixedDepositService {
   public FixedDepositDetails getFixedDepositDetails( ..... ) { ..... }


   @Transactional
   public boolean createFixedDeposit(FixedDepositDetails fixedDepositDetails) { ..... }
}
```

The above example listing shows that the FixedDepositService class doesn't implement or extend from any Spring-specific interface or class to use Spring's transaction management facility. The Spring Framework transparently provides transaction management feature to @Transactional annotated createFixedDeposit method. This shows that Spring is a *non-invasive* framework because it doesn't require your application objects to be dependent upon Spring-specific classes or interfaces. Also, you don't need to directly work with transaction management APIs to manage transactions.

Security

Security is an important aspect of any Java application. Spring Security (http://static.springsource.org/spring-security/site/) is a SpringSource's project that is built on top of Spring Framework. Spring Security provides authentication and authorization features that you can use for securing Java applications.

Let's say that the following 3 user roles have been identified for the MyBank application: LOAN_CUSTOMER, SAVINGS_ACCOUNT_CUSTOMER and APPLICATION_ADMIN. A customer *must* be associated with the SAVINGS_ACCOUNT_CUSTOMER or the APPLICATION_ADMIN role to invoke the createFixedDeposit method of FixedDepositService class (refer example listing 1-6). Using Spring Security you can easily address this requirement by annotating createFixedDeposit method with Spring Security's @Secured annotation, as shown in the following example listing:

Example listing 1-7 – Secured createFixedDeposit method

```
import org.springframework.transaction.annotation.Transactional;
import org.springframework.security.access.annotation.Secured;

public class FixedDepositService {
        public FixedDepositDetails getFixedDepositDetails( ..... ) { ..... }
```

```
    @Transactional
    @Secured({ "SAVINGS_ACCOUNT_CUSTOMER", "APPLICATION_ADMIN" })
    public boolean createFixedDeposit(FixedDepositDetails fixedDepositDetails) { ..... }
}
```

If you annotate a method with Spring Security's @Secured annotation, security feature is transparently applied to the method by the Spring Security framework. The above example listing shows that for implementing *method-level* security you don't need to extend or implement any Spring-specific classes or interfaces. Also, you don't need to write security-related code in your business methods.

Spring Security framework is discussed in detail in chapter 14.

JMX (Java Management Extensions)

Spring's JMX support simplifies incorporating JMX technology in your applications.

Let's say that the fixed deposit facility of MyBank application should only be available to customers from 9:00 AM to 6:00 PM everyday. To address this requirement, a variable is added to the FixedDepositService class, which acts as a flag indicating whether the fixed deposit service is active or inactive. The following example listing shows the FixedDepositService class that uses such a flag:

Example listing 1-8 – FixedDepositService with active variable

```
public class FixedDepositService {
    private boolean active;

    public FixedDepositDetails getFixedDepositDetails( ..... ) {
        if(active) { ..... }
    }
    public boolean createFixedDeposit(FixedDepositDetails fixedDepositDetails) {
        if(active) { ..... }
    }
    public void activateService() {
        active = true;
    }
    public void deactivateService() {
        active = false;
    }
}
```

The above example listing shows that a variable named active is added to the FixedDepositService class. If the value of the active variable is true, the getFixedDepositDetails and createFixedDeposit methods work as expected. If the value of the active variable is false, the getFixedDepositDetails and createFixedDeposit methods throw an exception indicating that the fixed deposit service is currently inactive. The activateService and deactivateService methods set the value of active variable to true and false, respectively.

Now, who calls the activateService and deactivateService methods? Let's say a separate scheduler application, *Bank App Scheduler*, runs at 9:00 AM and 6:00 PM to execute activateService and deactivateService methods, respectively. The Bank App Scheduler application uses JMX (Java Management Extensions) API to remotely interact with FixedDepositService instance.

> Refer to the following article to learn more about JMX: http://docs.oracle.com/javase/tutorial/jmx/index.html.

As Bank App Scheduler uses JMX to change the value of the active variable of the FixedDepositService instance, you need to register the FixedDepositService instance as a *managed bean* (or *MBean*) with an MBean server, and expose FixedDepositService's activateService and deactivateService methods as JMX operations. In Spring, you register instances of a class with the MBean server by annotating the class with Spring's @ManagedResource annotation, and expose the methods of the class as JMX operations using Spring's @ManagedOperation annotation.

The following example listing shows usage of @ManagedResource and @ManagedOperation annotations to register instances of the FixedDepositService class with the MBean server, and to expose its activateService and deactivateService methods as JMX operations:

Example listing 1-9 – FixedDepositService class that uses Spring's JMX support

```
import org.springframework.jmx.export.annotation.ManagedOperation;
import org.springframework.jmx.export.annotation.ManagedResource;

@ManagedResource(objectName = "fixed_deposit_service:name=FixedDepositService")
public class FixedDepositService {
   private boolean active;

   public FixedDepositDetails getFixedDepositDetails( ..... ) {
      if(active) { ..... }
   }
   public boolean createFixedDeposit(FixedDepositDetails fixedDepositDetails) {
      if(active) { ..... }
   }
```

```
    @ManagedOperation
    public void activateService() {
        active = true;
    }

    @ManagedOperation
    public void deactivateService() {
        active = false;
    }
}
```

The above example listing shows that the FixedDepositService class doesn't directly use JMX API to register its instances with the MBean server and to expose its methods as JMX operations.

JMS (Java Message Service)

Spring's JMS support simplifies sending and receiving messages from JMS providers.

In MyBank application, when a customer submits a request to receive details of their fixed deposits via email, the FixedDepositService sends the request details to a JMS messaging middleware (like ActiveMQ). The request is later processed by a message listener. Spring simplifies interaction with JMS providers by providing a layer of abstraction. The following example listing shows how FixedDepositService class sends request details to a JMS provider using Spring's JmsTemplate:

Example listing 1-10 – FixedDepositService that sends JMS messages

```
import org.springframework.beans.factory.annotation.Autowired;
import org.springframework.jms.core.JmsTemplate;

public class FixedDepositService {
    @Autowired
    private transient JmsTemplate jmsTemplate;
    .....
    public boolean submitRequest(Request request) {
        jmsTemplate.convertAndSend(request);
    }
}
```

The above example listing shows that the FixedDepositService defines a variable of type JmsTemplate, and is annotated with Spring's @Autowired annotation. For now, you can assume that the @Autowired annotation provides access to a JmsTemplate instance. The JmsTemplate instance knows about the JMS destination to which the JMS message is to be sent. How the

JmsTemplate is configured is described in detail in chapter 8. The FixedDepositService's submitRequest method invokes JmsTemplate's convertAndSend method to send request details (represented by Request argument of submitRequest method) as a JMS message to the JMS provider.

Once again, the above example listing shows that if you are using Spring Framework to send messages to JMS providers, then you don't need to directly deal with JMS API.

Caching

Spring's cache abstraction provides a consistent approach to use caching in your application.

It's common to use caching solutions to improve the performance of an application. MyBank application uses a caching product to improve the performance of *read* operations for fixed deposit details. Spring Framework simplifies interacting with different caching solutions by abstracting caching-related logic.

The following example listing shows that the FixedDepositService's getFixedDepositDetails method uses Spring's cache abstraction feature to cache fixed deposit details:

Example listing 1-11 – FixedDepositService that caches fixed deposit details

```
import org.springframework.cache.annotation.Cacheable;

public class FixedDepositService {

    @Cacheable("FixedDeposits")
    public FixedDepositDetails getFixedDepositDetails( ..... ) { ..... }

    public boolean createFixedDeposit(FixedDepositDetails fixedDepositDetails) { ..... }
}
```

In the above example listing, Spring's @Cacheable annotation indicates that the fixed deposit details returned by the getFixedDepositDetails method are *cached*. If the getFixedDepositDetails method is invoked with the same argument value(s), the getFixedDepositDetails method is *not* executed, and the fixed deposit details are returned from the cache. This shows that if you are using Spring Framework you don't need to write caching-related logic in your classes. Spring's cache abstraction is explained in detail in chapter 8.

In this section, we saw that Spring Framework simplifies developing enterprise applications by transparently providing services to POJOs, thereby shielding developers from lower level API details. Spring also provides easy integration with standard frameworks, like Hibernate, iBATIS, Quartz, JSF, Struts, EJB, and so on, which makes Spring an ideal choice for enterprise application development.

Now, that we have looked at some of the benefits of using Spring Framework, let's take a look at how to develop a simple Spring application.

1-5 A simple Spring application

In this section, we'll look at a simple Spring application that uses Spring's DI feature. To use Spring's DI feature in an application, follow these steps:

1. identify application objects and their dependencies
2. create POJO classes corresponding to the application objects identified in step 1
3. create *configuration metadata* that depicts application objects and their dependencies
4. create an instance of Spring IoC container and pass the configuration metadata to it
5. access application objects from the Spring IoC container instance

Let's now look at above mentioned steps in the context of MyBank application.

Identifying application objects and their dependencies

We discussed earlier that the MyBank application shows a form for creating a fixed deposit (refer figure 1-3) to its users for creating a fixed deposit. The following sequence diagram shows the application objects (and their interaction) that come into picture when the user submits the form:

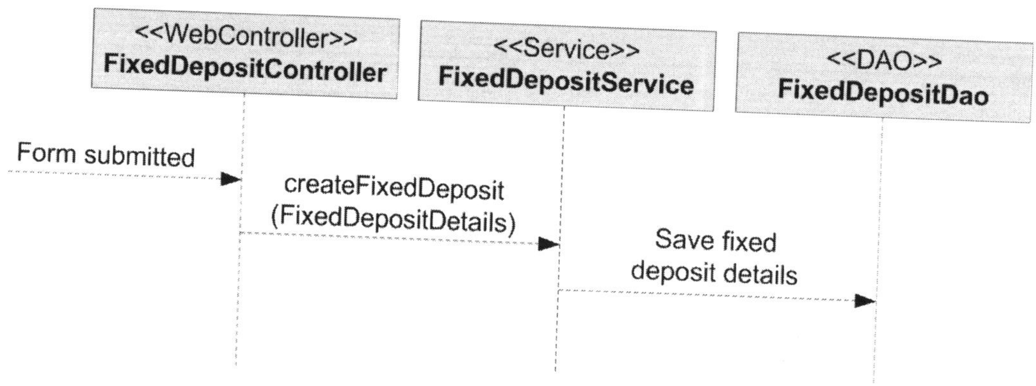

Figure 1-4 MyBank's application objects and their dependencies

In the above sequence diagram, FixedDepositController represents a web controller that receives the request when the form is submitted. The fixed deposit details are contained in the FixedDepositDetails object. The FixedDepositController invokes the createFixedDeposit method of FixedDepositService (a service layer object). Then, FixedDepositService invokes FixedDepositDao object (a data access object) to save the fixed deposit details in the application's data store.

So, we can interpret from the above diagram that FixedDepositService is a *dependency* of FixedDepositController object, and FixedDepositDao is a *dependency* of FixedDepositService object.

IMPORT **chapter 1/ch01-bankapp-xml** (This project shows a simple Spring application that uses Spring's DI feature. To run the application, execute the main method of the MyBankApp class of this project)

Creating POJO classes corresponding to identified application objects

Once you have identified application objects, the next step is to create POJO classes corresponding to these application objects. POJO classes corresponding to the FixedDepositController, FixedDepositService and FixedDepositDao application objects are available in ch01-bankapp-xml project. The ch01-bankapp-xml project represents a simplified version of MyBank application that uses Spring's DI feature. You should import the ch01-bankapp-xml project into your IDE as in the remaining steps we'll be looking at the files contained in this project.

In section 1-3 we discussed that a dependency is passed to an application object as a constructor argument or as a setter method argument. The following code listing shows that an instance of FixedDepositService (a dependency of FixedDepositController) is passed as a setter method argument to the FixedDepositController object:

Example listing 1-12 – FixedDepositController class
Project – ch01-bankapp-xml
Source location - src/main/java/sample/spring/chapter01/bankapp

```
package sample.spring.chapter01.bankapp;
.....
public class FixedDepositController {
  .....
  private FixedDepositService fixedDepositService;
  .....
  public void setFixedDepositService(FixedDepositService fixedDepositService) {
    logger.info("Setting fixedDepositService property");
    this.fixedDepositService = fixedDepositService;
  }
  .....
  public void submit() {
    fixedDepositService.createFixedDeposit(new FixedDepositDetails( 1, 10000,
      365, "someemail@something.com"));
  }
  .....
}
```

In the above example listing, FixedDepositService dependency is passed to FixedDepositController through setFixedDepositService method. We'll soon see that the setFixedDepositService setter method is invoked by Spring.

> If you look at the FixedDepositController, FixedDepositService and FixedDepositDao classes, you'll notice that none of these classes implement any Spring-specific interface or extend from any Spring-specific class.

Let's now look at how application objects and their dependencies are specified in the configuration metadata.

Creating the configuration metadata

We saw in section 1-3 that the configuration metadata specifies application objects and their dependencies, which is read by the Spring container to instantiate application objects and inject their dependencies. In this section, we'll first look at what other information is contained in the configuration metadata, followed by an in-depth look at how configuration metadata is specified in XML format.

The configuration metadata specifies information about the enterprise services (like transaction management, security and remote access) that are required by the application. For instance, if you want Spring to manage transactions, you need to configure an implementation of Spring's PlatformTransactionManager interface in the configuration metadata. The PlatformTransactionManager implementation is responsible for managing transactions (refer chapter 7 to know more about Spring's transaction management feature).

If your application interacts with messaging middlewares (like ActiveMQ), databases (like MySQL), e-mail servers, and so on, then Spring-specific objects that simplify interacting with these external systems are also defined in the configuration metadata. For instance, if your application sends or receives JMS messages from ActiveMQ, then you can configure Spring's JmsTemplate class in the configuration metadata to simplify interaction with ActiveMQ. We saw in example listing 1-10 that if you use JmsTemplate for sending messages to a JMS provider, then you don't need to deal with lower-level JMS API (refer chapter 8 to know more about Spring's support for interacting with JMS providers).

You can supply the configuration metadata to the Spring container via an XML file or through annotations in POJO classes. Starting with Spring 3.0, you can also supply the configuration metadata to the Spring container through Java classes annotated with Spring's @Configuration annotation. In this section, we'll see how configuration metadata is specified in XML format. In chapter 6, we'll see how configuration metadata is supplied via annotations in POJO classes and through @Configuration annotated Java classes.

You provide the configuration metadata for an application in XML format by creating an *application context XML* file that contains information about the application objects and their dependencies. Example listing 1-3 showed how an application context XML file looks like. The following XML shows the application context XML file of MyBank application that consists of FixedDepositController, FixedDepositService and FixedDepositDao objects (refer figure 1-4 to see how these objects interact with each other):

Example listing 1-13 – applicationContext.xml - MyBank's application context XML file
Project – ch01-bankapp-xml
Source location - src/main/resources/META-INF/spring

```
<?xml version="1.0" encoding="UTF-8" standalone="no"?>
<beans xmlns = "http://www.springframework.org/schema/beans"
   xmlns:xsi = "http://www.w3.org/2001/XMLSchema-instance"
   xsi:schemaLocation = "http://www.springframework.org/schema/beans
         http://www.springframework.org/schema/beans/spring-beans-4.0.xsd">

   <bean id="controller"
            class="sample.spring.chapter01.bankapp.FixedDepositController">
      <property name="fixedDepositService" ref="service" />
   </bean>

   <bean id="service" class="sample.spring.chapter01.bankapp.FixedDepositService">
      <property name="fixedDepositDao" ref="dao" />
   </bean>

   <bean id="dao" class="sample.spring.chapter01.bankapp.FixedDepositDao"/>
</beans>
```

The following are the important points to note about the application context XML file shown above:

- The <beans> element is the root element of the application context XML file, and is defined in spring-beans-4.0.xsd schema (also referred to as Spring's beans schema). The spring-beans-4.0.xsd schema is contained in spring-beans-4.0.0.RELEASE.jar JAR file that comes with the Spring Framework distribution.

- Each <bean> element configures an application object that is managed by the Spring container. In Spring Framework's terminology, a <bean> element represents a *bean definition*. The object that the Spring container creates based on the bean definition is referred to as a *bean*. The id attribute specifies a unique name for the bean, and the class attribute specifies the fully-qualified class name of the bean. You can also use the name attribute of <bean> element to specify *aliases* for the bean. In MyBank application, the application objects are FixedDepositController, FixedDepositService and FixedDepositDao; therefore, we have 3 <bean> elements - one for each application object. As application objects configured by <bean> elements are managed by the Spring container, the responsibility for creating them and injecting their dependencies is with the Spring container. Instead of directly creating instances of application objects defined by <bean> elements, you should obtain them from the Spring container. Later in this section, we'll look at how to obtain application objects managed by Spring container.

- No <bean> element is defined corresponding to the FixedDepositDetails domain object of MyBank application. This is because domain objects are *not* typically managed by the Spring container; they are created by the ORM framework (like Hibernate) used by the application, or you create them programmatically using the new operator.
- The <property> element specifies a dependency (or a configuration property) of the bean configured by the <bean> element. The <property> element corresponds to a *JavaBean-style setter* method in the bean class which is invoked by the Spring container to set a dependency (or a configuration property) of the bean.

Let's now look at how dependencies are injected via setter methods.

Injecting dependencies via setter methods

To understand how dependencies are injected via setter methods defined in the bean class, let's once again look at the FixedDepositController class of MyBank application:

Example listing 1-14 – FixedDepositController class
Project – ch01-bankapp-xml
Source location - src/main/java/sample/spring/chapter01/bankapp

```
package sample.spring.chapter01.bankapp;

import org.apache.log4j.Logger;

public class FixedDepositController {
  private static Logger logger = Logger.getLogger(FixedDepositController.class);

  private FixedDepositService fixedDepositService;

  public FixedDepositController() {
    logger.info("initializing");
  }

  public void setFixedDepositService(FixedDepositService fixedDepositService) {
    logger.info("Setting fixedDepositService property");
    this.fixedDepositService = fixedDepositService;
```

```
    }
    .....
}
```

The above example listing shows that the FixedDepositController class declares an instance variable named fixedDepositService of type FixedDepositService. The fixedDepositService variable is set by the setFixedDepositService method - a *JavaBean-style setter method* for fixedDepositService variable. This is an example of *setter-based DI*, wherein a setter method satisfies a dependency.

The following figure describes the bean definition for the FixedDepositController class in the applicationContext.xml file (refer example listing 1-13):

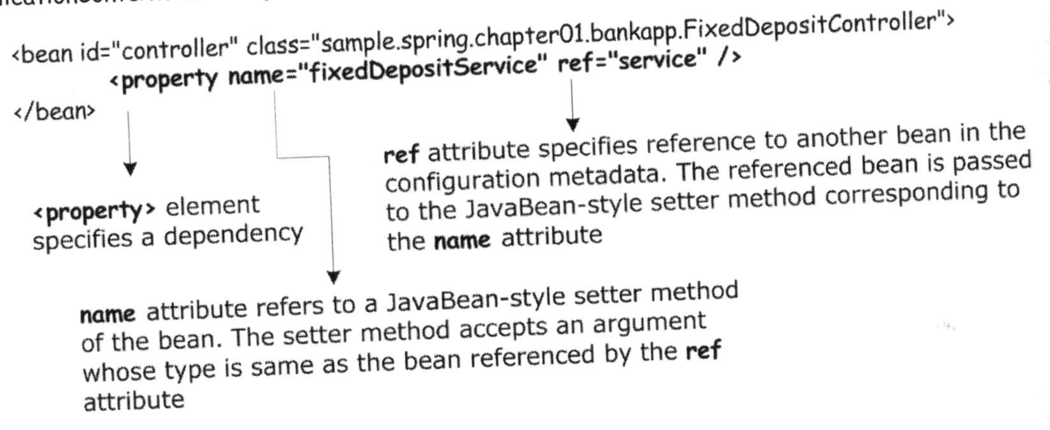

Figure 1-5 Defining dependencies using <property> elements

The above bean definition shows that the FixedDepositController bean defines its dependence on FixedDepositService bean via <property> element. The <property> element's name attribute corresponds to the JavaBean-style setter method in the bean class that is invoked by the Spring container at the time of bean creation. The <property> element's ref attribute identifies the Spring bean whose instance needs to be created and passed to the JavaBean-style setter method. The value of ref attribute must match the id attribute's value (or one of the names specified by the name attribute) of a <bean> element in the configuration metadata.

In figure 1-5, the value of <property> element's name attribute is fixedDepositService, which means that the <property> element corresponds to the setFixedDepositService setter method of FixedDepositController class (refer example listing 1-14). As the value of <property> element's ref attribute is service, the <property> element refers to the <bean> element whose id attribute's value is service. Now, the <bean> element whose id attribute's value is service is the FixedDepositService bean (refer example listing 1-13). Spring container creates an instance of FixedDepositService class (a dependency), and invokes the setFixedDepositService method (a

JavaBean-style setter method for fixedDepositService variable) of FixedDepositController (a dependent object), passing the FixedDepositService instance.

In the context of FixedDepositController application object, the following figure summarizes the purpose of name and ref attributes of <property> element:

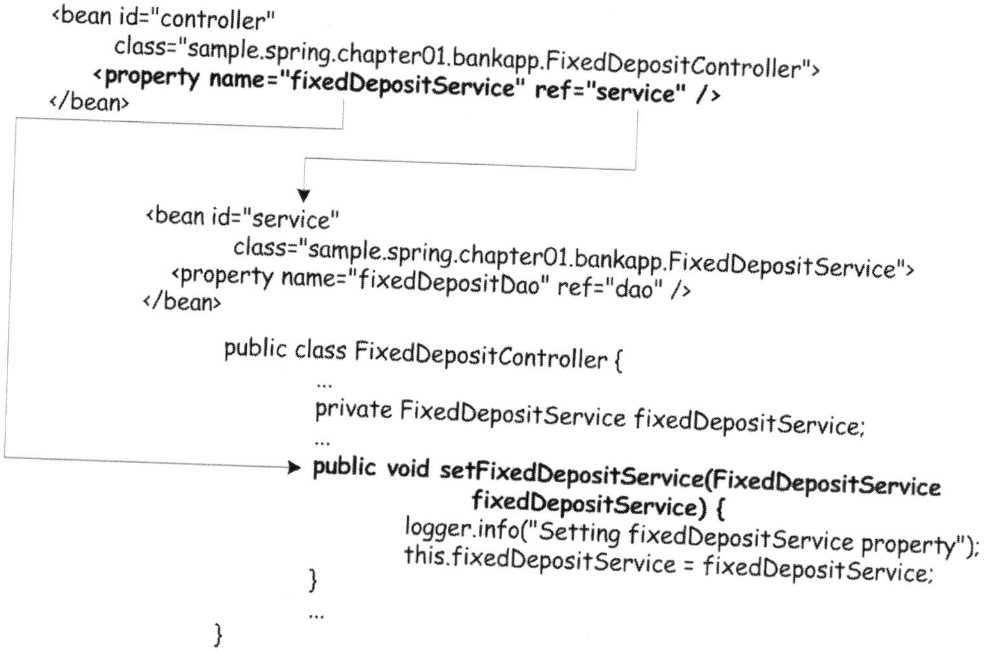

```
<bean id="controller"
      class="sample.spring.chapter01.bankapp.FixedDepositController">
    <property name="fixedDepositService" ref="service" />
</bean>

<bean id="service"
      class="sample.spring.chapter01.bankapp.FixedDepositService">
    <property name="fixedDepositDao" ref="dao" />
</bean>

public class FixedDepositController {
    ...
    private FixedDepositService fixedDepositService;
    ...
    public void setFixedDepositService(FixedDepositService
                fixedDepositService) {
        logger.info("Setting fixedDepositService property");
        this.fixedDepositService = fixedDepositService;
    }
    ...
}
```

Figure 1-6 <property> element's name attribute corresponds to a JavaBean-style setter method that satisfies a bean dependency, and ref attribute refers to another bean.

The above figure shows that fixedDepositService value of name attribute corresponds to the setFixedDepositService method of FixedDepositController class, and service value of ref attribute refers to the bean whose id is service.

> It is fairly common to refer to a bean definition by its name (which is id attribute's value) or type (which is class attribute's value) or the interface implemented by the bean class. For instance, you can refer to 'FixedDepositController bean' as 'controller bean'. And, if the FixedDepositController class implements FixedDepositControllerIntf interface, you can refer to 'FixedDepositController bean' as 'FixedDepositControllerIntf bean'.

The following diagram summarizes how the Spring container creates beans and injects their dependencies based on the configuration metadata supplied by the applicationContext.xml file (refer example listing 1-13) of MyBank application:

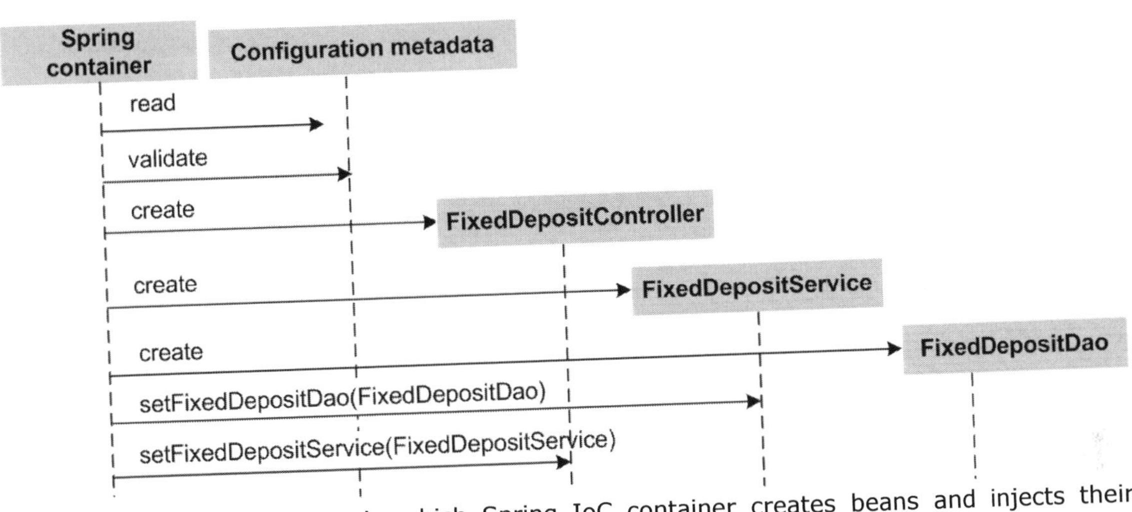

Figure 1-7 - The sequence in which Spring IoC container creates beans and injects their dependencies.

The above figure shows the sequence of steps followed by the Spring IoC container to create FixedDepositController, FixedDepositService and FixedDepositDao beans and inject their dependencies. Before attempting to create beans, the Spring container reads and validates the configuration metadata supplied by the applicationContext.xml file. The order in which the beans are created by the Spring container depends on the order in which they are defined in the applicationContext.xml file. Spring container ensures that the dependencies of a bean are completely configured before the setter method is invoked. For example, the FixedDepositController bean is dependent on FixedDepositService bean; therefore, Spring container configures the FixedDepositService bean before invoking the setFixedDepositService method of FixedDepositController bean.

The bean definitions that we have seen so far, instruct Spring container to create bean instances by invoking the *no-argument* constructor of the bean class, and inject dependencies using setter-based DI. In chapter 2, we'll look at bean definitions that instruct Spring container to create a bean instance via a *factory method* defined in a class. Also, we'll look at how to inject dependencies through constructor arguments (referred to as *constructor-based* DI), through arguments to the factory method that creates the bean instance, and by using setter-based DI on the bean instance returned by the factory method.

Let's now look at how to create an instance of Spring container and pass configuration metadata to it.

Creating an instance of Spring container

Spring's ApplicationContext object represents an instance of Spring container. Spring provides a few built-in implementations of ApplicationContext interface, like

ClassPathXmlApplicationContext, FileSystemXmlApplicationContext, XmlWebApplicationContext, XmlPortletApplicationContext, and so on. The choice of the ApplicationContext implementation depends on how you have defined the configuration metadata (using XML, annotations or Java code), and the type of your application (standalone, web or portlet application). For instance, ClassPathXmlApplicationContext and FileSystemXmlApplicationContext classes are suitable for *standalone* applications in which configuration metadata is supplied in XML format, XmlWebApplicationContext is suitable for *web* applications in which the configuration metadata is supplied in XML format, AnnotationConfigWebApplicationContext is suitable for *web* applications in which configuration metadata is supplied through Java code, and so on.

As MyBank application represents a standalone application, we can use either ClassPathXmlApplicationContext or FileSystemXmlApplicationContext class to create an instance of Spring container. You should note that the ClassPathXmlApplicationContext class loads an application context XML file from the specified *classpath* location, and the FileSystemXmlApplicationContext class loads an application context XML file from the specified location on the *filesystem*.

The following BankApp class of MyBank application shows that an instance of Spring container is created using the ClassPathXmlApplicationContext class:

Example listing 1-15 – BankApp class
Project – ch01-bankapp-xml
Source location - src/main/java/sample/spring/chapter01/bankapp

```
package sample.spring.chapter01.bankapp;

import org.springframework.context.ApplicationContext;
import org.springframework.context.support.ClassPathXmlApplicationContext;

public class BankApp {
   .....
   public static void main(String args[]) {
      ApplicationContext context = new ClassPathXmlApplicationContext(
          "classpath:META-INF/spring/applicationContext.xml");
      .....
   }
}
```

The above example listing shows the BankApp's main method, which is responsible for bootstrapping the Spring container. The classpath location of the application context XML file is passed to the constructor of ClassPathXmlApplicationContext class. The creation of ClassPathXmlApplicationContext instance results in creation of those beans in the application context XML file that are *singleton-scoped* and set to be *pre-instantiated*. In chapter 2, we'll discuss *bean scopes*, and what it means to have beans *pre-* or *lazily-instantiated* by Spring container. For now, you can assume that the beans defined in the applicationContext.xml file of MyBank application are singleton-scoped and set to be pre-instantiated. This means that the beans defined in the applicationContext.xml file are created when an instance of ClassPathXmlApplicationContext is created.

Now, that we have seen how to create an instance of the Spring container, let's look at how to retrieve bean instances from the Spring container.

Access beans from the Spring container

The application objects defined via <bean> elements are created and managed by the Spring container. You can access instances of these application objects by calling one of the getBean methods of the ApplicationContext interface.

The following example listing shows the main method of BankApp class that retrieves an instance of FixedDepositController bean from the Spring container and invokes its methods:

Example listing 1-16 – BankApp class
Project – ch01-bankapp-xml
Source location - src/main/java/sample/spring/chapter01/bankapp

```
package sample.spring.chapter01.bankapp;

import org.apache.log4j.Logger;
import org.springframework.context.ApplicationContext;
import org.springframework.context.support.ClassPathXmlApplicationContext;

public class BankApp {
   private static Logger logger = Logger.getLogger(BankApp.class);

   public static void main(String args[]) {
       ApplicationContext context = new ClassPathXmlApplicationContext(
         "classpath:META-INF/spring/applicationContext.xml");

         FixedDepositController fixedDepositController =
             (FixedDepositController) context.getBean("controller");
         logger.info("Submission status of fixed deposit : " + fixedDepositController.submit());
         logger.info("Returned fixed deposit info : " + fixedDepositController.get());
   }
}
```

At first, the ApplicationContext's getBean method is invoked to retrieve an instance of FixedDepositController bean from the Spring container, followed by invocation of submit and get methods of FixedDepositController bean. The argument passed to the getBean method is the name of the bean whose instance you want to retrieve from the Spring container. The name of the bean passed to the getBean method *must* be the value of the id or name attribute of the bean that you want to retrieve. If no bean with the specified name is registered with the Spring container, an exception is thrown by the getBean method.

In example listing 1-16, to configure the FixedDepositController instance, we didn't programmatically create an instance of FixedDepositService and set it on the FixedDepositController instance. Also, we didn't create an instance of FixedDepositDao and set it on the FixedDepositService instance. This is because the task of creating dependencies, and injecting them into the the dependent objects is handled by the Spring container.

If you go to ch01-bankapp-xml project and execute the main method of BankApp class, you'll see the following output on the console:

```
INFO  sample.spring.chapter01.bankapp.FixedDepositController - initializing
INFO  sample.spring.chapter01.bankapp.FixedDepositService - initializing
INFO  sample.spring.chapter01.bankapp.FixedDepositDao - initializing
INFO  sample.spring.chapter01.bankapp.FixedDepositService - Setting fixedDepositDao property
INFO sample.spring.chapter01.bankapp.FixedDepositController - Setting fixedDepositService property
INFO  sample.spring.chapter01.bankapp.BankApp - Submission status of fixed deposit : true
INFO  sample.spring.chapter01.bankapp.BankApp - Returned fixed deposit info : id :1, deposit amount :
10000.0, tenure : 365, email : someemail@something.com
```

The above output shows that Spring container creates an instance of each of the beans defined in the applicationContext.xml file of MyBank application. Also, Spring container uses setter-based DI to inject an instance of FixedDepositService into FixedDepositController instance, and an instance of FixedDepositDao into the FixedDepositService instance.

Let's now look at some of the frameworks that are built on top of Spring Framework.

1-6 Frameworks built on top of Spring

Though there are many frameworks from SpringSource that use Spring Framework as the foundation, we'll look at some of the widely popular ones. For a more comprehensive list of frameworks, and for more details about an individual framework, it's recommended that you visit the SpringSource website (www.springsource.org).

The following table provides a high-level overview of the frameworks from SpringSource that are built on top of Spring Framework:

Framework	Description
Spring Security	Authentication and authorization framework for enterprise applications. You need to configure a few beans in your application context XML file to incorporate authentication and authorization features into your application.
Spring Data	Provides a consistent programming model to interact with different types of databases. For instance, you can use it to interact with non-relational databases, like MongoDB or Neo4j, and you can also use it for accessing relational databases using JPA.
Spring Batch	If your application requires bulk processing, this framework is for you.
Spring Integration	Provides Enterprise Application Integration (EAI) capabilities to applications.
Spring Social	If your application requires interaction with social media websites, like Facebook and Twitter, then you'll find this framework highly useful.
Spring BlazeDS Integration	If you are developing an Adobe Flex based application, you can use this framework to connect Flex frontend with Spring-based business tier.

As the frameworks mentioned in the above table are built on top of Spring Framework, before using any of these frameworks make sure that they are compatible with the Spring Framework version that you are using.

1-7 Summary

In this chapter, we looked at the benefits of using Spring Framework. We also looked at a simple Spring application that showed how to specify configuration metadata in XML format, create the Spring container instance and retrieve beans from it. In the next chapter, we'll look at some of the foundation concepts of Spring Framework.

Chapter 2 – *Spring Framework basics*

2-1 Introduction

In the previous chapter, we saw that the Spring container invokes the no-argument constructor of a bean class to create a bean instance, and setter-based DI is used to set bean dependencies. In this chapter, we'll go a step further and look at:

- Spring's support for 'programming to interfaces' design principle
- different approaches to instantiating Spring beans
- constructor-based DI for passing bean dependencies as constructor arguments
- constructor- and setter-based DI for passing simple String values to beans, and
- bean scopes

Let's begin this chapter with looking at how Spring improves testability of applications by supporting 'programming to interfaces' design principle.

2-2 Programming to interfaces design principle

In section 1-5 of chapter 1, we saw that a dependent POJO class contained reference to the concrete class of the dependency. For example, the FixedDepositController class contained reference to the FixedDepositService class, and the FixedDepositService class contained reference to the FixedDepositDao class. If a dependent class has direct reference to the concrete class of the dependency, it results in tight coupling between the classes. This means that if you want to substitute a different implementation of the dependency, it'd require changing the dependent class.

Let's now look at a scenario in which a dependent class contains direct reference to the concrete class of the dependency.

Scenario: Dependent class contains reference to the concrete class of dependency

Let's say that the FixedDepositDao class makes use of plain JDBC to interact with the database. To simplify database interaction, you create another DAO implementation, FixedDepositHibernateDao, which uses Hibernate ORM for database interaction. Now, to switch from plain JDBC to Hibernate ORM implementation, you'll need to change FixedDepositService class to use FixedDepositHibernateDao class instead of FixedDepositDao, as shown in the following example listing:

Example listing 2-1 – FixedDepositService class

```
public class FixedDepositService {
  private FixedDepositHibernateDao fixedDepositDao;

  public void setFixedDepositDao(FixedDepositHibernateDao fixedDepositDao) {
     this.fixedDepositDao = fixedDepositDao;
  }

  public FixedDepositDetails getFixedDepositDetails(long id) {
     return fixedDepositDao.getFixedDepositDetails(id);
  }

  public boolean createFixedDeposit(FixedDepositDetails fixedDepositDetails) {
     return fixedDepositDao.createFixedDeposit(fixedDepositDetails);
  }
}
```

The above example listing shows that reference to FixedDepositDao class was replaced by FixedDepositHibernateDao so that Hibernate ORM can be used for database interaction. This shows that if a dependent class refers to the concrete implementation class of the dependency, then substituting a different implementation requires changes in the dependent class.

Let's now look at a scenario in which a dependent class contains reference to the interface implemented by the dependency.

Scenario: Dependent class contains reference to the interface implemented by the dependency

We know that a Java interface defines a contract to which the implementation classes conform. So, if a class depends on the interface implemented by the dependency, no change is required in the class if a different implementation of the dependency is substituted. The application design approach in which a class depends on the interface implemented by the dependency is referred to as 'programming to interfaces'. The interface implemented by the dependency class is referred to as a *dependency interface*.

As it is a good design practice to 'program to interfaces' than to 'program to classes', the following class diagram shows that it is a good design if ABean class depends on BBean interface and *not* on BBeanImpl class that implements BBean interface:

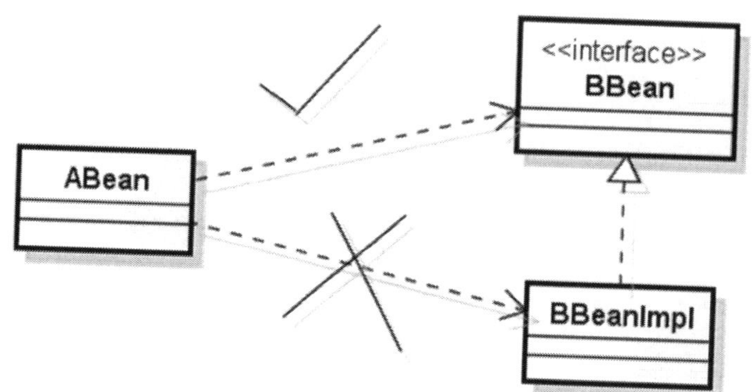

Figure 2-1 - 'Program to interfaces' is a good design practice than to 'program to classes'

The following class diagram shows how FixedDepositService class can make use of 'programming to interfaces' design approach to easily switch the strategy used for database interaction:

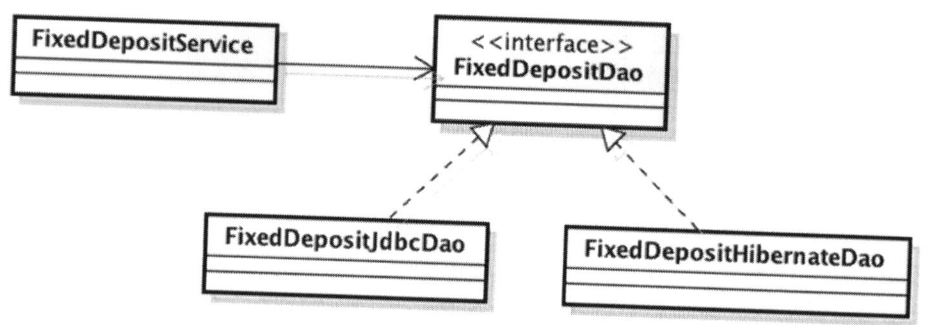

Figure 2-2 – The FixedDepositService depends on FixedDepositDao interface, which is implemented by FixedDepositJdbcDao and FixedDepositHibernateDao classes.

The above figure shows that the FixedDepositService class is not directly dependent on the FixedDepositJdbcDao or FixedDepositHibernateDao class. Instead, FixedDepositService depends on the FixedDepositDao interface (the dependency interface) implemented by FixedDepositJdbcDao and FixedDepositHibernateDao classes. Now, depending on whether you want to use plain JDBC or Hibernate ORM framework, you supply an instance of FixedDepositJdbcDao or FixedDepositHibernateDao to the FixedDepositService instance.

As FixedDepositService depends on FixedDepositDao interface, you can support other database interaction strategies in the future. Let's say that you decide to use iBATIS (now renamed to MyBatis) persistence framework for database interaction. You can use iBATIS without making any changes to FixedDepositService class by simply creating a new FixedDepositIbatisDao class that implements FixedDepositDao interface, and supplying an instance of FixedDepositIbatisDao to the FixedDepositService instance.

So far we have seen that 'programming to interfaces' design approach results in loose coupling between a dependent class and its dependencies. Let's now look at how this design approach improves testability of the dependent classes.

Improved testability of dependent classes

In figure 2-2, we saw that the FixedDepositService class holds reference to the FixedDepositDao interface. FixedDepositJdbcDao and FixedDepositHibernateDao are concrete implementation classes of FixedDepositDao interface. Now, to simplify unit testing of FixedDepositService class, you can substitute a mock implementation of FixedDepositDao interface that doesn't require a database.

If the FixedDepositService class had direct reference to FixedDepositJdbcDao or FixedDepositHibernateDao class, testing FixedDepositService class would have required setting up a database for testing purposes. This shows that by using a mock implementation of dependency interface, you can save the effort to setup the infrastructure for unit testing your dependent classes.

Let's now see how Spring supports 'programming to interfaces' design approach in applications.

Spring's support for 'programming to interfaces' design approach

To use 'programming to interfaces' design approach in your Spring application, you need to ensure the following things:

- the <bean> elements in the configuration metadata specify the concrete classes of the dependency
- the dependent bean classes refer to the dependency interface instead of the concrete class of the dependency

Let's now look at the modified MyBank application that uses 'programming to interfaces' design approach.

IMPORT **chapter 2/ch02-bankapp-interfaces** (This project shows how 'programming to interfaces' design approach is used in creating Spring applications. To run the application, execute the main method of the BankApp class of this project)

MyBank application that uses 'programming to interfaces' design approach

The following class diagram depicts the modified MyBank application that uses 'programming to interfaces' design approach:

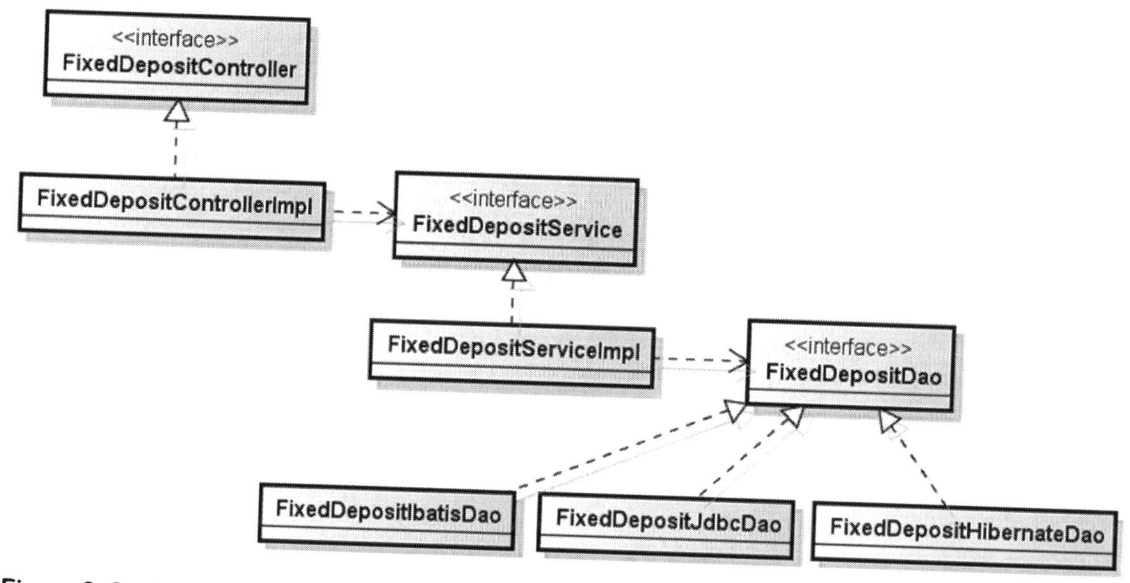

Figure 2-3 - MyBank application that uses 'program to interfaces' design approach

The above figure shows that a dependent class depends on the interface implemented by the dependency, and *not* on the concrete implementation class of the dependency. For instance, the FixedDepositControllerImpl class depends on the FixedDepositService interface, and the FixedDepositServiceImpl class depends on the FixedDepositDao interface.

The following example listing shows the FixedDepositServiceImpl class based on the design shown in figure 2-3:

Example listing 2-2 – FixedDepositService class
Project – ch02-bankapp-interfaces
Source location - src/main/java/sample/spring/chapter02/bankapp

```
package sample.spring.chapter02.bankapp;

public class FixedDepositServiceImpl implements FixedDepositService {
  private FixedDepositDao fixedDepositDao;
  .....
  public void setFixedDepositDao(FixedDepositDao fixedDepositDao) {
    this.fixedDepositDao = fixedDepositDao;
  }
```

```
  public FixedDepositDetails getFixedDepositDetails(long id) {
    return fixedDepositDao.getFixedDepositDetails(id);
  }

  public boolean createFixedDeposit(FixedDepositDetails fdd) {
    return fixedDepositDao.createFixedDeposit(fdd);
  }
}
```

The above example listing shows that the FixedDepositServiceImpl class contains reference to the FixedDepositDao interface. The FixedDepositDao implementation that you want to inject into the FixedDepositServiceImpl instance is specified in the application context XML file. As shown in figure 2-3, you can inject any one of the following concrete implementations of FixedDepositDao interface: FixedDepositIbatisDao, FixedDepositJdbcDao and FixedDepositHibernateDao.

The following example listing shows the applicationContext.xml file that caters to the design shown in figure 2-3:

Example listing 2-3 – applicationContext.xml - MyBank's application context XML file
Project – ch02-bankapp-interfaces
Source location - src/main/resources/META-INF/spring

```
<?xml version="1.0" encoding="UTF-8" standalone="no"?>
<beans .....>

  <bean id="controller"
      class="sample.spring.chapter02.bankapp.controller.FixedDepositControllerImpl">
    <property name="fixedDepositService" ref="service" />
  </bean>

  <bean id="service" class="sample.spring.chapter02.bankapp.service.FixedDepositServiceImpl">
      <property name="fixedDepositDao" ref="dao" />
  </bean>

  <bean id="dao" class="sample.spring.chapter02.bankapp.dao.FixedDepositHibernateDao"/>
</beans>
```

The above applicationContext.xml file shows that an instance of FixedDepositHibernateDao (an implementation of FixedDepositDao interface) is injected into FixedDepositServiceImpl. Now, if you decide to use iBATIS instead of Hibernate for persistence, then all you need to do is to change the class attribute of the dao bean definition in the applicationContext.xml file to refer to the fully-qualified name of the FixedDepositIbatisDao class.

Let's now look at different ways in which Spring container can instantiate beans.

2-3 Different approaches to instantiating Spring beans

So far we have seen bean definition examples that instruct Spring container to create bean instances by invoking the *no-argument* constructor of the bean class. Consider the following bean definition:

```
<bean id="myBean" class="mypackage.MyBean"/>
```

In the above bean definition, MyBean class represents a POJO class that defines a no-argument constructor. MyBean class doesn't implement any Spring-specific interface or extend from any Spring-specific class. This effectively means that the Spring container can create and manage instance of any class that provides a no-argument constructor.

> It is important to note that the Spring container can create and manage instance of any class, irrespective of whether the class provides a no-argument constructor or not. In section 2-4, we'll look at bean definitions in which the constructor of the bean class accepts one or more arguments.

If you have an existing project that uses factory classes to create object instances, you can still use Spring container to manage objects created by these factories. Let's now look at how Spring container invokes a *static* or an *instance* factory method of a class to manage the returned object instance.

Instantiating beans via *static* factory methods

In figure 2-3, we saw that the FixedDepositDao interface is implemented by FixedDepositHibernateDao, FixedDepositIbatisDao and FixedDepositJdbcDao classes. The following example listing shows a FixedDepositDaoFactory class that defines a *static* factory method for creating and returning an instance of FixedDepositDao based on the argument passed to the *static* method:

Example listing 2-4 – FixedDepositDaoFactory class

```
public class FixedDepositDaoFactory {
  private FixedDepositDaoFactory() { }

  public static FixedDepositDao getFixedDepositDao(String daoType) {
    FixedDepositDao fixedDepositDao = null;

    if("jdbc".equalsIgnoreCase(daoType)) {
        fixedDepositDao = new FixedDepositJdbcDao();
    }
```

```
        if("hibernate".equalsIgnoreCase(daoType)) {
            fixedDepositDao = new FixedDepositHibernateDao();
        }
        .....
        return fixedDepositDao;
    }
}
```

The above example listing shows that the FixedDepositDaoFactory class defines a getFixedDepositDao *static* method that creates and returns an instance of FixedDepositJdbcDao, FixedDepositHibernateDao or FixedDepositIbatisDao class, depending on the value of the daoType argument.

The following bean definition for the FixedDepositDaoFactory class instructs Spring container to invoke FixedDepositDaoFactory's getFixedDepositDao method to obtain an instance of FixedDepositJdbcDao class:

Example listing 2-5 – Bean definition for the FixedDepositDaoFactory class

```
<bean id="dao" class="sample.spring.FixedDepositDaoFactory"
        factory-method="getFixedDepositDao">
    <constructor-arg index="0" value="jdbc"/>
</bean>
```

In the above bean definition, class attribute specifies the fully-qualified name of the class that defines the *static* factory method. The factory-method attribute specifies the name of the *static* factory method that the Spring container invokes to obtain an instance of FixedDepositDao object. The <constructor-arg> element is defined in Spring's beans schema and is used for passing arguments to constructors, and *static* and *instance* factory methods. The index attribute refers to the location of the argument in the constructor, or in the *static* or *instance* factory method. In the above bean definition, the value 0 of index attribute means that the <constructor-arg> element is supplying value for the first argument, which is daoType, of the getFixedDepositDao factory method. The value attribute specifies the argument value. If a factory method accepts multiple arguments, you need to define a <constructor-arg> element for each of the arguments.

It is important to note that calling ApplicationContext's getBean method to obtain dao bean (refer example listing 2-5) will result in invocation of the FixedDepositDaoFactory's getFixedDepositDao factory method. This means that calling getBean("dao") returns the FixedDepositDao instance created by the getFixedDepositDao factory method, and *not* an instance of FixedDepositDaoFactory class.

Now, that we have seen the configuration of the factory class that creates an instance of FixedDepositDao, the following example listing shows how to inject an instance of FixedDepositDao into FixedDepositServiceImpl class:

Example listing 2-6 – Injecting object instances created by *static* factory method

```
<bean id="service" class="sample.spring.chapter02.bankapp.FixedDepositServiceImpl">
    <property name="fixedDepositDao" ref="dao" />
</bean>

<bean id="dao" class="sample.spring.chapter02.basicapp.FixedDepositDaoFactory"
      factory-method="getFixedDepositDao">
      <constructor-arg index="0" value="jdbc"/>
</bean>
```

In the above example listing, <property> element injects an instance of FixedDepositDao returned by FixedDepositDaoFactory's getFixedDepositDao factory method into FixedDepositServiceImpl instance. If you compare the bean definition for the FixedDepositServiceImpl class shown above with the one shown in example listing 2-3, you'll notice that they are exactly the same. This shows that the bean dependencies are specified the same way irrespective of how (using no-argument constructor or *static* factory method) the Spring container creates bean instances.

Let's now look at how Spring container instantiate beans by invoking an *instance* factory method.

Instantiating beans via *instance* factory methods

The following example listing shows the FixedDepositDaoFactory class that defines an *instance* factory method for creating and returning an instance of FixedDepositDao:

Example listing 2-7 – FixedDepositDaoFactory class

```
public class FixedDepositDaoFactory {
  public FixedDepositDaoFactory() {
  }

  public FixedDepositDao getFixedDepositDao(String daoType) {
    FixedDepositDao FixedDepositDao = null;

    if("jdbc".equalsIgnoreCase(daoType)) {
        FixedDepositDao = new FixedDepositJdbcDao();
    }
    if("hibernate".equalsIgnoreCase(daoType)) {
```

```
        FixedDepositDao = new FixedDepositHiberateDao();
    }
    .....
    return fixedDepositDao;
  }
}
```

If a class defines an *instance* factory method, the class must define a public constructor so that the Spring container can create an instance of that class. In the above example listing, the FixedDepositDaoFactory class defines a public no-argument constructor. The FixedDepositDaoFactory's getFixedDepositDao method is an *instance* factory method that creates and returns an instance of FixedDepositDao.

The following example listing shows how to instruct Spring container to invoke FixedDepositDaoFactory's getFixedDepositDao method to obtain an instance of FixedDepositDao:

Example listing 2-8 – Configuration to invoke FixedDepositDaoFactory's getFixedDepositDao method

```
<bean id="daoFactory" class="sample.spring.chapter02.basicapp.FixedDepositDaoFactory" />

<bean id="dao" factory-bean="daoFactory" factory-method="getFixedDepositDao">
    <constructor-arg index="0" value="jdbc"/>
</bean>

<bean id="service" class="sample.spring.chapter02.bankapp.FixedDepositServiceImpl">
    <property name="fixedDepositDao" ref="dao" />
</bean>
```

The above example listing shows that the FixedDepositDaoFactory class (a class that contains *instance* factory method) is configured like a regular Spring bean, and a separate <bean> element is used to configure the *instance* factory method details. To configure details of an *instance* factory method, factory-bean and factory-method attributes of <bean> element are used. The factory-bean attribute refers to the bean that defines the *instance* factory method, and the factory-method attribute specifies the name of the *instance* factory method. In the above example listing, <property> element injects an instance of FixedDepositDao returned by FixedDepositDaoFactory's getFixedDepositDao factory method into FixedDepositServiceImpl instance.

As with *static* factory methods, you can pass arguments to *instance* factory methods using <constructor-arg> element. It is important to note that invoking ApplicationContext's getBean method to obtain dao bean in the above example listing will result in invocation of the FixedDepositDaoFactory's getFixedDepositDao factory method.

So far we have looked at bean definition examples in which dependencies are injected into beans via setter methods. Let's now look at different DI mechanisms that you can use for injecting dependencies.

2-4 Dependency injection techniques

In Spring, dependency injection is performed by passing arguments to a bean's constructor and setter methods. If you are using a *static* or *instance* factory method to create bean instances, you can pass bean dependencies to the factory method or you can set them on the bean instance returned by the factory method.

We'll now look at examples that demonstrate different DI techniques.

Setter-based DI

So far in this book, we've seen examples of setter-based DI. In setter-based DI, <property> elements are used to specify bean dependencies. The <property> element is also used to pass *configuration information* (if any) required by the bean.

Let's say that the MyBank application contains a PersonalBankingService service that allows customers to retrieve bank account statement, check bank account details, update contact number, change password, and contact customer service. The PersonalBankingService class uses JmsMessageSender (for sending JMS messages), EmailMessageSender (for sending emails) and WebServiceInvoker (for invoking external web services) objects to accomplish it's intended functionality. The following example listing shows the PersonalBankingService class:

Example listing 2-9 – PersonalBankingService class

```
public class PersonalBankingService {
  private JmsMessageSender jmsMessageSender;
  private EmailMessageSender emailMessageSender;
  private WebServiceInvoker webServiceInvoker;
  .....
  public void setJmsMessageSender(JmsMessageSender jmsMessageSender) {
    this.jmsMessageSender = jmsMessageSender;
  }

  public void setEmailMessageSender(EmailMessageSender emailMessageSender) {
    this.emailMessageSender = emailMessageSender;
  }

  public void setWebServiceInvoker(WebServiceInvoker webServiceInvoker) {
    this.webServiceInvoker = webServiceInvoker;
  }
```

```
    .....
}
```

The above example listing shows that a setter method is defined for **JmsMessageSender**, **EmailMessageSender** and **WebServiceInvoker** dependencies of PersonalBankingService class.

We can use setter-based DI to inject the dependencies of the PersonalBankingService class, as shown here:

Example listing 2-10 – Bean definitions for PersonalBankingService class and its dependencies

```
<bean id="personalBankingService" class="PersonalBankingService">
    <property name="emailMessageSender" ref="emailMessageSender" />
    <property name="jmsMessageSender" ref="jmsMessageSender" />
    <property name="webServiceInvoker" ref="webServiceInvoker" />
</bean>

<bean id="jmsMessageSender" class="JmsMessageSender">
    .....
</bean>
<bean id="webServiceInvoker" class="WebServiceInvoker" />
    .....
</bean>
<bean id="emailMessageSender" class="EmailMessageSender" />
    .....
</bean>
```

The personalBankingService bean definition shows that a <property> element is specified for each dependency of PersonalBankingService class.

PersonalBankingService uses EmailMessageSender bean to send an email notification to the customer's email address in case customer changes his contact number. EmailMessageSender requires email server address, and username and password for authenticating with the email server. The following example listing shows that the <property> element can *also* be used for setting bean properties of type String:

Example listing 2-11 EmailMessageSender class and the corresponding bean definition

```
public class EmailMessageSender {
    private String host;
    private String username;
    private String password;
    .....
    public void setHost(String host) {
```

```
        this.host = host;
    }

    public void setUsername(String username) {
        this.username = username;
    }

    public void setPassword(String password) {
        this.password = password;
    }
    .....
}

<bean id="emailMessageSender" class="EmailMessageSender">
    <property name="host" value="smtp.gmail.com"/>
    <property name="username" value="myusername"/>
    <property name="password" value="mypassword"/>
</bean>
```

The above example listing shows that <property> elements have been used to set host, username and password properties of EmailMessageSender bean. The value attribute specifies the String value to be set for the bean property identified by the name attribute. The host, username and password properties represent configuration information required by EmailMessageSender bean. In chapter 3, we'll see how the <property> element is used to set primitive type (like int, long, and so on), collection type (like java.util.List, java.util.Map, and so on) and custom type (like Address) properties.

Setter-based DI is also used to inject dependencies into beans created by *static* and *instance* factory methods. Let's look at how to use setter-based DI in conjunction with *static* and *instance* factory methods.

Injecting dependencies into bean instances created by factory methods

You can use setter-based DI to inject dependencies of the bean instance returned by a *static* or *instance* factory method.

Consider the following FixedDepositJdbcDao class that defines a databaseInfo property:

Example listing 2-12 – FixedDepositJdbcDao class

```
public class FixedDepositJdbcDao {
    private DatabaseInfo databaseInfo;
    .....
    public FixedDepositJdbcDao() { }
```

```
    public void setDatabaseInfo(DatabaseInfo databaseInfo) {
        this. databaseInfo = databaseInfo;
    }
    .....
}
```

In the above example listing, the databaseInfo attribute represents a dependency of the FixedDepositJdbcDao class that is fulfilled by setDatabaseInfo method.

The following FixedDepositDaoFactory class defines a factory method responsible for creating and returning an instance of FixedDepositDaoJdbc class:

Example listing 2-13 – FixedDepositDaoFactory class

```
public class FixedDepositDaoFactory {
    public FixedDepositDaoFactory() {
    }

    public FixedDepositDao getFixedDepositDao(String daoType) {
        FixedDepositDao FixedDepositDao = null;

        if("jdbc".equalsIgnoreCase(daoType)) {
            FixedDepositDao = new FixedDepositJdbcDao();
        }
        if("hibernate".equalsIgnoreCase(daoType)) {
            FixedDepositDao = new FixedDepositHiberateDao();
        }
        .....
        return fixedDepositDao;
    }
}
```

In the above example listing, the getFixedDepositDao method is an *instance* factory method for creating FixedDepositDao instances. The getFixedDepositDao method creates an instance of FixedDepositJdbcDao instance if the value of daoType argument is jdbc. It is important to note that the getFixedDepositDao method doesn't set the databaseInfo property of the FixedDepositJdbcDao instance.

As we saw in example listing 2-8, the following bean definitions instruct Spring container to create an instance of FixedDepositJdbcDao by invoking the getFixedDepositDao *instance* factory method of FixedDepositDaoFactory class:

Example listing 2-14 – Configuration to invoke FixedDepositDaoFactory's getFixedDepositDao method

```
<bean id="daoFactory" class="FixedDepositDaoFactory" />

<bean id="dao" factory-bean="daoFactory" factory-method="getFixedDepositDao">
    <constructor-arg index="0" value="jdbc"/>
</bean>
```

The dao bean definition results in invocation of FixedDepositDaoFactory's getFixedDepositDao method, which creates and returns an instance of FixedDepositJdbcDao. But, the FixedDepositJdbcDao's databaseInfo property is not set. To set the databaseInfo dependency, you can perform setter-based DI on the FixedDepositJdbcDao instance returned by the getFixedDepositDao method, as shown here:

Example listing 2-15 – Configuration to invoke FixedDepositDaoFactory's getFixedDepositDao method and set databaseInfo property of returned FixedDepositJdbcDao instance

```
<bean id="daoFactory" class="FixedDepositDaoFactory" />

<bean id="dao" factory-bean="daoFactory" factory-method="getFixedDepositDao">
    <constructor-arg index="0" value="jdbc"/>
    <property name="databaseInfo" ref="databaseInfo"/>
</bean>

<bean id="databaseInfo" class="DatabaseInfo" />
```

The above bean definition shows that <property> element is used to set databaseInfo property of FixedDepositJdbcDao instance returned by getFixedDepositDao *instance* factory method. As with the *instance* factory method, you can use the <property> element to inject dependencies into the bean instance returned by the *static* factory method.

Let's now look at how to inject bean dependencies via constructor arguments.

Constructor-based DI

In constructor-based DI, dependencies of a bean are passed as arguments to the bean class's constructor. For instance, the following example listing shows PersonalBankingService class whose constructor accepts JmsMessageSender, EmailMessageSender and WebServiceInvoker objects:

Example listing 2-16 – PersonalBankingService class

```
public class PersonalBankingService {
  private JmsMessageSender jmsMessageSender;
  private EmailMessageSender emailMessageSender;
  private WebServiceInvoker webServiceInvoker;
  .....
  public PersonalBankingService(JmsMessageSender jmsMessageSender,
      EmailMessageSender emailMessageSender,
      WebServiceInvoker webServiceInvoker) {

    this.jmsMessageSender = jmsMessageSender;
    this.emailMessageSender = emailMessageSender;
    this.webServiceInvoker = webServiceInvoker;
  }
  .....
}
```

The arguments to the PersonalBankingService's constructor represent dependencies of the PersonalBankingService class. The following example listing shows how dependencies of PersonalBankingService instance are supplied via <constructor-arg> elements:

Example listing 2-17 – PersonalBankingService bean definition

```
<bean id="personalBankingService" class="PersonalBankingService">
  <constructor-arg index="0" ref="jmsMessageSender" />
  <constructor-arg index="1" ref="emailMessageSender" />
  <constructor-arg index="2" ref="webServiceInvoker" />
</bean>

<bean id="jmsMessageSender" class="JmsMessageSender">
  .....
</bean>
<bean id="webServiceInvoker" class="WebServiceInvoker" />
  .....
</bean>
<bean id="emailMessageSender" class="EmailMessageSender" />
  .....
</bean>
```

In the above example listing, <constructor-arg> elements specify details of the constructor arguments passed to the PersonalBankingService instance. The index attribute specifies the index of the constructor argument. If the index attribute value is 0, it means that the <constructor-arg> element corresponds to the first constructor argument, and if the index attribute value is 1, it means that the <constructor-arg> element corresponds to the second constructor argument, and so on. We saw earlier that ref attribute of <property> element is used for passing reference to a bean. Similarly, ref attribute of <constructor-arg> element is used for passing reference to a bean. Like the <property> element, the <constructor-arg> element is also used to pass *configuration information* (if any) required by the bean.

You should note that the <constructor-arg> element is also used for passing arguments to *static* and *instance* factory methods that create bean instances (refer section 2-3).

> Instead of using ref attribute of <property> and <constructor-arg> elements, you can use <ref> element inside the <property> and <constructor-arg> elements to set reference to beans. The ref attribute is preferred as it makes the XML less verbose.

The following example listing shows the EmailMessageSender class and the corresponding bean definition that demonstrates use of <constructor-arg> elements to supply values for String type constructor arguments:

Example listing 2-18 EmailMessageSender class and the corresponding bean definition

```
public class EmailMessageSender {
  private String host;
  private String username;
  private String password;
  .....
  public EmailMessageSender(String host, String username, String password) {
     this.host = host;
     this.username = username;
     this.password = password;
  }
  .....
}
  <bean id="emailMessageSender" class="EmailMessageSender">
       <constructor-arg index="0" value="smtp.gmail.com"/>
       <constructor-arg index="1" value="myusername"/>
       <constructor-arg index="2" value="mypassword"/>
  </bean>
```

So far we have seen that <constructor-arg> element is used for injecting bean dependencies and passing values for String type constructor arguments. In chapter 3, we'll see how the <constructor-arg> element is used to set primitive type (like int, long, and so on), collection type (like java.util.List, java.util.Map, and so on) and custom type (like Address) properties.

Let's now look at how we can use constructor-based DI along with setter-based DI.

Using a mix of constructor- and setter-based DI mechanisms

If a bean class requires both constructor- and setter-based DI mechanisms, you can use a combination of <constructor-arg> and <property> elements to inject dependencies.

The following example listing shows a bean class whose dependencies are injected as arguments to constructor and setter methods:

Example listing 2-19 – PersonalBankingService class

```
public class PersonalBankingService {
   private JmsMessageSender jmsMessageSender;
   private EmailMessageSender emailMessageSender;
   private WebServiceInvoker webServiceInvoker;
   .....
   public PersonalBankingService(JmsMessageSender jmsMessageSender,
            EmailMessageSender emailMessageSender) {
      this.jmsMessageSender = jmsMessageSender;
      this.emailMessageSender = emailMessageSender;
   }

   public void setWebServiceInvoker(WebServiceInvoker webServiceInvoker) {
      this.webServiceInvoker = webServiceInvoker;
   }
   .....
}
```

In the PersonalBankingService class, jmsMessageSender and emailMessageSender dependencies are injected as constructor arguments, and webServiceInvoker dependency is injected via the setWebServiceInvoker setter method. The following bean definition shows that both <constructor-arg> and <property> elements are used to inject dependencies of PersonalBankingService class:

Example listing 2-20 – Mixing constructor- and setter-based DI mechanisms

```
<bean id="dataSource" class="PersonalBankingService">
      <constructor-arg index="0" ref="jmsMessageSender" />
      <constructor-arg index="1" ref="emailMessageSender" />
      <property name="webServiceInvoker" ref="webServiceInvoker" />
</bean>
```

Now, that we have seen how to instruct Spring container to create beans and perform DI, let's look at different *scopes* that you can specify for beans.

2-5 Bean scopes

You may want to specify the scope of a bean to control whether a shared instance of the bean is created (singleton scope), or a new bean instance is created every time the bean is requested (prototype scope) from the Spring container. The scope of a bean is defined by the scope attribute of the <bean> element. If the scope attribute is not specified, it means that the bean is a singleton-scoped bean.

> In web application scenarios, Spring allows you to specify additional scopes: request, session and globalSession. These scopes determine the *lifetime* of the bean instance. For instance, a request-scoped bean's lifetime is limited to a single HTTP request. As in this chapter we'll *not* be discussing Spring Web MVC or Spring Portlet MVC, we'll restrict the discussion to singleton and prototype scopes. The request, session and globalSession scopes are described in chapter 10.

IMPORT **chapter 2/ch02-bankapp-scopes** (This project shows usage of singleton and prototype bean scopes. To run the application, execute the main method of the BankApp class of this project. The project also contains 2 JUnit tests, PrototypeTest and SingletonTest that you can execute)

Singleton

The singleton scope is the *default* scope for all the beans defined in the application context XML file. Instance of a singleton-scoped bean is created when the Spring container is created, and is destroyed when the Spring container is destroyed. Spring container creates a *single* instance of a singleton-scoped bean, which is shared by *all* the beans that depend on it.

The following example listing shows the applicationContext.xml file of ch02-bankapp-scopes project in which all the beans are singleton-scoped:

Example listing 2-21 – applicationContext.xml - Singleton-scoped beans
Project – ch02-bankapp-scopes
Source location - src/main/resources/META-INF/spring

```
<beans ..... >
  <bean id="controller"
      class="sample.spring.chapter02.bankapp.controller.FixedDepositControllerImpl">
    <property name="fixedDepositService" ref="service" />
  </bean>

  <bean id="service"
    class="sample.spring.chapter02.bankapp.service.FixedDepositServiceImpl">
    <property name="fixedDepositDao" ref="dao" />
  </bean>
```

```
    <bean id="dao" class="sample.spring.chapter02.bankapp.dao.FixedDepositDaoImpl" />
    .....
</beans>
```

In the above applicationContext.xml file, controller, service and dao beans are singleton-scoped because no scope attribute is specified for the <bean> elements. This means that only a single instance of FixedDepositControllerImpl, FixedDepositServiceImpl and FixedDepositDaoImpl classes is created by the Spring container. As these beans are singleton-scoped, Spring container returns the same instance of the bean every time we retrieve one of these beans using ApplicationContext's getBean method.

> If the scope attribute is not specified or the value of scope attribute is singleton, it means that the bean is singleton-scoped.

The following example listing shows the testInstances method of SingletonTest (a JUnit test class) class of ch02-bankapp-scopes project. The testInstances method tests whether multiple invocation of ApplicationContext's getBean method returns the same or different instance of the controller bean:

Example listing 2-22 – SingletonTest JUnit test class
Project – ch02-bankapp-scopes
Source location - src/test/java/sample/spring/chapter02/bankapp

```
package sample.spring.chapter02.bankapp;

import static org.junit.Assert.assertSame;
import org.junit.BeforeClass;
import org.junit.Test;

import sample.spring.chapter02.bankapp.controller.FixedDepositController;

public class SingletonTest {
    private static ApplicationContext context;

    @BeforeClass
    public static void init() {
        context = new ClassPathXmlApplicationContext(
                "classpath:META-INF/spring/applicationContext.xml");
    }

    @Test
    public void testInstances() {
```

```
        FixedDepositController controller1 = (FixedDepositController) context.getBean("controller");
        FixedDepositController controller2 = (FixedDepositController) context.getBean("controller");
        assertSame("Different FixedDepositController instances", controller1, controller2);
    }
    .....
}
```

In the above example listing, JUnit's @BeforeClass annotation specifies that the init method is invoked before any of the test methods (that is, methods annotated with JUnit's @Test annotation) in the class. This means that @BeforeClass annotated method is invoked only *once*, and @Test annotated methods are executed only *after* the execution of @BeforeClass annotated method. Note that the init method is a *static* method. The init method creates an instance of ApplicationContext object by passing the configuration metadata (shown in example listing 2-21) to the ClassPathXmlApplicationContext's constructor. The testInstances method obtains 2 instances of controller bean and checks whether both the instances are the same by using JUnit's assertSame assertion. As the controller bean is singleton-scoped, controller1 and controller2 bean instances are the same. For this reason, SingletonTest's testInstances test executes without any assertion errors.

The following figure shows that the Spring container returns the same instance of controller bean when you call the ApplicationContext's getBean method multiple times:

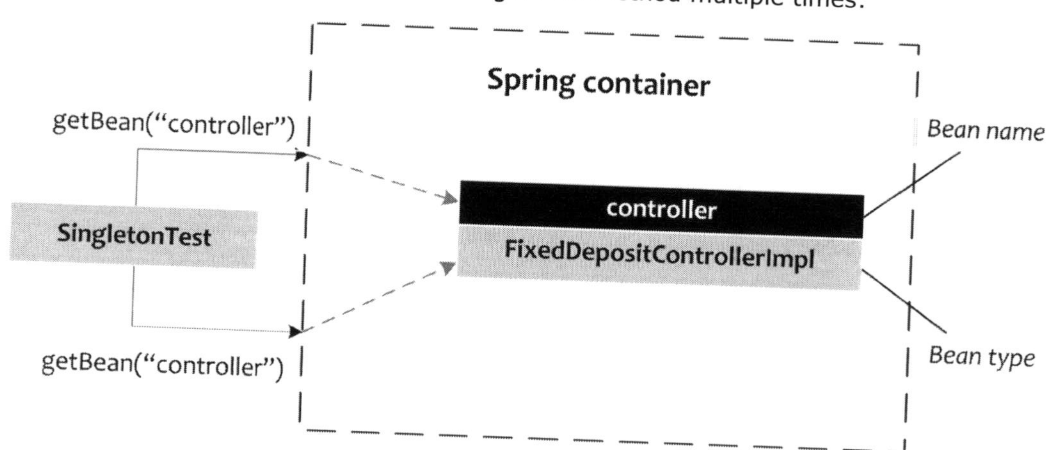

Figure 2-4 Multiple requests for a singleton-scoped bean results in the same bean instance returned by the Spring container

The above figure shows that multiple calls to obtain controller bean returns the *same* instance of the controller bean.

In figure 2-4, the controller bean instance is represented by a 2-compartment rectangle. The top compartment shows the *name* of the bean (that is, the value of the id attribute of the <bean> element) and the bottom compartment shows the *type* of the bean (that is, the value of the class attribute of the <bean> element). In the rest of this book, we'll use this convention to show bean instances inside a Spring container.

A singleton-scoped bean instance is shared amongst the beans that depend on it. The following example listing shows the testReference method of SingletonTest JUnit test class that checks if the FixedDepositDao instance referenced by the FixedDepositController instance is the same as the one obtained directly by calling getBean method of ApplicationContext:

Example listing 2-23 – testReference method of SingletonTest JUnit test class
Project – ch02-bankapp-scopes
Source location - src/test/java/sample/spring/chapter02/bankapp

```
package sample.spring.chapter02.bankapp;

import static org.junit.Assert.assertSame;
import org.junit.Test;

public class SingletonTest {
  private static ApplicationContext context;
  .....
  @Test
  public void testReference() {
    FixedDepositController controller = (FixedDepositController) context.getBean("controller");

    FixedDepositDao fixedDepositDao1 =
          controller.getFixedDepositService().getFixedDepositDao();
    FixedDepositDao fixedDepositDao2 = (FixedDepositDao) context.getBean("dao");
    assertSame("Different FixedDepositDao instances", fixedDepositDao1, fixedDepositDao2);
  }
}
```

In the above example listing, the testReference method first retrieves the FixedDepositDao instance (refer fixedDepositDao1 variable in the above example listing) referenced by the FixedDepositController bean, followed by directly retrieving another instance of FixedDepositDao bean (refer fixedDepositDao2 variable in the above example listing) using ApplicationContext's getBean method. If you execute the testReference test, you'll see that the test completes successfully because the fixedDepositDao1 and fixedDepositDao2 instances are the same.

Figure 2-5 shows that the FixedDepositDao instance referenced by FixedDepositController instance is the same as the one returned by invoking getBean("dao") method on ApplicationContext.

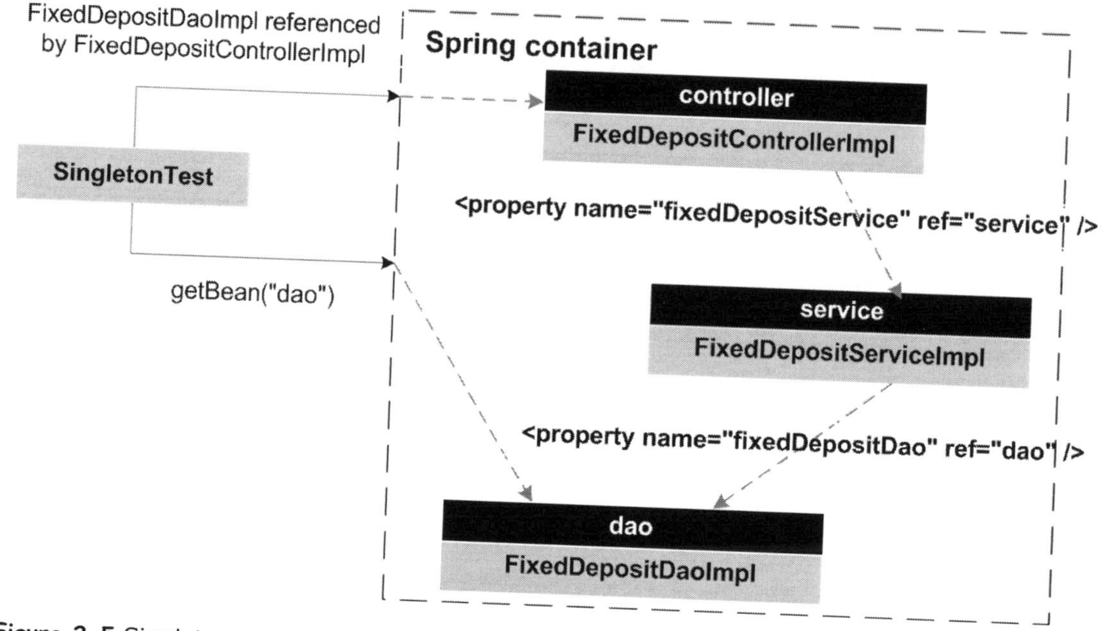

Figure 2-5 Singleton-scoped bean instance is shared between beans that depend on it

The above figure shows that the FixedDepositDao instance referenced by FixedDepositController bean instance and the one retrieved directly by calling ApplicationContext's getBean are same. If there are multiple beans dependent on a singleton-scoped bean, then all the dependent beans share the same singleton-scoped bean instance.

Let's now look at whether or not the same singleton-scoped bean instance is shared between multiple Spring container instances.

Singleton-scoped beans and multiple Spring container instances

The scope of a singleton-scoped bean instance is limited to the Spring container instance. This means that if you create 2 instances of the Spring container using the same configuration metadata, each Spring container has its own instances of the singleton-scoped beans.

The following example listing shows the testSingletonScope method of SingletonTest class, which tests whether the FixedDepositController bean instance retrieved from two different Spring container instances are same or different:

Example listing 2-24 – testSingletonScope method of SingletonTest JUnit test class
Project – ch02-bankapp-scopes
Source location - src/test/java/sample/spring/chapter02/bankapp

```
package sample.spring.chapter02.bankapp;

import static org.junit.Assert.assertNotSame;

public class SingletonTest {
  private static ApplicationContext context;
  .....
  @BeforeClass
  public static void init() {
      context = new ClassPathXmlApplicationContext(
            "classpath:META-INF/spring/applicationContext.xml");
  }

  @Test
  public void testSingletonScope() {
      ApplicationContext anotherContext = new ClassPathXmlApplicationContext(
            "classpath:META-INF/spring/applicationContext.xml");

     FixedDepositController fixedDepositController1 = (FixedDepositController) anotherContext
          .getBean("controller");

     FixedDepositController fixedDepositController2 =
           (FixedDepositController) context .getBean("controller");

     assertNotSame("Same FixedDepositController instances",
              fixedDepositController1, fixedDepositController2);
  }
}
```

The SingletonTest's init method (annotated with JUnit's @BeforeClass annotation) creates an instance of ApplicationContext (identified by context variable) before any @Test annotated method is executed. The testSingletonScope method creates one more instance of Spring container (identified by anotherContext variable) using the same applicationContext.xml file. An instance of FixedDepositController bean is retrieved from both the Spring containers and checked if they are *not* the same. If you execute the testSingletonScope test, you'll find that the test completes successfully because the FixedDepositController bean instance retrieved from context instance is different from the one retrieved from anotherContext instance.

The following figure depicts the behavior exhibited by the testSingletonScope method:

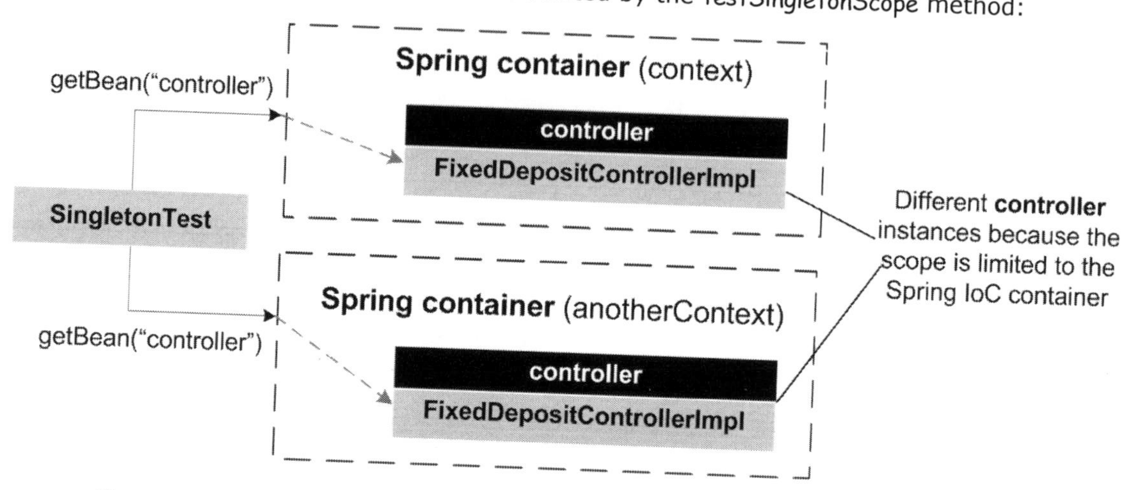

Figure 2-6 Each Spring container creates its own instance of a singleton-scoped bean

The above figure shows that each Spring container creates its own instance of controller bean. This is the reason why context and anotherContext instances return different instances of controller bean when you call getBean("controller") method.

The testSingletonScope method showed that each Spring container creates its own instance of a singleton-scoped bean. It is important to note that Spring container creates an instance of a singleton-scoped bean for *each* bean definition. The following example listing shows multiple bean definitions for the FixedDepositDaoImpl class:

Example listing 2-25 – applicationContext.xml - Multiple bean definitions for the same class
Project – ch02-bankapp-scopes
Source location - src/main/resources/META-INF/spring

```
<bean id="dao" class="sample.spring.chapter02.bankapp.dao.FixedDepositDaoImpl" />
<bean id="anotherDao"
          class="sample.spring.chapter02.bankapp.dao.FixedDepositDaoImpl" />
```

The bean definitions shown in the above example listing are for FixedDepositDaoImpl class. As scope attribute is *not* specified, bean definitions shown in the above example listing represent singleton-scoped beans. Even if multiple bean definitions are defined for a class, Spring container creates a bean instance corresponding to each bean definition. This means that Spring container creates distinct instances of FixedDepositDaoImpl class corresponding to dao and anotherDao bean definitions. The following example listing shows SingletonScope's testSingletonScopePerBeanDef method that tests whether the FixedDepositDaoImpl instances corresponding to dao and anotherDao bean definitions are same or different:

Example listing 2-26 – testSingletonScopePerBeanDef method of SingletonTest JUnit test class
Project – ch02-bankapp-scopes
Source location - src/test/java/sample/spring/chapter02/bankapp

```
package sample.spring.chapter02.bankapp;

import static org.junit.Assert.assertNotSame;

public class SingletonTest {
  private static ApplicationContext context;
  .....
  @Test
  public void testSingletonScopePerBeanDef() {
    FixedDepositDao fixedDepositDao1 = (FixedDepositDao) context.getBean("dao");
    FixedDepositDao fixedDepositDao2 = (FixedDepositDao) context.getBean("anotherDao");
    assertNotSame("Same FixedDepositDao instances", fixedDepositDao1, fixedDepositDao2);
  }
}
```

In the above example listing, fixedDepositDao1 and fixedDepositDao2 variables represent instances of FixedDepositDaoImpl class that Spring container creates corresponding to the dao and anotherDao bean definitions, respectively. If you execute the testSingleScopePerBeanDef test, it'll execute without any assertion errors because the fixedDepositDao1 instance (corresponding to dao bean definition) and fixedDepositDao2 instance (corresponding to anotherDao bean definition) are distinct.

The following figure summarizes that a singleton-scoped bean is created *per bean definition*:

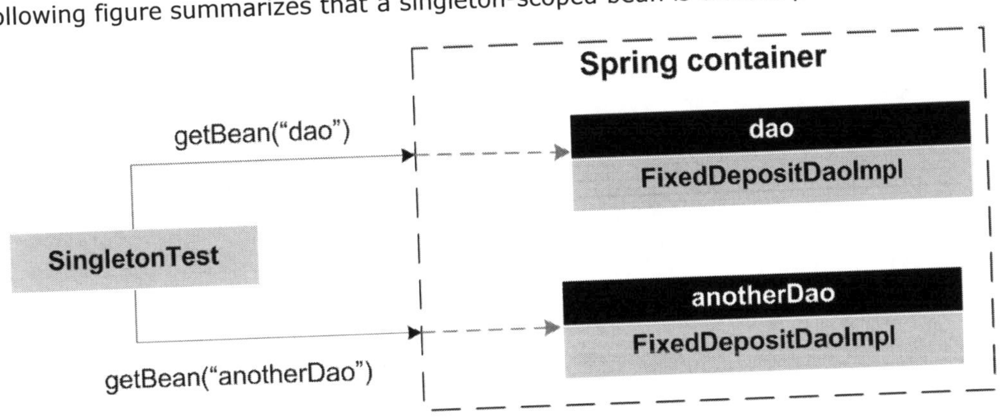

Figure 2-7 There is one singleton-scoped bean instance per bean definition

The above figure shows that there exists one instance of singleton-scoped bean *per bean definition* in the Spring container.

We mentioned earlier that a singleton-scoped bean is *pre-instantiated* by default, which means an instance of a singleton-scoped bean is created when you create an instance of the Spring container. Let's now look at how you can *lazily* initialize a singleton-scoped bean.

Lazily initializing a singleton-scoped bean

You can instruct Spring container to create an instance of a singleton-scoped bean only when it is requested for the *first* time. The following lazyExample bean definition shows how to instruct Spring container to lazy initialize lazyBean bean:

Example listing 2-27 – Lazily initializing a singleton-scoped bean

```
<bean id="lazyBean" class="example.LazyBean" lazy-init="true"/>
```

The <bean> element's lazy-init attribute specifies whether the bean instance is created lazily or eagerly. If the value is true (as in case of the bean definition shown above), the bean instance is initialized by the Spring container when it receives the request for the bean for the *first* time.

The following sequence diagram shows how lazy-init attribute affects the creation of a singleton-scoped bean instance:

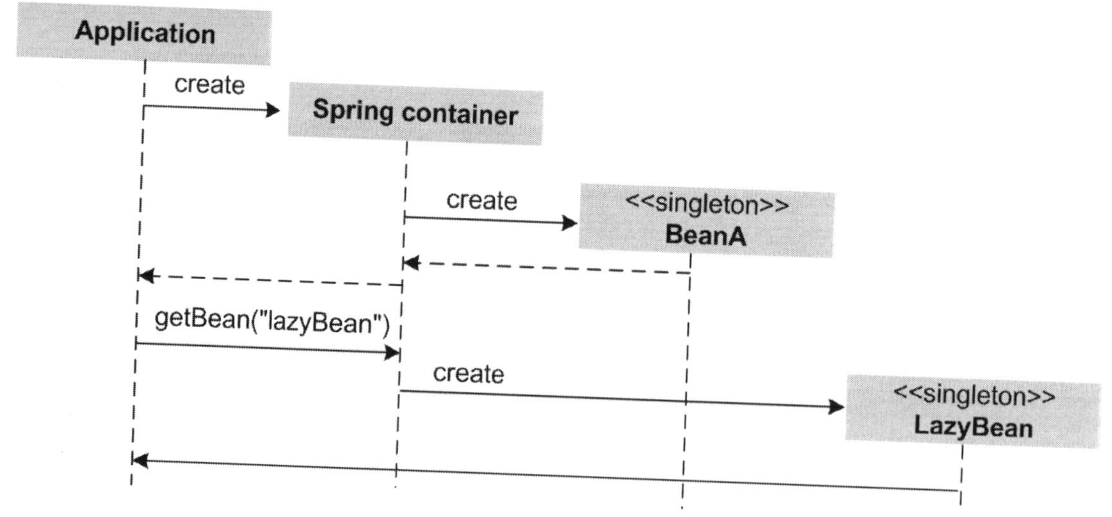

Figure 2-8 A lazily-initialized singleton-scoped bean instance is created when it is requested for the first time by the application

In the above diagram, BeanA represents a singleton-scoped bean instance that is *not* set to be lazily-initialized, and LazyBean represents a singleton-scoped bean that is set to be lazily-initialized. When the Spring container instance is created, BeanA is also instantiated because it is *not* set to be lazily-initialized. On the other hand, LazyBean is instantiated when

ApplicationContext's getBean method is invoked for the time first time to retrieve an instance of LazyBean from the Spring container.

> You can use <beans> element's default-lazy-init attribute to specify default initialization strategy for beans defines in the application context XML file. If the <bean> element's lazy-init attribute specifies a different value than the <beans> element's default-lazy-init, the value specified by the lazy-init attribute applies to the bean.

As a singleton-scoped bean can be lazily-initialized or pre-instantiated by the Spring container, you may be thinking at this time whether you should define your singleton-scoped beans to be lazily-initialized or pre-instantiated. In most application scenarios, it is beneficial to pre-instantiate singleton-scoped beans to discover configuration issues at the time of creation of the Spring container. The following example listing shows a aBean singleton-scoped bean that is set to be lazily-initialized, and that depends on bBean bean:

Example listing 2-28 – A lazily-initialized singleton-scoped bean

```
public class ABean {
   private BBean bBean;

   public void setBBean(BBean bBean) {
      this.bBean = bBean;
   }
   .....
}

<bean id="aBean" class="ABean" lazy-init="true">
   <property name="bBean" value="bBean" />
</bean>

<bean id="bBean" class="BBean" />
```

In the above example listing, ABean's bBean property refers to the BBean bean. Notice that instead of ref attribute, value attribute of <property> element has been used to set ABean's bBean property. If you create an ApplicationContext instance by passing it the XML file containing the above bean definition, no errors will be reported. But, when you try to fetch the aBean bean by invoking ApplicationContext's getBean method, you'll get the following error message:

```
Caused by: java.lang.IllegalStateException: Cannot convert value of type [java.lang.String] to required type [BBean] for property 'bBean: no matching editors or conversion strategy found
```

The above error message is shown because the Spring container fails to convert the *String* value of ABean's bBean property to BBean type. This highlights a simple configuration issue in which instead of specifying <bean> element's ref attribute, value attribute was specified. If the aBean bean was defined as pre-instantiated (instead of lazily-initialized), the above configuration issue could have been caught at the time we created an instance of ApplicationContext, and not when we tried to obtain an instance of aBean bean from the ApplicationContext.

Let's now look at *prototype-scoped* beans in Spring.

Prototype

A prototype-scoped bean is different from a singleton-scoped bean in the sense that the Spring container always returns a *new* instance of a prototype-scoped bean. Another distinctive feature of prototype-scoped beans is that they are *always* lazily-initialized.

The following FixedDepositDetails bean in the applicationContext.xml file of ch02-bankapp-scopes project represents a prototype-scoped bean:

Example listing 2-29 – applicationContext.xml - A prototype-scoped bean example
Project – ch02-bankapp-scopes
Source location - src/main/resources/META-INF/spring

```
<bean id="FixedDepositDetails"
    class="sample.spring.chapter02.bankapp.domain.FixedDepositDetails"
      scope="prototype" />
```

The above example listing shows that the <bean> element's scope attribute value is set to prototype. This means that the FixedDepositDetails bean is a prototype-scoped bean.

The following testInstances method of PrototypeTest JUnit test class shows that the 2 instances of FixedDepositDetails bean retrieved from the Spring container are different:

Example listing 2-30 – testInstances method of PrototypeTest JUnit test class
Project – ch02-bankapp-scopes
Source location - src/test/java/sample/spring/chapter02/bankapp

```
package sample.spring.chapter02.bankapp;

import static org.junit.Assert.assertNotSame;

public class PrototypeTest {
  private static ApplicationContext context;
  .....
  @Test
```

```
public void testInstances() {
    FixedDepositDetails fixedDepositDetails1 =
          (FixedDepositDetails)context.getBean("fixedDepositDetails");
    FixedDepositDetails fixedDepositDetails2 =
          (FixedDepositDetails) context.getBean("fixedDepositDetails");

    assertNotSame("Same FixedDepositDetails instances",
          fixedDepositDetails1, fixedDepositDetails2);
  }
}
```

If you execute the testInstances test, it'll complete without any assertion errors because the 2 FixedDepositDetails instances (fixedDepositDetails1 and fixedDepositDetails2) obtained from the ApplicationContext are different.

Let's now look at how to choose the right scope (singleton or prototype) for a bean.

Choosing the right scope for your beans

If a bean doesn't maintain any conversational state (that is, it is stateless in nature), it should be defined as a singleton-scoped bean. If a bean maintains conversational state, it should be defined as a prototype-scoped bean. FixedDepositServiceImpl, FixedDepositDaoImpl and FixedDepositControllerImpl beans of MyBank application are stateless in nature; therefore, they are defined as singleton-scoped beans. FixedDepositDetails bean (a *domain object*) of MyBank application maintains conversational state; therefore, it is defined as a prototype-scoped bean.

> If you are using an ORM framework (like Hibenate or iBATIS) in your application, the domain objects are created either by the ORM framework or you create them programmatically in your application code using the new operator. It is because of this reason domain objects are not defined in the application context XML file if the application uses an ORM framework for persistence.

2-6 Summary

In this chapter, we discussed some of the basics of Spring Framework. We looked at 'programming to interfaces' design approach, different approaches to create bean instances, constructor-based DI and bean scopes. In the next chapter, we'll look at how to set different types (like int, long, Map, Set, and so on) of bean properties and constructor arguments.

Chapter 3 - *Configuring beans*

3-1 Introduction

In previous chapters, we touched upon some of the basic concepts of Spring Framework. We saw how Spring beans and their dependencies are specified in the application context XML file. We also looked at singleton- and prototype-scoped beans, and discussed the implications of assigning these scopes to beans.

In this chapter, we'll look at:

- bean definition inheritance
- how arguments to a bean class's constructor are resolved
- how to configure bean properties and constructor arguments of primitive type (like `int`, `float`, and so on), collection type (like `java.util.List`, `java.util.Map`, and so on), custom type (like `Address`), and so on
- how you can make the application context XML file less verbose by using p-namespace and c-namespace to specify bean properties and constructor arguments, respectively
- Spring's `FactoryBean` interface that allows you to write your own factory class for creating bean instances

3-2 Bean definition inheritance

We saw in chapter 1 and 2 that a bean definition in the application context XML file specifies the fully-qualified name of the bean class and its dependencies. In some scenarios, to make a bean definition less verbose, you may want a bean definition to *inherit* configuration information from another bean definition. Let's look at one such scenario in MyBank application.

IMPORT **chapter 3/ch03-bankapp-inheritance** (This project shows the MyBank application that uses *bean definition inheritance*. To run the application, execute the `main` method of the `BankApp` class of this project)

MyBank – Bean definition inheritance example

In the previous chapter, we saw that the MyBank application accesses database through DAOs. Let's say that the MyBank application defines a `DatabaseOperations` class that simplifies interacting with the database. So, all the DAOs in the MyBank application depend on `DatabaseOperations` class to perform database operations, as shown in the following figure:

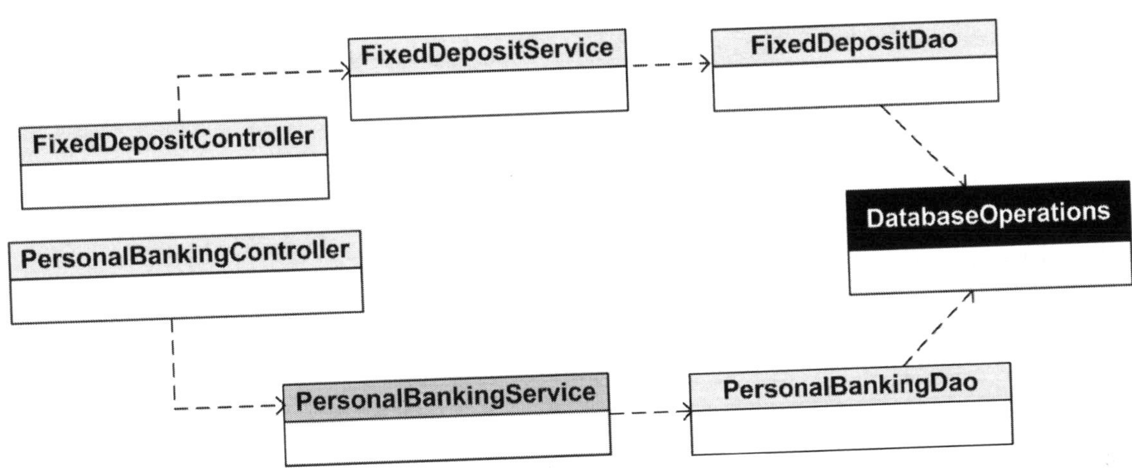

Figure 3-1 - DAO classes in MyBank application make use of DatabaseOperations class to perform database interaction

The above figure shows that the FixedDepositDao and PersonalBankingDao classes are dependent on the DatabaseOperations class. The following application context XML file shows the bean definitions for these classes:

Example listing 3-1 – DAO beans are dependent on DatabaseOperations bean

```
<bean id="databaseOperations"
   class="sample.spring.chapter01.bankapp.utils.DatabaseOperations" />

<bean id="personalBankingDao"
   class="sample.spring.chapter01.bankapp.dao.PersonalBankingDaoImpl">
      <property name="databaseOperations" ref="databaseOperations" />
</bean>

<bean id="FixedDepositDao"
   class="sample.spring.chapter01.bankapp.dao.FixedDepositDaoImpl">
      <property name="databaseOperations" ref="databaseOperations" />
</bean>
```

Both the personalBankingDao and FixedDepositDao bean definitions use the <property> element to perform dependency injection of the DatabaseOperations instance. As the name of the property that refers to the DatabaseOperations instance is databaseOperations in both the bean definitions, it implies that both PersonalBankingDaoImpl and FixedDepositDaoImpl classes define a setDatabaseOperations method to allow Spring container to inject DatabaseOperations instance.

If multiple beans in your application share a common set of configuration (properties, constructor arguments, and so on), you can create a bean definition that acts as a parent for other bean definitions. In case of personalBankingDao and fixedDepositDao bean definitions, the common configuration is the databaseOperations property. The following example listing shows that the personalBankingDao and fixedDepositDao bean definitions make use of bean definition inheritance:

Example listing 3-2 – applicationContext.xml - MyBank's application context XML file
Project – ch03-bankapp-inheritance
Source location - src/main/resources/META-INF/spring

```
<bean id="databaseOperations"
   class="sample.spring.chapter03.bankapp.utils.DatabaseOperations" />

<bean id="daoTemplate" abstract="true">
    <property name="databaseOperations" ref="databaseOperations" />
</bean>

<bean id="FixedDepositDao" parent="daoTemplate"
   class="sample.spring.chapter03.bankapp.dao.FixedDepositDaoImpl" />

<bean id="personalBankingDao" parent="daoTemplate"
   class="sample.spring.chapter03.bankapp.dao.PersonalBankingDaoImpl" />
```

In the above example listing, the daoTemplate bean definition defines the common configuration shared by both the fixedDepositDao and personalBankingDao bean definitions. As both the fixedDepositDao and personalBankingDao bean definitions require the databaseOperations dependency (refer example listing 3-1), the daoTemplate bean definition defines the databaseOperations dependency using the <property> element. The <bean> element's parent attribute specifies the name of the bean definition from which the configuration is inherited. As the parent attribute value is daoTemplate for fixedDepositDao and personalBankingDao bean definitions, they inherit databaseOperations property from the daoTemplate bean definition. The example listings 3-1 and 3-2 are same, except that the example listing 3-2 makes use of bean definition inheritance.

If the <bean> element's abstract attribute value is set to true, it means that the bean definition is *abstract*. It is important to note that the Spring container *doesn't* attempt to create a bean corresponding to an *abstract* bean definition. It is important to note that you can't define a bean to be dependent on an *abstract* bean, that is, you can't use <property> or <constructor-arg> element to refer to an *abstract* bean.

In example listing 3-2, daoTemplate bean definition is *abstract*. You may have noticed that the daoTemplate bean definition doesn't specify the class attribute. If a parent bean definition doesn't specify the class attribute, child bean definitions (like the fixedDepositDao and personalBankingDao) specify the class attribute. It is important to note that if you don't specify the class attribute, you must define the parent bean definition as *abstract* so that Spring container doesn't attempt to create a bean instance corresponding to it.

To verify that the fixedDepositDao and personalBankingDao bean definitions inherit daoTemplate bean definition's databaseOperations property, execute the main method of BankApp class of ch03-bankapp-inheritance project. BankApp's main method invokes methods on the fixedDepositDao and personalBankingDao beans; those beans in turn invoke methods on the DatabaseOperations instance. If a DatabaseOperations instance is *not* injected into the fixedDepositDao and personalBankingDao beans, java.lang.NullPointerException will be thrown.

The following diagram summarizes how bean definition inheritance works in case of FixedDepositDao and personalBankingDao bean definitions:

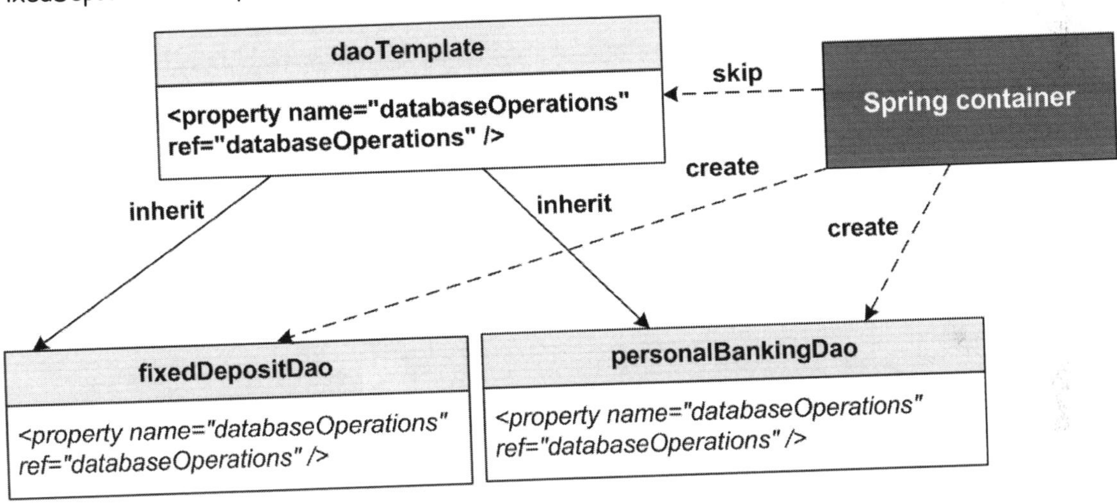

Figure 3-2 – Bean definition inheritance in MyBank application

The above figure shows that the fixedDepositDao and personalBankingDao bean definitions inherit the databaseOperations property (shown in *italics* in the boxes labeled fixedDepositDao and personalBankingDao) from the daoTemplate bean definition. The above figure also depicts that the Spring container doesn't attempt to create a bean instance corresponding to the daoTemplate bean definition because it is marked as *abstract*.

Let's now look at what configuration information gets inherited from the parent bean definition.

What gets inherited ?

A child bean definition inherits the following configuration information from the parent bean definition:

- properties – specified via <property> elements

- constructor arguments – specified via <constructor-arg> elements
- method overrides (discussed in section 4-5 of chapter 4)
- initialization and destroy methods (discussed in chapter 5), and
- factory methods – specified via factory-method attribute of <bean> element (refer section 2-3 of chapter 2 to know how *static* and *instance* factory methods are used for creating beans)

IMPORT **chapter 3/ch03-bankapp-inheritance-example** (This project shows the MyBank application that uses bean definition inheritance. In this project, you'll see multiple scenarios in which bean definition inheritance is used. To run the application, execute the main method of the BankApp class of this project)

Let's now look at some of the bean definition inheritance examples.

Bean definition inheritance example – parent bean definition is *not* abstract

The following example listing shows a bean inheritance example in which the parent bean definition is *not* abstract, and the child bean definitions define an additional dependency:

Example listing 3-3 – applicationContext.xml - Bean definition inheritance – parent bean definition is *not* abstract
Project – ch03-bankapp-inheritance-examples
Source location - src/main/resources/META-INF/spring

```
<bean id="serviceTemplate"
      class="sample.spring.chapter03.bankapp.base.ServiceTemplate">
   <property name="jmsMessageSender" ref="jmsMessageSender" />
   <property name="emailMessageSender" ref="emailMessageSender" />
   <property name="webServiceInvoker" ref="webServiceInvoker" />
</bean>

<bean id="fixedDepositService" class=".....FixedDepositServiceImpl"
      parent="serviceTemplate">
   <property name="fixedDepositDao" ref="fixedDepositDao" />
</bean>

<bean id="personalBankingService" class=".....PersonalBankingServiceImpl"
      parent="serviceTemplate">
   <property name="personalBankingDao" ref="personalBankingDao" />
</bean>

<bean id="userRequestController" class=".....UserRequestControllerImpl">
   <property name="serviceTemplate" ref="serviceTemplate" />
```

```
</bean>
```

A little background before we delve into the details of the above listed configuration: a service in the MyBank application may send JMS messages to a messaging-middleware or send emails to an email server or it may invoke an external web service. In the above example listing, the jmsMessageSender, emailMessageSender and webServiceInvoker beans simplify these tasks by providing a layer of abstraction. The serviceTemplate bean provides access to jmsMessageSender, emailMessageSender and webServiceInvoker beans. This is the reason why the serviceTemplate bean is dependent on the jmsMessageSender, emailMessageSender and webServiceInvoker beans.

Example listing 3-3 shows that the serviceTemplate bean definition is the parent bean definition of fixedDepositService and personalBankingService bean definitions. Notice that the serviceTemplate bean definition is not *abstract*; the class attribute specifies ServiceTemplate as the class. In our previous bean definition inheritance example (refer example listing 3-2), child bean definitions didn't define any properties. In the above example listing, notice that the fixedDepositService and personalBankingService child bean definitions define fixedDepositDao and personalBankingDao properties, respectively.

As parent bean definition's properties are inherited by the child bean definitions, FixedDepositServiceImpl and PersonalBankingServiceImpl classes *must* define setter methods for jmsMessageSender, emailMessageSender and webServiceInvoker properties. You have the option to either define setter methods in FixedDepositServiceImpl and PersonalBankingServiceImpl classes or make FixedDepositServiceImpl and PersonalBankingServiceImpl classes as subclasses of ServiceTemplate class. In ch03-bankapp-inheritance-examples, the FixedDepositServiceImpl and PersonalBankingServiceImpl classes are subclasses of ServiceTemplate class.

The following example listing shows the PersonalBankingServiceImpl class:

Example listing 3-4 – PersonalBankingServiceImpl class
Project – ch03-bankapp-inheritance-examples
Source location - src/main/java/sample/spring/chapter03/bankapp/service

```
package sample.spring.chapter03.bankapp.service;

public class PersonalBankingServiceImpl extends ServiceTemplate implements
        PersonalBankingService {

  private PersonalBankingDao personalBankingDao;

  public void setPersonalBankingDao(PersonalBankingDao personalBankingDao) {
    this.personalBankingDao = personalBankingDao;
  }
```

```
    @Override
    public BankStatement getMiniStatement() {
        return personalBankingDao.getMiniStatement();
    }
}
```

In example listing 3-3, we saw that the personalBankingService bean definition specifies personalBankingDao as a dependency. In the above example listing, the setPersonalBankingDao setter method corresponds to the personalBankingDao dependency. Also, notice that the PersonalBankingServiceImpl class is a subclass of the ServiceTemplate class.

The following diagram shows that a parent bean definition (like serviceTemplate) need not be *abstract*, child bean definitions (like fixedDepositService and personalBankingService) may define additional properties, and classes represented by parent (like ServiceTemplate class) and child bean definitions (like FixedDepositServiceImpl and PersonalBankingServiceImpl) may themselves be related by inheritance:

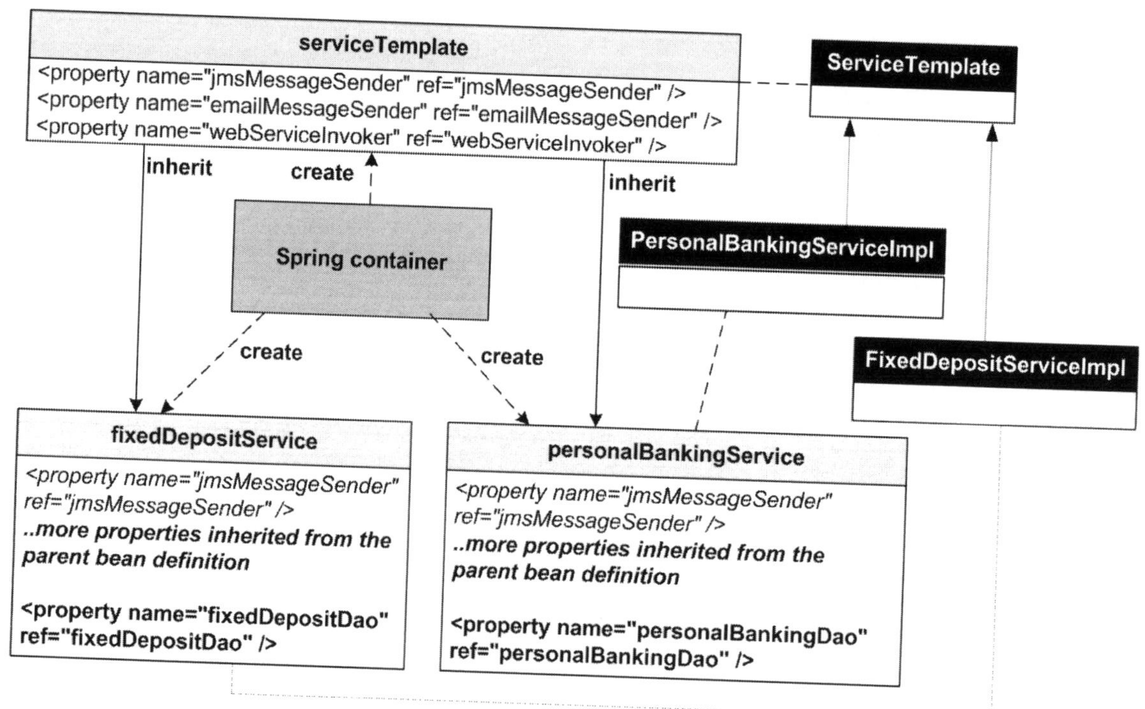

Figure 3-3 – Child bean definitions add additional properties, parent bean definition is *not* abstract, and parent-child relationship exists between the classes represented by the parent and child bean definitions

Figure 3-3 shows:

- Spring container creates an instance of serviceTemplate bean because it's *not* defined as abstract
- FixedDepositServiceImpl and PersonalBankingServiceImpl classes (corresponding to the child bean definitions) are subclasses of ServiceTemplate class – the class corresponding to the serviceTemplate parent bean definition.
- And, fixedDepositService and personalBankingService bean definitions define additional properties, fixedDepositDao and personalBankingDao, respectively. You should note that the child bean definitions can also define additional constructor arguments and *method overrides* (discussed in section 4-5).

As serviceTemplate bean definition is *not* abstract, other beans can define serviceTemplate bean as their dependency. For instance, in example listing 3-3, the serviceTemplate bean is a dependency of userRequestController bean. You can infer from this discussion that if a parent bean definition is not abstract, the functionality offered by the parent bean can be utilized not only by child beans but also by other beans in the application context.

Bean definition inheritance example – inheriting factory method configuration

Child bean definitions can use bean definition inheritance to inherit factory method configuration from the parent bean definition. Let's look at an example that shows factory method configurations are inherited by child bean definitions.

The following ControllerFactory class defines a getController *instance* factory method:

Example listing 3-5 – ControllerFactory class
Project – ch03-bankapp-inheritance-examples
Source location - src/main/java/sample/spring/chapter03/bankapp/controller

```
package sample.spring.chapter03.bankapp.controller;

public class ControllerFactory {

  public Object getController(String controllerName) {
    Object controller = null;
    if ("fixedDepositController".equalsIgnoreCase(controllerName)) {
      controller = new FixedDepositControllerImpl();
    }
    if ("personalBankingController".equalsIgnoreCase(controllerName)) {
      controller = new PersonalBankingControllerImpl();
    }
```

```
        return controller;
    }
}
```

The above example listing shows that the getController factory method creates an instance of FixedDepositControllerImpl or PersonalBankingControllerImpl class, depending upon the value of the controllerName argument passed to it. If the value of controllerName argument is fixedDepositController, the getController method creates an instance of FixedDepositControllerImpl class. And, if the value of controllerName argument is personalBankingController, the getController method creates an instance of PersonalBankingControllerImpl class.

The following bean definitions in the applicationContext.xml file of ch03-bankapp-inheritance-example project show that the child bean definitions inherit the getController *instance* factory method configuration from the parent bean definition:

Example listing 3-6 – applicationContext.xml - Bean definition inheritance – inheriting the factory method configuration
Project – ch03-bankapp-inheritance-examples
Source location - src/main/resources/META-INF/spring

```
<bean id="controllerFactory"
    class="sample.spring.chapter03.bankapp.controller.ControllerFactory" />

<bean id="controllerTemplate" factory-bean="controllerFactory"
    factory-method="getController" abstract="true">
</bean>

<bean id="fixedDepositController" parent="controllerTemplate">
  <constructor-arg index="0" value="fixedDepositController" />
  <property name="fixedDepositService" ref="fixedDepositService" />
</bean>

<bean id="personalBankingController" parent="controllerTemplate">
  <constructor-arg index="0" value="personalBankingController" />
  <property name="personalBankingService" ref="personalBankingService" />
</bean>
```

In the above example listing, the ControllerFactory class represents a factory class that defines a getController *instance* factory method. The controllerTemplate bean definition specifies that the ControllerFactory's getController factory method is used for creating bean instances. The getController method (refer example listing 3-5) creates an instance of FixedDepositControllerImpl or PersonalBankingControllerImpl bean, depending on the argument passed to the getController method.

As the controllerTemplate bean definition has been defined as *abstract*, it is up to the fixedDepositController and personalBankingController child bean definitions to use the getController factory method configuration. The fixedDepositController bean definition would like to pass an argument to the ControllerFactory's getController factory method so that it creates an instance of FixedDepositControllerImpl bean. And, personalBankingController bean definition would like to pass an argument to the ControllerFactory's getController factory method so that it creates an instance of PersonalBankingControllerImpl bean. We saw in section 2-3 of chapter 2 that the <constructor-arg> element is used to pass an argument to an *instance* factory method. In example listing 3-6, the <constructor-arg> element has been used by fixedDepositController and personalBankingController child bean definitions to pass 'fixedDepositService' and 'personalBankingService' values, respectively, to the getController factory method.

It is recommended that you now run the main method of BankApp class of ch03-bankapp-inheritance-examples project to see usage of the bean definition inheritance examples discussed in this section.

Let's now look at how constructor arguments are matched.

3-3 Constructor argument matching

In the previous chapter, we saw that the constructor arguments are specified in the bean definitions using the <constructor-arg> element. In this section, we'll look at how Spring container matches a constructor argument specified by a <constructor-arg> element to the corresponding constructor argument specified in the bean class's constructor.

Before we go into the details of constructor argument matching, let's look back at how we pass arguments to a bean class's constructor.

IMPORT chapter 3/ch03-bankapp-constructor-args-by-type (This project shows the MyBank application in which bean class's constructor arguments are matched *by type* (explained later in this section). To run the application, execute the main method of the BankApp class of this project)

Passing simple values and bean references using <constructor-arg> element

If a constructor argument is of simple Java type (like int, String, and so on), the <constructor-arg> element's value attribute is used to specify the value of the constructor argument. If a constructor argument is a reference to a bean, you specify the name of the bean using the <constructor-arg> element's ref attribute.

The following example listing shows the UserRequestControllerImpl class of ch03-bankapp-constructor-args-by-type project whose constructor accepts an argument of type ServiceTemplate:

Example listing 3-7 – UserRequestControllerImpl class
Project – ch03-bankapp-constructor-args-by-type
Source location - src/main/java/sample/spring/chapter03/bankapp/controller

```
package sample.spring.chapter03.bankapp.controller;

public class UserRequestControllerImpl implements UserRequestController {
  private ServiceTemplate serviceTemplate;

  public UserRequestControllerImpl(ServiceTemplate serviceTemplate) {
    this.serviceTemplate = serviceTemplate;
  }

  @Override
  public void submitRequest(Request request) {
    //-- do something using ServiceTemplate
    serviceTemplate.getJmsMessageSender(); //-- For ex., send JMS message
    .....
  }
}
```

The following example listing shows that a reference to ServiceTemplate instance (represented by serviceTemplate bean definition) is passed to UserRequestControllerImpl's constructor using ref attribute of <constructor-arg> element:

Example listing 3-8 – applicationContext.xml - Passing reference to a Spring bean as constructor argument
Project – ch03-bankapp-constructor-args-by-type
Source location - src/main/resources/META-INF/spring

```
<bean id="serviceTemplate" class="sample.spring.chapter03.bankapp.base.ServiceTemplate">
  .....
</bean>

<bean id="userRequestController"
    class="sample.spring.chapter03.bankapp.controller.UserRequestControllerImpl">
  <constructor-arg index="0" ref="serviceTemplate" />
</bean>
```

With this background information on how to pass simple values and bean references as constructor arguments, let's now look at how Spring container matches constructor argument *types* to locate the bean's constructor to be invoked.

Constructor argument matching based on type

If the <constructor-arg> element's index attribute is *not* specified, Spring container locates the constructor to be invoked by matching the types referenced by the <constructor-arg> elements with the argument types specified in the bean class's constructor(s).

Let's first look at how Spring container matches constructor arguments when the constructor arguments are Spring beans that are *not* related by inheritance.

Constructor arguments representing distinct Spring beans

The following example listing shows the ServiceTemplate class that defines a constructor that accepts references to JmsMessageSender, EmailMessageSender and WebServiceInvoker beans:

Example listing 3-9 – ServiceTemplate class
Project – ch03-bankapp-constructor-args-by-type
Source location - src/main/java/sample/spring/chapter03/bankapp/base

```
package sample.spring.chapter03.bankapp.base;

public class ServiceTemplate {
   .....
   public ServiceTemplate(JmsMessageSender jmsMessageSender,
        EmailMessageSender emailMessageSender,
        WebServiceInvoker webServiceInvoker) {
     .....
   }
}
```

The following example listing shows the bean definitions for the ServiceTemplate class and the beans referenced by ServiceTemplate:

Example listing 3-10 – applicationContext.xml - Bean definition for the ServiceTemplate class and its dependencies
Project – ch03-bankapp-constructor-args-by-type
Source location - src/main/resources/META-INF/spring

```
<bean id="serviceTemplate" class="sample.spring.chapter03.bankapp.base.ServiceTemplate">
   <constructor-arg ref="emailMessageSender" />
   <constructor-arg ref="jmsMessageSender" />
   <constructor-arg ref="webServiceInvoker" />
</bean>

<bean id="jmsMessageSender" class="sample.spring.chapter03.bankapp.base.JmsMessageSender" />
<bean id="emailMessageSender" class="sample.spring.chapter03.bankapp.base.EmailMessageSender" />
```

```
<bean id="webServiceInvoker" class="sample.spring.chapter03.bankapp.base.WebServiceInvoker" />
```

In the above example listing, the <constructor-arg> elements of serviceTemplate bean *don't* specify the index attribute. The order in which the constructor arguments are specified by the <constructor-arg> elements is: EmailMessageSender, JmsMessageSender, WebServiceInvoker. The order in which constructor arguments are specified in the ServiceTemplate class's constructor is: JmsMessageSender, EmailMessageSender, WebServiceInvoker. As you can see, the order in which constructor arguments are defined by the <constructor-arg> elements is different from the order specified by the ServiceTemplate class's constructor.

If you execute the main method of BankApp class of ch03-bankapp-constructor-args-by-type project, you'll find that the Spring container successfully creates an instance of ServiceTemplate bean. This is because JmsMessageSender, EmailMessageSender and WebServiceInvoker classes are distinct in nature (that is, they are not related by inheritance), which makes it easier for the Spring container to inject their instances into the ServiceTemplate class's constructor in the correct order.

If the constructor argument types are related by inheritance, Spring container needs extra instructions to help resolve constructor arguments. Let's now look at how Spring container matches constructor arguments when beans referenced by the constructor arguments are related by inheritance.

Constructor arguments representing related Spring beans

Consider the following SampleBean bean class whose constructor accepts argument types that are related by inheritance:

Example listing 3-11 – SampleBean class

```
public class SampleBean {
   public SampleBean(ABean aBean, BBean bBean) { ..... }
   .....
}
```

The above example listing shows that the SampleBean class's constructor accepts ABean and BBean types as arguments. ABean and BBean represent Spring beans that are related by inheritance; BBean is a subclass of ABean.

The following application context XML file shows the bean definitions for SampleBean, ABean and BBean classes:

Example listing 3-12 – Bean definitions for SampleBean, ABean and BBean classes

```
<bean id="aBean" class="example.ABean"/>
<bean id="bBean" class="example.BBean"/>

<bean id="sampleBean" class="example.SampleBean">
   <constructor-arg ref="bBean"/>
   <constructor-arg ref="aBean"/>
</bean>
```

As aBean and bBean beans are related by inheritance, Spring container applies constructor arguments to the SampleBean's constructor in the order in which <constructor-arg> elements appear in the bean definition for the SampleBean class. In the above sampleBean bean definition, the first <constructor-arg> element refers to bBean bean and the second <constructor-arg> element refers to aBean bean. This means that bBean is passed as the first constructor argument and aBean is passed as the second constructor argument to the SampleBean constructor. As instance of ABean (the superclass) can't be passed where BBean (the subclass) instance is expected, the second <constructor-arg> element in the sampleBean bean definition results in exception being thrown by the Spring container. To handle such scenarios, you can use <constructor-arg> element's index or type attribute to identify the constructor argument to which <constructor-arg> element applies. For instance, the following sampleBean bean definition makes use of type attribute to indicate the type of the constructor argument to which the <constructor-arg> element applies:

Example listing 3-13 – <constructor-arg> element's type attribute identifies the type of the constructor argument

```
<bean id="sampleBean" class="example.SampleBean">
   <constructor-arg type="sample.spring.chapter03.bankapp.controller.BBean" ref="bBean"/>
   <constructor-arg type="sample.spring.chapter03.bankapp.controller.ABean" ref="aBean"/>
</bean>
```

The <constructor-arg> element's type attribute specifies the fully-qualified name of the type to which the <constructor-arg> element applies. In the above example listing, the first <constructor-arg> applies to the constructor argument of type BBean, and the second <constructor-arg> element applies to the constructor argument of type ABean. Specifying the type attribute takes away the ambiguity that arises when constructor arguments are related by inheritance.

> If two or more constructor arguments are of the same type, the only option is to use index attribute to identify the constructor argument to which each <constructor-arg> element applies.

So far we have looked at constructor argument type matching scenarios in which constructor arguments represented distinct or related Spring beans. We'll now look at how constructor argument types are matched for standard Java types (like int, long, boolean, String, Date, and so on) and custom types.

Constructor arguments representing standard Java types and custom types

If the type of a constructor argument is a primitive type (like int, long, boolean, and so on) or a String type or a custom type (like Address), the <constructor-arg> element's value attribute is used to specify the value. If there are 2 or more constructor arguments into which the string value specified by the value attribute can be converted, it'll not be possible for the Spring container to derive the type (for example, whether the value represents an int or long or String) of the constructor argument. In such scenarios, you need to explicitly specify the type of the constructor argument using the type attribute.

The following example listing shows the TransferFundsServiceImpl class that defines a constructor which accepts arguments of types String, boolean, long and int:

Example listing 3-14 – TransferFundsServiceImpl class
Project – ch03-bankapp-constructor-args-by-type
Source location - src/main/java/sample/spring/chapter03/bankapp/service

```
package sample.spring.chapter03.bankapp.service;

public class TransferFundsServiceImpl implements TransferFundsService {
    public TransferFundsServiceImpl(String webServiceUrl, boolean active, long timeout,
        int numberOfRetrialAttempts) {.....}
    .....
}
```

As the above example listing shows, TransferFundsServiceImpl constructor accepts the following arguments: webServiceUrl, active, timeout and numberOfRetrialAttempts. The following bean definition for the TransferFundsServiceImpl class shows how constructor argument values can be passed to the TransferFundsServiceImpl's constructor:

Example listing 3-15 – Bean definition for the TransferFundsServiceImpl class

```
<bean id="transferFundsService"
    class="sample.spring.chapter03.bankapp.service.TransferFundsServiceImpl">
    <constructor-arg value="http://someUrl.com/xyz" />
    <constructor-arg value="true" />
    <constructor-arg value="5" />
    <constructor-arg value="200" />
</bean>
```

Let's assume that the 3rd <constructor-arg> element (value attribute's value is '5') is supposed to supply value for the numberOfRetrialAttempts constructor argument, and the 4th <constructor-arg> element (value attribute's value is '200') is supposed to supply value for the timeout constructor argument. Spring container applies <constructor-arg> elements to the TransferFundsServiceImpl's constructor in the order in which <constructor-arg> elements appear in the transferFundsService bean definition. This means that the 3rd <constructor-arg> element applies to timeout argument, and the 4th <constructor-arg> element applies to numberOfRetrialAttempts argument. To handle such ambiguities, you can specify the *type* of a constructor argument via <constructor-arg> element's type attribute, as shown in the following example listing:

Example listing 3-16 – applicationContext.xml - <constructor-arg> element's type attribute
Project – ch03-bankapp-constructor-args-by-type
Source location - src/main/resources/META-INF/spring

```
<bean id="transferFundsService"
   class="sample.spring.chapter03.bankapp.service.TransferFundsServiceImpl">
   <constructor-arg type="java.lang.String" value="http://someUrl.com/xyz" />
   <constructor-arg type="boolean" value="true" />
   <constructor-arg type="int" value="5" />
   <constructor-arg type="long" value="200" />
</bean>
```

In the above bean definition for the TransferFundsServiceImpl class, type attribute is used to specify the constructor argument type. Spring container can now use type matching to correctly apply constructor arguments.

> If two or more constructor arguments are of the same type, the only option is to use index attribute for identifying the constructor argument to which each <constructor-arg> element applies.

In this section, we saw how type matching is performed by Spring to resolve constructor arguments. Let's now look at how you can instruct Spring to perform constructor argument matching based on constructor argument's name.

IMPORT **chapter 3/ch03-bankapp-constructor-args-by-name** (This project shows the MyBank application in which bean class's constructor arguments are matched *by name*. To run the application, execute the main method of the BankApp class of this project)

Constructor argument matching based on name

The <constructor-arg> element's name attribute is used for specifying the name of the constructor argument to which the <constructor-arg> element applies. The following example listing shows once again the TransferFundsServiceImpl class whose constructor accepts multiple arguments:

Example listing 3-17 – TransferFundsServiceImpl class
Project – ch03-bankapp-constructor-args-by-name
Source location - src/main/java/sample/spring/chapter03/bankapp/service

```
package sample.spring.chapter03.bankapp.service;

public class TransferFundsServiceImpl implements TransferFundsService {
  .....
  public TransferFundsServiceImpl(String webServiceUrl, boolean active, long timeout,
      int numberOfRetrialAttempts) { ..... }
}
```

The above example listing shows that the names of the constructor arguments defined by TransferFundsServiceImpl's constructor are: webServiceUrl, active, timeout and numberOfRetrialAttempts.

> The TransferFundsServiceImpl class's constructor accepts arguments that are simple Java types (like, int, long, boolean, String, and so on), but the concept explained in this section also applies to scenarios in which constructor arguments are references to Spring beans.

The following bean definition for the TransferFundsServiceImpl class uses <constructor-arg> element's name attribute to specify the name of the constructor argument to which the <constructor-arg> element applies:

Example listing 3-18 – applicationContext.xml - <constructor-arg> element's name attribute
Project – ch03-bankapp-constructor-args-by-name
Source location - src/main/resources/META-INF/spring

```
<bean id="transferFundsService"
   class="sample.spring.chapter03.bankapp.service.TransferFundsServiceImpl">

   <constructor-arg name="webServiceUrl" value="http://someUrl.com/xyz" />
   <constructor-arg name="active" value="true" />
   <constructor-arg name="numberOfRetrialAttempts" value="5" />
   <constructor-arg name="timeout" value="200" />
</bean>
```

The above configuration will work only if TransferFundsServiceImpl class is compiled with *debug flag* enabled (refer to -g option of javac). When the debug flag is enabled, names of constructor arguments are preserved in the generated .class file. If you don't compile your classes with debug flag enabled, the constructor argument names are lost during compilation, and Spring has no way to locate the constructor argument corresponding to the constructor argument name specified by the <constructor-arg> element's name attribute.

If you don't want to compile your classes using debug flag enabled, you can use @ConstructorProperties annotation (introduced in Java SE 6) to clearly spell out names of the constructor arguments, as shown here for TransferFundsServiceImpl class:

Example listing 3-19 – @ConstructorProperties annotation
Project – ch03-bankapp-constructor-args-by-name
Source location - src/main/java/sample/spring/chapter03/bankapp/service

```
package sample.spring.chapter03.bankapp.service;

import java.beans.ConstructorProperties;

public class TransferFundsServiceImpl implements TransferFundsService {

    @ConstructorProperties({"webServiceUrl","active","timeout","numberOfRetrialAttempts"})
    public TransferFundsServiceImpl(String webServiceUrl, boolean active, long timeout,
          int numberOfRetrialAttempts) { ..... }
}
```

In the above example listing, @ConstructorProperties annotation specifies the names of constructor arguments in the order in which they appear in the bean class's constructor. You *must* ensure that you use the same constructor argument names in the <constructor-arg> elements.

Let's now look at how the @ConstructorProperties annotation affects bean definition inheritance.

@ConstructorProperties annotation and bean definition inheritance

If the constructor of the class corresponding to the *parent* bean definition is annotated with @ConstructorProperties annotation, the bean class corresponding to the *child* bean definition *must* also be annotated with @ConstructorProperties annotation.

The following example listing shows the serviceTemplate (parent bean definition) and FixedDepositService (child bean definition) bean definitions:

Example listing 3-20 – applicationContext.xml - Parent and child bean definitions
Project – ch03-bankapp-constructor-args-by-name
Source location - src/main/resources/META-INF/spring

```
<bean id="serviceTemplate"
    class="sample.spring.chapter03.bankapp.base.ServiceTemplate">
        <constructor-arg name="emailMessageSender" ref="emailMessageSender" />
        <constructor-arg name="jmsMessageSender" ref="jmsMessageSender" />
        <constructor-arg name="webServiceInvoker" ref="webServiceInvoker" />
</bean>

<bean id="FixedDepositService"
    class="sample.spring.chapter03.bankapp.service.FixedDepositServiceImpl"
    parent="serviceTemplate">
        <property name="fixedDepositDao" ref="FixedDepositDao" />
</bean>
```

The above example listing shows that the serviceTemplate bean definition is *not* abstract, which means that the Spring container will create an instance of serviceTemplate bean. The serviceTemplate bean definition specifies 3 <constructor-arg> elements, corresponding to the 3 arguments defined by the ServiceTemplate class (refer example listing 3-21). As we have specified constructor arguments *by name* in the serviceTemplate bean definition, the ServiceTemplate class's constructor is annotated with the @ConstructorProperties annotation to ensure that constructor argument names are available to Spring at runtime, as shown here:

Example listing 3-21 – ServiceTemplate class
Project – ch03-bankapp-constructor-args-by-name
Source location - src/main/java/sample/spring/chapter03/bankapp/base

```
package sample.spring.chapter03.bankapp.base;

import java.beans.ConstructorProperties;

public class ServiceTemplate {
   .....
   @ConstructorProperties({"jmsMessageSender","emailMessageSender","webServiceInvoker"})
   public ServiceTemplate(JmsMessageSender jmsMessageSender,
         EmailMessageSender emailMessageSender,
         WebServiceInvoker webServiceInvoker) { ..... }
}
```

As FixedDepositService is a child bean definition of serviceTemplate, the <constructor-arg> configuration in serviceTemplate bean definition is inherited by the FixedDepositService bean definition. This means that the FixedDepositServiceImpl class *must* define a constructor that accepts the same set of arguments as defined by the ServiceTemplate class, and it *must* also be annotated with @ConstructorProperties annotation. If you don't annotate FixedDepositServiceImpl's constructor with @ConstructorProperties annotation, Spring container will *not* be able to match the inherited <constructor-arg> elements with the constructor arguments specified in the FixedDepositServiceImpl's constructor.

You can't use @ConstructorProperties annotation for passing arguments by name to a *static* or *instance* factory method, as explained next.

@ConstructorProperties annotation and factory methods

We saw in section 2-3 of chapter 2 that the <constructor-arg> elements are also used for passing arguments to *static* and *instance* factory methods. You might think that you can pass arguments by name to *static* and *instance* factory methods by specifying the <constructor-arg> element's name attribute and annotating the factory method with @ConstructorProperties annotation. You should note that @ConstructorProperties annotation is meant *only* for constructors; you can't annotate methods with @ConstructorProperties annotation. So, if you want to pass arguments by name to a *static* or *instance* factory method, the only option you have is to compile classes with debug flag enabled.

> If you compile classes with debug flag enabled, it results in .class files that are larger in size, but has no impact on the runtime performance of the application. It only results in increased loading time for the classes.

Let's now look at how to enable or disable debug flag in Eclipse IDE.

Enabling (or disabling) the debug flag in Eclipse IDE

In Eclipse IDE, follow these steps to enable the debug flag for projects:

1. Go to Windows → Preferences and select the option Java → Compiler
2. You'll now see a section titled 'Classfile Generation'. In this section, if you check the checkbox labeled *'Add variable attributes to generated class files (used by the debugger)'*, the debug flag is *enabled*. Unchecking this checkbox will *disable* the debug flag.

So far we have mostly seen bean definition examples in which bean properties and constructor arguments were references to other beans. We'll now look at bean definition examples in which bean properties and constructor arguments are of primitive type, collection type, java.util.Date, java.util.Properties, and so on.

3-4 Configuring different types of bean properties and constructor arguments

In real world application development scenarios, properties and constructor arguments of a Spring bean could range from a String type to reference to another bean to any other standard (like java.util.Date, java.util.Map) or custom (like Address) type. So far we have seen examples of how to supply value for String type bean properties (using value attribute of <property> element) and String type constructor arguments (using value attribute of <constructor-arg> element). We also looked at how to inject dependencies via bean properties (using ref attribute of <property> element) and constructor arguments (using ref attribute of <constructor-arg> elements).

In this section, we'll look at built-in PropertyEditor implementations in Spring that simplify passing bean properties and constructor arguments of types java.util.Date, java.util.Currency, primitive type, and so on. We'll also look at how to specify values for collection types (like java.util.List and java.util.Map) in the application context XML file, and how to register a custom PropertyEditor implementation with Spring.

Let's now look at bean definition examples that demonstrate use of built-in PropertyEditor implementations.

IMPORT **chapter 3/ch03-simple-types-examples** (This project shows a Spring application in which bean properties and constructor arguments are of primitive type, java.util.Date, java.util.List, java.util.Map, and so on. This project also shows how to register a custom PropertyEditor implementation with Spring container. To run the application, execute the main method of the SampleApp class of this project)

Built-in property editors in Spring

JavaBeans PropertyEditors provide the necessary logic for converting a Java type to a string value, and vice versa. Spring provides a couple of built-in PropertyEditors that are used for converting string value of a bean property or a constructor argument (specified via value attribute of <property> and <constructor-arg> elements) to the actual Java type of the property or constructor argument.

Before we look at examples involving built-in PropertyEditors, let's first understand the importance of PropertyEditors in setting values of bean properties or constructor arguments.

Consider the following BankDetails class that we want to configure as a singleton-scoped bean with pre-defined values for its attributes:

Example listing 3-22 – BankDetails class

```
public class BankDetails {
   private String bankName;

   public void setBankName(String bankName) {
      this.bankName = bankName;
   }
}
```

In the above example listing, bankName is an attribute of the BankDetails class, and is of type String. The following bean definition for the BankDetails class shows how to set the value of bankName attribute to 'My Personal Bank':

Example listing 3-23 – Bean definition for the BankDetails class

```
<bean id= "bankDetails" class= "BankDetails">
   <property name= "bankName" value= "My Personal Bank"/>
</bean>
```

In the above bean definition, the <property> element's value attribute specifies a string value for the bankName property. As you can see, if a bean property is of type String, you can simply set that property value using <property> element's value attribute. Similarly, if a constructor argument is of type String, you can set the constructor argument value using <constructor-arg> element's value attribute.

Let's say that the following attributes (along with their setter methods) are added to the BankDetails class: a bankPrimaryBusiness attribute of type byte[], a headOfficeAddress attribute of type char[], a privateBank attribute of type char, a primaryCurrency attribute of type java.util.Currency, a dateOfInception attribute of type java.util.Date, and a branchAddresses attribute of type java.util.Properties. The following example listing shows the modified BankDetails class:

Example listing 3-24 – BankDetails class containing different types of properties
Project – ch03-simple-types-examples
Source location - src/main/java/sample/spring/chapter03/beans

```
package sample.spring.chapter03.beans;
.....
public class BankDetails {
   private String bankName;
   private byte[] bankPrimaryBusiness;
   private char[] headOfficeAddress;
   private char privateBank;
```

```
    private Currency primaryCurrency;
    private Date dateOfInception;
    private Properties branchAddresses;
    .....
    public void setBankName(String bankName) {
        this.bankName = bankName;
    }
    //-- more setter methods
}
```

You can configure the BankDetails class as a Spring bean by specifying string values for the properties, and letting the Spring container convert these string values into the corresponding Java types of the properties by using registered JavaBeans PropertyEditor implementations.

The following bean definition for the BankDetails class shows that simple string values are specified for different property types:

Example listing 3-25 – applicationContext.xml - Bean definition for the BankDetails class
Project – ch03-simple-types-examples
Source location - src/main/resources/META-INF/spring

```
<bean id="bankDetails" class="sample.spring.chapter03.beans.BankDetails">
    <property name="bankName" value="My Personal Bank" />
    <property name="bankPrimaryBusiness" value="Retail banking" />
    <property name="headOfficeAddress" value="Address of head office" />
    <property name="privateBank" value="Y" />
    <property name="primaryCurrency" value="INR" />
    <property name="dateOfInception" value="30-01-2012"></property>
    <property name="branchAddresses">
        <value>
            x = Branch X's address
            y = Branch Y's address
        </value>
    </property>
</bean>
```

The above example listing shows that string values are specified for properties of types java.util.Date, java.util.Currency, char[], byte[], char and java.util.Properties. Spring container uses registered PropertyEditors for converting the string value of the property or constructor argument to the corresponding Java type of the property or constructor argument. For instance, Spring container converts the value '30-01-2012' of dateOfInception property to java.util.Date type using CustomDateEditor (a built-in PropertyEditor implementation for java.util.Date type).

If you look at how branchAddresses property (of type java.util.Properties) is configured in example listing 3-25, you'll notice that instead of <property> element's value attribute, <value> sub-element of <property> element has been used to specify the value for the property. In case of single-valued properties, the use of <property> element's value attribute is preferred over <value> sub-element. But, if you need to specify multiple values for a property or the values need to be specified on separate lines (as in the case of branchAddresses property), the <value> sub-element is preferred over value attribute. In the next section, you'll see that values for properties (or constructor arguments) of type java.util.Properties can also be specified using <props> sub-element of <property> (or <constructor-arg>) element.

Spring comes with couple of built-in PropertyEditor implementations that perform the task of converting values specified in the application context XML file to the Java type of the bean property or constructor argument. The following table describes some of the built-in PropertyEditor implementations in Spring:

Built-in PropertyEditor implementation	Description
CustomBooleanEditor	converts string value to Boolean or boolean type
CustomNumberEditor	converts string value to a number (like int, long, and so on)
ChracterEditor	converts string value to char type
ByteArrayPropertyEditor	converts string value to byte[]
CustomDateEditor	converts string value to java.util.Date type
PropertiesEditor	converts string value to java.util.Properties type

The above table shows only a subset of built-in PropertyEditor implementations in Spring. For a complete list, refer to the org.springframework.beans.propertyeditors package of Spring. It is important to note that not all built-in PropertyEditor implementations in Spring are registered with the Spring container by default. For instance, you need to explicitly register CustomDateEditor to allow Spring container to perform conversion from a string value to a java.util.Date type. Later in this section, we'll look at how you can register property editors with Spring container.

Let's now look at how to specify values for bean properties (or constructor arguments) of types java.util.List, java.util.Set and java.util.Map.

Specifying values for different collection types

The <list>, <map> and <set> sub-elements (defined in Spring's beans schema) of <property> and <constructor-arg> elements are used to set properties and constructor arguments of type java.util.List, java.util.Map and java.util.Set, respectively.

> Spring's util schema also provides <list>, <set> and <map> elements that simplify setting properties and constructor arguments of different collection types. Later in this chapter, we'll look at Spring's util schema elements in detail.

The following DataTypesExample class shows that its constructor accepts arguments of different types:

Example listing 3-26 – DataTypesExample class
Project – ch03-simple-types-examples
Source location - src/main/java/sample/spring/chapter03/beans

```
package sample.spring.chapter03.beans;

import java.beans.ConstructorProperties;
.....
public class DataTypesExample {
  private static Logger logger = Logger.getLogger(DataTypesExample.class);

  @SuppressWarnings("rawtypes")
  @ConstructorProperties({ "byteArrayType", "charType", "charArray",
      "classType", "currencyType", "booleanType", "dateType", "longType",
      "doubleType", "propertiesType", "listType", "mapType", "setType",
      "anotherPropertiesType" })
  public DataTypesExample(byte[] byteArrayType, char charType,
      char[] charArray, Class classType, Currency currencyType,
      boolean booleanType, Date dateType, long longType,
      double doubleType, Properties propertiesType, List<Integer> listType,
      Map mapType, Set setType, Properties anotherPropertiesType) {
    .....
    logger.info("classType " + classType.getName());
    logger.info("listType " + listType);
    logger.info("mapType " + mapType);
    logger.info("setType " + setType);
    logger.info("anotherPropertiesType " + anotherPropertiesType);
  }
}
```

The above example listing shows that the DataTypesExample class's constructor accepts arguments of types java.util.List, java.util.Map, java.util.Set and java.util.Properties, and so on, and logs the value of each constructor argument.

The following example listing shows the bean definition for the DataTypesExample class:

Example listing 3-27 – applicationContext.xml - Bean definition for DataTypesExample class
Project – ch03-simple-types-examples
Source location - src/main/resources/META-INF/spring

```
<bean id="dataTypes" class="sample.spring.chapter03.beans.DataTypesExample">
   .....
   <constructor-arg name="anotherPropertiesType">
       <props>
          <prop key="book">Getting started with the Spring Framework</prop>
       </props>
   </constructor-arg>
   <constructor-arg name="listType" value-type="java.lang.Integer" >
       <list>
          <value>1</value>
          <value>2</value>
       </list>
   </constructor-arg>
   <constructor-arg name="mapType">
       <map>
          <entry>
             <key>
                <value>map key 1</value>
             </key>
             <value>map key 1's value</value>
          </entry>
       </map>
   </constructor-arg>
   <constructor-arg name="setType">
       <set>
          <value>Element 1</value>
          <value>Element 2</value>
       </set>
   </constructor-arg>
</bean>
```

The above example listing shows:

- the value of anotherPropertiesType (of type java.util.Properties) is specified using the <props> sub-element of <constructor-arg> element. Each <prop> element specifies a key-value pair; the key attribute specifies the key value and the content of <prop> element is the value for the key. Instead of using <props> element, you can use <value> sub-element of <constructor-arg> element to specify the value for anotherPropertiesType argument.

- the value of listType constructor argument (of type java.util.List) is specified using the <list> sub-element of <constructor-arg>. The <value> sub-elements of <list> element specify items contained in the list. The <list> element's value-type attribute specifies the Java type of the elements that the java.util.List type constructor argument accepts. As the listType constructor argument is of type List<Integer> (refer example listing 3-26), the value-type attribute's value is specified as java.lang.Integer. The value-type attribute is *optional*, and is particularly useful if you are using a *parameterized* List type, like List<Integer>. If you specify the value-type attribute, Spring container uses the registered property editors to perform conversion of values to the type specified by the value-type attribute, followed by converting (if required) the values to the type accepted by the parameterized List type. If you don't specify the value-type attribute, Spring container simply uses the registered property editors to perform conversion of values to the type accepted by the parameterized List type.

- the value of mapType constructor argument (of type java.util.Map) is specified using the <map> sub-element of <constructor-arg>. The <entry> sub-element of <map> specifies a key-value pair contained in the Map; the <key> element specifies the key and the <value> element specifies the value for the key. The key-type and value-type attributes of <map> element specify the Java type of keys and values that java.util.Map accepts. The key-type and value-type attributes are optional, and especially useful if you are using parameterized Map type, like Map<Integer, Integer>. Spring container uses registered property editors to perform conversion of keys and values to the types specified by the key-type and value-type attributes, and to the types accepted by the parameterized Map type.

- the value of the setType constructor argument (of type java.util.Set) is specified using the <set> sub-element of <constructor-arg>. Each <value> sub-element of <set> specifies an element contained in the Set. The value-type attribute of <set> element specifies the Java type of elements that java.util.Set accepts. The value-type attribute is optional, and is useful if you are using parameterized Set type, like Set<Integer>. Spring container uses registered property editors to perform conversion of values to the type specified by the value-type attribute, and to the type accepted by the parameterized Set type.

In DataTypesExample class (refer example listing 3-26 and 3-27), constructor arguments of type List, Map and Set contained elements of type String or Integer. In an application, a collection may contain elements of type Map, Set, Class, Properties, or any other Java type. The elements contained in the collection can also be bean references. To address such scenarios, Spring allows you to use elements like <map>, <set>, <list>, <props>, <ref>, and so on, as sub-elements of <list>, <map> and <set> elements. Let's now look at examples that demonstrate how to add different types of elements to Map, List and Set type constructor arguments and bean properties.

Adding elements of type List, Map, Set and Properties to collection types

If a bean property or constructor argument is of type List<List>, simply use a nested <list> element, as shown here:

Example listing 3-28 – Configuration example: List inside a List

```
<constructor-arg name="nestedList">
  <list>
    <list>
      <value>A simple String value in the nested list</value>
      <value>Another simple String value in nested list</value>
    </list>
  </list>
</constructor-arg>
```

The <constructor-arg> element shown in the above example listing supplies value for a constructor argument named nestedList which is of type List<List>. The nested <list> element represents an element of type List. Similarly, you can use <map>, <set> and <props> elements inside a <list> element to set value of properties or constructor arguments of type List<Map>, List<Set> and List<Properties>, respectively. As with the <list> element, a <set> element can contain <set>, <list>, <map> or <props> element. In case of a <map> element, you can use <map>, <set>, <list> or <props> element to specify key and value of an entry.

The following example listing shows how you can specify values for a Map<List, Set> type constructor argument:

Example listing 3-29 – Configuration example: Map containing List type as key and Set type as value

```
<constructor-arg name="nestedListAndSetMap">
    <map>
      <entry>
        <key>
          <list>
```

```
            <value>a List element</value>
          </list>
        </key>
        <set>
          <value>a Set element</value>
        </set>
      </entry>
    </map>
</constructor-arg>
```

The above example listing shows that the nestedListAndSetMap constructor argument is of Map type whose key is of type List and value is of type Set. The <key> element can have either of the following elements as its sub-element: <map>, <set>, <list> and <props>. The value for the key can be defined using <map>, <set>, <list> or <props> element.

Adding bean references to collection types

You can use <ref> elements inside <list> and <set> elements to add references to beans into properties and constructor arguments of type List and Set, respectively.

The following example listing shows how references to beans are added to a List type constructor argument:

Example listing 3-30 – Configuration example: List containing reference to beans

```
<bean .....>
  <constructor-arg name="myList">
    <list>
      <ref bean="aBean" />
      <ref bean="bBean" />
    </list>
  </constructor-arg>
</bean>

<bean id="aBean" class="somepackage.ABean" />
<bean id="bBean" class="somepackage.BBean" />
```

The above example listing shows that the myList constructor argument is of type List and it contains 2 elements - a reference to aBean bean and a reference to bBean bean. The <ref> element's bean attribute specifies the name of the bean referenced by the <ref> element.

As with the <list> element, you can use <ref> elements inside <set> element to add bean references to a Set type constructor argument or bean property. In case of <map> element, you can use <ref> element inside a <key> element to specify a bean reference as a key, and use the

<ref> element to specify a bean reference as a value for the key. The following example listing shows a Map type constructor argument that contains a single key-value pair in which both key and value are references to beans:

Example listing 3-31 – Configuration example: Map containing bean references as keys and values

```
<bean .....>
  <constructor-arg name="myMapWithBeanRef">
    <map>
      <entry>
        <key>
          <ref bean="aBean" />
        </key>
        <ref bean="bBean" />
      </entry>
    </map>
  </constructor-arg>
</bean>

<bean id="aBean" class="somepackage.ABean" />
<bean id="bBean" class="somepackage.BBean" />
```

The above example listing shows that myMapWithBeanRef constructor argument is of type Map and it contains a key-value pair in which the key is a reference to aBean bean and corresponding value is a reference to bBean bean.

Adding bean names to collection types

If you want to add a bean name (as specified by the id attribute of <bean> element) to a List, Map or Set type constructor argument or bean property, you can use the <idref> element inside <map>, <set> and <list> elements. The following example listing shows a Map type constructor argument that contains a single key-value pair, where bean name is the key and bean reference is the value:

Example listing 3-32 – Configuration example: Map containing bean name as key and bean reference as value

```
<constructor-arg name="myExample">
  <map>
    <entry>
      <key>
        <idref bean="sampleBean" />
      </key>
```

```
            <ref bean="sampleBean" />
        </entry>
    </map>
</constructor-arg>

<bean id="sampleBean" class="somepackage.SampleBean" />
```

The above example listing shows that the myExample constructor argument is of type Map whose key is the string value 'sampleBean' and value is the sampleBean bean. We could have used <value> element to set 'sampleBean' string value as the key, but <idref> element is used because Spring container verifies existence of the sampleBean bean when the application is deployed.

> You can use the <idref> element inside a <property> or <constructor-arg> element to set a bean name as the value of a bean property or constructor argument.

Adding null values to collection types

You can add a null value to collections of type Set and List using <null> element. The following example listing shows how to add a null value to a Set type constructor argument using <null> element:

Example listing 3-33 – Configuration example: Set containing a null element

```
<constructor-arg name="setWithNullElement">
    <set>
        <value>Element 1</value>
        <value>Element 2</value>
        <null />
    </set>
</constructor-arg>
```

In the above example listing, setWithNullElement constructor argument contains 3 elements: Element 1, Element 2 and null.

To add a null key to a Map type constructor argument or property, you can use <null> element inside the <key> element. And, to add a null value, you can add a <null> element inside the <entry> element. The following example listing shows a Map type constructor argument that contains a null key and a null value:

Example listing 3-34 – Configuration example: Map containing a null key and a null value

```
<constructor-arg name="mapType">
    <map>
```

```
        <entry>
          <key>
              <null />
          </key>
          <null />
        </entry>
    </map>
</constructor-arg>
```

The above example listing shows that an element with null key and null value is added to the mapType constructor argument using <null> element.

> You can also use <null> element inside <property> and <constructor-arg> elements to set null values for properties and constructor arguments, respectively.

Let's now look at how to specify values for array type properties and constructor arguments.

Specifying values for arrays

If a bean class defines an array type property, you can set its value using the <array> sub-element of <property> element. Similarly, you can set an array type constructor argument using the <array> sub-element of <constructor-arg> element.

The following example listing shows how you can set a bean property of type int[]:

Example listing 3-35 – Configuration example: Setting value of a bean property of type int[]

```
<property name="numbersProperty">
      <array>
          <value>1</value>
          <value>2</value>
      </array>
</property>
```

In the above example listing, each <value> sub-element of the <array> element represents an element in the numbersProperty array. The property editors registered with the Spring container are used to convert the string value specified by each of the <value> element to int type. You can use <array> element inside <list>, <set> and <map> elements. You can also use <list>, <set>, <map>, <props> and <ref> elements inside an <array> element to create arrays of List, Set, Map, Properties and bean references, respectively. If you want to create an array of arrays, you can use <array> elements inside an <array> element.

We discussed that <list>, <map> and <set> elements are used to set properties or constructor arguments of type List, Map and Set, respectively. Let's now look at the default collection implementation that is created by Spring for each of these elements.

Default collection implementation for <list>, <set> and <map> elements

The following table shows the default collection implementation that is created by Spring for <list>, <set> and <map> elements:

Collection element	Default collection implementation created by Spring
<list>	java.util.ArrayList
<set>	java.util.LinkedHashSet
<map>	java.util.LinkedHashMap

The above table suggests:

- if a property's (or a constructor argument's) value is specified using <list> element, Spring creates an instance of ArrayList and assigns it to the property (or the constructor argument).

- if a property's (or a constructor argument's) value is specified using <set> element, Spring creates an instance of LinkedHashSet and assigns it to the property (or the constructor argument).

- if a property's (or a constructor argument's) value is specified using <map> element, Spring creates an instance of LinkedHashMap and assigns it to the property (or the constructor argument).

It is likely that you may want to substitute a different implementation of List, Set or Map to a bean property or a constructor argument. For instance, instead of java.util.ArrayList, you may want to assign an instance of java.util.LinkedList to a bean property of type List. In such scenarios, it is recommended to use <list>, <map> and <set> elements of Spring's util schema (explained in section 3-8). The <list>, <set> and <map> elements of Spring's util schema provide the option to specify the fully-qualified name of the concrete collection class that you want to assign to the property or constructor argument of the bean.

Let's now look at some of the built-in property editors provided by Spring.

3-5 Built-in property editors

Spring provides a couple of built-in property editors that are useful when setting bean properties and constructor arguments. Let's take a quick look at CustomCollectionEditor,

CustomMapEditor and CustomDateEditor built-in property editors. To view the complete list of built-in property editors, refer to org.springframework.beans.propertyeditors package.

CustomCollectionEditor

CustomCollectionEditor property editor is responsible for converting a source Collection (like, java.util.LinkedList) type to the target Collection (like, java.util.ArrayList) type. By default, CustomCollectionEditor is registered for Set, SortedSet and List types.

Consider the following CollectionTypesExample class that defines attributes (and corresponding setter methods) of type Set and List:

Example listing 3-36 – CollectionTypesExample class
Project – ch03-simple-types-examples
Source location - src/main/java/sample/spring/chapter03/beans

```
package sample.spring.chapter03.beans;

import java.util.List;
import java.util.Set;

public class CollectionTypesExample {
  private Set setType;
  private List listType;
   .....
   //-- setter methods for attributes
   public void setSetType(Set setType) {
      this.setType = setType;
   }
   .....
}
```

CollectionTypesExample class defines setType and listType attributes of type Set and List, respectively. The following example listing shows the bean definition for CollectionTypesExample class:

Example listing 3-37 – applicationContext.xml - Bean definition for CollectionTypesExample class
Project – ch03-simple-types-examples
Source location - src/main/resources/META-INF/spring

```
<bean class="sample.spring.chapter03.beans.CollectionTypesExample">
   <property name="listType">
       <set>
           <value>set element 1</value>
```

```
            <value>set element 2</value>
        </set>
    </property>
    <property name="setType">
        <list>
            <value>list element 1</value>
            <value>list element 2</value>
        </list>
    </property>
    .....
</bean>
```

You might think that the above configuration is incorrect because <set> element has been used to set the value of listType property (of type List), and <list> element has been used to set the value of setType property (of type Set).

The above configuration is completely legal, and the Spring container does *not* complain. This is because CustomCollectionEditor converts the ArrayList instance (created corresponding to the <list> type element) to LinkedHashSet type (an implementation of Set type) *before* setting the setType property. Also, CustomCollectionEditor converts the LinkedHashSet instance (created corresponding to the <set> type element) to ArrayList type (an implementation of List type) *before* setting the listType property.

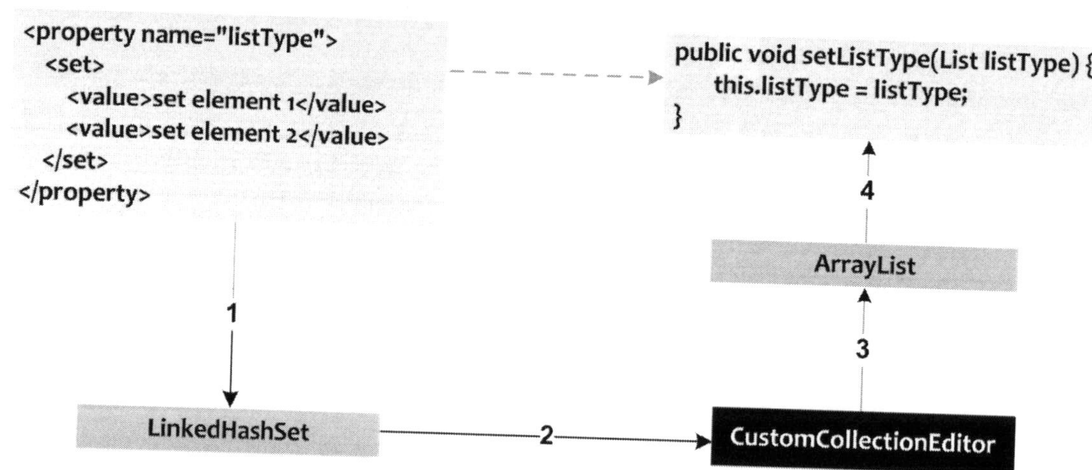

Figure 3-4 – CustomCollectionEditor converts the LinkedHashSet to ArrayList type

Figure 3-4 shows that the CustomCollectionEditor converts the LinkedHashSet type to ArrayList to set the value of CollectionTypesExample's listType property. The figure shows the sequence of steps that are performed by Spring to set the value of listType property. First, Spring creates an instance of LinkedHashSet corresponding to the <set> element. As the listType property is of type List (refer example listing 3-36), the CustomCollectionEditor comes into picture for setting the listType property's value. If the type of the bean property is List, CustomCollectionEditor creates an instance of ArrayList and populates it with the elements from the LinkedHashSet. In the end, the value of the listType variable is set to the ArrayList implementation created by CustomCollectionEditor.

It is important to note that if a property or constructor argument type is a concrete collection class (like LinkedList), CustomCollectionEditor simply creates an instance of the concrete collection class and adds elements to it from the source collection. The following figure shows a scenario in which the bean property is of type java.util.Vector (a concrete collection class):

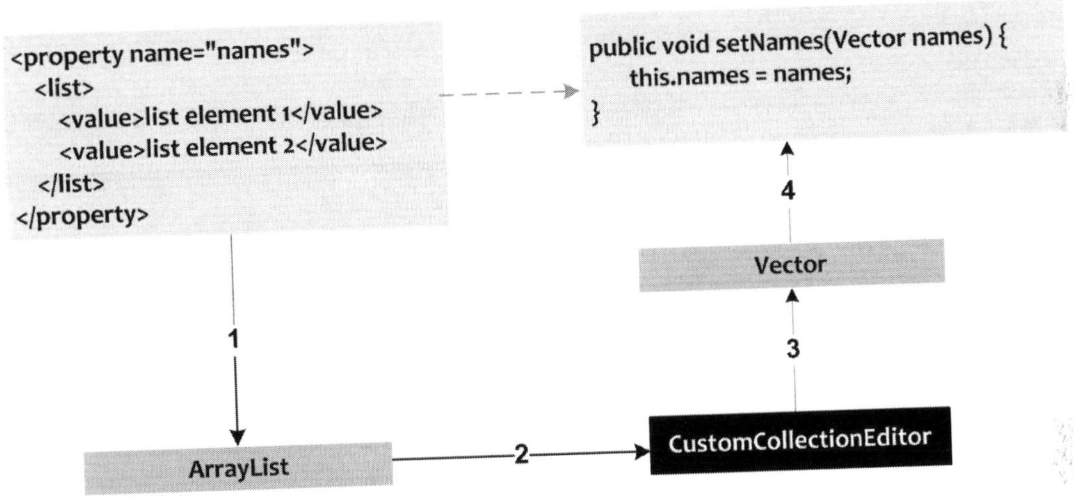

Figure 3-5 CustomCollectionEditor converts the ArrayList to Vector type

The above figure shows that the CustomCollectionEditor creates an instance of Vector (a concrete collection class) and adds elements to it from the source collection, ArrayList.

Let's now look at CustomMapEditor property editor.

CustomMapEditor

CustomMapEditor property editor deals with converting a source Map type (like HashMap) to a target Map type (like TreeMap). By default, CustomMapEditor is registered only for SortedMap type.

Figure 3-6 shows a scenario in which CustomMapEditor converts LinkedHashMap (the source Map type) to TreeMap (an implementation of SortedMap type).

Figure 3-6 shows the sequence of steps performed by Spring to set the value of mapType property. First, Spring creates an instance of LinkedHashMap corresponding to the <map>

element. As the mapType property is of type SortedMap, CustomMapEditor comes into picture while setting the value of mapType property. CustomMapEditor creates an instance of TreeMap (a concrete implementation of SortedSet interface), adds key-value pairs from LinkedHashMap to the newly created TreeMap instance and assigns the TreeMap instance to the mapType property.

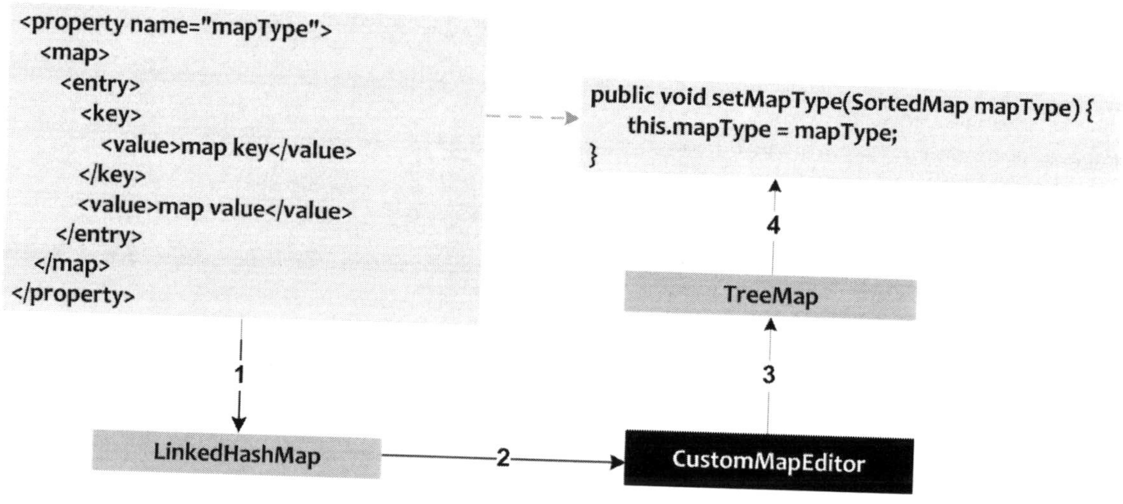

Figure 3-6 CustomMapEditor converts the LinkedHashMap (the source Map type) to TreeMap (the target Map type) type

CustomDateEditor

CustomDateEditor is a property editor for java.util.Date type bean properties and constructor arguments. CustomDateEditor supports a custom java.text.DateFormat that is used for formatting a date/time string to a java.util.Date type object, and parsing a java.util.Date type object to a date/time string. In the next section, we'll see how CustomDateEditor is used for setting bean properties and constructor arguments of type java.util.Date. In ch03-simple-types-examples project, CustomDateEditor converts the string value of a bean property (refer dateOfInception attribute of BankDetails class) or constructor argument (refer dateType constructor argument of DataTypesExample class) to java.util.Date type.

In ch03-simple-types-examples project, some of the other built-in property editors that are utilized by beans include: ByteArrayPropertyEditor - for converting a string value to byte[] (refer bankPrimaryBusiness attribute of BankDetails class), CurrencyEditor – for converting a currency code to a java.util.Currency object (refer primaryCurrency attribute of BankDetails class), CharacterArrayPropertyEditor – for converting a string value to a char[] (refer headOfficeAddress attribute of BankDetails class), and so on.

Let's now look at how to register property editors with the Spring container.

3-6 Registering property editors with the Spring container

Spring's BeanWrapperImpl class registers a couple of built-in property editors with the Spring container. For instance, CustomCollectionEditor, CustomMapEditor, CurrencyEditor, ByteArrayPropertyEditor and CharacterArrayEditor property editors are registered by default with the Spring container. But, CustomDateEditor property editor is *not* registered by default with the Spring container. To register property editors with the Spring container, you can use Spring's CustomEditorConfigurer *special* bean. CustomEditorConfigurer class implements Spring's BeanFactoryPostProcessor interface (explained in detail in section 5-4 of chapter 5), and it is automatically detected and executed by the Spring container.

In ch03-simple-types-examples project, BankDetails class (refer example listing 3-24) defines a dateOfInception property of type java.util.Date. The value specified for the dateOfInception property is '30-01-2012' (refer example listing 3-25). To convert the string value '30-01-2012' to java.util.Date type, you *must* register a custom property editor for java.util.Date type or you can register Spring's built-in CustomDateEditor property editor with the Spring container.

To register property editors with the Spring container, you need to do the following:

1. Create a class that implements Spring's PropertyEditorRegistrar interface. This class is responsible for registering property editors with the Spring container.
2. Configure the PropertyEditorRegistrar implementation as a Spring bean in the application context XML file.
3. Configure Spring's CustomEditorConfigurer *special* bean in the application context XML file, and provide it with reference to the PropertyEditorRegistrar implementation (that you created in step 1 and configured in step 2).

Let's now see how CustomDateEditor is registered with the Spring container in ch03-simple-types-examples project.

Creating a PropertyEditorRegistrar implementation

The following example listing shows the MyPropertyEditorRegistrar class that implements PropertyEditorRegistrar interface:

Example listing 3-38 – MyPropertyEditorRegistrar class
Project – ch03-simple-types-examples
Source location - src/main/java/sample/spring/chapter03/beans

```
package sample.spring.chapter03.beans;

import java.text.SimpleDateFormat;
import java.util.Date;
```

```
import org.springframework.beans.PropertyEditorRegistrar;
import org.springframework.beans.PropertyEditorRegistry;
import org.springframework.beans.propertyeditors.CustomDateEditor;

public class MyPropertyEditorRegistrar implements PropertyEditorRegistrar {

  @Override
   public void registerCustomEditors(PropertyEditorRegistry registry) {
    registry.registerCustomEditor(Date.class, new CustomDateEditor(
          new SimpleDateFormat("dd-MM-yyyy"), false));
  }
}
```

The above example listing shows that the MyPropertyEditorRegistrar class implements Spring's PropertyEditorRegistrar interface, and provides implementation for registerCustomEditors method defined in the PropertyEditorRegistrar interface. The PropertyEditorRegistry instance passed to the registerCustomEditors method is used for registering property editors. PropertyEditorRegistry's registerCustomEditor method is used for registering a PropertyEditor implementation with the Spring container. In the above example listing, PropertyEditorRegistry's registerCustomEditor is used for registering a CustomDateEditor property editor with the Spring container.

Configuring the CustomEditorConfigurer class

The following example listing shows how the CustomEditorConfigurer class is configured in the application context XML file:

Example listing 3-39 – applicationContext.xml - CustomEditorConfigurer configuration
Project – ch03-simple-types-examples
Source location - src/main/resources/META-INF/spring

```
  <bean id=" myPropertyEditorRegistrar"
        class="sample.spring.chapter03.beans.MyPropertyEditorRegistrar " />

 <bean id="editorConfigurer"
      class="org.springframework.beans.factory.config.CustomEditorConfigurer">
    <property name="propertyEditorRegistrars">
      <list>
        <ref bean="myPropertyEditorRegistrar"/>
      </list>
    </property>
</bean>
```

In the above example listing, myPropertyEditorRegistrar bean definition configures MyPropertyEditorRegistrar class as a Spring bean. MyPropertyEditorRegistrar class implements Spring's PropertyEditorRegistrar interface, and is responsible for registering additional property editors with Spring container. CustomEditorConfigurer's propertyEditorRegistrars property specifies a list of PropertyEditorRegistrar implementations. In the above example listing, myPropertyEditorRegistrar is specified as one of the values of propertyEditorRegistrars property. CustomEditorConfigurer bean is automatically detected and executed by the Spring container, resulting in registration of property editors by the MyPropertyEditorRegistrar instance.

Let's now look at how to use p-namespace (for bean properties) and c-namespace (for constructor arguments) to write concise bean definitions in application context XML files.

3-7 Concise bean definitions with p and c namespaces

To make bean definitions less verbose in application context XML files, Spring provides p and c namespaces to specify values for bean properties and constructor arguments, respectively. The p and c namespaces are alternatives to using <property> and <constructor-arg> elements, respectively.

Let's first look at p-namespace.

IMPORT chapter 3/ch03-namespaces-example (This project shows a Spring application in which bean properties and constructor arguments are set using p- and c-namespaces, respectively. To run the application, execute the main method of the SampleApp class of this project)

p-namespace

To use p-namespace to set bean properties, specify bean properties as attributes of the <bean> element, and specify each bean property to be in the p-namespace.

The following bean definition shows how to use p-namespace to set bean properties:

Example listing 3-40 – applicationContext.xml - p-namespace example
Project – ch03-namespaces-example
Source location - src/main/resources/META-INF/spring

```
<beans xmlns="http://www.springframework.org/schema/beans"
    xmlns:p="http://www.springframework.org/schema/p" xsi:schemaLocation=".....">

  <bean id="bankDetails" class="sample.spring.chapter03.beans.BankDetails"
     p:bankName="My Personal Bank" p:bankPrimaryBusiness="Retail banking"
     p:headOfficeAddress="Address of head office" p:privateBank="Y"
     p:primaryCurrency="INR" p:dateOfInception="30-01-2012"
     p:branchAddresses-ref="branchAddresses"/>
```

```
    .....
</beans>
```

In the application context XML file shown above, p-namespace is specified via xmlns attribute. The bankDetails bean definition makes use of the p prefix for the p-namespace to specify bean properties. If you compare the above example listing with the example listing 3-25, you'll notice that the above example listing is *less* verbose. Even though it is possible to use a mix of <property> elements and p-namespace to specify bean properties, it's recommended that you choose one style for specifying bean properties and use it consistently in bean definitions.

> As p-namespace is implemented as part of Spring, there is *no* schema corresponding to p-namespace. For this reason, you don't see any schema reference corresponding to p-namespace in example listing 3-40. If you want your IDE to autocomplete bean property names when using p-namespace, consider using IntelliJ IDEA or SpringSource Tool Suite (STS).

If a bean property is *not* a reference to another bean, it is specified using the following syntax:

```
p:<property-name>="<property-value>"
```

here, *<property-name>* is the name of the bean property, and *<property-value>* is the value of the bean property.

If a bean property is a reference to another bean, it is specified using the following syntax:

```
p:<property-name>-ref="<bean-reference>"
```

here, *<property-name>* is the name of the bean property, and *<bean-reference>* is the id (or name) of the referenced bean. It is important to note that the name of the bean property is followed by --ref. As the branchAddresses property of BankDetails bean represents a reference to the branchAddresses bean, the branchAddresses property is specified as p:branchAddresses-ref in example listing 3-40.

Let's now look at how c-namespace is used for setting constructor arguments.

c-namespace

To use c-namespace to supply values for constructor arguments, specify constructor arguments as attributes of the <bean> element, and specify each constructor argument to be in the c-namespace.

The following example listing shows the BankStatement class that we'll configure as a Spring bean using c-namespace.

Example listing 3-41 – BankStatement class
Project – ch03-namespaces-example
Source location - src/main/java/sample/spring/chapter03/beans

```
package sample.spring.chapter03.beans;

import java.beans.ConstructorProperties;

public class BankStatement {
  .....
  @ConstructorProperties({ "transactionDate", "amount", "transactionType",
      "referenceNumber" })
   public BankStatement(Date transactionDate, double amount,
          String transactionType, String referenceNumber) {
    this.transactionDate = transactionDate;
    this.amount = amount;
    .....
  }
  .....
}
```

The following bean definition for the BankStatement class shows usage of c-namespace for setting values of constructor arguments:

Example listing 3-42 – applicationContext.xml - c-namespace example
Project – ch03-namespaces-example
Source location - src/main/resources/META-INF/spring

```
<beans xmlns="http://www.springframework.org/schema/beans"
  xmlns:c="http://www.springframework.org/schema/c"
  xsi:schemaLocation=".....">
  .....
  <bean id="bankStatement" class="sample.spring.chapter03.beans.BankStatement"
    c:transactionDate = "30-01-2012"
    c:amount = "1000"
    c:transactionType = "Credit"
    c:referenceNumber = "1110202" />
  .....
</beans>
```

In the above example listing, c-namespace is specified via xmlns attribute. The bankStatement bean definition makes use of the c prefix for the c-namespace to specify constructor arguments. The syntax followed for specifying constructor arguments using c-namespace is similar to what we saw in case of p-namespace.

> As c-namespace is implemented as part of Spring, there is *no* schema corresponding to c-namespace. For this reason, you don't see any schema reference corresponding to c-namespace in example listing 3-42. If you want your IDE to autocomplete constructor argument names when using c-namespace, consider using IntelliJ IDEA or SpringSource Tool Suite (STS).

If a constructor argument is *not* a reference to another bean, it is specified using the following syntax:

```
c:<constructor-argument-name>="<constructor-argument-value>"
```

here, *<constructor-argument-name>* is the name of the constructor argument, and *<constructor-argument-value>* is the value of the constructor argument.

If a constructor argument is a reference to another bean, it is specified using the following syntax:

```
c:<constructor-argument-name>-ref="<bean-reference>"
```

here, *<constructor-argument-name>* is the name of the constructor argument, and *<bean-reference>* is the id (or name) of the referenced bean. It is important to note that the name of the constructor argument is followed by --ref. For instance, if a constructor argument named myargument represents a reference to a bean with id 'x', you specify myargument constructor argument as:

```
c:myargument-ref = "x"
```

As mentioned earlier, if a class is compiled with debug flag enabled, constructor argument names are preserved in the generated *.class* file. If the BankStatement class is *not* compiled with the debug flag enabled, the configuration shown in example listing 3-42 will not work. In such cases, you supply values for constructor arguments using their index, as shown here:

Example listing 3-43 – Supplying values for constructor arguments using their index

```
<beans xmlns="http://www.springframework.org/schema/beans"
  xmlns:c="http://www.springframework.org/schema/c"
  xsi:schemaLocation=".....">
  .....
  <bean id="bankStatement" class="sample.spring.chapter03.beans.BankStatement"
    c:_0 = "30-01-2012"
    c:_1 = "1000"
    c:_2 = "Credit"
    c:_3 = "1110202" />
```

```
.....
</beans>
```

The above example listing shows bean definition for the BankStatement class, which uses constructor argument index instead of constructor arguments name to supply values. It is important to note that the index of the constructor argument is prefixed with an *underscore* because attribute names in XML *cannot* begin with a numeric value. If a constructor argument is a reference to another bean, -ref *must* be added to the index of the constructor argument. For instance, if the constructor argument at index 0 represents reference to another bean, it is specified as c:_0-ref. Even though it's possible to use a combination of <constructor-arg> elements and c-namespace to specify constructor arguments, it's recommended that you choose one style of specifying constructor arguments and use it consistently in bean definitions.

We saw earlier how <list>, <map> and <set> elements are used to set properties or constructor arguments of type List, Map and Set, respectively. Let's now look at Spring's util schema that simplifies creating collection types, Properties type, constants, and so on, and exposing them as a Spring beans.

3-8 Spring's util schema

Spring's util schema simplifies configuring beans by providing a concise way to perform common configuration tasks. The following table describes the various elements of util schema:

Element	Description
<list>	Creates a java.util.List type, and exposes it as a bean
<map>	Creates a java.util.Map type, and exposes it as a bean
<set>	Creates a java.util.Set type, and exposes it as a bean
<constant>	Exposes a public static field on a type as a bean
<property-path>	Exposes a bean property as a bean
<properties>	Creates a java.util.Properties from a properties file, and exposes it as a bean

All the elements of Spring's util schema accept a scope attribute that identifies whether the exposed bean is a singleton- or prototype-scoped.

Spring provides a FactoryBean interface that can be implemented to create a factory object responsible for creating bean instances. Instead of using util schema's elements mentioned in the above table, you can use an out-of-the-box FactoryBean implementation provided by Spring to perform the same functionality. In this section, we'll look at the util schema's elements and the built-in FactoryBean implementations that you can use instead of util schema's elements.

IMPORT **chapter 3/ch03-util-schema-examples** (This project shows a Spring application that makes use of Spring's util schema elements to create shared instances of List, Set, Map, and so on. To run the application, execute the main method of the SampleApp class of this project)

Let's first look at the <list> element.

<list>

The <list> element of Spring's util schema is used for creating objects of type java.util.List, as shown here:

Example listing 3-44 – applicationContext.xml - util schema's <list> element
Project – ch03-util-schema-examples
Source location - src/main/resources/META-INF/spring

```
<beans xmlns="http://www.springframework.org/schema/beans"
        xmlns:util="http://www.springframework.org/schema/util"
        xsi:schemaLocation="..... http://www.springframework.org/schema/util
        http://www.springframework.org/schema/util/spring-util-4.0.xsd">

  <bean id="dataTypes" class="sample.spring.chapter03.beans.DataTypesExample">
    .....
    <constructor-arg name="listType" ref="listType" />
    .....
  </bean>

  <util:list id="listType" list-class="java.util.ArrayList">
      <value>A simple String value in list</value>
      <value>Another simple String value in list</value>
  </util:list>
</beans>
```

First, you need to include Spring's util schema to access its elements. In the above example listing, the <list> element of util schema creates an instance of java.util.ArrayList and exposes it as a bean. The id attribute specifies the bean id with which the java.util.ArrayList instance is exposed, and list-class attribute specifies the concrete implementation of java.util.List that you want to create. If you don't specify the list-class attribute, an instance of java.util.ArrayList is created by default. The <value> element of Spring's beans schema is used to specify individual elements of the list.

As util schema's <list> element exposes a List instance as a bean, you can refer to the exposed List instance from other beans. For instance, in the above example listing, the listType constructor argument (of type java.util.List) of DataTypesExample bean specifies listType as the value of the ref attribute to refer to the List instance created by the util schema's <list> element.

If you compare the util schema's <list> element shown in the above example listing with the beans schema's <list> element (refer example listing 3-27), you'll notice that the util schema's <list> element gives you control over the List implementation to create. For instance, if you want to create a Vector instead of an ArrayList instance, specify java.util.Vector as the value of the list-class attribute.

Let's now look at Spring's ListFactoryBean which you can use instead of util schema's <list> element.

ListFactoryBean

An alternative to using util schema's <list> element is Spring's ListFactoryBean – a factory that is used for creating instances of java.util.List and making them available as Spring beans.

The following example listing shows how the ListFactoryBean can be used instead of the util schema's <list> element:

Example listing 3-45 – ListFactoryBean example

```
<beans .....>

  <bean id="dataTypes" class="sample.spring.chapter03.beans.DataTypesExample">
    .....
    <constructor-arg name="listType" ref="listType" />
    .....
  </bean>

  <bean id="listType" class=" org.springframework.beans.factory.config.ListFactoryBean">
      <property name="sourceList">
        <list>
          <value>A simple String value in list</value>
          <value>Another simple String value in list</value>
        </list>
      </property>
  </bean>
```

```
</beans>
```

In the above example listing, the sourceList property of ListFactoryBean specifies the elements in the list. By default, ListFactoryBean creates an instance of java.util.ArrayList. If you want the ListFactoryBean to create an instance of any other List implementation (like Vector), set the ListFactoryBean's targetListClass property. The targetListClass property specifies the fully-qualified name of the concrete implementation class of java.util.List interface that should be created by the ListFactoryBean.

If you compare example listings 3-44 and 3-45, you'll notice that using util schema's <list> element is a lot simpler than using the ListFactoryBean to create a List instance and expose it as a bean.

<map>

The <map> element of Spring's util schema is used for creating an object of type java.util.Map and exposing it as a bean, as shown here:

Example listing 3-46 – applicationContext.xml - util schema's <map> element
Project – ch03-util-schema-examples
Source location - src/main/resources/META-INF/spring

```
<beans .....
    xmlns:util="http://www.springframework.org/schema/util"
    xsi:schemaLocation="..... http://www.springframework.org/schema/util
    http://www.springframework.org/schema/util/spring-util-4.0.xsd">

  <bean id="dataTypes" class="sample.spring.chapter03.beans.DataTypesExample">
    .....
    <constructor-arg name="mapType" ref="mapType" />
    .....
  </bean>

  <util:map id="mapType" map-class="java.util.TreeMap">
      <entry key="map key 1" value="map key 1's value"/>
  </util:map>
  .....
</beans>
```

In the above example listing, util schema's <map> element creates an instance of java.util.TreeMap and exposes it as a bean. The id attribute specifies the id with which the bean is made available to other beans, and map-class attribute specifies the fully-qualified name of the concrete implementation class of java.util.Map interface that should be created by the <map>

element. The <entry> element of Spring's beans schema specifies a key-value pair in the created Map instance.

As the <map> element exposes a Map instance as a bean, the exposed Map instance can be referenced from other beans. For instance, in the above example listing, DataTypesExample's mapType constructor argument (of type java.util.Map) specifies value of ref attribute as mapType to refer to the TreeMap instance created by the <map> element.

> We saw earlier in this chapter that <key> and <value> sub-elements of <entry> are used to specify a key-value pair contained in the Map instance. The example listing 3-46 shows that you can also specify a key-value pair contained in the Map instance by using <entry> element's key and value attributes.

If you compare the util schema's <map> element shown in the above example listing with the beans schema's <map> element in example listing 3-27, you'll notice that the util schema's <map> element gives you control over the Map implementation to create. For instance, if you want to use LinkedHashMap instead of TreeMap, specify java.util.LinkedHashMap as the value of map-class attribute. If you don't specify the map-class attribute, Spring container creates an instance of java.util.LinkedHashMap by default.

Let's now look at Spring's MapFactoryBean that you can use instead of util schema's <map> element.

MapFactoryBean

Instead of using util schema's <map> element, you can use Spring's MapFactoryBean – a factory that is used for creating instances of java.util.Map and making them available as Spring beans.

The following example listing shows how MapFactoryBean is used:

Example listing 3-47 – MapFactoryBean example

```
<beans .....>

  <bean id="dataTypes" class="sample.spring.chapter03.beans.DataTypesExample">
    .....
    <constructor-arg name="mapType" ref="mapType" />
    .....
  </bean>

  <bean id="mapType" class="org.springframework.beans.factory.config.MapFactoryBean">
     <property name="sourceMap">
        <map>
           <entry key="map key 1" value="map key 1's value"/>
```

```
        </map>
      </property>
    </bean>
    .....
</beans>
```

In the above example listing, MapFactoryBean's sourceMap property specifies the key-value pairs contained in the Map instance created by the MapFactoryBean. By default, MapFactoryBean creates an instance of java.util.LinkedHashMap. You can control the Map instance created by MapFactoryBean by setting the targetMapClass property. The targetMapClass specifies the fully-qualified name of the concrete implementation class of java.util.Map interface. For instance, if you specify java.util.HashMap as the value of targetMapClass, MapFactoryBean creates an instance of java.util.HashMap.

If you compare example listings 3-46 and 3-47, you'll notice that using util schema's <map> element results in a more concise configuration than MapFactoryBean for creating Map instances.

<set>

The <set> element of Spring's util schema is used for creating an object of type java.util.Set and exposing it as a bean, as shown here:

Example listing 3-48 – applicationContext.xml - util schema's <set> element
Project – ch03-util-schema-examples
Source location - src/main/resources/META-INF/spring

```
<beans .....
    xmlns:util="http://www.springframework.org/schema/util"
    xsi:schemaLocation="..... http://www.springframework.org/schema/util
    http://www.springframework.org/schema/util/spring-util-4.0.xsd">

  <bean id="dataTypes" class="sample.spring.chapter03.beans.DataTypesExample">
    .....
    <constructor-arg name="setType" ref="setType" />
  </bean>
  <util:set id="setType" set-class="java.util.HashSet">
    <value>Element 1</value>
    <value>Element 2</value>
  </util:set>
  .....
</beans>
```

In the above example listing, util schema's <set> element creates an instance of HashSet and exposes it as a Spring bean with id as setType. The id attribute specifies the id with which the bean is made available to other beans, and the set-class attribute specifies the concrete implementation class of java.util.Set interface that should be created by the <set> element. The <value> element of Spring's beans schema specifies an element in the created Set instance.

The Set instance created by the <set> element can be referenced from other beans. For instance, in the above example listing, DataTypesExample's setType constructor argument (of type java.util.Set) refers to the HashSet instance created by the <set> element.

Instead of using util schema's <set> element, you can use Spring's SetFactoryBean to create a Set instance and expose it as a Spring bean.

SetFactoryBean

Spring's SetFactoryBean is a factory object for creating instances of java.util.Set type.

The following example listing shows how you can use SetFactoryBean to perform the same function as the util schema's <set> element:

Example listing 3-49 – SetFactoryBean example

```
<beans .....>

  <bean id="dataTypes" class="sample.spring.chapter03.beans.DataTypesExample">
    .....
    <constructor-arg name="setType" ref="setType" />
    .....
  </bean>

  <bean id="setType" class="org.springframework.beans.factory.config.SetFactoryBean">
       <property name="sourceSet">
          <set>
               <value>Element 1</value>
               <value>Element 2</value>
          </set>
       </property>
  </bean>
  .....
</beans>
```

In the above example listing, SetFactoryBean's sourceSet property specifies the elements contained in the Set instance created by the SetFactoryBean. SetFactoryBean's targetSetClass property specifies the fully-qualified name of the class that implements java.util.Set interface.

If the targetSetClass property is specified, SetFactoryBean creates an instance of the class specified by the targetSetClass property and makes it available as a Spring bean. For instance, if you specify java.util.HashSet as the value of targetSetClass, SetFactoryBean creates an instance of java.util.HashSet. If the targetSetClass property is unspecified, SetFactoryBean creates an instance of java.util.LinkedHashSet.

The above example listing shows that using util schema's <set> element results in a more concise configuration than using SetFactoryBean for creating Set instances.

<properties>

The util schema's <properties> element is useful if you want to create an instance of java.util.Properties object from a properties file, and expose the java.util.Properties object as a bean.

The following example listing shows how the <properties> element is used:

Example listing 3-50 – applicationContext.xml - util schema's <properties> element
Project – ch03-util-schema-examples
Source location - src/main/resources/META-INF/spring

```
<beans .....
   xmlns:util="http://www.springframework.org/schema/util"
   xsi:schemaLocation=".....http://www.springframework.org/schema/util
   http://www.springframework.org/schema/util/spring-util-4.0.xsd">

  <bean id="bankDetails" class="sample.spring.chapter03.beans.BankDetails">
     .....
     <property name="branchAddresses" ref="branchAddresses" />
  </bean>
  .....
  <util:properties id="branchAddresses"
       location="classpath:META-INF/addresses.properties" />
</beans>
```

In the above example listing, <properties> element creates an instance of java.util.Properties containing properties loaded from the addresses.properties file (specified by the location attribute), and exposes the java.util.Properties instance as a bean with branchAddresses as the id (specified by the id attribute). The above example listing also shows that the branchAddresses property (of type java.util.Properties) of BankDetails bean refers to the branchAddresses bean created by the util schema's <properties> element.

An alternative to using the <properties> element is Spring's PropertiesFactoryBean.

PropertiesFactoryBean

Spring's PropertiesFactoryBean is a factory for creating instances of java.util.Properties.

The following example listing shows how you can use PropertiesFactoryBean to perform the same function as the util schema's <properties> element:

Example listing 3-51 – PropertiesFactoryBean example

```
<beans .....>

  <bean id="bankDetails" class="sample.spring.chapter03.beans.BankDetails">
     .....
     <property name="branchAddresses" ref="branchAddresses" />
  </bean>

  <bean id="branchAddresses"
        class="org.springframework.beans.factory.config.PropertiesFactoryBean">
      <property name="location" value="classpath:META-INF/addresses.properties"/>
  </bean>
  .....
</beans>
```

In the above example listing, bean definition for Spring's PropertiesFactoryBean creates an instance of java.util.Properties from the properties loaded from addresses.properties file (specified by location property), and exposes the java.util.Properties instance as a bean with branchAddresses as the id.

<constant>

The util schema's <constant> element is used for exposing an object's public static field as a Spring bean.

The following example listing shows an example usage of <constant> element:

Example listing 3-52 – applicationContext.xml - util schema's <constant> element
Project – ch03-util-schema-examples
Source location - src/main/resources/META-INF/spring

```
<beans ..... xmlns:util="http://www.springframework.org/schema/util"
     xsi:schemaLocation="..... http://www.springframework.org/schema/util
     http://www.springframework.org/schema/util/spring-util-4.0.xsd">

  <bean id="dataTypes" class="sample.spring.chapter03.beans.DataTypesExample">
     .....
```

```
        <constructor-arg name="booleanType" ref="booleanTrue" />
        .....
    </bean>

    <util:constant id="booleanTrue" static-field="java.lang.Boolean.TRUE" />
    .....
</beans>
```

The util schema's <constant> element exposes the value specified by its static-field attribute as a Spring bean. In the above example listing, <constant> element exposes a bean whose value is java.lang.Boolean.TRUE and id is booleanTrue. You can specify any public static field as the value of the static-field attribute and refer to it from other beans in the Spring container. For instance, in the above example listing, booleanType bean is referenced by DataTypesExample's booleanType constructor argument of type boolean.

A rather less concise way to expose public static fields as Spring beans is to use Spring's FieldRetrievingFactoryBean.

FieldRetrievingFactoryBean

Spring's FieldRetrievingFactoryBean is a factory for retrieving value of a public static field specified by the FieldRetrievingFactoryBean's staticField property. The value retrieved by the FieldRetrievingFactoryBean is exposed as a bean. You can also use the FieldRetrievingFactoryBean to retrieve a non-static field value.

The following example listing shows an example usage of FieldRetrievingFactoryBean:

Example listing 3-53 – FieldRetrievingFactoryBean example

```
<beans .....>

   <bean id="dataTypes" class="sample.spring.chapter03.beans.DataTypesExample">
      .....
      <constructor-arg name="booleanType" ref="booleanTrue" />
      .....
   </bean>

   <bean id="booleanTrue"
          class="org.springframework.beans.factory.config.FieldRetrievingFactoryBean">
      <property name="staticField" value=" java.lang.Boolean.TRUE"/>
   </bean>
   .....
</beans>
```

In the above example listing, FieldRetrievingFactoryBean retrieves the value of java.lang.Boolean.TRUE field and exposes it as a bean. The bean exposed by the FieldRetrievingFactoryBean is referenced by DataTypesExample's booleanType constructor argument of type boolean.

<property-path>

The util schema's <property-path> element is used to expose a bean property value as a bean.

The following example listing shows an example usage of <property-path> element:

Example listing 3-54 – applicationContext.xml - util schema's <property-path> element
Project – ch03-util-schema-examples
Source location - src/main/resources/META-INF/spring

```
<beans .....
    xmlns:util="http://www.springframework.org/schema/util"
    xsi:schemaLocation="..... http://www.springframework.org/schema/util
    http://www.springframework.org/schema/util/spring-util-4.0.xsd">

  <bean id="bankDetails" class="sample.spring.chapter03.beans.BankDetails">
     .....
     <property name="dateOfInception" ref="dateType" />
     .....
  </bean>

  <util:property-path id="dateType" path="dataTypes.dateType" />

  <bean id="dataTypes" class="sample.spring.chapter03.beans.DataTypesExample">
     .....
     <property name="dateType" value="30-01-2012" />
     .....
  </bean>
</beans>
```

In the above example listing, DataTypesExample's dateType property (of type java.util.Date) value is specified as '30-01-2012'. The <property-path> element retrieves the DataTypesExample's dateType property and exposes it as a bean with id as dateType. The path attribute of <property-path> element has the following syntax:

```
<bean-name>.<bean-property>
```

Here, *<bean-name>* is the id or name of the bean, and *<bean-property>* is the name of the property.

As <property-path> element exposes a bean, the exposed bean can be referenced by other beans in the Spring container. For instance in the above example listing, dateType bean is referenced by dateOfInception property of BankDetails bean.

Instead of using <property-path> element, you can use Spring's PropertyPathFactoryBean to expose a bean property value as a bean.

PropertyPathFactoryBean

PropertyPathFactoryBean is a factory used for creating bean instances that represent a bean property value.

The following example listing shows how to use PropertyPathFactoryBean:

Example listing 3-55 – PropertyPathFactoryBean example

```
<beans .....
   xmlns:util="http://www.springframework.org/schema/util"
   xsi:schemaLocation="..... http://www.springframework.org/schema/util
   http://www.springframework.org/schema/util/spring-util-4.0.xsd">

  <bean id="bankDetails" class="sample.spring.chapter03.beans.BankDetails">
     .....
     <property name="dateOfInception" ref="dateType" />
     .....
  </bean>

  <bean id="dataType"
   class="org.springframework.beans.factory.config.PropertyPathFactoryBean">
      <property name="targetBeanName" value="dataTypes"/>
      <property name="propertyPath" value="dateType"/>
  </bean>

  <bean id="dataTypes" class="sample.spring.chapter03.beans.DataTypesExample">
     .....
     <property name="dateType" value="30-01-2012" />
     .....
  </bean>
</beans>
```

In the above example listing, PropertyPathFactoryBean is used to create an instance of a bean that represents the value of dateType property of dataTypes bean. PropertyPathFactoryBean's targetBeanName attribute specifies the id or name of the bean that contains the property, and PropertyPathFactoryBean's propertyPath attribute specifies the name of the property whose value is to be exposed as a bean. The bean instance created by PropertyPathFactoryBean can be accessed by other beans in the Spring container. In the above example listing, the dataType bean created by PropertyPathFactoryBean is referenced by dateOfInception property (of type java.util.Date) of BankDetails bean.

Now, that we have taken an in-depth look at util schema elements, let's look at Spring's FactoryBean interface.

3-9 FactoryBean interface

Spring's FactoryBean interface is implemented by classes that act as a factory for creating bean instances. In the previous section, we saw that the classes that implement the FactoryBean interface are configured in the application context XML file like any other bean. FactoryBean is particularly useful if you want to perform complicated conditional checks to decide on which bean type to create, and to execute complex bean initialization logic.

Let's now look at an application scenario in which we'll use FactoryBean for selecting a bean type, and then creating it.

MyBank application – Storing events in the database

In MyBank application, important events, like credit and debit transactions, open and liquidate fixed deposits, and so on, are saved in the database. MyBank may directly save these events in the database or indirectly by first sending the events to a messaging middleware or a web service. The following table describes the classes that are defined by the MyBank application for directly or indirectly saving events:

Class	Description
DatabaseEventSender	Class that contains the functionality for saving events in the database
MessagingEventSender	Class that contains the functionality for sending events to a messaging middleware
WebServiceEventSender	Class that contains the functionality for sending events to a remote web service

The decision to directly save the events in the database or to send them to a messaging middleware or a web service is based on configuration. For instance, if MyBank finds that there exists a database.properties file, MyBank reads the configuration information (like database url, username and password) from the database.properties file and creates the DatabaseEventSender instance. Similarly, if a messging.properties file exists, MyBank creates an instance of

MessagingEventSender instance, and if a webservice.properties file exists, an instance of WebServiceEventSender is created.

Initializing DatabaseEventSender, MessagingEventSender and WebServiceEventSender instances may require executing complex initialization logic. For instance, you need to create (or obtain from JNDI) javax.jms.ConnectionFactory and javax.jms.Destination instances and set them on the MessagingEventSender instance so that the MessagingEventSender can send JMS messages to the messaging middleware.

The following class diagram shows that the FixedDepositServiceImpl class of MyBank uses either DatabaseEventSender or MessagingEventSender or WebServiceEventSender instance to directly or indirectly save events related to fixed deposits in the database:

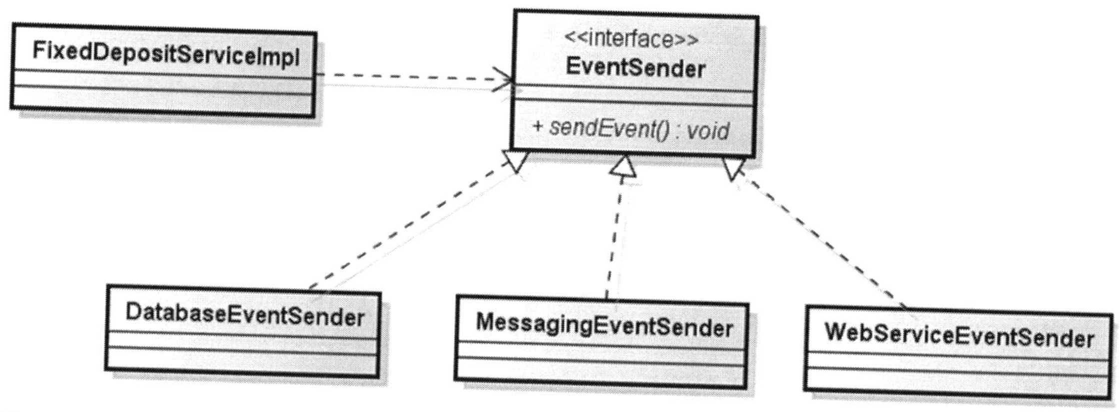

Figure 3-7 FixedDepositServiceImpl class uses one of the implementations of EventSender interface.

In the above class diagram, sendEvent method of EventSender interface defines the contract for directly or indirectly saving events in the database. DatabaseEventSender, MessagingEventSender and WebServiceEventSender classes implement the EventSender interface and provide an appropriate implementation for the sendEvent method.

Let's now look at how FactoryBean simplifies choosing the right implementation of EventSender interface and initializing it.

IMPORT **chapter 3/ch03-bankapp-factorybean** (This project shows the MyBank application that uses a FactoryBean implementation to create objects of type EventSender. To run the application, execute the main method of the BankApp class of this project)

MyBank – FactoryBean example

In MyBank, selecting the right EventSender implementation and initializing it is an involved task; therefore, it represents an ideal scenario for using a FactoryBean implementation. FactoryBean interface defines the following methods that you need to implement:

- getObjectType: returns the *type* of the object managed by the FactoryBean implementation. In case of MyBank, the FactoryBean implementation creates and returns objects of type EventSender.

- getObject: returns the object managed by the FactoryBean implementation. In case of MyBank, the getObject method returns an instance of DatabaseEventSender or MessagingEventSender or WebServiceEventSender.

- isSingleton: returns true if the FactoryBean implementation is a factory for singleton-scoped objects. If the isSingleton method returns true, the object returned by the getObject method is cached by the Spring container and the same instance is returned on subsequent requests. If the FactoryBean implementation is a factory for prototype-scoped objects, return false from the isSingleton method. If the isSingleton method returns false, a fresh instance is created by getObject method on every request. In case of MyBank, FactoryBean implementation returns an instance of DatabaseEventSender or MessagingEventSender or WebServiceEventSender class. Once created, the same instance is used throughout the lifetime of the MyBank application; therefore, the isSingleton method returns true in case of MyBank.

The following example listing shows the EventSenderFactoryBean – the FactoryBean implementation that creates and returns objects of type EventSender:

Example listing 3-56 – EventSenderFactoryBean class
Project – ch03-bankapp-factorybean
Source location - src/main/java/sample/spring/chapter03/bankapp/event

```
package sample.spring.chapter03.bankapp.event;

import org.springframework.beans.factory.FactoryBean;
import org.springframework.beans.factory.FactoryBeanNotInitializedException;
import org.springframework.core.io.ClassPathResource;
.....
public class EventSenderFactoryBean implements FactoryBean<EventSender> {
    private String databasePropertiesFile;
    private String webServicePropertiesFile;
    private String messagingPropertiesFile;
    .....
    public EventSender getObject() throws Exception {
```

```
        EventSender eventSender = null;
      Properties properties = new Properties();

      ClassPathResource databaseProperties = null;
      if(databasePropertiesFile != null) {
               databaseProperties = new ClassPathResource(databasePropertiesFile);
      }
      .....
      if (databaseProperties != null && databaseProperties.exists()) {
        InputStream inStream = databaseProperties.getInputStream();
        properties.load(inStream);
        eventSender = new DatabaseEventSender(properties);
      }
      else if (webServiceProperties != null  && webServiceProperties.exists()) {.....}
      else if (messagingProperties != null  && messagingProperties.exists()) {.....}

      return eventSender;
    }

    public Class<?> getObjectType() {
      return EventSender.class;
    }

    public boolean isSingleton() {
      return true;
    }
}
```

The above example listing shows that the EventSenderFactoryBean implements FactoryBean interface. The EventSender parameter in FactoryBean<EventSender> indicates that the FactoryBean's getObject returns objects of type EventSender. The databasePropertiesFile, webServicePropertiesFile and messagingPropertiesFile are properties of the EventSenderFactoryBean class, and they represent the location of database.properties, webservice.properties and messaging.properties files in the classpath.

The getObject method uses Spring's ClassPathResource class to verify whether the specified properties file exists in the classpath or not. If the properties file exists, properties from that file are loaded and passed as to the EventSender implementation class's constructor. For instance, in the above example listing, if database.properties file (represented by databasePropertiesFile property) exists, properties are loaded from the database.properties file and passed as an argument to the DatabaseEventSender's constructor. The getObjectType method returns EventSender type because the EventSenderFactoryBean's getObject method returns objects of type EventSender. The isSingleton method returns true, which means that the object returned by getObject method is cached by Spring and the same instance is returned every time EventSenderFactoryBean's getObject method is invoked.

Now, that you have seen how EventSenderFactoryBean class is implemented in the MyBank, you can guess how Spring's built-in FactoryBean implementations, like ListFactoryBean (for creating instances of List type), MapFactoryBean (for creating instances of Map type), SetFactoryBean (for creating instances of Set type), and so on, are implemented.

The following example listing shows how EventSenderFactoryBean is configured in the application context XML file:

Example listing 3-57 – applicationContext.xml - EventSenderFactoryBean configuration
Project – ch03-bankapp-factorybean
Source location - src/main/resources/META-INF/spring

```
<beans .....>

  <bean id="service"
     class="sample.spring.chapter03.bankapp.service.FixedDepositServiceImpl">
     .....
     <property name="eventSender" ref="eventSenderFactory" />
  </bean>
  .....
  <bean id="eventSenderFactory"
        class="sample.spring.chapter03.bankapp.event.EventSenderFactoryBean">
      <property name="databasePropertiesFile" value="META-INF/config/database.properties"/>
  </bean>
</beans>
```

The above example listing shows that the EventSenderFactoryBean is configured like any other Spring bean. Even though a FactoryBean implementation is configured like any other Spring bean, it is treated *differently* by the Spring container. One of the most important differences is that if a bean is dependent on a FactoryBean implementation, the Spring container invokes the getObject method of the FactoryBean implementation and injects the returned object into the dependent bean.

> You should note that FactoryBean's getObject method is invoked only once by the Spring container if the isSingleton method returns true.

In the above example listing, bean definition for the FixedDepositServiceImpl class shows that it is dependent on the EventSenderFactoryBean – a FactoryBean implementation. So, the Spring container invokes the EventSenderFactoryBean's getObject method and injects the returned EventSender object into the FixedDepositServiceImpl instance.

The following example listing shows the FixedDepositServiceImpl class that requires EventSender instance created by EventSenderFactoryBean:

Example listing 3-58 – FixedDepositServiceImpl class
Project – ch03-bankapp-factorybean
Source location - src/main/java/sample/spring/chapter03/bankapp/service

```
package sample.spring.chapter03.bankapp.service;

import sample.spring.chapter03.bankapp.event.EventSender;

public class FixedDepositServiceImpl implements FixedDepositService {
  .....
  private EventSender eventSender;

  public void setEventSender(EventSender eventSender) {
     this.eventSender = eventSender;
  }
  .....
  public void createFixedDeposit(FixedDepositDetails fixedDepositDetails) {
    .....
    eventSender.sendEvent(event);
  }
}
```

The above example listing shows that the FixedDepositServiceImpl class depends on an EventSender instance and *not* on the EventSenderFactoryBean instance. The Spring container obtains the EventSender instance by invoking EventSenderFactoryBean's getObject method, and injects the obtained EventSender instance into the FixedDepositServiceImpl instance.

Let's now look at how to access the FactoryBean itself and *not* the bean it creates and returns via the getObject method.

Accessing the FactoryBean instance

If you want to obtain the FactoryBean itself from the Spring container, prefix the name (or id) of the factory bean with ampersand '&'.

Let's say that the FixedDepositServiceImpl class requires access to the EventSenderFactoryBean itself, as shown here:

Example listing 3-59 – FixedDepositServiceImpl class that depends on the EventSenderFactoryBean itself

```
package sample.spring.chapter03.bankapp.service;

import sample.spring.chapter03.bankapp.event.EventSenderFactoryBean;
import sample.spring.chapter03.bankapp.event.EventSender;

public class FixedDepositServiceImpl implements FixedDepositService {
  .....
  private EventSenderFactoryBean eventSenderFactoryBean;

  public void setEventSenderFactoryBean (EventSenderFactoryBean eventSenderFactoryBean) {
    this. eventSenderFactoryBean = eventSenderFactoryBean;
  }
  .....
  public void createFixedDeposit(FixedDepositDetails fixedDepositDetails) {
    .....
    EventSender eventSender = eventSenderFactoryBean.getObject();
    evenSender.sendEvent(event);
  }
}
```

In the above example listing, the FixedDepositServiceImpl class depends on the EventSenderFactoryBean itself, and uses its getObject method to obtain an instance of EventSender object.

We saw in example listing 3-57 that when you define the EventSenderFactoryBean bean as a dependency of FixedDepositServiceImpl bean, the Spring container invokes the getObject method of EventSenderFactoryBean and injects the returned EventSender object into the FixedDepositServiceImpl bean. To instruct the Spring container to inject the EventSenderFactoryBean itself, add ampersand '&' prefix to the id (or name) of the bean specified by the ref attribute, as shown in the following example listing:

Example listing 3-60 – Injecting the EventSenderFactoryBean instance into the FixedDepositServiceImpl bean

```
<beans .....>

  <bean id="service" class="sample.spring.chapter03.bankapp.service.FixedDepositServiceImpl">
    .....
    <property name="eventSenderFactoryBean" ref="&amp;eventSenderFactory" />
  </bean>
  .....
```

```
    <bean id="eventSenderFactory"
          class="sample.spring.chapter03.bankapp.event.EventSenderFactoryBean">
       <property name="databasePropertiesFile" value="META-INF/config/database.properties"/>
    </bean>
</beans>
```

In the above example listing, the following <property> element specifies that the FixedDepositServiceImpl bean is dependent on EventSenderFactoryBean:

```
<property name="eventSenderFactoryBean" ref="&amp;eventSenderFactory" />
```

Notice that the ref attribute's value is "&eventSenderFactory". The & prefix instructs the Spring container to inject the EventSenderFactoryBean instance itself into the FixedDepositServiceImpl bean.

The use of ampersand '&' is also required when you want to retrieve the FactoryBean instance itself using ApplicationContext's getBean method. The following example listing shows the BankApp class of MyBank application that retrieves the EventSender object created by the EventSenderFactoryBean, and the EventSenderFactoryBean instance itself:

Example listing 3-61 – BankApp class
Project – ch03-bankapp-factorybean
Source location - src/main/java/sample/spring/chapter03/bankapp

```
package sample.spring.chapter03.bankapp;
.....
public class BankApp {
   private static Logger logger = Logger.getLogger(BankApp.class);

   public static void main(String args[]) {
      ApplicationContext context = new ClassPathXmlApplicationContext(
      .....
      logger.info("Invoking getBean(\"eventFactory\") returns : " +
            context.getBean("eventSenderFactory"));
      logger.info("Invoking getBean(\"&eventFactory\") returns : " +
            context.getBean("&eventSenderFactory"));
   }
}
```

If you execute the main method of the BankApp class shown above, you'll find that calling getBean("eventSenderFactory") returns an instance of DatabaseEventSender class, and getBean("&eventSenderFactory") returns EventSenderFactoryBean instance.

3-10 Summary

In this chapter, we saw how you can use bean definition inheritance to create less verbose and easily manageable bean definitions. The majority of this chapter focused on how to set different types of bean properties and constructor arguments using built-in FactoryBean implementations, Spring's util schema, and p- and c-namespaces. We also looked at some of the built-in PropertyEditor implementations in Spring and how to register additional property editors with the Spring container. In the next chapter, we'll take an in-depth look at dependency injection feature of Spring.

Chapter 4 - *Dependency injection*

4-1 Introduction

In the previous chapter, we looked at how to configure beans using Spring's util schema, p- and c-namespaces, FactoryBean implementations, and so on. In this chapter we focus on different dependency injection scenarios which we typically come across in real world application development efforts and how Spring addresses these scenarios.

We'll begin this chapter with a look at *inner beans* - an alternative to using the ref attribute of <property> and <constructor-arg> elements. We'll then look at depends-on attribute of the <bean> element. In the second half of this chapter, we'll look at issues that may arise when singleton- and prototype-scoped beans collaborate to provide application behavior. We'll wrap this chapter with an in-depth look at Spring's *autowiring* feature.

IMPORT **chapter 4/ch04-bankapp-dependencies** (This project shows usage of inner beans and <bean> element's depends-on attribute. This project also shows implications of defining dependence of singleton-scoped beans on prototype-scoped beans, and vice versa. To run the application, execute the main method of the BankApp class of this project)

4-2 Inner beans

If a dependency of a bean is *not* shared by multiple beans, you can consider defining the dependency as an *inner bean*. An inner bean is defined inside a <property> or <constructor-arg> element by using the <bean> element of Spring's beans schema. You should note that an inner bean is only accessible to the bean definition enclosing it, and *not* to other beans registered with the Spring container.

The following example listing shows how we generally represent bean dependencies:

Example listing 4-1 – Dependency specified using <property> element's ref attribute

```
<bean id="service"
   class="sample.spring.chapter04.bankapp.service.FixedDepositServiceImpl">
  <property name="fixedDepositDao" ref="dao" />
</bean>

<bean id="dao" class="sample.spring.chapter04.bankapp.dao.FixedDepositDaoImpl" />
```

The above example listing shows that the service bean is dependent on dao bean. If service bean is the only bean that is dependent on the dao bean, then you can define the dao bean as an *inner bean* of service bean.

Example listing 4-2 – applicationContext.xml - Inner bean example
Project – ch04-bankapp-dependencies
Source location - src/main/resources/META-INF/spring

```
<bean id="service"
      class="sample.spring.chapter04.bankapp.service.FixedDepositServiceImpl">
   <property name="fixedDepositDao">
        <bean class="sample.spring.chapter04.bankapp.dao.FixedDepositDaoImpl" />
   </property>
</bean>
```

In the above example listing, the bean definition for the FixedDepositDaoImpl class is inside the <property> element of service bean. If you compare the above example listing with 4-1, you'll notice that the <property> element no longer specifies the ref attribute, and the <bean> element corresponding to FixedDepositDaoImpl class doesn't have the id attribute anymore.

The <bean> element corresponding to an inner bean definition doesn't specify an id attribute because an inner bean is *not* registered with the Spring container. If you specify an id attribute for an inner bean definition, it is ignored by the Spring container. An inner bean is *always* prototype-scoped; therefore, if the <bean> element corresponding to an inner bean definition specifies the scope attribute, then it is ignored by the Spring container. It is important to note that an inner bean is *anonymous* in nature, and it's not accessible to other beans (except the bean that contains the inner bean definition) in the Spring container.

> As in case of normal bean definition, you can use <property>, <constructor-arg>, and so on, elements inside the <bean> element of the inner bean definition.

In the previous chapter, we saw that Spring's util schema elements are used to create beans that represent a List, Set, Map, and so on. We saw that the beans created by Spring's util schema elements are referenced by other beans. The concept of inner beans makes it possible to use Spring's util schema elements inside <property> and <constructor-arg> elements also, as shown in the following example listing:

Example listing 4-3 – util schema's <list> element defines an inner bean

```
<beans xmlns="http://www.springframework.org/schema/beans"
          xmlns:util="http://www.springframework.org/schema/util"
          xsi:schemaLocation="..... http://www.springframework.org/schema/util
                 http://www.springframework.org/schema/util/spring-util-4.0.xsd">

   <bean id="someBean" class="com.sample.SomeBean">
      .....
      <constructor-arg name="listType">
```

```
            <util:list list-class="java.util.ArrayList">
                <value>A simple String value in list</value>
                <value>Another simple String value in list</value>
            </util:list>
        </constructor-arg>
        .....
    </bean>
</beans>
```

In the above example listing, the listType constructor argument is of type java.util.List. The value passed to the listType constructor argument is specified by the util schema's <list> element. Note that we didn't specify the *id* attribute of the <list> element because Spring container ignores ids of inner beans.

Let's now look at depends-on attribute of <bean> element.

4-3 Explicitly controlling the bean initialization order with depends-on attribute

In section 1-4 of chapter 1, we discussed that beans are created in the order in which they are defined in the application context XML file. The order in which beans are created is also decided based on the inter-dependencies of beans. For instance, if bean A accepts an instance of bean B as a constructor argument, the Spring container will create bean B *before* bean A irrespective of the order in which they are defined in the application context XML file. This behavior of the Spring container ensures that the dependencies of a bean (bean B is a dependency in our example) are completely configured before they are injected into the dependent bean (bean A is a dependent bean in our example).

In some application scenarios, bean dependencies are not explicitly specified via <property> and <constructor-arg> elements. If the bean dependencies are *not* explicit, you can use <bean> element's depends-on attribute to explicitly specify dependencies of a bean. Spring container ensures that bean dependencies specified by the depends-on attribute are initialized *before* the bean that specifies the depends-on attribute.

Let's now look at an example scenario in which depends-on attribute is used to control the initialization order of beans.

MyBank – implied dependencies between beans

In the MyBank application of the previous chapter, a FactoryBean implementation created an EventSender object that was used by the FixedDepositServiceImpl instance to directly or indirectly store events in the database (refer section 3-9 of chapter 3 for details). Let's say that instead of using a FactoryBean implementation for creating an EventSender implementation, the approach shown in the following diagram is adopted:

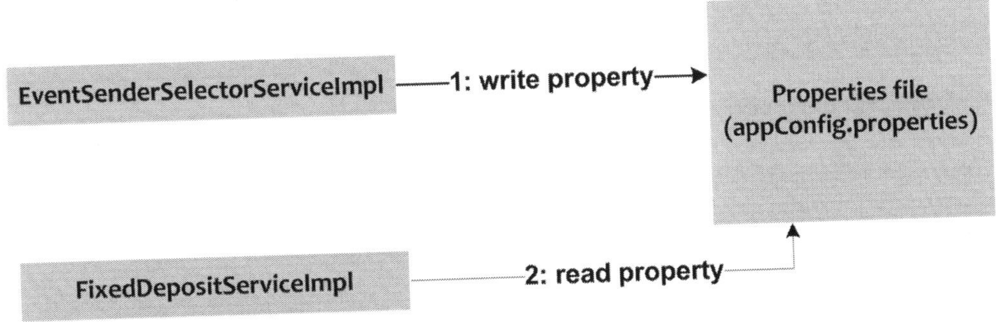

Figure 4-1 – EventSenderSelectorServiceImpl class writes the name of the EventSender implementation in the appConfig.properties file, which is later read by the FixedDepositServiceImpl instance

The above diagram shows that:

- an EventSenderSelectorServiceImpl class is used to decide on the EventSender implementation (DatabaseEventSender or WebServiceEventSender or MessagingEventSender) to be used by the FixedDepositServiceImpl class

- EventSenderSelectorServiceImpl class stores the fully-qualified name of the EventSender implementation in the appConfig.properties file

- FixedDepositServiceImpl class reads the fully-qualified name of the EventSender implementation from the appConfig.properties file, creates the EventSender object and uses it for storing fixed deposit events in the database

The above approach suggests that the FixedDepositServiceImpl instance won't work correctly if EventSenderSelectorServiceImpl fails to save the fully-qualified name of the EventSender implementation in the appConfig.properties file. This means that the FixedDepositServiceImpl class is implicitly dependent on the EventSenderSelectorServiceImpl class.

Let's now look at the implication of implicit dependence of FixedDepositServiceImpl instance on the EventSenderSelectorServiceImpl instance.

Implicit dependency problem

Consider the following application context XML file that contains bean definitions for FixedDepositServiceImpl and EventSenderSelectorServiceImpl classes:

Example listing 4-4 – applicationContext.xml - Implicit dependency example
Project – ch04-bankapp-dependencies
Source location - src/main/resources/META-INF/spring

```
<beans .....>
  <bean id="service"
     class="sample.spring.chapter04.bankapp.service.FixedDepositServiceImpl">
     .....
    <constructor-arg index="0" value="META-INF/config/appConfig.properties" />
  </bean>

  <bean id="eventSenderSelectorService"
      class="sample.spring.chapter04.bankapp.service.EventSenderSelectorServiceImpl">
    <constructor-arg index="0" value="META-INF/config/appConfig.properties" />
  </bean>
</beans>
```

The above application context XML file shows that both FixedDepositServiceImpl and EventSenderSelectorServiceImpl class's constructor accept location of the appConfig.properties file. The EventSenderSelectorServiceImpl instance uses the appConfig.properties file for communicating the fully-qualified name of the EventSender implementation class to the FixedDepositServiceImpl instance. As an explicit dependence *doesn't* exist between service and eventSenderSelectorService beans, Spring container creates their instances in the order in which they are defined in the application context XML file. As the service bean is defined *before* the eventSenderSelectorService bean, FixedDepositServiceImpl instance is created *before* EventSenderSelectorServiceImpl instance. We'll soon see that if FixedDepositServiceImpl instance is created *before* EventSenderSelectorServiceImpl instance, the FixedDepositServiceImpl instance will *not* be able to read the name of the fully-qualified EventSender implementation class from the appConfig.properties file.

Let's now take an in-depth look at the EventSenderSelectorServiceImpl and FixedDepositServiceImpl classes, and the **appConfig.properties** file.

EventSenderSelectorServiceImpl – the writer

The following example listing shows the EventSenderSelectorServiceImpl class:

Example listing 4-5 – EventSenderSelectorServiceImpl class
Project – ch04-bankapp-dependencies
Source location - src/main/java/sample/spring/chapter04/bankapp/service

```
package sample.spring.chapter04.bankapp.service;

import org.springframework.core.io.ClassPathResource;
```

```
import sample.spring.chapter04.bankapp.Constants;

public class EventSenderSelectorServiceImpl {

  public EventSenderSelectorServiceImpl(String configFile) throws Exception {
    ClassPathResource resource = new ClassPathResource(configFile);
    OutputStream os = new FileOutputStream(resource.getFile());

    Properties properties = new Properties();
    properties
      .setProperty(Constants.EVENT_SENDER_CLASS_PROPERTY,
         "sample.spring.chapter04.bankapp.event.DatabaseEventSender");
    properties.store(os, null);
    .....
  }
}
```

The above example listing shows that the location of appConfig.properties file is passed as a constructor argument to the EventSenderSelectorServiceImpl class's constructor. The EventSenderSelectorServiceImpl class's constructor writes a property named eventSenderClass (which is the value of EVENT_SENDER_CLASS_PROPERTY constant defined in the Constants class) to the appConfig.properties file. The eventSenderClass property specifies the fully-qualified name of the EventSender implementation to be used by the FixedDepositServiceImpl instance for directly or indirectly saving events in the database. For the sake of simplicity, EventSenderSelectorServiceImpl class's constructor sets the fully-qualified name of the DatabaseEventSender class as the value of eventSenderClass property.

appConfig.properties

The following is the entry that gets added to the appConfig.properties file by EventSenderSelectorServiceImpl class:

```
eventSenderClass=sample.spring.chapter04.bankapp.event.DatabaseEventSender
```

FixedDepositServiceImpl – the reader

The eventSenderClass property written by the EventSenderSelectorServiceImpl instance is read by the FixedDepositServiceImpl instance, as shown in the following example listing:

Example listing 4-6 – FixedDepositServiceImpl class
Project – ch04-bankapp-dependencies
Source location - src/main/java/sample/spring/chapter04/bankapp/service

```
package sample.spring.chapter04.bankapp.service;
```

```
import org.springframework.core.io.ClassPathResource;
import sample.spring.chapter04.bankapp.Constants;

public class FixedDepositServiceImpl implements FixedDepositService {
  private FixedDepositDao fixedDepositDao;
  private EventSender eventSender;

  public FixedDepositServiceImpl(String configFile) throws Exception {
    ClassPathResource configProperties = new ClassPathResource(configFile);

    if (configProperties.exists()) {
       InputStream inStream = configProperties.getInputStream();
       Properties properties = new Properties();
       properties.load(inStream);

       String eventSenderClassString =
           properties.getProperty(Constants.EVENT_SENDER_CLASS_PROPERTY);

       if (eventSenderClassString != null) {
           Class<?> eventSenderClass = Class.forName(eventSenderClassString);
           eventSender = (EventSender) eventSenderClass.newInstance();
           logger.info("Created EventSender class");
       } else {
           logger.info("appConfig.properties file doesn't contain the information " +
                          "about EventSender class");
       }
    }
  }

  public void createFixedDeposit(FixedDepositDetails fixedDepositDetails) throws Exception {
    .....
    eventSender.sendEvent(event);
  }
}
```

The above example listing shows following sequence of actions are performed by the constructor of FixedDepositServiceImpl class:

- loads properties from the appConfig.properties file. The configFile constructor argument represents the location of the appConfig.properties file.
- obtains property named eventSenderClass (represented by EVENT_SENDER_CLASS_PROPERTY constant defined in the Constants class) from the

properties loaded from the appConfig.properties file. The value of eventSenderClass property is the fully-qualified name of the EventSender implementation class that FixedDepositServiceImpl needs to use. The value of eventSenderClass property is stored in the eventSenderClassString local variable.

- creates an instance of the EventSender implementation class whose fully-qualified name is stored in the eventSenderClassString variable, and stores the newly created instance into an instance variable named eventSender. The eventSender variable is later used by the FixedDepositServiceImpl's createFixedDeposit method (refer to the createFixedDeposit method in the above example listing) to directly or indirectly store events in the database.

You should note that if a property named eventSenderClass is *not* found in the appConfig.properties file, the eventSenderClassString variable is *not* set. In this case, the FixedDepositServiceImpl's constructor prints the following message on the console: *'appConfig.properties file doesn't contain the information about EventSender class'*.

In example listing 4-4, we looked at bean definitions for EventSenderSelectorServiceImpl and FixedDepositServiceImpl classes, and concluded that the FixedDepositServiceImpl instance is created before EventSenderSelectorServiceImpl instance because Spring container initializes beans in the order in which they appear in the application context XML file. We saw in example listing 4-5 that the creation of EventSenderSelectorServiceImpl instance results in writing an eventSenderClass property to the appConfig.properties file. So, if the FixedDepositServiceImpl instance is created *before* the EventSenderSelectorServiceImpl instance, the FixedDepositServiceImpl instance will *not* find any eventSenderClass property in the appConfig.properties file. This shows that the FixedDepositServiceImpl class is *implicitly* dependent on the EventSenderSelectorServiceImpl class; therefore, the EventSenderSelectorServiceImpl instance *must* be created *before* the FixedDepositServiceImpl instance.

How to address implicit dependency problem?

We can solve the implicit dependency problem in two ways:

- we change the order in which bean definitions for EventSenderSelectorServiceImpl and FixedDepositServiceImpl classes are defined in the application context XML file. If the bean definition for the EventSenderSelectorServiceImpl class appears *before* the bean definition for the FixedDepositServiceImpl class, the EventSenderSelectorServiceImpl instance will be created *before* the FixedDepositServiceImpl instance.

- use <bean> element's depends-on attribute to *explicitly* specify that the service bean (corresponding to the FixedDepositServiceImpl class) is dependent on the eventSenderSelectorService bean (corresponding to the EventSenderSelectorServiceImpl class).

The following example listing shows the usage of <bean> element's depends-on attribute:

Example listing 4-7 – <bean> element's depends-on attribute

```
<beans .....>
   <bean id="service"
        class="sample.spring.chapter04.bankapp.service.FixedDepositServiceImpl"
      depends-on="eventSenderSelectorService">
        .....
   </bean>

   <bean id="eventSenderSelectorService"
        class="sample.spring.chapter04.bankapp.service.EventSenderSelectorServiceImpl">
      .....
   </bean>
</beans>
```

In the above example listing, the service bean uses depends-on attribute to explicitly specify that it is dependent on the eventSenderSelectorService bean. The depends-on attribute specifies the ids or names of the beans on which the bean is dependent. As the service bean specifies that it is dependent on the eventSenderSelectorService bean, Spring container creates eventSenderSelectorService bean (corresponding to the EventSenderSelectorServiceImpl class) instance *before* service bean (corresponding to the FixedDepositServiceImpl class) instance.

> If you execute the main method of the BankApp class of ch04-bankapp-dependencies project, you'll find that the FixedDepositServiceImpl instance is created *before* EventSenderSelectServiceImpl instance. For this reason, the following message is printed on the console: *'appConfig.properties file doesn't contain the information about EventSender class'.*

Multiple implicit dependencies

If a bean has multiple implicit dependencies, you can specify ids or names of all those dependencies as the value of depends-on attribute, as shown here:

Example listing 4-8 – depends-on attribute example - multiple implicit dependencies

```
<beans .....>
  <bean id="abean" ..... depends-on="bBean, cBean">
     .....
  </bean>
  .....
```

```
</beans>
```

The above example listing shows that you can specify multiple bean ids or names as the value of depends-on attribute.

depends-on attribute and bean definition inheritance

It is important to note that the depends-on attribute is *not* inherited by child bean definitions. The following example listing shows an *abstract* serviceTemplate parent bean definition that uses the depends-on attribute to specify baseService bean as a dependency:

Example listing 4-9 – depends-on attribute – bean definition inheritance

```
<bean id="serviceTemplate" class=".....ServiceTemplate" depends-on="baseService"
      abstract="true"/>

<bean id="someService" class=".....SomeServiceImpl" parent="serviceTemplate"/>

<bean id="someOtherService" class=".....SomeOtherServiceImpl" parent="serviceTemplate"/>

<bean id="baseService" class=".....BaseServiceImpl" />
```

In the above example listing, someService and someOtherService child bean definitions don't inherit the depends-on attribute from the serviceTemplate parent bean definition. As the Spring container creates beans in the order in which they are defined in the application context XML file, the baseService bean is created *after* the creation of someService and someOtherService beans.

Let's now look at how the Spring container manages dependencies of singleton- and prototype-scoped beans.

4-4 Singleton- and prototype-scoped bean's dependencies

A singleton-scoped bean (and its singleton-scoped dependencies) is created when the ApplicationContext instance is created. And, a prototype-scoped bean (and its prototype-scoped dependencies) is created each time ApplicationContext's getBean method is invoked to obtain the prototype-scoped bean.

If a singleton-scoped bean is dependent on a prototype-scoped bean, or vice versa, things get a bit complicated. For instance, if a singleton-scoped bean is dependent on a prototype-scoped bean, you might ask the question whether the Spring container will create the prototype-scoped bean (the dependency) *before* the singleton-scoped bean (the dependent bean)? or the Spring container will create and inject the prototype-scoped bean instance only when you call the ApplicationContext's getBean method to retrieve the singleton-scoped bean instance? The answers to these questions lies in the way singleton- and prototype-scoped dependencies of a bean are managed by the Spring container, as explained next.

Singleton-scoped bean's dependencies

The following example listing shows the singleton-scoped customerRequestService bean of MyBank application, and its dependencies:

Example listing 4-10 – applicationContext.xml - Dependencies of customerRequestService bean
Project – ch04-bankapp-dependencies
Source location - src/main/resources/META-INF/spring

```
<bean id="customerRequestService"
    class="sample.spring.chapter04.bankapp.service.CustomerRequestServiceImpl">
        <constructor-arg name="customerRequestDetails" ref="customerRequestDetails" />
        <constructor-arg name="customerRequestDao" ref="customerRequestDao" />
</bean>

<bean id="customerRequestDetails"
    class="sample.spring.chapter04.bankapp.domain.CustomerRequestDetails"
    scope="prototype" />

<bean id="customerRequestDao"
    class="sample.spring.chapter04.bankapp.dao.CustomerRequestDaoImpl" />
```

The above example listing shows that the customerRequestService (singleton-scoped) bean depends on customerRequestDetails (prototype-scoped) and customerRequestDao (singleton-scoped) beans. CustomerRequestService object (represented by the customerRequestService bean) represents a service that is invoked when a bank customer creates a new request, like a cheque book request. CustomerRequestService puts the details of the customer request into a CustomerRequestDetails object (represented by the customerRequestDetails bean) and saves it in the data store using CustomerRequestDao object (represented by the customerRequestDao bean).

The following example listing shows the main method of BankApp class that loads the bean definitions shown in example listing 4-10:

Example listing 4-11 – BankApp class
Project – ch04-bankapp-dependencies
Source location - src/main/java/sample/spring/chapter04/bankapp

```
package sample.spring.chapter04.bankapp;

import org.springframework.context.ApplicationContext;
import org.springframework.context.support.ClassPathXmlApplicationContext;
```

```
public class BankApp {
  private static Logger logger = Logger.getLogger(BankApp.class);

  public static void main(String args[]) throws Exception {
    ApplicationContext context = new ClassPathXmlApplicationContext(
          "classpath:META-INF/spring/applicationContext.xml");
    .....
    logger.info("Beginning with accessing CustomerRequestService");
    CustomerRequestService customerRequestService_1
          = context.getBean(CustomerRequestService.class);
    .....
    CustomerRequestService customerRequestService_2
          = context.getBean(CustomerRequestService.class);
    .....
    logger.info("Done with accessing CustomerRequestService");
  }
}
```

The above example listing shows that after the ApplicationContext instance is created, ApplicationContext's getBean method is invoked twice to obtain reference to the customerRequestService bean.

If you execute the main method of the BankApp class, you'll see the following output:

```
Created CustomerRequestDetails instance
Created CustomerRequestDaoImpl instance
Created CustomerRequestServiceImpl instance
.....
Beginning with accessing CustomerRequestService
Done with accessing CustomerRequestService
```

The *'Created.....'* messages shown in the above output are printed by the constructors of the respective bean classes. The above output shows that the customerRequestDetails (prototype-scoped) and customerRequestDao (singleton-scoped) dependencies of the customerRequestService (singleton-scoped) bean are created and injected into the customerRequestService instance when the Spring container is created. As no *'Created .....'* message was printed on the console between *'Beginning .....'* and *'Done .....'* messages, no bean instances were created by the Spring container when ApplicationContext's getBean method was invoked to retrieve the customerRequestService bean.

Figure 4-2 shows the sequence diagram that depicts the sequence of events that occur when BankApp's main method (refer example listing 4-11) is executed. Figure 4-2 shows that when Spring container is created, the customerRequestDetails (prototype-scoped) and customerRequestDao (singleton-scoped) beans are first created, followed by creation of customerRequestService (singleton-scoped). Constructor-based DI is used to inject the customerRequestDetails and customerRequestDao beans into the customerRequestService bean. As a singleton-scoped bean is created *only once* by the Spring container, the Spring container has *only one* opportunity to inject customerRequestService bean's dependencies. For this reason, the Spring container injects prototype-scoped customerRequestDetails bean instance into the customerRequestService bean *only once*. The implication of this behavior is that the customerRequestService bean ends up holding reference to the *same* customerRequestDetails bean during its lifetime.

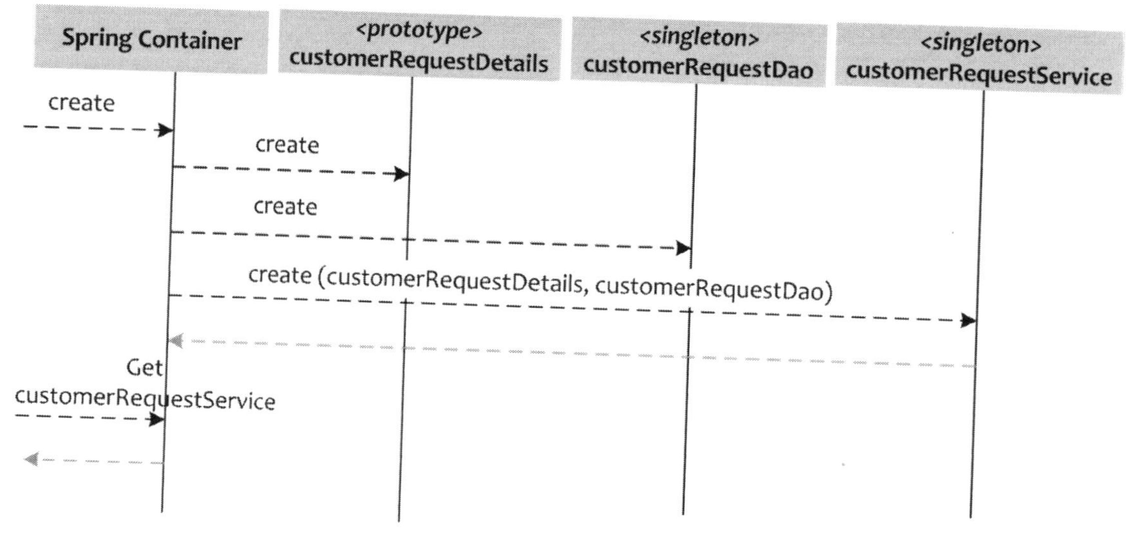

Figure 4-2 - The sequence of events that occur when the Spring container is created and the customerRequestService bean is retrieved from the Spring container

It is important to note that even if setter-based DI was used to inject the prototype-scoped customerRequestDetails dependency of the customerRequestService bean, the Spring container would have called the setter method *only once* during the lifetime of the customerRequestService bean. This means that irrespective of whether setter- or constructor-based DI is used, a singleton bean is created and configured only once during it's lifetime.

Now, once the Spring container is created, any request for the singleton-scoped customerRequestService bean returns the same cached instance of the customerRequestService bean. For this reason, no *'Created .....'* message was written out to the console between *'Beginning .....'* and *'Done .....'* messages when we executed BankApp's main method (refer example listing 4-11).

As the singleton-scoped customerRequestService bean always holds reference to the *same* prototype-scoped customerRequestDetails bean, it may adversely affect the behavior of MyBank application. For instance, if multiple customers simultaneously submit request to the CustomerRequestServiceImpl instance, all the requests will result in modifying the same instance of the CustomerRequestDetails object held by the CustomerRequestService. Ideally, CustomerRequestServiceImpl should create a new instance of CustomerRequestDetails object on every request. In section 4-5, we'll see what modifications we need to make to the bean class of a singleton-scoped bean so that it can retrieve a new instance of a prototype-scoped bean on every method call.

Let's now look at how the Spring container manages prototype- and singleton-scoped dependencies of a prototype-scoped bean.

Prototype-scoped bean's dependencies

In MyBank, a customer registers with the MyBank application by following a sequence of steps. For instance, a customer first enters personal information and his account details, and if the MyBank application finds a matching record, the customer is asked for his debit card details. The CustomerRegistrationServiceImpl class of MyBank application contains the necessary business logic to register customers. As the customers follow a sequence of steps to register with the MyBank application, the CustomerRegistrationServiceImpl object maintains conversational state between method calls.

The following example listing shows the prototype-scoped customerRegistrationService bean (representing the CustomerRegistrationServiceImpl class) of MyBank application, and its dependencies:

Example listing 4-12 – applicationContext.xml - customerRegistrationService bean and its dependencies
Project – ch04-bankapp-dependencies
Source location - src/main/resources/META-INF/spring

```
<bean id="customerRegistrationService"
   class="sample.spring.chapter04.bankapp.service.CustomerRegistrationServiceImpl"
   scope="prototype">
     <constructor-arg name="customerRegistrationDetails" ref="customerRegistrationDetails" />
     <constructor-arg name="customerRegistrationDao" ref="customerRegistrationDao" />
</bean>
<bean id="customerRegistrationDetails"
   class="sample.spring.chapter04.bankapp.domain.CustomerRegistrationDetails"
   scope="prototype" />

<bean id="customerRegistrationDao"
   class="sample.spring.chapter04.bankapp.dao.CustomerRegistrationDaoImpl" />
```

The above example listing shows that the customerRegistrationService (prototype-scoped) bean depends on customerRegistrationDetails (prototype-scoped) and customerRegistrationDao (singleton-scoped) beans.

CustomerRegistrationServiceImpl instance maintains progress of the registration process, and stores information provided by the customer during the registration process in a CustomerRegistrationDetails object (represented by the customerRegistrationDetails bean). As both CustomerRegistrationServiceImpl and CustomerRegistrationDetails objects are stateful in nature, both customerRegistrationService and customerRegistrationDetails beans are defined as prototype-scoped beans.

The following example listing shows the main method of BankApp class that loads customer registration related beans (refer example listing 4-12) and performs registrations for 2 customers:

Example listing 4-13 – BankApp class
Project – ch04-bankapp-dependencies
Source location - src/main/java/sample/spring/chapter04/bankapp

```
package sample.spring.chapter04.bankapp;

import org.springframework.context.ApplicationContext;
import org.springframework.context.support.ClassPathXmlApplicationContext;

public class BankApp {
  private static Logger logger = Logger.getLogger(BankApp.class);

  public static void main(String args[]) throws Exception {
     ApplicationContext context = new ClassPathXmlApplicationContext(
        "classpath:META-INF/spring/applicationContext.xml");
     .....
     logger.info("Beginning with accessing CustomerRegistrationService");

     CustomerRegistrationService customerRegistrationService_1 = context
         .getBean(CustomerRegistrationService.class);
     customerRegistrationService_1.setAccountNumber("account_1");
     customerRegistrationService_1.setAddress("address_1");
     customerRegistrationService_1.setDebitCardNumber("debitCardNumber_1");
     customerRegistrationService_1.register();
     logger.info("registered customer with id account_1");

     CustomerRegistrationService customerRegistrationService_2 = context
         .getBean(CustomerRegistrationService.class);
```

```
        .....
        logger.info("registered customer with id account_2");
        logger.info("Done with accessing CustomerRegistrationService");
    }
}
```

The above example listing shows that the BankApp's main method calls ApplicationContext's getBean method twice to obtain reference to customerRegistrationService bean. Once the customerRegistrationService bean instance is retrieved, the setAccountNumber, setAddress, setDebitCardNumber and register methods are invoked on it. If you execute BankApp's main method, you'll see the following output on the console:

```
Created CustomerRegistrationDaoImpl instance
.....
Beginning with accessing CustomerRegistrationService
Created CustomerRegistrationDetails instance
Created CustomerRegistrationServiceImpl instance
registered customer with id account_1
Created CustomerRegistrationDetails instance
Created CustomerRegistrationServiceImpl instance
registered customer with id account_2
Done with accessing CustomerRegistrationService
```

The *'Created.....'* messages shown in the above output are printed by the constructors of the respective bean classes. The above output shows that the singleton-scoped customerRegistrationDao bean (representing the CustomerRegistrationDaoImpl class) is created *only once* when the ApplicationContext instance is created. The *'Created.....'* messages between *'Beginning.....'* and *'Done.....'* messages indicate that each time ApplicationContext's getBean method is invoked to obtain the prototype-scoped customerRegistrationService bean, a new instance of the customerRegistrationService bean and its prototype-scoped dependency (the customerRegistrationDetails bean) is created by the Spring container.

Figure 4-3 shows the sequence diagram that depicts the sequence of events that occur when BankApp's main method (refer example listing 4-13) is executed. The figure shows that the singleton-scoped customerRegistrationDao bean is created *only once* when ApplicationContext instance is created. When the prototype-scoped customerRegistrationService bean is requested from the Spring container, the Spring container first creates an instance of customerRegistrationDetails bean (which is the prototype-scoped dependency of the customerRegistrationService bean), followed by the creation of the customerRegistrationService bean. This shows that if a prototype-scoped bean X is dependent on another prototype-scoped bean Y, Spring container will create a new instance of X and Y each time you request bean X from the Spring container.

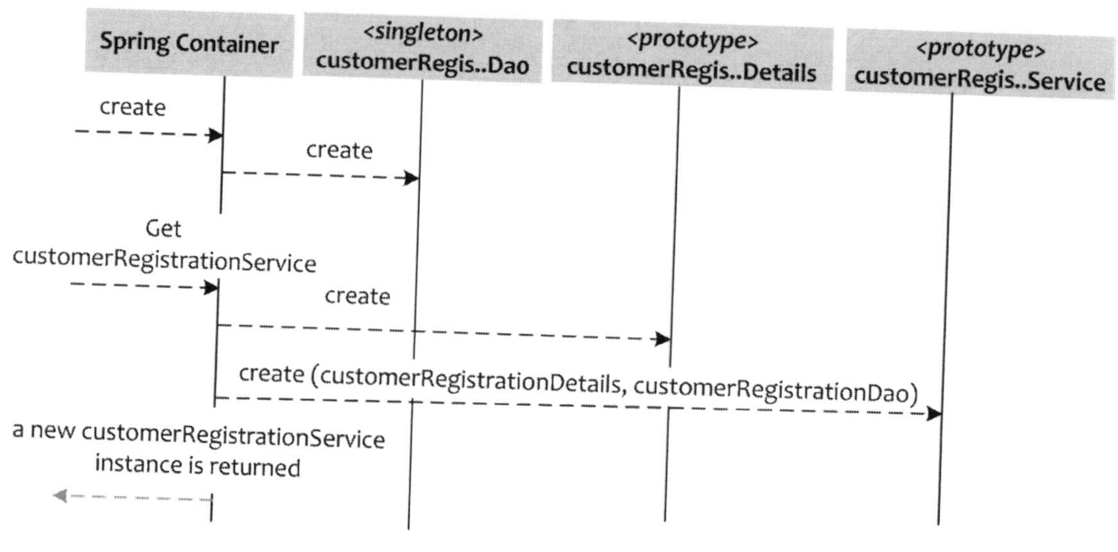

Figure 4-3 – The sequence of events that occur when the Spring container is created and the customerRegistrationService bean is retrieved from the Spring container

Earlier in this section, we saw that if a singleton-scoped bean is dependent on a prototype-scoped bean, then throughout its lifetime the singleton-scoped bean is associated with the *same* instance of the prototype-scoped bean. Let's now look at different ways in which a singleton-scoped bean can retrieve a new instance of a prototype-scoped bean from the Spring container.

4-5 Obtaining new instances of prototype beans inside singleton beans

In the previous section, we saw that the prototype-scoped dependency of a singleton-scoped bean is injected at the time of creation of the singleton-scoped bean (refer figure 4-2). Spring container creates instance of a singleton-scoped bean *only once*; therefore, the singleton-scoped bean holds reference to the *same* prototype-scoped bean instance during its lifetime. A singleton-scoped bean's methods can retrieve a new instance of their prototype-scoped dependency from the Spring container using any one of the following approaches:

- make the singleton-scoped bean's class implement Spring's ApplicationContextAware interface
- use the <lookup-method> element of Spring's beans schema
- use the <replaced-method> element of Spring's beans schema

> It is possible to use the new keyword to create an instance of the prototype-scoped bean's class in a singleton-scoped bean's method and use it. As the responsibility of creating a bean instance is with the Spring container, we should *not* attempt to directly create a bean instance using the new keyword.

IMPORT **chapter 4/ch04-bankapp-context-aware** (This project shows a scenario in which a singleton-scoped bean implements Spring's ApplicationContextAware interface to obtain instances of a prototype-scoped bean from the Spring container. To run the application, execute the main method of the BankApp class of this project)

Let's first begin by looking at the ApplicationContextAware interface.

ApplicationContextAware interface

Spring's ApplicationContextAware interface is implemented by beans that require access to the ApplicationContext instance in which they are running. ApplicationContextAware interface defines a single method, setApplicationContext, which provides the implementing beans with an instance of the ApplicationContext object.

ApplicationContextAware interface is a *lifecycle interface*, which means that the Spring container calls the beans implementing the ApplicationContextAware interface at appropriate times during their lifetime. For instance, ApplicationContextAware's setApplicationContext method is called by the Spring container *after* the bean instance is created but *before* the bean instance is completely initialized. A bean instance is considered completely initialized only after its *initialization method* (refer section 5-2 of chapter 5) is called by the Spring container. It is important to note that after a bean instance is completely initialized, it is injected into the dependent bean instances by the Spring container. In chapter 5, we'll look at some more lifecycle interfaces in Spring.

A bean that implements the ApplicationContextAware interface can access other beans registered with the ApplicationContext instance by calling ApplicationContext's getBean method. This means that if the bean class of a singleton-scoped bean implements ApplicationContextAware interface, it can fetch a new instance of a prototype-scoped bean from the Spring container by calling ApplicationContext's getBean method. As the singleton-scoped bean explicitly obtains its prototype-scoped dependency from the Spring container by calling ApplicationContext's getBean method, you don't need to define the prototype-scoped bean as a dependency of the singleton-scoped bean in the application context XML file.

The following example listing shows the CustomerRequestServiceImpl class that needs a new instance of CustomerRequestDetails object each time CustomerRequestServiceImpl's submitRequest method is called:

Example listing 4-14 – CustomerRequestServiceImpl class
Project – ch04-bankapp-context-aware
Source location - src/main/java/sample/spring/chapter04/bankapp/service

```
package sample.spring.chapter04.bankapp.service;

import sample.spring.chapter04.bankapp.dao.CustomerRequestDao;
import sample.spring.chapter04.bankapp.domain.CustomerRequestDetails;

public class CustomerRequestServiceImpl implements CustomerRequestService {
  private CustomerRequestDetails customerRequestDetails;
  private CustomerRequestDao customerRequestDao;

  @ConstructorProperties({ "customerRequestDetails", "customerRequestDao" })
  public CustomerRequestServiceImpl(CustomerRequestDetails customerRequestDetails,
      CustomerRequestDao customerRequestDao) {
    this.customerRequestDetails = customerRequestDetails;
    this.customerRequestDao = customerRequestDao;
  }

  public void submitRequest(String requestType, String requestDescription) {
    // -- populate CustomerRequestDetails object and save it
    customerRequestDetails.setType(requestType);
    customerRequestDetails.setDescription(requestDescription);
    customerRequestDao.submitRequest(customerRequestDetails);
  }
}
```

The above example listing shows that the CustomerRequestDetails and CustomerRequestDao objects are passed as arguments to the CustomerRequestServiceImpl class's constructor. The submitRequest method populates the CustomerRequestDetails instance and saves it into the database by calling CustomerRequestDao's submitRequest method. If multiple customers simultaneously submit request, the submitRequest method will end up modifying the same instance of the CustomerRequestDetails object, resulting in undesired behavior of MyBank application. To address this issue, the submitRequest *must* obtain a new instance of the CustomerRequestDetails object from the Spring container on each invocation.

The following example listing shows the CustomerRequestServiceContextAwareImpl class (a modified version of CustomerRequestServiceImpl class that we saw in example listing 4-14) that implements the ApplicationContextAware interface:

Example listing 4-15 – CustomerRequestServiceContextAwareImpl class that implements Spring's ApplicationContextAware interface
Project – ch04-bankapp-context-aware
Source location - src/main/java/sample/spring/chapter04/bankapp/service

```
package sample.spring.chapter04.bankapp.service;

import org.springframework.context.ApplicationContext;
import org.springframework.context.ApplicationContextAware;

public class CustomerRequestServiceContextAwareImpl implements
   CustomerRequestService, ApplicationContextAware {

   private CustomerRequestDao customerRequestDao;
   private ApplicationContext applicationContext;

   @ConstructorProperties({ "customerRequestDao" })
   public CustomerRequestServiceContextAwareImpl(CustomerRequestDao customerRequestDao) {
      this.customerRequestDao = customerRequestDao;
   }

   public void setApplicationContext(ApplicationContext applicationContext)
         throws BeansException {
      this.applicationContext = applicationContext;
   }

   public void submitRequest(String requestType, String requestDescription) {
      CustomerRequestDetails customerRequestDetails = applicationContext
            .getBean(CustomerRequestDetails.class);
      customerRequestDetails.setType(requestType);
      customerRequestDetails.setDescription(requestDescription);
      customerRequestDao.submitRequest(customerRequestDetails);
   }
}
```

In the above example listing, setApplicationContext method provides CustomerRequestServiceContextAwareImpl with an instance of ApplicationContext object. The ApplicationContext instance is later used by the submitRequest method to obtain an instance of CustomerRequestDetails object from the Spring container.

As the CustomerRequestServiceContextAwareImpl class explicitly obtains CustomerRequestDetails object from the Spring container, you *don't* need to use Spring's DI mechanism to inject CustomerRequestDetails instance into the CustomerRequestServiceContextAwareImpl instance. For this reason, CustomerRequestServiceContextAwareImpl class's constructor (refer example listing 4-15) doesn't specify CustomerRequestDetails object as an argument. If you now go to ch04-bankapp-context-aware project and execute BankApp's main method, you'll find that on each invocation of submitRequest method a new instance of CustomerRequestDetails object is fetched from the Spring container.

In the context of MyBank, we saw that the ApplicationContextAware interface is useful if a bean requires access to other beans. The downside of implementing the ApplicationContextAware interface is that it couples your bean class to Spring Framework. You can avoid coupling your bean classes with Spring Framework and still access other beans from the Spring container by using *method injection* techniques offered by <lookup-method> and <replaced-method> elements of Spring's beans schema.

Let's first look at the <lookup-method> element.

IMPORT **chapter 4/ch04-bankapp-lookup-method** (This project shows the MyBank application that uses <lookup-method> element of Spring's beans schema. To run the application, execute the main method of the BankApp class of this project)

<lookup-method> element

If a bean class defines a *bean lookup method* whose return type represents a bean, the <lookup-method> element instructs the Spring container to provide implementation for this method. The method implementation provided by the Spring container is responsible for retrieving the bean instance from the Spring container and returning it.

The <lookup-method> element's bean attribute specifies the name of the bean to be looked-up and returned by the method implementation, and the name attribute specifies the name of the method whose implementation is to be provided by the Spring container. It is important to note that the bean lookup method defined by the bean class can be an abstract or a concrete method.

> The use of <lookup-method> element to instruct the Spring container to provide implementation for a bean lookup method is referred to as a *'Method Injection techinique'* because the <lookup-method> element injects a bean lookup method implementation into the bean class.

The following example listing shows CustomerRequestServiceImpl's getCustomerRequestDetails *abstract* method that returns an instance of CustomerRequestDetails instance:

Example listing 4-16 – CustomerRequestServiceImpl class – defining a bean lookup method
Project – ch04-bankapp-lookup-method
Source location - src/main/java/sample/spring/chapter04/bankapp/service

```
package sample.spring.chapter04.bankapp.service;

public abstract class CustomerRequestServiceImpl implements CustomerRequestService {
  private CustomerRequestDao customerRequestDao;

  @ConstructorProperties({ "customerRequestDao" })
  public CustomerRequestServiceImpl(CustomerRequestDao customerRequestDao) {
    this.customerRequestDao = customerRequestDao;
  }

  public abstract CustomerRequestDetails getCustomerRequestDetails();

  @Override
  public void submitRequest(String requestType, String requestDescription) {
    // -- populate CustomerRequestDetails object and save it
    CustomerRequestDetails customerRequestDetails = getCustomerRequestDetails();
    .....
  }
}
```

The above example listing shows that the CustomerRequestServiceImpl class is defined as abstract because it contains an abstract bean lookup method, getCustomerRequestDetails. Instead of abstract, we could have very well defined the getCustomerRequestDetails method as a concrete method. The submitRequest method invokes the getCustomerRequestDetails method to access a CustomerRequestDetails instance.

The following example listing shows bean definitions for CustomerRequestServiceImpl and CustomerRequestDetails classes:

Example listing 4-17 – applicationContext.xml - <lookup-method> element usage
Project – ch04-bankapp-lookup-method
Source location - src/main/resources/META-INF/spring

```
<bean id="customerRequestService"
   class="sample.spring.chapter04.bankapp.service.CustomerRequestServiceImpl">
   <constructor-arg name="customerRequestDao" ref="customerRequestDao" />
   <lookup-method bean="customerRequestDetails" name="getCustomerRequestDetails"/>
</bean>

<bean id="customerRequestDetails"
```

```
class="sample.spring.chapter04.bankapp.domain.CustomerRequestDetails"
scope="prototype" />
```

The above example listing shows that the bean definition for the CustomerRequestServiceImpl class contains a <lookup-method> element. The value of <lookup-method> element's name attribute is getCustomerRequestDetails, which instructs the Spring container to provide implementation for the getCustomerRequestDetails lookup method (refer example listing 4-16) of CustomerRequestServiceImpl class. The value of <lookup-method> element's bean attribute is customerRequestDetails, which means that the implementation of getCustomerRequestDetails method retrieves a bean with id (or name) as customerRequestDetails from the Spring container and returns it to the calling method. As the customerRequestDetails bean represents a CustomerRequestDetails object (refer to the customerRequestDetails bean definition in example listing 4-17), the implementation of getCustomerRequestDetails method returns a CustomerRequestDetails object.

In example listing 4-16, the CustomerRequestService's submitRequest method invokes the getCustomerRequestDetails bean lookup method to obtain a CustomerRequestDetails instance. As CustomerRequestDetails class is represented as a prototype-scoped bean in the application context XML file (refer example listing 4-17), each invocation of the submitRequest method results in retrieval of a new instance of CustomerRequestDetails object from the Spring container.

To check that the <lookup-method> element provides correct implementation for the CustomerRequestService's getCustomerRequestDetails bean lookup method, the main method of BankApp class obtains an instance of CustomerRequestService from the Spring container and invokes its submitRequest method multiple times. If each invocation of the submitRequest method results in retrieval of a fresh instance of CustomerRequestDetails object from the Spring container, then it means that the <lookup-method> element provides correct implementation for the CustomerRequestService's getCustomerRequestDetails method.

The following example listing shows the BankApp's main method that invokes CustomerRequestService's submitRequest method multiple times:

Example listing 4-18 – BankApp class
Project – ch04-bankapp-lookup-method
Source location - src/main/java/sample/spring/chapter04/bankapp

```
package sample.spring.chapter04.bankapp;
.....
public class BankApp {
  private static Logger logger = Logger.getLogger(BankApp.class);

  public static void main(String args[]) throws Exception {
```

```
    ApplicationContext context = new ClassPathXmlApplicationContext(
          "classpath:META-INF/spring/applicationContext.xml");
    .....
    logger.info("Beginning with accessing CustomerRequestService");
    CustomerRequestService customerRequestService_1 = context
          .getBean(CustomerRequestService.class);
    customerRequestService_1.submitRequest("checkBookRequest",
          "Request to send a 50-leaf check book");
    customerRequestService_1.submitRequest("checkBookRequest",
          "Request to send a 100-leaf check book");
    .....
    logger.info("Done with accessing CustomerRequestService");
  }
}
```

If you execute the BankApp's main method, you'll see the following output on the console:

```
Beginning with accessing CustomerRequestService
Created CustomerRequestDetails instance
Created CustomerRequestDetails instance
.....
Done with accessing CustomerRequestService
```

The *'Created.....'* messages shown in the above output are printed by the constructors of the respective bean classes. The above output shows that each invocation of CustomerRequestService's submitRequest method resulted in retrieval of a new CustomerRequestDetails instance from the Spring container.

As the implementation of the bean lookup method is provided by the Spring container, some restrictions apply to the signature of the bean lookup methods. For instance, the bean lookup method *must* be defined as public or protected, and it *must not* accept any arguments. As the bean class containing the bean lookup method is subclassed at runtime by the Spring container to provide the implementation for the bean lookup method, the bean class and the bean lookup method *must not* be defined as final.

> As the bean class containing the bean lookup method needs to be subclassed at runtime by the Spring container to provide implementation for the bean lookup method, the Spring container uses CGLIB (http://cglib.sourceforge.net/) library to perform subclassing of the bean class. Starting with Spring 3.2, the CGLIB classes are packaged within the spring-core JAR file itself; therefore, you don't need to explicitly specify that your project is dependent on CGLIB JAR file.

The <lookup-method> element provides a method injection technique in which a bean class defines a bean lookup method whose implementation is provided by the Spring container. Instead of using <lookup-method> element, you can consider using <replaced-method> element of Spring's beans schema to perform method injection.

IMPORT chapter 4/ch04-bankapp-replaced-method (This project shows the MyBank application that uses <replaced-method> element of Spring's beans schema. To run the application, execute the main method of the BankApp class of this project)

<replaced-method> element

The <replaced-method> element allows you to replace any arbitrary method in a bean class with a different implementation. The following example listing shows the CustomerRequestServiceImpl class that we'll be using as an example to demonstrate use of <replaced-method> element:

Example listing 4-19 – CustomerRequestServiceImpl class
Project – ch04-bankapp-replaced-method
Source location - src/main/java/sample/spring/chapter04/bankapp/service

```
package sample.spring.chapter04.bankapp.service;
.....
public class CustomerRequestServiceImpl implements CustomerRequestService {
   private CustomerRequestDao customerRequestDao;
   .....
   public Object getMyBean(String beanName) {
      return null;
   }

   @Override
   public void submitRequest(String requestType, String requestDescription) {
      // -- populate CustomerRequestDetails object and save it
      CustomerRequestDetails customerRequestDetails =
          (CustomerRequestDetails) getMyBean("customerRequestDetails");
      customerRequestDetails.setType(requestType);
      customerRequestDetails.setDescription(requestDescription);
      customerRequestDao.submitRequest(customerRequestDetails);
   }
}
```

The above example listing shows that the CustomerRequestServiceImpl class defines a getMyBean method. The getMyBean method accepts name of a bean as an argument, and instead of returning the bean instance corresponding to the bean name argument, the getMyBean method returns null. The submitRequest method passes customerRequestDetails string as argument to the getMyBean method and assumes that the getMyBean method returns an instance of customerRequestDetails bean. Using <replaced-method> element, you can override the getMyBean method with a method that returns the bean instance corresponding to the bean name argument.

The <replaced-method> element needs information about the *overridden* method (which is CustomerRequestServiceImpl getMyBean method in our example scenario) and the *overriding* method. The overriding method is provided by the class that implements Spring's MethodReplacer interface. The following example listing shows MyMethodReplacer class that implements the MethodReplacer interface:

Example listing 4-20 – MyMethodReplacer class
Project – ch04-bankapp-replaced-method
Source location - src/main/java/sample/spring/chapter04/bankapp/service

```
package sample.spring.chapter04.bankapp.service;

import org.springframework.beans.factory.support.MethodReplacer;
import org.springframework.context.ApplicationContextAware;

public class MyMethodReplacer implements MethodReplacer, ApplicationContextAware {
   private ApplicationContext applicationContext;

   @Override
   public Object reimplement(Object obj, Method method, Object[] args) throws Throwable {
      return applicationContext.getBean((String) args[0]);
   }

   @Override
   public void setApplicationContext(ApplicationContext applicationContext)
         throws BeansException {
      this.applicationContext = applicationContext;
   }
}
```

Spring's MethodReplacer interface defines a reimplement method whose implementation is provided by the MyMethodReplacer class. The reimplement method represents the *overriding* method. MyMethodReplacer class also implements Spring's ApplicationContextAware interface so that the reimplement method can access the ApplicationContext instance. The reimplement method uses the ApplicationContext's getBean method to retrieve beans from the Spring container.

The reimplement method accepts the following arguments:

- Object obj – identifies the object whose method we are overriding. In our example scenario, the obj object is the CustomerRequestServiceImpl object.
- Method method – identifies the bean class's method that is overridden by the reimplement method. In our example scenario, this is CustomerRequestServiceImpl's getMyBean method.
- Object[] args – identifies arguments passed to the method that we are overriding. In our example scenario, args represents the arguments passed to the CustomerRequestServiceImpl's getMyBean method. In example listing 4-20, args[0] in the reimplement method refers the bean name argument passed to the CustomerRequestServiceImpl's getMyBean method.

If you now look at MyMethodReplacer's reimplement method in example listing 4-20, you can infer that it uses args argument to first obtain bean name passed to the CustomerRequestServiceImpl's getMyBean method, and then calls ApplicationContext's getBean method to obtain the corresponding bean instance. As MyMethodReplacer's reimplement method overrides CustomerRequestServiceImpl's getMyBean method, call to getMyBean method at runtime returns the bean instance whose name was passed to the getMyBean method.

The <replaced-method> element informs the Spring container that MyMethodReplacer's reimplement method overrides CustomerRequestServiceImpl's getMyBean method, as shown in the following example listing:

Example listing 4-21 – applicationContext.xml - <replaced-method> element usage
Project – ch04-bankapp-replaced-method
Source location - src/main/resources/META-INF/spring

```
<bean id="customerRequestService"
   class="sample.spring.chapter04.bankapp.service.CustomerRequestServiceImpl">
   <constructor-arg name="customerRequestDao" ref="customerRequestDao" />
   <replaced-method name="getMyBean" replacer="methodReplacer" />
</bean>

<bean id="methodReplacer"
   class="sample.spring.chapter04.bankapp.service.MyMethodReplacer" />
```

The above example listing shows bean definitions for MyMethodReplacer and CustomerRequestServiceImpl classes. The <replace-method> element's name attribute specifies name of the method that you want to override, and the replacer attribute specifies reference to the bean that implements the MethodReplacer interface. The method specified by the name attribute is overridden by the reimplement method of the bean referenced by the replacer attribute.

As in case of <lookup-method> element, the main method of the BankApp class of ch04-bankapp-replaced-method project validates whether or not the <replaced-method> element overrides the CustomerRequestService's getMyBean method with the MyMethodReplacer's reimplement method. BankApp class of ch04-bankapp-replaced-method project is same as the one we saw in example listing 4-18 for ch04-bankapp-lookup-method project. If you execute the main method of the BankApp class, you'll find that <replaced-method> element overrides CustomerRequestServiceImpl's getMyBean method with MyMethodReplacer's reimplement method; therefore, a fresh instance of CustomerRequestDetails instance is retrieved from the Spring container each time CustomerRequestServiceImpl's submitRequest method (refer example listing 4-19) is invoked.

It is important to note that you can use <replaced-method> element to replace an abstract or concrete method of a bean class with a different method implementation. For instance, we could have defined getMyBean method as an abstract method and used the <replaced-method> element in the same way as described in this section.

> As the bean class needs to be subclassed at runtime by the Spring container to replace a bean method with a different method, the Spring container uses CGLIB (http://cglib.sourceforge.net/) library to perform subclassing of the bean class. Starting with Spring 3.2, the CGLIB classes are packaged within the spring-core JAR file itself; therefore, you don't need to explicitly specify that your project is dependent on CGLIB JAR file.

Let's now look at how <replaced-method> element uniquely identifies the bean method to be overridden.

Uniquely identifying the bean method

You may come across scenarios in which the bean method that you want to replace using <replaced-method> element can't be uniquely identified by name. For instance, the following example listing shows a bean class that contains overloaded perform methods:

Example listing 4-22 – Overloaded methods in a bean class

```
public class MyBean {
        public void perform(String task1, String task2) { ..... }
        public void perform(String task) { ..... }
        public void perform(my.Task task) { ..... }
}
```

In the above example listing, the MyBean class contains multiple methods named perform. To uniquely identify the bean method to be overridden, the <replaced-method> element uses <arg-type> sub-elements to specify method argument types. For instance, the following example listing shows how <replaced-method> element specifies that the perform(String, String) method of MyBean class should be replaced:

Example listing 4-23 – <replaced-method> element with <arg-type> sub-element

```
<bean id="mybean" class="MyBean">
   <replaced-method name="perform " replacer=".....">
      <arg-type>java.lang.String</arg-type>
      <arg-type>java.lang.String</arg-type>
   </replaced-method>
</bean>
```

Instead of using the fully-qualified name as the value of <arg-type> element, you can use a substring of the fully-qualified name as the value. For instance, instead of using java.lang.String, you can specify Str or String as the value of <arg-type> element in the above example listing.

Let's now look at Spring's autowiring feature that saves you the effort of specifying bean dependencies in the application context XML file.

4-6 Autowiring dependencies

In Spring, you have the option to either explicitly specify bean dependencies using <property> and <constructor-arg> elements or let Spring automatically resolve bean dependencies. The process in which dependencies are automatically resolved by Spring is referred to as 'autowiring'.

IMPORT **chapter 4/ch04-bankapp-autowiring** (This project shows the MyBank application that uses Spring's *autowiring* feature for dependency injection. To run the application, execute the main method of the BankApp class of this project)

The <bean> element's autowire attribute specifies how a bean's dependencies are automatically resolved by Spring. The autowire attribute can take any one of the following values: default, byName, byType, constructor and no. Let's now look at each of these attribute values in detail.

> You should note that the <bean> element's autowire attribute is not inherited by child bean definitions.

byType

If you specify autowire attribute's value as byType, Spring autowires bean properties based on their type. For instance, if a bean A defines a property of type X, Spring finds a bean of type X in the ApplicationContext and injects it into bean A. Let's look at an example usage of byType autowiring in the MyBank application.

The following example listing shows the MyBank application's CustomerRegistrationServiceImpl class:

Example listing 4-24 – CustomerRegistrationServiceImpl class
Project – ch04-bankapp-autowiring
Source location - src/main/java/sample/spring/chapter04/bankapp/service

```
package sample.spring.chapter04.bankapp.service;

public class CustomerRegistrationServiceImpl implements CustomerRegistrationService {

  private CustomerRegistrationDetails customerRegistrationDetails;
  private CustomerRegistrationDao customerRegistrationDao;
  ....
  public void setCustomerRegistrationDetails(
        CustomerRegistrationDetails customerRegistrationDetails) {
     this.customerRegistrationDetails = customerRegistrationDetails;
  }
  public void setCustomerRegistrationDao(
        CustomerRegistrationDao customerRegistrationDao) {
     this.customerRegistrationDao = customerRegistrationDao;
  }
  .....
}
```

The above example listing shows that the CustomerRegistrationServiceImpl class defines properties named customerRegistrationDetails (of type CustomerRegistrationDetails) and customerRegistrationDao (of type CustomerRegistrationDao). This means that the CustomerRegistrationDetails and CustomerRegistrationDao objects are dependencies of CustomerRegistrationServiceImpl object.

The following example listing shows bean definitions for CustomerRegistrationServiceImpl, CustomerRegistrationDetails and CustomerRegistrationDaoImpl (an implementation of CustomerRegistrationDao interface) classes:

Example listing 4-25 – applicationContext.xml - autowiring byType configuration
Project – ch04-bankapp-autowiring
Source location - src/main/resources/META-INF/spring

```
<bean id="customerRegistrationService"
      class="sample.spring.chapter04.bankapp.service.CustomerRegistrationServiceImpl"
      scope="prototype" autowire="byType" />

<bean id="customerRegistrationDetails"
      class="sample.spring.chapter04.bankapp.domain.CustomerRegistrationDetails"
      scope="prototype" />

<bean id="customerRegistrationDao"
      class="sample.spring.chapter04.bankapp.dao.CustomerRegistrationDaoImpl" />
```

In the above example listing, the customerRegistrationService bean definition doesn't contain <property> elements for setting customerRegistrationDetails and customerRegistrationDao properties (refer example listing 4-24). Instead, the <bean> element specifies autowire attribute's value as byType to instruct Spring to automatically resolve dependencies of the customerRegistrationService bean based on their *type*. Spring looks for beans of types CustomerRequestDetails and CustomerRegistrationDao in the ApplicationContext, and injects them into the customerRegistrationService bean. As customerRegistrationDetails and customerRegistrationDao beans represent beans of types CustomerRegistrationDetails and CustomerRegistrationDao, the Spring container injects customerRegistrationDetails and customerRegistrationDao beans into customerRegistrationService bean.

It may happen that Spring doesn't find any bean registered with the ApplicationContext whose type matches the property type. In such cases, no exception is thrown and the bean property is *not* set. For instance, if a bean defines a property x of type Y, and there is no bean of type Y registered with the ApplicationContext instance, the property x is not set. If Spring finds multiple beans in the ApplicationContext that match the property type, an exception is thrown. In such cases, instead of using autowiring feature, use <property> elements to explicitly identify bean dependencies or set a bean as the *primary candidate* for autowiring by setting the value of primary attribute of <bean> element to true.

constructor

If you specify autowire attribute's value as constructor, Spring autowires bean class's constructor arguments based on their type. For instance, if bean *A*'s constructor accepts arguments of type X and Y, Spring finds beans of types X and Y in the ApplicationContext and injects them as arguments to bean *A*'s constructor. Let's look at an example usage of constructor autowiring in the MyBank application.

The following example listing shows the MyBank application's CustomerRequestServiceImpl class:

Example listing 4-26 – CustomerRequestServiceImpl class
Project – ch04-bankapp-autowiring
Source location - src/main/java/sample/spring/chapter04/bankapp/service

```
package sample.spring.chapter04.bankapp.service;

public class CustomerRequestServiceImpl implements CustomerRequestService {
  private CustomerRequestDetails customerRequestDetails;
  private CustomerRequestDao customerRequestDao;

  @ConstructorProperties({ "customerRequestDetails", "customerRequestDao" })
  public CustomerRequestServiceImpl(
        CustomerRequestDetails customerRequestDetails,
        CustomerRequestDao customerRequestDao) {
    this.customerRequestDetails = customerRequestDetails;
    this.customerRequestDao = customerRequestDao;
  }
  .....
}
```

The CustomerRequestServiceImpl class defines a constructor that accepts arguments of type CustomerRequestDetails and CustomerRequestDao.

The following example listing shows bean definitions for CustomerRequestServiceImpl, CustomerRequestDetails and CustomerRequestDaoImpl (an implementation of CustomerRequestDao interface) classes:

Example listing 4-27 – applicationContext.xml - constructor autowiring
Project – ch04-bankapp-autowiring
Source location - src/main/resources/META-INF/spring

```
<bean id="customerRequestService"
  class="sample.spring.chapter04.bankapp.service.CustomerRequestServiceImpl"
  autowire="constructor">
</bean>

<bean id="customerRequestDetails"
  class="sample.spring.chapter04.bankapp.domain.CustomerRequestDetails" scope="prototype" />

<bean id="customerRequestDao"
  class="sample.spring.chapter04.bankapp.dao.CustomerRequestDaoImpl" />
```

In the above example listing, the customerRequestService bean definition specifies autowire attribute's value as constructor, which means that Spring locates beans of types CustomerRequestDetails and CustomerRequestDao in the ApplicationContext, and passes them as arguments to CustomerRequestServiceImpl class's constructor. As customerRequestDetails and customerRequestDao beans are of type CustomerRequestDetails and CustomerRequestDao, Spring automatically injects instances of these beans into customerRequestService bean.

If Spring doesn't find any bean in the ApplicationContext whose type matches the constructor argument type, the constructor argument is not set. If Spring finds multiple beans in the ApplicationContext that match the constructor argument type, an exception is thrown; therefore, in such scenarios use <constructor-arg> elements to explicitly identify bean dependencies or set a bean as the *primary candidate* for autowiring by setting value of primary attribute of <bean> element to true.

byName

If you specify autowire attribute's value as byName, Spring autowires bean properties based on their names. For instance, if a bean *A* defines a property named x, Spring finds a bean named x in the ApplicationContext and injects it into bean *A*. Let's look at an example usage of byName autowiring in the MyBank application.

The following example listing shows the MyBank application's FixedDepositServiceImpl class:

Example listing 4-28 – FixedDepositServiceImpl class
Project – ch04-bankapp-autowiring
Source location - src/main/java/sample/spring/chapter04/bankapp/service

```
package sample.spring.chapter04.bankapp.service;

import sample.spring.chapter04.bankapp.dao.FixedDepositDao;
import sample.spring.chapter04.bankapp.domain.FixedDepositDetails;

public class FixedDepositServiceImpl implements FixedDepositService {
  private FixedDepositDao myFixedDepositDao;

  public void setMyFixedDepositDao(FixedDepositDao myFixedDepositDao) {
    this.myFixedDepositDao = myFixedDepositDao;
  }
  .....
}
```

The above example listing shows that FixedDepositServiceImpl class defines a property named myFixedDepositDao of type FixedDepositDao.

The following example listing shows bean definitions for FixedDepositServiceImpl and FixedDepositDaoImpl (an implementation of FixedDepositDao interface) classes:

Example listing 4-29 – applicationContext.xml - byName autowiring
Project – ch04-bankapp-autowiring
Source location - src/main/resources/META-INF/spring

```
<bean id="FixedDepositService"
   class="sample.spring.chapter04.bankapp.service.FixedDepositServiceImpl"
   autowire="byName" />

<bean id="myFixedDepositDao"
    class="sample.spring.chapter04.bankapp.dao.FixedDepositDaoImpl" />
```

In the above example listing, FixedDepositService bean definition specifies autowire attribute's value as byName, which means properties of FixedDepositService bean are automatically resolved by Spring based on their names. In listing 4-28, we saw that the FixedDepositServiceImpl class defines a property named myFixedDepositDao; therefore, Spring looks for a bean named myFixedDepositDao in the ApplicationContext and injects it into FixedDepositService bean. In the above example listing, myFixedDepositDao bean definition represents the FixedDepositDaoImpl class, which means that an instance of FixedDepositDaoImpl is injected for property named myFixedDepositDao in the FixedDepositService bean.

default / no

If you specify autowire attribute's value as default or no, autowiring feature is *disabled* for the bean. As Spring's default behavior is to use *no* autowiring for beans, specifying autowire attribute's value as default means no autowiring will be performed for the bean. You can explicitly specify that a bean *must not* use Spring's autowiring feature by specifying autowire attribute's value as no.

> You can change the default autowiring behavior of beans by setting the default-autowire attribute of <beans> element. For instance, if you set default-autowire attribute's value to byType, it effectively means setting value of autowire attribute of all the <bean> elements in the application context XML file to byType. You should note that if a <bean> element's autowire attribute specifies a different value than the <beans> element's default-autowire attribute, the <bean> element's autowire attribute value applies to the bean.

The following example listing shows the bean definition for the MyBank application's CustomerRegistrationServiceImpl class that specifies autowire attribute's value as no:

Example listing 4-30 – applicationContext.xml - no autowiring
Project – ch04-bankapp-autowiring
Source location - src/main/resources/META-INF/spring

```
<bean id="customerRegistrationService_"
    class="sample.spring.chapter04.bankapp.service.CustomerRegistrationServiceImpl"
    scope="prototype" autowire="no" />
```

Example listing 4-24 showed that the CustomerRegistrationServiceImpl class defines customerRegistrationDetails (of type CustomerRegistrationDetails) and customerRegistrationDao (of type CustomerRegistrationDao) properties. As the autowire attribute's value is specified as no for customerRegistrationService_ bean, autowiring is disabled for customerRegistrationService_ bean. This means that the customerRegistrationDetails and customerRegistrationDao properties of customerRegistrationService_ bean are *not* set by Spring.

So far in this section we have seen different ways in which bean dependencies can be autowired by Spring. Let's now look at how we can make a bean *unavailable* for autowiring purposes using <bean> element's autowire-candidate attribute.

Making beans unavailable for autowiring

The default behavior of the Spring container is to make beans available for autowiring. You can make a bean unavailable to other beans for autowiring purposes by setting autowire-candidate attribute's value to false.

In MyBank application, the AccountStatementServiceImpl class defines a property of type AccountStatementDao. The following example listing shows the AccountStatementServiceImpl class:

Example listing 4-31 – AccountStatementServiceImpl class
Project – ch04-bankapp-autowiring
Source location - src/main/java/sample/spring/chapter04/bankapp/service

```
package sample.spring.chapter04.bankapp.service;

import sample.spring.chapter04.bankapp.dao.AccountStatementDao;
import sample.spring.chapter04.bankapp.domain.AccountStatement;

public class AccountStatementServiceImpl implements AccountStatementService {
  private AccountStatementDao accountStatementDao;

  public void setAccountStatementDao(AccountStatementDao accountStatementDao) {
    this.accountStatementDao = accountStatementDao;
  }
```

```
    .....
}
```

The following example listing shows bean definitions for AccountStatementServiceImpl and AccountStatementDaoImpl (an implementation of AccountStatementDao interface) classes:

Example listing 4-32 – applicationContext.xml - autowire-candidate attribute
Project – ch04-bankapp-autowiring
Source location - src/main/resources/META-INF/spring

```
<bean id="accountStatementService"
      class="sample.spring.chapter04.bankapp.service.AccountStatementServiceImpl"
      autowire="byType" />

<bean id="accountStatementDao"
      class="sample.spring.chapter04.bankapp.dao.AccountStatementDaoImpl"
      autowire-candidate="false" />
```

In the above example listing, the accountStatementService bean definition specifies autowire attribute's value as byType, which means AccountStatementDao property type of accountStatementService bean is autowired by type. As accountStatementDao bean is of type AccountStatementDao, you might think that Spring will inject accountStatementDao bean instance into accountStatementService bean. But, Spring won't consider accountStatementDao bean for autowiring purposes because the accountStatementDao bean definition specifies autowire-candidate attribute's value as false.

> You should note that a bean that is unavailable to other beans for autowiring purposes can itself make use of Spring's autowiring feature to automatically resolve it's dependencies.

As mentioned earlier, the default behavior of the Spring container is to make beans available for autowiring purposes. To make only only a select set of beans available for autowiring purposes, set <beans> element's default-autowire-candidates attribute. The default-autowire-candidates attribute specifies a bean name *pattern*, and only beans whose names match the specified pattern are made available for autowiring. The following example listing shows an example usage of default-autowire-candidates attribute:

Example listing 4-33 – default-autowire-candidates attribute example

```
<beans default-autowire-candidates="*Dao" >
    .....
    <bean id="customerRequestDetails"
        class="sample.spring.chapter04.bankapp.domain.CustomerRequestDetails"
        scope="prototype" autowire-candidate="true"/>
```

```
<bean id="customerRequestDao"
    class="sample.spring.chapter04.bankapp.dao.CustomerRequestDaoImpl" />

<bean id="customerRegistrationDao"
    class="sample.spring.chapter04.bankapp.dao.CustomerRegistrationDaoImpl" />
.....
</beans>
```

In the above example listing, default-autowire-candidates value is set to *Dao, which means that beans whose names end with Dao (like customerRequestDao and customerRegistrationDao beans) will be available for autowiring purposes. If a bean name doesn't match the pattern specified by the default-autowire-candidates attribute (like customerRequestDetails bean), you can still make it available for autowiring purposes by setting the autowire-candidate attribute of the corresponding <bean> element to true.

Let's now look at limitations of using autowiring in applications.

Autowiring limitations

We saw that autowiring feature saves the effort to explicitly specify bean dependencies using <property> and <constructor-arg> elements. The downsides of using autowiring feature are:

- You can't use autowiring to set properties or constructor arguments that are of simple Java types (like int, long, boolean, String, Date, and so on). You can autowire arrays, typed collections and maps if the autowire attribute's value is set to byType or constructor.

- As bean dependencies are automatically resolved by Spring, it results in hiding the overall structure of the application. If you use <property> and <constructor-arg> elements to specify bean dependencies, it results in explicitly documenting the overall structure of the application. You can easily understand and maintain an application in which bean dependencies are explicitly documented. For this reason, it is not recommended to use autowiring in large applications.

4-7 Summary

In this chapter, we looked at how Spring caters to different dependency injection scenarios. We looked at how you can use ApplicationContextAware interface, <replaced-method> and <lookup-method> sub-elements of <bean> element to programmatically retrieve a bean instance from the ApplicationContext. We also looked at how Spring's autowiring feature can save the effort for explicitly specifying bean dependencies in the application context XML file. In the next chapter, we'll look at how to customize beans and bean definitions.

Chapter 5 - *Customizing beans and bean definitions*

5-1 Introduction

So far in this book we have seen examples in which the Spring container created a bean instance based on the bean definition specified in the application context XML file. In this chapter, we'll go a step further and look at:

- how to incorporate custom initialization and destruction logic for a bean
- how to interact with a newly created bean instance by implementing Spring's BeanPostProcessor interface
- how to modify bean definitions by implementing Spring's BeanFactoryPostProcessor interface

5-2 Customizing bean's initialization and destruction logic

We saw in earlier chapters that the Spring container is responsible for creating a bean instance and injecting its dependencies. After creating a bean instance by invoking the constructor of the bean class, the Spring container sets bean properties by invoking bean's setter methods. If you want to execute custom initialization logic (like opening a file, creating a database connection, and so on) *after* the bean properties are set but *before* the bean is completely initialized by the Spring container, you can do so by specifying the name of the initialization method as the value of init-method attribute of <bean> element. Similarly, if you want to execute custom cleanup logic *before* the Spring container containing the bean instance is destroyed, you can specify the name of the cleanup method as the value of destroy-method attribute of <bean> element.

IMPORT chapter 5/ch05-bankapp-customization (This project shows the MyBank application that uses <bean> element's init-method and destroy-method elements to specify custom initialization and destruction methods. To test whether the initialization method is executed, execute the main method of the BankApp class of this project. To test whether the destruction method is executed, execute the main method of the BankAppWithHook class of this project.)

The following example listing shows the MyBank's FixedDepositDaoImpl class that defines an initialization method named initializeDbConnection for obtaining connection to MyBank's database, and a destruction method named releaseDbConnection for releasing the connection:

Example listing 5-1 – FixedDepositDaoImpl class - Custom initialization and destruction logic
Project – ch05-bankapp-customization
Source location - src/main/java/sample/spring/chapter05/bankapp/dao

```
package sample.spring.chapter05.bankapp.dao;
```

```
public class FixedDepositDaoImpl implements FixedDepositDao {
  private static Logger logger = Logger.getLogger(FixedDepositDaoImpl.class);
  private DatabaseConnection connection;

  public FixedDepositDaoImpl() {
    logger.info("FixedDepositDaoImpl's constructor invoked");
  }

  public void initializeDbConnection() {
    logger.info("FixedDepositDaoImpl's initializeDbConnection method invoked");
    connection = DatabaseConnection.getInstance();
  }

  public boolean createFixedDeposit(FixedDepositDetails fixedDepositDetails) {
    logger.info("FixedDepositDaoImpl's createFixedDeposit method invoked");
    // -- save the fixed deposits and then return true
    return true;
  }

  public void releaseDbConnection() {
    logger.info("FixedDepositDaoImpl's releaseDbConnection method invoked");
    connection.releaseConnection();
  }
}
```

In the above example listing, the DatabaseConnection object is used for interacting with the MyBank's database. FixedDepositDaoImpl class defines an initializeDbConnection method that initializes the DatabaseConnection object, which is later used by the createFixedDeposit method for saving fixed deposit details in the MyBank's database.

The following example listing shows the MyBank's FixedDepositServiceImpl class that uses FixedDepositDaoImpl instance to create new fixed deposits:

Example listing 5-2 – FixedDepositServiceImpl class
Project – ch05-bankapp-customization
Source location - src/main/java/sample/spring/chapter05/bankapp/service

```
package sample.spring.chapter05.bankapp.service;

public class FixedDepositServiceImpl implements FixedDepositService {
  private static Logger logger = Logger.getLogger(FixedDepositServiceImpl.class);
  private FixedDepositDao myFixedDepositDao;

  public void setMyFixedDepositDao(FixedDepositDao myFixedDepositDao) {
```

```
        logger.info("FixedDepositServiceImpl's setMyFixedDepositDao method invoked");
        this.myFixedDepositDao = myFixedDepositDao;
    }

    @Override
    public void createFixedDeposit(FixedDepositDetails fixedDepositDetails) throws Exception {
        // -- create fixed deposit
        myFixedDepositDao.createFixedDeposit(fixedDepositDetails);
    }
}
```

The above example listing shows that the FixedDepositDaoImpl instance is a dependency of FixedDepositServiceImpl, and is passed as an argument to the setMyFixedDepositDao setter-method. And, if FixedDepositServiceImpl's createFixedDeposit method is invoked, it results in invocation of FixedDepositDaoImpl's createFixedDeposit method.

The following example listing shows bean definitions for FixedDepositDaoImpl and FixedDepositServiceImpl classes:

Example listing 5-3 – applicationContext.xml – usage of init-method and destroy-method attributes
Project – ch05-bankapp-customization
Source location - src/main/resources/META-INF/spring

```
<beans .....>
    <bean id="FixedDepositService"
        class="sample.spring.chapter05.bankapp.service.FixedDepositServiceImpl">
        <property name="myFixedDepositDao" ref="myFixedDepositDao" />
    </bean>

    <bean id="myFixedDepositDao"
        class="sample.spring.chapter05.bankapp.dao.FixedDepositDaoImpl"
        init-method="initializeDbConnection" destroy-method="releaseDbConnection" />
</beans>
```

The above example listing shows that the <bean> element corresponding to the FixedDepositDaoImpl class specifies initializeDbConnection and releaseDbConnection as the values of init-method and destroy-method attributes, respectively.

> It is important to note that the initialization and destruction methods specified by the init-method and destroy-method attributes of <bean> element *must not* accept any arguments, but can be defined to throw exceptions.

The following example listing shows BankApp class whose main method retrieves FixedDepositServiceImpl instance from the ApplicationContext and invokes FixedDepositServiceImpl's createFixedDeposit method:

Example listing 5-4 – BankApp class
Project – ch05-bankapp-customization
Source location - src/main/java/sample/spring/chapter05/bankapp

```
package sample.spring.chapter05.bankapp;

public class BankApp {
  public static void main(String args[]) throws Exception {
    ApplicationContext context = new ClassPathXmlApplicationContext(
        "classpath:META-INF/spring/applicationContext.xml");

    FixedDepositService FixedDepositService = context.getBean(FixedDepositService.class);
    FixedDepositService.createFixedDeposit(new FixedDepositDetails(1, 1000,
        12, "someemail@somedomain.com"));
  }
}
```

If you now execute the BankApp's main method, you'll see the following output on the console:

```
FixedDepositDaoImpl's constructor invoked
FixedDepositDaoImpl's initializeDbConnection method invoked
FixedDepositServiceImpl's setMyFixedDepositDao method invoked
FixedDepositDaoImpl's createFixedDeposit method invoked
```

The above output shows that the Spring container first creates FixedDepositDaoImpl's instance, and then invokes initializeDbConnection method. After the invocation of initializeDbConnection method, the FixedDepositDaoImpl instance is injected into the FixedDepositServiceImpl instance. This shows that the Spring container injects a dependency (the FixedDepositDaoImpl instance) into the dependent bean (the FixedDepositServiceImpl instance) *after* the initialization method of the dependency is invoked by the Spring container.

You may have noticed that the output from executing BankApp's main method didn't contain the following message: *FixedDepositDaoImpl's releaseDbConnection method invoked* (refer FixedDepositDaoImpl's releaseDbConnection method in example listing 5-1). This means that the FixedDepositDaoImpl's releaseDbConnection method was not called by the Spring container when BankApp's main method exited. In a real world application development scenario, this means that the database connection held by FixedDepositDaoImpl instance is never released. Let's now see how you can make Spring gracefully destroy singleton-scoped bean instances by calling the cleanup method specified by the <bean> element's destroy-method attribute.

Making Spring invoke cleanup method specified by the destory-method attribute

The web version of ApplicationContext implementation is represented by Spring's WebApplicationContext object. WebApplicationContext implementation has the necessary logic to invoke the cleanup method (specified by the destroy-method attribute) of singleton-scoped bean instances *before* the web application is shutdown.

> The approach described in this section on making Spring gracefully destroy singleton-scoped bean instances by calling the cleanup method is specific to standalone applications.

The following example listing shows the BankAppWithHook class (a modified version of BankApp class shown in example listing 5-4) whose main method ensures that cleanup methods (specified by <bean> element's destroy-method attribute) of all singleton-scoped beans registered with the Spring container are invoked when the main method exits:

Example listing 5-5 – BankAppWithHook class – registering a shutdown hook with JVM
Project – ch05-bankapp-customization
Source location - src/main/java/sample/spring/chapter05/bankapp

```
package sample.spring.chapter05.bankapp;

public class BankAppWithHook {
  public static void main(String args[]) throws Exception {
    AbstractApplicationContext context = new ClassPathXmlApplicationContext(
          "classpath:META-INF/spring/applicationContext.xml");

    context.registerShutdownHook();

    FixedDepositService FixedDepositService = context.getBean(FixedDepositService.class);
    FixedDepositService.createFixedDeposit(new FixedDepositDetails(1, 1000,
          12, "someemail@somedomain.com"));
  }
}
```

Spring's AbstractionApplicationContext class implements ApplicationContext interface and defines a registerShutdownHook method that registers a shutdown hook with the JVM. The shutdown hook is responsible for closing the ApplicationContext when the JVM is shutdown. In the above example listing, you'll notice that the ClassPathXmlApplicationContext instance is assigned to AbstractionApplicationContext type, and the AbstractionApplicationContext's registerShutdownHook is called to register a shutdown hook with the JVM. When the BankAppWithHook's main method exists, the shutdown hook destroys all cached singleton bean instances and closes the ApplicationContext instance.

If you execute BankAppWithHook's main method of ch05-bankapp-customization project, you'll see the following output on the console:

```
FixedDepositDaoImpl's constructor invoked
FixedDepositDaoImpl's initializeDbConnection method invoked
FixedDepositServiceImpl's setMyFixedDepositDao method invoked
FixedDepositDaoImpl's releaseDbConnection method invoked
```

The message *'FixedDepositDaoImpl's releaseDbConnection method invoked'* on the console confirms that the FixedDepositDaoImpl's releaseDbConnection method (refer FixedDepositDaoImpl's releaseDbConnection method in example listing 5-1) was invoked. As you can see, registering a shutdown hook with the JVM resulted in invocation of the cleanup method of the singleton-scoped myFixedDepositDao bean (corresponding to the FixedDepositDaoImpl class).

Let's now look at the impact of shutdown hook on prototype-scoped beans.

Cleanup methods and prototype-scoped beans

In case of prototype-scoped beans, destroy-method attribute is ignored by the Spring container. The destroy-method attribute is ignored because the Spring container expects that the object that fetches the prototype-scoped bean instance from the ApplicationContext is responsible for explicitly calling the cleanup method on the prototype-scoped bean instance.

> Lifecycles of prototype- and singleton-scoped beans are same, except that the Spring container will *not* call the cleanup method (specified by the destroy-init attribute) of the prototype-scoped bean instance.

Let's now look at how you can specify default initialization and destruction methods for all the beans contained in the application context XML file.

Specifying default bean initialization and destruction methods for all beans

You can use the default-init-method and default-destroy-method attributes of <beans> element to specify default initialization and destruction methods for beans, as shown in the following example listing:

Example listing 5-6 – default-init-method and default-destroy-method attributes

```
<beans ..... default-init-method="initialize" default-destroy-method="release">
  <bean id="A" class="....." init-method="initializeService" />
  <bean id="B" class="....." />
</beans>
```

If multiple beans define initialization or cleanup methods with the same name, it makes sense to use default-init-method and default-destroy-method attributes. By specifying init-method and destroy-method attributes, a <bean> element can override the values specified by <beans> element's default-init-method and default-destroy-method attributes. For instance, in the above example listing, bean A specifies init-method attribute value as initializeService, which means initializeService method (and not initialize method specified by the default-init-method attribute of <beans> element) is the initialization method of bean A.

Instead of using init-method and destroy-method attributes of <bean> element to specify custom initialization and destruction methods, you can use Spring's InitializingBean and DisposableBean lifecycle interfaces.

InitializingBean and DisposableBean lifecycle interfaces

A bean that implements lifecycle interfaces, like ApplicationContextAware (refer section 4-5 of chapter 4), InitializingBean and DisposableBean, receives callbacks from the Spring container to give a chance to the bean instance to perform some action, or to provide bean instance with some information. For instance, if a bean implements ApplicationContextAware interface, container invokes setApplicationContext method of the bean instance to provide the bean with a reference to the ApplicationContext in which the bean is deployed.

InitializingBean interface defines an afterPropertiesSet method that is invoked by the Spring container after the bean properties are set. Beans perform initialization work in the afterPropertiesSet method, like obtaining connection to a database, opening a flat file for reading, and so on. DisposableBean interface defines a destroy method that is invoked by the Spring container when the bean instance is destroyed.

> As with the ApplicationContextAware lifecycle interface, beans should avoid implementing InitializingBean and DisposableBean interfaces because it couples application code with Spring.

Let's now look at JSR 250's @PostConstruct and @PreDestroy annotations for specifying bean initialization and destruction methods.

JSR 250's @PostConstruct and @PreDestroy annotations

JSR 250 (Common Annotations for the Java Platform) defines standard annotations that are used across different Java technologies. JSR 250's @PostConstruct and @PreDestroy annotations identify initialization and destruction methods of an object. A bean class in Spring can set a method as an initialization method by annotating it with @PostConstruct, and set a method as a destruction method by annotating it with @PreDestroy annotation.

> Refer JSR 250 home page (http://jcp.org/en/jsr/detail?id=250) for more details.

IMPORT **chapter 5/ch05-bankapp-jsr250** (This project shows the MyBank application that uses JSR 250's @PostConstruct and @PreDestroy annotations to identify custom initialization and destruction methods, respectively. To test whether the initialization method is executed, execute the main method of the BankApp class of this project. To test whether the destruction method is executed, execute the main method of the BankAppWithHook class of this project.)

The following example listing shows the FixedDepositDaoImpl class of ch05-bankapp-jsr250 project that uses @PostConstruct and @PreDestroy annotations:

Example listing 5-7 – FixedDepositDaoImpl class - @PostConstruct and @PreDestroy annotations
Project – ch05-bankapp-jsr250
Source location - src/main/java/sample/spring/chapter05/bankapp/dao

```
package sample.spring.chapter05.bankapp.dao;

import javax.annotation.PostConstruct;
import javax.annotation.PreDestroy;

public class FixedDepositDaoImpl implements FixedDepositDao {
  private DatabaseConnection connection;
  .....
  @PostConstruct
  public void initializeDbConnection() {
    logger.info("FixedDepositDaoImplís initializeDbConnection method invoked");
    connection = DatabaseConnection.getInstance();
  }
  .....
  @PreDestroy
  public void releaseDbConnection() {
    logger.info("FixedDepositDaoImpl's releaseDbConnection method invoked");
    connection.releaseConnection();
  }
}
```

In the above example listing, the FixedDepositDaoImpl class uses @PostConstruct and @PreDestroy annotations to identify initialization and destruction methods. You should note that @PostConstruct and @PreDestroy annotations are not specific to Spring.

> Java SE 6 provides annotations defined by JSR 250; if you are using Java SE 6 or later, you don't need to include JSR 250 JAR file in your application's classpath. If you are using Java SE 5, you need to include JSR 250 JAR file and the related JAR files in your application's classpath.

To use @PostConstruct and @PreDestroy annotations in your application, you need to configure Spring's CommonAnnotationBeanPostProcessor class in the application context XML file, as shown here:

Example listing 5-8 – applicationContext.xml – CommonAnnotationBeanPostProcessor configuration
Project – ch05-bankapp-jsr250
Source location - src/main/resources/META-INF/spring

```
<beans .....>
  <bean id="FixedDepositService"
    class="sample.spring.chapter05.bankapp.service.FixedDepositServiceImpl">
    <property name="myFixedDepositDao" ref="myFixedDepositDao" />
  </bean>

  <bean id="myFixedDepositDao"
    class="sample.spring.chapter05.bankapp.dao.FixedDepositDaoImpl" />

  <bean
    class="org.springframework.context.annotation.CommonAnnotationBeanPostProcessor"/>
</beans>
```

CommonAnnotationBeanPostProcessor implements Spring's BeanPostProcessor interface (explained in the next section), and is responsible for processing JSR 250 annotations.

If you execute the main method of BankApp and BankAppWithHook classes, you'll notice that the @PostConstruct and @PreDestroy annotated methods of FixedDepositDaoImpl class are executed at creation and destruction of FixedDepositDaoImpl instance, respectively.

We'll now look at Spring's BeanPostProcessor interface that allows you to interact with newly created bean instances *before* or *after* they are initialized by the Spring container.

5-3 Interacting with newly created bean instances using BeanPostProcessor

BeanPostProcessor is used to interact with newly created bean instances *before* and/or *after* their initialization method (refer section 5-2) is invoked by the Spring container. You can use BeanPostProcessor to execute custom logic *before* and/or *after* bean's initialization method is invoked by the Spring container.

> A bean that implements Spring's BeanPostProcessor interface is a special bean type; the Spring container automatically detects and executes a BeanPostProcessor bean.

BeanPostProcessor interface defines the following methods:

- Object postProcessBeforeInitialization(Object bean, String beanName) – this method is invoked *before* the initialization method of a bean instance is invoked
- Object postProcessAfterInitialization(Object bean, String beanName) – this method is invoked *after* the initialization method of a bean instance is invoked

BeanPostProcessor's methods accept newly created bean instance and its name as arguments, and return the same or modified bean instance. For instance, if you have configured a FixedDepositDaoImpl class as a bean with id value as myFixedDepositDao in the application context XML file (refer example listing 5-8), the BeanPostProcessor's methods receive an instance of FixedDepositDaoImpl class and myFixedDepositDao string value as arguments. The BeanPostProcessor's methods may return the original bean instance as-is or they may modify the bean instance or they may return an object that wraps the original bean instance.

You configure a BeanPostProcessor implementation in the application context XML file like any other Spring bean. Spring container automatically detects beans that implement BeanPostProcessor interface, and creates their instance *before* creating instance of any other bean defined in the application context XML file. Once the BeanPostProcessor beans are created, the Spring container invokes each BeanPostProcessor's postProcessBeforeInitialization and postProcessAfterInitialization methods for each bean instance created by the Spring container.

Let's say that you have defined a singleton-scoped bean ABean and a BeanPostProcessor bean, MyBeanPostProcessor, in the application context XML file. Figure 5-1 shows a sequence diagram that depicts the sequence in which MyBeanPostProcessor's methods are invoked by the Spring container.

The init method call in the sequence diagram represents a call to the initialization method of the bean. The sequence diagram shows that the MyBeanPostProcessor instance is created before the ABean bean instance is created. As a BeanPostProcessor implementation is configured like any other bean, if MyBeanPostProcessor defines an initialization method, container invokes the initialization method of the MyBeanPostProcessor instance. After ABean's instance is created, setter methods of the ABean instance are invoked by the Spring container to satisfy its dependencies, and to provide the bean instance with the required configuration information. After properties are set, but *before* ABean's initialization method is invoked, the Spring container invokes MyBeanPostProcessor's postProcessBeforeInitialization method. After ABean's initialization method is invoked, MyBeanPostProcessor's postProcessAfterInitialization method is called by the Spring container.

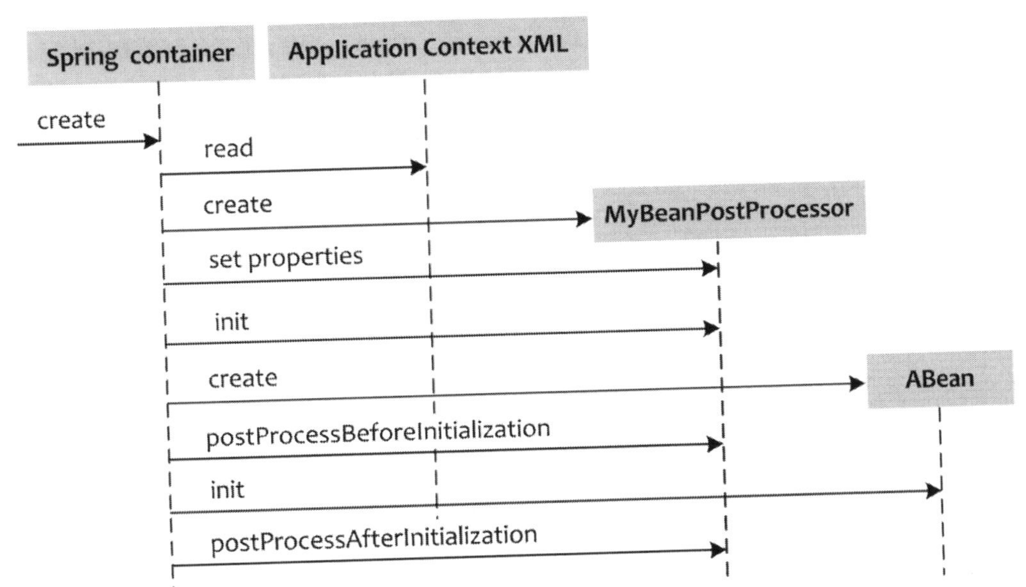

Figure 5-1 – The Spring container invokes MyBeanPostProcessor's methods *before* and *after* the initialization of ABean's initialization method

It's only after invocation of postProcessAfterInitialization method, a bean instance is considered completely initialized by the Spring container. For instance, if a BBean bean is dependent on ABean, container will inject ABean instance into BBean only after MyBeanPostProcessor's postProcessAfterInitialization is invoked for both ABean and BBean instances.

You should note that if the bean definition for a BeanPostProcessor bean specifies that it should be lazily created (refer <bean> element's lazy-init attribute or <beans> element's default-lazy-init attribute in section 2-5 of chapter 2), the Spring container ignores lazy initialization configuration and creates the BeanPostProcessor bean instance *before* creating instances of singleton-scoped beans defined in the application context XML file. You should note that the beans that implement BeanFactoryPostProcessor interface (explained in section 5-4) are created *before* the beans that implement BeanPostProcessor interface.

Let's now look at some example scenarios in which you can use Spring's BeanPostProcessor.

IMPORT **chapter 5/ch05-bankapp-beanpostprocessor** (This project shows the MyBank application that uses BeanPostProcessor implementations to validate bean instances and to resolve bean dependencies. To verify that the BeanPostProcessor implementations function correctly, execute the main method of the BankApp class of this project.)

BeanPostProcessor example – Validating bean instances

In a Spring application, you may want to verify that a bean instance is configured correctly before it is injected into dependent beans or accessed by other objects in the application. Let's see how we can use a BeanPostProcessor implementation to give an opportunity to each bean instance to validate its configuration before the bean instance is made available to dependent beans or other application objects.

The following example listing shows the MyBank's InstanceValidator interface that must be implemented by beans whose configuration we want to validate using a BeanPostProcessor implementation:

Example listing 5-9 – InstanceValidator interface
Project – ch05-bankapp-beanpostprocessor
Source location - src/main/java/sample/spring/chapter05/bankapp/common

```
package sample.spring.chapter05.bankapp.common;

public interface InstanceValidator {
   void validateInstance();
}
```

InstanceValidator interface defines a validateInstance method that verifies whether the bean instance was correctly initialized or not. We'll soon see that the validateInstance method is invoked by a BeanPostProcessor implementation.

The following example listing shows the FixedDepositDaoImpl class that implements InstanceValidator interface:

Example listing 5-10 – FixedDepositDaoImpl class
Project – ch05-bankapp-beanpostprocessor
Source location - src/main/java/sample/spring/chapter05/bankapp/dao

```
package sample.spring.chapter05.bankapp.dao;

import org.apache.log4j.Logger;
import sample.spring.chapter05.bankapp.common.InstanceValidator;

public class FixedDepositDaoImpl implements FixedDepositDao, InstanceValidator {
   private static Logger logger = Logger.getLogger(FixedDepositDaoImpl.class);
   private DatabaseConnection connection;

   public FixedDepositDaoImpl() {
      logger.info("FixedDepositDaoImpl's constructor invoked");
```

```
}

public void initializeDbConnection() {
  logger.info("FixedDepositDaoImplís initializeDbConnection method invoked");
  connection = DatabaseConnection.getInstance();
}

@Override
public void validateInstance() {
  logger.info("Validating FixedDepositDaoImpl instance");
  if(connection == null) {
    logger.error("Failed to obtain DatabaseConnection instance");
  }
}
}
```

In the above example listing, the initializeDbConnection method is the initialization method that retrieves an instance of DatabaseConnection by calling getInstance *static* method of DatabaseConnection class. The connection attribute is null if FixedDepositDaoImpl instance fails to retrieve an instance of DatabaseConnection. If connection attribute is null, the validateInstance method logs an error message indicating that the FixedDepositDaoImpl instance is not correctly initialized. As the initializeDbConnection initialization method sets the value of connection attribute, the validateInstance method *must* be invoked *after* the initializeDbConnection method. In a real world application development scenario, if a bean instance is not configured correctly, the validateInstance method may take some corrective action or throw a runtime exception to stop the application from starting up. For simplicity, the validateInstance method logs an error message if a bean instance is not configured correctly.

The following example listing shows the InstanceValidationBeanPostProcessor class that implements Spring's BeanPostProcessor interface, and is responsible for invoking validateInstance method of newly created beans:

Example listing 5-11 – InstanceValidationBeanPostProcessor class
Project – ch05-bankapp-beanpostprocessor
Source location - src/main/java/sample/spring/chapter05/bankapp/postprocessor

```
package sample.spring.chapter05.bankapp.postprocessor;

import org.springframework.beans.BeansException;
import org.springframework.beans.factory.config.BeanPostProcessor;
import org.springframework.core.Ordered;

public class InstanceValidationBeanPostProcessor implements BeanPostProcessor, Ordered {
```

```
    private static Logger logger = Logger.getLogger(InstanceValidationBeanPostProcessor.class);
    private int order;

    public InstanceValidationBeanPostProcessor() {
      logger.info("Created InstanceValidationBeanPostProcessor instance");
    }

    @Override
    public Object postProcessBeforeInitialization(Object bean, String beanName)
          throws BeansException {
      logger.info("postProcessBeforeInitialization method invoked");
      return bean;
    }

    @Override
    public Object postProcessAfterInitialization(Object bean, String beanName)
          throws BeansException {
      logger.info("postProcessAfterInitialization method invoked");
      if (bean instanceof InstanceValidator) {
        ((InstanceValidator) bean).validateInstance();
      }
      return bean;
    }

    public void setOrder(int order) {
      this.order = order;
    }

    @Override
    public int getOrder() {
      return order;
    }
}
```

The above example listing shows that the InstanceValidationBeanPostProcessor class implements Spring's BeanPostProcessor and Ordered interfaces. The postProcessBeforeInitialization method simply returns the bean instance passed to the method. In the postProcessAfterInitialization method, if the bean instance is found to be of type InstanceValidator, the bean instance's validateInstance method is invoked. This means that if a bean implements InstanceValidator interface, InstanceValidationBeanPostProcessor calls validateInstance method of the bean instance *after* the initialization method of the bean instance is invoked by the Spring container.

The Ordered interface defines a getOrder method which returns an integer value. The integer value returned by the getOrder method determines the priority of a BeanPostProcessor implementation with respect to other BeanPostProcessor implementations configured in the application context XML file. A BeanPostProcessor with *higher* order value is considered at a *lower* priority, and is executed *after* the BeanPostProcessor implementations with *lower* order values are executed. As we want the integer value returned by the getOrder method to be configured as a bean property, a setOrder method and an order instance variable are defined in the InstanceValidationBeanPostProcessor class.

The following example listing shows bean definitions for InstanceValidationBeanPostProcessor class:

Example listing 5-12 – InstanceValidationBeanPostProcessor bean definition
Project – ch05-bankapp-beanpostprocessor
Source location - src/main/resources/META-INF/spring

```
<bean class="......bankapp.postprocessor.InstanceValidationBeanPostProcessor">
      <property name="order" value="1" />
</bean>
```

In the above bean definition, <bean> element's id attribute is *not* specified because we typically don't want InstanceValidationBeanPostProcessor to be a dependency of any other bean. The <property> element sets the value of order property to 1.

Let's now look at a BeanPostProcessor implementation that is used for resolving bean dependencies.

BeanPostProcessor example – Resolving bean dependencies

In chapter 4, we saw that if a bean implements Spring's ApplicationContextAware interface, it can programmatically obtain bean instances using ApplicationContext's getBean method. Implementing ApplicationContextAware interface couples the application code with Spring, and for that reason it is not recommended to implement ApplicationContextAware interface. In this section, we'll look at a BeanPostProcessor implementation that provides beans with an object that wraps an ApplicationContext instance, resulting in application code that is *not* directly dependent on ApplicationContextAware and ApplicationContext interfaces of Spring.

The following example listing shows the MyBank's DependencyResolver interface that is implemented by beans who want to programmatically retrieve their dependencies from the ApplicationContext:

Example listing 5-13 – DependencyResolver interface
Project – ch05-bankapp-beanpostprocessor
Source location - src/main/java/sample/spring/chapter05/bankapp/common

```
package sample.spring.chapter05.bankapp.common;

public interface DependencyResolver {
  void resolveDependency(MyApplicationContext myApplicationContext);
}
```

DependencyResolver defines a resolveDependency method that accepts a MyApplicationContext object – a wrapper around ApplicationContext object. We'll soon see that the resolveDependency method is invoked by a BeanPostProcessor implementation.

The following example listing shows the FixedDepositServiceImpl class that implements DependencyResolver interface:

Example listing 5-14 – FixedDepositServiceImpl class
Project – ch05-bankapp-beanpostprocessor
Source location - src/main/java/sample/spring/chapter05/bankapp/service

```
package sample.spring.chapter05.bankapp.service;

import sample.spring.chapter05.bankapp.common.DependencyResolver;
import sample.spring.chapter05.bankapp.common.MyApplicationContext;

public class FixedDepositServiceImpl implements FixedDepositService, DependencyResolver {
  private FixedDepositDao fixedDepositDao;
  .....
  @Override
  public void resolveDependency(MyApplicationContext myApplicationContext) {
    FixedDepositDao = myApplicationContext.getBean(FixedDepositDao.class);
  }
}
```

The FixedDepositServiceImpl class defines a FixedDepositDao attribute of type FixedDepositDao. The resolveDependency method is responsible for obtaining an instance of FixedDepositDao object from MyApplicationContext (a wrapper around Spring's ApplicationContext object) and assigning it to the FixedDepositDao attribute.

The following example listing shows that the DependencyResolutionBeanPostProcessor class invokes resolveDependency method on beans that implement DependencyResolver interface:

Example listing 5-15 – DependencyResolutionBeanPostProcessor class
Project – ch05-bankapp-beanpostprocessor
Source location - src/main/java/sample/spring/chapter05/bankapp/postprocessor

```
package sample.spring.chapter05.bankapp.postprocessor;

import org.springframework.beans.factory.config.BeanPostProcessor;
import org.springframework.core.Ordered;
import sample.spring.chapter05.bankapp.common.MyApplicationContext;

public class DependencyResolutionBeanPostProcessor implements BeanPostProcessor,
    Ordered {
  private MyApplicationContext myApplicationContext;
  private int order;

  public void setMyApplicationContext(MyApplicationContext myApplicationContext) {
    this.myApplicationContext = myApplicationContext;
  }

  public void setOrder(int order) {
    this.order = order;
  }

  @Override
  public int getOrder() {
    return order;
  }

  @Override
  public Object postProcessBeforeInitialization(Object bean, String beanName)
      throws BeansException {
    if (bean instanceof DependencyResolver) {
      ((DependencyResolver) bean).resolveDependency(myApplicationContext);
    }
    return bean;
  }

  @Override
  public Object postProcessAfterInitialization(Object bean, String beanName)
      throws BeansException {
    return bean;
  }
}
```

The DependencyResolutionBeanPostProcessor class implements Spring's BeanPostProcessor and Ordered interfaces. The myApplicationContext attribute (of type MyApplicationContext) represents a dependency of DependencyResolutionBeanPostProcessor. The postProcessBeforeInitialization method invokes resolveDependency method on bean instances that implement DependencyResolver interface, passing the MyApplicationContext object as argument. The postProcessAfterInitialization method simply returns the bean instance passed to the method.

The following example listing shows the MyApplicationContext class that acts as a wrapper around Spring's ApplicationContext object:

Example listing 5-16 – MyApplicationContext class
Project – ch05-bankapp-beanpostprocessor
Location - src/main/java/sample/spring/chapter05/bankapp/common

```
package sample.spring.chapter05.bankapp.common;

import org.springframework.context.ApplicationContext;
import org.springframework.context.ApplicationContextAware;

public class MyApplicationContext implements ApplicationContextAware {
  private ApplicationContext applicationContext;

  @Override
  public void setApplicationContext(ApplicationContext applicationContext)
       throws BeansException {
    this.applicationContext = applicationContext;
  }

  public <T> T getBean(Class<T> klass) {
    return applicationContext.getBean(klass);
  }
}
```

The MyApplicationContext class implements Spring's ApplicationContextAware interface to obtain reference to the ApplicationContext object in which the bean is deployed. The MyApplicationContext class defines a getBean method that returns a bean instance with the given name from the ApplicationContext instance.

The following example listing shows the bean definitions for DependencyResolutionBeanPostProcessor and MyApplicationContext classes:

Example listing 5-17 – applicationContext.xml
Project – ch05-bankapp-beanpostprocessor
Source location - src/main/resources/META-INF/spring

```
<bean class=".....postprocessor.DependencyResolutionBeanPostProcessor">
    <property name="myApplicationContext" ref="myApplicationContext" />
    <property name="order" value="0" />
</bean>

<bean id="myApplicationContext" class=".....bankapp.common.MyApplicationContext" />
```

The bean definition for DependencyResolutionBeanPostProcessor class shows that its order property value is set to 0. Example listing 5-12 showed that the InstanceValidationBeanPostProcessor's order property value is 1. As *lower* order property value means *higher* priority, the Spring container applies DependencyResolutionBeanPostProcessor to a bean instance, followed by applying the InstanceValidationBeanPostProcessor.

The following example listing shows the main method of BankApp class that checks the functionality of DependencyResolutionBeanPostProcessor and InstanceValidationBeanPostProcessor:

Example listing 5-18 – BankApp class
Project – bankapp-beanpostprocessor
Location - src/main/java/sample/spring/chapter05/bankapp

```
package sample.spring.chapter05.bankapp;

public class BankApp {
    public static void main(String args[]) throws Exception {
        AbstractApplicationContext context = new ClassPathXmlApplicationContext(
              "classpath:META-INF/spring/applicationContext.xml");
        context.registerShutdownHook();

        FixedDepositService FixedDepositService = context.getBean(FixedDepositService.class);
        FixedDepositService.createFixedDeposit(new FixedDepositDetails(1, 1000, 12,
            "someemail@somedomain.com"));
        .....
    }
}
```

BankApp's main method retrieves an instance of FixedDepositService from the ApplicationContext and executes FixedDepositService's createFixedDeposit method. When you execute BankApp's main method, you'll notice that the Spring container creates instance of DependencyResolutionBeanPostProcessor and InstanceValidationBeanPostProcessor beans *before* creating instance of any other bean defined in the application context XML file. And, the

DependencyResolutionBeanPostProcessor (order value 0) is applied to a newly created bean instance *before* the InstanceValidationBeanPostProcessor (order value 1) is applied.

You should note that the Spring container doesn't apply a BeanPostProcessor implementation to other BeanPostProcessor implementations. For instance, in the MyBank application, DependencyResolutionBeanPostProcessor's postProcessBeforeInitialization and postProcessAfterInitialization methods are *not* invoked by the Spring container when an instance of InstanceValidationBeanPostProcessor is created.

Let's now look at the behavior of a BeanPostProcessor implementation for a bean that implements FactoryBean interface.

BeanPostProcessor behavior for FactoryBeans

In section 3-9 of chapter 3, we discussed that a bean that implements Spring's FactoryBean interface represents a factory for creating bean instances. The question that you might be asking at this time is whether a BeanPostProcessor implementation applies to a FactoryBean implementation or to the bean instances created by the FactoryBean implementation. Later in this section, we'll see that a BeanPostProcessor's postProcessBeforeInitialization and postProcessAfterInitialization methods are invoked for a FactoryBean instance created by the Spring container. And, *only* postProcessAfterInitialization method is invoked for bean instances created by a FactoryBean.

The following example listing shows the EventSenderFactoryBean (a FactoryBean implementation) class of MyBank application that creates instances of EventSender bean:

Example listing 5-19 – EventSenderFactoryBean class
Project – ch05-bankapp-beanpostprocessor
Location - src/main/java/sample/spring/chapter05/bankapp/factory

```
package sample.spring.chapter05.bankapp.factory;

import org.springframework.beans.factory.FactoryBean;
import org.springframework.beans.factory.InitializingBean;

public class EventSenderFactoryBean implements FactoryBean<EventSender>, InitializingBean {
  .....
  @Override
  public EventSender getObject() throws Exception {
    logger.info("getObject method of EventSenderFactoryBean invoked");
    return new EventSender();
  }

  @Override
```

```
  public Class<?> getObjectType() {
    return EventSender.class;
  }

  @Override
  public boolean isSingleton() {
    return false;
  }

  @Override
  public void afterPropertiesSet() throws Exception {
    logger.info("afterPropertiesSet method of EventSenderFactoryBean invoked");
  }
}
```

EventSenderFactoryBean class implements Spring's InitializingBean and FactoryBean interfaces. The getObject method returns an instance of EventSender object. As the isSingleton method returns false, EventSenderFactoryBean's getObject method is invoked each time EventSenderFactoryBean receives request for an EventSender object.

The following example listing shows the main method of BankApp class of ch05-bankapp-beanpostprocessor project that retrieves EventSender instances from the EventSenderFactoryBean:

Example listing 5-20 – BankApp class
Project – ch05-bankapp-beanpostprocessor
Location - src/main/java/sample/spring/chapter05/bankapp

```
package sample.spring.chapter05.bankapp;

public class BankApp {
  public static void main(String args[]) throws Exception {
    AbstractApplicationContext context = new ClassPathXmlApplicationContext(
        "classpath:META-INF/spring/applicationContext.xml");
    context.registerShutdownHook();
    .....
    context.getBean("eventSenderFactory");
    context.getBean("eventSenderFactory");
  }
}
```

In the above example listing, the ApplicationContext's getBean method is called twice to retrieve two distinct EventSender instances from the EventSenderFactoryBean. If you execute BankApp's main method, you'll see the following messages printed on the console:

Created EventSenderFactoryBean

DependencyResolutionBeanPostProcessor's **postProcessBeforeInitialization** method invoked for.....EventSenderFactoryBean

InstanceValidationBeanPostProcessor's **postProcessBeforeInitialization** method invoked for .....EventSenderFactoryBean

afterPropertiesSet method of EventSenderFactoryBean invoked

DependencyResolutionBeanPostProcessor's **postProcessAfterInitialization** method invoked for.....EventSenderFactoryBean

InstanceValidationBeanPostProcessor's **postProcessAfterInitialization** method invoked for bean .....EventSenderFactoryBean

The above output shows that a BeanPostProcessor's postProcessBeforeInitialization and postProcessAfterInitialization methods are invoked for the EventSenderFactoryBean instance created by the Spring container.

Execution of BankApp's main method also shows the following output on the console:

getObject method of EventSenderFactoryBean invoked

DependencyResolutionBeanPostProcessor's **postProcessAfterInitialization** method invoked for.....EventSender

getObject method of EventSenderFactoryBean invoked

DependencyResolutionBeanPostProcessor's **postProcessAfterInitialization** method invoked for.....EventSender

The above output shows that *only* the postProcessAfterInitialization method of a BeanPostProcessor is invoked for the EventSender instance created by the EventSenderFactoryBean. If you want, you can make modifications to an EventSender instance in the postProcessAfterInitialization method.

Let's now look at Spring's built-in RequiredAnnotationBeanPostProcessor that you can use to ensure that *required* (or mandatory) bean properties are configured in the application context XML file.

RequiredAnnotationBeanPostProcessor

If the setter-method for a bean property is annotated with Spring's @Required annotation, Spring's RequiredAnnotationBeanPostProcessor (a BeanPostProcessor implementation) checks if the bean property is configured in the application context XML file.

> You should note that the RequiredAnnotationBeanPostProcessor is not automatically registered with the Spring container, you need to register it explicitly by defining it in the application context XML file.

The following example listing shows an example usage of @Required annotation:

Example listing 5-21 – @Required annotation usage

```
import org.springframework.beans.factory.annotation.Required;

public class FixedDepositServiceImpl implements FixedDepositService {
   private FixedDepositDao fixedDepositDao;

   @Required
   public void setFixedDepositDao(FixedDepositDao fixedDepositDao) {
      this.fixedDepositDao = fixedDepositDao;
   }
   .....
}
```

In the above example listing, the setFixedDepositDao setter-method for FixedDepositDao property is annotated with @Required annotation. If you have defined RequiredAnnotationBeanPostProcessor in the application context XML file, the RequiredAnnotationBeanPostProcessor will check if you have specified a <property> element (or used p-namespace) to set the value of FixedDepositDao property. If you haven't configured the FixedDepositDao property in the bean definition for the FixedDepositServiceImpl class in the application context XML file, it'll result in an exception. This shows that you can use RequiredAnnotationBeanPostProcessor to ensure that all bean instances in your application are configured properly in the application context XML file.

RequiredAnnotationBeanPostProcessor only ensures that a bean property is configured in the bean definition. It *doesn't* ensure that the configured property value is correct. For instance, you can configure a property's value as null, instead of a valid value. For this reason, beans may still need to implement initialization methods to check if the properties are correctly set.

Let's now look at Spring's DestructionAwareBeanPostProcessor interface that is a sub-interface of Spring's BeanPostProcessor interface.

DestructionAwareBeanPostProcessor

So far we have seen that a BeanPostProcessor implementation is used for interacting with newly created bean instances. In some scenarios you may also want to interact with a bean instance before it is destroyed. To interact with a bean instance before it is destroyed, configure a bean that implements Spring's DestructionAwareBeanPostProcessor interface in the application context XML file. DestructionAwareBeanPostProcessor is a sub-interface of BeanPostProcessor interface and defines the following method:

```
void postProcessBeforeDestruction(Object bean, String beanName)
```

The postProcessBeforeDestruction method accepts the bean instance, which is about to be destroyed by the Spring container, and its name as arguments. Spring container invokes the postProcessBeforeDestruction method for each singleton-scoped bean instance *before* the bean instance is destroyed by the Spring container. Usually, the postProcessBeforeDestruction method is used to invoke custom destruction methods on the bean instances. It is important to note that the postProcessBeforeDestruction method is *not* called for prototype-scoped beans.

We'll now look at Spring's BeanFactoryPostProcessor interface, which allows you to make modifications to bean definitions.

5-4 Modifying bean definitions using BeanFactoryPostProcessor

Spring's BeanFactoryPostProcessor interface is implemented by classes that want to make modifications to bean definitions. A BeanFactoryPostProcessor is executed *after* bean definitions are loaded by the Spring container, but before any bean instance is created. A BeanFactoryPostProcessor is created *before* any other bean defined in the application context XML file, giving the BeanFactoryPostProcessor an opportunity to make modifications to bean definitions of other beans. You configure a BeanFactoryPostProcessor implementation in the application context XML file like any other Spring bean.

> Instead of bean definitions, if you want to modify or interact with bean instances, use a BeanPostProcessor (refer to section 5-3) and not a BeanFactoryPostProcessor.

BeanFactoryPostProcessor interface defines a single method - postProcessBeanFactory. This method accepts an argument of type ConfigurableListableBeanFactory that can be used to obtain and modify bean definitions loaded by the Spring container. It is possible to create a bean instance inside postProcessBeanFactory method itself by calling ConfigurableListableBeanFactory's getBean method, but bean creation inside postProcessBeanFactory method is *not* recommended. It is important to note that BeanPostProcessors (refer section 5-3) are *not* executed for bean instances created inside postProcessBeanFactory method.

It is important to note that a ConfigurableListableBeanFactory provides access to the Spring container just like the ApplicationContext object. ConfigurableListableBeanFactory additionally allows you to configure the Spring container, iterate over beans, and modify bean definitions. For instance, using ConfigurableListableBeanFactory object you can register

PropertyEditorRegistrars (refer section 3-6 of chapter 3), register BeanPostProcessors, and so on. Later in this section, we'll see how ConfigurableListableBeanFactory object is used to modify bean definitions.

Let's now look at how we can use a BeanFactoryPostProcessor to modify bean definitions.

IMPORT **chapter 5/ch05-bankapp-beanfactorypostprocessor** (This project shows the MyBank application that uses a BeanFactoryPostProcessor implementation to disable autowiring across the application, and log an error message if a singleton-scoped bean is found to be dependent on a prototype-scoped bean. To verify that the BeanFactoryPostProcessor implementation functions correctly, execute the main method of the BankApp class of this project.)

BeanFactoryPostProcessor example

In the previous chapter, we saw that autowiring hides the overall structure of the application (refer section 4-6 of chapter 4). We also discussed that instead of using <property> element to specify that a singleton-scoped bean is dependent on a prototype-scoped bean, you should use <lookup-method> or <replaced-method> element (refer section 4-4 and 4-5 of chapter 4 for more details) to programmatically obtain a prototype-scoped dependency of a singleton-bean. We'll now look at a BeanFactoryPostProcessor implementation that makes beans *unavailable* for autowiring (refer <bean> element's autowire-candidate attribute described in section 4-6 of chapter 4) and logs an error message if it finds a singleton-scoped bean is dependent on a prototype-scoped bean. For simplicity, we assume that a singleton-scoped bean uses <property> element to specify that it is dependent on a prototype-scoped bean.

> A bean that implements Spring's BeanFactoryPostProcessor interface is a *special* bean type; the Spring container automatically detects and executes a BeanFactoryPostProcessor bean.

The following example listing shows the MyBank's ApplicationConfigurer class that implements BeanFactoryPostProcessor interface:

Example listing 5-22 – ApplicationConfigurer class – a BeanFactoryPostProcessor implementation
Project – ch05-bankapp-beanfactorypostprocessor
Source location - src/main/java/sample/spring/chapter05/bankapp/postprocessor

```
package sample.spring.chapter05.bankapp.postprocessor;

import org.springframework.beans.factory.config.BeanDefinition;
import org.springframework.beans.factory.config.BeanFactoryPostProcessor;
import org.springframework.beans.factory.config.ConfigurableListableBeanFactory;

public class ApplicationConfigurer implements BeanFactoryPostProcessor {
```

```
    public ApplicationConfigurer() {
      logger.info("Created ApplicationConfigurer instance");
    }

    @Override
    public void postProcessBeanFactory(
        ConfigurableListableBeanFactory beanFactory) throws BeansException {
      String[] beanDefinitionNames = beanFactory.getBeanDefinitionNames();

      // -- get all the bean definitions
      for (int i = 0; i < beanDefinitionNames.length; i++) {
        String beanName = beanDefinitionNames[i];
        BeanDefinition beanDefinition = beanFactory.getBeanDefinition(beanName);
        beanDefinition.setAutowireCandidate(false);

        // -- obtain dependencies of a bean
        if (beanDefinition.isSingleton()) {
          if (hasPrototypeDependency(beanFactory, beanDefinition)) {
            logger.error("Singleton-scoped " + beanName
                + " bean is dependent on a prototype-scoped bean.");
          }
        }
      }
    }
    .....
}
```

The following sequence of actions is performed by the postProcessBeanFactory method:

1. First, the postProcessBeanFactory method calls ConfigurableListableBeanFactory's getBeanDefinitionNames method to obtain names of all the bean definitions loaded by the Spring container. You should note that the name of a bean definition is the value of <bean> element's id attribute.

2. Once the names of all the bean definitions are obtained, the postProcessBeanFactory method invokes ConfigurableListableBeanFactory's getBeanDefinition method to obtain the BeanDefinition object corresponding to each bean definition. The getBeanDefinition method accepts a bean definition name (obtained in step 1) as argument.

3. A BeanDefinition object represents a bean definition, and can be used to modify bean configuration. For each bean definition loaded by the Spring container, the postProcessBeanFactory method invokes BeanDefinition's setAutowireCandidate method to make *all* the beans unavailable for autowiring.

4. BeanDefinition's isSingleton method returns true if a bean definition is for a singleton-scoped bean. If a bean definition is for a singleton-scoped bean, the postProcessBeanFactory method invokes hasPrototypeDependency method to check if the singleton-scoped bean is dependent on any prototype-scoped bean. And, if the singleton-scoped bean is dependent on a prototype-scoped bean, the postProcessBeanFactory method logs an error message.

The following example listing shows the implementation of ApplicationConfigurer's hasPrototypeDependency method that returns true if a bean is dependent on a prototype-scoped bean:

Example listing 5-23 – ApplicationConfigurer's hasPrototypeDependency method
Project – ch05-bankapp-beanfactorypostprocessor
Source location - src/main/java/sample/spring/chapter05/bankapp/postprocessor

```
import org.springframework.beans.MutablePropertyValues;
import org.springframework.beans.PropertyValue;
import org.springframework.beans.factory.config.RuntimeBeanReference;

public class ApplicationConfigurer implements BeanFactoryPostProcessor {
  .....
  private boolean hasPrototypeDependency(ConfigurableListableBeanFactory beanFactory,
       BeanDefinition beanDefinition) {
    boolean isPrototype = false;
    MutablePropertyValues mutablePropertyValues = beanDefinition.getPropertyValues();
    PropertyValue[] propertyValues = mutablePropertyValues.getPropertyValues();

    for (int j = 0; j < propertyValues.length; j++) {
      if (propertyValues[j].getValue()   instanceof   RuntimeBeanReference) {
        String dependencyBeanName = ((RuntimeBeanReference) propertyValues[j]
             .getValue()).getBeanName();
        BeanDefinition dependencyBeanDef = beanFactory
                                         .getBeanDefinition(dependencyBeanName);
        if (dependencyBeanDef.isPrototype()) {
          isPrototype = true;
          break;
        }
      }
    }
    return isPrototype;
  }
}
```

The hasPrototypeDependency method checks if the bean represented by BeanDefinition argument is dependent on a prototype-scoped bean. The ConfigurableListableBeanFactory argument provides access to bean definitions loaded by the Spring container. The following sequence of actions is performed by hasPrototypeDependency method to find if the bean represented by the BeanDefinition argument has a prototype-scoped dependency:

1. First, hasPrototypeDependency method calls BeanDefinition's getPropertyValues method to obtain bean properties defined by <property> elements. BeanDefinition's getPropertyValues returns an object of type MutablePropertyValues which you can use to modify bean properties. For instance, you can add additional properties to the bean definition by using addPropertyValue and addPropertyValues methods of MutablePropertyValues.

2. As we want to iterate over all the bean properties and check if any bean property refers to a prototype-scoped bean, the getPropertyValues method of MutablePropertyValues is invoked to retrieve an array of PropertyValue objects. A PropertyValue object holds information about a bean property.

3. If a bean property refers to a Spring bean, calling PropertyValue's getValue method returns an instance of RuntimeBeanReference object that holds name of the referenced bean. As we are interested in bean properties that reference Spring beans, the return value of PropertyValue's getValue method is checked if it represents an instance of RuntimeBeanReference type. If it does, the object returned by PropertyValue's getValue method is cast to RuntimeBeanReference type, and the name of the referenced bean is obtained by calling the RuntimeBeanReference's getBeanName method.

4. Now, that we have the name of the bean referenced by the bean property, the BeanDefinition object for the referenced bean is obtained by calling ConfigurableListableBeanFactory's getBeanDefinition method. You can check if the referenced bean is a prototype-scoped bean by calling BeanDefinition's isPrototype method.

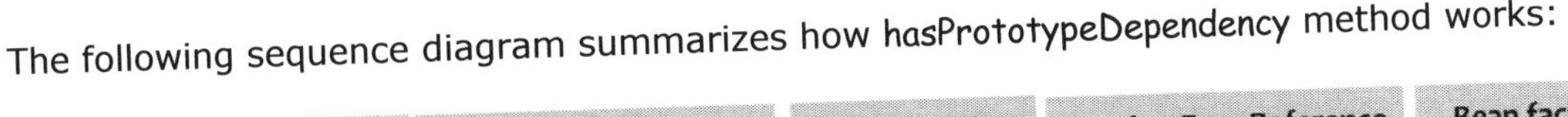

The following sequence diagram summarizes how hasPrototypeDependency method works:

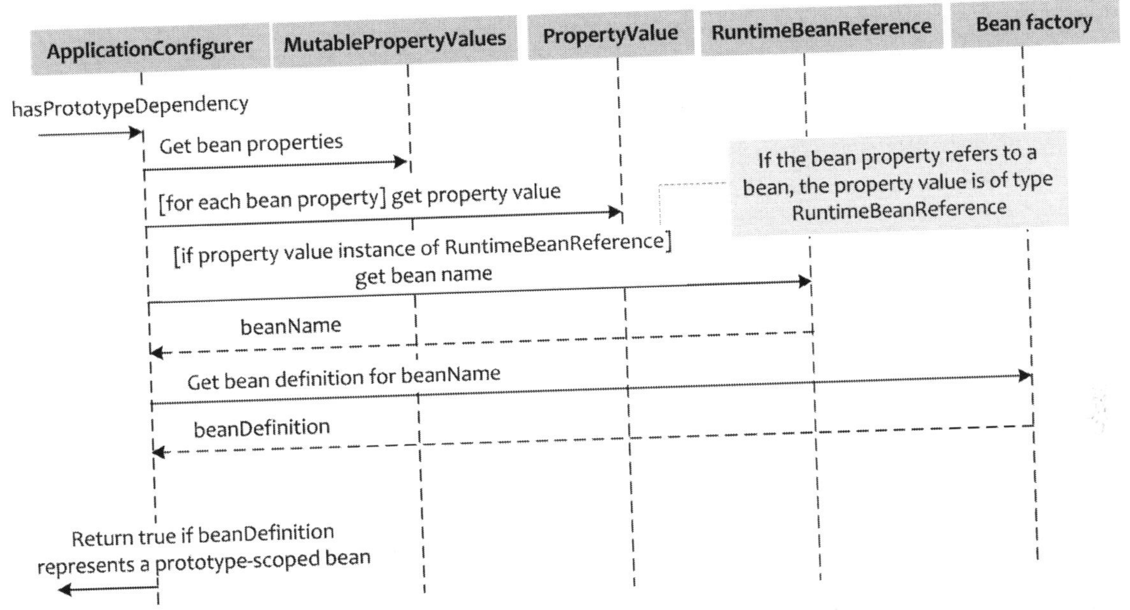

Figure 5-2 - hasPrototypeDependency method iterates over bean definitions of dependencies, and returns true if a prototype-scoped dependency is found

In the above sequence diagram ConfigurableListableBeanFactory object has been depicted as 'Bean factory' object.

The following example listing shows the application context XML file of ch05-bankapp-beanfactorypostprocessor project that contains bean definitions for ApplicationConfigurer class (a BeanFactoryPostProcessor implementation), InstanceValidationBeanPostProcessor class (a BeanPostProcessor implementation), along with bean definitions for application-specific objects:

Example listing 5-24 – applicationContext.xml - BeanFactoryPostProcessor bean definition
Project – ch05-bankapp-beanfactorypostprocessor
Source location - src/main/resources/META-INF/spring

```
<beans .....>
  .....
  <bean id="FixedDepositDao"
     class="sample.spring.chapter05.bankapp.dao.FixedDepositDaoImpl"..... >
     <property name="fixedDepositDetails" ref="FixedDepositDetails" />
  </bean>

  <bean id="FixedDepositDetails"
     class="sample.spring.chapter05.bankapp.domain.FixedDepositDetails"
```

```
    scope="prototype" />

  <bean class=".....postprocessor.InstanceValidationBeanPostProcessor">
    <property name="order" value="1" />
  </bean>

  <bean
    class="sample.spring.chapter05.bankapp.postprocessor.ApplicationConfigurer" />
</beans>
```

In the bean definitions shown above, the singleton-scoped FixedDepositDao bean is dependent on the prototype-scoped FixedDepositDetails bean.

If you execute the main method of BankApp class of ch05-bankapp-beanfactorypostprocessor project, you'll see the following output on the console:

```
Created ApplicationConfigurer instance
Singleton-scoped FixedDepositDao bean is dependent on a prototype-scoped bean.
Created InstanceValidationBeanPostProcessor instance
```

The above output shows that the Spring container creates ApplicationConfigurer (a BeanFactoryPostProcessor) and executes ApplicationConfigurer's postProcessBeanFactory method *before* creating InstanceValidationBeanPostProcessor (a BeanPostProcessor) instance. It is important to note that the beans that implement the BeanFactoryPostProcessor interface are processed *before* beans that implement the BeanPostProcessor interface. For this reason, you *can't* use a BeanPostProcessor to make modifications to a BeanFactoryPostProcessor instance. The BeanFactoryPostProcessor gives you the opportunity to modify bean definitions loaded by the Spring container, and the BeanFactoryPostProcessor gives you the opportunity to make modifications to newly created bean instances.

Let's now look at some of the similarities between BeanPostProcessors and BeanFactoryPostProcessors:

- you can configure multiple BeanFactoryPostProcessors in the application context XML file. To control the order in which BeanFactoryPostProcessors are executed by the Spring container, implement Spring's Ordered interface (refer section 5-3 to know more about Ordered interface).

- even if you specify that a BeanFactoryPostProcessor implementation is lazily initialized by the Spring container, BeanFactoryPostProcessors are created when the Spring container instance is created.

In chapter 3, we looked at CustomEditorConfigurer – a BeanFactoryPostProcessor implementation that Spring provides out-of-the-box for registering custom property editors. Let's now look at some more BeanFactoryPostProcessor implementations that Spring provides out-of-the-box.

PropertySourcesPlaceholderConfigurer

So far we have seen bean definition examples in which <property> or <constructor-arg> element's value attribute is used to specify the actual string value of a bean property or a constructor argument. PropertySourcesPlaceholderConfigurer (a BeanFactoryPostProcessor) let's you specify the actual string value of bean properties and constructor arguments in a properties file. In the bean definition, you only specify *property placeholders* (of the form ${*<property_name_in_properties_file>*}) as the value of <property> or <constructor-arg> element's value attribute. When bean definitions are loaded by the Spring container, the PropertySourcesPlaceholderConfigurer pulls the actual values from the properties file and replaces the property placeholders in the bean definitions with actual values.

IMPORT **chapter 5/ch05-propertySourcesPlaceholderConfigurer-example** (This project shows a Spring application that uses Spring's PropertySourcesPlaceholderConfigurer to set bean properties from the properties specified in external properties files. To verify that the PropertySourcesPlaceholderConfigurer functions correctly, execute the main method of the SampleApp class of this project.)

The following example listing shows bean definitions for DataSource and WebServiceConfiguration classes that use property placeholders:

Example listing 5-25 – applicationContext.xml - Bean definitions that use property placeholders
Project – ch05-propertySourcesPlaceholderConfigurer-example
Source location - src/main/resources/META-INF/spring

```
<bean id="datasource" class="sample.spring.chapter05.domain.DataSource">
   <property name="url" value="${database.url}" />
   <property name="username" value="${database.username}" />
   <property name="password" value="${database.password}" />
   <property name="driverClass" value="${database.driverClass}" />
</bean>

<bean id="webServiceConfiguration"
      class="sample.spring.chapter05.domain.WebServiceConfiguration">
   <property name="webServiceUrl" value="${webservice.url}" />
</bean>
```

The above example listing shows that each <property> element's value attribute specifies a property placeholder. When bean definitions are loaded by the Spring container, PropertySourcesPlaceholderConfigurer replaces property placeholders with values from a properties file. For instance, if a database.username property is defined in a properties file, the value of database.username property replaces the ${database.username} property placeholder of dataSource bean.

The bean definition for the PropertySourcesPlaceholderConfigurer specifies properties files to be searched for finding replacement for a property placeholder, as shown in the following example listing:

Example listing 5-26 – applicationContext.xml-PropertySourcesPlaceholderConfigurer bean definition
Project – ch05-propertySourcesPlaceholderConfigurer-example
Source location - src/main/resources/META-INF/spring

```
<bean
   class="org.springframework.context.support.PropertySourcesPlaceholderConfigurer">
   <property name="locations">
      <list>
         <value>classpath:database.properties</value>
         <value>classpath:webservice.properties</value>
      </list>
   </property>
   <property name="ignoreUnresolvablePlaceholders" value="false" />
</bean>
```

PropertySourcesPlaceholderConfigurer's locations property specifies properties files to be searched for finding the value for a property placeholder. In the above example listing, PropertySourcesPlaceholderConfigurer looks for the value of a property placeholder in database.properties and webservice.properties files. The ignoreUnresolvablePlaceholders property specifies whether PropertySourcesPlaceholderConfigurer silently ignores or throws an exception in case a property placeholder value is not found in any of the properties files specified by the locations property. The value false indicates that the PropertySourcesPlaceholderConfigurer will throw an exception if value for a property placeholder is not found in database.properties or webservice.properties files.

The following example listing shows the properties defined in database.properties and webservice.properties files:

Example listing 5-27 – Properties defined in database.properties and webservice.properties files
Project – ch05-propertySourcesPlaceholderConfigurer-example
Source location - src/main/resources/META-INF

```
---------------- database.properties file ------------------
database.url=some_url
database.username=some_username
```

```
database.password=some_password
database.driverClass=some_driverClass

---------------- webservice.properties file ------------------
webservice.url=some_url
```

If you compare the properties defined in database.properties and webservice.properties files with the property placeholders specified in datasource and webServiceConfiguration bean definitions (refer example listing 5-25), you'll notice that for each property placeholder a property is defined in one of the properties files.

The main method of SampleApp class of ch05-propertySourcesPlaceholderConfigurer-example project retrieves WebServiceConfiguration and DataSource beans from the ApplicationContext and prints their properties on the console. If you execute SampleApp's main method, you'll see the following output on the console:

```
DataSource [url=some_url, username=some_username, password=some_password,
driverClass=some_driverClass]
WebServiceConfiguration [webServiceUrl=some_url]
```

The above output shows:

- DataSource's url property is set to some_url, username to some_username, password to some_password and driverClass to some_driverClass.
- WebServiceConfiguration's webServiceUrl property is set to some_url.

If you remove a property from either database.properties or webservice.properties file, executing SampleApp's main method will result in an exception.

Let's now look at localOverride property of PropertySourcesPlaceholderConfigurer.

localOverride property

If you want local properties (set via <props> element) to override properties read from properties file, you can set PropertySourcesPlaceholderConfigurer's localOverride property to true.

IMPORT **chapter 5/ch05-localoverride-example** (This project shows a Spring application that uses PropertySourcesPlaceholderConfigurer's localOverride property. To run the application, execute the main method of the SampleApp class of this project.)

The following example listing shows bean definitions for DataSource and WebServiceConfiguration classes:

Example listing 5-28 – applicationContext.xml - Bean definitions that use property placeholders
Project – ch05-localOverride-example
Source location - src/main/resources/META-INF/spring

```
<bean id="datasource" class="sample.spring.chapter05.domain.DataSource">
    <property name="url" value="${database.url}" />
    <property name="username" value="${database.username}" />
    <property name="password" value="${database.password}" />
    <property name="driverClass" value="${database.driverClass}" />
</bean>

<bean id="webServiceConfiguration"
        class="sample.spring.chapter05.domain.WebServiceConfiguration">
    <property name="webServiceUrl" value="${webservice.url}" />
</bean>
```

The bean definitions for DataSource and WebServiceConfiguration classes are same as we saw in example listing 5-25.

The following example listing shows the properties defined in database.properties and webservice.properties files:

Example listing 5-29 – Properties defined in database.properties and webservice.properties files
Project – ch05-localOverride-example
Source location - src/main/resources/META-INF

```
--------------- database.properties file -----------------
database.url=some_url
database.username=some_username

--------------- webservice.properties file -----------------
webservice.url=some_url
```

If you compare the properties defined in database.properties and webservice.properties files with the property placeholders specified in datasource and webServiceConfiguration bean definitions (refer example listing 5-28), you'll notice that properties are not defined for ${database.password} and ${database.driverClass} placeholders in the database.properties file.

The following example listing shows the bean definition for PropertySourcesPlaceholderConfigurer class:

Example listing 5-30 – applicationContext.xml - PropertySourcesPlaceholderConfigurer bean definition
Project – ch05-localOverride-example
Source location - src/main/resources/META-INF/spring

```
<bean
  class="org.springframework.context.support.PropertySourcesPlaceholderConfigurer">
  <property name="locations">
    <list>
      <value>classpath:database.properties</value>
      <value>classpath:webservice.properties</value>
    </list>
  </property>
  <property name="properties">
    <props>
      <prop key="database.password">locally-set-password</prop>
      <prop key="database.driverClass">locally-set-driverClass</prop>
      <prop key="webservice.url">locally-set-webServiceUrl</prop>
    </props>
  </property>
  <property name="ignoreUnresolvablePlaceholders" value="false" />
  <property name="localOverride" value="true" />
</bean>
```

The properties property of PropertySourcesPlaceholderConfigurer defines *local* properties. The database.password, database.driverClass and webservice.url properties are local properties. The localOverride property specifies whether local properties take precedence over properties read from external properties files. As the value of localOverride property is true, local properties take precedence.

The main method of SampleApp class in ch05-localOverride-example project retrieves WebServiceConfiguration and DataSource beans from the ApplicationContext and prints their properties on the console. If you execute SampleApp's main method, you'll see the following output on the console:

```
DataSource [url=some_url, username=some_username, password=locally-set-password,
driverClass=locally-set-driverClass]
WebServiceConfiguration [webServiceUrl=locally-set-webServiceUrl]
```

The output shows that the value of DataSource's password and driverClass properties are locally-set-password and locally-set-driverClass, respectively. This means that the values for DataSource's password and driverClass properties come from the local properties defined by the PropertySourcesPlaceholderConfigurer bean (refer example listing 5-30). This shows that if the PropertySourcesPlaceholderConfigurer can't find a property for a placeholder in the external properties files, it searches for the property in the local properties defined by PropertySourcesPlaceholderConfigurer bean. The output also shows that the WebServiceConfiguration's webServiceUrl property value comes from the local properties defined by the PropertySourcesPlaceholderConfigurer bean (refer example listing 5-30). The value of PropertySourcesPlaceholderConfigurer's localOverride property is set to true; therefore, the locally defined webservice.url property takes *precedence* over the webservice.url property read from the webservice.properties file.

> Instead of using PropertySourcesPlaceholderConfigurer's properties property, you can use <properties> element of Spring's util schema (refer section 3-8 of chapter 3) or PropertiesFactoryBean (refer section 3-8 of chapter 3) to define local properties.

Instead of directly configuring the PropertySourcesPlaceholderConfigurer bean in your application context XML file, you can use the <property-placeholder> element of Spring's context schema. The <property-placeholder> element configures a PropertySourcesPlaceholderConfigurer instance. Let's now look at the <property-placeholder> element in detail.

IMPORT **chapter 5/ch05-property-placeholder-element-example** (This project shows a Spring application that uses the <property-placeholder> element. To run the application, execute the main method of the SampleApp class of this project.)

<property-placeholder> element

The following example listing shows how the <property-placeholder> element is used to configure a PropertySourcesPlaceholderConfigurer instance with the same configuration as the one we configured in example listing 5-30:

Example listing 5-31 – applicationContext.xml - <property-placeholder> element
Project – ch05-property-placeholder-element-example
Source location - src/main/resources/META-INF/spring

```
<beans xmlns="http://www.springframework.org/schema/beans"
   xmlns:context="http://www.springframework.org/schema/context"
  xmlns:util="http://www.springframework.org/schema/util" .....>
  .....
  <context:property-placeholder ignore-unresolvable="false"
     location="classpath:database.properties, classpath:webservice.properties"
     local-override="true" order="1" properties-ref="localProps" />

  <util:properties id="localProps">
     <prop key="database.password">locally-set-password</prop>
     <prop key="database.driverClass">locally-set-driverClass</prop>
     <prop key="webservice.url">locally-set-webServiceUrl</prop>
  </util:properties>
```

```
</beans>
```

In the above example listing, reference to Spring's context schema is included so that its elements are accessible. The above example listing shows that the use of <property-placeholder> element results in a less verbose configuration of PropertySourcesPlaceholderConfigurer. The ignore-unresolvable, location and local-override attributes correspond to ignoreUnresolvablePlaceholders, locations and localOverride properties of PropertySourcesPlaceholderConfigurer. As the PropertySourcesPlaceholderConfigurer class implements Spring's Ordered interface, the order attribute's value is used to set the order property of PropertySourcesPlaceholderConfigurer instance. The properties-ref attribute refers to a java.util.Properties object that represents the *local properties*. In the above example listing, the <properties> element of Spring's util schema (refer section 3-8 of chapter 3) creates an instance of java.util.Properties object, which is referenced by the properties-ref attribute of <property-placeholder> element.

Let's now look at Spring's PropertyOverrideConfigurer (a BeanFactoryPostProcessor) which allows you to specify values for bean properties in external properties files.

PropertyOverrideConfigurer

PropertyOverrideConfigurer is similar to PropertySourcesPlaceholderConfigurer in the sense that it allows you to specify a bean property value in external properties file. When using PropertyOverrideConfigurer, bean property value is specified in the following format in external properties files:

```
<bean-name>.<bean-property-name>=<value>
```

here, *<bean-name>* is the name of the bean, *<bean-property-name>* is the name of the bean property, and *<value>* is the value that you want to assign to the bean property.

The notable differences between PropertyOverrideConfigurer and PropertySourcesPlaceholderConfigurer classes are:

- You can use PropertyOverrideConfigurer only for externalizing values of bean properties, that is, you can't use PropertyOverrideConfigurer to externalize values of constructor arguments.
- PropertySourcesPlaceholderConfigurer *doesn't* provide you with an option to specify default values for properties. But, PropertyOverrideConfigurer allows you to specify default values for bean properties.

Let's now look at an example usage of PropertyOverrideConfigurer.

IMPORT **chapter 5/ch05-propertyOverrideConfigurer-example** (This project shows a Spring application that uses Spring's PropertyOverrideConfigurer. To run the application, execute the main method of the SampleApp class of this project.)

PropertyOverrideConfigurer example

The following example listing shows bean definitions for DataSource and WebServiceConfiguration classes whose properties we'll set using PropertyOverrideConfigurer:

Example listing 5-32 – applicationContext.xml - Bean definitions for DataSource and WebServiceConfiguration
Project – ch05-propertyOverrideConfigurer-example
Source location - src/main/resources/META-INF/spring

```
<bean id="datasource" class="sample.spring.chapter05.domain.DataSource">
   <property name="url" value="test url value" />
   <property name="username" value="test username value" />
   <property name="password" value="test password value" />
   <property name="driverClass" value="test driverClass value" />
</bean>

<bean id="webServiceConfiguration"
      class="sample.spring.chapter05.domain.WebServiceConfiguration">
   <property name="webServiceUrl" value="this webservice url needs to be replaced" />
</bean>
```

In the above example listing, the <bean> element's value attribute specifies default value of a bean property.

The following example listing shows the bean definition for the PropertyOverrideConfigurer class that replaces the default values of bean properties (shown in example listing 5-32) with values read from database.properties and webservice.properties files:

Example listing 5-33 – applicationContext.xml - PropertyOverrideConfigurer configuration
Project – ch05-propertyOverrideConfigurer-example
Source location - src/main/resources/META-INF/spring

```
<bean
   class="org.springframework.beans.factory.config.PropertyOverrideConfigurer">
   <property name="locations">
      <list>
         <value>classpath:database.properties</value>
         <value>classpath:webservice.properties</value>
      </list>
```

```
    </property>
  </bean>
```

In the above example listing, PropertyOverrideConfigurer's locations property specifies the properties files that contain values for bean properties.

> Instead of directly configuring PropertyOverrideConfigurer, you can use <property-override> element of Spring's context schema to configure a PropertyOverrideConfigurer instance.

The following example listing shows database.properties and webservice.properties files that contain values of bean properties:

Example listing 5-34 – Properties defined in database.properties and webservice.properties
Project – ch05-propertyOverrideConfigurer-example
Source location - src/main/resources/META-INF

```
---------------- database.properties file ------------------
datasource.url=some_url
datasource.username=some_username
datasource.password=some_password

---------------- webservice.properties file ------------------
webServiceConfiguration.webServiceUrl=some_url
```

The entries in the database.properties and webservice.properties files show that the property name follows the pattern: *<bean-name>.<property-name>*. When bean definitions are loaded by the Spring container, PropertyOverrideConfigurer replaces the default value of a bean property with the value read for that bean property from the database.properties and webservice.properties files. For instance, the url property of datasource bean is set to the value of datasource.url property defined in the database.properties file. Similarly, webServiceUrl property of webServiceConfiguration bean is set to the value of webServiceConfiguration.webServiceUrl property defined in the webservice.properties file.

If no value is found for a bean property in the external properties files, the bean property retains its default value. Example listing 5-32 shows that the driverClass property of datasource bean has the default value 'test driverClass value'. Example listing 5-34 shows that there is no property named datasource.driverClass defined in the database.properties or webservice.properties file; therefore, the driverClass bean property retains its default value.

The main method of SampleApp class of ch05-propertyOverrideConfigurer-example project retrieves WebServiceConfiguration and DataSource beans from the ApplicationContext and prints their properties on the console. If you execute SampleApp's main method, you'll see the following output on the console:

```
DataSource [url=some_url, username=some_username, password=some_password, driverClass=test driverClass value]

WebServiceConfiguration [webServiceUrl=some_url]
```

The above output shows that the default values of all bean properties, except that of driverClass, are replaced by the property values specified in the external properties files.

As PropertyOverrideConfigurer and PropertySourcesPlaceholderConfigurer inherit from Spring's PropertyResourceConfigurer class, you'll notice that both of these classes share many common configuration options. For instance, you can set PropertyOverrideConfigurer's localOverride property to control whether the local properties get precedence over properties read from external properties files, you can set PropertyOverrideConfigurer's properties property to define local properties, and so on.

5-5 Summary

In this chapter, we saw how to add custom initialization and destruction logic to a bean instance. We also looked at how you can modify newly created bean instances using BeanPostProcessor implementations, and modify bean definitions using BeanFactoryPostProcessor implementations. Spring internally makes use of BeanPostProcessors and BeanFactoryPostProcessors to provide many framework features. In the next chapter, we'll look at Spring's support for annotation-driven development.

Chapter 6- *Annotation-driven development with Spring*

6-1 Introduction

In previous chapters, we saw that the bean definitions contained in the application context XML file are used as a blueprint by the Spring container to create bean instances. A bean definition specifies information about bean dependencies, initialization and destruction methods of a bean, lazy or eager initialization strategy for the bean instance, bean scope, and so on. In this section, we'll look at annotations that you can use to specify the same information in the bean class itself, thereby saving the effort to explicitly configure a bean in the application context XML file. We'll also touch upon *Spring Expression Language* (SpEL) and how to validate objects using Spring's Validator interface and through JSR 303 annotations. We'll end this chapter with a quick look at how to programmatically define Spring beans using Spring's @Configuration and @Bean annotations.

Let's first begin with looking at Spring's @Component annotation that indicates that a particular class represents a Spring component.

6-2 Identifying Spring components with @Component

Spring's @Component annotation is a type-level annotation, which indicates that a class represents a Spring component. It is recommended that you use more specialized forms of @Component annotation to annotate controllers, services and data access objects (DAOs) of your application. For instance, annotate controllers with @Controller, services with @Service, and DAOs with @Repository annotation.

IMPORT **chapter 6/ch06-bankapp-annotations** (This project shows the MyBank application that uses annotations for registering beans with the Spring container and for autowiring dependencies. To run the application, execute the main method of the BankApp class of this project.)

The following example listing shows the MyBank's FixedDepositServiceImpl class that makes use of @Service annotation:

Example listing 6-1 – FixedDepositServiceImpl class - @Service annotation usage
Project – ch06-bankapp-annotations
Source location - src/main/java/sample/spring/chapter06/bankapp/service

```
package sample.spring.chapter06.bankapp.service;

import org.springframework.stereotype.Service;
```

```
@Service(value="FixedDepositService")
public class FixedDepositServiceImpl implements FixedDepositService { ..... }
```

As FixedDepositSerivceImpl class is annotated with @Service annotation, FixedDepositServiceImpl class represents a Spring component. @Service annotation accepts a value attribute that specifies the name with which the component is registered as a bean with the Spring container. For instance, FixedDepositServiceImpl class is registered with Spring container as a bean with the name FixedDepositService. The value attribute serves the same purpose as the <bean> element's id attribute.

Like @Service annotation, @Component, @Repository and @Controller annotations specify the name of the component via value attribute. You can specify the name of a Spring component without explicitly specifying the value attribute. This means that @Service(value="FixedDepositService") is same as @Service("FixedDepositService"). If you don't specify a name for the component, Spring assumes name of the component is same as the name of the component class. Only difference is that the name of the component begins with a *lowercase* letter. You should specify a custom name for a component because it's particularly helpful when autowiring dependencies 'by name'.

If you enable classpath-scanning feature of Spring, bean classes annotated with @Component, @Controller, @Service or @Repository annotations are automatically registered with the Spring container. You enable classpath scanning feature of Spring by using the <component-scan> element of Spring's context schema.

The following example listing shows usage of <component-scan> element:

Example listing 6-2 – applicationContext.xml
Project – ch06-bankapp-annotations
Source location - src/main/resources/META-INF/spring

```
<beans xmlns="http://www.springframework.org/schema/beans"
  xmlns:context="http://www.springframework.org/schema/context"
  xsi:schemaLocation=".....http://www.springframework.org/schema/context
      http://www.springframework.org/schema/context/spring-context-4.0.xsd">

  <context:component-scan base-package="sample.spring"/>
</beans>
```

In the above example listing, reference to Spring's context schema is included so that its elements are accessible. The <component-scan> element's base-package attribute specifies comma-separated list of packages that should be searched for Spring components. As the base-package attribute's value is sample.spring, Spring components are searched inside sample.spring package and its sub-packages. As the FixedDepositServiceImpl class shown in example listing 6-1 is annotated with @Service annotation and is located in package sample.spring.chapter06.bankapp.service, the <component-scan> element in the above example listing automatically registers FixedDepositServiceImpl class as a bean with the Spring container. This is equivalent to the following bean definition for the FixedDepositServiceImpl class in the application context XML file:

Example listing 6-3 – Bean definition for the FixedDepositServiceImpl class

```
<bean id="FixedDepositService"
        class="sample.spring.chapter06.bankapp.service.FixedDepositServiceImpl" />
```

If you want to filter the component classes that should be considered for automatic registration with the Spring container, use the resource-pattern attribute of <component-scan> element. The default value of resource-pattern attribute is **/*.class, which means all the component classes under the package(s) specified by the base-package attribute will be considered for automatic registration. The <include-filter> and <exclude-filter> sub-elements of <component-scan> element provide a more concise way to specify component classes that should be considered for automatic registration, and the classes that should be ignored. For instance, the following example listing shows an example usage of <include-filter> and <exclude-filter> elements:

Example listing 6-4 – <include-filter> and <exclude-filter> elements

```
<beans .....>
  <context:component-scan base-package="sample.example">
      <context:include-filter type="annotation" expression="example.annotation.MyAnnotation"/>
      <context:exclude-filter type="regex" expression=".*Details"/>
  </context:component-scan>
</beans>
```

The <exclude-filter> and <include-filter> elements define a type attribute that specifies the strategy used for filtering component classes, and the expression attribute specifies the corresponding filter expression. In the above example listing, the <include-filter> element specifies that the component classes that are annotated with MyAnnotation type-level annotation are automatically registered with the Spring container, and the <exclude-filter> element specifies that the component classes whose names end with Details are ignored by the <component-scan> element.

The following table describes the possible values that the type attributes of <include-filter> and <exclude-filter> elements can accept:

Value of type attribute	Description
annotation	If the type attribute's value is annotation, the expression attribute specifies the fully-qualified class name of the annotation that a component class *must* be annotated with. For instance, if the expression attribute's value is example.annotation.MyAnnotation, component classes that are annotated with MyAnnotation annotation are considered for inclusion (in case of <include-filter> element) or exclusion (in case of <exclude-filter> element).
assignable	If the type attribute's value is assignable, the expression attribute specifies the fully-qualified name of a class or interface to which a component class must be assignable.
aspectj	If the type attribute's value is aspectj, the expression attribute specifies an AspectJ expression that is used for filtering the component classes.
regex	If the type attribute's value is regex, the expression attribute specifies a regular expression that is used for filtering component classes by their names.
custom	If the type attribute's value is custom, an implementation of org.springframework.core.type.TypeFilter interface is specified by the expression attribute for filtering the component classes.

> In this section, we looked at an example usage of @Service annotation. @Component, @Controller and @Repository annotations are specified the same way as @Service annotation. Refer CustomerRegistrationDetails and CustomerRequestDetails classes of ch06-bankapp-annotations project to see usage of @Component annotation. Refer DAO classes contained in ch06-bankapp-annotations project to see usage of @Repository annotation.

As Spring components are *not* defined in the application context XML file, you don't have the option to use <property> or <constructor-arg> element to specify their dependencies. For this reason, Spring components make use of annotations like @Autowired, @Inject, and so on, to specify their dependencies.

Let's now look at Spring's @Autowired annotation.

6-3 @Autowired - autowiring dependencies *by type*

@Autowired annotation is used to autowire dependencies 'by type'. Spring's @Autowired annotation provides the same functionality as the Spring's autowiring feature that we discussed in chapter 4, but @Autowired annotation offers a more cleaner and flexible approach to autowiring bean dependencies. @Autowired annotation can be used at *constructor-level*, *method-level* and *field-level*.

The following example listing shows the AccountStatementServiceImpl class that uses the @Autowired annotation at the field-level:

Example listing 6-5 – AccountStatementServiceImpl class - @Autowired annotation usage at the field-level
Project – ch06-bankapp-annotations
Source location - src/main/java/sample/spring/chapter06/bankapp/service

```
package sample.spring.chapter06.bankapp.service;

import org.springframework.beans.factory.annotation.Autowired;
import org.springframework.stereotype.Service;

@Service(value="accountStatementService")
public class AccountStatementServiceImpl implements AccountStatementService {

   @Autowired
   private AccountStatementDao accountStatementDao;

   @Override
   public AccountStatement getAccountStatement(Date from, Date to) {
      return accountStatementDao.getAccountStatement(from, to);
   }
}
```

In the above example listing, the accountStatementDao field (of type AccountStatementDao) is annotated with @Autowired annotation. When an instance of AccountStatementServiceImpl is created, Spring's AutowiredAnnotationBeanPostProcessor (a BeanPostProcessor implementation) is responsible for autowiring accountStatementDao field. The AutowiredAnnotationBeanPostProcessor retrieves reference to an AccountStatementDao type bean from the Spring container and assigns it to the accountStatementDao field. It is important to note that the field annotated with @Autowired annotation need *not* be public or have a corresponding public setter method.

> Spring's AutowiredAnnotationBeanPostProcessor performs autowiring of fields, methods and constructors that are annotated with Spring's @Autowired or JSR 330's @Inject (explained in section 6-5) annotation.

The following example listing shows the CustomerRegistrationServiceImpl class that uses the @Autowired annotation at the method-level:

Example listing 6-6 – CustomerRegistrationServiceImpl class - @Autowired annotation usage at the method-level
Project – ch06-bankapp-annotations
Source location - src/main/java/sample/spring/chapter06/bankapp/service

```
package sample.spring.chapter06.bankapp.service;

@Service("customerRegistrationService")
@Scope(value = ConfigurableBeanFactory.SCOPE_PROTOTYPE)
public class CustomerRegistrationServiceImpl implements CustomerRegistrationService {

  private CustomerRegistrationDetails customerRegistrationDetails;
  .....
  @Autowired
  public void obtainCustomerRegistrationDetails(
        CustomerRegistrationDetails customerRegistrationDetails) {
    this.customerRegistrationDetails = customerRegistrationDetails;
  }
  .....
  @Override
  public void setAccountNumber(String accountNumber) {
    customerRegistrationDetails.setAccountNumber(accountNumber);
  }
  .....
}
```

In the above example listing, obtainCustomerRegistrationDetails method is annotated with @Autowired annotation. If a method is annotated with @Autowired annotation, the arguments of the method are autowired. As obtainCustomerRegistrationDetails method is annotated with @Autowired annotation, its CustomerRegistrationDetails argument is autowired *by type*. It is important to note that an @Autowired annotated method need *not* be public.

> A method annotated with @Autowired annotation is invoked after the component instance is created, and the fields annotated with @Autowired annotation are injected with matching bean instances.

The following example listing shows the CustomerRequestServiceImpl class that defines a constructor annotated with @Autowired annotation:

Example listing 6-7 – CustomerRequestServiceImpl class - @Autowired annotation usage at constructor-level
Project – ch06-bankapp-annotations
Source location - src/main/java/sample/spring/chapter06/bankapp/service

```
package sample.spring.chapter06.bankapp.service;

@Service(value="customerRequestService")
public class CustomerRequestServiceImpl implements CustomerRequestService {
   private CustomerRequestDetails customerRequestDetails;
   private CustomerRequestDao customerRequestDao;

   @Autowired
   public CustomerRequestServiceImpl(CustomerRequestDetails customerRequestDetails,
         CustomerRequestDao customerRequestDao) {
      this.customerRequestDetails = customerRequestDetails;
      this.customerRequestDao = customerRequestDao;
   }
   .....
}
```

In the above example listing, the CustomerRequestServiceImpl's constructor is annotated with @Autowired annotation. If a constructor is annotated with @Autowired annotation, the arguments of the constructor are autowired. As CustomerRequestServiceImpl's constructor is annotated with @Autowired annotation, its CustomerRequestDetails and CustomerRequestDao arguments are autowired *by type*. It is important to note that an @Autowired annotated constructor need *not* be public.

When using the @Autowired annotation, exception is thrown if a bean matching the required type is *not* found. For instance, in example listing 6-7, if a bean of type CustomerRequestDetails or CustomerRequestDao is not found to be registered with the Spring container, an exception is thrown while creating the CustomerRequestServiceImpl instance. @Autowired's required attribute specifies whether it is mandatory or optional to autowire dependencies. If you set @Autowired's required attribute value to false, autowiring of dependencies is considered *optional*. This means that if the required attribute's value is set to false, exception is not thrown if no bean matching the required type is found in the Spring container. By default, value of required attribute is true; dependencies must be satisfied by the Spring container.

If a component class defines an @Autowired annotated constructor with required attribute's value set to true, it *can't* have another @Autowired annotated constructor. For instance, consider the following example listing that defines 2 constructors annotated with the @Autowired annotation:

Example listing 6-8 – A component class that defines 2 @Autowired annotated constructors

```
@Service(value="customerRequestService")
public class CustomerRequestServiceImpl implements CustomerRequestService {
  .....
  @Autowired(required=false)
  public CustomerRequestServiceImpl(CustomerRequestDetails customerRequestDetails) { ..... }

  @Autowired
  public CustomerRequestServiceImpl(CustomerRequestDetails customerRequestDetails,
        CustomerRequestDao customerRequestDao) { ..... }
}
```

As autowiring of dependencies is required (@Autowired's required attribute is set to true) for one of the constructors and optional (@Autowired's required attribute is set to false) for the other in the above example listing, it results in an exception thrown by Spring.

A component class can define multiple @Autowired annotated constructors with required attribute's value set to false. In such a case, one of the constructors will be invoked by Spring to create an instance of the component class. The following example listing shows a component class that defines 2 constructors annotated with @Autowired (required = false), and a default constructor:

Example listing 6-9 – A component class that defines multiple @Autowired annotated constructors with required attribute value set to false

```
@Service(value="customerRequestService")
public class CustomerRequestServiceImpl implements CustomerRequestService {
  public CustomerRequestServiceImpl() {
    .....
  }
  @Autowired(required=false)
  public CustomerRequestServiceImpl(CustomerRequestDetails customerRequestDetails) {
    .....
  }
```

```
    @Autowired(required=false)
    public CustomerRequestServiceImpl(CustomerRequestDetails customerRequestDetails,
          CustomerRequestDao customerRequestDao) {
       .....
    }
}
```

In the above example listing, both the @Autowired annotated constructors are candidates for autowiring by Spring to create an instance of the CustomerRequestServiceImpl class. The constructor with the largest number of satisfied dependencies is chosen. In case of CustomerRequestServiceImpl class, if beans of types CustomerRequestDetails and CustomerRequestDao are registered with the Spring container, Spring invokes CustomerRequestServiceImpl(CustomerRequestDetails, CustomerRequestDao) constructor. If a bean of type CustomerRequestDetails is registered with container but no bean of type CustomerRequestDao is registered, CustomerRequestServiceImpl(CustomerRequestDetails) constructor is invoked. In case none of the dependencies are found, the default constructor of CustomerRequestServiceImpl class is invoked.

Let's now look at how you can use Spring's @Qualifier annotation along with @Autowired annotation to autowire dependencies *by name*.

6-4 @Qualifier – autowiring dependencies *by name*

You can use Spring's @Qualifier annotation along with @Autowired annotation to autowire dependencies *by name*. The @Qualifier annotation can be used at field-level, method-parameter-level and constructor-argument-level.

The following example listing shows the FixedDepositServiceImpl class that uses @Qualifier annotation:

Example listing 6-10 – FixedDepositServiceImpl class - @Qualifier annotation usage
Project – ch06-bankapp-annotations
Source location - src/main/java/sample/spring/chapter06/bankapp/service

```
package sample.spring.chapter06.bankapp.service;

import org.springframework.beans.factory.annotation.Autowired;
import org.springframework.beans.factory.annotation.Qualifier;

@Service(value="FixedDepositService")
public class FixedDepositServiceImpl implements FixedDepositService {

    @Autowired
    @Qualifier(value="myFixedDepositDao")
```

```
    private FixedDepositDao myFixedDepositDao;
    .....
}
```

In the above example listing, myFixedDepositDao field is annotated with @Autowired and @Qualifier annotations. @Qualifier annotation's value attribute specifies the name of the bean to be assigned to the myFixedDepositDao field.

Spring first finds autowiring candidates 'by type' for the fields, constructors and methods that are annotated with @Autowired annotation. Then, Spring uses the bean name specified by @Qualifier annotation to locate a *unique* bean from the list of autowiring candidates. For example, in example listing 6-10, Spring first finds beans of type FixedDepositDao for myFixedDepositDao field, and then locates the bean named myFixedDepositDao from the list of autowiring candidates. If a bean named myFixedDepositDao is found, Spring assigns it to the myFixedDepositDao field.

> @Qualifier(value="myFixedDepositDao") is same as @Qualifier("myFixedDepositDao"); you don't need to use the value attribute to specify the name of the bean to be autowired.

The following example listing shows usage of @Qualifier annotation at method-parameter-level and constructor-argument-level:

Example listing 6-11 – @Qualifier usage at method-parameter-level and constructor-argument-level

```
public class Sample {

    @Autowired
    public Sample(@Qualifier("aBean") ABean bean) { .... }

    @Autowired
    public void doSomething(@Qualifier("bBean") BBean bean, CBean cBean) { ..... }
}
```

In the above example listing, @Qualifier annotation is specified for a constructor argument and a method argument. When creating an instance of Sample class, Spring finds a bean of type ABean with name aBean and passes it as an argument to the Sample class's constructor. When calling Sample's doSomething method, Spring finds a bean of type BBean (whose name is bBean) and another bean of type CBean, and passes both these beans as arguments to the doSomething method. It is important to note that the BBean dependency is autowired *by name*, and CBean dependency is autowired *by type*.

Let's now look at JSR 330's @Inject and @Named annotations that you can use instead of Spring's @Autowired and @Qualifier annotations.

6-5 JSR 330's @Inject and @Named annotations

JSR 330 (Dependency Injection for Java) standardizes dependency injection annotations for the Java platform. JSR 330 defines @Inject and @Named annotations that are similar to Spring's @Autowired and @Qualifier annotations, respectively. Spring provides support for @Inject and @Named annotations.

IMPORT **chapter 6/ch06-bankapp-jsr330** (This project shows the MyBank application that uses JSR 330's @Inject and @Named annotations for autowiring dependencies. To run the application, execute the main method of the BankApp class of this project.)

The following example listing shows the FixedDepositServiceImpl class that makes use of JSR 330's @Inject and @Named annotations:

Example listing 6-12 – FixedDepositServiceImpl class
Project – ch06-bankapp-jsr330
Source location - src/main/java/sample/spring/chapter06/bankapp/service

```
package sample.spring.chapter06.bankapp.service;

import javax.inject.Inject;
import javax.inject.Named;

@Named(value="FixedDepositService")
public class FixedDepositServiceImpl implements FixedDepositService {

    @Inject
    @Named(value="myFixedDepositDao")
    private FixedDepositDao myFixedDepositDao;
    .....
}
```

If you compare the FixedDepositServiceImpl class shown in the above example listing with the FixedDepositServiceImpl class in example listing 6-10, you'll notice that JSR 330's @Named annotation has been used in place of @Service and @Qualifier annotations, and JSR 330's @Inject annotation has been used in place of @Autowired annotation.

@Autowired and @Inject annotations have the same semantics; they are used for autowiring dependencies *by type*. Like @Autowired annotation, @Inject can be used at method-level, constructor-level and field-level. Dependency injection of constructors is performed first, followed by fields, and then methods. We saw earlier that @Autowired annotation's required attribute specifies whether it is mandatory or optional to autowire dependencies. @Inject doesn't have any equivalent of @Autowired annotation's required attribute.

If @Named annotation is used at the type-level, it acts like Spring's @Component annotation. And, if @Named annotation is used at the method-parameter-level or constructor-argument-level, it acts like Spring's @Qualifier annotation. If a class is annotated with @Named annotation, <component-scan> element of Spring's context schema treats it like a component class annotated with @Component annotation.

To use @Named and @Inject annotations, you need to include JSR 330 JAR file in your project. The ch06-bankapp-jsr330 project includes JSR 330 JAR file through the following <dependency> element in the pom.xml file:

```
<dependency>
    <groupId>javax.inject</groupId>
    <artifactId>javax.inject</artifactId>
    <version>1</version>
</dependency>
```

In chapter 5, we looked at JSR 250's @PostConstruct and @PreDestroy annotations that are used to identify initialization and destruction methods of a bean. Let's now look at JSR 250's @Resource annotation that you can use for autowiring dependencies *by name*.

6-6 JSR 250's @Resource annotation

Spring supports autowiring 'by name' of fields and methods via JSR 250's @Resource annotation. @Resource annotation's name attribute specifies the name of the bean to be autowired. It is important to note that you can't use @Resource annotation for autowiring constructor arguments.

The following example listing shows how FixedDepositServiceImpl class from example listing 6-12 can be rewritten using @Resource annotation:

Example listing 6-13 – @Resource annotation usage at field-level

```
import javax.annotation.Resource;

@Named(value="FixedDepositService")
public class FixedDepositServiceImpl implements FixedDepositService {

    @Resource(name="myFixedDepositDao")
    private FixedDepositDao myFixedDepositDao;
    .....
}
```

In the above example listing, @Resource annotation has been used for autowiring myFixedDepositDao field. As the value of name attribute is myFixedDepositDao, Spring locates a bean named myFixedDepositDao in the Spring container and assigns it to myFixedDepositDao field.

Instead of using @Autowired and @Qualifier annotations, you should use @Resource annotation for autowiring dependencies 'by name'. As mentioned earlier, if you are using @Autowired-@Qualifier combination to perform autowiring 'by name', Spring first finds beans based on the type of the field (or the type of the method argument or constructor argument) to be autowired, followed by narrowing down to a unique bean based on the bean name specified by @Qualifier annotation. But, if you are using @Resource annotation, Spring uses bean name specified by @Resource annotation to locate a unique bean. This means that when you use @Resource annotation, type of the field (or setter method argument) to be autowired is *not* taken into consideration by Spring.

> As @Autowired, @Inject and @Resource annotations are processed by BeanPostProcessors, you should not use these annotations in component classes that implement BeanFactoryPostProcessor or BeanPostProcessor interface.

Let's now look at @Scope, @Lazy, @DependsOn and @Primary annotations.

6-7 @Scope, @Lazy, @DependsOn and @Primary annotations

You specify the scope (prototype or singleton) of a Spring component using Spring's @Scope annotation. By default, Spring components are singleton-scoped. If you want a Spring component to be prototype-scoped, you have to specify so via @Scope annotation. @Scope annotation plays the same role as the <bean> element's scope attribute (refer section 2-5 of chapter 2 to know more about the scope attribute).

The following example listing shows the CustomerRequestDetails class that uses @Scope annotation:

Example listing 6-14 – @Scope annotation usage
Project – ch06-bankapp-jsr330
Source location - src/main/java/sample/spring/chapter06/bankapp/domain

```
package sample.spring.chapter06.bankapp.domain;

import javax.inject.Named;
import org.springframework.beans.factory.config.ConfigurableBeanFactory;
import org.springframework.context.annotation.Scope;

@Named(value="customerRequestDetails")
@Scope(value=ConfigurableBeanFactory.SCOPE_PROTOTYPE)
```

```
public class CustomerRequestDetails { ..... }
```

The @Scope annotation accepts a value attribute that specifies the scope of the component. You can set value attribute's value to prototype or singleton to indicate whether the component is singleton-scoped or prototype-scoped, or you can set value attribute's value to ConfigurableBeanFactory's SCOPE_SINGLETON (value is singleton) or SCOPE_PROTOTYPE (value is prototype) constants.

By default, singleton-scoped Spring components are *eagerly* initialized, that is, they are instantiated when the Spring container is created. If you want a singleton-scoped component to be lazily created, annotate the component class of a singleton-scoped component with @Lazy annotation.

> @Lazy annotation serves the same purpose as the <bean> element's lazy-init attribute. Refer section 2-5 of chapter 2 to know more about lazy-init attribute.

The following example listing shows usage of @Lazy annotation:

Example listing 6-15 – @Lazy annotation usage

```
@Lazy(value=true)
@Component
public class Sample { ..... }
```

@Lazy annotation's value attribute specifies whether the component is lazily or eagerly initialized. If the value attribute's value is true, it means that the component is lazily initialized.

You specify implicit bean dependencies using @DependsOn annotation. The following example listing shows usage of @DependsOn annotation:

Example listing 6-16 – @DependsOn annotation usage

```
@DependsOn(value = {"beanA", "beanB"})
@Component
public class Sample { ..... }
```

In the above example listing, @DependsOn annotation on the Sample class instructs the Spring container to create beanA and beanB beans before creating an instance of Sample class.

> @DependsOn annotation serves the same purpose as the <bean> element's depends-on attribute. Refer section 4-3 of chapter 4 to know more about depends-on attribute.

If multiple autowiring candidates are available for a dependency, @Primary annotation designates a bean as a primary candidate for autowiring. The following example listing shows usage of @Primary annotation:

Example listing 6-17 – @Primary annotation usage

```
@Primary
@Component
public class Sample { ..... }
```

> @Primary annotation serves the same purpose as the <bean> element's primary attribute. Refer section 4-6 of chapter 4 to know more about primary attribute.

Let's now look at Spring's @Value annotation that simplifies configuring component classes.

6-8 Simplifying component configuration using @Value annotation

In previous chapters, we saw examples in which configuration information required by beans was specified via value attribute of <property> and <constructor-arg> elements. As Spring components are not defined in the application context XML file, Spring's @Value annotation is used to serve the same purpose as the value attribute of <property> and <constructor-arg> elements. You should note that the @Value annotation can be used at field-level, method-level, method-parameter-level and constructor-argument-level.

IMPORT **chapter 6/ch06-value-annotation** (This project shows an application that uses Spring's @Value annotation to configure Spring components. To run the application, execute the main method of the SampleApp class of this project.)

The following example listing shows an example usage of @Value annotation at field-level:

Example listing 6-18 – Sample class - @Value annotation usage
Project – ch06-value-annotation
Source location - src/main/java/sample/spring/chapter06/beans

```
package sample.spring.chapter06.beans;

import org.springframework.beans.factory.annotation.Value;

@Component(value="sample")
public class Sample {
   @Value("Some currency")
   private String currency;
   .....
}
```

In the above example listing, currency field is annotated with @Value annotation. The @Value annotation's value attribute specifies the default value for the field. It is optional to specify the value attribute; therefore, @Value(value="Some currency") is same as @Value("Some currency").

You can also use a *Spring Expression Language* (SpEL) expression as the value of @Value annotation. SpEL is an *expression language* that you can use to query and manipulate objects at runtime. The following example listing shows @Value annotations that make use of SpEL expressions:

Example listing 6-19 – Sample class - @Value annotation that uses SpEL expressions
Project – ch06-value-annotation
Source location - src/main/java/sample/spring/chapter06/beans

```
package sample.spring.chapter06.beans;

import org.springframework.beans.factory.annotation.Value;

@Component(value="sample")
public class Sample {
  @Value("#{configuration.environment}")
  private String environment;
  .....
  @Value("#{configuration.getCountry()}")
  private String country;

  @Value("#{configuration.state}")
  private String state;
  .....
}
```

The above example listing shows that the @Value annotation specifies a value that has the syntax #{<spel-expression>}. The SpEL expression specified by @Value annotation is processed by a BeanPostProcessor. The SpEL expressions can make use of <beanName>.<field or property or method> format to obtain its value. For instance, #{configuration.environment} means obtain value of environment property of bean named configuration, and #{configuration.getCountry()} means invoke getCountry method of bean named configuration.

The following example listing shows the Java class of the configuration bean referenced by SpEL expressions shown in example listing 6-19:

Example listing 6-20 – Configuration component class
Project – ch06-value-annotation
Source location - src/main/java/sample/spring/chapter06/beans

```
package sample.spring.chapter06.beans;

import org.springframework.stereotype.Component;

@Component("configuration")
public class Configuration {
  public static String environment = "DEV";

  public String getCountry() {
    return "Some country";
  }

  public String getState() {
    return "Some state";
  }

  public String[] splitName(String name) {
    return name.split(" ");
  }

  public String getCity() {
    return "Some city";
  }
}
```

The above example listing shows that the Configuration class represents a Spring component that defines fields and methods. If you compare example listing 6-19 with 6-20, you'll notice that #{configuration.environment} expression refers to the static environment variable defined in the Configuration class, #{configuration.getCountry()} expression refers to Configuration's getCountry method, and #{configuration.state} expression refers to Configuration's getState method.

The main method of SampleApp class in ch06-value-annotation project retrieves an instance of Sample bean from the ApplicationContext and prints the value of various attributes of Sample bean instance. If you execute SampleApp's main method, you'll see the following output:

```
Sample [environment=DEV, currency=Some currency, country=Some country, state=Some state, splitName=[FirstName, LastName], city=Some city]
```

The above output shows:

- #{configuration.environment} expression results in Sample's environment field value set to DEV, which is the value specified by public static field environment of Configuration class.
- #{configuration.getCountry()} expression results in Sample's country field value set to Some country, which is the value returned by invoking Configuration's getCountry method.
- #{configuration.state} expression results in Sample's state field value set to Some state, which is the value returned by invoking Configuration's getState method.

The above example shows that you can use SpEL to retrieve configuration information from other beans.

> SpEL is a very powerful expression language, and it offers many more capabilities than described in this book. It is recommended that you refer to Spring reference documentation to know about SpEL.

The following example listing shows usage of @Value annotation at method-level and method-parameter-level:

Example listing 6-21 – Sample class - @Value annotation usage at method-level and method-parameter-level
Project – ch06-value-annotation
Source location - src/main/java/sample/spring/chapter06/beans

```
package sample.spring.chapter06.beans;

import org.springframework.beans.factory.annotation.Autowired;
import org.springframework.beans.factory.annotation.Value;

@Component(value="sample")
public class Sample {
  .....
  private String[] splitName;
  private String city;

  @Autowired
  public void splitName(@Value("#{configuration.splitName('FirstName LastName')}")
                        String[] splitName) {
    this.splitName = splitName;
  }

  @Autowired
  @Value("#{configuration.getCity()}")
```

```
  public void city(String city) {
    this.city = city;
  }
  .....
}
```

The above example listing shows that the methods that are annotated with @Autowired annotation make use of @Value annotation at method-level and method-parameter-level. You should note that the @Value annotation can be used at method-level and method-parameter-level *only if* the method is annotated with @Autowired or @Resource or @Inject annotation. SpEL expression #{configuration.splitName('FirstName LastName')} results in invocation of Configuration's splitName method with 'FirstName LastName' as argument. This shows that SpEL expressions can be used to invoke methods that accept arguments.

> @Value annotation is processed by a BeanPostProcessor; therefore, you should not use @Value annotation in component classes that implement BeanFactoryPostProcessor or BeanPostProcessor interface.

Usage of SpEL is *not* limited to @Value annotations, you can also use SpEL in bean definitions contained in the application context XML file.

IMPORT **chapter 6/ch06-spel-example** (This project shows an application that uses SpEL expressions in bean definitions. To run the application, execute the main method of the SampleApp class of this project.)

The following example listing shows how SpEL is used in bean definitions:

Example listing 6-22 – applicationContext.xml – SpEL expressions in bean definitions
Project – ch06-spel-example
Source location - src/main/resources/META-INF/spring

```
<beans ..... >
  <bean id="sample" class="sample.spring.chapter06.beans.Sample">
    <property name="environment" value="#{configuration.environment}" />
    <property name="currency" value="Some currency" />
    <property name="country" value="#{configuration.getCountry()}" />
    <property name="state" value="#{configuration.state}" />
  </bean>

  <bean id="configuration" class="sample.spring.chapter06.beans.Configuration" />
</beans>
```

The above example listing shows that the bean definition for the *Sample* class makes use of SpEL expressions (that refer to *Configuration* bean) to set default values for *environment*, *currency*, *country* and *state* properties.

Let's now look at how you can perform validation of objects in Spring applications using Spring's *Validator* interface.

6-9 Validating objects using Spring's Validator interface

Spring's *Validator* interface is part of Spring Validation API that allows you to perform validation of objects. You can use the *Validator* interface for performing validation of objects in any of the application layers. For instance, you can use the *Validator* interface to validate objects in the web layer as well as in the persistence layer.

> An alternative to using the *Validator* interface is to use JSR 303 annotations to specify constraints that apply on an object. JSR 303 annotations are explained in the next section.

IMPORT **chapter 6/ch06-validator-interface** (This project shows the MyBank application that uses Spring's *Validator* interface to validate *FixedDepositDetails* object. To run the application, execute the *main* method of the *BankApp* class of this project.)

The *FixedDepositDetails* object of MyBank application represents details of a fixed deposit. The following example listing shows the *FixedDepositDetails* class:

Example listing 6-23 – FixedDepositDetails class
Project – ch06-validator-interface
Source location - src/main/java/sample/spring/chapter06/bankapp/domain

```
package sample.spring.chapter06.bankapp.domain;

public class FixedDepositDetails {
  private long id;
  private float depositAmount;
  private int tenure;
  private String email;

  public FixedDepositDetails(long id, float depositAmount, int tenure,
        String email) {
     this.id = id;
     this.depositAmount = depositAmount;
     this.tenure = tenure;
     this.email = email;
  }
```

```
    .....
    //-- getters and setters for instance variables
    public float getDepositAmount() {
        return depositAmount;
    }
    .....
}
```

The above example listing shows that the FixedDepositDetails class defines id, depositAmount, tenure and email instance variables. Let's say that before the fixed deposit details are saved in the system, we need to make sure that the fixed deposit amount (represented by the depositAmount instance variable) is not 0.

To validate the FixedDepositDetails object's depositAmount property, we need to create an implementation of Spring's Validator interface. The following example listing shows a validator for objects of type FixedDepositDetails:

Example listing 6-24 – FixedDepositValidator class – Spring's Validator interface implementation
Project – ch06-validator-interface
Source location - src/main/java/sample/spring/chapter06/bankapp/validator

```
package sample.spring.chapter06.bankapp.validator;

import org.springframework.validation.Errors;
import org.springframework.validation.Validator;

public class FixedDepositValidator implements Validator {

    @Override
    public boolean supports(Class<?> clazz) {
        return FixedDepositDetails.class.isAssignableFrom(clazz);
    }

    @Override
    public void validate(Object target, Errors errors) {
        FixedDepositDetails fixedDepositDetails = (FixedDepositDetails) target;
        if (fixedDepositDetails.getDepositAmount() == 0) {
            errors.reject("zeroDepositAmount");
        }
    }
}
```

The Validator interface defines supports and validate methods. The supports method checks if the supplied object instance (represented by the clazz attribute) can be validated. If the supports method returns true, the validate method is used to validate the object. In the above example listing, the FixedDepositValidator's supports method checks if the supplied object instance is of type FixedDepositDetails. If the supports method returns true, the FixedDepositValidator's validate method validates the object. The validate method accepts the object instance to be validated, and an Errors instance. The Errors instance's reject method is used to store errors that occur during validation. You can later inspect the Errors instance to know more about validation errors.

The following example listing shows that the FixedDepositServiceImpl's createFixedDeposit method uses the FixedDepositValidator (refer example listing 6-24) to validate FixedDepositDetails objects:

Example listing 6-25 – FixedDepositServiceImpl class – Validating FixedDepositDetails object
Project – ch06-validator-interface
Source location - src/main/java/sample/spring/chapter06/bankapp/service

```
package sample.spring.chapter06.bankapp.service;

import org.springframework.validation.BeanPropertyBindingResult;
import sample.spring.chapter06.bankapp.validator.FixedDepositValidator;

@Service(value="FixedDepositService")
public class FixedDepositServiceImpl implements FixedDepositService {

  @Autowired
  @Qualifier(value="myFixedDepositDao")
  private FixedDepositDao myFixedDepositDao;

  @Override
  public void createFixedDeposit(FixedDepositDetails fixedDepositDetails) throws Exception {
    BeanPropertyBindingResult bindingResult =
            new BeanPropertyBindingResult(fixedDepositDetails, "Errors");
    FixedDepositValidator validator = new FixedDepositValidator();
    validator.validate(fixedDepositDetails, bindingResult);

    if(bindingResult.getErrorCount() > 0) {
       logger.error("Errors were found while validating FixedDepositDetails instance");
    } else {
       myFixedDepositDao.createFixedDeposit(fixedDepositDetails);
       logger.info("Created fixed deposit");
    }
  }
}
```

FixedDepositServiceImpl's createFixedDeposit method validates the FixedDepositDetails object (represented by fixedDepositDetails argument) before it is saved into the data store by FixedDepositDao. The createFixedDeposit method shown in the above example listing performs the following tasks:

- creates an instance of FixedDepositValidator and Spring's BeanPropertyBindingResult - a default implementation of Errors interface provided out-of-the-box by Spring
- invokes FixedDepositValidator's validate method, passing FixedDepositDetails object and the BeanPropertyBindingResult instance
- invokes BeanPropertyBindingResult's getErrorCount method to check if any validation errors were reported. If no validation errors are reported, FixedDepositDao's createFixedDeposit method is called to save fixed deposit details in the data store.

The following example listing shows BankApp's main method that invokes FixedDepositServiceImpl's createFixedDeposit method (refer example listing 6-25) to check if the validation is performed correctly by FixedDepositValidator's validate method:

Example listing 6-26 – BankApp class
Project – ch06-validator-interface
Source location - src/main/java/sample/spring/chapter06/bankapp

```
package sample.spring.chapter06.bankapp;

public class BankApp {
  public static void main(String args[]) throws Exception {
    ApplicationContext context = new ClassPathXmlApplicationContext(
        "classpath:META-INF/spring/applicationContext.xml");

    FixedDepositService FixedDepositService = context.getBean(FixedDepositService.class);

    FixedDepositService.createFixedDeposit(new FixedDepositDetails(1, 0,
        12, "someemail@somedomain.com"));
    FixedDepositService.createFixedDeposit(new FixedDepositDetails(1, 1000,
        12, "someemail@somedomain.com"));
  }
}
```

First, FixedDepositService's createFixedDeposit method is passed a FixedDepositDetails object with depositAmount value as 0, followed by a FixedDepositDetails object with depositAmount value as 1000.

If you execute BankApp's main method, you'll see the following output on the console:

```
Errors were found while validating FixedDepositDetails instance
Created fixed deposit
```

The output *'Errors were found while validating FixedDepositDetails instance'* shows that FixedDepositValidator reported errors when the FixedDepositDetails instance with 0 as the depositAmount value was validated. The output *'Created fixed deposit'* shows that the no errors were reported when the FixedDepositDetails instance with 1000 as the depositAmount value was validated.

> Spring's Validator interface is typically used in Spring MVC based web applications while binding information entered by a user in the HTML form to the corresponding form-backing object.

Let's now look at how you can specify constraints on bean properties using JSR 303 annotations, and let Spring perform the validation.

6-10 Specifying constraints using JSR 303 annotations

JSR 303 (Bean Validation API) allows you to use annotations to specify constraints on JavaBeans components. When using JSR 303 with Spring, you annotate bean properties with JSR 303 annotations, and Spring takes care of validating the bean and providing the validation result.

IMPORT **chapter 6/ch06-jsr303-validation** (This project shows the MyBank application that uses JSR 303 annotations. To run the application, execute the main method of the BankApp class of this project.)

The following example listing shows the FixedDepositDetails class that makes use of JSR 303 annotations:

Example listing 6-27 – FixedDepositDetails class – JSR 303 annotations
Project – ch06-jsr303-validation
Source location - src/main/java/sample/spring/chapter06/bankapp/domain

```
package sample.spring.chapter06.bankapp.domain;

import javax.validation.constraints.*;
import org.hibernate.validator.constraints.NotBlank;

public class FixedDepositDetails {
    @NotNull
    private long id;

    @Min(1000)
```

```
    @Max(500000)
    private float depositAmount;

    @Min(6)
    private int tenure;

    @NotBlank
    @Size(min=5, max=100)
    private String email;

    public FixedDepositDetails(long id, float depositAmount, int tenure, String email) {
        this.id = id;
        this.depositAmount = depositAmount;
        this.tenure = tenure;
        this.email = email;
    }
    .....
}
```

@NotNull, @Min, @Max, @NotBlank and @Size are some of the annotations defined by JSR 303 Bean Validation API. The above example listing shows that by using JSR 303 annotations FixedDepositDetails class clearly specifies the constraints that apply on its fields. On the other hand, if you are using Spring Validation API to validate an object, constraint information is contained in the Validator implementation (refer example listing 6-24).

The following table describes the constraints enforced by JSR 303 annotations on the FixedDepositDetails object shown in example listing 6-27:

JSR 303 annotation	Constraint description
@NotNull	The annotated field must not be null. For instance, FixedDepositDetails' id field must not be null.
@Min	The annotated field's value must be greater than or equal to the specified minimum value. For instance, @Min(1000) annotation on depositAmount field of FixedDepositDetails object means that depositAmount's value must be greater than or equal to 1000.
@Max	The annotated field's value must be less than or equal to the specified value.

	For instance, @Max(500000) annotation on depositAmount field of FixedDepositDetails object means that the depositAmount's value must be less than or equal to 500000.
@NotBlank	The annotated field's value must not be null or empty. For instance, FixedDepositDetails' email field must not be empty or null.
@Size	The annotated field's size must be between the specified min and max attributes. For instance, @Size(min=5, max=100) annotation on email field of FixedDepositDetails object means that the size of the email field must be greater than or equal to 5 and less than or equal to 100.

> To use JSR 303 annotations, ch06-jsr303-validation project specifies dependency on JSR 303 API JAR file (validation-api-1.0.0.GA) and Hibernate Validator framework (hibernate-validation-4.3.0.Final). The Hibernate Validator framework provides the reference implementation for JSR 303.

If you look at the import statements in example listing 6-27, you'll notice that the @NotBlank annotation is defined by Hibernate Validator framework, and not by JSR 303. Hibernate Validator framework provides additional annotations that you can use along with JSR 303 annotations.

Now, that we have specified JSR 303 constraints on FixedDepositDetails class, let's look at how to validate FixedDepositDetails object using Spring.

JSR 303 support in Spring

Spring supports validating objects that make use of JSR 303 constraints. Spring's LocalValidatorFactoryBean class is responsible for detecting the presence of a JSR 303 provider (like Hibernate Validator) in the application's classpath and initializing it. It is important to note that the LocalValidatorFactoryBean implements JSR 303's Validator and ValidatorFactory interfaces, and also Spring's Validator interface.

The following example listing shows the configuration of LocalValidatorFactoryBean class in the application context XML file:

Example listing 6-28 – applicationContext.xml – Spring's LocalValidatorFactoryBean configuration
Project – ch06-jsr303-validation
Source location - src/main/resources/META-INF/spring

```
<bean id="validator"
```

```
class="org.springframework.validation.beanvalidation.LocalValidatorFactoryBean" />
```

As you can see, LocalValidatorFactoryBean is configured like any other Spring bean. Now that we have configured LocalValidatorFactoryBean, let's see how it is used to perform validation.

The following example listing shows the FixedDepositServiceImpl class which requires that the FixedDepositDetails object is validated before fixed deposit details are saved in the data store:

Example listing 6-29 – FixedDepositServiceImpl class – validating FixedDepositDetails object
Project – ch06-jsr303-validation
Source location - src/main/java/sample/spring/chapter06/bankapp/service

```
package sample.spring.chapter06.bankapp.service;

import org.springframework.validation.BeanPropertyBindingResult;
import org.springframework.validation.Validator;
.....
@Service(value="FixedDepositService")
public class FixedDepositServiceImpl implements FixedDepositService {

    @Autowired
    private Validator validator;

    @Autowired
    @Qualifier(value="myFixedDepositDao")
    private FixedDepositDao myFixedDepositDao;

    @Override
    public void createFixedDeposit(FixedDepositDetails fixedDepositDetails) throws Exception {
        BeanPropertyBindingResult bindingResult =
              new BeanPropertyBindingResult(fixedDepositDetails, "Errors");
        validator.validate(fixedDepositDetails, bindingResult);

        if(bindingResult.getErrorCount() > 0) {
            logger.error("Errors were found while validating FixedDepositDetails instance");
        } else {
            myFixedDepositDao.createFixedDeposit(fixedDepositDetails);
            logger.info("Created fixed deposit");
        }
    }
}
```

The above example listing shows that Spring's Validator implementation is referenced by the validator field. As LocalValidatorFactoryBean implements Spring's Validator interface,

LocalValidatorFactoryBean instance is assigned to the validator field. FixedDepositServiceImpl's createFixedDeposit method invokes Validator's validate method to perform validation of FixedDepositDetails object.

One of the interesting things to notice in example listing 6-29 is that we are *not* dealing with JSR 303 API to perform validation of FixedDepositDetails object. Instead, we have used Spring Validation API to perform validation. This is possible because LocalValidatorFactoryBean implements validate method of Spring's Validator interface to use JSR 303 API to perform validation of objects, shielding developers from JSR 303-specific API details.

As LocalValidatorFactoryBean implements JSR 303's Validator and ValidatorFactory interfaces, you have the option to use JSR 303 API to perform validation of FixedDepositDetails object. The following example listing shows an alternative implementation of FixedDepositServiceImpl class that makes use of JSR 303's Validator to perform validation:

Example listing 6-30 – FixedDepositServiceImplJsr303 class - validating FixedDepositDetails object
Project – ch06-jsr303-validation
Source location - src/main/java/sample/spring/chapter06/bankapp/service

```
package sample.spring.chapter06.bankapp.service;

import javax.validation.ConstraintViolation;
import javax.validation.Validator;

@Service(value = "FixedDepositServiceJsr303")
public class FixedDepositServiceJsr303Impl implements FixedDepositService {
  .....
  @Autowired
  private Validator validator;

  @Autowired
  @Qualifier(value = "myFixedDepositDao")
  private FixedDepositDao myFixedDepositDao;

  @Override
  public void createFixedDeposit(FixedDepositDetails fixedDepositDetails) throws Exception {
    Set<ConstraintViolation<FixedDepositDetails>> violations =
        validator.validate(fixedDepositDetails);

    Iterator<ConstraintViolation<FixedDepositDetails>> itr = violations.iterator();

    if (itr.hasNext()) {
      logger.error("Errors were found while validating FixedDepositDetails instance");
```

```
    } else {
        myFixedDepositDao.createFixedDeposit(fixedDepositDetails);
        logger.info("Created fixed deposit");
    }
  }
}
```

The above example listing shows that JSR 303's Validator implementation is referenced by the validator field. As LocalValidatorFactoryBean implements JSR 303's Validator interface, LocalValidatorFactoryBean instance is assigned to the validator field. The createFixedDeposit method validates FixedDepositDetails object by calling Validator's validate method. The validate method returns a java.util.Set object that contains the constraint violations reported by JSR 303 provider. You can check the java.util.Set object returned by the validate method to know if any constraint violations were reported. For instance, in the above example listing, the createFixedDeposit method calls FixedDepositDao's createFixedDeposit method only if java.util.Set doesn't contain any constraint violations.

In this section, we saw how to use Spring's support for JSR 303 to perform validation of objects. We only looked at constraints, like @NotNull, @Size, and so on, that are provided out-of-the-box by JSR 303. It is important to note that JSR 303 allows you to create custom constraints and use them in your application. For instance, you can create a @MyConstraint custom constraint and a corresponding validator to enforce that constraint on objects.

Let's now look at annotations that you can use to programmatically configure Spring beans.

6-11 Programmatically configuring Spring beans using @Configuration and @Bean annotations

You can use @Configuration and @Bean annotations to programmatically configure Spring beans. If you annotate a class with @Configuration annotation, it indicates that the class contains @Bean annotated methods that return bean instances meant to be registered with the Spring container.

> To use @Configuration annotated classes for defining beans, CGLIB library is required because Spring extends @Configuration annotated classes to add behavior to the @Bean annotated methods. Starting with Spring 3.2, the CGLIB classes are packaged within the spring-core JAR file itself; therefore, you don't need to explicitly specify that your project is dependent on CGLIB JAR file.

IMPORT **chapter 6/ch06-bankapp-configuration** (This project shows the MyBank application that uses @Configuration and @Bean annotations to programmatically configure beans. To run the application, execute the main method of the BankApp class of this project.)

The following example listing shows the BankAppConfiguration class that is annotated with @Configuration annotation:

Example listing 6-31 – BankAppConfiguration class - @Configuration and @Bean annotations
Project – ch06-bankapp-configuration
Source location - src/main/java/sample/spring/chapter06/bankapp

```
package sample.spring.chapter06.bankapp;

import org.springframework.context.annotation.Bean;
import org.springframework.context.annotation.Configuration;
import org.springframework.context.annotation.Scope;
.....
@Configuration
public class BankAppConfiguration {
  .....
  @Bean(name = "customerRegistrationService")
  @Scope(value = ConfigurableBeanFactory.SCOPE_PROTOTYPE)
  public CustomerRegistrationService customerRegistrationService() {
    return new CustomerRegistrationServiceImpl();
  }
  .....
}
```

BankAppConfiguration class defines @Bean annotated methods that return bean instances. @Bean's name attribute specifies the name with which the returned bean instance is registered with the Spring container. @Scope annotation specifies the scope (singleton or prototype) of the returned bean instance.

> @Scope annotation is also used at the type-level to specify the scope of a Spring component. Refer example listing 6-14 that shows usage of @Scope annotation at type-level.

In example listing 6-31, the customerRegistrationService method returns an instance of CustomerRegistrationService bean that is registered with the Spring container as a prototype-scoped bean named customerRegistrationService. The customerRegistrationService method has the same effect as the following bean definition in the application context XML file:

```
<bean id="customerRegistrationService" scope="prototype"
      class="sample.spring.chapter06.bankapp.service.CustomerRegistrationServiceImpl" />
```

The following table describes the attributes of @Bean annotation that you can use to configure the bean instance:

Value of type attribute	Description
Autowire	Same as <bean> element's autowire attribute (refer section 4-6 of chapter 4 to know more about autowire attribute). If the bean returned by the @Bean annotated method is dependent on other beans, you can use autowire attribute to instruct Spring to perform autowiring of dependencies by name or type.
initMethod	Same as <bean> element's init-method attribute (refer section 5-2 of chapter 5 to know more about init-method attribute)
destroyMethod	Same as <bean> element's destroy-method attribute (refer section 5-2 of chapter 5 to know more about destroy-method attribute)

It is important to note that @Bean annotated methods may also be annotated with @Lazy, @DependsOn, @Primary and @Scope annotations. These annotations apply to the object instance returned by the @Bean annotated method. For instance, @DependsOn annotation specifies the implicit dependencies of the object instance returned by the @Bean annotated method. Also, if the bean instance returned by @Bean annotated method implements lifecycle interfaces (like InitializingBean and DisposableBean), and Spring's *Aware interfaces (like ApplicationContextAware, BeanNameAware, and so on), it'll receive callbacks from the Spring container.

In the examples that we have seen so far, we created an instance of ClassPathXmlApplicationContext class (an implementation of ApplicationContext interface) to represent the Spring container. If you are using an @Configuration annotated class as the source of beans, you need to create an instance of AnnotationConfigApplicationContext class (another implementation of ApplicationContext interface) to represent the Spring container.

The following example listing shows the BankApp class that creates an instance of AnnotationConfigApplicationContext class and retrieves beans from the newly created AnnotationConfigApplicationContext instance:

Example listing 6-32 – BankApp class - AnnotationConfigApplicationContext usage
Project – ch06-bankapp-configuration
Source location - src/main/java/sample/spring/chapter06/bankapp

```
package sample.spring.chapter06.bankapp;

import org.springframework.context.annotation.AnnotationConfigApplicationContext;

public class BankApp {
```

```
  public static void main(String args[]) throws Exception {
    AnnotationConfigApplicationContext context =
        new AnnotationConfigApplicationContext(BankAppConfiguration.class);
    .....
    FixedDepositService FixedDepositService = context.getBean(FixedDepositService.class);
    FixedDepositService.createFixedDeposit(new FixedDepositDetails(1, 1000,
        12, "someemail@somedomain.com"));
    .....
  }
}
```

In the above example listing, the BankAppConfiguration class is passed as an argument to the AnnotationConfigApplicationContext's constructor. As AnnotationConfigApplicationContext class implements ApplicationContext interface, you can access registered beans in the same way as in case of ClassPathXmlApplicationContext.

You should note that @Bean annotated methods can also be defined in @Component and JSR 330's @Named annotated classes. In case you have defined beans in multiple @Configuration, @Component and @Named annotated classes, pass all these classes to the AnnotationConfigApplicationContext's constructor.

The following example listing shows @Bean annotated methods of BankAppConfiguration class that return a BeanFactoryPostProcessor and a BeanPostProcessor implementation:

Example listing 6-33 – BankAppConfiguration class – defining BeanFactoryPostProcessor and BeanPostProcessor beans
Project – ch06-bankapp-configuration
Source location - src/main/java/sample/spring/chapter06/bankapp

```
package sample.spring.chapter06.bankapp;

import org.springframework.context.annotation.Bean;

@Configuration
public class BankAppConfiguration {
  .....
  @Bean
  public ExampleBeanPostProcessor exampleBeanPostProcessor() {
    return new ExampleBeanPostProcessor();
  }

  @Bean
  public static BeanNamePrinterBeanFactoryPostProcessor applicationConfigurer() {
```

```
        return new BeanNamePrinterBeanFactoryPostProcessor();
    }
}
```

In the above example listing, ExampleBeanPostProcessor instance represents a BeanPostProcessor that prints a message on the console *before* and *after* a newly created bean instance is initialized, and BeanNamePrinterBeanFactoryPostProcessor instance represents a BeanFactoryPostProcessor implementation that prints names of all the beans registered with the Spring container.

If you go to ch06-bankapp-configuration project and execute BankApp's main method, you'll notice that the BeanNamePrinterBeanFactoryPostProcessor is invoked before any bean defined in @Configuration annotated class is created by the Spring container, and the ExampleBeanPostProcessor is invoked each time a new bean instance is created by the Spring container. This shows that whether you configure beans declaratively (via application context XML file) or programmatically (via @Configuration annotated class), beans that implement callback interfaces (like ApplicationContextAware, BeanNameAware, InitializingBean, DisposableBean, BeanFactoryPostProcessor, and so on) receive callback from the Spring container.

6-12 Summary

This chapter looked at annotations that you can use to simplify developing Spring applications. We looked at how to designate a bean class as a Spring component using Spring's @Component, @Service, @Repository and @Controller annotations, perform classpath scanning to automatically register Spring components with container, validate objects using Spring Validation API and JSR 303's annotations, perform dependency injection using Spring's @Autowired, JSR 330's @Inject and JSR 250's @Resource annotations, and use @Configuration and @Bean annotations to configure beans programmatically. The next chapter shows how Spring simplifies interacting with databases.

Chapter 7 - *Database interaction using Spring*

7-1 Introduction

Spring simplifies interaction with databases by providing a layer of abstraction on top of JDBC. Spring also simplifies using ORM (Object Relational Mapping) frameworks, like Hibernate (http://www.hibernate.org/) and MyBatis (http://www.mybatis.org), for database interaction. In this chapter, we'll look at examples that demonstrate how Spring simplifies developing applications that interact with databases.

> The examples described in this chapter make use of Hibernate 4. If you are using Hibernate 3, the changes that you'll need to make to the configuration are specified at relevant places.

We'll begin this chapter by looking at a sample application that uses Spring's JDBC abstraction to interact with MySQL database. After that, we we'll develop the same application using Spring's support for Hibernate framework. We'll wrap this chapter by looking at Spring's support for programmatic and declarative transaction management.

Let's first look at the MyBank application's requirements that we'll be developing in this chapter.

7-2 MyBank application's requirements

MyBank application is an internet banking application that allows bank customers to check bank account details, generate bank statement, create fixed deposits, request cheque book, and so on. The following figure shows the BANK_ACCOUNT_DETAILS and FIXED_DEPOSIT_DETAILS tables in which MyBank application's data is stored:

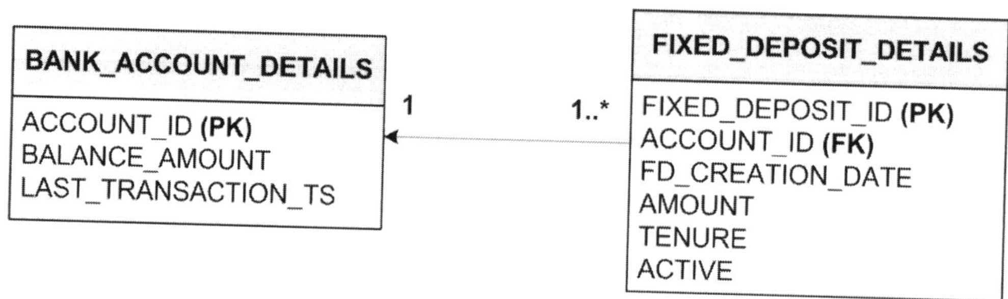

Figure 7-1 Database tables used by the MyBank application

BANK_ACCOUNT_DETAILS table contains information about bank accounts, and FIXED_DEPOSIT_DETAILS table contains information about fixed deposits. The above figure shows that there is many-to-one relationship between FIXED_DEPOSIT_DETAILS and BANK_ACCOUNT_DETAILS tables. When a bank customer opens a new fixed deposit, the fixed deposit amount is deducted from the BANK_ACCOUNT_DETAILS table's BALANCE_AMOUNT column, and the fixed deposit details are saved in the FIXED_DEPOSIT_DETAILS table.

The columns of BANK_ACCOUNT_DETAILS table are:

- ACCOUNT_ID – account identifier that uniquely identifies a customer's bank account.
- BALANCE_AMOUNT – holds the current balance in the bank account. When a customer requests for opening a fixed deposit, the fixed deposit amount is deducted from this column.
- LAST_TRANSACTION_TS – specifies the date/time when the last transaction was performed on this account.

The columns of FIXED_DEPOSIT_DETAILS table are:

- FIXED_DEPOSIT_ID – fixed deposit identifier that uniquely identifies a fixed deposit. When a customer opens a fixed deposit, a unique fixed deposit identifier is generated by the MyBank for future reference by the customer. The value of FIXED_DEPOSIT_ID column is auto-generated by MySQL database.
- ACCOUNT_ID – foreign key that identifies the bank account with which the fixed deposit is associated. Every quarter, interest generated by the fixed deposit is credited into the bank account identified by this column.
- FD_CREATION_DATE – the date on which the fixed deposit was created
- AMOUNT – fixed deposit amount
- TENURE – fixed deposit tenure (in months). Fixed deposit tenure must be greater than or equal to 12 months and less than or equal to 60 months.
- ACTIVE – indicates whether the fixed deposit is currently active or not. An active fixed deposit generates interest on the fixed deposit amount.

Let's now look at how we can create the MyBank application using Spring's JDBC module.

7-3 Developing the MyBank application using Spring's JDBC module

Spring's JDBC module simplifies interaction with data sources by taking care of lower level details of opening and closing connections, managing transactions, processing exceptions, and so on. In this section, we'll develop the MyBank application (as described in the previous section) using Spring's JDBC module. For the sake of simplicity, we'll develop only the services and DAOs that form part of the MyBank application.

IMPORT **chapter 7/ch07-bankapp-jdbc** (This project shows the MyBank application that uses Spring's JDBC module to interact with the database. To run the application, execute the main method of the BankApp class of this project. Before executing BankApp's main method, install MySQL database and execute the spring_bank_app_db.sql SQL script contained in the sql folder of ch07-bankapp-jdbc project. Executing spring_bank_app_db.sql script creates SPRING_BANK_APP_DB database and adds BANK_ACCOUNT_DETAILS and FIXED_DEPOSIT_DETAILS tables to the SPRING_BANK_APP_DB database. Also, modify the src/main/resources/META-INF/spring/database.properties file to point to your MySQL installation.)

In MyBank application, you first need to configure a javax.sql.DataSource object that identifies the data source with which the MyBank application interacts, followed by implementing DAOs that use Spring's JDBC module classes to interact with the data source. Let's look at each of these steps in detail.

Configuring a data source

If you are using Spring to develop a standalone application, you can configure the data source in the application context XML file. If you are developing an enterprise application, you can define a data source that is bound to the application server's JNDI, and retrieve the JNDI-bound data source in the application context XML file for use by the application. In case of ch07-bankapp-jdbc project, the data source is configured in the application context XML file.

The following example listing shows how MyBank application's data source is configured in the application context XML file:

Example listing 7-1 – applicationContext.xml – data source configuration
Project – ch07-bankapp-jdbc
Source location - src/main/resources/META-INF/spring

```
<context:property-placeholder location="classpath*:META-INF/spring/database.properties" />

<bean id="dataSource"
   class="org.apache.commons.dbcp.BasicDataSource" destroy-method="close" >
   <property name="driverClassName" value="${database.driverClassName}" />
   <property name="url" value="${database.url}" />
   <property name="username" value="${database.username}" />
   <property name="password" value="${database.password}" />
</bean>
```

In the above example listing, the <property-placeholder> element (refer section 5-4 of chapter 5 for more details) of Spring's context schema loads properties from the META-INF/spring/database.properties file and makes them available to bean definitions in the application context XML file. The dataSource bean represents a javax.sql.DataSource object that acts as a factory for creating connections to the data source. BasicDataSource class is an implementation of javax.sql.DataSource interface that supports connection pooling feature. BasicDataSource class is part of Apache Commons DBCP project (http://commons.apache.org/dbcp/) and supports database connection pooling feature. The values for driverClassName, url, username and password properties of BasicDataSource class comes from the properties defined in the database.properties file. The close method of BasicDataSource class closes all idle connections in the pool. As the bean definition for the BasicDataSource class specifies value of destroy-method attribute as close, all idle connections in the pool are closed when the dataSource bean instance is destroyed by the Spring container.

Configuring a data source in Java EE environments

If you are developing an enterprise application that is deployed in an application server, you can use Spring's jee schema's <jndi-lookup> element to make the JNDI-bound data source available as a Spring bean in the ApplicationContext:

```
<jee:jndi-lookup jndi-name="java:comp/env/jdbc/bankAppDb" id="dataSource" />
```

here, jndi-name attribute specifies the JNDI name with which the javax.sql.DataSource object is bound to the JNDI, and id attribute specifies the name with which the javax.sql.DataSource object is registered as a bean in the ApplicationContext.

Let's now look at some of the Spring's JDBC module classes that you can use in your DAOs to interact with the database.

Creating DAOs that use Spring's JDBC module classes

Spring's JDBC module defines multiple classes that simplify database interaction. We'll first look at the JdbcTemplate class that is at the heart of Spring's JDBC module. The other classes that we'll discuss in this section are NamedParameterJdbcTemplate and SimpleJdbcInsert. To learn about other Spring's JDBC module classes, refer to Spring's reference documentation.

JdbcTemplate

JdbcTemplate class takes care of managing Connection, Statement and ResultSet objects, catching JDBC exceptions and translating them into easily understandable exceptions (like IncorrectResultSetColumnCountException and CannotGetJdbcConnectionException), performing batch operations, and so on. An application developer only needs to provide SQL to the JdbcTemplate class, and extract results after the SQL is executed.

As JdbcTemplate acts as a wrapper around javax.sql.DataSource object, you don't need to directly deal with a javax.sql.DataSource object. A JdbcTemplate instance is typically initialized with reference to the javax.sql.DataSource object from which it needs to obtain connections, as shown in the following example listing:

Example listing 7-2 – applicationContext.xml – JdbcTemplate configuration
Project – ch07-bankapp-jdbc
Source location - src/main/resources/META-INF/spring

```
<bean id="jdbcTemplate" class="org.springframework.jdbc.core.JdbcTemplate">
   <property name="dataSource" ref="dataSource" />
</bean>

<bean id="dataSource" class="org.apache.commons.dbcp.BasicDataSource".....>
   .....
</bean>
```

The above example listing shows that the JdbcTemplate class defines a dataSource property that refers to a javax.sql.DataSource object.

If your application uses a JNDI-bound data source, use the <jndi-lookup> element of jee schema to register the JNDI-bound data source as a bean with the Spring container. Now, the the JdbcTemplate class can refer to the javax.sql.DataSource bean registered by the <jndi-lookup> element, as shown in the following example listing:

Example listing 7-3 – JdbcTemplate configuration for JNDI-bound data source

```
<beans .....
      xmlns:jee="http://www.springframework.org/schema/jee"
      xsi:schemaLocation=".....
         http://www.springframework.org/schema/jee
         http://www.springframework.org/schema/jee/spring-jee-4.0.xsd">

   <bean id="jdbcTemplate" class="org.springframework.jdbc.core.JdbcTemplate">
      <property name="dataSource" ref="dataSource" />
   </bean>

   <jee:jndi-lookup jndi-name="java:comp/env/jdbc/bankAppDb" id="dataSource" />
   .....
</beans>
```

In the above example listing, reference to Spring's jee schema is included in the application context XML file. The <jndi-lookup> element retrieves javax.sql.DataSource object from JNDI and exposes it as a bean named dataSource, which is referenced by the JdbcTemplate class.

JdbcTemplate instance is thread-safe, which means multiple DAOs of your application can share the same instance of JdbcTemplate class to interact with the database. The following example listing shows FixedDepositDaoImpl's createFixedDeposit method that makes use of JdbcTemplate to save fixed deposit details in the database:

Example listing 7-4 – FixedDepositDaoImpl class – saving data using JdbcTemplate
Project – ch07-bankapp-jdbc
Source location - src/main/java/sample/spring/chapter07/bankapp/dao

```
package sample.spring.chapter07.bankapp.dao;

import java.sql.*;
import org.springframework.jdbc.core.JdbcTemplate;
import org.springframework.jdbc.core.PreparedStatementCreator;
import org.springframework.jdbc.support.GeneratedKeyHolder;
import org.springframework.jdbc.support.KeyHolder;
import org.springframework.stereotype.Repository;

@Repository(value = "FixedDepositDao")
public class FixedDepositDaoImpl implements FixedDepositDao {

    @Autowired
    private JdbcTemplate jdbcTemplate;
  .....
  public int createFixedDeposit(final FixedDepositDetails fixedDepositDetails) {
    final String sql =
      "insert into fixed_deposit_details(account_id, fixedDeposit_creation_date, amount,
          tenure, active) values(?, ?, ?, ?, ?)";

    KeyHolder keyHolder = new GeneratedKeyHolder();

    jdbcTemplate.update(new PreparedStatementCreator() {

      @Override
      public PreparedStatement createPreparedStatement(Connection con)
          throws SQLException {
        PreparedStatement ps = con.prepareStatement(sql, new String[] {
              "fixed_deposit_id" });
        ps.setInt(1, fixedDepositDetails.getBankAccountId());
```

```
            ps.setDate(2,
                new java.sql.Date(fixedDepositDetails.getFixedDepositCreationDate().getTime()));
            .....
            return ps;
        }
    }, keyHolder);

    return keyHolder.getKey().intValue();
  }
  .....
}
```

In the above example listing, the FixedDepositDaoImpl class is annotated with Spring's @Repository annotation because the FixedDepositDaoImpl class represents a DAO class. JdbcTemplate instance that we configured in the application context XML file (refer example listing 7-2) is autowired into the FixedDepositDaoImpl class. JdbcTemplate's update method accepts an instance of PreparedStatementCreator and an instance of KeyHolder. PreparedStatementCreator is used to perform insert, update or delete operation on the database. Spring's KeyHolder interface represents a holder for the keys that are auto-generated when insert SQL statements are executed. GeneratedKeyHolder class is the default implementation of KeyHolder interface.

Once the INSERT SQL statement is successfully executed, the auto-generated keys are added to the GeneratedKeyHolder instance. You can extract the auto-generated keys from the GeneratedKeyHolder by calling the getKey method. In example listing 7-4, the createFixedDeposit method inserts fixed deposit details into the FIXED_DEPOSIT_DETAILS table and returns the auto-generated key. Example listing 7-4 shows that you don't need to worry about catching SQLException that may be thrown by the execution of PreparedStatement. This is because JdbcTemplate is responsible for catching SQLExceptions and handling them.

Let's now look at NamedParameterJdbcTemplate class.

NamedParameterJdbcTemplate

As shown in example listing 7-4, if you are using JdbcTemplate class for database interaction, parameters to be passed to the SQL statement are specified using ? placeholders. Spring's NamedParameterJdbcTemplate is a wrapper around JdbcTemplate instance that allows you to use named parameters in the SQL statement rather than using ? .

The following example listing shows how the NamedParameterJdbcTemplate class is configured in the application context XML file:

Example listing 7-5 – applicationContext.xml – NamedParameterJdbcTemplate configuration
Project – ch07-bankapp-jdbc
Source location - src/main/resources/META-INF/spring

```
<bean id="namedJdbcTemplate"
   class="org.springframework.jdbc.core.namedparam.NamedParameterJdbcTemplate">
   <constructor-arg index="0" ref="dataSource" />
</bean>

<bean id="dataSource" class="org.apache.commons.dbcp.BasicDataSource".....>
   .....
</bean>
```

The above example listing shows that the NamedParameterJdbcTemplate class accepts javax.sql.DataSource object as constructor argument.

The following example listing shows the FixedDepositDaoImpl class that uses NamedParameterJdbcTemplate to fetch fixed deposit details from the FIXED_DEPOSIT_DETAILS table:

Example listing 7-6 – FixedDepositDaoImpl class – NamedParameterJdbcTemplate usage
Project – ch07-bankapp-jdbc
Source location - src/main/java/sample/spring/chapter07/bankapp/dao

```
package sample.spring.chapter07.bankapp.dao;

import java.sql.ResultSet;
import org.springframework.jdbc.core.RowMapper;
import org.springframework.jdbc.core.namedparam.MapSqlParameterSource;
import org.springframework.jdbc.core.namedparam.NamedParameterJdbcTemplate;
import org.springframework.jdbc.core.namedparam.SqlParameterSource;
.....
@Repository(value = "FixedDepositDao")
public class FixedDepositDaoImpl implements FixedDepositDao {
   .....
   @Autowired
   private NamedParameterJdbcTemplate namedParameterJdbcTemplate;
   .....
   public FixedDepositDetails getFixedDeposit(final int FixedDepositId) {
      final String sql = "select * from fixed_deposit_details where fixed_deposit_id
               = :FixedDepositId";

      SqlParameterSource namedParameters = new MapSqlParameterSource(
               "FixedDepositId", FixedDepositId);
```

```
    return namedParameterJdbcTemplate.queryForObject(sql, namedParameters,
        new RowMapper<FixedDepositDetails>() {
            public FixedDepositDetails mapRow(ResultSet rs, int rowNum) throws SQLException {
                FixedDepositDetails fixedDepositDetails = new FixedDepositDetails();
                fixedDepositDetails.setActive(rs.getString("active"));
                .....
                return fixedDepositDetails;
            }
        });
    }
}
```

NamedParameterJdbcTemplate instance that we configured in the application context XML file (refer example listing 7-5) is autowired into FixedDepositDaoImpl class. In the above example listing, the SQL query passed to NamedParameterJdbcTemplate's queryForObject method contains a named parameter FixedDepositId. The named parameter values are supplied via an implementation of Spring's SqlParameterSource interface. MapSqlParameterSource class is an implementation of SqlParameterSource interface that stores named parameters (and their values) in a java.util.Map. In the above example listing, MapSqlParameterSource instance holds value of FixedDepositId named parameter. NamedParameterJdbcTemplate's queryForObject method executes the supplied SQL query and returns a single object. Spring's RowMapper object is used for mapping each returned row to an object. In the above example listing, RowMapper maps the returned row in the ResultSet to a FixedDepositDetails object.

Let's now look at Spring's SimpleJdbcInsert class.

SimpleJdbcInsert

SimpleJdbcInsert class makes use of database metadata to simplify creating a basic SQL insert statement for a table.

The following example listing shows the BankAccountDaoImpl class that makes use of SimpleJdbcInsert to insert bank account details into BANK_ACCOUNT_DETAILS table:

Example listing 7-7 – BankAccountDaoImpl class – SimpleJdbcInsert usage
Project – ch07-bankapp-jdbc
Source location - src/main/java/sample/spring/chapter07/bankapp/dao

```
package sample.spring.chapter07.bankapp.dao;

import javax.sql.DataSource;
import org.springframework.jdbc.core.simple.SimpleJdbcInsert;
.....
```

```
@Repository(value = "bankAccountDao")
public class BankAccountDaoImpl implements BankAccountDao {
   private SimpleJdbcInsert insertBankAccountDetail;

   @Autowired
   private void setDataSource(DataSource dataSource) {
      this.insertBankAccountDetail = new SimpleJdbcInsert(dataSource)
            .withTableName("bank_account_details")
            .usingGeneratedKeyColumns("account_id");
   }

   @Override
   public int createBankAccount(final BankAccountDetails bankAccountDetails) {
      Map<String, Object> parameters = new HashMap<String, Object>(2);
      parameters.put("balance_amount", bankAccountDetails.getBalanceAmount());
      parameters.put("last_transaction_ts", new java.sql.Date(
            bankAccountDetails.getLastTransactionTimestamp().getTime()));

      Number key = insertBankAccountDetail.executeAndReturnKey(parameters);
      return key.intValue();
   }
   .....
}
```

As the setDataSource method is annotated with @Autowired annotation, javax.sql.DataSource object is passed as an argument to the setDataSource method. In the setDataSource method, an instance of SimpleJdbcInsert is created by passing reference to javax.sql.DataSource object to the SimpleJdbcInsert constructor.

SimpleJdbcInsert's withTableName method sets the name of the table into which you want to insert record(s). As we want to insert bank account details into BANK_ACCOUNT_DETAILS table, 'bank_account_details' string value is passed as argument to the withTableName method. SimpleJdbcInsert's usingGeneratedKeyColumns method sets names of table columns that contain auto-generated keys. In case of BANK_ACCOUNT_DETAILS table, ACCOUNT_ID column contains the auto-generated key; therefore, 'account_id' string value is passed to the usingGeneratedKeyColumns method. The actual insert operation is performed by calling SimpleJdbcInsert's executeAndReturnKey method. The executeAndReturnKey method accepts a java.util.Map type argument that contains table column names and their corresponding values, and returns the generated key value. You should note that the SimpleJdbcInsert class internally uses JdbcTemplate to execute the actual SQL insert operation.

If you look at BankAccountDaoImpl class of ch07-bankapp-jdbc project, you'll notice that it makes use of both SimpleJdbcInsert and JdbcTemplate classes to interact with the database.

Similarly, FixedDepositDaoImpl class of ch07-bankapp-jdbc project uses both JdbcTemplate and NamedParameterJdbcTemplate classes for database interaction. This shows that you can use a combination of Spring's JDBC module classes to interact with a database.

> As ch07-bankapp-jdbc project makes use of Spring's JDBC module and uses Spring's Transaction Management feature (explained in section 7-5), the pom.xml file of ch07-bankapp-jdbc project depends on spring-jdbc and spring-tx JAR files.

Let's now look at BankApp class of ch07-bankapp-jdbc project that creates a bank account and opens a fixed deposit corresponding to it.

BankApp class

BankApp class of ch07-bankapp-jdbc project runs the MyBank application as a standalone Java application. BankApp's main method creates a bank account in the BANK_ACCOUNT_DETAILS table and creates a fixed deposit (corresponding to the newly created bank account) in the FIXED_DEPOSIT_DETAILS table.

The following example listing shows the BankApp class:

Example listing 7-8 – BankApp class
Project – ch07-bankapp-jdbc
Source location - src/main/java/sample/spring/chapter07/bankapp

```
package sample.spring.chapter07.bankapp;
.....
public class BankApp {
  private static Logger logger = Logger.getLogger(BankApp.class);

  public static void main(String args[]) throws Exception {
    ApplicationContext context = new ClassPathXmlApplicationContext(
        "classpath:META-INF/spring/applicationContext.xml");

    BankAccountService bankAccountService = context.getBean(BankAccountService.class);
    BankAccountDetails bankAccountDetails = new BankAccountDetails();
    .....
    int bankAccountId = bankAccountService.createBankAccount(bankAccountDetails);
    .....
    FixedDepositService FixedDepositService = context.getBean(FixedDepositService.class);
    FixedDepositDetails fixedDepositDetails = new FixedDepositDetails();
    .....
    int FixedDepositId = FixedDepositService.createFixedDeposit(fixedDepositDetails);
    .....
  }
```

```
}
```

In the above example listing, the BankAccountService object interacts with BankAccountDaoImpl (refer example listing 7-7) to create a bank account, and FixedDepositService object interacts with FixedDepositDaoImpl (refer example listing 7-4 and 7-6) object to open a fixed deposit corresponding to the newly created bank account. If you execute BankApp's main method, you'll find that a new record is inserted into both BANK_ACCOUNT_DETAILS and FIXED_DEPOSIT_DETAILS tables.

In this section, we looked at how Spring's JDBC module simplifies updating or fetching data from databases. Spring's JDBC module can also be used for the following purposes:

- executing stored procedures and functions. For instance, you can use Spring's SimpleJdbcCall class for executing stored procedures and functions
- executing prepared statements in batches
- accessing relational databases in an object-oriented manner. For instance, you can extend Spring's MappingSqlQuery class to create an SQL query and map the returned ResultSet to a domain object.
- configuring an embedded database instance. For instance, you can Spring's jdbc schema to create an instance of HSQL, H2 or Derby databases, and register the database instance with the Spring container as a bean of type javax.sql.DataSource.

Let's now look at how we can use Spring's support for Hibernate ORM framework to interact with databases.

7-4 Developing the MyBank application using Hibernate

Spring's ORM module provides integration with Hibernate, Java Persistence API (JPA), MyBatis, and Java Data Objects (JDO). In this section, we'll see how Spring simplifies using Hibernate framework for database interaction. As Hibernate itself is a JPA provider, we'll use JPA annotations to map our persistent entity classes to database tables.

IMPORT **chapter 7/ch07-bankapp-hibernate** (This project shows the MyBank application that uses Hibernate to interact with the database. To run the application, execute the main method of the BankApp class of this project.)

Let's first look at how to configure Hibernate's SessionFactory instance.

Configuring SessionFactory instance

SessionFactory is a factory for creating Hibernate's Session object. It is the Session object that is used by DAOs to perform create, read, delete and update operations on persistent entities.

Spring's org.springframework.orm.hibernate4.LocalSessionFactoryBean (a FactoryBean implementation) creates a *SessionFactory* instance that can be used by DAO classes for obtaining a *Session* instance.

> If you want to use JPA's EntityManager in your application's DAOs for database interaction, configure Spring's LocalContainerEntityManagerFactoryBean instead of org.springframework.orm.hibernate4.LocalSessionFactoryBean.

The following example listing shows how the LocalSessionFactoryBean class is configured in the application context XML file:

Example listing 7-9 – applicationContext.xml - LocalSessionFactoryBean configuration
Project – ch07-bankapp-hibernate
Source location - src/main/java/sample/spring/chapter07/bankapp

```
<bean id="sessionFactory"
    class=" org.springframework.orm.hibernate4.LocalSessionFactoryBean">
    <property name="dataSource" ref="dataSource" />
    <property name="packagesToScan" value="sample.spring" />
</bean>
```

The dataSource property specifies reference to a bean of type javax.sql.DataSource. The packagesToScan property specifies the package(s) under which Spring looks for persistent classes. For instance, the above example listing specifies that if a persistent class is annotated with JPA's @Entity annotation, and is located inside sample.spring package (or its sub-packages), it is automatically detected by org.springframework.orm.hibernate4.LocalSessionFactoryBean. An alternative to using packagesToScan property is to explicitly specify all the persistent classes using annotatedClasses property, as shown in the following example listing:

Example listing 7-10 LocalSessionFactoryBean's annotatedClasses property

```
<bean id="sessionFactory"
   class="org.springframework.orm.hibernate4.LocalSessionFactoryBean">
   <property name="dataSource" ref="dataSource" />
   <property name="annotatedClasses">
      <list>
         <value>sample.spring.chapter07.bankapp.domain.BankAccountDetails</value>
         <value>sample.spring.chapter07.bankapp.domain.FixedDepositDetails</value>
      </list>
   </property>
</bean>
```

In the above example listing, annotatedClasses property (of type java.util.List) lists down all the persistent classes in the application.

> If you are using Hibernate 3, use Spring's org.springframework.orm.hibernate3.annotation.AnnotationSessionFactoryBean instead of org.springframework.orm.hibernate4.LocalSessionFactoryBean to create a SessionFactory instance.

As we have configured LocalSessionFactoryBean, let's now look at DAOs that make use of SessionFactory instance created by LocalSessionFactoryBean to perform database operations.

Creating DAOs that use Hibernate API for database interaction

To interact with the database, DAOs need access to Hibernate's *Session* object. To access Hibernate's *Session* object, inject the *SessionFactory* instance created by LocalSessionFactoryBean bean (refer example listing 7-9) into DAOs, and use the injected SessionFactory instance to obtain a *Session* instance.

The following example listing shows the FixedDepositDaoImpl class that uses Hibernate API for saving and retrieving the FixedDepositDetails persistent entity:

Example listing 7-11 – FixedDepositDaoImpl class - Hibernate API usage
Project – ch07-bankapp-hibernate
Source location - src/main/java/sample/spring/chapter07/bankapp/dao

```
package sample.spring.chapter07.bankapp.dao;

import org.hibernate.SessionFactory;
.....
@Repository(value = "FixedDepositDao")
public class FixedDepositDaoImpl implements FixedDepositDao {

    @Autowired
    private SessionFactory sessionFactory;

    public int createFixedDeposit(final FixedDepositDetails fixedDepositDetails) {
        sessionFactory.getCurrentSession().save(fixedDepositDetails);
        return fixedDepositDetails.getFixedDepositId();
    }

    public FixedDepositDetails getFixedDeposit(final int FixedDepositId) {
        String hql = "from FixedDepositDetails as FixedDepositDetails where "
                + "FixedDepositDetails.FixedDepositId ="
                + FixedDepositId;
```

```
        return (FixedDepositDetails) sessionFactory.getCurrentSession()
                .createQuery(hql).uniqueResult();
    }
}
```

The above example listing shows that an instance of SessionFactory is autowired into FixedDepositDaoImpl instance, which is later used by createFixedDeposit and getFixedDeposit methods to save and retrieve FixedDepositDetails persistent entity. Autowiring of SessionFactory instance shows that you can autowire an object created by Spring's FactoryBean implementation by simply defining the type created by the FactoryBean and annotating it with @Autowired annotation (refer section 3-9 of chapter 3 to know more about Spring's FactoryBean interface). The createFixedDeposit and getFixedDeposit methods call SessionFactory's getCurrentSession method to obtain an instance of Session. It is important to note that the call to getCurrentSession method returns the Session object associated with the *current transaction* or *thread*. Using getCurrentSession method is useful if you want Spring to manage transactions, which is the case in MyBank application.

Let's now look at Spring's programmatic and declarative transaction management feature.

7-5 Transaction management using Spring

Spring Framework supports both programmatic and declarative transaction management. In programmatic transaction management, Spring's transaction management abstraction is used to explicitly start, end and commit transactions. In declarative transaction management, you annotate methods that execute within a transaction with Spring's @Transactional annotation.

Let's first look at the transaction management requirement of MyBank application described in section 7-2.

MyBank's transaction management requirements

In section 7-2, it was mentioned that when a bank customer opens a new fixed deposit, the fixed deposit amount is deducted from the BANK_ACCOUNT_DETAILS table's BALANCE_AMOUNT column, and the fixed deposit details are saved in the FIXED_DEPOSIT_DETAILS table.

The following sequence diagram shows that the createFixedDeposit method of FixedDepositServiceImpl class saves the fixed deposit details in FIXED_DEPOSIT_DETAILS table and deducts the fixed deposit amount from the corresponding bank account in BANK_ACCOUNT_DETAILS table:

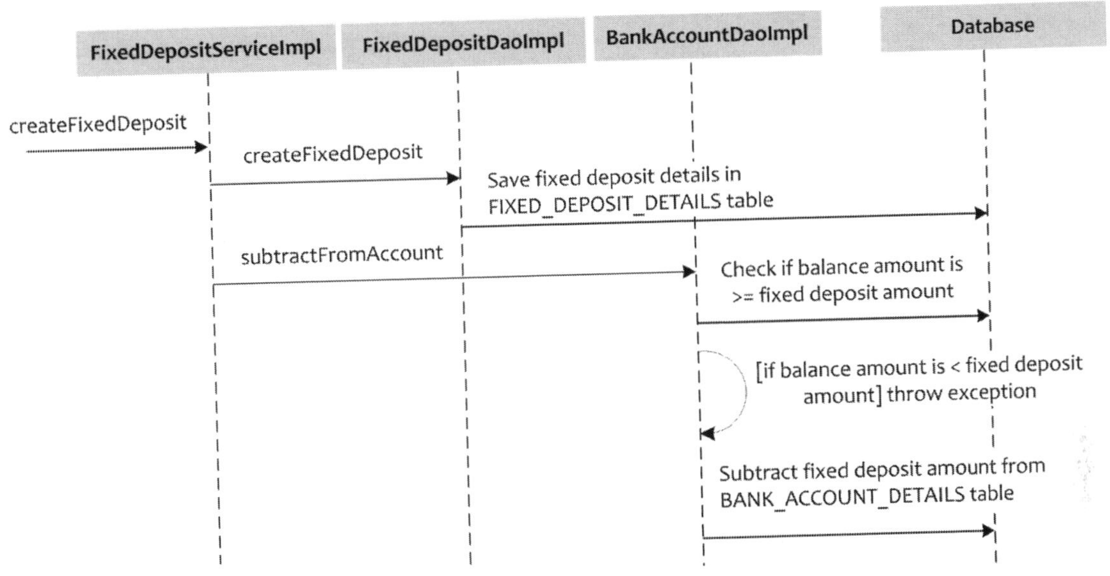

Figure 7-2 The sequence of actions performed by MyBank application when a customer opens a new fixed deposit

The above sequence diagram shows that FixedDepositServiceImpl's createFixedDeposit method calls FixedDepositDaoImpl's createFixedDeposit method and BankAccountDaoImpl's subtractFromAccount method. FixedDepositDaoImpl's createFixedDeposit method saves the fixed deposit details in the FIXED_DEPOSIT_DETAILS table. BankAccountDaoImpl's subtractFromAccount method first checks that the customer's bank account contains sufficient balance to create the fixed deposit of the specified amount. If sufficient balance is available in customer's bank account, the subtractFromAccount method deducts the fixed deposit amount from the customer's bank account. If sufficient balance isn't available, an exception is thrown by BankAccountDaoImpl's subtractFromAccount method. If FixedDepositDaoImpl's createFixedDeposit or BankAccountDaoImpl's subtractFromAccount method fails for some reason, the system will be left in an inconsistent state; therefore, both the methods must be executed within a *transaction*.

Let's now look at how you can use Spring to programmatically manage transactions in the MyBank application.

Programmatic transaction management

You can programmatically manage transactions by using Spring's TransactionTemplate class or by using an implementation of Spring's PlatformTransactionManager interface. TransactionTemplate class simplifies transaction management by taking care of *initiating* and *committing* transactions. You only need to provide an implementation of Spring's TransactionCallback interface that contains the code to be executed within a transaction.

IMPORT **chapter 7/ch07-bankapp-tx-jdbc** (This project shows the MyBank application that uses Spring's TransactionTemplate class for programmatically managing transactions. To run the application, execute the main method of the BankApp class of this project. Create SPRING_BANK_APP_DB database, and BANK_ACCOUNT_DETAILS and FIXED_DEPOSIT_DETAILS tables as described for ch07-bankapp-jdbc project)

The following example listing shows how the TransactionTemplate class is configured in the application context XML file:

Example listing 7-12 – applicationContext.xml - TransactionTemplate configuration
Project – ch07-bankapp-tx-jdbc
Source location - src/main/resources/META-INF/spring

```
<bean id="dataSource" class="org.apache.commons.dbcp.BasicDataSource".....>
   .....
</bean>

<bean id="txManager"
   class="org.springframework.jdbc.datasource.DataSourceTransactionManager">
   <property name="dataSource" ref="dataSource" />
</bean>

<bean id="transactionTemplate"
   class="org.springframework.transaction.support.TransactionTemplate">
   <property name="transactionManager" ref="txManager"/>
   <property name="isolationLevelName" value="ISOLATION_READ_UNCOMMITTED" />
   <property name="propagationBehaviorName" value="PROPAGATION_REQUIRED" />
</bean>
```

TransactionTemplate's transactionManager property refers to Spring's PlatformTransactionManager implementation that is responsible for managing transactions.

TransactionTemplate's isolationLevelName property specifies the transaction isolation level to be set for the transactions managed by the transaction manager. The value of isolationLevelName property refers to a constant defined by Spring's TransactionDefinition interface. For instance, ISOLATION_READ_UNCOMMITTED is a constant defined by TransactionDefinition interface that indicates that the *uncommitted* changes by a transaction *can* be read by other transactions.

TransactionTemplate's propagationBehaviorName property specifies the transaction propagation behavior. The value of propagationBehaviorName property refers to a constant defined by Spring's TransactionDefinition interface. For instance, PROPAGATION_REQUIRED is a constant defined by TransactionDefinition interface that indicates:

- if a method is *not* invoked within a transaction, the transaction manager starts a new transaction and executes the method in the newly created transaction

- if a method is invoked within a transaction, the transaction manager executes the method in the *same* transaction

Spring provides a couple of built-in PlatformTransactionManager implementations that you can choose from, depending upon the data access technology used by your application. For instance, DataSourceTransactionManager is appropriate for managing transactions in applications that use JDBC for interacting with a database, HibernateTransactionManager is appropriate when Hibernate is used for database interaction and JpaTransactionManager when JPA's EntityManager is used for data access. In example listing 7-12, TransactionTemplate's transactionManager property refers to a DataSourceTransactionManager instance because the MyBank application of ch07-bankapp-tx-jdbc project uses JDBC for data access. The example listing 7-12 shows that DataSourceTransactionManager's dataSource property refers to a javax.sql.DataSource object that represents the database whose transactions are managed by the DataSourceTransactionManager instance.

The following example listing shows the FixedDepositServiceImpl class that uses TransactionTemplate instance for transaction management:

Example listing 7-13 – FixedDepositServiceImpl class that uses TransactionTemplate
Project – ch07-bankapp-tx-jdbc
Source location - src/main/java/sample/spring/chapter07/bankapp/service

```
package sample.spring.chapter07.bankapp.service;

import org.springframework.transaction.TransactionStatus;
import org.springframework.transaction.support.TransactionCallback;
import org.springframework.transaction.support.TransactionTemplate;
.....
@Service(value = "FixedDepositService")
public class FixedDepositServiceImpl implements FixedDepositService {

  @Autowired
  private TransactionTemplate transactionTemplate;
  .....
  @Override
  public int createFixedDeposit(final FixedDepositDetails fixedDepositDetails) throws Exception {
    transactionTemplate.execute(new TransactionCallback<FixedDepositDetails>() {
          public FixedDepositDetails doInTransaction(TransactionStatus status) {
            try {
              myFixedDepositDao.createFixedDeposit(fixedDepositDetails);
              bankAccountDao.subtractFromAccount(
```

```
                    fixedDepositDetails.getBankAccountId(),
                           fixedDepositDetails.getFixedDepositAmount()
                  );
              } catch (Exception e) { status.setRollbackOnly(); }
              return fixedDepositDetails;
          }
       });
    return fixedDepositDetails.getFixedDepositId();
  }
  .....
}
```

The above example listing shows FixedDepositServiceImpl's createFixedDeposit method (refer figure 7-2 for more details) that saves fixed deposit details in the FIXED_DEPOSIT_DETAILS table, and deducts the fixed deposit amount from the corresponding bank account in the BANK_ACCOUNT_DETAILS table.

You create an implementation of TransactionCallback interface to define the actions that you want to execute within a transaction. And, TransactionTemplate's execute method executes the actions contained in the TransactionCallback instance within a transaction. TransactionCallback interface defines a doInTransaction method that you implement to provide the actions that should be executed within a transaction. TransactionCallback's doInTransaction method is invoked within a transaction by TransactionTemplate's execute method. The doInTransaction method accepts a TransactionStatus object that you can use to control the outcome of the transaction. In example listing 7-13, TransactionCallback's doInTransaction method contains calls to FixedDepositDaoImpl's createFixedDeposit method and BankAccountDaoImpl's subtractFromAccount method because we want both the methods to be executed within a single transaction. As we'd want to roll back the transaction if either of the methods fails, the setRollbackOnly method of TransactionStatus is invoked in case of an exception. If you call TransactionStatus's setRollbackOnly method, the TransactionTemplate instance roll backs the transaction. A transaction will be automatically rolled back if the actions contained in the doInTransaction method result in a java.lang.RuntimeException.

TransactionCallback instance accepts a *generic type* argument which refers to the object type returned by the doInTransaction method. In example listing 7-13, a FixedDepositDetails object is returned by the doInTransaction method. If you don't want the doInTransaction method to return any object, use the TransactionCallbackWithoutResult abstract class that implements the TransactionCallback interface. The TransactionCallbackWithoutResult class allows you to create TransactionCallback implementations in which doInTransaction method doesn't return a value.

The following example listing shows the main method of BankApp class that calls BankAccountServiceImpl's createBankAccount method to create a bank account, and

FixedDepositServiceImpl's createFixedDeposit method to create a fixed deposit corresponding to the newly created bank account:

Example listing 7-14 – BankApp class
Project – ch07-bankapp-tx-jdbc
Source location - src/main/java/sample/spring/chapter07/bankapp

```
package sample.spring.chapter07.bankapp;

public class BankApp {
  .....
  public static void main(String args[]) throws Exception {
    ApplicationContext context = new ClassPathXmlApplicationContext(
        "classpath:META-INF/spring/applicationContext.xml");

    BankAccountService bankAccountService = context.getBean(BankAccountService.class);
    FixedDepositService FixedDepositService = context.getBean(FixedDepositService.class);

    BankAccountDetails bankAccountDetails = new BankAccountDetails();
    bankAccountDetails.setBalanceAmount(1000);
    .....
    int bankAccountId = bankAccountService.createBankAccount(bankAccountDetails);

    FixedDepositDetails fixedDepositDetails = new FixedDepositDetails();
    fixedDepositDetails.setFixedDepositAmount(1500);
    fixedDepositDetails.setBankAccountId(bankAccountId);
    .....
    int FixedDepositId = FixedDepositService.createFixedDeposit(fixedDepositDetails);
    .....
  }
}
```

The above example listing shows that a bank account is first created with a balance amount of 1000, followed by creating a fixed deposit of amount 1500. As fixed deposit amount is greater than the balance in the bank account, BankAccountDaoImpl's subtractFromAccount method throws an exception (refer BankAccountDaoImpl's subtractFromAccount method or figure 7-2).

If you execute BankApp's main method, you'll notice that the fixed deposit is *not* created in the FIXED_DEPOSIT_DETAILS table, and 1500 amount is *not* deducted from the BANK_ACCOUNT_DETAILS table. This shows that both FixedDepositDaoImpl's createFixedDeposit and BankAccountDaoImpl's subtractFromAccount are executed in the same transaction.

Instead of using TransactionTemplate class, you can directly use a PlatformTransactionManager implementation to programmatically manage transactions. When using PlatformTransactionManager implementation, you are required to explicitly initiate and commit (or roll back) transactions. For this reason, it is recommended to use TransactionTemplate instead of directly using a PlatformTransactionManager implementation.

Let's now look at declarative transaction management feature of Spring.

Declarative transaction management

Programmatic transaction management couples your application code with Spring-specific classes. On the other hand, declarative transaction management requires you to only annotate methods or classes with Spring's @Transactional annotation. If you want to execute a method within a transaction, annotate the method with @Transactional annotation. If you want to execute *all* the methods of a class within a transaction, annotate the class with @Transactional annotation.

> Instead of using @Transactional annotation for declarative transaction management, you can use Spring's tx schema elements to identify transactional methods. As using Spring's tx schema results in verbose application context XML file, we'll be only looking at using @Transactional annotation for declarative transaction management.

IMPORT **chapter 7/ch07-bankapp-jdbc** and **chapter 7/ch07-bankapp-hibernate** (The ch07-bankapp-jdbc project shows the MyBank application that uses Spring's JDBC module for database interaction (refer section 7-3 to learn more about ch07-bankapp-jdbc project). The ch07-bankapp-hibernate project shows the MyBank application that uses Hibernate to interact with the database (refer section 7-4 to learn more about ch07-bankapp-hibernate project).

You enable declarative transaction management using <annotation-driven> element of Spring's tx schema. The following example listing shows the <annotation-driven> element's usage in ch07-bankapp-jdbc project:

Example listing 7-15 – applicationContext.xml - <annotation-driven> element
Project – ch07-bankapp-jdbc
Source location - src/main/resources/META-INF/spring

```
<beans ..... xmlns:tx="http://www.springframework.org/schema/tx"
  xsi:schemaLocation=".....http://www.springframework.org/schema/tx
    http://www.springframework.org/schema/tx/spring-tx-4.0.xsd">
  .....
  <tx:annotation-driven transaction-manager="txManager" />

  <bean id="txManager"
```

```
    class="org.springframework.jdbc.datasource.DataSourceTransactionManager">
    <property name="dataSource" ref="dataSource" />
  </bean>
  .....
</beans>
```

In the above example listing, Spring's tx schema is included so that its elements are accessible in the application context XML file. The <annotation-driven> element enables declarative transaction management. The <annotation-driven> element's transaction-manager attribute specifies reference to the PlatformTransactionManager implementation to use for transaction management. The above example listing shows that the DataSourceTransactionManager is used as the transaction manager in ch07-bankapp-jdbc project.

The following example listing shows how you can use declarative transaction management in ch07-bankapp-hibernate project that uses Hibernate ORM for data access:

Example listing 7-16 – applicationContext.xml - <annotation-driven> element
Project – ch07-bankapp-hibernate
Source location - src/main/resources/META-INF/spring

```
<beans ..... xmlns:tx="http://www.springframework.org/schema/tx"
  xsi:schemaLocation=".....http://www.springframework.org/schema/tx
    http://www.springframework.org/schema/tx/spring-tx-4.0.xsd">
  .....
  <tx:annotation-driven transaction-manager="txManager" />

  <bean id="txManager"
    class="org.springframework.orm.hibernate4.HibernateTransactionManager">
    <property name="sessionFactory" ref="sessionFactory"/>
  </bean>
  .....
</beans>
```

If you compare the above example listing with 7-15, you'll notice that the only difference is in the PlatformTransactionManager implementation referenced by the transaction-manager attribute of <annotation-driven> element. The above example listing shows that if Hibernate ORM is used for database interaction, the org.springframework.orm.hibernate4.HibernateTransactionManager implementation of PlatformTransactionManager is used for managing transactions.

> If you are using Hibernate 3, set transaction-manager attribute to org.springframework.orm.hibernate3.HibernateTransactionManager instead of org.springframework.orm.hibernate4.HibernateTransactionManager.

The following example listing shows the FixedDepositServiceImpl class that makes use of declarative transaction management:

Example listing 7-17 – FixedDepositServiceImpl class - @Transactional annotation usage
Project – ch07-bankapp-jdbc
Source location - src/main/java/sample/spring/chapter07/bankapp/service

```
package sample.spring.chapter07.bankapp.service;

import org.springframework.transaction.annotation.Transactional;
.....
@Service(value = "FixedDepositService")
public class FixedDepositServiceImpl implements FixedDepositService {
  .....
  @Transactional
  public int createFixedDeposit(FixedDepositDetails fixedDepositDetails) throws Exception {
    bankAccountDao.subtractFromAccount(fixedDepositDetails.getBankAccountId(),
      fixedDepositDetails.getFixedDepositAmount());
    return myFixedDepositDao.createFixedDeposit(fixedDepositDetails);
  }
  .....
}
```

In the above example listing, the createFixedDeposit method is annotated with @Transactional annotation. This means that the createFixedDeposit method is executed within a transaction. The transaction manager specified via the transaction-manager attribute of <annotation-driven> element (refer example listing 7-15 and 7-16) is used for managing the transaction. If a java.lang.RuntimeException is thrown during execution of createFixedDeposit method, the transaction is automatically rolled back.

@Transactional annotation defines attributes that you can use to configure the behavior of the transaction manager. For instance, you can use the rollbackFor attribute to specify exception classes that result in transaction roll back. The exception classes specified by rollbackFor attribute *must* be subclasses of java.lang.Throwable class. Similarly, you can use isolation attribute to specify the transaction isolation level.

In case your application defines multiple transaction managers, you can use @Transactional annotation's value attribute to specify the bean name of the PlatformTransactionManager implementation that you want to use for managing transactions. The following example listing shows that 2 transaction managers, tx1 and tx2, are defined in the application context XML file. The tx1 transaction manager is used by SomeServiceImpl's methodA and tx2 transaction manager is used by SomeServiceImpl's methodB:

Example listing 7-18 – @Transactional's value attribute usage

```
---------------------- SomeServiceImpl class ----------------------

@Service
public class SomeServiceImpl implements SomeService {
    .....
    @Transactional(value = "tx1")
    public int methodA() {.....}

    @Transactional(value = "tx2")
    public int methodB() {.....}
}
---------------------- application context XML file ----------------------

<tx:annotation-driven />

<bean id="tx1"
    class="org.springframework.orm.hibernate4.HibernateTransactionManager">
    <property name="sessionFactory1" ref="sessionFactory1"/>
</bean>

<bean id="tx2"
    class="org.springframework.jdbc.datasource.DataSourceTransactionManager">
    <property name="dataSource" ref="dataSource" />
</bean>
```

In the above example listing, the <annotation-driven> element of Spring's tx schema doesn't specify the transaction-manager attribute because the transaction manager to use for managing transactions is specified by the @Transactional annotation itself. In the above example listing, @Transactional annotation's value attribute specifies the transaction manager to use for managing transactions. This means that SomeServiceImpl's methodA executes under tx1 transaction manager and SomeServiceImpl's methodB executes under tx2 transaction manager.

Let's now look at Spring's support for JTA (Java Transaction API) transactions.

Spring's support for JTA

In chapter 1, we discussed that when multiple transactional resources are involved in a transaction, JTA is used for transaction management. Spring provides a generic JtaTransactionManager class (a PlatformTransactionManager implementation) that you can use in applications to manage JTA transactions.

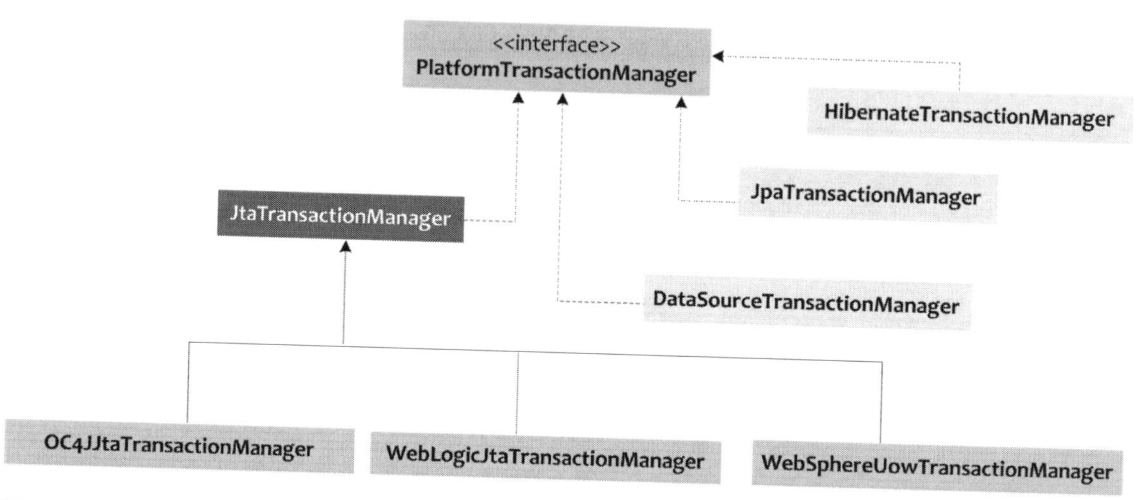

Figure 7-3 JTA transaction managers and resource-specific transaction managers implement PlatformTransactionManager interface

In most application server environments, the JtaTransactionManager will meet your requirements. But, Spring also provides vendor-specific PlatformTransactionManager implementations that leverage application server-specific features to manage JTA transactions. The vendor-specific JTA transaction managers provided by Spring are: OC4JJtaTransactionManager (for Oracle OC4J), WebLogicJtaTransactionManager (for WebLogic application server), WebSphereUowTransactionManager (for WebSphere application server). Figure 7-3 summarizes how JTA transaction managers and resource-specific transaction managers are related to the PlatformTransactionManager interface. The figure shows that the PlatformTransactionManager is implemented by both JTA transaction manager classes and resource-specific transaction manager classes.

Let's now look at how Spring simplifies configuring a JTA transaction manager in application context XML file.

Configuring a JTA transaction manager using <jta-transaction-manager> element

Spring's tx schema provides a <jta-transaction-manager> element that automatically detects the application server in which the application is deployed and configures an appropriate JTA transaction manager. This saves the effort for explicitly configuring an application server-specific JTA transaction manager in the application context XML file. For instance, if you deploy an application in WebSphere application server, the <jta-transaction-manager> element configures an instance of WebSphereUowTransactionManager instance. If the same application is deployed in WebLogic application server, the <jta-transaction-manager> element configures an instance of WebLogicJtaTransactionManager instance. If the application is deployed in any application server other than OC4J, WebSphere or WebLogic, the <jta-transaction-manager> element configures an instance of JtaTransactionManager instance.

7-6 Summary

In this chapter, we saw that Spring supports database interaction using JDBC and Hibernate ORM framework. We also saw how we can use Spring to manage transactions programmatically and declaratively. In the next chapter, we'll look at how Spring simplifies sending emails, interaction with messaging middlewares, and perform transparent caching of data.

Chapter 8 - *Messaging, emailing, asynchronous method execution, and caching using Spring*

8-1 Introduction

In the previous chapter, we saw that Spring simplifies database interaction. In the context of MyBank application, this chapter goes a step further and shows how Spring simplifies:

- sending and receiving JMS messages from a JMS provider, like ActiveMQ
- sending email messages
- asynchronously executing methods
- storing and retrieving data from cache

Let's first look at the MyBank application's requirements that we'll implement in this chapter.

8-2 MyBank application's requirements

MyBank application allows its customers to open fixed deposits and retrieve details of their existing fixed deposits. Figure 8-1 shows the sequence of events that occur when a customer requests for opening a new fixed deposit.

First, FixedDepositService's createFixedDeposit method is invoked that sends 2 JMS messages – a message containing customer's email id, and a message that contains fixed deposit details. EmailMessageListener retrieves the JMS message containing the email id of the customer and sends an email to the customer informing that the request for opening a fixed deposit has been received. FixedDepositMessageListener retrieves the JMS message containing fixed deposit details and saves the fixed deposit details in the database.

A scheduled job runs every 5 seconds to check if any new fixed deposits have been created in the database. If the job finds any new fixed deposits, it subtracts the fixed deposit amount from the bank account of the customer and sends an email to the customer informing that the fixed deposit request has been successfully processed.

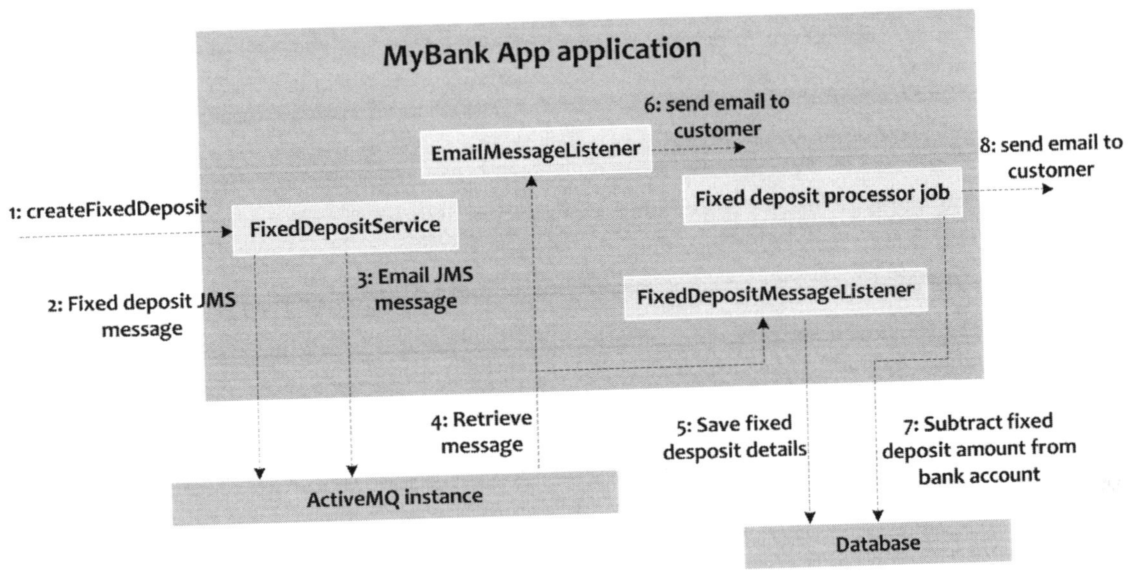

Figure 8-1 MyBank application behavior when a customer requests for opening a new fixed deposit

The following diagram shows the behavior of MyBank application when `FixedDepositService`'s `findFixedDepositsByBankAccount` method is invoked to retrieve all fixed deposits corresponding to a bank account:

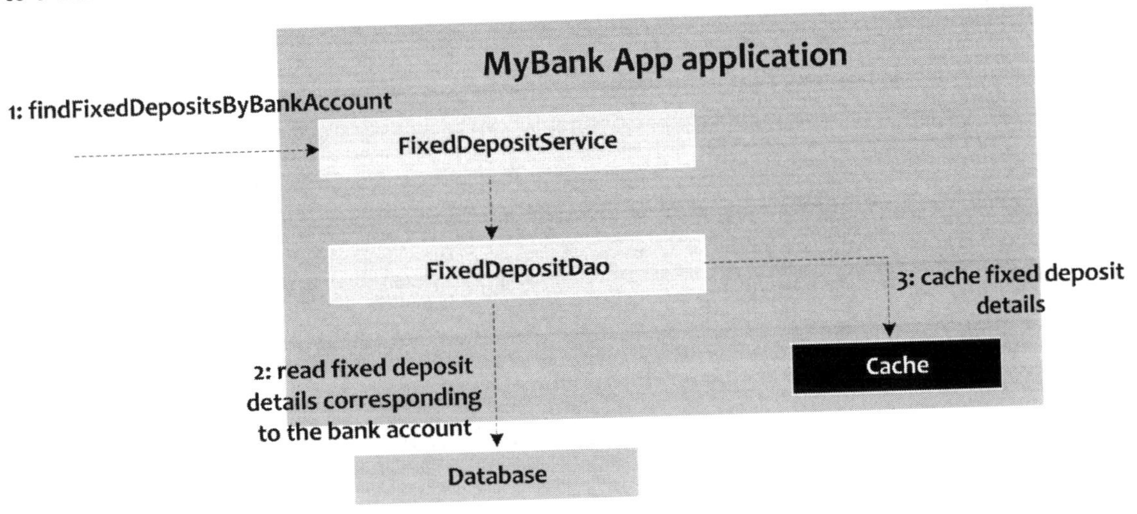

Figure 8-2 MyBank application behavior when a customer requests for the details of all his fixed deposits

The above figure shows that when FixedDepositService's findFixedDepositsByBankAccount method is invoked, the fixed deposit information is fetched from the database and cached into memory. If you can FixedDepositService's findFixedDepositsByBankAccount again, the fixed deposit information is fetched from the cache and not from the database.

Let's now look at how Spring is used in the MyBank application to send JMS messages to JMS destinations configured in ActiveMQ.

IMPORT **chapter 8/ch08-bankapp** (To get the most of out of this chapter, install MySQL database and execute the spring_bank_app_db.sql SQL script contained in the sql folder of ch08-bankapp project. Executing spring_bank_app_db.sql script creates SPRING_BANK_APP_DB database and adds BANK_ACCOUNT_DETAILS and FIXED_DEPOSIT_DETAILS tables to the SPRING_BANK_APP_DB database. Modify the src/main/resources/META-INF/spring/database.properties to point to your MySQL installation. To get the email feature working, modify src/main/resources/META-INF/spring/email.properties to specify the email server and the email account to use for sending emails. Modify the BankApp class to specify the email id of the customer to whom the emails are sent)

8-3 Sending JMS messages

Spring simplifies interaction with JMS providers by providing a layer of abstraction on top of JMS API. In the context of MyBank application, this section shows how to *synchronously* and *asynchronously* send and receive messages from an ActiveMQ broker using Spring. For the sake of simplicity, the ActiveMQ broker is configured to run in *embedded* mode in ch08-bankapp project.

> In Spring, JMS support classes are defined in spring-jms JAR file; therefore, you must define that your application depends on spring-jms JAR file to use Spring's support for JMS.

Configuring ActiveMQ broker to run in embedded mode

An embedded ActiveMQ broker runs in the *same* JVM as the application. You can use ActiveMQ's XML schema to configure an embedded ActiveMQ broker in a Spring application. The following example listing shows how ActiveMQ's XML schema is used to configure an embedded ActiveMQ broker in MyBank application:

Example listing 8-1 – applicationContext.xml – embedded ActiveMQ broker configuration
Project – ch08-bankapp
Source location - src/main/resources/META-INF/spring

```
<beans .....
  xmlns:amq="http://activemq.apache.org/schema/core"
  xsi:schemaLocation=".....http://activemq.apache.org/schema/core
```

```
    http://activemq.apache.org/schema/core/activemq-core-5.7.0.xsd.....">

  <amq:broker>
    <amq:transportConnectors>
      <amq:transportConnector uri="tcp://localhost:61616" />
    </amq:transportConnectors>
  </amq:broker>
  .....
</beans>
```

In the above example listing, the amq namespace refers to ActiveMQ's XML schema (activemq-core-5.7.0.xsd) that allows you to configure an embedded ActiveMQ broker. The <broker> element configures an embedded ActiveMQ broker with name localhost. The <transportConnectors> element specifies the transport connectors on which the embedded ActiveMQ broker allows clients to connect. In the above example listing, the <transportConnector> sub-element of <transportConnectors> specifies that clients can connect to the embedded ActiveMQ broker on port number 61616 using a TCP socket.

Let's now look at how to configure a JMS ConnectionFactory for creating connections to the embedded ActiveMQ instance.

Configuring a JMS ConnectionFactory

The following example listing shows how a JMS ConnectionFactory is configured in the application context XML file:

Example listing 8-2 – applicationContext.xml – JMS ConnectionFactory configuration
Project – ch08-bankapp
Source location - src/main/resources/META-INF/spring

```
<beans .....
  xmlns:amq="http://activemq.apache.org/schema/core"
  xsi:schemaLocation=".....http://activemq.apache.org/schema/core
    http://activemq.apache.org/schema/core/activemq-core-5.7.0.xsd.....">
  .....
  <amq:connectionFactory brokerURL="vm://localhost" id="jmsFactory" />

  <bean class="org.springframework.jms.connection.CachingConnectionFactory"
    id="cachingConnectionFactory">
    <property name="targetConnectionFactory" ref="jmsFactory" />
  </bean>
  .....
</beans>
```

In the above example listing, the <connectionFactory> element of amq schema creates a JMS ConnectionFactory instance that is used for creating connections to the embedded ActiveMQ instance (refer example listing 8-1). The brokerUrl attribute specifies the URL for connecting to the ActiveMQ broker. As we are using embedded ActiveMQ broker, the brokerUrl specifies that VM protocol (specified by vm://) is used to connect to the ActiveMQ broker instance.

Spring's CachingConnectionFactory is an adapter for the JMS ConnectionFactory (specified by the targetConnectionFactory property), that provides the additional feature of caching instances of JMS *Session*, MessageProducer and MessageConsumer.

Let's now look at how to use Spring's JmsTemplate class to send JMS messages.

Sending JMS messages using JmsTemplate

Spring's JmsTemplate class simplifies *synchronously* sending and receiving JMS messages. For the purpose of this chapter, we'll only look at how to send JMS messages using JmsTemplate. Like TransactionTemplate (refer section 7-5 of chapter 7) and JdbcTemplate (refer section 7-3 of chapter 7) classes, the JmsTemplate class provides a layer of abstraction so that you don't have to deal with lower-level JMS API.

The following example listing shows how the JmsTemplate class is configured in the application context XML file of MyBank application to send messages to the embedded ActiveMQ instance:

Example listing 8-3 – applicationContext.xml –JmsTemplate configuration
Project – ch08-bankapp
Source location - src/main/resources/META-INF/spring

```
<beans .....
    xmlns:amq="http://activemq.apache.org/schema/core"
   xsi:schemaLocation=".....http://activemq.apache.org/schema/core
     http://activemq.apache.org/schema/core/activemq-core-5.7.0.xsd.....">
   .....
   <bean class="org.springframework.jms.core.JmsTemplate" id="jmsTemplate">
      <property name="connectionFactory" ref="cachingConnectionFactory" />
      <property name="defaultDestination" ref="FixedDepositDestination" />
   </bean>

   <amq:queue id="FixedDepositDestination" physicalName="aQueueDestination" />
   <amq:queue id="emailQueueDestination" physicalName="emailQueueDestination" />
   .....
</beans>
```

JmsTemplate's connectionFactory property specifies the JMS ConnectionFactory that is used for creating a connection with the JMS provider. JmsTemplate's defaultDestination property refers to the default JMS destination to which the JmsTemplate sends JMS messages. In the above example listing, connectionFactory property refers to the CachingConnectionFactory instance (refer example listing 8-2), and defaultDestination property refers to the JMS queue destination created by amq schema's <queue> element.

The amq schema's <queue> element creates a JMS queue destination in ActiveMQ. In example listing 8-3, the first <queue> element creates a JMS queue destination named aQueueDestination in ActiveMQ, and the second <queue> element creates a JMS queue destination named emailQueueDestination in ActiveMQ. The physicalName attribute refers to the name with which the JMS queue destination is created in ActiveMQ, and id attribute refers to the name with which the JMS queue destination is accessed by other beans in the Spring container. In example listing 8-3, JmsTemplate's defaultDestination property refers to the id attribute of the <queue> element that creates the aQueueDestination JMS destination; therefore, the aQueueDestination is the default JMS destination to which the JmsTemplate instance sends JMS messages.

JMS Session used by JmsTemplate has the acknowledgement mode set to *auto-acknowledge* and is *not transacted* in nature. If you want JmsTemplate to use *transacted* Sessions, set JmsTemplate's transacted property to true. In case of transacted Sessions, a new transaction begins when the Session is created by the application, or when the transaction is committed or rolled back. This means that a transacted JMS Session is *always* associated with a transaction. You can use a transacted JMS Session to send and receive JMS messages within a transaction. If you use JmsTemplate with Spring's JmsTransactionManager, the JmsTemplate instance will always get a transacted JMS Session.

Let's now look at how JmsTransactionManager is configured, and JMS messages are sent by JmsTemplate within a transaction.

Sending JMS messages within a transaction

In chapter 7, we saw that Spring provides a couple of PlatformTransactionManager implementations that provide resource-specific transaction management. In your JMS applications, you can use Spring's JmsTransactionManager (an implementation of PlatformTransactionManager) class for managing transactions for a single JMS ConnectionFactory. As JmsTransactionManager implements PlatformTransactionManager, you can use TransactionTemplate for programmatically managing JMS transactions or you can use @Transactional annotation for declaratively managing JMS transactions.

The following example listing shows the configuration of Spring's JmsTransactionManager in application context XML file:

Example listing 8-4 – applicationContext.xml – JmsTransactionManager configuration
Project – ch08-bankapp
Source location - src/main/resources/META-INF/spring

```
<bean id="jmsTxManager" class="org.springframework.jms.connection.JmsTransactionManager">
    <property name="connectionFactory" ref="cachingConnectionFactory" />
</bean>
```

JmsTransactionManager's connectionFactory property specifies reference to the JMS ConnectionFactory for which the JmsTransactionManager manages transactions. In the above example listing, reference to Spring's CachingConnectionFactory bean (refer example listing 8-2) is specified as the value for connectionFactory property. As the CachingConnectionFactory caches JMS Sessions, using CachingConnectionFactory with JmsTransactionManager results in reduced utilization of resources.

If you want to programmatically manage JMS transactions using TransactionTemplate class, configure the TransactionTemplate class in the application context XML file. If you want to use declarative transaction management, use <annotation-driven> element of Spring's tx schema.

The following example listing shows the FixedDepositServiceImpl class that makes use of JmsTemplate to send messages to the embedded ActiveMQ broker:

Example listing 8-5 – FixedDepositServiceImpl class – send JMS messages using JmsTemplate
Project – ch08-bankapp
Source location - src/main/java/sample/spring/chapter08/bankapp/service

```
package sample.spring.chapter08.bankapp.service;

import javax.jms.*;
import org.springframework.jms.core.JmsTemplate;
import org.springframework.jms.core.MessageCreator;

@Service(value = "FixedDepositService")
public class FixedDepositServiceImpl implements FixedDepositService {
  @Autowired
  private JmsTemplate jmsTemplate;
  .....
  @Override
  @Transactional("jmsTxManager")
  public void createFixedDeposit(final FixedDepositDetails fixedDepositDetails)throws Exception {

    jmsTemplate.send("emailQueueDestination", new MessageCreator() {
      public Message createMessage(Session session) throws JMSException {
        TextMessage textMessage = session.createTextMessage();
```

```
            textMessage.setText(fixedDepositDetails.getEmail());
            return textMessage;
        }
    });
    // --this JMS message goes to the default destination configured for the JmsTemplate
    jmsTemplate.send(new MessageCreator() {
        public Message createMessage(Session session) throws JMSException {
            ObjectMessage objectMessage = session.createObjectMessage();
            objectMessage.setObject(fixedDepositDetails);
            return objectMessage;
        }
    });
  }
  .....
}
```

The above example listing shows that JmsTemplate's send method is used to send messages to emailQueueDestination and aQueueDestination JMS destinations. Refer example listing 8-3 to see how these JMS destinations are configured in the application context XML file. The name of the JMS destination passed to JmsTemplate's send method is resolved to the actual JMS Destination object by Spring's DynamicDestinationResolver instance (an implementation of Spring's DestinationResolver interface). If you have configured JMS destinations in the application context XML file using amq schema's <queue> (or <topic>) element, the JMS destination name passed to the JmsTemplate's send message is the value of id attribute of the <queue> (or <topic>) element corresponding to the JMS destination to which you want to send messages.

In example listing 8-5, the FixedDepositServiceImpl's createFixedDeposit method is annotated with @Transactional("jmsTxManager"), which means that the createFixedDeposit method executes within a transaction, and the transaction is managed by jmsTxManager transaction manager (refer example listing 8-4 to see how jmsTxManager is configured). JmsTemplate's send method accepts the name of the JMS destination (to which the JMS message is to be sent) and a MessageCreator instance. If you don't specify the JMS destination, the send method sends the JMS message to the *default* destination that you configured for the JmsTemplate using defaultDestination property (refer example listing 8-3).

In MessageCreator's createMessage method you create the JMS message that you want to send. You don't need to explicitly handle checked exceptions thrown by JMS API, as they are taken care by the JmsTemplate itself. Example listing 8-5 shows that if you are using JmsTemplate, you don't need to explicitly obtain Connection from ConnectionFactory, create Session from Connection, and so on, for sending JMS messages. So, using JmsTemplate hides the lower-level JMS API details from the developers.

In example listing 8-5, the TextMessage and ObjectMessage instances represent JMS messages. Both, TextMessage and ObjectMessage classes implement javax.jms.Message interface. In the MyBank application, the TextMessage instance has been used to send the email id (a simple string value) of the customer requesting to open a fixed deposit, and the ObjectMessage instance has been used to send FixedDepositDetails object (a Serializable object) that contains fixed deposit information. As the FixedDepositServiceImpl's createFixedDeposit method executes within a JMS transaction, either both the messages are sent to the ActiveMQ instance or none.

Instead of using @Transactional annotation, you can programmatically manage JMS transactions by using the TransactionTemplate class (refer section 7-5 of chapter 7). The following example listing shows how you can configure the TransactionTemplate class to use JmsTransactionManager for transaction management:

Example listing 8-6 – TransactionTemplate configuration

```
<bean id="jmsTxManager"
    class="org.springframework.jms.connection.JmsTransactionManager">
    <property name="connectionFactory" ref="cachingConnectionFactory" />
</bean>

<bean id="transactionTemplate"
    class="org.springframework.transaction.support.TransactionTemplate">
    <property name="transactionManager" ref="jmsTxManager" />
</bean>
```

In the above example listing, TransactionTemplate's transactionManager property refers to the JmsTransactionManager bean.

Once you have configured the TransactionTemplate class, you can use it to manage JMS transactions. The following example listing shows a variant of FixedDepositServiceImpl's createFixedDeposit method that uses TransactionTemplate for managing JMS transactions:

Example listing 8-7 – Programmatically managing JMS transactions using TransactionTemplate

```
package sample.spring.chapter08.bankapp.service;

import javax.jms.*;
import org.springframework.jms.core.JmsTemplate;
import org.springframework.jms.core.MessageCreator;

@Service(value = "FixedDepositService")
public class FixedDepositServiceImpl implements FixedDepositService {
  @Autowired
```

```
private JmsTemplate jmsTemplate;

@Autowired
private TransactionTemplate transactionTemplate;
.....
public void createFixedDeposit(final FixedDepositDetails fixedDepositDetails)throws Exception {

    transactionTemplate.execute(new TransactionCallbackWithoutResult() {
      protected void doInTransactionWithoutResult(TransactionStatus status) {
            jmsTemplate.send("emailQueueDestination", new MessageCreator() { ..... });
            jmsTemplate.send(new MessageCreator() { ..... });
      }
    });
  }
  .....
}
```

The above example listing shows that JMS messages are sent from within the doInTransaction method of TransactionCallbackWithoutResult class so that they are in the same JMS transaction. This is similar to how we programmatically managed JDBC transactions (refer section 7-5 of chapter 7) using TransactionTemplate.

So far we have seen examples in which JmsTemplate is used to send messages to a *pre-configured* JMS destination. Let's now look at how to configure JmsTemplate class if an application uses dynamic JMS destinations.

Dynamic JMS destinations and JmsTemplate configuration

If your application uses dynamic JMS destinations (that is, JMS destinations are created by the application at runtime), you must specify the JMS destination type (queue or topic) using pubSubDomain property of JmsTemplate. The pubSubDomain property is used to determine the JMS destination type to which the JmsTemplate sends JMS messages. If you don't specify the pubSubDomain property, by default JMS queue is assumed to be the destination type.

The following example listing shows the JmsTemplate that sends messages to a dynamically created JMS topic:

Example listing 8-8 – Using JmsTemplate for sending messages to dynamic JMS topic destinations

```
-------------------------- applicationContext.xml ---------------------

  <bean class="org.springframework.jms.core.JmsTemplate" id="jmsTemplate">
      <property name="connectionFactory" ref="cachingConnectionFactory" />
```

```
    <property name="defaultDestination" ref="FixedDepositDestination" />
    <property name="pubSubDomain" value="true" />
</bean>

------------------ Dynamic topic creation ------------------

jmsTemplate.send("dynamicTopic", new MessageCreator() {
  public Message createMessage(Session session) throws JMSException {
     session.createTopic("dynamicTopic");
     ObjectMessage objectMessage = session.createObjectMessage();
     objectMessage.setObject(someObject);
     return objectMessage;
  }
});
```

In the above example listing, JmsTemplate's pubSubDomain property is set to true, which means that when dynamic destinations are used, Spring resolves a dynamic destination's name to a JMS *topic*. Notice that the name of the JMS destination passed to JmsTemplate's send method is dynamicTopic, and a JMS topic with the same name is created by MessageCreator's createMessage method. As no dynamicTopic JMS destination is configured in the application context XML file, Spring doesn't know whether the dynamicTopic JMS destination is a queue or a topic. As JmsTemplate's pubSubDomain property is set to true, Spring's DynamicDestinationResolver resolves dynamicTopic JMS destination name to the dynamicTopic JMS topic created at runtime by MessageCreator's createMessage method. If you had *not* set JmsTemplate's pubSubDomain property, Spring's DynamicDestinationResolver would have tried resolving dynamicTopic JMS destination name to a dynamicTopic JMS *queue*.

Let's now look at how JmsTemplate simplifies sending Java objects as JMS messages.

JmsTemplate and message conversion

JmsTemplate defines multiple convertAndSend methods that convert and send a Java object as a JMS message. By default, JmsTemplate is configured with a SimpleMessageConverter instance (an implementation of Spring's MessageConverter interface) that converts Java objects to JMS messages, and vice versa.

MessageConverter interface defines the following methods:

- Object toMessage(Object object, Session session) – converts the Java object (represented by object argument) to a JMS Message using the supplied JMS Session (represented by session argument)

- Object fromMessage(Message message) - converts Message argument to Java object

Spring's SimpleMessageConverter class provides conversion between String and JMS TextMessage, byte[] and JMS BytesMessage, Map and JMS MapMessage, and Serializable object and JMS ObjectMessage. If you want to modify the JMS Message created by JmsTemplate's convertAndSend method, you can use a MessagePostProcessor implementation to make modifications.

The following example listing shows a scenario in which a MessagePostProcessor implementation is used to modify the JMS message created by JmsTemplate's convertAndSend method:

Example listing 8-9 – JmsTemplate's convertAndSend method usage

```
jmsTemplate.convertAndSend("aDestination", "Hello, World !!",
    new MessagePostProcessor() {
      public Message postProcessMessage(Message message)throws JMSException {
        message.setBooleanProperty("printOnConsole", true);
        return message;
      }
    });
```

In the above example listing, 'Hello, World !!' string is passed to the convertAndSend method. The convertAndSend method creates a JMS TextMessage instance and makes it available to the MessagePostProcessor implementation to perform any post processing of the message before it is sent. In the above example listing, MessagePostProcessor's postProcessMessage method sets a printOnConsole property on the JMS message before it is sent to aDestination.

So far we have seen how to send JMS messages to JMS destinations using JmsTemplate. Let's now look at how to receive JMS messages from JMS destinations using JmsTemplate and Spring's *message listener containers*.

8-4 Receiving JMS messages

You can receive JMS messages *synchronously* using JmsTemplate and *asynchronously* using Spring's message listener containers.

Synchronously receiving JMS messages using JmsTemplate

JmsTemplate defines multiple receive methods that you can use to *synchronously* receive JMS messages. It is important to note that call to JmsTemplate's receive method causes the calling thread to block until a JMS message is obtained from the JMS destination. To ensure that the calling thread is not blocked indefinitely, you must specify an appropriate value for JmsTemplate's receiveTimeout property. The receiveTimeout property specifies the amount of time (in milliseconds) the calling thread should wait before giving up.

JmsTemplate also defines multiple receiveAndConvert methods that automatically convert the received JMS message to a Java object. By default, JmsTemplate uses SimpleMessageConverter for performing conversions.

Asynchronously receiving JMS messages using message listener containers

You can use Spring's message listener containers to *asynchronously* receive JMS messages. A message listener container takes care of transaction and resource management aspects, so that you can focus on writing the message processing logic.

A message listener container receives messages from JMS destinations and dispatches them to JMS MessageListener implementations for processing. The following example listing shows how to configure a message listener container using <listener-container> element of Spring's jms schema:

Example listing 8-10 – applicationContext.xml – message listener container configuration
Project – ch08-bankapp
Source location - src/main/resources/META-INF/spring

```
<beans ..... xmlns:jms="http://www.springframework.org/schema/jms"
   xsi:schemaLocation=".....
      http://www.springframework.org/schema/jms
      http://www.springframework.org/schema/jms/spring-jms-4.0.xsd">
   .....
   <jms:listener-container connection-factory="cachingConnectionFactory"
     destination-type="queue"  transaction-manager="jmsTxManager">

        <jms:listener destination="aQueueDestination" ref="FixedDepositMessageListener" />
        <jms:listener destination="emailQueueDestination" ref="emailMessageListener" />
   </jms:listener-container>

   <bean class="sample.spring.chapter08.bankapp.jms.EmailMessageListener"
      id="emailMessageListener" />

   <bean class="sample.spring.chapter08.bankapp.jms.FixedDepositMessageListener"
      id="FixedDepositMessageListener" />
   .....
</beans>
```

In the above example listing, Spring's jms schema is included so that its elements are available in the application context XML file. The <listener-container> element configures a message listener container for each of the MessageListener implementations defined by <listener> sub-elements. The connection-factory attribute specifies reference to the JMS ConnectionFactory bean that the message listener container uses to obtain connections to the

JMS provider. As we are using Spring's CachingConnectionFactory in the MyBank application, the connection-factory attribute refers to the cachingConnectionFactory bean defined in the application context XML file of MyBank application (refer example listing 8-2). The destination-type attribute specifies the JMS destination type with which the message listener container is associated with. The possible values that the destination-type attribute can accept are: queue, topic and durableTopic.

The transaction-manager attribute of <listener-container> element specifies a PlatformTransactionManager implementation that ensures JMS message reception and message processing by MessageListener happens within a transaction. In the above example listing, the value of transaction-manager attribute refers to the JmsTransactionManager implementation (refer example listing 8-4) configured for the MyBank application. If a MessageListener implementation interacts with other transactional resources also, consider using Spring's JtaTransactionManager instead of JmsTransactionManager. In a standalone application, you can use embedded transaction managers, like Atomikos (http://www.atomikos.com/), to perform JTA transactions in your application.

> By default, the <listener-container> element creates an instance of Spring's DefaultMessageListenerContainer class corresponding to each JMS MessageListener implementation specified by <listener> sub-elements.

Each <listener> element specifies a JMS MessageListener implementation which is *asynchronously* invoked by the message listener container. The <listener> element's destination attribute specifies the JMS destination name from which MessageListener implementation receives its messages via the message listener container. The <listener> element's ref attribute specifies reference to the MessageListener implementation responsible for processing the JMS messages received from the destination. Example listing 8-10 shows that the FixedDepositMessageListener (a MessageListener implementation) is responsible for processing messages received from aQueueDestination destination, and the EmailMessageListener (a MessageListener implementation) is responsible for processing messages received from emailQueueDestination destination.

MessageListener interface defines an onMessage method that is *asynchronously* invoked by the message listener container. The message listener container passes the JMS Message received from the JMS destination to the onMessage method. The onMessage method is responsible for processing the received JMS message. The following example listing shows implementation of MyBank application's FixedDepositMessageListener that is responsible for retrieving FixedDepositDetails object from the JMS Message, and then saving the fixed deposit information contained in the FixedDepositDetails object into the database:

Example listing 8-11 – FixedDepositMessageListener class – processing JMS message
Project – ch08-bankapp
Source location - src/main/java/sample/spring/chapter08/bankapp/jms

```
package sample.spring.chapter08.bankapp.jms;

import javax.jms.MessageListener;
import javax.jms.ObjectMessage;
import sample.spring.chapter08.bankapp.domain.FixedDepositDetails;
.....
public class FixedDepositMessageListener implements MessageListener {
  @Autowired
  @Qualifier(value = "FixedDepositDao")
  private FixedDepositDao myFixedDepositDao;

  @Autowired
  private BankAccountDao bankAccountDao;

  @Transactional
   public int createFixedDeposit(FixedDepositDetails fixedDepositDetails) {
    bankAccountDao.subtractFromAccount(fixedDepositDetails.getBankAccountId(),
       fixedDepositDetails.getFixedDepositAmount());
    return myFixedDepositDao.createFixedDeposit(fixedDepositDetails);
  }

  @Override
  public void onMessage(Message message) {
    ObjectMessage objectMessage = (ObjectMessage) message;
    FixedDepositDetails fixedDepositDetails = null;
    try {
      fixedDepositDetails = (FixedDepositDetails) objectMessage.getObject();
    } catch (JMSException e) {
      e.printStackTrace();
    }
    if (fixedDepositDetails != null) {
      createFixedDeposit(fixedDepositDetails);
    }
  }
}
```

In the above example listing, FixedDepositMessageListener's onMessage method obtains the FixedDepositDetails object from the JMS message and saves the fixed deposit details into the database. FixedDepositMessageListener's createFixedDeposit method is responsible for saving the fixed deposit information into the database. As the createFixedDeposit method is annotated with @Transactional annotation, it is executed under the transaction managed by DataSourceTransactionManager (refer the applicationContext.xml file of ch08-bankapp project). The message listener container receives the JMS message and executes FixedDepositMessageListener's onMessage method under the transaction managed by JmsTransactionManager (refer example listing 8-10).

As onMessage and createFixedDeposit methods execute under different transaction managers, the database update is *not* rolled back if the JMS transaction fails for some reason, and the JMS message is *not* redelivered to the MessageListener if the database update fails for some reason. If you want JMS message reception (and processing) and the database update to be part of the same transaction, you should use JTA transactions.

In this section, we looked at how to send and receive JMS messages using Spring. Let's now look at how Spring simplifies sending emails.

8-5 Sending emails

Spring simplifies sending emails from an application by providing a layer of abstraction on top of JavaMail API. Spring takes care of resource management and exception handling aspects, so that you can focus on writing the necessary logic required to prepare the email message.

To send emails using Spring, you first need to configure Spring's JavaMailSenderImpl class in your application context XML file. The JavaMailSenderImpl class acts as a wrapper around JavaMail API. The following example listing shows how JavaMailSenderImpl class is configured in MyBank application:

Example listing 8-12 – applicationContext.xml – JavaMailSenderImpl class configuration
Project – ch08-bankapp
Source location - src/main/resources/META-INF/spring

```
<bean id="mailSender" class="org.springframework.mail.javamail.JavaMailSenderImpl">
   <property name="host" value="${email.host}" />
   <property name="protocol" value="${email.protocol}" />
   .....
   <property name="javaMailProperties">
      <props>
         <prop key="mail.smtp.auth">true</prop>
         <prop key="mail.smtp.starttls.enable">true</prop>
      </props>
   </property>
</bean>
```

JavaMailSenderImpl class defines properties, like host, port, protocol, and so on, that provide information about the mail server. The javaMailProperties property specifies configuration information that is used by JavaMailSenderImpl instance for creating a JavaMail Session object. The mail.smtp.auth property value is set to true, which means that SMTP (Simple Mail Transfer Protocol) is used for authentication with the mail server. The mail.smtp.starttls.enable property value is set to true, which means TLS-protected connection is used for authenticating with the mail server.

Example listing 8-12 shows that the values of some of the properties of JavaMailSenderImpl class are specified using property placeholders. For instance, host property value is specified as ${email.host} and protocol property value as ${email.protocol}. The value of these property placeholders comes from email.properties file located in src/main/resources/META-INF/spring directory. The following example listing shows the contents of email.properties file:

Example listing 8-13 – email.properties
Project – ch08-bankapp
Source location - src/main/resources/META-INF/spring

```
email.host=smtp.gmail.com
email.port=587
email.protocol=smtp
email.username=<enter-email-id>
email.password=<enter-email-password>
```

The above example listing shows that email.properties file contains mail server information, communication protocol information, and the mail account to use for connecting to the mail server. The properties specified in the email.properties file are used to configure the JavaMailSenderImpl instance (refer example listing 8-12).

> The classes that provide abstraction on top of JavaMail API are defined in spring-context-support JAR file. So, to use Spring's support for sending emails, you must define that your application depends on spring-context-support JAR file.

Spring's SimpleMailMessage class represents a simple email message. SimpleMailMessage defines properties, like to, cc, subject, text, and so on, that you can set to construct the email message that you want to send from your application.

The following example listing shows the MyBank's application context XML file that configures two SimpleMailMessage instances corresponding to the two email messages that we send from the MyBank application:

Example listing 8-14 – applicationContext.xml – SimpleMailMessage configuration
Project – ch08-bankapp
Source location - src/main/resources/META-INF/spring

```
<bean class="org.springframework.mail.SimpleMailMessage" id="requestReceivedTemplate">
   <property name="subject" value="${email.subject.request.received}" />
   <property name="text" value="${email.text.request.received}" />
</bean>

<bean class="org.springframework.mail.SimpleMailMessage" id="requestProcessedTemplate">
   <property name="subject" value="${email.subject.request.processed}" />
   <property name="text" value="${email.text.request.processed}" />
</bean>
```

In the above example listing, the requestReceivedTemplate bean represents the email message that is sent to the customer informing that the request for opening a fixed deposit has been received, and requestProcessedTemplate bean represents the email message that is sent to the customer informing that the request for opening the fixed deposit has been successfully processed. SimpleMailMessage's subject property specifies the subject line of the email, and text property specifies the body of the email. The values for these properties are defined in the emailtemplate.properties file, as shown in the following example listing:

Example listing 8-15 – emailtemplate.properties
Project – ch08-bankapp
Source location - src/main/resources/META-INF/spring

```
email.subject.request.received=Fixed deposit request received
email.text.request.received=Your request for creating the fixed deposit has been received

email.subject.request.processed=Fixed deposit request processed
email.text.request.processed=Your request for creating the fixed deposit has been processed
```

We have so far seen how to configure JavaMailSenderImpl and SimpleMailMessage classes in the application context XML file. Let's now look at how to send email messages.

The following example listing shows the MyBank application's EmailMessageListener class (a JMS MessageListener implementation) that retrieves customer's email address from the JMS message and sends an email to the customer informing that the request for opening a fixed deposit has been received:

Example listing 8-16 – EmailMessageListener class – sending emails using MailSender
Project – ch08-bankapp
Source location - src/main/java/sample/spring/chapter08/bankapp/jms

```
package sample.spring.chapter08.bankapp.jms;

import org.springframework.mail.MailSender;
import org.springframework.mail.SimpleMailMessage;
.....
public class EmailMessageListener implements MessageListener {
  @Autowired
  private transient MailSender mailSender;

  @Autowired
  @Qualifier("requestReceivedTemplate")
  private transient SimpleMailMessage simpleMailMessage;

  public void sendEmail() {
    mailSender.send(simpleMailMessage);
  }

  public void onMessage(Message message) {
    TextMessage textMessage = (TextMessage) message;
    try {
      simpleMailMessage.setTo(textMessage.getText());
    } catch (Exception e) {
      e.printStackTrace();
    }
    sendEmail();
  }
}
```

The above example listing shows that the MailSender's send method sends the email message represented by the SimpleMailMessage instance. As JavaMailSenderImpl class implements Spring's MailSender interface, the JavaMailSenderImpl instance (refer example listing 8-12) is autowired into the EmailMessageListener instance. SimpleMailMessage instance named requestReceivedTemplate (refer example listing 8-14) is also autowired into the EmailMessageListener instance. As SimpleMailMessage's to property identifies the email recipient, the onMessage method retrieves the email id of the customer from the JMS message and sets it as the value of to property.

Spring's MailSender interface represents a generic interface that is independent of JavaMail API, and is suited for sending simple email messages. Spring's JavaMailSender interface (a sub-interface of MailSender) is dependent on JavaMail API, and defines the functionality for sending MIME messages. A MIME message is used if you want to send emails containing inline images, attachments, and so on. A MIME message is represented by a MimeMessage class in JavaMail API. Spring provides a MimeMessageHelper class and a MimeMessagePreparator callback interface that you can use to create and populate a MimeMessage instance.

The following example listing shows the MyBank application's FixedDepositProcessorJob class that subtracts the fixed deposit amount from the customer's bank account and sends an email to the customer informing that the request for opening the fixed deposit has been processed:

Example listing 8-17 – FixedDepositProcessorJob class – JavaMailSender usage
Project – ch08-bankapp
Source location - src/main/java/sample/spring/chapter08/bankapp/job

```
package sample.spring.chapter08.bankapp.job;

import javax.mail.internet.MimeMessage;
import org.springframework.mail.javamail.JavaMailSender;

public class FixedDepositProcessorJob {
  .....
  @Autowired
  private transient JavaMailSender mailSender;

  @Autowired
  @Qualifier("requestProcessedTemplate")
  private transient SimpleMailMessage simpleMailMessage;

  private List<FixedDepositDetails> getInactiveFixedDeposits() {
    return myFixedDepositDao.getInactiveFixedDeposits();
  }

  public void sendEmail() throws AddressException, MessagingException {
    List<FixedDepositDetails> inactiveFixedDeposits = getInactiveFixedDeposits();

    for (FixedDepositDetails fixedDeposit : inactiveFixedDeposits) {
      MimeMessage mimeMessage = mailSender.createMimeMessage();
      MimeMessageHelper mimeMessageHelper = new MimeMessageHelper(mimeMessage);
      mimeMessageHelper.setTo(fixedDeposit.getEmail());
      mimeMessageHelper.setSubject(simpleMailMessage.getSubject());
      mimeMessageHelper.setText(simpleMailMessage.getText());
      mailSender.send(mimeMessage);
    }
```

```
        myFixedDepositDao.setFixedDepositsAsActive(inactiveFixedDeposits);
    }
}
```

The above example listing shows that JavaMailSender's send method is used to send a MIME message. As JavaMailSenderImpl instance implements Spring's JavaMailSender interface, JavaMailSenderImpl instance (refer example listing 8-12) is autowired into the FixedDepositProcessorJob instance. SimpleMailMessage instance named requestProcessedTemplate (refer example listing 8-14) is also autowired into the FixedDepositProcessorJob instance. The mailSender instance variable is defined of type JavaMailSender (and not MailSender) because the FixedDepositProcessorJob creates and sends MIME messages. FixedDepositProcessorJob's sendEmail method creates an instance of a MimeMessage using JavaMailSender's createMimeMessage method. Spring's MimeMessageHelper is then used to populate the MimeMessage instance with to, subject and text properties.

The following example listing shows how the FixedDepositProcessorJob's sendEmail method can be written using Spring's MimeMessagePreparator callback interface instead of MimeMessageHelper:

Example listing 8-18 – MimeMessagePreparator usage

```
import javax.mail.Message;
import javax.mail.internet.InternetAddress;
import org.springframework.mail.javamail.MimeMessagePreparator;

public class FixedDepositProcessorJob {
  .....
  public void sendEmail_() throws AddressException, MessagingException {
    List<FixedDepositDetails> inactiveFixedDeposits = getInactiveFixedDeposits();
    for (final FixedDepositDetails fixedDeposit : inactiveFixedDeposits) {
      mailSender.send(new MimeMessagePreparator() {
        @Override
        public void prepare(MimeMessage mimeMessage) throws Exception {
          mimeMessage.setRecipient(Message.RecipientType.TO,
              new InternetAddress(fixedDeposit.getEmail()));
          mimeMessage.setSubject(simpleMailMessage.getText());
          mimeMessage.setText(simpleMailMessage.getText());
        }
      });
    }
    myFixedDepositDao.setFixedDepositsAsActive(inactiveFixedDeposits);
  }
}
```

The above example shows that a MimeMessagePreparator instance is passed to JavaMailSender's send method to prepare a MimeMessage instance for sending. MimeMessagePreparator's prepare method provides a new instance of MimeMessage that you need to populate. In the above example listing, notice that setting the MimeMessage's recipient property requires you to deal with lower-level JavaMail API. In example listing 8-17, MimeMessageHelper's setTo method accepted an email id of the recipient as a string argument to set the MimeMessage's recipient property. For this reason, you should consider using MimeMessageHelper to populate the MimeMessage instance passed to the prepare method of MimeMessagePreparator.

Let's now look at how you can use Spring to execute a task asynchronously, and to schedule execution of a task in the future.

8-6 Task scheduling and asynchronous execution

You can asynchronously execute java.lang.Runnable tasks using Spring's TaskExecutor, and you can schedule execution of java.lang.Runnable tasks using Spring's TaskScheduler. Instead of directly using TaskExecutor and TaskScheduler, you can use Spring's @Async and @Scheduled annotations to execute a method asynchronously and to schedule execution of a method, respectively.

Let's first look at TaskExecutor and TaskScheduler interfaces.

TaskExecutor interface

Java 5 introduced the concept of *executors* for executing java.lang.Runnable tasks. An executor implements java.util.concurrent.Executor interface that defines a single method, execute(Runnable runnable). Spring's TaskExecutor extends java.util.concurrent.Executor interface. Spring also provides a couple of TaskExecutor implementations that you can choose from depending upon your application's requirements. Depending upon the TaskExecutor implementation you choose, the Runnable task may be executed synchronously or asynchronously, using a thread pool or CommonJ, and so on. Some of the TaskExecutor implementations provided by Spring are: ThreadPoolTaskExecutor (asynchronously executes tasks using a thread from a thread pool), SyncTaskExecutor (executes tasks synchronously) and SimpleAsyncTaskExecutor (asynchronously executes each task in a new thread).

ThreadPoolTaskExecutor is the most commonly used TaskExecutor implementation that uses Java 5's ThreadPoolExecutor to execute tasks. The following example listing shows how to configure a ThreadPoolTaskExecutor instance in the application context XML file:

Example listing 8-19 –ThreadPoolTaskExecutor configuration

```
<bean id="myTaskExecutor"
    class="org.springframework.scheduling.concurrent.ThreadPoolTaskExecutor">
  <property name="corePoolSize" value="5" />
```

```
    <property name="maxPoolSize" value="10" />
    <property name="queueCapacity" value="15" />
    <property name="rejectedExecutionHandler" ref="abortPolicy"/>
</bean>

<bean id="abortPolicy" class="java.util.concurrent.ThreadPoolExecutor.AbortPolicy"/>
```

The corePoolSize property specifies the minimum number of threads in the thread pool. The maxPoolSize property specifies the maximum number of threads that can be accommodated in the thread pool. The queueCapacity property specifies the maximum number of tasks that can wait in the queue if all the threads in the thread pool are busy executing tasks. The rejectedExecutionHandler property specifies a handler for tasks rejected by the ThreadPoolTaskExecutor. A task is rejected by ThreadPoolTaskExecutor if the queue is full and there is no thread available in the thread pool for executing the submitted task. The rejectedExecutionHandler property refers to an instance of java.util.concurrent.RejectedExecutionHandler object.

In example listing 8-19, the rejectedExecutionHandler property refers to java.util.concurrent.ThreadPoolExecutor.AbortPolicy instance that always throws RejectedExecutionException. The other possible handlers for rejected tasks are: java.util.concurrent.ThreadPoolExecutor.CallerRunsPolicy (the rejected task is executed in caller's thread), java.util.concurrent.ThreadPoolExecutor.DiscardOldestPolicy (the handler discards the oldest task from the queue and retries executing the rejected task), and java.util.concurrent.ThreadPoolExecutor.DiscardPolicy (the handler simply discards the rejected task).

The <executor> element of Spring's task schema simplifies configuring a ThreadPoolTaskExecutor instance, as shown in the following example listing:

Example listing 8-20 –ThreadPoolTaskExecutor configuration using Spring's task schema

```
<beans ..... xmlns:task="http://www.springframework.org/schema/task"
  xsi:schemaLocation=".....http://www.springframework.org/schema/task
     http://www.springframework.org/schema/task/spring-task-4.0.xsd">

  <task:executor id=" myTaskExecutor" pool-size="5-10"
     queue-capacity="15" rejection-policy="ABORT" />
</beans>
```

In the above example listing, the <executor> element configures a ThreadPoolTaskExecutor instance. The pool-size attribute specifies the core pool size and the maximum pool size. In the above example listing, 5 is the core pool size and 10 is the maximum pool size. The queue-capacity attribute sets the queueCapacity property, and rejection-policy attribute specifies the handler for rejected tasks. The possible values of rejection-policy attribute are ABORT, CALLER_RUNS, DISCARD_OLDEST, and DISCARD.

Once you have configured a ThreadPoolTaskExecutor instance by explicitly defining it as a Spring bean (refer example listing 8-19) or by using Spring's task schema (refer example listing 8-20), you can inject the ThreadPoolTaskExecutor instance into beans that want to asynchronously execute java.lang.Runnable tasks, as shown in the following example listing:

Example listing 8-21 –Executing tasks using ThreadPoolTaskExecutor

```
import org.springframework.beans.factory.annotation.Autowired;
import org.springframework.core.task.TaskExecutor;

@Component
public class Sample {
   @Autowired
   private TaskExecutor taskExecutor;

   public void executeTask(Runnable task) {
      taskExecutor.execute(task);
   }
}
```

In the above example listing, an instance of ThreadPoolTaskExecutor is autowired into the Sample class, and is later used by Sample's executeTask method to execute a java.lang.Runnable task.

TaskExecutor executes a java.lang.Runnable task immediately after it is submitted, and the task is executed only once. If you want to schedule execution of a java.lang.Runnable task, and you want the task to be executed periodically, you should use a TaskScheduler implementation.

TaskScheduler interface

Spring's TaskScheduler interface provides the abstraction to schedule execution of java.lang.Runnable tasks. Spring's Trigger interface abstracts the time when a java.lang.Runnable task is executed. You associate a TaskScheduler instance with a Trigger instance to schedule execution of java.lang.Runnable tasks. PeriodicTrigger (an implementation of Trigger interface) is used if you want *periodic* execution of tasks. CronTrigger (another implementation of Trigger interface) accepts a *cron expression* that indicates the date/time when the task is executed.

ThreadPoolTaskScheduler is one of the most commonly used implementations of TaskScheduler that internally uses Java 5's ScheduledThreadPoolExecutor (an implementation of Java 5's ScheduledExecutorService interface) to schedule task execution. You can configure a ThreadPoolTaskScheduler implementation and associate it with a Trigger implementation to schedule task execution. The following example listing shows how ThreadPoolTaskScheduler is configured and used:

Example listing 8-22 –ThreadPoolTaskExecutor configuration and usage

```
----------- ThreadPoolTaskScheduler configuration --------------------

  <bean id="myScheduler"
          class="org.springframework.scheduling.concurrent.ThreadPoolTaskScheduler">
    <property name="poolSize" value="5"/>
  </bean>

-------------- ThreadPoolTaskScheduler usage --------------------

import org.springframework.scheduling.TaskScheduler;
import org.springframework.scheduling.support.PeriodicTrigger;

@Component
public class Sample {
  @Autowired
  @Qualifier("myScheduler")
  private TaskScheduler taskScheduler;

  public void executeTask(Runnable task) {
    taskScheduler.schedule(task, new PeriodicTrigger(5000));
  }
}
```

In the above example listing, ThreadPoolTaskScheduler's poolSize property specifies the number of threads in the thread pool. To schedule a task for execution, ThreadPoolTaskScheduler's schedule method is called, passing the java.lang.Runnable task and a Trigger instance. In the above example listing, PeriodicTrigger instance is passed to ThreadPoolTaskScheduler's schedule method. The argument to the PeriodicTrigger constructor specifies the time interval (in milliseconds) between task executions.

The <scheduler> element of Spring's task schema simplifies configuring a ThreadPoolTaskScheduler instance. The ThreadPoolTaskScheduler instance created by the <scheduler> element can be used by the <scheduled-tasks> element of Spring's task schema to schedule execution of bean methods. The following example listing shows how <scheduler> and <scheduled-tasks> elements are used by MyBank application to execute FixedDepositProcessorJob's sendEmail method every 5 seconds:

Example listing 8-23 –<scheduler> and <scheduled-tasks> elements
Project – ch08-bankapp
Source location - src/main/java/sample/spring/chapter08/bankapp/job

```
<task:scheduler id="emailScheduler" pool-size="10" />

<task:scheduled-tasks scheduler="emailScheduler">
   <task:scheduled ref="FixedDepositProcessorJob" method="sendEmail" fixed-rate="5000" />
</task:scheduled-tasks>

<bean id="FixedDepositProcessorJob"
   class="sample.spring.chapter08.bankapp.job.FixedDepositProcessorJob" />
```

In the above example listing, the <scheduler> element configures a ThreadPoolTaskScheduler instance. The id attribute of the <scheduler> element specifies the name with which the ThreadPoolTaskScheduler instance is accessed by other beans in the Spring container. The <scheduled-tasks> element's scheduler attribute specifies reference to the ThreadPoolTaskScheduler instance that is used for scheduling execution of bean methods. In the above example listing, the ThreadPoolTaskScheduler instance created by the <scheduler> element is referenced by the <scheduled-tasks> element's scheduled attribute.

The <scheduled-tasks> element contains one or more <scheduled> elements. The <scheduled> element contains information about the bean method to be executed and the trigger for the bean method execution. The ref attribute specifies reference to a Spring bean, the method attribute specifies a method of the bean referenced by the ref attribute, and the fixed-rate attribute (an interval-based trigger) specifies the time interval between successive method executions. In example listing 8-23, the <scheduled> element specifies that FixedDepositProcessorJob's sendEmail method is executed every 5 seconds.

Instead of using fixed-rate attribute of the <scheduled> element, you can use fixed-delay (an interval-based trigger) or cron (a cron-based trigger) or trigger (reference to a Trigger implementation) attribute, to specify a trigger for the bean method execution.

Let's now look at Spring's @Async and @Scheduled annotations.

@Async and @Scheduled annotations

If you annotate a bean method with Spring's @Async annotation, it is asynchronously executed by Spring. If you annotate a bean method with Spring's @Scheduled annotation, it is scheduled for execution by Spring.

Use of @Async and @Scheduled annotations is enabled by <annotation-driven> element of Spring's task schema, as shown in the following example listing:

Example listing 8-24 – Enabling @Async and @Scheduled annotations

```
<task:annotation-driven executor="anExecutor" scheduler="aScheduler"/>

<task:executor id="anExecutor"/>

<task:scheduled-tasks scheduler="aScheduler">
   <task:scheduled ref="sampleJob" method="doSomething" fixed-rate="5000" />
</task:scheduled-tasks>
```

The <annotation-driven> element's executor attribute specifies reference to a Spring's TaskExecutor (or Java 5's Executor) instance that is used for executing @Async annotated methods. The scheduler attribute specifies reference to a Spring's TaskScheduler (or Java 5's ScheduledExecutorService) instance that is used for executing @Scheduled annotated methods.

Let's now look at @Async annotation in detail.

@Async annotation

The following example listing highlights some of the important points that you need to know when using @Async annotation:

Example listing 8-25 –@Async annotation usage

```
import java.util.concurrent.Future;
import org.springframework.scheduling.annotation.Async;
import org.springframework.scheduling.annotation.AsyncResult;
import org.springframework.stereotype.Component;

@Component
public class Sample {
  @Async
  public void doA() { ..... }

  @Async(value="someExecutor")
  public void doB(String str) { ..... }

  @Async
  public Future<String> doC() {
     return new AsyncResult<String>("Hello");
  }
}
```

@Async annotation's value attribute specifies the Spring's TaskExecutor (or Java 5's Executor) instance to use for asynchronously executing the method. As the @Async annotation on the doA method doesn't specify the executor to use, Spring's SimpleAsyncTaskExector is used for asynchronously executing the doA method. @Async annotation on the doB method specifies the value attribute's value as someExecutor, which means the bean named someExecutor (of type TaskExecutor or Java 5's Executor) is used for asynchronously executing the doB method. @Async annotated methods can accept arguments, like the doB method in the above example listing. @Async annotated methods can either return void (like the doA and doB methods) or a Future instance (like the doC method). To return a Future instance, you'll need to wrap the value that you want to return into an AsyncResult object, and return the AsyncResult object.

Let's now look at @Scheduled annotation in detail.

@Scheduled annotation

The following example listing highlights some of the important points that you need to know when using @Scheduled annotation:

Example listing 8-26 –@Scheduled annotation usage

```
import org.springframework.scheduling.annotation.Scheduled;

@Component
public class Sample {
   @Scheduled(cron="0 0 9-17 * * MON-FRI")
   public void doA() { ..... }

   @Scheduled(fixedRate = 5000)
   public void doB() { ..... }
}
```

A method annotated with @Scheduled annotation *must* return void and *must not* be defined to accept any arguments. You *must* specify cron, fixedRate or fixedDelay attribute of @Scheduled annotation.

It is important to note that if the @Async (or @Scheduled) annotation is specified on one or more methods of a class, you are required to include CGLIB JAR file in your application's classpath. If the @Async (or @Scheduled) annotation is specified only on the methods defined in an interface, you don't need to include CGLIB JAR file. Starting with Spring 3.2, the CGLIB classes are packaged within the spring-core JAR file itself; therefore, you don't need to explicitly specify that your project is dependent on CGLIB JAR file.

> If you want to use the Quartz Scheduler (http://quartz-scheduler.org/) in your Spring application, you can use the integration classes provided by Spring that simplify using the Quartz Scheduler.

Spring simplifies using caching in an application by providing an abstraction on top of java.util.concurrent.ConcurrentMap and Ehcache (http://ehcache.org/).

8-7 Caching

If you want to use caching in your application, you can consider using Spring's cache abstraction. Spring's cache abstraction shields developers from directly dealing with the underlying caching implementation's API. Starting with Spring 3.2, cache abstraction is available out-of-the-box for java.util.concurrent.ConcurrentMap, Ehcache and for caching solutions that implement JSR 107 – Java Temporary Caching API (referred to as JCACHE).

> If you are using a caching solution which is not currently supported by Spring's cache abstraction, you have the option to either directly use the API of the caching solution or create adapters that map Spring's cache abstraction to the caching solution.

Spring provides a *CacheManager* interface that defines methods for managing a collection of *Cache* instances. A *CacheManager* instance acts as a wrapper around the cache manager provided by the underlying caching solution. For instance, *EhCacheCacheManager* is a wrapper around Ehcache's *net.sf.ehcache.CacheManager*, *JCacheCacheManager* is a wrapper around JSR 107 provider's *javax.cache.CacheManager* implementation, and so on. A *Cache* instance is a wrapper around the underlying cache, and it provides methods for interacting with the underlying cache. For instance, *EhCacheCache* (a *Cache* implementation) is a wrapper around *net.sf.ehcache.Ehcache*, and *JCacheCache* (a *Cache* implementation) is a wrapper around JSR 107 provider's *javax.cache.Cache* instance.

Spring also provides a *ConcurrentMapCacheManager* that you can use if you want to use *java.util.concurrent.ConcurrentMap* as the underlying cache. The *Cache* instance managed by *ConcurrentMapCacheManager* is a *ConcurrentMapCache*. The following diagram summarizes relationship between *CacheManager* and *Cache* interfaces provided by Spring's caching abstraction:

> If you want to use Spring's caching abstraction for a caching solution that is not currently supported by Spring's caching abstraction, all you need to do is to provide *CacheManager* and *Cache* implementations for the caching solution.

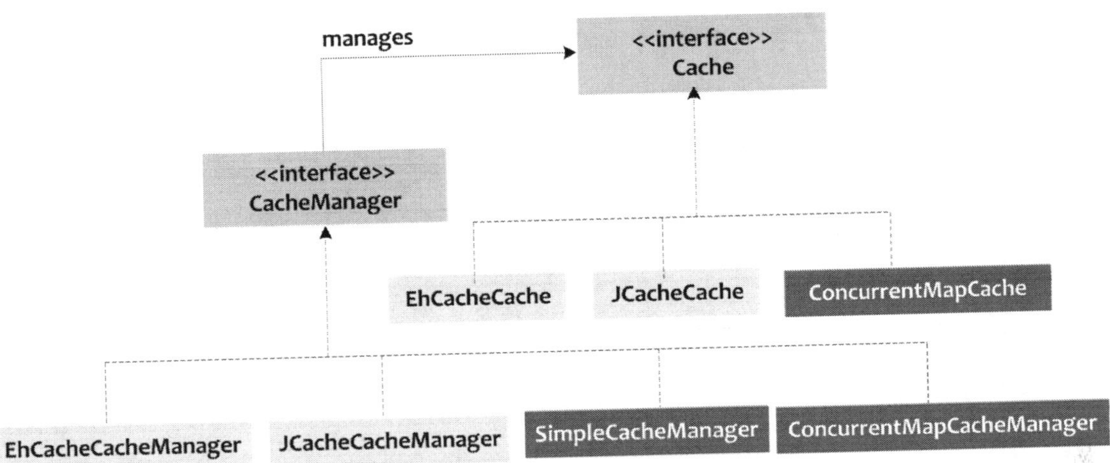

Figure 8-3 A *CacheManager* implementation acts as wrapper around the cache manager of the underlying caching solution, and a *Cache* implementation provides operations to interact with the underlying cache.

The above figure shows that *CacheManager* manages *Cache* instances. *EhCacheCacheManager* manages *EhCacheCache* instances (underlying cache store is Ehcache), *JCacheCacheManager* manages *JCacheCache* instances (underlying cache store is a caching solution that implements JSR 107), *ConcurrentMapCacheManager* manages *ConcurrentMapCache* instances (underlying cache store is *java.util.concurrent.ConcurrentMap*), and so on.

Figure 8-3 shows a *SimpleCacheManager* class that implements *CacheManager* interface. *SimpleCacheManager* is useful for simple caching scenarios and for testing purposes. For instance, if you want to use *java.util.concurrent.ConcurrentMap* as the underlying cache store, you can use *SimpleCacheManager*, instead of *ConcurrentMapCacheManager*, to manage the cache.

Let's now look at how a *CacheManager* is configured in the application context XML file.

Configuring a CacheManager

In MyBank application, a collection of *java.util.concurrent.ConcurrentMap* instances are used as the underlying cache store; therefore, *SimpleCacheManager* is used to manage the cache.

The following example listing shows how a *SimpleCacheManager* instance is configured in MyBank application:

Example listing 8-27 – SimpleCacheManager configuration
Project – ch08-bankapp
Source location - src/main/resources/META-INF/spring/

```
<bean id="myCacheManager"
```

```
   class="org.springframework.cache.support.SimpleCacheManager">
   <property name="caches">
     <set>
       <bean
         class="org.springframework.cache.concurrent.ConcurrentMapCacheFactoryBean">
         <property name="name" value="FixedDepositList" />
       </bean>
       <bean
         class="org.springframework.cache.concurrent.ConcurrentMapCacheFactoryBean">
         <property name="name" value="FixedDeposit" />
       </bean>
     </set>
   </property>
</bean>
```

SimpleCacheManager's caches property specifies a collection of caches managed by the SimpleCacheManager instance. ConcurrentMapCacheFactoryBean is a FactoryBean implementation that simplifies configuring a ConcurrentMapCache instance - a Cache instance that uses a java.util.concurrent.ConcurrentHashMap instance (an implementation of java.util.concurrent.ConcurrentMap interface) as the underlying cache store. ConcurrentMapCacheFactoryBean's name property specifies a name for the cache. In the above example listing, the FixedDepositList and FixedDeposit caches are managed by the SimpleCacheManager instance.

Let's now look at how to use Spring's caching annotations in applications.

Caching annotations - @Cacheable, @CacheEvict and @CachePut

After you have configured an appropriate CacheManager for your application, you need to choose how you want to use Spring's cache abstraction. You can use Spring's cache abstraction either by using caching annotations (like @Cacheable, @CacheEvict and @CachePut) or by using Spring's cache schema. As using Spring's cache schema for caching results in a verbose application context XML file, we'll be only looking at using caching annotations for declarative caching.

To use caching annotations, you need to configure <annotation-driven> element of Spring's cache schema, as shown here for the MyBank application:

Example listing 8-28 – Enable caching annotations using <annotation-driven>
Project – ch08-bankapp
Source location - src/main/resources/META-INF/spring/

```
<beans .....xmlns:cache="http://www.springframework.org/schema/cache"
    xsi:schemaLocation=".....
```

```
    http://www.springframework.org/schema/cache
    http://www.springframework.org/schema/cache/spring-cache.xsd">

    <cache:annotation-driven cache-manager="myCacheManager"/>
    .....
</beans>
```

In the above example listing, Spring's cache schema is included so that its elements are accessible in the application context XML file. The <annotation-driven> element's cache-manager attribute refers to the CacheManager bean that is used for managing the cache. You don't need to specify the cache-manager attribute if the CacheManager bean is named cacheManager.

Now, that we have enabled caching annotations, let's look at different caching annotations.

@Cacheable

@Cacheable annotation on a method indicates that the value returned by the method is cached. Spring's DefaultKeyGenerator class is used by default to generate the key with which the method's return value is stored in the cache. DefaultKeyGenerator uses method signature and method arguments to compute the key. You can use a custom key generator by providing an implementation of Spring's KeyGenerator interface, and specifying it as the value of key-generator attribute of <annotation-driven> element.

The following example listing shows the usage of @Cacheable annotation to cache the value returned by FixedDepositService's findFixedDepositsByBankAccount method in the MyBank application:

Example listing 8-29 – @Cacheable annotation
Project – ch08-bankapp
Source location - src/main/java/sample/spring/chapter08/bankapp/service

```
package sample.spring.chapter08.bankapp.service;

import org.springframework.cache.annotation.Cacheable;
.....
@Service(value = "FixedDepositService")
public class FixedDepositServiceImpl implements FixedDepositService {
    .....
    @Cacheable(value = { "FixedDepositList" })
    public List<FixedDepositDetails> findFixedDepositsByBankAccount(int bankAccountId) {
        logger.info("findFixedDepositsByBankAccount method invoked");
        return myFixedDepositDao.findFixedDepositsByBankAccount(bankAccountId);
    }
}
```

@Cacheable annotation's value attribute specifies the cache region into which the returned value is cached. In listing 8-27, we created a cache region named FixedDepositList for the MyBank application. In the above example listing, the @Cacheable annotation specifies that the value returned by the findFixedDepositsByBankAccount method is stored in the FixedDepositList cache. It is important to note that @Cacheable annotated method is not invoked if the same set of argument values are passed to the method. But, @Cacheable annotated method will be invoked if you pass a different value for at least one of the arguments.

@CacheEvict

If you want to evict data from the cache when a method is called, annotate the method with the @CacheEvict annotation. In the MyBank application, when a new fixed deposit is created, the fixed deposit details cached by FixedDepositServiceImpl's findFixedDepositsByBankAccount method *must* be evicted from the cache. This ensures that when the next time findFixedDepositsByBankAccount method is invoked, the newly created fixed deposit is also fetched from the database. The following example listing shows usage of @CacheEvict annotation:

Example listing 8-30 – @CacheEvict annotation
Project – ch08-bankapp
Source location - src/main/java/sample/spring/chapter08/bankapp/service

```
package sample.spring.chapter08.bankapp.service;

import org.springframework.cache.annotation.CacheEvict;
.....
@Service(value = "FixedDepositService")
public class FixedDepositServiceImpl implements FixedDepositService {
  .....
  @Transactional("jmsTxManager")
  @CacheEvict(value = { "FixedDepositList" }, allEntries=true, beforeInvocation = true)
  public void createFixedDeposit(final FixedDepositDetails fixedDepositDetails) throws Exception {
..... }
  .....
}
```

In the above example listing, the @CacheEvict annotation on the createFixedDeposit method instructs Spring to remove all the cached entries from the cache region named FixedDepositList. The value attribute specifies the cache region from which to evict the cached item, and allEntries attribute specifies whether or not all entries from the specified cache region are evicted. If you want to evict a particular cached item, use the key attribute to specify the key with which the item is cached. You can also specify conditional eviction of items by using the condition attribute. The condition and key attributes support specifying values using SpEL (refer section 6-8 of chapter 6 for more details), making it possible to perform sophisticated cache evictions. The beforeInvocation attribute specifies whether the cache eviction is performed *before* or after the method execution. As the value of beforeInvocation attribute is set to true, cache is evicted before the createFixedDeposit method is invoked.

@CachePut

Spring also provides a @CachePut annotation that indicates that a method is *always* invoked, and the value returned by the method is put into the cache. @CachePut annotation is different from the @Cacheable annotation in the sense that @Cacheable annotation instructs Spring to skip the method invocation if the method is called with the same set of argument values.

The following example listing shows usage of @CachePut annotation by FixedDepositServiceImpl class of MyBank application:

Example listing 8-31 – @CachePut annotation
Project – ch08-bankapp
Source location - src/main/java/sample/spring/chapter08/bankapp/service

```
package sample.spring.chapter08.bankapp.service;

import org.springframework.cache.annotation.CachePut;
import org.springframework.cache.annotation.Cacheable;
.....
@Service(value = "FixedDepositService")
public class FixedDepositServiceImpl implements FixedDepositService {
  .....
  @CachePut(value={"FixedDeposit"}, key="#FixedDepositId")
  public FixedDepositDetails getFixedDeposit(int FixedDepositId) {
    logger.info("getFixedDeposit method invoked with FixedDepositId " + FixedDepositId);
    return myFixedDepositDao.getFixedDeposit(FixedDepositId);
  }

  @Cacheable(value={"FixedDeposit"}, key="#FixedDepositId")
  public FixedDepositDetails getFixedDepositFromCache(int FixedDepositId) {
    logger.info("getFixedDepositFromCache method invoked with FixedDepositId "
      + FixedDepositId);
    throw new RuntimeException("This method throws exception because "
      + "FixedDepositDetails object must come from the cache");
  }
  .....
}
```

In the above example listing, the getFixedDeposit method is annotated with @CachePut annotation, which means that the getFixedDeposit method is always invoked, and the returned FixedDepositDetails object is stored into the cache named FixedDeposit. The value attribute specifies the name of the cache into which the FixedDepositDetails object is stored. The key attribute specifies the key to be used for storing the returned FixedDepositDetails object into the cache. As you can see, key attribute makes use of SpEL to specify the key. The #FixedDepositId value of key attribute refers to the FixedDepositId argument passed to the getFixedDeposit method. To summarize, the FixedDepositDetails object returned by the getFixedDeposit method is stored in the cache named FixedDeposit, and the value of FixedDepositId method argument is used as the key.

In example listing 8-31, FixedDepositServiceImpl's getFixedDepositFromCache method retrieves the FixedDepositDetails object from the cache based on the key attribute value specified by the @Cacheable annotation. Notice that the body of the getFixedDepositFromCache method does nothing but throw a RuntimeException. The key attribute value refers to the FixedDepositId argument passed to the getFixedDepositFromCache method. If the FixedDepositDetails object is not found in the cache, the getFixedDepositFromCache method is invoked, which will result in RuntimeException.

Let's now look at what happens when you run the MyBank application of ch08-bankapp project.

8-8 Running the MyBank application

BankApp class of MyBank application defines the main method of the application. The main method accesses methods of FixedDepositService and BankAccountService instances to demonstrate different features that we discussed in this chapter.

The following example listing shows the MyBank application's BankApp class:

Example listing 8-32 – BankApp class
Project – ch08-bankapp
Source location - src/main/java/sample/spring/chapter08/bankapp

```
package sample.spring.chapter08.bankapp;

import org.springframework.context.ApplicationContext;
import org.springframework.context.support.ClassPathXmlApplicationContext;

public class BankApp {
  public static void main(String args[]) throws Exception {
    ApplicationContext context = new ClassPathXmlApplicationContext(
        "classpath:META-INF/spring/applicationContext.xml");

    BankAccountService bankAccountService = context.getBean(BankAccountService.class);
```

```
    BankAccountDetails bankAccountDetails = new BankAccountDetails();
    .....
    int bankAccountId = bankAccountService.createBankAccount(bankAccountDetails);

    FixedDepositService FixedDepositService = context.getBean(FixedDepositService.class);
    FixedDepositDetails fixedDepositDetails = new FixedDepositDetails();
    .....
    fixedDepositDetails.setEmail("someUser@someDomain.com");
    FixedDepositService.createFixedDeposit(fixedDepositDetails);
    .....
    FixedDepositService.findFixedDepositsByBankAccount(bankAccountId);
    FixedDepositService.findFixedDepositsByBankAccount(bankAccountId);

    FixedDepositService.createFixedDeposit(fixedDepositDetails);
    .....
    List<FixedDepositDetails> FixedDepositDetailsList = FixedDepositService
        .findFixedDepositsByBankAccount(bankAccountId);

    for (FixedDepositDetails detail : FixedDepositDetailsList) {
      FixedDepositService.getFixedDeposit(detail.getFixedDepositId());
    }

    for (FixedDepositDetails detail : FixedDepositDetailsList) {
      FixedDepositService.getFixedDepositFromCache(detail.getFixedDepositId());
    }
    .....
  }
}
```

In the above example listing, following sequence of actions are performed by the main method:

Step 1. First, a bank account is created in the BANK_ACCOUNT_DETAILS table by calling BankAccountService's createBankAccount method.

Step 2. Corresponding to the newly created bank account, a fixed deposit is created in the FIXED_DEPOSIT_DETAILS table by calling FixedDepositService's createFixedDeposit method. You should make sure that email property of FixedDepositDetails object is set to the email id where you can check the emails. The createFixedDeposit method sends 2 JMS messages (refer example listing 8-5). One JMS message contains the email id specified by the FixedDepositDetails object's email property, and is processed by EmailMessageListener (refer example listing 8-16) that sends an email to the customer. The other JMS message is processed by FixedDepositMessageListener (refer example listing 8-11) that saves the fixed deposit details in the FIXED_DEPOSIT_DETAILS table. You should also note that

FixedDepositServiceImpl's createFixedDeposit method is annotated with @CacheEvict annotation (refer example listing 8-30) that results in removing all the items cached in FixedDepositList cache.

Step 3. FixedDepositService's findFixedDepositsByBankAccount method is invoked that retrieves fixed deposits corresponding to the bank account that we created in Step 1. As the findFixedDepositsByBankAccount method is annotated with @Cacheable annotation (refer example listing 8-29), fixed deposits returned by the findFixedDepositsByBankAccount method are stored in the cache named FixedDepositList. Listing 8-29 showed that findFixedDepositsByBankAccount method writes the following message to the console '*findFixedDepositsByBankAccount method invoked*'. In the above example listing, the findFixedDepositsByBankAccount is called twice for the same bankAccountId argument, but you'll notice that only once '*findFixedDepositsByBankAccount method invoked*' is written to the console. This is because the second call to the findFixedDepositsByBankAccount results in retrieving fixed deposit details from the cache named FixedDepositList, and the findFixedDepositsByBankAccount method is *not* executed.

Step 4. Corresponding to the bank account created in Step 1, another fixed deposit is created in the FIXED_DEPOSIT_DETAILS table by calling FixedDepositService's createFixedDeposit method. Now, the FixedDepositServiceImpl's createFixedDeposit method is annotated with @CacheEvict annotation (refer example listing 8-30) that results in removing all the items cached in FixedDepositList cache.

Step 5. FixedDepositService's findFixedDepositsByBankAccount method is invoked once again. This time findFixedDepositsByBankAccount is executed because the previous call to createFixedDeposit method (refer Step 4) resulted in evicting all the items from the FixedDepositList cache. At this time, you'll once again see '*findFixedDepositsByBankAccount method invoked*' message written on the console. The fixed deposits returned by the findFixedDepositsByBankAccount method are cached in FixedDepositList cache because the method is annotated with @Cacheable annotation.

Step 6. For each fixed deposit retrieved in Step 5, FixedDepositService's getFixedDeposit method (refer example listing 8-31) is invoked. The getFixedDeposit method accepts the fixed deposit identifier and returns the fixed deposit information from the database. The getFixedDeposit method is annotated with @CachePut, which means it is *always* invoked. The fixed deposit returned by the getFixedDeposit method is cached in the FixedDeposit cache.

Step 7. For each fixed deposit retrieved in Step 5, FixedDepositService's getFixedDepositFromCache method (refer example listing 8-31) is invoked. The getFixedDepositFromCache method accepts the fixed deposit identifier and throws a RuntimeException on execution. The getFixedDepositFromCache method is annotated with @Cacheable, and is executed only when the fixed deposit is not found in the FixedDeposit cache. As all the fixed deposits were cached by the getFixedDeposit method in Step 6, the getFixedDepositFromCache method is never executed.

Step 8. Every 5 seconds, the FixedDepositProcessorJob (refer example listing 8-17) checks if any new fixed deposits have been created in the database. If new fixed deposits are found in the database, the FixedDepositProcessorJob activates the fixed deposit and sends an email to the customer, confirming that the fixed deposit request has been successfully processed.

8-9 Summary

In this chapter, we touched upon some of the frequently used features of Spring. We saw that Spring simplifies sending and receiving JMS messages, sending emails, asynchronously invoking bean methods, scheduling bean methods for execution, and caching data. In the next chapter, we'll look at Spring's support for AOP (Aspect-oriented programming).

Chapter 9 - *Aspect-oriented programming*

9-1 Introduction

Aspect-oriented programming (AOP) is a programming approach in which responsibilities that are distributed across multiple classes are encapsulated into a separate class, referred to as an 'aspect'. The responsibilities that are distributed across multiple classes are referred to as 'cross-cutting concerns'. Logging, transaction management, caching, security, and so on, are examples of cross-cutting concerns.

Spring provides an AOP framework that is used internally by Spring for implementing declarative services, like transaction management (refer chapter 7) and caching (refer chapter 8). Instead of using Spring AOP framework, you can consider using AspectJ (http://www.eclipse.org/aspectj/) as the AOP framework for your application. As Spring AOP framework is sufficient for most AOP scenarios, and provides integration with the Spring container, this chapter focuses on Spring AOP framework.

Let's begin this chapter by looking at an example usage of AOP.

9-2 A simple AOP example

Let's say that for auditing purposes we want to capture the arguments passed to the methods of classes defined in the service layer of MyBank application. A simple approach to log details of method arguments is to write the logging logic inside each method. But, this would mean that each method is *additionally* responsible for logging details of method arguments. As the responsibility to log details of method arguments is distributed across multiple classes and methods, it represents a *cross-cutting concern*.

To address a cross-cutting concern using AOP, you need to follow these steps:

- create a Java class (referred to as an *aspect*)
- add implementation of the cross-cutting concern to the Java class, and
- use a regular expression to specify the methods to which the cross-cutting concern applies

In terms of AOP terminology, the methods of an aspect that implement cross-cutting concerns are referred to as *advices*. And, each advice is associated with a *pointcut* that identifies the methods to which the advice applies. The methods to which an advice applies are referred to as *join points*.

In Spring AOP, you have the option to develop an aspect using AspectJ *annotation-style* or XML *schema-style*. In AspectJ annotation-style, AspectJ annotations, like @Aspect, @Pointcut, @Before, and so on, are used to develop an aspect. In XML schema-style, elements of Spring's aop schema are used to configure a Spring bean as an aspect.

IMPORT **chapter 9/ch09-simple-aop** (The ch09-simple-aop project shows the MyBank application that uses Spring AOP to log details of method arguments passed to the methods defined by the classes in the service layer of MyBank application. To run the application, execute the main method of the BankApp class of this project)

The following example listing shows the logging aspect that logs details of the arguments passed to service methods in MyBank application:

Example listing 9-1 – LoggingAspect class
Project – ch09-simple-aop
Source location - src/main/java/sample/spring/chapter09/bankapp/aspects

```
package sample.spring.chapter09.bankapp.aspects;

import org.aspectj.lang.JoinPoint;
import org.aspectj.lang.annotation.Aspect;
import org.aspectj.lang.annotation.Before;
import org.springframework.stereotype.Component;

@Aspect
@Component
public class LoggingAspect {
  private Logger logger = Logger.getLogger(LoggingAspect.class);

  @Before(value = "execution(* sample.spring.chapter09.bankapp.service.*Service.*(..))")
  public void log(JoinPoint joinPoint) {
    logger.info("Entering "
        + joinPoint.getTarget().getClass().getSimpleName() + "'s "
        + joinPoint.getSignature().getName());

    Object[] args = joinPoint.getArgs();
    for (int i = 0; i < args.length; i++) {
      logger.info("args[" + i + "] -->" + args[i]);
    }
  }
}
```

In example listing 9-1:

- AspectJ's @Aspect type-level annotation specifies that the LoggingAspect class is an AOP *aspect*

- AspectJ's @Before method-level annotation specifies that the log method represents an *advice* that is applied *before* the methods matched by the value attribute are executed. Refer section 9-5 to learn about different advice types that you can create.

- @Before annotation's value attribute specifies a *pointcut expression* that is used by Spring AOP framework to identify methods (referred to as *target methods*) to which an advice applies. In section 9-4, we'll take an in-depth look at pointcut expressions. For now, you can assume that the pointcut expression execution(* sample.spring.chapter09.bankapp.service.*Service.*(..)) specifies that LoggingAspect's log method is applied to *all* the public methods defined by classes (or interfaces) in sample.spring.chapter09.bankapp.service package, and whose names end with Service.

- The log method's JoinPoint argument represents the target method to which the advice is being applied. The log method uses JoinPoint instance to retrieve information about the arguments passed to the target method. In example listing 9-1, JoinPoint's getArgs method is invoked to retrieve the method arguments being passed to the target method.

You need to register an aspect with the Spring container so that the Spring AOP framework is made aware of the aspect. In example listing 9-1, the LoggingAspect class is annotated with Spring's @Component annotation so that it is automatically registered with the Spring container.

The following example listing shows the BankApp class that invokes methods of BankAccountServiceImpl (implements BankAccountService interface) and FixedDepositServiceImpl (implements FixedDepositService interface) classes of MyBank application:

Example listing 9-2 – BankApp class
Project – ch09-simple-aop
Source location - src/main/java/sample/spring/chapter09/bankapp

```
package sample.spring.chapter09.bankapp;
.....
public class BankApp {
   public static void main(String args[]) throws Exception {
      ApplicationContext context = new ClassPathXmlApplicationContext(
            "classpath:META-INF/spring/applicationContext.xml");

      BankAccountService bankAccountService = context.getBean(BankAccountService.class);
      BankAccountDetails bankAccountDetails = new BankAccountDetails();
```

```
        bankAccountDetails.setBalanceAmount(1000);
        bankAccountDetails.setLastTransactionTimestamp(new Date());
        bankAccountService.createBankAccount(bankAccountDetails);

        FixedDepositService FixedDepositService = context.getBean(FixedDepositService.class);
        FixedDepositService.createFixedDeposit(new FixedDepositDetails(1, 1000,
                12, "someemail@somedomain.com"));
    }
}
```

In the above example listing, BankAccountService's createBankAccount and FixedDepositService's createFixedDeposit methods are invoked by BankApp's main method. If you execute BankApp's main method, you'll see the following output on the console:

```
INFO  LoggingAspect - Entering BankAccountServiceImpl's createBankAccount
INFO  LoggingAspect - args[0] -->BankAccountDetails [accountId=0, balanceAmount=1000,
lastTransactionTimestamp=Sat Oct 27 16:48:11 IST 2012]
INFO  BankAccountServiceImpl - createBankAccount method invoked
INFO  LoggingAspect - Entering FixedDepositServiceImpl's createFixedDeposit
INFO  LoggingAspect - args[0] -->id :1, deposit amount : 1000.0, tenure : 12, email :
someemail@somedomain.com
INFO  FixedDepositServiceImpl - createFixedDeposit method invoked
```

The above output shows that LoggingAspect's log method is executed before the execution of BankAccountService's createBankAccount and FixedDepositService's createFixedDeposit method.

In the context of LoggingAspect, let's look at how Spring AOP framework works.

> To use AspectJ annotation-style aspects, ch09-simple-aop project defines dependency on spring-aop, aopalliance, aspectjrt and aspectjweaver JAR files. Please refer to the pom.xml file of ch09-simple-aop project for details.

9-3 Spring AOP framework

Spring AOP framework is *proxy-based*; a *proxy object* is created for objects that are target of an advice. A proxy is an intermediary object, introduced by the AOP framework, between the calling object and the target object. At runtime, calls to the target object are intercepted by the proxy, and advices that apply to the target method are executed by the proxy. In Spring AOP, a target object is a bean instance registered with the Spring container.

The following diagram shows how the LoggingAspect's log method (refer example listing 9-1) is applied to the methods of BankAccountService and FixedDepositService objects (refer example listing 9-2):

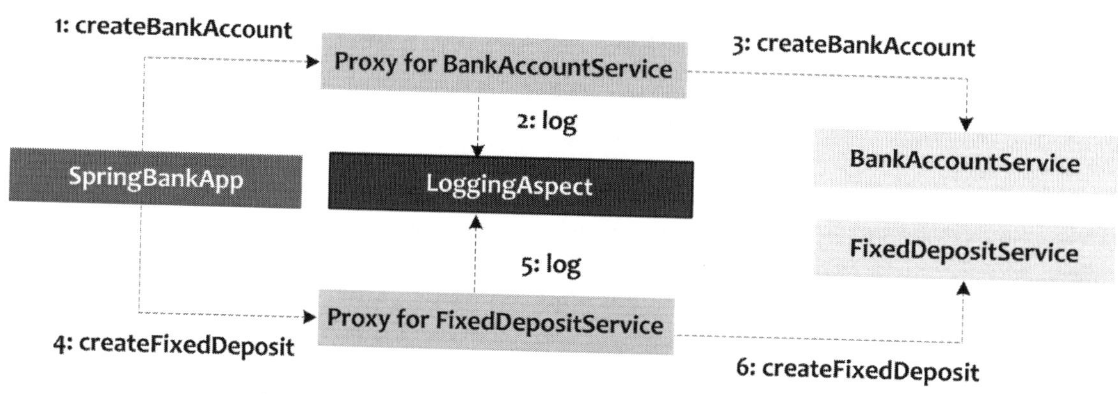

Figure 9-1 The proxy object is responsible for intercepting method calls to the target object and executing the advices that apply to the target method.

The above diagram shows that a proxy is created for both BankAccountService and FixedDepositService objects. The proxy for BankAccountService intercepts the call to BankAccountService's createBankAccount method, and the proxy for FixedDepositService intercepts the call to FixedDepositService's createFixedDeposit method. The proxy for BankAccountService first executes LoggingAspect's log method, followed by BankAccountService's createBankAccount method invocation. Similarly, the proxy for FixedDepositService first executes LoggingAspect's log method, followed by FixedDepositService's createFixedDeposit method invocation.

The timing of the execution of an advice (like the log method of LoggingAspect aspect) depends on the *type* of the advice. In AspectJ annotation-style, type of an advice is specified by the AspectJ annotation on the advice. For instance, AspectJ's @Before annotation specifies that the advice is executed *before* the invocation of the target method, @After annotation specifies that the advice is executed *after* the invocation of the target method, @Around annotation specifies that the advice is executed both *before* and *after* the execution of the target method, and so on. As LoggingAspect's log method is annotated with @Before annotation, log method is executed *before* the execution of the target object's method.

Let's now look at how Spring AOP framework creates a proxy object.

Proxy creation

When using Spring AOP, you have the option to explicitly create AOP proxies via Spring's ProxyFactoryBean (refer to org.springframework.aop.framework package) or you can let Spring automatically create AOP proxies. The automatic generation of AOP proxies by Spring AOP is referred to as *autoproxying*.

If you want to use AspectJ annotation-style for creating aspects, you need to enable support for using AspectJ annotation-style by specifying Spring aop schema's <aspectj-autoproxy> element. The <aspectj-autoproxy> element also instructs Spring AOP framework to automatically create AOP proxies for target objects. The following example listing shows usage of <aspectj-autoproxy> element in ch09-simple-aop project:

Example listing 9-3 – applicationContext.xml - <aspectj-autoproxy> element
Project – ch09-simple-aop
Source location - src/main/resources/META-INF/spring

```
<beans .....
   xmlns:context="http://www.springframework.org/schema/context"
   xmlns:aop="http://www.springframework.org/schema/aop"
   xsi:schemaLocation=".....http://www.springframework.org/schema/aop
        http://www.springframework.org/schema/aop/spring-aop-4.0.xsd">

   <context:component-scan base-package="sample.spring" />
   <aop:aspectj-autoproxy proxy-target-class="false" expose-proxy="true"/>

</beans>
```

The <aspectj-autoproxy> element's proxy-target-class attribute specifies whether JavaSE- or CGLIB-based proxies are created for target objects, and expose-proxy attribute specifies whether the AOP proxy itself is available to the target object. If expose-proxy's value is set to true, the target object's method can access the AOP proxy by calling AopContext's currentProxy static method.

Spring AOP framework creates a CGLIB- or JavaSE-based proxy. If the target object doesn't implement any interface, Spring AOP creates a CGLIB-based proxy. If the target object implements one or more interfaces, Spring AOP creates a JavaSE-based proxy. If the value of <aspectj-autoproxy> element's proxy-target-class attribute is set to false, it instructs Spring AOP to create a JavaSE-based proxy if the target object implements one or more interface. If you set proxy-target-class attribute's value to true, it instructs Spring AOP to create CGLIB-based proxies even if a target object implements one or more interfaces.

> Starting with Spring 3.2, the CGLIB classes are packaged within the spring-core JAR file itself; therefore, you don't need to explicitly include CGLIB JAR file in your application to allow Spring AOP framework to create CGLIB-based proxies for target objects.

Let's now look at a scenario in which you'd prefer to set expose-proxy attribute of <aspectj-autoproxy> element to true.

IMPORT **chapter 9/ch09-aop-proxy** (The ch09-aop-proxy project shows the MyBank application in which AopProxy's currentProxy method is used by a target method to retrieve the AOP proxy object created by Spring AOP framework. To run the application, execute the main method of the BankApp class of this project)

expose-proxy attribute

The following example listing shows a modified BankAccountServiceImpl class in which the createBankAccount method invokes the isDuplicateAccount method to check if a bank account with same details already exists in the system:

Example listing 9-4 – BankAccountServiceImpl class

```
@Service(value = "bankAccountService")
public class BankAccountServiceImpl implements BankAccountService {
  @Autowired
  private BankAccountDao bankAccountDao;

  @Override
  public int createBankAccount(BankAccountDetails bankAccountDetails) {
    if(!isDuplicateAccount(bankAccountDetails)) {
      return bankAccountDao.createBankAccount(bankAccountDetails);
    } else {
      throw new BankAccountAlreadyExistsException("Bank account already exists");
    }
  }

  @Override
  public boolean isDuplicateAccount(BankAccountDetails bankAccountDetails) { ..... }
}
```

The above example listing shows that the createBankAccount method invokes the isDuplicateAccount method to check if the bank account already exists in the system.

Now, the question arises that whether the LoggingAspect's log method (refer example listing 9-1) will be executed when the isDuplicateAccount method is invoked by the createBankAccount method? Even though the isDuplicateAccount method matches the pointcut expression specified by @Before annotation on the LoggingAspect's log method (refer example listing 9-1), the LoggingAspect's log method is *not* invoked. This is because methods invoked by the target object on itself are *not* proxied by the AOP proxy. As the method invocation doesn't go through the AOP proxy object, any advice that is associated with the target method is *not* executed.

To ensure that the call to isDuplicateAccount method goes to the target object through the AOP proxy, retrieve the AOP proxy object in the createBankAccount method and invoke the isDuplicateAccount method on the AOP proxy object. The following example listing shows how to retrieve AOP proxy object inside the createBankAccount method:

Example listing 9-5 – BankAccountServiceImpl class
Project – ch09-aop-proxy
Source location - src/main/java/sample/spring/chapter09/bankapp/service

```
package sample.spring.chapter09.bankapp.service;

import org.springframework.aop.framework.AopContext;
.....
@Service(value = "bankAccountService")
public class BankAccountServiceImpl implements BankAccountService {
   .....
   @Override
   public int createBankAccount(BankAccountDetails bankAccountDetails) {
      //-- obtain the proxy and invoke the isDuplicateAccount method via proxy
      boolean isDuplicateAccount =
         ((BankAccountService)AopContext.currentProxy()).isDuplicateAccount(bankAccountDetails);

      if(!isDuplicateAccount) { ..... }
      .....
   }

   @Override
   public boolean isDuplicateAccount(BankAccountDetails bankAccountDetails) { ..... }
}
```

In the above example listing, call to AopContext's currentProxy method returns the AOP proxy that made the call to the createBankAccount method. If the createBankAccount method is not invoked through Spring AOP framework or the value of expose-proxy attribute of <aspectj-autoproxy> element is false, call to the currentProxy method will result in throwing java.lang.IllegalStateException. As the AOP proxy implements the same interface as the target object, the above example listing shows that the AOP proxy returned by the currentProxy method is cast to BankAccountService type and BankAccountService's isDuplicateAccount method is invoked.

If you now go to ch09-aop-proxy project and execute BankApp's main method, you'll notice that LoggingAspect's log method is executed when isDuplicateAccount method is invoked by the createBankAccount method.

Let's now take at an in-depth look at pointcut expressions.

9-4 Pointcut expressions

When using Spring AOP, a pointcut expression identifies the *join points* to which an advice is applied. In Spring AOP, join points are *always* bean methods. If you want to apply an advice to fields, constructors, non-public methods, and to objects that are not Spring beans, you should use AspectJ instead of Spring AOP framework. If you want to develop aspects using AspectJ annotation-style, you have the option to specify a pointcut expression using AspectJ's @Pointcut annotation or by using AspectJ's @Before, @After, and so on, annotations that specify the advice type.

Pointcut expressions use *pointcut designators*, like execution, args, within, this, and so on, to find matching methods to which an advice is applied. For instance, in example listing 9-1, @Before annotation made use of execution pointcut designator to find methods to which the LoggingAspect's log method is applied.

Let's now look at how pointcut expressions are specified using @Pointcut annotation.

IMPORT **chapter 9/ch09-aop-pointcuts** (The ch09-aop-pointcuts project shows the MyBank application that uses AspectJ's @Pointcut annotation to specify a pointcut expression. To run the application, execute the main method of the BankApp class of this project)

@Pointcut annotation

@Pointcut annotation's value attribute specifies the pointcut expression. To use @Pointcut annotation, create an *empty* method and annotate it with @Pointcut annotation. The empty method *must* be defined to return void. An advice that refers to the name of the @Pointcut annotated method is applied to the methods matched by the pointcut expression specified by the @Pointcut annotation.

> Using @Pointcut annotation is particularly useful if a pointcut expression is shared by multiple advices in the same or different aspects.

The following example listing shows a modified version of LoggingAspect (refer example listing 9-1) class that uses @Pointcut annotation:

Example listing 9-6 – LoggingAspect class
Project – ch09-aop-pointcuts
Source location - src/main/java/sample/spring/chapter09/bankapp/aspects

```
package sample.spring.chapter09.bankapp.aspects;

import org.aspectj.lang.annotation.Before;
import org.aspectj.lang.annotation.Pointcut;

@Aspect
@Component
public class LoggingAspect {
   @Pointcut(value = "execution(* sample.spring.chapter09.bankapp.service.*Service.*(..))")
   private void invokeServiceMethods() { }

   @Before(value = "invokeServiceMethods()")
   public void log(JoinPoint joinPoint) {
      logger.info("Entering " + joinPoint.getTarget().getClass().getSimpleName() + "'s "
            + joinPoint.getSignature().getName());
      .....
   }
}
```

In the above example listing, the invokeServiceMethods method is annotated with @Pointcut annotation, and @Before annotation's value attribute refers to the invokeServiceMethods method. This means that the log method is applied to the methods that match the pointcut expression specified by the @Pointcut annotation on the invokeServiceMethods method.

As the execution and args pointcut designators are mostly used when specifying pointcut expressions, let's look at execution and args pointcut designators in detail.

execution and args pointcut designators

The execution pointcut designator has the following format:

execution(*<access-modifier-pattern>* *<return-type-pattern>* *<declaring-type-pattern>* *<method-name-pattern>*(*<method-param-pattern>*) *<throws-pattern>*)

If you compare an execution expression to a method declaration, you'll notice that an execution expression is similar to a method declaration.

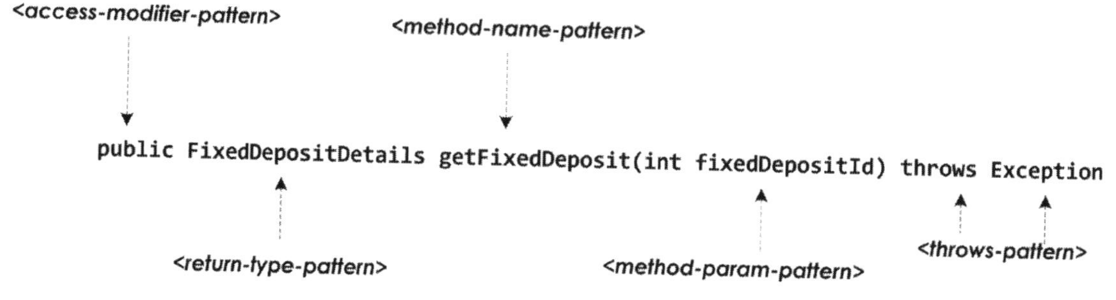

Figure 9-2 Different parts of an *execution* expression map to different parts of a method declaration.

Figure 9-2 shows how the different parts of an *execution* expression map to a method declaration:

Spring AOP framework matches different parts of an *execution* expression with different parts of a method declaration (as shown above) to find the methods to which an advice is applied. The *<declaring-type-pattern>* is not shown in the above figure because *<declaring-type-pattern>* is only used when you want to refer to methods contained in a particular type or package.

The following table describes different parts of an *execution* expression:

Expression part	Description
access-modifier-pattern	Specifies the access modifier of the target method. In Spring AOP, the only value that can be specified for this expression part is public. This part of *execution* expression is *optional*.
return-type-pattern	Specifies the fully-qualified name of the return type of the target method. A value of * means that the return type of a method doesn't matter.
declaring-type-pattern	Specifies the fully-qualified name of the type that contains the target method. This part of *execution* expression is *optional*. A value of * means that all types (classes and interfaces) in the application are considered by the pointcut expression.
method-name-pattern	Specifies the method name pattern. For instance, a value of *save** means that the methods whose names begin with *save* are target of advice.
method-param-pattern	Specifies the method parameter pattern. If the value is (..), it means target method can contain any number of arguments or no arguments at all.

throws-pattern	Specifies the exception(s) thrown by the target method. This part of execution expression is *optional*.

The *args* pointcut designator specifies the arguments that must be accepted by the target method *at runtime*. For instance, if you want pointcut expression to locate methods that accept an instance of java.util.List at runtime, then the *args* expression looks like: args(java.util.List). Later in this section, we'll see how *args* pointcut designator can be used to make arguments passed to the target method available to an advice.

Let's now look at some pointcut expressions that use execution and *args* pointcut designators:

Example 1

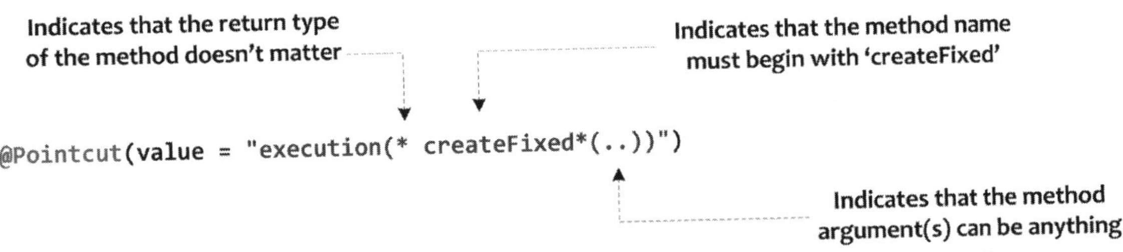

Figure 9-3 execution expression that uses a method name pattern

The methods matched by the above pointcut expression are the methods whose names start with createFixed. The return type is specified as *, which means the target method may return any type. The (..) specifies that the target method may accept zero or more arguments.

Example 2

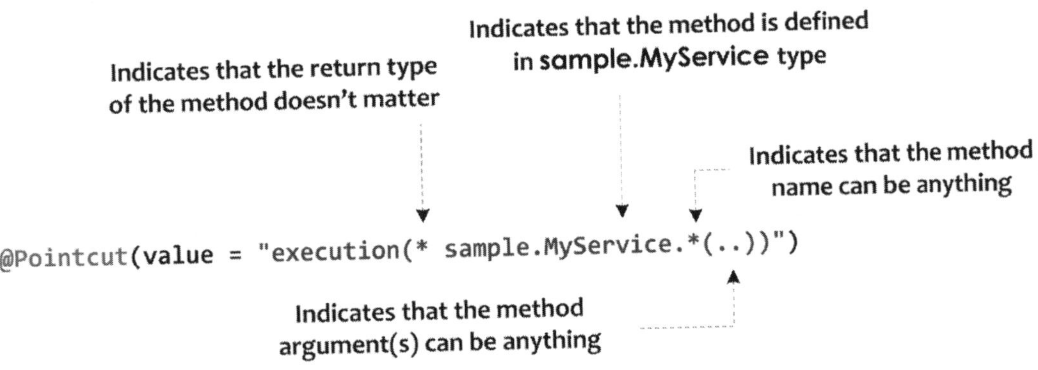

Figure 9-4 execution expression that specifies the *type* (class or interface) containing the target method(s)

The methods matched by the above pointcut expression are the methods defined by the MyService type in sample package.

Example 3

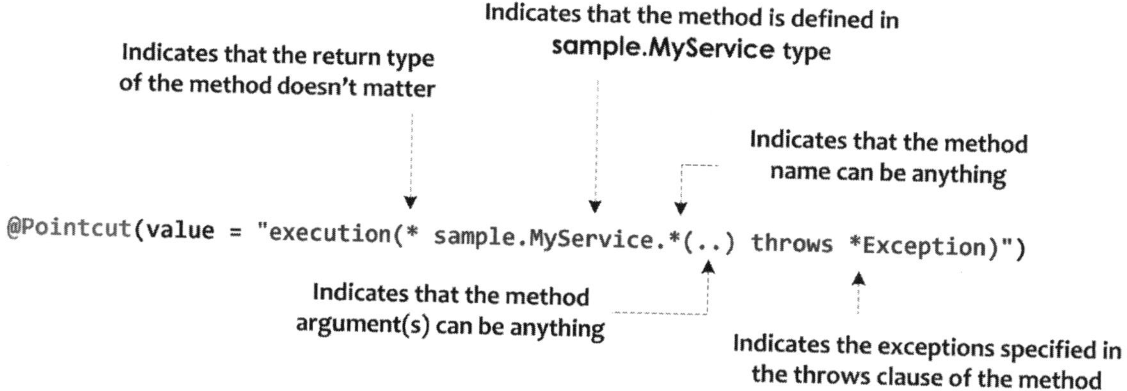

Figure 9-5 execution expression that specifies an exception pattern for the method

The methods matched by the above pointcut expression are the methods of sample.MyService type that specify a throws clause.

Example 4

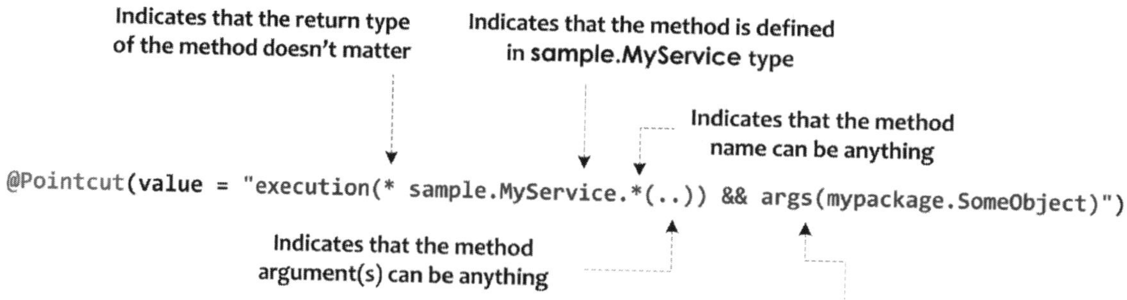

Figure 9-6 args pointcut designator specifies the object *instance* passed to the target method

In the above pointcut expression, combinations of execution and args pointcut designators have been used. You can combine pointcut designators using && and|| operators to create complex pointcut expressions. The methods matched by the above pointcut expression are the methods defined in sample.MyService type that accept an instance of SomeObject at runtime. The && in the above pointcut expression specifies that the target method *must* match the expressions specified by the execution and args pointcut designators.

If you want an advice to have access to one or more method arguments passed to the target method, specify names of the method arguments in the args expression, as shown here:

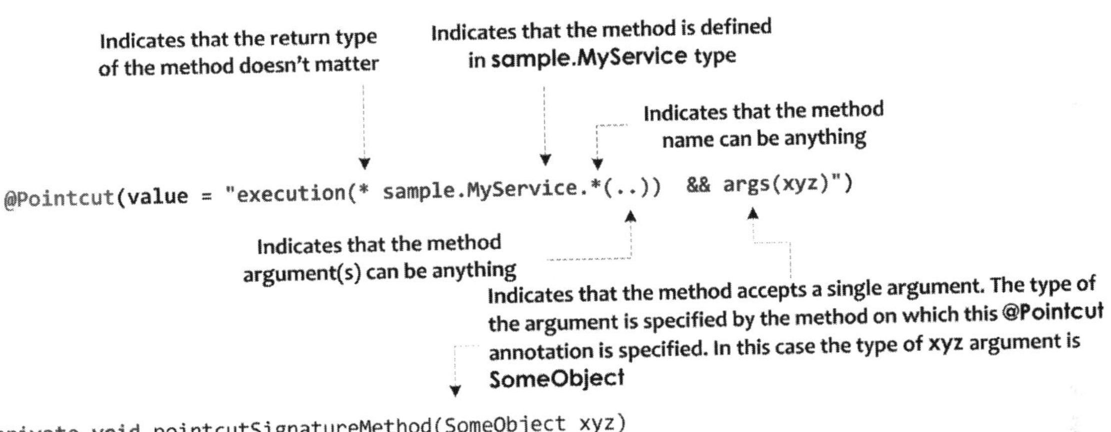

Figure 9-7 args pointcut designator specifies the target method's argument(s) that *must* be made available to the advice

In the above pointcut expression, args expression specifies that the target method *must* accept an argument of type SomeObject, and that argument is available to advice via xyz parameter. Let's see, a real example that makes use of this feature to pass arguments to the advice.

Passing target method's arguments to an advice

The following example listing shows a modified version of LoggingAspect in which log method is executed only if the method argument passed to the target method is an instance of FixedDepositDetails, and that FixedDepositDetails instance is also made available to the log method:

Example listing 9-7 – LoggingAspect class – passing target method's arguments to an advice

```
import org.aspectj.lang.annotation.Before;
import org.aspectj.lang.annotation.Pointcut;
```

```
@Aspect
@Component
public class LoggingAspect {
  .....
  @Pointcut(value =
    "execution(* sample.spring.chapter09.bankapp.service.*Service.*(..))
    && args(FixedDepositDetails) ")
  private void invokeServiceMethods(FixedDepositDetails FixedDepositDetails) {
  }

  @Before(value = "invokeServiceMethods(FixedDepositDetails)")
  public void log(JoinPoint joinPoint, FixedDepositDetails FixedDepositDetails) {
    .....
  }
}
```

In the above example listing, the args expression specifies that the FixedDepositDetails instance passed to the target method is available to log method (an advice) via FixedDepositDetails parameter. As the args expression provides log method with an instance of FixedDepositDetails object, the log method has been modified to accept an additional argument of type FixedDepositDetails.

Pointcut designators, like execution, args, within, this, target, and so on, are defined by AspectJ. Spring AOP defines a bean pointcut designator that is specific to Spring AOP framework. Let's take a quick look at bean pointcut designator.

bean pointcut designator

The bean pointcut designator is for limiting the target methods to the specified bean id (or name). You can specify the exact bean id or name, or you can specify a pattern. Let's look at a few examples of bean pointcut designator:

Example 1

Name or id of the bean whose methods are target of the advice

```
@Pointcut(value = "bean(someBean)")
```

Figure 9-8 bean pointcut designator specifies the bean id or name whose methods are target of the advice

The methods matched by the above pointcut expression are the methods defined by the bean named *someBean*.

Example 2

Advice is applied to methods of beans whose name or id begins with someBean

```
@Pointcut(value = "bean(someBean*)")
```

Figure 9-9 bean pointcut designator specifies that an advice is applied to the methods of the beans whose id or name begin with *someBean*.

In the above pointcut expression, bean pointcut designator specifies that an advice is applied to the methods of the beans whose id or name begin with *someBean*.

> Like any other pointcut designator, you can combine bean pointcut designator with other pointcut designators using && and ||operators to form complex pointcut expressions.

Let's now look at pointcut designators that perform matching based on annotations.

Annotations-based pointcut designators

AspectJ also provides pointcut designators, like *@annotation*, *@target*, *@within* and *@args* that you can use with Spring AOP to find target methods. Let's look at couple of examples that show usage of these pointcut designators:

Example 1

Advice is applied to methods that are annotated with Spring's @Cacheable annotation

```
@Pointcut(value = "@annotation(org.springframework.cache.annotation.Cacheable)")
```

Figure 9-10 *@annotation* pointcut designator specifies that an advice is applied to the methods annotated with Spring's *Cacheable* annotation

The methods matched by the above pointcut expression are the methods annotated with Spring's *@Cacheable* annotation.

Example 2

Advice is applied to methods that are contained in an object annotated with Spring's @Component annotation

```
@Pointcut(value = "@target(org.springframework.stereotype.Component)")
```

Figure 9-11 @target pointcut designator specifies that advice is applied to the methods of objects annotated with Spring's @Component annotation

The methods matched by the above pointcut expression are the methods contained in an object annotated with Spring's @Component annotation.

In this section, we looked at some of the pointcut designators defined by AspectJ. It is important to note that *not* all pointcut designators defined by AspectJ are supported by Spring AOP framework. If you use an unsupported pointcut designator in pointcut expressions, Spring AOP framework throws a java.lang.IllegalArgumentException. For instance, if you use call, set and get pointcut designators in pointcut expressions, Spring AOP will throw java.lang.IllegalArgumentException.

Let's now look at different advice types and how to create them.

9-5 Advice types

So far in this chapter, we've seen examples of *before* advice type. A before advice type is created by annotating a method of an aspect with @Before annotation (refer listing 9-1, 9-6 and 9-7). The other advice types that you can create are *after*, *after returning*, *after throwing*, *after* and *around*.

IMPORT **chapter 9/ch09-aop-advices** (The ch09-aop-advices project shows the MyBank application that uses different advice types. To run the application, execute the main method of the BankApp class of this project)

Let's now look at salient features of various advice types, and how to create them.

Before advice

A *before* advice is executed before the target method is executed. If a before advice doesn't throw an exception, the target method will *always* be invoked. You can control whether the target method is executed or not, by using an *around* advice (explained later in this section). As discussed earlier, AspectJ's @Before annotation is used to indicate that an advice is a *before* advice.

@Before annotated method may define its first argument to be of type JoinPoint. You can use the JoinPoint argument inside the advice to retrieve information about the target method. For instance, listing 9-1 showed that the JoinPoint instance can be used to obtain the class name of the target object and the arguments passed to the target method.

After returning advice

An *after returning* advice is executed *after* the target method returns. You should note that an *after returning* advice is not executed if the target method throws an exception. An *after returning* advice is annotated with AspectJ's @AfterReturning annotation. An *after returning* advice can access the value returned by the target method, and modify it before it is returned to the calling object.

The SampleAspect class of ch09-aop-advices project represents an AOP aspect. The following example listing shows that the SampleAspect class defines an *after returning* advice that prints the value returned by BankAccountService's createBankAccount method:

Example listing 9-8 – SampleAspect class – *after returning* advice
Project – ch09-aop-advices
Source location - src/main/java/sample/spring/chapter09/bankapp/aspects

```
package sample.spring.chapter09.bankapp.aspects;

import org.aspectj.lang.annotation.AfterReturning;
.....
@Aspect
public class SampleAspect {
   private Logger logger = Logger.getLogger(SampleAspect.class);

   @Pointcut(value = "execution(* sample.spring..BankAccountService.createBankAccount(..))")
   private void createBankAccountMethod() {}

   @AfterReturning(value = "createBankAccountMethod()", returning = "aValue")
   public void afterReturningAdvice(JoinPoint joinPoint, int aValue) {
      logger.info("Value returned by " + joinPoint.getSignature().getName()
            + " method is " + aValue);
   }
   .....
}
```

In the above example listing, afterReturningAdvice method represents an *after returning* advice. The pointcut expression specified by the @Pointcut annotation limits the join point to BankAccountService's createBankAccount method. The .. in the execution expression specifies that the sample.spring package and its sub-packages are searched to find the BankAccountService type.

In example listing 9-8, SampleAspect's afterReturningAdvice method is invoked after the invocation of BankAccountService's createBankAccount method. The returning attribute of @AfterReturning annotation specifies the name with which the return value of the target method is available to the advice. In the above example listing, the value returned by the createBankAccount method is made available to the afterReturningAdvice method via aValue argument. The type of the aValue argument has been specified as int because the createBankAccount method returns an int value. You should note that if you specify the returning attribute, the advice is applied only to methods that return the specified type. If an *after returning* advice is applied to methods that return different value types (including void), you can specify argument type of the returned value as Object.

As shown in example listing 9-8, a @AfterReturning annotated method may define its first argument to be of type JoinPoint to access target method information.

After throwing advice

An *after throwing* advice is executed when the target method throws an exception. An *after throwing* advice can access the exception thrown by the target method. An *after throwing* advice is annotated with AspectJ's @AfterThrowing annotation.

The following example listing shows an *after throwing* advice that is executed when an exception is thrown by target methods:

Example listing 9-9 – SampleAspect class – *after throwing* advice
Project – ch09-aop-advices
Source location - src/main/java/sample/spring/chapter09/bankapp/aspects

```
package sample.spring.chapter09.bankapp.aspects;

import org.aspectj.lang.annotation.AfterThrowing;
.....
@Aspect
public class SampleAspect {
  private Logger logger = Logger.getLogger(SampleAspect.class);
  .....
  @Pointcut(value = " execution(* sample.spring..FixedDepositService.*(..)) ")
  private void exceptionMethods() {}
  .....
  @AfterThrowing(value = "exceptionMethods()", throwing = "exception")
  public void afterThrowingAdvice(JoinPoint joinPoint, Throwable exception) {
    logger.info("Exception thrown by " + joinPoint.getSignature().getName()
```

```
        + " Exception type is : " + exception);
    }
}
```

In the above example listing, SampleAspect's afterThrowingAdvice method represents an *after throwing* advice. The afterThrowingAdvice method is executed when an exception is thrown by any of the FixedDepositService object's methods. In the above example listing, the throwing attribute of @AfterThrowing annotation specifies the name with which the exception thrown by the target method is made available to the afterThrowingAdvice method. As the throwing attribute's value is exception, the exception is passed to the afterThrowingAdvice method via argument named exception. Notice that the type of the exception argument is java.lang.Throwable, which means that the afterThrowingAdvice method is executed for all exceptions thrown by the target method. If you want afterThrowingAdvice method is executed only when a specific exception type is thrown by the target method, change the type of the exception argument. For instance, if you want the afterThrowingAdvice method is executed only when the target method throws java.lang.IllegalStateException, specify java.lang.IllegalStateException as the type of the exception argument.

As shown in example listing 9-9, @AfterThrowing annotated method may define its first argument to be of type JoinPoint to access target method information.

After advice

An *after* advice is executed after the target method is executed, irrespective of whether the target method completes normally or throws an exception. An *after* advice is annotated with AspectJ's @After annotation.

The following example listing shows an *after* advice that is executed for BankAccountService's createBankAccount method, and for the methods defined by the FixedDepositService interface:

Example listing 9-10 – SampleAspect class – *after* advice
Project – ch09-aop-advices
Source location - src/main/java/sample/spring/chapter09/bankapp/aspects

```
package sample.spring.chapter09.bankapp.aspects;

import org.aspectj.lang.annotation.After;
.....
@Aspect
public class SampleAspect {
    private Logger logger = Logger.getLogger(SampleAspect.class);

    @Pointcut(value = "execution(* sample.spring..BankAccountService.createBankAccount(..))")
    private void createBankAccountMethod() {}
```

```
    @Pointcut(value = "execution(* sample.spring..FixedDepositService.*(..))")
    private void exceptionMethods() {}
    .....
    @After(value = "exceptionMethods() || createBankAccountMethod()")
    public void afterAdvice(JoinPoint joinPoint) {
        logger.info("After advice executed for " + joinPoint.getSignature().getName());
    }
}
```

In the above example listing, SampleAspect's afterAdvice method represents an *after* advice. The afterAdvice method is executed after the target method is executed. Notice that the @After annotation's value attribute uses || operator to combine pointcut expressions represented by the createBankAccountMethod and exceptionMethods methods to form a new pointcut expression.

As shown in example listing 9-10, @After annotated method may define its first argument to be of type JoinPoint, to access target method information.

Around advice

An *around* advice is executed both *before* and *after* the execution of the target method. Unlike other advices, an *around* advice can control whether the target method is executed or not. An *around* advice is annotated with AspectJ's @Around annotation.

The following example listing shows an *around* advice defined by SampleAspect class of ch09-aop-advices project:

Example listing 9-11 – SampleAspect class – *around* advice
Project – ch09-aop-advices
Source location - src/main/java/sample/spring/chapter09/bankapp/aspects

```
package sample.spring.chapter09.bankapp.aspects;

import org.aspectj.lang.ProceedingJoinPoint;
import org.aspectj.lang.annotation.Around;
import org.springframework.util.StopWatch;
.....
@Aspect
public class SampleAspect {
    .....
    @Around(value = "execution(* sample.spring..*Service.*(..))")
    public Object aroundAdvice(ProceedingJoinPoint pjp) {
        Object obj = null;
```

```
    StopWatch watch = new StopWatch();
    watch.start();
    try {
      obj = pjp.proceed();
    } catch (Throwable throwable) {
      // -- perform any action that you want
    }
    watch.stop();
    logger.info(watch.prettyPrint());
    return obj;
  }
}
```

In the above example listing, the aroundAdvice method represents an *around* advice. The ProceedingJoinPoint argument to the aroundAdvice method is meant for controlling the invocation of the target method. It is important to note that ProceedingJoinPoint argument *must* be the first argument passed to an *around* advice. When you invoke ProceedingJoinPoint's proceed method, the target method is invoked. This means that if you don't invoke the ProceedingJoinPoint's proceed method, the target method is *not* invoked. If you pass an Object[] to the proceed method, the values contained in the Object[] are passed as arguments to the target method. If an around advice chooses *not* to invoke the target method, the around advice may itself return a value.

As the target method is invoked only when you call ProceedingJoinPoint's proceed method, around advice allows you to perform actions *before* and *after* the invocation of the target method, and to share information between these action. In example listing 9-11, the aroundAdvice method records the time taken for the target method to execute. The aroundAdvice method starts a stop watch (represented by Spring's StopWatch object) before calling ProceedingJoinPoint's proceed method, and stops the stop watch after calling ProceedingJoinPoint's proceed method. StopWatch's prettyPrint method is then used to print the time taken by the target method to execute.

If you want to modify the value returned by the target method, cast the returned value of ProceedingJoinPoint's proceed method to the return type of the target method and modify it. A calling method sees the value returned by the around advice; therefore, you *must* define the return type of an advice method as Object or the type that is returned by the target method. An advice method has the option to return the value returned by the target method, or to return a different value altogether. For instance, instead of invoking the target method, an around advice may inspect the argument(s) being passed to the target method and return a value from the cache if a cache entry exists for the same set of arguments.

So far we have looked at examples that showed how to use AspectJ annotation-style to create aspects. Let's now look at how to use a regular Spring bean as an AOP aspect.

9-6 Spring AOP - XML schema-style

In XML schema-style, a regular Spring bean acts as an aspect. A method defined in an aspect is associated with an advice type and a pointcut expression using Spring's aop schema.

IMPORT **chapter 9/ch09-aop-xml-schema** (The ch09-aop-xml-schema project is same as ch09-aop-advices project, except that ch09-aop-xml-schema's SampleAspect class is a simple Java class that doesn't use AspectJ's annotations)

The following example listing shows the SampleAspect class of ch09-aop-xml-schema project that defines advices:

Example listing 9-12 – SampleAspect class
Project – ch09-aop-xml-schema
Source location - src/main/java/sample/spring/chapter09/bankapp/aspects

```
package sample.spring.chapter09.bankapp.aspects;
.....
public class SampleAspect {
  .....
  public void afterReturningAdvice(JoinPoint joinPoint, int aValue) {
    logger.info("Value returned by " + joinPoint.getSignature().getName()+ " method is " + aValue);
  }
  public void afterThrowingAdvice(JoinPoint joinPoint, Throwable exception) {
    logger.info("Exception thrown by " + joinPoint.getSignature().getName()
          + " Exception type is : " + exception);
  }
  .....
}
```

The above example listing shows that the SampleAspect class defines methods that represent AOP advices. Notice that the SampleAspect class is *not* annotated with @Aspect annotation and the methods are not annotated with @After, @AfterReturning, and so on, annotations.

Let's now look at how <config> element of Spring's aop schema is used to configure a regular Spring bean as an AOP aspect.

Configuring an AOP aspect

In XML schema-style, AOP-specific configurations are enclosed within <config> element of Spring's aop schema. And, an AOP aspect is configured using <aspect> sub-element of <config> element.

The following example listing shows how the SampleAspect class is configured using <aspect> sub-element of <config> element:

Example listing 9-13 – applicationContext.xml – Spring's aop schema usage
Project – **ch09-aop-xml-schema**
Source location - src/main/resources/META-INF/spring

```
<beans ..... xmlns:aop="http://www.springframework.org/schema/aop" ..... >
  .....
  <bean id="sampleAspect"
    class="sample.spring.chapter09.bankapp.aspects.SampleAspect" />

  <aop:config proxy-target-class="false" expose-proxy="true">
    <aop:aspect id="sampleAspect" ref="sampleAspect">
      .....
    </aop:aspect>
  </aop:config>
</beans>
```

As the <config> element relies on autoproxying, the <config> element defines proxy-target-class and expose-proxy attributes. If you remember, the same attributes were defined by <aspectj-autoproxy> element of Spring's aop schema. Refer section 9-3 to know more about proxy-target-class and expose-proxy attributes.

In example listing 9-13, the sampleAspect bean definition defines SampleAspect class as a bean. The <aspect> element configures the sampleAspect bean as an AOP aspect. The <aspect> element's id attribute specifies a unique identifier for an aspect, and the ref attribute specifies the Spring bean that you want to configure as an AOP aspect.

Now, that we have configured an AOP aspect, let's look at how to map methods defined in an AOP aspect to different advice types and pointcut expressions.

Configuring an advice

You configure an advice using one of the following sub-elements of <aspect> element: <before> (for configuring a *before* advice type), <after-returning> (for configuring an *after returning* advice type), <after-throwing> (for configuring an *after throwing* advice type), <after> (for configuring an *after* advice type) and <around> (for configuring an *around* advice type).

Let's now look at how the advices defined in the SampleAspect class of **ch09-aop-xml-schema** project are configured in the application context XML file.

Configuring an *after returning* advice

The following figure shows how the SampleAspect's afterReturningAdvice method is configured as an *after returning* advice using <after-returning> element:

```
public void afterReturningAdvice(JoinPoint joinPoint, int aValue) {
        logger.info("Value returned by " + joinPoint.getSignature().getName()
                        + " method is " + aValue);
}

                    ↓ ↓

<aop:after-returning method="afterReturningAdvice" returning="aValue"
pointcut="execution(*sample.spring..BankAccountService.createBankAccount(..))" />
```

Figure 9-12 afterReturningAdvice method of SampleAspect class is configured as an *after returning* advice using <after-returning> element of Spring's aop schema

The <after-returning> element's method attribute specifies the name of the method which you want to configure as an *after returning* advice. The returning attribute serves the same purpose as the @AfterReturning annotation's returning attribute; it makes the returned value from the target method available to the advice. The pointcut attribute specifies the pointcut expression used for finding the methods to which the advice is applied.

Configuring an *after throwing* advice

The following figure shows how the SampleAspect's afterThrowingAdvice method is configured as an *after throwing* advice using <after-throwing> element:

```
public void afterThrowingAdvice(JoinPoint joinPoint, Throwable exception) {
        logger.info("Exception thrown by " + joinPoint.getSignature().getName()
                        + " Exception type is : " + exception);
}

                    ↓ ↓

<aop:after-throwing method="afterThrowingAdvice" throwing="exception"
pointcut="execution(* sample.spring..FixedDepositService.*(..))" />
```

Figure 9-13 afterThrowingAdvice method of SampleAspect class is configured as an *after throwing* advice using <after-throwing> element of Spring's aop schema

The <after-throwing> element's method attribute specifies the name of the method which you want to configure as an *after throwing* advice. The throwing attribute serves the same purpose as the @AfterThrowing annotation's throwing attribute; it makes the exception thrown by the target method available to the advice. The pointcut attribute specifies the pointcut expression used for finding the methods to which the advice is applied.

The other advice types (*before*, *after* and *around*) are configured the same way as the *after returning* and *after throwing* advices that we just saw.

Let's now look at different ways in which you can associate a pointcut expression with an advice.

Associating a pointcut expression with an advice

The <after>, <after-returning>, <after-throwing>, <before> and <around> elements of Spring's aop schema define a pointcut attribute that you can use to specify the pointcut expression associated with the advice. If you want to share pointcut expressions between different advices, you can use the <pointcut> sub-element of the <config> element to define pointcut expressions.

The following example listing shows that the <pointcut> element is used for defining pointcut expressions:

Example listing 9-14 – application context XML - <pointcut> element

```
<beans ..... xmlns:aop="http://www.springframework.org/schema/aop" ..... >
  .....
  <bean id="sampleAspect"
    class="sample.spring.chapter09.bankapp.aspects.SampleAspect" />

  <aop:config proxy-target-class="false" expose-proxy="true">
    <aop:pointcut expression="execution(* sample.spring..*Service.*(..))" id="services" />

    <aop:aspect id="sampleAspect" ref="sampleAspect">
      <aop:after method="afterAdvice" pointcut-ref="services" />
      <aop:around method="aroundAdvice" pointcut-ref="services"/>
    </aop:aspect>
  </aop:config>
</beans>
```

In the above example listing, the <pointcut> element specifies a pointcut expression. The expression attribute specifies the pointcut expression, and the id attribute specifies a unique identifier for the pointcut expression. The pointcut expression defined by a <pointcut> element is referenced by <after>, <after-returning>, and so on, advice type elements using pointcut-ref attribute. For instance, in the above example listing, <after> and <around> elements use pointcut-ref attribute to refer to the services pointcut expressions.

9-7 Summary

In this chapter, we looked at AOP concepts and how Spring AOP can be used to address cross-cutting concerns in Spring applications. We saw how to create aspects using AspectJ annotation-style and XML schema-style. We also discussed how to create and configure different advice types. We touched upon the pointcut expressions that you can create to find matching methods in the application. For a more comprehensive coverage of Spring AOP please refer to Spring reference documentation. In the next chapter, we'll look at how to develop web applications using Spring Web MVC module of Spring Framework.

Chapter 10 – *Spring Web MVC basics*

10-1 Introduction

The Spring Web MVC module of Spring Framework provides an MVC (Model-View-Controller) framework that you can use for developing servlet-based web applications. Spring Web MVC is a *non-intrusive* framework that provides a clear *separation of concerns* between application objects that form the web layer. For instance, a *controller* object is used for processing the request, a *validator* object is used for performing validation, and a *command* object is used for storing form data, and so on. It is important to note that none of these application objects implement or extend from any Spring-specific interface or class.

In this chapter, we'll first look at the directory structure that will be followed by all the sample *web* projects discussed in this chapter. We'll then look at a simple 'Hello World' web application developed using Spring Web MVC. In the rest of this chapter, we'll look at some of the Spring Web MVC annotations in the context of our MyBank web application. This chapter sets the stage for discussing more advanced Spring Web MVC features in the next chapter.

IMPORT **chapter 10/ch10-helloworld** (This project shows a simple 'Hello World' web application that uses Spring Web MVC. Refer appendix A to learn how to deploy sample web projects on Tomcat server. Once you have deployed the application, go to the following URL: http://localhost:8080/ch10-helloworld/helloworld/sayhello. If the application is deployed successfully, it will show you 'Hello World !!' message.)

10-2 Directory structure of sample web projects

Figure 10-1 describes the important directories of ch10-helloworld web project. Some of the important points that you need to remember are:

- The src/main/resources/META-INF/spring folder contains the *root web application context XML* file that defines beans that are shared by all the servlets and filters of the web application. The root web application context XML file typically defines data sources, services, DAOs, transaction managers, and so on. The root web application context XML file is loaded by Spring's ContextLoaderListener (a javax.servlet.ServletContextListener implementation). Refer section 10-10 to learn about how ContextLoaderListener is configured in web.xml file.

- The src/main/webapp/WEB-INF/spring folder contains the *web application context XML* file that defines beans that form part of the *web* layer of the application. The web application context XML file typically defines *controllers* (also referred to as *handlers*), *handler mappings*, *view resolvers*, *exception resolvers*, and so on. We'll learn about these objects later in this chapter.

- The beans defined in the root web application context XML file are *available* to the beans defined in the web application context XML file. This means, a bean defined in the web application context XML file can be dependent on a bean defined in the root web application context XML file, but *not* the other way round.

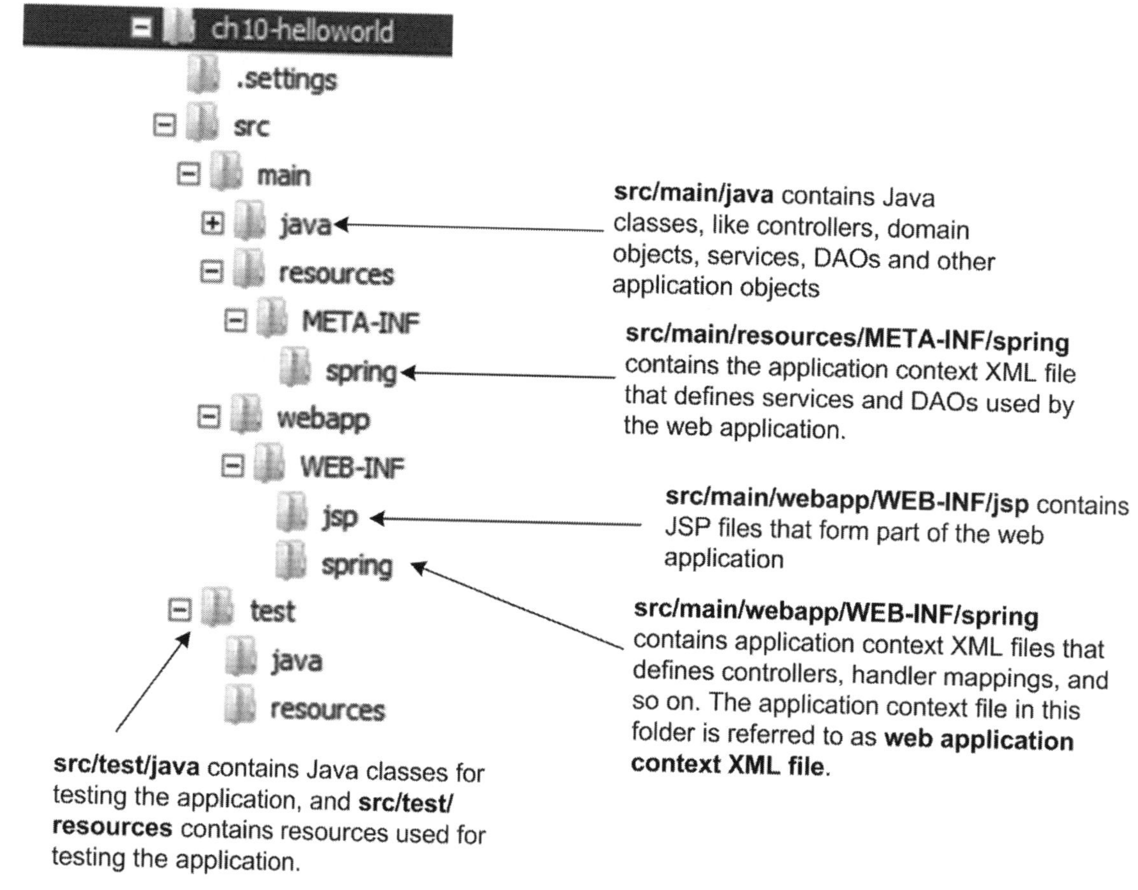
ch10-helloworld
.settings
src
main
java
resources
META-INF
spring
webapp
WEB-INF
jsp
spring
test
java
resources
src/main/java contains Java classes, like controllers, domain objects, services, DAOs and other application objects
src/main/resources/META-INF/spring contains the application context XML file that defines services and DAOs used by the web application.
src/main/webapp/WEB-INF/jsp contains JSP files that form part of the web application
src/main/webapp/WEB-INF/spring contains application context XML files that defines controllers, handler mappings, and so on. The application context file in this folder is referred to as web application context XML file.
src/test/java contains Java classes for testing the application, and src/test/resources contains resources used for testing the application.

Figure 10-1 Directory structure of ch10-helloworld project

Let's now look at the configuration files and the classes that form the ch10-helloworld project.

10-3 Understanding the 'Hello World' web application

If you right-click on the ch10-helloworld project in your Eclipse IDE and select Build Path → Configure Build Path option, you'll notice that the project depends on spring-beans, spring-context, spring-core, spring-expression, spring-web and spring-webmvc JAR files. These JAR files are required for building a basic Spring Web MVC application.

The following table describes the configuration files and the Java source files that constitute the ch10-helloworld project. Later in this section, we'll take a closer look at these files and classes.

Configuration file or Java source file	Description
HelloWorldController.java	Spring Web MVC *controller* that is responsible for request handling. You'll find this file inside sample.spring.chapter10.web package of src/main/java folder.
helloworld.jsp	JSP file that shows the 'Hello World !!' message You'll find this file inside src/main/webapp/WEB-INF/jsp folder
myapp-config.xml	Web application context XML file that contains bean definitions for controllers, handler mappings, and so on. You'll find this file inside src/main/webapp/WEB-INF/spring folder
web.xml	Web application deployment descriptor You'll find this file inside src/main/webapp/WEB-INF folder

Apart from the files shown in the above table, the ch10-helloworld project also contains log4j.properties file that contains Log4j configuration, and pom.xml file that goes as input to the maven build tool. To know more about these files refer to Log4j (http://logging.apache.org/log4j/1.2/) and Maven (http://maven.apache.org/index.html) documentation.

Let's now take a closer look at each of the files described in the above table.

HelloWorldController.java – Hello World web application's controller class

In Spring Web MVC applications, the request handling logic is contained in controller classes. The following example listing shows the HelloWorldController controller class of ch10-helloworld project:

Example listing 10-1 – HelloWorldController class
Project – ch10-helloworld
Source location - src/main/java/sample/spring/chapter10/web

```
package sample.spring.chapter10.web;
```

```
import org.springframework.web.servlet.ModelAndView;
import org.springframework.web.servlet.mvc.Controller;
.....

public class HelloWorldController implements Controller {

  @Override

  public ModelAndView handleRequest(HttpServletRequest request,
        HttpServletResponse response) throws Exception {
    Map<String, String> modelData = new HashMap<String, String>();
    modelData.put("msg", "Hello World !!");
    return new ModelAndView("helloworld", modelData);
  }
}
```

The above example listing shows that the HelloWorldController class implements Spring's Controller interface. The Controller interface defines a handleRequest method, which you need to implement to provide the request handling logic. The handleRequest method returns a ModelAndView object that contains the following information:

- the data (referred to as *model* data) to be shown to the user, and
- logical name of the JSP page (referred to as *view*) that shows the model data

The model data is usually represented as a java.util.Map type object, and each entry in the java.util.Map object represents a *model attribute*. The name of the view (the JSP page) to be shown to the user is specified as a String value.

Example listing 10-1 shows that the HelloWorldController's handleRequest method returns a ModelAndView object that contains helloworld (a String value) as the view name and modelData (a java.util.Map type object) as the model data. The modelData contains a msg model attribute whose value is the 'Hello World !!' message. We'll soon see that the msg model attribute is used by the helloworld view (a JSP page) to show the 'Hello World !!' message to the users.

The following diagram summarizes how HelloWorldController's handleRequest method renders a JSP page:

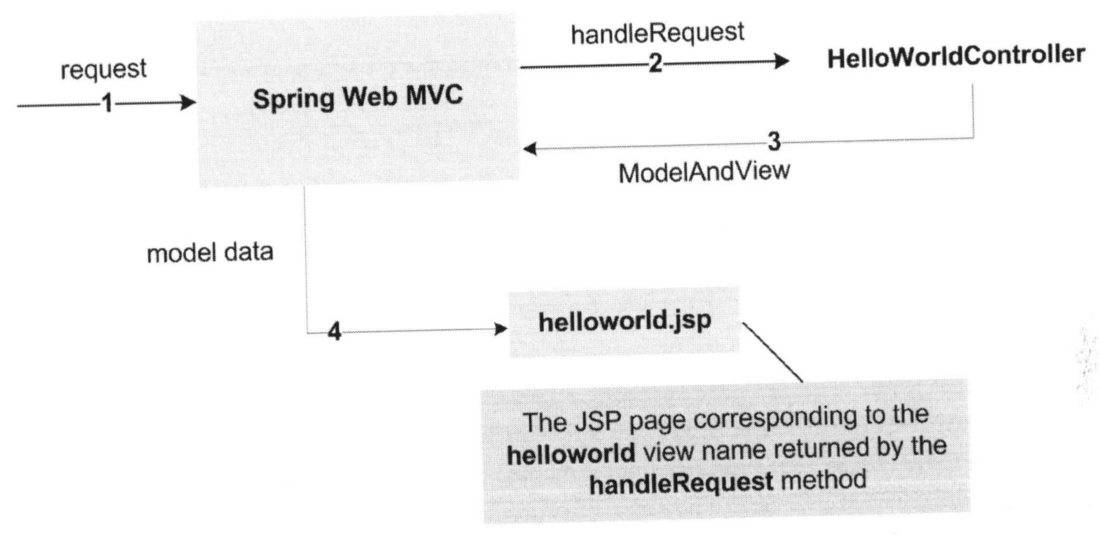

Figure 10-2 Spring Web MVC framework invokes the HelloWorldController's handleRequest method and uses the returned ModelAndView object to render the helloworld.jsp page

The above figure shows that the Spring Web MVC framework intercepts an incoming HTTP request and invokes the HelloWorldController's handleRequest method. The handleRequest method returns a ModelAndView object that contains the model data and the view information. After receiving the ModelAndView object from the handleRequest method, the Spring Web MVC framework dispatches the HTTP request to the helloworld.jsp page and makes the model attributes available to the helloworld.jsp page as *request attributes*.

> Spring Web MVC makes the model attributes available to the view technology (like JSP and Velocity) in a format that is suitable for the view technology. For instance, if you are using JSP as the view technology, model attributes are made available to the JSP pages as request attributes.

helloworld.jsp – JSP page that shows the 'Hello World !!' message

The following example listing shows the helloworld.jsp page of ch10-helloworld project:

Example listing 10-2 – helloworld.jsp JSP page
Project – ch10-helloworld
Source location - src/main/webapp/WEB-INF/jsp

```
<%@taglib uri="http://java.sun.com/jsp/jstl/core" prefix="c" %>
```

```
<c:out value="${msg}"/>
```

In the above example listing, <c:out> prints the value of msg request attribute. The msg request attribute refers to the msg model attribute returned by HelloWorldController's handleRequest method (refer example listing 10-1). As the value of msg model attribute is 'Hello World !!', helloworld.jsp JSP page shows 'Hello World !!' message.

myapp-config.xml – Web application context XML file

The following example listing shows the beans configured in myapp-config.xml file of ch10-helloworld project:

Example listing 10-3 – myapp-config.xml
Project – ch10-helloworld
Source location - src/main/webapp/WEB-INF/spring

```
<beans xmlns="http://www.springframework.org/schema/beans"
  xmlns:xsi="http://www.w3.org/2001/XMLSchema-instance"
  xsi:schemaLocation="http://www.springframework.org/schema/beans
 http://www.springframework.org/schema/beans/spring-beans.xsd">

  <bean name="helloWorldController"
       class="sample.spring.chapter10.web.HelloWorldController" />

  <bean id="handlerMapping"
     class="org.springframework.web.servlet.handler.SimpleUrlHandlerMapping">
     <property name="urlMap">
        <map>
            <entry key="/sayhello" value-ref="helloWorldController" />
        </map>
     </property>
  </bean>

  <bean id="viewResolver"
     class="org.springframework.web.servlet.view.InternalResourceViewResolver">
     <property name="prefix" value="/WEB-INF/jsp/" />
     <property name="suffix" value=".jsp" />
  </bean>
</beans>
```

The above example listing shows that apart from the HelloWorldController, Spring's SimpleUrlHandlerMapping and InternalResourceViewResolver beans are also configured in the myapp-config.xml file.

SimpleUrlHandlerMapping bean (an implementation of Spring's HandlerMapping interface) maps an incoming HTTP request to the controller responsible for handling the request. SimpleUrlHandlerMapping bean uses the URL path to map a request to a controller. The urlMap property (of type java.util.Map) specifies URL path to controller bean mapping. In example listing 10-3, the "/sayhello" URL path (specified by the key attribute) is mapped to the HelloWorldController bean (specified by the value-ref attribute). You should note that the URL path specified by the key attribute is *relative* to the URL path to which Spring's DispatcherServlet (a servlet) is mapped in the web application deployment descriptor. DispatcherServlet is discussed later in this section.

InternalResourceViewResolver bean (an implementation of Spring's ViewResolver interface) locates the actual view (like, JSP or servlet) based on the view name contained in the ModelAndView object. The actual view is located by *prepending* the value of prefix property and *appending* the value of suffix property to the view name. The example listing 10-3 shows that the value of prefix property is /WEB-INF/jsp, and the value of suffix property is .jsp. As the HelloWorldController's handleRequest method returns a ModelAndView object which contains helloworld as the view name, the actual view is /WEB-INF/jsp/helloworld.jsp (a string that is obtained by prepending /WEB-INF/jsp and appending .jsp to the helloworld view name).

The following figure shows the role played by SimpleUrlHandlerMapping and InternalResourceViewResolver beans in the 'Hello World' web application:

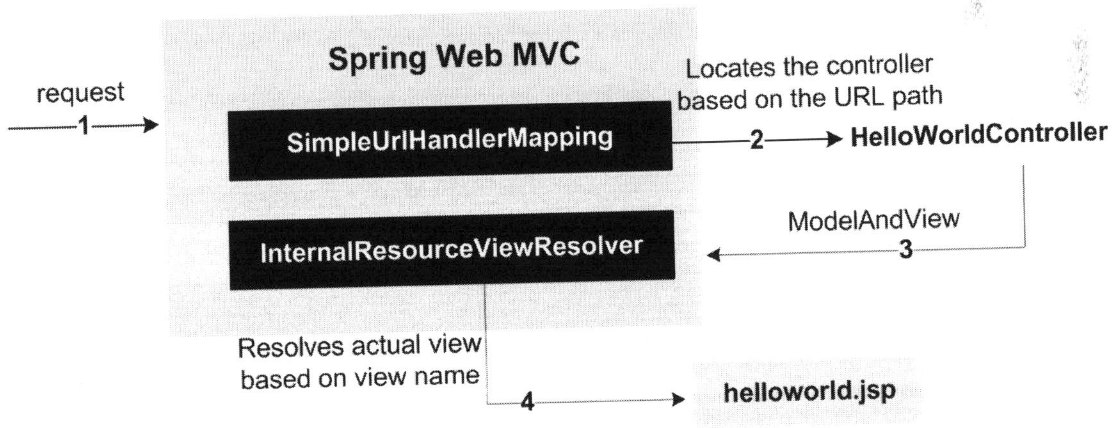

Figure 10-3 SimpleUrlHandlerMapping locates the controller to be invoked and InternalResourceViewResolver resolves the actual view based on the view name

SimpleUrlHandlerMapping and InternalResourceViewResolver beans are *automatically* detected by Spring Web MVC and used for finding the controller for request handling and resolving views, respectively.

web.xml – Web application deployment descriptor

In Spring Web MVC based applications, requests are intercepted by a DispatcherServlet (a servlet provided by Spring Web MVC) that is responsible for dispatching requests to the appropriate controller.

The following example listing shows the configuration of DispatcherServlet in web.xml file of ch10-helloworld project:

Example listing 10-4 – web.xml
Project – ch10-helloworld
Source location - src/main/webapp/WEB-INF/spring

```
<web-app xmlns="java.sun.com/xml/ns/javaee"
  xmlns:xsi="w3.org/2001/XMLSchema-instance"
  xsi:schemaLocation="java.sun.com/xml/ns/javaee java.sun.com/xml/ns/javaee/web-app_3_0.xsd"
  version="3.0">

  <servlet>
    <servlet-name>hello</servlet-name>
    <servlet-class>org.springframework.web.servlet.DispatcherServlet</servlet-class>
    <init-param>
       <param-name>contextConfigLocation</param-name>
       <param-value>/WEB-INF/spring/myapp-config.xml</param-value>
    </init-param>
    <load-on-startup>1</load-on-startup>
  </servlet>

  <servlet-mapping>
    <servlet-name>hello</servlet-name>
    <url-pattern>/helloworld/*</url-pattern>
  </servlet-mapping>
</web-app>
```

A DispatcherServlet is associated with a web application context XML file which is identified by the contextConfigLocation servlet initialization parameter. In the above example listing, the contextConfigLocation initialization parameter refers to the myapp-config.xml file (refer example listing 10-3).

If you don't specify the contextConfigLocation parameter, the DispatcherServlet looks for the web application context XML file named <name-of-DispatcherServlet>-servlet.xml file in the WEB-INF directory of the web application. Here, the value of <name-of-DispatcherServlet> is the servlet name specified by the <servlet-name> sub-element of <servlet> that configures the DispatcherServlet. For instance, if we had *not* specified the contextConfigLocation parameter in example listing 10-3, the DispatcherServlet would have looked for a file named hello-servlet.xml in the WEB-INF directory.

The HandlerMapping and ViewResolver beans defined in the web application context XML file are used by the DispatcherServlet for request processing. DispatcherServlet uses the HandlerMapping implementation for finding the appropriate controller for the request, and uses the ViewResolver implementation for resolving the actual view based on the view name returned by the controller.

In the context of 'Hello World' web application, the following figure summarizes the role played by the DispatcherServlet servlet in request processing:

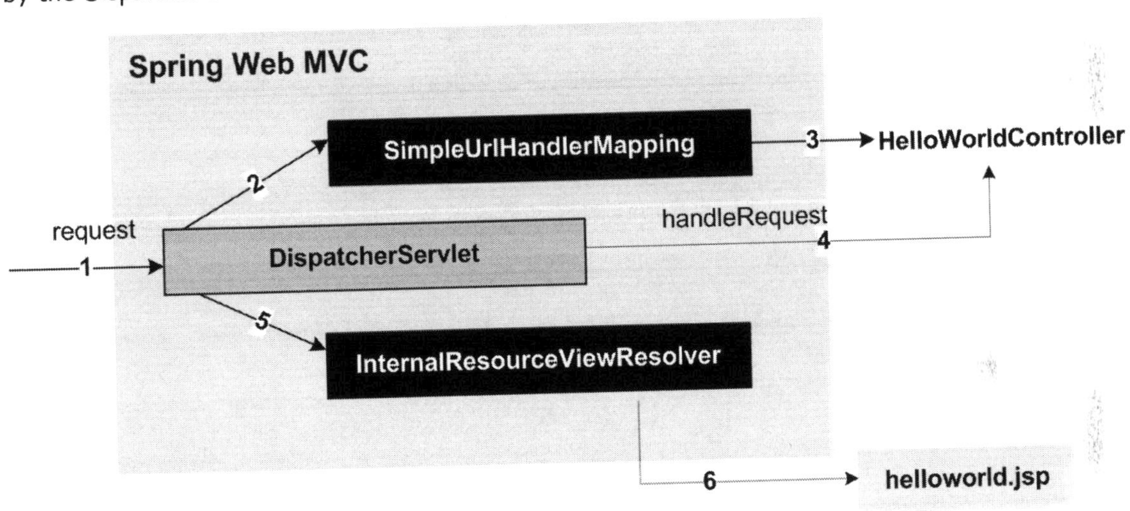

Figure 10-4 DispatcherServlet uses HandlerMapping and ViewResolver beans for request processing.

The above figure shows that the following sequence of activities are performed by Spring Web MVC during request processing:

- request is first intercepted by the DispatcherServlet servlet
- DispatcherServlet uses the HandlerMapping bean (which is SimpleUrlHandlerMapping bean in case of 'Hello World' web application) to find an appropriate controller for handling the request
- DispatcherServlet calls the request handling method of the controller (which is HelloWorldController's handleRequest method in case of 'Hello World' web application)

- DispatcherServlet sends the view name returned by the controller to the ViewResolver bean (which is InternalResourceViewResolver bean in case of 'Hello World' web application) to find the actual view (JSP or servlet) to be rendered

- DispatcherServlet dispatches the request to the actual view (JSP or servlet). The model data returned by the controller are made available to the view as request attributes.

The DispatcherServlet of 'Hello World' web application is mapped to /helloworld/* pattern (refer example listing 10-4), and SimpleUrlHandlerMapping maps /sayhello URL path to HelloWorldController bean (refer example listing 10-3). If you access the URL http://localhost:8080/ch10-helloworld/helloworld/sayhello, it results in invocation of handleRequest method of HelloWorldController controller. The following figure shows how Spring Web MVC maps the URL http://localhost:8080/ch10-helloworld/helloworld/sayhello to the HelloWorldController controller:

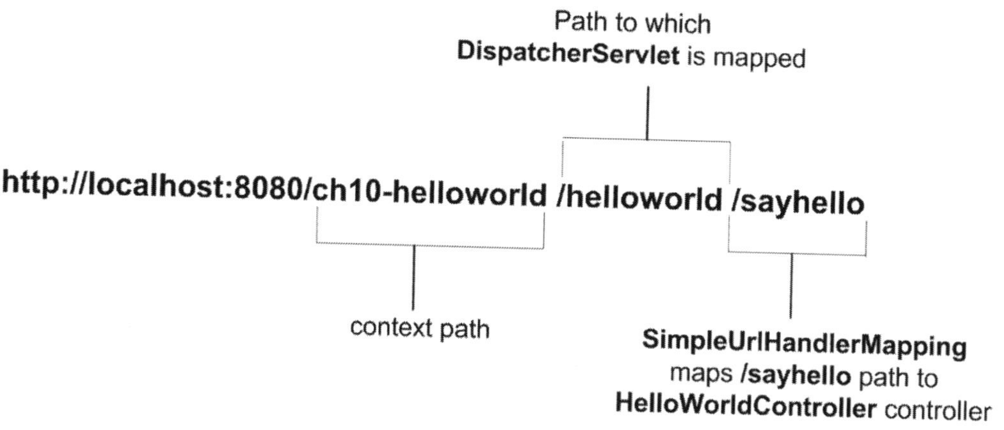

Figure 10-5 How the URL path http://localhost:8080/ch10-helloworld/helloworld/sayhello is mapped to the HelloWorldController by Spring Web MVC

In the above figure, the /ch10-helloworld part of the URL represents the context path of the 'Hello World' web application, the /helloworld part of the URL maps to the DispatcherServlet servlet (refer example listing 10-4), and the /sayhello part of the URL maps to the HelloWorldController controller (refer example listing 10-3).

In this section, we saw how a simple 'Hello World' web application is developed using Spring Web MVC. Let's now take a closer look at the DispatcherServlet servlet that acts a *front controller* in a Spring Web MVC application.

10-4 DispatcherServlet – the front controller

In the previous section, we saw that the DispatcherServlet acts as a *front controller* that interacts with the HandlerMapping and ViewResolver beans defined in the web application context XML file to process requests. In this section, we'll look at how DispatcherServlet works behind the scenes.

At the time of initialization, a DispatcherServlet loads the corresponding web application context XML file (which could be specified via contextConfigLocation initialization parameter, or is named as <name-of-DispatcherServlet>-servlet.xml file and placed in the WEB-INF directory), and creates an instance of Spring's WebApplicationContext object. WebApplicationContext is a sub-interface of ApplicationContext interface that provides features that are specific to web applications. For instance, beans in the WebApplicationContext can have additional scopes, like request and session. You can think of WebApplicationContext object as an object that represents a Spring container instance in Spring Web MVC applications.

The following table describes the additional scopes that you can specify for beans configured in the web application context XML file:

Bean scope	Description
request	Spring container creates a *new* bean instance for every HTTP request. The bean instance is destroyed by the Spring container when the HTTP request completes. This scope is valid only for ApplicationContext implementations that are applicable in web application scenarios. For instance, if you are using XmlWebApplicationContext or AnnotationConfigWebApplicationContext, only then you can specify the request scope for a bean.
session	Spring container creates a *new* bean instance when an HTTP Session is created. The bean instance is destroyed by the Spring container when the HTTP Session is destroyed. This scope is valid only for ApplicationContext implementations that are applicable in web application scenarios. For instance, if you are using XmlWebApplicationContext or AnnotationConfigWebApplicationContext, only then you can specify the session scope for a bean.
globalSession	This scope is applicable only in case of portlet applications.

If your web application consists of multiple modules, you may define a DispatcherServlet for each of the modules in the web.xml file. In such a scenario, each DispatcherServlet has its own web application context XML file that contains beans (like controllers, view resolvers, and so on) specific to that module. You should note that these beans are *not* shared between DispatcherServlet instances. The beans that are shared between DispatcherServlet instances are defined in the *root* web application context XML file. As mentioned earlier, the *root* web application context XML file defines data sources, services and DAOs, and so on, that are typically shared by different modules of a web application. Refer to section 10-10 to learn about how the root web application context XML file is loaded.

The following figure shows relationship between beans defined by the web application context XML file associated with a DispatcherServlet and the beans defined by the root web application context XML file:

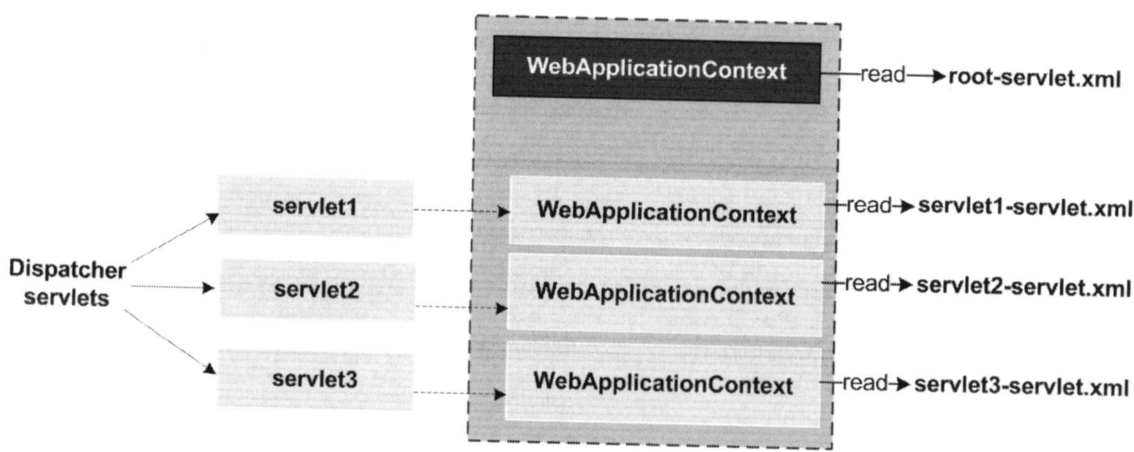

Figure 10-6 Beans in the root WebApplicationContext are inherited by the WebApplicationContext instance associated with a DispatcherServlet

In the above figure, servlet1, servlet2 and servlet3 are the names of DispatcherServlet instances configured in the web.xml file. And, servlet1-servlet.xml, servlet2-servlet.xml and servlet3-servlet.xml are web application context XML files that are loaded by servlet1, servlet2 and servlet3, respectively. When DispatcherServlet instances are initialized, an instance of WebApplicationContext is created corresponding to each servlet1-servlet.xml, servlet2-servlet.xml and servlet3-servlet.xml files and associated with the DispatcherServlet instance. A WebApplicationContext instance is also created corresponding to the *root* web application context XML file, root-servlet.xml. The beans contained in the root WebApplicationContext instance are available to all the WebApplicationContext instances associated with DispatcherServlets.

Let's now look at how a controller or any other Spring bean defined in a web application context XML file can access ServletContext and ServletConfig objects.

Accessing ServletContext and ServletConfig objects

In some scenarios, beans defined in the web application context XML file may require access to the ServletContext or ServletConfig object associated with the web application.

ServletContext is a Servlet API object that a bean can use to communicate with the servlet container. For instance, you can use it to get and set context attributes, obtain context initialization parameters, and so on. If a bean class implements Spring's ServletContextAware interface (a callback interface), the Spring container provides the bean instance with an instance of ServletContext object.

ServletConfig is a Servlet API object that a bean can use to obtain configuration information about the DispatcherServlet that intercepted the request. For instance, you can use it to obtain initialization parameters passed to the DispatcherServlet and the name with which the DispatcherServlet is configured in web.xml. If a bean class implements Spring's ServletConfigAware interface (a callback interface), the Spring container provides the bean instance with an instance of ServletConfig object.

The following example listing shows a bean class that implements ServletContextAware and the ServletConfigAware interface:

Example listing 10-5 – ServletContextAware and ServletConfigAware usage

```
import javax.servlet.ServletConfig;
import javax.servlet.ServletContext;
import org.springframework.web.context.ServletConfigAware;
import org.springframework.web.context.ServletContextAware;

public class ABean implements ServletContextAware, ServletConfigAware {
    private ServletContext servletContext;
    private ServletConfig servletConfig;

    @Override
    public void setServletContext(ServletContext servletContext) {
        this.servletContext = servletContext;
    }

    @Override
    public void setServletConfig(ServletConfig servletConfig) {
        this.servletConfig = servletConfig;
    }

    public void doSomething() {
        //--use ServletContext and ServletConfig objects
```

```
    }
}
```

The above example listing shows that the ABean class implements ServletContextAware and ServletConfigAware interface. The ServletContextAware interface defines a setServletContext method which is invoked by the Spring container to provide ABean instance with an instance of ServletContext object. The ServletConfigAware interface defines a setServletConfig method which is invoked by the Spring container to provide ABean instance with an instance of ServletConfig object.

We saw earlier that you can create a controller by implementing the Controller interface. Let's now look at @Controller and @RequestMapping annotations that simplify developing controllers.

10-5 Developing controllers using @Controller and @RequestMapping annotations

Spring Web MVC provides classes, like MultiActionController, UrlFilenameViewController, AbstractController, and so on, that you can extend to create your controller implementation. If you extend a Spring-specific class or implement a Spring-specific interface to create a controller, the controller class becomes tightly coupled with Spring. Spring 2.5 introduced annotations like @Controller, @RequestMapping, @ModelAttribute, and so on, that allow you to create controllers with flexible method signatures. In this section, we'll look at different Spring Web MVC annotations for developing annotated controllers.

Let's first look at a 'Hello World' web application that uses an annotated controller to show the 'Hello World !!' message.

IMPORT **chapter 10/ch10-annotation-helloworld** (This project shows a simple 'Hello World' web application that uses an annotated controller to show 'Hello World !!' message. If you deploy the project on Tomcat server and access the URL http://localhost:8080/ch10-annotation-helloworld/helloworld/saySomething/sayhello, you'll see the 'Hello World !!' message.)

Developing a 'Hello World' web application using an annotated controller

The ch10-annotation-helloworld project is similar to ch10-helloworld, except that the ch10-annotation-helloworld project uses an annotated controller to show 'Hello World !!' message. The web.xml and helloworld.jsp files in both the projects are exactly the same, but HelloWorldController.java and myapp-config.xml files are different. For this reason, we'll restrict our discussion to HelloWorldController.java and myapp-config.xml files in this section.

Let's first look at how to create a controller using @Controller and @RequestMapping annotations.

@Controller and @RequestMapping annotations

You designate a particular class as a Spring Web MVC controller by annotating it with @Controller annotation. And, you use @RequestMapping annotation to map an incoming request to the appropriate method of a controller.

The following example listing shows the HelloWorldController class that uses @Controller and @RequestMapping annotations:

Example listing 10-6 – HelloWorldController class - @Controller and @RequestMapping usage

```
package sample.spring.chapter10.web;

import org.springframework.stereotype.Controller;
import org.springframework.web.bind.annotation.RequestMapping;
import org.springframework.web.servlet.ModelAndView;
.....
@Controller(value="sayHelloController")
@RequestMapping("/saySomething")
public class HelloWorldController {

    @RequestMapping("/sayhello")
    public ModelAndView sayHello() {
      Map<String, String> modelData = new HashMap<String, String>();
      modelData.put("msg", "Hello World !!");
      return new ModelAndView("helloworld", modelData);
    }
}
```

In the above example listing, the HelloWorldController class is annotated with @Controller and @RequestMapping annotations, and the sayHello method is annotated with @RequestMapping annotation. @Controller annotation is a specialized form of @Component annotation (refer chapter 6) that indicates that the HelloWorldController is a controller component.

Like @Service (refer chapter 6) and @Repository (refer chapter 7) annotated classes, @Controller annotated classes are automatically registered with the Spring container; you don't need to explicitly define a @Controller annotated class in the web application context XML file. The value attribute of @Controller annotation specifies the name with which the class is registered with the Spring container. The value attribute serves the same purpose as the <bean> element's id attribute. If the value attribute is not specified, the name (beginning with lowercase first letter) of the class is used to register the class with the Spring container.

@RequestMapping annotation maps incoming web requests to appropriate controllers and/or controller methods. @RequestMapping annotation at the type-level maps a request to the appropriate controller. For instance, @RequestMapping("/saySomething") on HelloWorldController class indicates that all requests to /saySomething request path are handled by the HelloWorldController controller.

@RequestMapping at the method-level narrows down the @RequestMapping at the type-level to a specific method in the controller class. For instance, @RequestMapping("/sayhello") annotation on sayHello method in example listing 10-6 specifies that the sayHello method is invoked when the request path is /saySomething/sayhello. Notice that the HelloWorldController's sayHello method doesn't accept any arguments and returns a ModelAndView object. This is possible because annotated controllers can have flexible method signatures. In section 10-7, we'll look at possible arguments and return types @RequestMapping annotated methods can define.

@RequestMapping annotation at the type-level usually specifies a request path or a path pattern. And, @RequestMapping annotation at the method-level usually specifies an HTTP method or a request parameter to further narrow down the mapping specified by the type-level @RequestMapping annotation. The following figure shows how http://localhost:8080/ch10-annotation-helloworld/helloworld/saySomething/sayhello URL will result in invocation of HelloWorldController's sayHello method by Spring Web MVC:

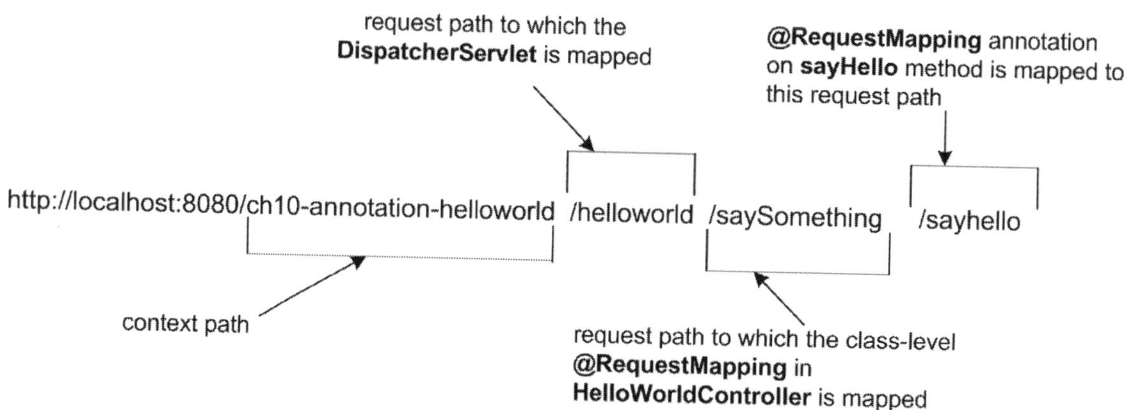

Figure 10-7 How a request URL is mapped to an appropriate @RequestMapping annotated method of a controller

The above figure shows how a particular request URL results in invocation of HelloWorldController's sayHello method.

Let's now look at how annotation-driven development of Spring Web MVC controllers is enabled in an application.

Enabling Spring Web MVC annotations

To use annotated controllers in your Spring Web MVC application, you need to enable Spring Web MVC annotations using `<annotation-driven>` element of Spring's `mvc` schema, as shown in the following example listing:

Example listing 10-7 – myapp-config.xml
Project – ch10-annotation-helloworld
Source location - src/main/webapp/WEB-INF/spring

```
<beans .....
   xmlns:mvc="http://www.springframework.org/schema/mvc"
   xsi:schemaLocation=".....http://www.springframework.org/schema/mvc
     http://www.springframework.org/schema/mvc/spring-mvc-4.0.xsd.....">

   <mvc:annotation-driven />
   <context:component-scan base-package="sample.spring.chapter10.web" />

   <bean id="viewResolver"
      class="org.springframework.web.servlet.view.InternalResourceViewResolver">
      <property name="prefix" value="/WEB-INF/jsp/" />
      <property name="suffix" value=".jsp" />
   </bean>
</beans>
```

In the above example listing, `<mvc:annotation-driven>` element of Spring's `mvc` schema enables use of Spring Web MVC annotations in implementing controllers. Also, `<component-scan>` element (refer section 6-2 for more details) of `context` schema is used to automatically register `@Controller` annotated classes with the Spring container.

In this section, we saw how to develop a simple 'Hello World' web application using `@Controller` and `@RequestMapping` annotations. Let's now look at the requirements of the MyBank web application that we'll develop in this chapter using Spring Web MVC annotations.

10-6 MyBank web application's requirements

The following figure shows the home page of MyBank web application that displays a list of currently active fixed deposits in the system:

ID	Deposit amount	Tenure	Email	Action
1	10000	24	a1email@somedomain.com	Close Edit
2	20000	36	a2email@somedomain.com	Close Edit
3	30000	36	a3email@somedomain.com	Close Edit
4	50000	36	a4email@somedomain.com	Close Edit
5	15000	36	a5email@somedomain.com	Close Edit

Create new Fixed Deposit

Figure 10-8 MyBank web application's home page shows fixed deposit details. The web page provides the option to close, edit and create a fixed deposit.

In the above figure, the ID column shows the unique identifier for a fixed deposit. The ID value is assigned to a fixed deposit when it is created by a user. *Close* and *Edit* hyperlinks allow a user to remove or edit details of a fixed deposit. The *Create new Fixed Deposit* button shows the '*Open fixed deposit*' form for entering details of the fixed deposit to be opened, as shown in the following figure:

Open fixed deposit

Amount (in USD):	100	must be greater than or equal to 1000
Tenure (in months):	6	must be greater than or equal to 12
Email:	xyz	not a well-formed email address

Save Go Back

Figure 10-9 '*Open fixed deposit*' form for opening fixed deposits. *Amount*, *Tenure* and *Email* fields are mandatory.

In the above figure, clicking the *Save* button saves the fixed deposit details in the data store, and *Go Back* hyperlink takes the user back to the web page that shows the fixed deposit list (refer figure 10-8). The above figure shows that appropriate error messages are displayed if the entered data doesn't meet the constraints set on Amount, Tenure and Email fields.

When you click the Edit hyperlink in figure 10-8, a form similar to figure 10-9 is shown for modifying details of the selected fixed deposit. And, clicking the Close hyperlink in figure 10-8 removes the selected fixed deposit from the list of fixed deposits.

Now, that we know the MyBank web application requirements, let's look at how we implement it using Spring Web MVC annotations.

10-7 Spring Web MVC annotations - @RequestMapping and @RequestParam

In section 10-5, we saw that we can use @Controller and @RequestMapping annotations to develop a simple controller. In this section, we'll take a closer look at @RequestMapping and other Spring Web MVC annotations that simplify developing annotated controllers.

IMPORT **chapter 10/ch10-bankapp** (This project shows the MyBank web application that allows its user to manage fixed deposits. If you deploy the project on Tomcat server and access the URL http://localhost:8080/ch10-bankapp, you'll see the list of fixed deposits (as shown in figure 10-8) in the system.)

Let's begin by looking at the @RequestMapping annotation.

Mapping requests to controllers or controller methods using @RequestMapping

In section 10-5, we saw that the @RequestMapping annotation is used at the *type* and *method*-level to map requests to controllers and its methods. In this section, we'll first look at how Spring Web MVC maps a web request to a particular controller method that uses @RequestMapping annotation. We'll then look at the attributes of @RequestMapping annotation, and the arguments and return types that @RequestMapping annotated methods can have.

@RequestMapping annotation and RequestMappingHandlerMapping

The following example listing shows @RequestMapping annotation usage in SomeController (a Spring Web MVC controller) class:

Example listing 10-8 – SomeController class - @RequestMapping usage

```
@Controller
@RequestMapping("/type_Level_Url")
public class SomeController {

  @RequestMapping("/methodA_Url")
```

```
    public ModelAndView methodA() { ..... }

    @RequestMapping("/methodB_Url")
    public ModelAndView methodB() { ..... }
}
```

The <annotation-driven> element of Spring's mvc schema creates an instance of RequestMappingHandlerMapping (a HandlerMapping implementation) that is responsible for mapping a web request to an appropriate @RequestMapping annotated method. RequestMappingHandlerMapping considers controller methods as endpoints, and is responsible for *uniquely* mapping a request to a controller method based on the @RequestMapping annotations at type- and method-level. In case of SomeController, if the request path is /type_Level_Url/methodA_Url, methodA is invoked, and if the request path is /type_Level_Url/methodB_Url, methodB is invoked. You should note that if a request cannot be mapped uniquely to a controller method, then a HTTP 404 (which means, resource not found) status code is returned.

The attributes of @RequestMapping annotation are used to narrow down the mapping of a request to a particular controller or a controller method. You can specify these attributes at both type- and method-level @RequestMapping annotations. Let's now look at the attributes of @RequestMapping annotation.

Mapping requests based on request path

@RequestMapping's value attribute specifies the request path to which a controller or controller method is mapped. You can specify the request path without explicitly specifying the value attribute in the @RequestMapping annotation. For instance, you can specify @RequestMapping(value = "/type_Level_Url") as @RequestMapping("/type_Level_Url").

You can also specify Ant-style path patterns as the value of value attribute. For instance, you can specify patterns, like /myUrl/*, /myUrl/** and /myUrl/*.do, as the value of value attribute. The following example listing shows a @RequestMapping annotation that specifies /myUrl/** as the path pattern:

Example listing 10-9 – SomeController class – Ant-style request path pattern usage

```
@Controller
@RequestMapping("/myUrl/**")
public class SomeController { ..... }
```

In the above example listing, @RequestMapping("/myUrl/**") annotation at the type-level specifies that the SomeController controller handles all requests that begin with /myUrl path. For instance, requests to /myUrl/abc, /myUrl/xyz and /myUrl/123/something paths are handled by SomeController controller.

Mapping requests based on HTTP methods

@RequestMapping's method attribute specifies the HTTP method that is handled by the controller or controller method. So, if the method attribute specifies an HTTP GET method, the controller or the controller method handles *only* HTTP GET requests.

The following example listing shows the FixedDepositController's listFixedDeposits method that is responsible for rendering the list of fixed deposits in the system:

Example listing 10-10 – @RequestMapping's method attribute usage
Project – ch10-bankapp
Source location - src/main/java/sample/spring/chapter10/web

```
package sample.spring.chapter10.web;

import org.springframework.web.bind.annotation.RequestMethod;
.....
@Controller
@RequestMapping(value="/fixedDeposit")
public class FixedDepositController {
  .....
  @RequestMapping(value = "/list", method = RequestMethod.GET)
  public ModelAndView listFixedDeposits() { ..... }
  .....
}
```

In the above example listing, @RequestMapping annotation on the listFixedDeposits method specifies value of method attribute as RequestMethod.GET. The RequestMethod is an enum that defines HTTP request methods, like GET, POST, PUT, DELETE, and so on. As the value of the method attribute is RequestMethod.GET, the listFixedDeposits method is invoked only if an HTTP GET request is sent to /fixedDeposit/list path. For instance, if you send an HTTP POST request to /fixedDeposit/list path, application will return an HTTP 405 (which means, the HTTP method is not supported) status code.

You can also specify an array of HTTP methods as the value of method attribute, as shown in the following example listing:

Example listing 10-11 – Specifying multiple HTTP methods as the value of method attribute

```
@Controller
@RequestMapping(value="/sample")
public class MyController {

  @RequestMapping(value = "/action" method={ RequestMethod.GET, RequestMethod.POST })
```

```
  public ModelAndView action() { ..... }
}
```

In the above example listing, the action method is annotated with @RequestMapping annotation whose method attribute's value is { RequestMethod.GET, RequestMethod.POST }. This means that the action method is invoked if an HTTP GET or POST request is sent to /sample/action path.

Mapping requests based on request parameters

@RequestMapping's params attribute typically specifies the name and value of the request parameter that *must* be present in the request. The following example listing shows the FixedDepositController's showOpenFixedDepositForm method that is responsible for showing the form for creating a fixed deposit:

Example listing 10-12 – @RequestMapping's params attribute usage
Project – ch10-bankapp
Source location - src/main/java/sample/spring/chapter10/web

```
package sample.spring.chapter10.web;

import org.springframework.web.bind.annotation.RequestMethod;
.....
@Controller
@RequestMapping(value="/fixedDeposit")
public class FixedDepositController {
  .....
  @RequestMapping(params = "fdAction=createFDForm", method = RequestMethod.POST)
  public ModelAndView showOpenFixedDepositForm() { ..... }
  .....
}
```

In the above example listing, @RequestMapping annotation on the showOpenFixedDepositForm method specifies the value of params attribute as fdAction=createFDForm. As the FixedDepositController is mapped to /fixedDeposit path, the showOpenFixedDepositForm method is invoked if an HTTP POST request containing request parameter named fdAction with value createFDForm is sent to /fixedDeposit path.

If you want to map requests to a controller or controller method based on the values of multiple request parameters, you can specify an array of request parameter name-value pairs as the value of params attribute, as shown in the following example listing:

Example listing 10-13 – Specifying multiple request parameter name-value pairs as the value of params attribute

```
  @RequestMapping(params = { "x=a", "y=b" })
```

```
public void perform() { ..... }
```

In the above example listing, the perform method is invoked only if the request contains parameters named x and y with values a and b, respectively.

You can also map requests to a controller or controller method based on the existence of a request parameter in the request. All you need to do is to simply specify the name of the request parameter as the value of params attribute. For instance, the perform method shown here is invoked irrespective of the value of request parameter x:

Example listing 10-14 – perform method is invoked if request parameter x is found

```
@RequestMapping(params = "x")
public void perform() { ..... }
```

To map requests to a controller or controller method if a request parameter does *not* exist, use the ! operator. For example, the following perform method is invoked if request parameter named x is *not* found in the request:

Example listing 10-15 – perform method is invoked if request parameter x is *not* found

```
@RequestMapping(params = "!x")
public void perform() { ..... }
```

You can use != operator to map requests to a controller or controller method if the value of a request parameter is *not* equal to the specified value, as shown here:

Example listing 10-16 – perform method is invoked if the value of request parameter x is *not equal* to a

```
@RequestMapping(params = "x != a")
public void perform() { ..... }
```

In the above example listing, perform method is invoked only if the request contains a request parameter named x, and the value of x is *not equal* to a.

Mapping requests based on the MIME type of the request

The Content-Type request header specifies the MIME type of the request. @RequestMapping's consumes attribute specifies the MIME type of the request that a controller or a controller method handles. So, if the value of consumes attribute matches the value of the Content-Type request header, the request is mapped to that particular controller or controller method.

The following example listing shows that the perform method is invoked if the Content-Type request header's value is application/json:

Example listing 10-17 – perform method is invoked if the value of Content-Type header is application/json

```
@RequestMapping(consumes = "application/json")
public void perform() { ..... }
```

As with the params attribute, you can use ! operator to specify the condition that a Content-Type header value is *not* present. For instance, the following perform method is invoked if the Content-Type header's value is *not* application/json:

Example listing 10-18 – perform method is invoked if the value of Content-Type header is *not* application/json

```
@RequestMapping(consumes = "!application/json")
public void perform() { ..... }
```

You can specify an array of values in the consumes attribute, in which case the request is mapped to the controller or the controller method if the Content-Type value matches one of the values specified by the consumes attribute. In the following example listing, the perform method is invoked if the Content-Type is application/json or text/plain:

Example listing 10-19 – perform method is invoked if Content-Type is application/json or text/plain

```
@RequestMapping(consumes = { "application/json", "text/plain")
public void perform() { ..... }
```

Mapping requests based on the acceptable MIME type of the response

The Accept request header specifies the acceptable MIME type of the response. @RequestMapping's produces attribute specifies the acceptable MIME type of the response. So, if the value of produces attribute value matches the Accept request header, the request is mapped to that particular controller or controller method.

The following example listing shows that the perform method is invoked if the Accept request header's value is application/json:

Example listing 10-20 – perform method is invoked if the value of Accept header is application/json

```
@RequestMapping(produces = "application/json")
public void perform() { ..... }
```

As with the consumes attribute, you can use ! operator to specify the condition that an Accept header value is *not* present in the request. If you specify an array of values for the produces attribute, request is mapped to the controller or the controller method if the Accept header value matches one of the values specified by the produces attribute.

Mapping requests based on a request header value

To map requests based on request headers, you can use @RequestMapping's headers attribute. The following example listing shows that the request is mapped to the perform method if the value of Content-Type header is text/plain:

Example listing 10-21 – perform method is invoked if the value of Content-Type header is text/plain

```
@RequestMapping(headers = "Content-Type=text/plain")
public void perform() { ..... }
```

As with the params attribute, you can use ! and != operators while specifying value of headers attribute. For instance, the following example listing shows that the request is mapped to the perform method if the value of Content-Type header is *not equal* to application/json, the Cache-Control header *doesn't exist* in the request, and the From header *exists* in the request with any value:

Example listing 10-22 – Using ! and != operators for specifying value of headers attribute

```
@RequestMapping(headers = { "Content-Type != application/json", "!Cache-Control", "From"} )
public void perform() { ..... }
```

Now, that we have looked at the attributes of @RequestMapping annotation, let's look at the arguments that you can pass to @RequestMapping annotated methods.

@RequestMapping annotated methods arguments

@RequestMapping annotated methods can have flexible method signatures. The argument types that can be passed to @RequestMapping annotated methods include HttpServletRequest, HttpSession, java.security.Principal, org.springframework.validation.BindingResult, org.springframework.web.bind.support.SessionStatus, org.springframework.ui.Model, and so on. To view a complete list of arguments that can be passed to @RequestMapping annotated method, please refer to @RequestMapping Javadoc.

As we discuss different Spring Web MVC features in this book, we'll come across scenarios which require us to pass different argument types to @RequestMapping annotated methods. For now, we'll look at a scenario in which we need to send HttpServletRequest object as an argument.

The following example listing shows the FixedDepositController's viewFixedDepositDetails method that accepts an argument of type HttpServletRequest:

Example listing 10-23 – FixedDepositController class - passing HttpServletRequest argument
Project – ch10-bankapp
Source location - src/main/java/sample/spring/chapter10/web

```
package sample.spring.chapter10.web;

import javax.servlet.http.HttpServletRequest;
.....
public class FixedDepositController {
  .....
  @RequestMapping(params = "fdAction=view", method = RequestMethod.GET)
  public ModelAndView viewFixedDepositDetails(HttpServletRequest request) {
     FixedDepositDetails fixedDepositDetails = fixedDepositService
           .getFixedDeposit(Integer.parseInt(request.getParameter("fixedDepositId")));
     .....
  }
  .....
}
```

The viewFixedDepositDetails method is invoked when you click the Edit hyperlink corresponding to a fixed deposit (refer figure 10-8). HttpServletRequest is used by the viewFixedDepositDetails method to obtain the fixedDepositId request parameter that uniquely identifies a fixed deposit in the system.

Let's now look at the return types that are supported for @RequestMapping annotated methods.

@RequestMapping annotated methods return types

The supported return types for @RequestMapping annotated methods include ModelAndView, org.springframework.web.servlet.View, String, java.util.concurrent.Callable, void, and so on. To view a complete list of return types supported for @RequestMapping annotated methods, please refer to @RequestMapping Javadoc.

As we discuss different Spring Web MVC features in this book, we'll come across scenarios which require @RequestMapping annotated methods to have different return types. In this section, we'll only look at examples that show methods that have String or ModelAndView as return types.

The following example listing shows FixedDepositController's showOpenFixedDepositForm method that renders the HTML form for opening a new fixed deposit (refer figure 10-9):

Example listing 10-24 – FixedDepositController class - ModelAndView return type example
Project – ch10-bankapp
Source location - src/main/java/sample/spring/chapter10/web

```
package sample.spring.chapter10.web;

import org.springframework.ui.ModelMap;
.....
public class FixedDepositController {
  .....
  @RequestMapping(params = "fdAction=createFDForm", method = RequestMethod.POST)
  public ModelAndView showOpenFixedDepositForm() {
    FixedDepositDetails fixedDepositDetails = new FixedDepositDetails();
    fixedDepositDetails.setEmail("You must enter a valid email");
    ModelMap modelData = new ModelMap();
    modelData.addAttribute(fixedDepositDetails);
    return new ModelAndView("createFixedDepositForm", modelData);
  }
  .....
}
```

The showOpenFixedDepositForm method returns a ModelAndView object that contains an instance of FixedDepositDetails as a model attribute and createFixedDepositForm string value as the view name.

If you compare the above example listing with 10-1 and 10-6, you'll notice that the showOpenFixedDepositForm method uses Spring's ModelMap object instead of java.util.Map to store model attributes. ModelMap is an implementation of java.util.Map interface that allows you to store model attributes without explicitly specifying their names. ModelMap automatically generates the name of the model attribute based on a pre-defined strategy. For instance, if you add a custom Java object as a model attribute, the name (beginning with lowercase first letter) of the object's class is used as the name of the model attribute. In the above example listing, when an instance of FixedDepositDetails is added to the ModelMap, it is stored in the ModelMap with the name fixedDepositDetails.

When a @RequestMapping annotated method returns a string value, it is considered as the name of the view that is resolved to an actual view (like, JSP page or servlet) by the ViewResolver configured for the web application. The following example listing shows the configuration of InternalResourceViewResolver in ch10-bankapp project:

Example listing 10-25 – bankapp-config.xml – ViewResolver configuration
Project – ch10-bankapp
Source location - src/main/webapp/WEB-INF/spring

```
<bean id="viewResolver"
    class="org.springframework.web.servlet.view.InternalResourceViewResolver">
    <property name="prefix" value="/WEB-INF/jsp/" />
    <property name="suffix" value=".jsp" />
</bean>
```

The above configuration suggests that when a string value xyz is returned, it is resolved to /WEB-INF/jsp/xyz.jsp. Refer section 10-3 to learn more about the InternalResourceViewResolver configuration shown above.

If the string value returned by the @RequestMapping annotated method has the prefix redirect:, it is treated as a redirect URL and *not* as a view name. The following example listing shows FixedDepositController's closeFixedDeposit method that is responsible for closing a fixed deposit when a user clicks the Close button (refer figure 10-9):

Example listing 10-26 – FixedDepositController class - String return type example
Project – ch10-bankapp
Source location - src/main/java/sample/spring/chapter10/web

```
@RequestMapping(params = "fdAction=close", method = RequestMethod.GET)
public String closeFixedDeposit(..... int fdId) {
    fixedDepositService.closeFixedDeposit(fdId);
    return "redirect:/fixedDeposit/list";
}
```

FixedDepositController's closeFixedDeposit method closes the fixed deposit identified by the fdId argument and returns redirect:/fixedDeposit/list string value. As the returned string value is prefixed with redirect:, the user is redirected to the /fixedDeposit/list URL that shows the list of fixed deposits (refer figure 10-8).

Let's now look at the @RequestParam annotation that allows you to assign a request parameter value to a controller method argument.

Passing request parameters to controller methods using @RequestParam

We saw in example listing 10-23 that we can pass HttpServletRequest object to a controller method and use it to retrieve request parameters. Instead of passing HttpServletRequest object to a controller method, you can annotate a method argument with @RequestParam annotation to assign value of a request parameter to the method argument.

> You should note that the @RequestParam annotation can only be used if the method is annotated with @RequestMapping or @ModelAttribute (explained in chapter 11) annotation.

The following example listing shows FixedDepositController's closeFixedDeposit method that is invoked when a user clicks the Close button (refer figure 10-8) to close a fixed deposit:

Example listing 10-27 – FixedDepositController class - @RequestParam usage
Project – ch10-bankapp
Source location - src/main/java/sample/spring/chapter10/web

```
package sample.spring.chapter10.web;

import org.springframework.web.bind.annotation.RequestParam;
.....
public class FixedDepositController {
    .....
    @RequestMapping(params = "fdAction=close", method = RequestMethod.GET)
    public String closeFixedDeposit(@RequestParam(value = "fixedDepositId") int fdId) {
        fixedDepositService.closeFixedDeposit(fdId);
        return "redirect:/fixedDeposit/list";
    }
    .....
}
```

@RequestParam's value attribute specifies the name of the request parameter whose value is assigned to the method argument. In the above example listing, @RequestParam annotation is used to assign the value of fixedDepositId request parameter to fdId method argument. As the type of the fdId argument is int, Spring is responsible for converting the fixedDepositId request parameter to int type. By default, Spring automatically provides type conversion for simple Java types, like int, long, java.util.Date, and so on. To convert request parameters to custom Java types (like Address), you need to register custom PropertyEditors with Spring's WebDataBinder instance or org.springframework.format.Formatters with Spring's FormattingConversionService instance. We'll learn more about WebDataBinder in chapter 11, and Formatter and FormattingConversionService in chapter 13.

Let's now look at how you can access all the request parameters in a controller method.

Passing all the request parameters to a controller method

To pass *all* the request parameters to a controller method, define an argument of type Map<String, String> or MultiValueMap<String, String> (an object provided by Spring that implements java.util.Map interface) and annotate it with @RequestParam annotation.

The following example listing shows FixedDepositController's openFixedDeposit method that creates a fixed deposit when a user enters fixed deposit details and clicks the *Save* button on the 'Open fixed deposit' form for opening fixed deposits (refer figure 10-9):

Example listing 10-28 – FixedDepositController class – accessing all request parameters
Project – ch10-bankapp
Source location - src/main/java/sample/spring/chapter10/web

```
package sample.spring.chapter10.web;

import java.util.Map;
.....
@RequestMapping(value = "/fixedDeposit")
public class FixedDepositController {
  .....
  @RequestMapping(params = "fdAction=create", method = RequestMethod.POST)
  public ModelAndView openFixedDeposit(@RequestParam Map<String, String> params) {
    String depositAmount = params.get("depositAmount");
    String tenure = params.get("tenure");
    .....
  }
}
```

In the above example listing, params argument of type Map<String, String> is annotated with @RequestParam annotation. Notice that the value attribute of @RequestParam annotation is *not* specified. If @RequestParam's value attribute is not specified and the type of the method argument is Map<String, String> or MultiValueMap<String, String>, Spring copies all the requests parameters into the method argument. Each request parameter's value is stored in the Map (or MultiValueMap) with the name of the request parameter as the key.

The following example listing shows FixedDepositController's editFixedDeposit method that is responsible for making changes to an existing fixed deposit:

Example listing 10-29 – FixedDepositController class – accessing all request parameters
Project – ch10-bankapp
Source location - src/main/java/sample/spring/chapter10/web

```
package sample.spring.chapter10.web;

import org.springframework.util.MultiValueMap;
.....
public class FixedDepositController {
  .....
  @RequestMapping(params = "fdAction=edit", method = RequestMethod.POST)
```

```
public ModelAndView editFixedDeposit(@RequestParam MultiValueMap<String, String> params) {
      String depositAmount = params.get("depositAmount").get(0);
      String tenure = params.get("tenure").get(0);
      .....
  }
}
```

In the above example listing, editFixedDeposit's params argument is of type MultiValueMap<String, String>, and is annotated with @RequestParam annotation. If an object is of type MultiValueMap<K, V>, then it means that K is the type of the key and List<V> is the type of the value. As the params argument is of type MultiValueMap<String, String>, it means that the key is of type String and the value is of type List<String>. When storing request parameters in MultiValueMap<String, String> type, Spring uses request parameter's name as key and the value of the request parameter is added to the List<String> value. MultiValueMap is particularly useful if you have multiple request parameters with the same name.

As the value corresponding to a request parameter is of type List<String>, calling params.get(String key) returns a List<String> type. For this reason, get(0) is called on the returned List<String> to get the value of request parameters depositAmount, tenure, and so on. Alternatively, you can use getFirst(String key) method of MultiValueMap to obtain the first element from the List<String> value.

Let's now take a closer look at the various attributes of @RequestParam annotation.

Specifying request parameter name using value attribute

We saw earlier that @RequestParam's value attribute specifies the name of the request parameter whose value is assigned to the method argument. If you don't specify the name of a request parameter, method argument name is considered as the name of the request parameter name. For instance, in the following example listing, value of request parameter named param is assigned to the param argument:

Example listing 10-30 – @RequestParam usage - unspecified request parameter name

```
@RequestMapping(.....)
public String doSomething(@RequestParam String param) { ..... }
```

In the above example listing, @RequestParam doesn't specify the name of the request parameter whose value is assigned to the param argument; therefore, param is considered as the name of the request parameter.

Specifying request parameter is optional or mandatory by using required attribute

By default, request parameter specified by the @RequestParam annotation is mandatory; if the specified request parameter is not found in the request, an exception is thrown. You can specify that the request parameter is optional by setting the value of required attribute to false, as shown here:

Example listing 10-31 – @RequestParam's required attribute

```
@RequestMapping(.....)
public String perform(@RequestParam(value = "myparam", required = false) String param) { ..... }
```

In the above example listing, @RequestParam's required attribute value is set to false, which means that the myparam request parameter is optional. Now, if the myparam request parameter is not found in the request, it'll not result in an exception. Instead, a null value is assigned to the param method argument.

Specifying default value for a request parameter using defaultValue attribute

@RequestParam's defaultValue attribute specifies the default value for a request parameter. If the request parameter specified by @RequestParam's value attribute is not found in the request, the value specified by the defaultValue attribute is assigned to the method argument. The following example listing shows usage of defaultValue attribute:

Example listing 10-32 – @RequestParam's defaultValue attribute

```
@RequestMapping(.....)
public String perform(@RequestParam(value = "location", defaultValue = "earth") String param) {
  .....
}
```

In the above example listing, if request parameter named location is not found in the request, the value earth is assigned to the param method argument.

In this section, we looked at @RequestMapping and @RequestParam annotations to create the FixedDepositController of MyBank application. Let's now look at how validation of form data is performed in the FixedDepositController class.

10-8 Validation

We saw earlier that FixedDepositController's showOpenFixedDepositForm method (refer example listing 10-24) renders createFixedDepositForm.jsp JSP page that shows the form for opening a new fixed deposit. When the form is submitted, the data entered in the form is validated by FixedDepositController's openFixedDeposit method (refer example listing 10-28). If errors are reported during validation, the createFixedDepositForm.jsp JSP page is rendered again with validation error messages and the original form data that was entered by the user (refer figure 10-9).

The following example listing shows the <form> element of createFixedDepositForm.jsp JSP page:

Example listing 10-33 – createFixedDepositForm.jsp – <form> element
Project – ch10-bankapp
Source location - src/main/webapp/WEB-INF/jsp

```
<form name="createFixedDepositForm" method="POST"
    action="${pageContext.request.contextPath}/fixedDeposit?fdAction=create">
      .....
    <input type="submit" value="Save" />
</form>
```

In the above example listing, <form> element's method attribute specifies POST as the HTTP method, and action attribute specifies /fixedDeposit?fdAction=create as the URL to which the form is submitted when the user clicks the Save button. Submission of the form results in the invocation of FixedDepositController's openFixedDeposit method.

The following example listing shows how the validation is performed by the openFixedDeposit method, and how the original form data entered by the user is shown again in case of validation errors:

Example listing 10-34 – FixedDepositController's openFixedDeposit method
Project – ch10-bankapp
Source location - src/main/java/sample/spring/chapter10/web

```
package sample.spring.chapter10.web;
.....
import org.apache.commons.lang3.math.NumberUtils;
@RequestMapping(value = "/fixedDeposit")
public class FixedDepositController {
  .....
  @RequestMapping(params = "fdAction=create", method = RequestMethod.POST)
  public ModelAndView openFixedDeposit(@RequestParam Map<String, String> params) {
    String depositAmount = params.get("depositAmount");
    .....
    Map<String, Object> modelData = new HashMap<String, Object>();

    if (!NumberUtils.isNumber(depositAmount)) {
      modelData.put("error.depositAmount", "enter a valid number");
    } else if (NumberUtils.toInt(depositAmount) < 1000) {
      modelData.put("error.depositAmount", "must be greater than or equal to 1000");
    }
    .....
```

```
    FixedDepositDetails fixedDepositDetails = new FixedDepositDetails();
    fixedDepositDetails.setDepositAmount(depositAmount);
    .....
    if (modelData.size() > 0) { // --this means there are validation errors
      modelData.put("fixedDepositDetails", fixedDepositDetails);
      return new ModelAndView("createFixedDepositForm", modelData);
    } else {
      fixedDepositService.saveFixedDeposit(fixedDepositDetails);
      return new ModelAndView("redirect:/fixedDeposit/list");
    }
  }
  .....
}
```

The openFixedDeposit method validates deposit amount, tenure and email information entered by the user. Notice that to simplify validation of data, NumberUtils class of Apache Commons Lang (http://commons.apache.org/proper/commons-lang/) library has been used. The modelData variable is a java.util.Map object that stores model attributes that we want to pass to the createFixedDepositForm.jsp JSP page in case of validation errors.

As we want to show validation error messages and the original form data if validation fails, the validation error messages and the original form data are stored in modelData. For instance, if the deposit amount entered by the user fails validation, an appropriate validation error message is stored in the modelData with name error.depositAmount. The values entered by the user are set on a new instance of FixedDepositDetails object. If validation errors are reported, the newly created FixedDepositDetails instance is added to the modelData with name fixedDepositDetails, and the createFixedDepositForm.jsp JSP page is rendered. Alternatively, if no validation errors are reported, the newly created FixedDepositDetails object is saved in the data source, and the page that shows the complete list of fixed deposits is rendered.

As we are using FixedDepositDetails object to store the original form data entered by the user, all the attributes of FixedDepositDetails have been defined of type String, as shown here:

Example listing 10-35 – FixedDepositDetails class
Project – ch10-bankapp
Source location - src/main/java/sample/spring/chapter10/domain

```
package sample.spring.chapter10.domain;

public class FixedDepositDetails {
  private long id; //-- id value is set by the system
  private String depositAmount;
  private String tenure;
  private String email;
```

```
  //--getters and setters for fields
  .....
}
```

As depositAmount and tenure fields are defined of type String, we had to write extra logic to convert them into numeric values for performing numerical comparisons. In chapter 11, we'll look at how Spring Web MVC simplifies binding form data to *form backing* objects (like FixedDepositDetails) and re-displaying the original form data in case of validation errors.

The following fragments from the createFixedDepositForm.jsp JSP page demonstrate how validation error messages and the original form data are displayed in the MyBank application:

Example listing 10-36 – createFixedDepositForm.jsp
Project – ch10-bankapp
Source location - src/main/webapp/WEB-INF/jsp

```
<%@taglib uri="http://java.sun.com/jsp/jstl/core" prefix="c"%>

<form name="createFixedDepositForm" method="POST"
    action="${pageContext.request.contextPath}/fixedDeposit?fdAction=create">
        .....
        <td class="td"><b>Amount (in USD):</b></td>
        <td class="td">
            <input type="text" name="depositAmount"
                value="${requestScope.fixedDepositDetails.depositAmount}"/>
            <font style="color: #C11B17;">
                <c:out value="${requestScope['error.depositAmount']}"/></font>
        </td>
        .....
    <input type="submit" value="Save" />
</form>
```

In the above example listing, the value of depositAmount form field is specified as ${requestScope.fixedDepositDetails.depositAmount}. In the openFixedDeposit method (refer example listing 10-34), we added a FixedDepositDetails instance as a model attribute named fixedDepositDetails; therefore, the ${requestScope.fixedDepositDetails.depositAmount} expression shows the original value that the user entered for the depositAmount field.

The expression ${requestScope['error.depositAmount']} refers to the error.depositAmount request attribute. In the openFixedDeposit method (refer example listing 10-34), we saw that the error.depositAmount contains validation error message corresponding to the fixed deposit amount entered by the user; therefore, the <c:out value=

"${requestScope['error.depositAmount']}"/> element shows the validation error message corresponding to the fixed deposit amount entered by the user.

Let's now look at how to handle exceptions in Spring Web MVC applications.

10-9 Handling exceptions using @ExceptionHandler annotation

@ExceptionHandler annotation is used in an annotated controller to identify the method responsible for handling exceptions thrown by the controller. Spring's HandlerExceptionResolver is responsible for mapping an exception to an appropriate controller method responsible for handling the exception. You should note that the <annotation-driven> element of Spring's mvc schema configures an instance of ExceptionHandlerExceptionResolver (a HandlerExceptionResolver implementation) that maps an exception to an appropriate @ExceptionHandler annotated method.

The following example listing shows usage of @ExceptionHandler annotation in ch10-bankapp project:

Example listing 10-37 – @ExceptionHandler annotation usage
Project – ch10-bankapp
Source location - src/main/java/sample/spring/chapter10/web

```
package sample.spring.chapter10.web;

import org.springframework.web.bind.annotation.ExceptionHandler;
.....
@Controller
@RequestMapping(value = "/fixedDeposit")
public class FixedDepositController {
  .....
  @ExceptionHandler
  public String handleException(Exception ex) {
    return "error";
  }
}
```

The above example listing shows that the FixedDepositController's handleException method is annotated with @ExceptionHandler annotation. This means that the handleException method is invoked by Spring Web MVC to handle exceptions thrown during execution of FixedDepositController controller. @ExceptionHandler methods typically render an error page containing error details. An @ExceptionHandler annotation's value attribute specifies the list of exceptions that the @ExceptionHandler annotated method handles. If the value attribute is *not* specified, the exception types specified as method arguments are handled by the

@ExceptionHandler annotated method. In the above example listing, the handleException method handles exceptions of type java.lang.Exception.

Like @RequestMapping methods, @ExceptionHandler methods can have flexible method signatures. The return types supported for @ExceptionHandler methods include ModelAndView, View, String, void, Model, and so on. The argument types supported for @ExceptionHandler methods include HttpServletRequest, HttpServletResponse, HttpSession, and so on. Refer to @ExceptionHandler Javadoc for the complete list of supported arguments and return types.

The view information returned by an @ExceptionHandler annotated method is used by the DispatcherServlet to render an appropriate error page. For instance, in example listing 10-37, the error string value returned by the handleException method is used by the DispatcherServlet to render /WEB-INF/jsp/error.jsp page. If the @ExceptionHandler method doesn't return any view information (that is, the return type is void or Model), Spring's RequestToViewNameTranslator class (refer section 11-2 of chapter 11 for details) is used to determine the view to be rendered.

You can define multiple @ExceptionHandler annotated methods in your controller class for handling different exception types. The value attribute of @ExceptionHandler annotation allows you to specify the exception types that are handled by the method. The following example listing shows that the myExceptionHandler method handles exceptions of type IOException and FileNotFoundException, and myOtherExceptionHandler method handles exceptions of type TimeoutException:

Example listing 10-38 – Specifying the type of exceptions handled by an @ExceptionHandler method

```
@Controller
.....
public class MyController {
  .....
  @ExceptionHandler(value = {IOException.class, FileNotFoundException.class})
  public String myExceptionHandler() {
    return "someError";
  }

  @ExceptionHandler(value = TimeoutException.class)
  public String myOtherExceptionHandler() {
    return "otherError";
  }
}
```

If MyController throws an exception of type IOException or FileNotFoundException (or an exception that is a subtype of IOException or FileNotFoundException), the myExceptionHandler method is invoked to handle the exception. If MyController throws an exception of type TimeoutException (or an exception that is a subtype of TimeoutException), the myOtherExceptionHandler method is invoked to handle the exception.

Let's now look at how Spring's ContextLoaderListener is used to load root web application context XML file(s).

10-11 Loading root web application context XML file(s)

As mentioned at the beginning of this chapter, the root web application context file defines beans that are shared by all the servlets and filters of the web application. The following example listing shows the configuration of ContextLoaderListener:

Example listing 10-39 – ContextLoaderListener configuration
Project – ch10-bankapp
Source location - src/main/webapp/WEB-INF/web.xml

```
<context-param>
   <param-name>contextConfigLocation</param-name>
   <param-value>classpath*:/META-INF/spring/applicationContext.xml</param-value>
</context-param>

<listener>
   <listener-class>org.springframework.web.context.ContextLoaderListener</listener-class>
</listener>
```

In the above example listing, <listener> element configures the ContextLoaderListener (a ServletContextListener) that is responsible for loading the root web application context XML file(s) specified by the contextConfigLocation servlet context initialization parameter. The <context-param> element is used to specify a servlet context initialization parameter. ContextLoaderListener creates an instance of the root WebApplicationContext with which the beans loaded from the root web application context XML file(s) are registered.

In the above example listing, contextConfigLocation parameter specifies /META-INF/spring/applicationContext.xml file as the root web application context XML file. You can specify multiple application context XML files separated by comma or newline or whitespace or semicolon. If you don't specify the contextConfigLocation parameter, the ContextLoaderListener treats /WEB-INF/applicationContext.xml file as the root web application context XML file.

10-12 Summary

In this chapter, we looked at some of the important objects of a simple Spring Web MVC application. We also looked at how to use @Controller, @RequestMapping, @RequestParam and @ExceptionHandler annotations to create annotated controllers. In the next chapter, we'll look at how Spring transparently *binds* request parameters to form backing objects and performs validation.

Chapter 11 – *Validation and data binding in Spring Web MVC*

11-1 Introduction

In the previous chapter, we looked at the MyBank web application that was developed using @Controller, @RequestMapping and @RequestParam annotations. We saw that the form data was retrieved from the request (refer example listing 10-23, 10-28 and 10-29) and *explicitly* set on the form backing object (which was FixedDepositDetails object). Also, the validation logic was written in the controller method itself (refer example listing 10-34).

In this chapter, we'll discuss:

- @ModelAttribute and @SessionAttributes annotations that are useful when dealing with model attributes
- how Spring's WebDataBinder simplifies binding form data to form backing objects
- validating form backing objects using Spring Validation API and JSR 303's constraint annotations
- Spring's form tag library that simplifies writing JSP pages

Let's first look at the @ModelAttribute annotation that is used for adding and retrieving model attributes to and from Spring's Model object.

11-2 Adding and retrieving model attributes using @ModelAttribute annotation

In the previous chapter, we saw that a @RequestMapping method stores model attributes in a HashMap (or ModelMap) instance and returns these model attributes via ModelAndView object. The model attributes returned by a @RequestMapping method are stored in Spring's Model object.

A model attribute may represent a form backing object or a *reference data*. FixedDepositDetails object in the MyBank web application is an example of a form backing object; when the form for opening a new fixed deposit is submitted, the information contained in the form is stored in the FixedDepositDetails object. Typically, *domain* objects or entities in an application are used as form backing objects. *Reference data* refers to the additional information (other than the form backing object) required by the view. For instance, if you add a user category (like military personnel, senior citizen, and so on) to each fixed deposit, the form for opening new fixed deposits would need to show a combo box displaying the list of categories. The list of categories would be the *reference data* needed for displaying the form for opening new fixed deposits.

@ModelAttribute annotation is used on methods and method arguments to store and retrieve model attributes from Spring's Model object, respectively. @ModelAttribute annotation on a method indicates that the method adds one or more model attributes to the Model object. And, @ModelAttribute annotation on a method argument is used to retrieve a model attribute from the Model object and assign it to the method argument.

IMPORT **chapter 11/ch11-bankapp** (This project shows the MyBank web application that uses @ModelAttribute annotation and Spring's form tag library. The MyBank web application functionality offered by ch11-bankapp and ch10-bankapp projects is the same. If you deploy the project on Tomcat server and access the URL http://localhost:8080/ch11-bankapp, you'll see the list of fixed deposits in the system.)

Let's first look at @ModelAttribute annotated methods.

Adding model attributes using method-level @ModelAttribute annotation

The following example listing shows FixedDepositController's getNewFixedDepositDetails method that is annotated with @ModelAttribute annotation:

Example listing 11-1 – @ModelAttribute annotation usage at method level
Project – ch11-bankapp
Source location - src/main/java/sample/spring/chapter11/web

```
package sample.spring.chapter11.web;

import org.springframework.web.bind.annotation.ModelAttribute;
import sample.spring.chapter11.domain.FixedDepositDetails;
.....
@Controller
@RequestMapping(value = "/fixedDeposit")
.....
public class FixedDepositController {
    private static Logger logger = Logger.getLogger(FixedDepositController.class);
    .....
    @ModelAttribute(value = "newFixedDepositDetails")
    public FixedDepositDetails getNewFixedDepositDetails() {
        FixedDepositDetails fixedDepositDetails = new FixedDepositDetails();
        fixedDepositDetails.setEmail("You must enter a valid email");
        logger.info("getNewFixedDepositDetails() method: Returning a new instance of
              FixedDepositDetails");
        return fixedDepositDetails;
```

```
  }
  .....
}
```

The getNewFixedDepositDetails method creates and returns a new instance of FixedDepositDetails object. As the getNewFixedDepositDetails method is annotated with @ModelAttribute annotation, the returned FixedDepositDetails instance is added to the Model object. @ModelAttribute's value attribute specifies that the returned FixedDepositDetails object is stored with name newFixedDepositDetails in the Model object. Notice that the getNewFixedDepositDetails method logs the following message - 'getNewFixedDepositDetails() method: Returning a new instance of FixedDepositDetails'.

> You should note that the scope of model attributes is *request*. This means that the model attributes are lost when a request completes, or if a request is *redirected*.

Later in this section, we'll see how the createFixedDepositForm.jsp JSP page (refer src/main/webapp/WEB-INF/jsp/createFixedDepositForm.jsp file) of ch11-bankapp project uses Spring's form tag library to access the FixedDepositDetails object named newFixedDepositDetails from the Model object.

If you don't specify @ModelAttribute's value attribute, the returned object is stored in the Model object using the simple name of the returned object's *type*. In the following example listing, the Sample object returned by the getSample method is stored with name sample in the Model object:

Example listing 11-2 – @ModelAttribute usage – value attribute is *not* specified

```
import org.springframework.ui.Model;
.....
public class SampleController {

  @ModelAttribute
  public Sample getSample() {
      return new Sample();
  }
}
```

A @ModelAttribute annotated method accepts same types of arguments as a @RequestMapping method. The following example listing shows a @ModelAttribute annotated method that accepts an argument of type HttpServletRequest:

Example listing 11-3 – @ModelAttribute annotated method that accepts HttpServletRequest as argument

```
@ModelAttribute(value = "myObject")
public SomeObject doSomething(HttpServletRequest request) { ..... }
```

In chapter 10, we saw that the @RequestParam annotation is used to pass request parameters to a @RequestMapping annotated method. @RequestParam annotation can also be used to pass request parameters to a @ModelAttribute annotated method, as shown in the following example listing:

Example listing 11-4 – Passing request parameters to a @ModelAttribute annotated method

```
@ModelAttribute(value = "myObject")
public SomeObject doSomething(@RequestParam("someArg") String myarg) { ..... }
```

As @RequestMapping and @ModelAttribute annotated methods can accept Model objects as argument, you can *directly* add model attributes to the Model object in a @ModelAttribute or @RequestMapping annotated method. The following example listing shows a @ModelAttribute method that directly adds model attributes to the Model object:

Example listing 11-5 – Adding model attributes directly to Model object

```
import org.springframework.ui.Model;
.....
public class SampleWebController {

   @ModelAttribute
   public void doSomething(Model model) {
       model.addAttribute("myobject", new MyObject());
       model.addAttribute("otherobject", new OtherObject());
   }
}
```

In the above example listing, the Model object is passed as an argument to the doSomething method that directly adds model attributes to the Model object. As the doSomething method adds model attributes directly to the Model object, the doSomething method's return type is specified as void, and the @ModelAttribute's value attribute is *not* specified.

It is possible to have a single method annotated with both @RequestMapping and @ModelAttribute annotations. The following example listing shows FixedDepositController's listFixedDeposits method that is annotated with both @RequestMapping and @ModelAttribute annotations:

Example listing 11-6 – @ModelAttribute and @RequestMapping annotations on the same method
Project – ch11-bankapp
Source location - src/main/java/sample/spring/chapter11/web

```
package sample.spring.chapter11.web;
.....
@Controller
@RequestMapping(value = "/fixedDeposit")
.....
public class FixedDepositController {
   private static Logger logger = Logger.getLogger(FixedDepositController.class);

   @RequestMapping(value = "/list", method = RequestMethod.GET)
   @ModelAttribute(value = "fdList")
   public List<FixedDepositDetails> listFixedDeposits() {
      logger.info("listFixedDeposits() method: Getting list of fixed deposits");
      return fixedDepositService.getFixedDeposits();
   }
   .....
}
```

The listFixedDeposits method renders the list.jsp JSP page (refer src/main/webapp/WEB-INF/jsp/fixedDeposit/list.jsp file of ch11-bankapp project) that shows the list of fixed deposits in the system. When a method is annotated with both @RequestMapping and @ModelAttribute annotations, the value returned by the method is considered as a model attribute, and *not* as a view name. In such a scenario, view name is determined by Spring's RequestToViewNameTranslator class that determines the view to render based on the request URI of the incoming request. Later in this chapter, we'll discuss RequestToViewNameTranslator in detail. In example listing 11-6, notice that the listFixedDeposits method logs the following message – 'listFixedDeposits() method: Getting list of fixed deposits'.

It is important to note that you can define multiple methods annotated with @ModelAttribute annotation in a controller. When a request is dispatched to a @RequestMapping annotated method of a controller, *all* the @ModelAttribute annotated methods of that controller are invoked *before* the @RequestMapping annotated method is invoked. The following example listing shows a controller that defines @RequestMapping and @ModelAttribute annotated methods:

Example listing 11-7 – @RequestMapping method is invoked after all the @ModelAttribute methods are invoked

```
@RequestMapping("/mycontroller")
public class MyController {
```

```
  @RequestMapping("/perform")
  public String perform() { ..... }

  @ModelAttribute(value = "a")
  public A getA() { ..... }

  @ModelAttribute(value = "b")
  public B getB() { ..... }
}
```

In the above example listing, if a request is mapped to MyController's perform method, Spring Web MVC will first invoke getA and getB methods, followed by invoking the perform method.

If a method is annotated with both @RequestMapping and @ModelAttribute annotations, the method is invoked only *once* for processing the request. The following example listing shows a controller that defines a method that is annotated with both @RequestMapping and @ModelAttribute annotations:

Example listing 11-8 – Method annotated with both @RequestMapping and @ModelAttribute annotations is invoked only *once* for processing the request

```
@RequestMapping("/mycontroller")
public class MyController {

  @RequestMapping("/perform")
  @ModelAttribute
  public String perform() { ..... }

  @ModelAttribute(value = "a")
  public A getA() { ..... }

  @ModelAttribute(value = "b")
  public B getB() { ..... }
}
```

In the above example listing, if a request is mapped to MyController's perform method, Spring Web MVC will first invoke getA and getB methods, followed by invoking the perform method. As the perform method is annotated with both @RequestMapping and @ModelAttribute annotations, Spring's RequestToViewNameTranslator class is used for determining the name of the view to render after the perform method is executed.

If you now deploy the ch11-bankapp project on Tomcat and go to http://localhost:8080/ch11-bankapp/fixedDeposit/list URL, you'll see a web page showing the list of fixed deposits. Also, you'll see the following sequence of messages on the console:

```
INFO sample.spring.chapter11.web.FixedDepositController - getNewFixedDepositDetails() method: Returning a new instance of FixedDepositDetails
INFO sample.spring.chapter11.web.FixedDepositController - listFixedDeposits() method: Getting list of fixed deposits
```

The above output shows that the getNewFixedDepositDetails method (which is annotated with @ModelAttribute annotation) is invoked first, followed by the listFixedDeposits (which is annotated with both @ModelAttribute and @RequestMapping annotation).

Let's now look at how model attributes are retrieved from the Model object using @ModelAttribute annotation on a method argument.

Retrieving model attributes using @ModelAttribute annotation

You can use @ModelAttribute annotation on arguments of a @RequestMapping annotated method to retrieve model attributes from the Model object.

The following example listing shows FixedDepositController's openFixedDeposit method that uses @ModelAttribute annotation to retrieve newFixedDepositDetails object from the Model object:

Example listing 11-9 – @ModelAttribute annotation on a method argument
Project – ch11-bankapp
Source location - src/main/java/sample/spring/chapter11/web

```
package sample.spring.chapter11.web;
.....
@Controller
@RequestMapping(value = "/fixedDeposit")
.....
public class FixedDepositController {
  .....
  @ModelAttribute(value = "newFixedDepositDetails")
  public FixedDepositDetails getNewFixedDepositDetails() {
    .....
    logger.info("getNewFixedDepositDetails() method: Returning a new instance of
          FixedDepositDetails");
    .....
  }
  .....
  @RequestMapping(params = "fdAction=create", method = RequestMethod.POST)
  public String openFixedDeposit(
    @ModelAttribute(value = "newFixedDepositDetails")
        FixedDepositDetails fixedDepositDetails,.....) {
      .....
```

```
        fixedDepositService.saveFixedDeposit(fixedDepositDetails);
        logger.info("openFixedDeposit() method: Fixed deposit details successfully saved.
          Redirecting to show the list of fixed deposits.");
        .....
    }
  }
  .....
}
```

In the above example listing, @ModelAttribute annotated getNewFixedDepositDetails method is invoked *before* @RequestMapping annotated openFixedDeposit method. When the getNewFixedDepositDetails method is invoked, the returned FixedDepositDetails instance is stored in the Model object with name newFixedDepositDetails. Now, the openFixedDeposit method's fixedDepositDetails argument is annotated with @ModelAttribute(value="newFixedDepositDetails"); therefore, the newFixedDepositDetails object is obtained from the Model object and assigned to the fixedDepositDetails argument.

If you look at the FixedDepositController's openFixedDeposit method, you'll notice that we have *not* written any logic to obtain values of tenure, amount and email fields from the request and populate the newFixedDepositDetails instance. This is because the Spring's WebDataBinder object (explained later in this chapter) is responsible for transparently retrieving request parameters from the request and populating the fields (with matching names) of newFixedDepositDetails instance. For instance, if a request parameter named tenure is found in the request, WebDataBinder sets the value of tenure field of newFixedDepositDetails instance to the value of tenure request parameter.

Figure 11-1 summarizes the sequence of actions that are performed by Spring when a request is dispatched to FixedDepositController's openFixedDeposit method.

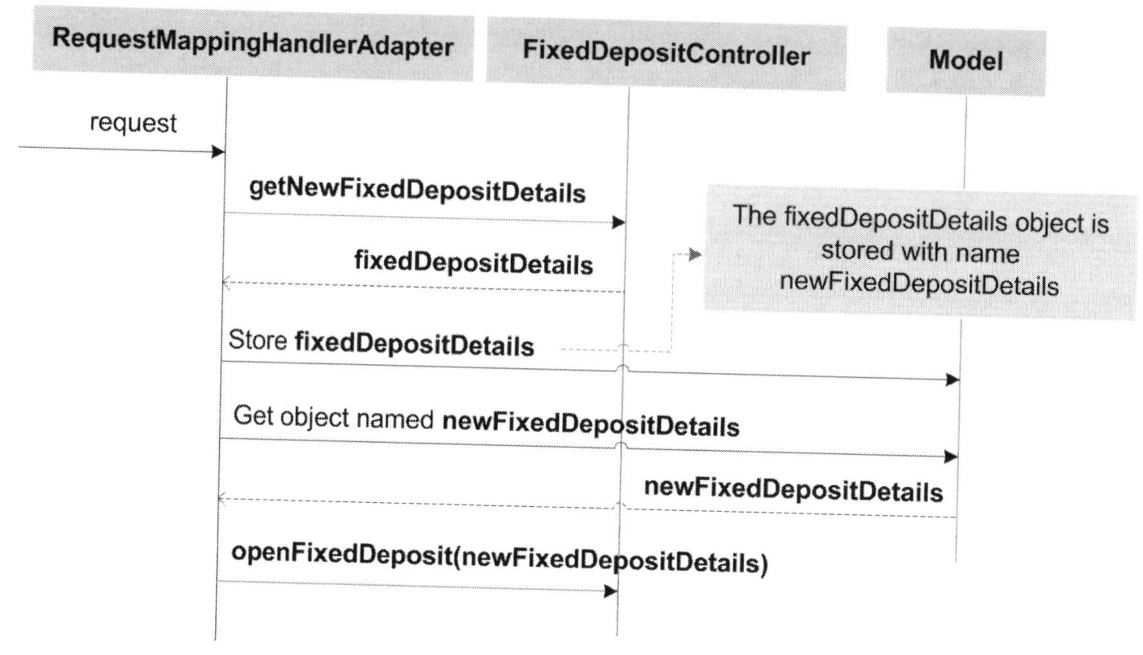

Figure 11-1 Order in which @ModelAttribute and @RequestMapping annotated methods of FixedDepositController are invoked

In the above figure, the RequestMappingHandlerAdapter object of Spring Web MVC is responsible for invoking @ModelAttribute and @RequestMapping annotated methods of a controller. At first, the getNewFixedDepositDetails method is invoked and the returned FixedDepositDetails instance is stored in the Model object with name newFixedDepositDetails. Next, the newFixedDepositDetails instance is retrieved from the Model and passed as an argument to the openFixedDeposit method.

Let's now look at what times during the processing of a request a @ModelAttribute annotated method is invoked.

Request processing and @ModelAttribute annotated methods

In example listing 11-6, we saw that the execution of listFixedDeposits method logs the following message:

```
listFixedDeposits() method: Getting list of fixed deposits
```

In example listing 11-9, we saw that the execution of getNewFixedDepositDetails method logs the following message:

```
getNewFixedDepositDetails() method: Returning a new instance of FixedDepositDetails
```

And, the openFixedDeposit method logs the following message:

openFixedDeposit() method: Fixed deposit details successfully saved. Redirecting to show the list of fixed deposits

To see the order in which the listFixedDeposits, getNewFixedDepositDetails and openFixedDeposit methods are invoked, deploy the ch11-bankapp project and follow these steps:

1. Go to http://localhost:8080/ch11-bankapp/fixedDeposit/list URL. You'll see the list of fixed deposits in the system and the 'Create new Fixed Deposit' button (refer figure 10-8 of chapter 10).
2. Click the 'Create new Fixed Deposit' button that shows the HTML form for opening a new fixed deposit (refer figure 10-9 of chapter 10).
3. Enter fixed deposit details and click the 'Save' button. If no validation errors are found in the entered data, the fixed deposit details are successfully saved and the list of fixed deposits in the system (which includes the newly created fixed deposit) is displayed once again.

The following table describes the actions performed by you and the corresponding messages that are printed by the MyBank application on the console:

Action	Messages printed on the console
Go to http://localhost:8080/ch11-bankapp/fixedDeposit/list URL	**getNewFixedDepositDetails()** method: Returning a new instance of FixedDepositDetails **listFixedDeposits()** method: Getting list of fixed deposits
Click the 'Create new Fixed Deposit' button	**getNewFixedDepositDetails()** method: Returning a new instance of FixedDepositDetails **showOpenFixedDepositForm()** method: Showing form for opening a new fixed deposit
Enter fixed deposit details and click the 'Save' button	**getNewFixedDepositDetails()** method: Returning a new instance of FixedDepositDetails **openFixedDeposit()** method: Fixed deposit details successfully saved. Redirecting to show the list of fixed deposits. **getNewFixedDepositDetails()** method: Returning a new instance of FixedDepositDetails **listFixedDeposits()** method: Getting list of fixed deposits

The above table shows that the @ModelAttribute annotated getNewFixedDepositDetails method is called *before each* invocation of @RequestMapping annotated method of the FixedDepositController class. As the getNewFixedDepositDetails method creates a new instance of FixedDepositDetails object, a new instance of FixedDepositDetails object is created each time a request is handled by the FixedDepositController.

If a @ModelAttribute annotated method fires SQL queries or invokes an external web service to populate the model attribute returned by the method, multiple invocations of @ModelAttribute annotated method will adversely affect the performance of the application. Later in this chapter, we'll see that you can use *@SessionAttributes* annotation to avoid multiple invocations of a @ModelAttribute annotated method. *@SessionAttributes* annotation instructs Spring to cache the object returned by the @ModelAttribute annotated method.

Let's now look at a scenario in which the model attribute referred by the @ModelAttribute annotated method argument is *not* found in the Model object.

Behavior of @ModelAttribute annotated method arguments

We saw earlier that the @ModelAttribute annotation can be used on a method argument to retrieve a model attribute from the Model object. If the model attribute specified by the @ModelAttribute annotation is *not* found in the Model, Spring automatically creates a new instance of the method argument type, assigns it to the method argument and also puts it into the Model object. To allow Spring to create an instance of the method argument type, the Java class of the method argument type *must* provide a no-argument constructor.

Let's consider the following SomeController controller that defines a single @RequestMapping method, doSomething:

Example listing 11-10 – @ModelAttribute argument is *not* available in the Model object

```
@Controller
@RequestMapping(value = "/some")
public class SomeController {
  .....
  @RequestMapping("/do")
  public void doSomething(@ModelAttribute("myObj") MyObject myObject) {
    logger.info(myObject);
    .....
  }
}
```

The above example listing shows that the SomeController class doesn't define any @ModelAttribute annotated method that adds an object named myObj of type MyObject in the Model. For this reason, when a request for doSomething method is received, Spring creates an instance of MyObject, assigns it to the myObject argument and also puts the newly created MyObject instance into the Model object.

Let's now look at Spring's RequestToViewNameTranslator object.

RequestToViewNameTranslator

RequestToViewNameTranslator determines the view to be rendered when a @RequestMapping annotated method doesn't explicitly specify the view to be rendered.

We saw earlier that when a @RequestMapping method is also annotated with @ModelAttribute annotation, the value returned by the method is considered as a model attribute. In such a situation, the RequestToViewNameTranslator object is responsible for determining the view to be rendered based on the incoming web request. Similarly, if a @RequestMapping annotated method returns void, org.springframework.ui.Model or java.util.Map, the RequestToViewNameTranslator object determines the view to be rendered.

DefaultRequestToViewNameTranslator is an implementation of RequestToViewNameTranslator that is used by default by DispatcherServlet to determine the view to be rendered when no view is explicitly returned by a @RequestMapping method. DefaultRequestToViewNameTranslator uses the request URI to determine the name of the logical view to render. DefaultRequestToViewNameTranslator removes the leading and trailing slashes and the file extension from the URI to determine the view name. For instance, if the URL is http://localhost:8080/doSomething.htm, the view name becomes doSomething.

In case of MyBank web application, the FixedDepositController's listFixedDeposits method (refer example listing 11-6 or FixedDepositController.java file of ch11-bankapp project) is annotated with both @RequestMapping and @ModelAttribute; therefore, RequestToViewNameTranslator is used by the DispatcherServlet to determine the view to render. As the listFixedDeposits method is mapped to request URI /fixedDeposit/list, RequestToViewNameTranslator returns /fixedDeposit/list as the view name. The ViewResolver configured in the web application context XML file of MyBank web application (refer bankapp-config.xml file of ch11-bankapp project) maps /fixedDeposit/list view name to /WEB-INF/jsp/fixedDeposit/list.jsp JSP view.

Let's now look at @SessionAttributes annotation.

11-3 Caching model attributes using @SessionAttributes annotation

In the previous section, we saw that *all* the @ModelAttribute annotated methods of a controller are *always* invoked before the @RequestMapping annotated method. This behavior may not be acceptable in situations in which @ModelAttribute methods obtain data from the database or from an external web service to populate the model attribute. In such scenarios, you can annotate your controller class with @SessionAttributes annotation that specifies the model attributes that are stored in HttpSession between requests.

If @SessionAttributes annotation is used, a @ModelAttribute annotated method is invoked only if the model attribute specified by the @ModelAttribute annotation is *not* found in the HttpSession. Also, @ModelAttribute annotation on a method argument will result in creation of a new instance of model attribute only if the model attribute is not found in the HttpSession.

IMPORT **chapter 11/ch11-session-attributes** (This project shows a modified version of ch11-bankapp project that uses @SessionAttributes annotation to temporarily store model attributes in HttpSession. The MyBank web application functionality offered by ch11-session-attributes and ch10-bankapp projects are the same. If you deploy the project on Tomcat server and access the URL http://localhost:8080/ch11-session-attributes, you'll see the list of fixed deposits in the system.)

The following example listing shows usage of @SessionAttributes annotation in ch11-session-attributes project to temporarily store newFixedDepositDetails and editableFixedDepositDetails model attributes in HttpSession:

Example listing 11-11 – @SessionAttributes annotation usage
Project – ch11-session-attributes
Source location - src/main/java/sample/spring/chapter11/web

```
package sample.spring.chapter11.web;

import org.springframework.web.bind.annotation.SessionAttributes;
.....
@SessionAttributes(value = { "newFixedDepositDetails", "editableFixedDepositDetails" })
public class FixedDepositController {
  .....
  @ModelAttribute(value = "newFixedDepositDetails")
  public FixedDepositDetails getNewFixedDepositDetails() {
    FixedDepositDetails fixedDepositDetails = new FixedDepositDetails();
    fixedDepositDetails.setEmail("You must enter a valid email");
    return fixedDepositDetails;
  }
  .....
  @RequestMapping(params = "fdAction=create", method = RequestMethod.POST)
  public String openFixedDeposit(
      @ModelAttribute(value = "newFixedDepositDetails") FixedDepositDetails fixedDepositDetails,
       .....) { ..... }
  .....
  @RequestMapping(params = "fdAction=view", method = RequestMethod.GET)
  public ModelAndView viewFixedDepositDetails(
      @RequestParam(value = "fixedDepositId") int fixedDepositId) {
    FixedDepositDetails fixedDepositDetails = fixedDepositService
       .getFixedDeposit(fixedDepositId);
```

```
        Map<String, Object> modelMap = new HashMap<String, Object>();
        modelMap.put("editableFixedDepositDetails", fixedDepositDetails);
        .....
        return new ModelAndView("editFixedDepositForm", modelMap);
    }
}
```

@SessionAttributes annotation's value attribute specifies *names* of the model attributes that are temporarily stored in HttpSession. In the above example listing, model attributes named newFixedDepositDetails and editableFixedDepositDetails are stored in HttpSession between requests. The newFixedDepositDetails model attribute is returned by @ModelAttribute annotated getNewFixedDepositDetails method, and the editableFixedDepositDetails model attribute is returned by the @RequestMapping annotated viewFixedDepositDetails method.

A controller contributes model attributes via @ModelAttribute annotated methods, @RequestMapping methods (that return ModelAndView, Model or Map), and by directly adding model attributes to the Model object. The model attributes contributed by the controller through *any* approach are candidate for storage in the HttpSession by @SessionAttributes annotation.

When using @SessionAttributes annotation, you should ensure that the model attributes stored in the HttpSession are removed when they are no longer required. For instance, the newFixedDepositDetails model attribute represents an instance of FixedDepositDetails that is used by the 'Open fixed deposit' form to show the default value(s) of Email form field as 'You must enter a valid email' (refer getNewFixedDepositDetails method in example listing 11-11). Also, when the user clicks the 'Save' button on the 'Open fixed deposit' form, the fixed deposit details entered by the user are set on the newFixedDepositDetails instance (refer openFixedDeposit method in example listing 11-11). After the fixed deposit is successfully created, the newFixedDepositDetails instance is no longer required; therefore, it must be removed from the HttpSession. Similarly, editableFixedDepositDetails model attribute is not required after you have successfully modified details of a fixed deposit.

You can instruct Spring to remove *all* the model attributes stored in HttpSession by calling setComplete method of Spring's SessionStatus object. The following example listing shows FixedDepositController's openFixedDeposit and editFixedDeposit methods that invoke SessionStatus's setComplete method after a fixed deposit is successfully created or modified:

Example listing 11-12 – Removing model attributes from HttpSession using SessionStatus object
Project – ch11-session-attributes
Source location - src/main/java/sample/spring/chapter11/web

```
package sample.spring.chapter11.web;
```

```
import org.springframework.web.bind.support.SessionStatus;
.....
@SessionAttributes(value = { "newFixedDepositDetails", "editableFixedDepositDetails" })
public class FixedDepositController {
  .....
  @RequestMapping(params = "fdAction=create", method = RequestMethod.POST)
  public String openFixedDeposit(
        @ModelAttribute(value = "newFixedDepositDetails") FixedDepositDetails fixedDepositDetails,
        ....., SessionStatus sessionStatus) {
        fixedDepositService.saveFixedDeposit(fixedDepositDetails);
        sessionStatus.setComplete();
    }
  }

  @RequestMapping(params = "fdAction=edit", method = RequestMethod.POST)
  public String editFixedDeposit(
        @ModelAttribute("editableFixedDepositDetails") FixedDepositDetails fixedDepositDetails,
        ....., SessionStatus sessionStatus) {
        fixedDepositService.editFixedDeposit(fixedDepositDetails);
        sessionStatus.setComplete();
        .....
    }
  }
  .....
}
```

The above example listing shows that both openFixedDeposit and editFixedDeposit methods are defined to accept an argument of type SessionStatus. When a @RequestMapping annotated method specifies an argument of type SessionStatus, Spring supplies an instance of SessionStatus to the method. The call to setComplete method instructs Spring to remove the *current* controller's model attributes from the HttpSession object.

In example listing 11-11 and 11-12, we saw that the @SessionAttributes's value attribute specifies the names of model attributes that are temporarily stored in HttpSession. If you want that only certain *types* of model attributes are stored in HttpSession, you can use @SessionAttributes's types attribute. For instance, the following @SessionAttributes annotation specifies that attributes named x and y, and *all* model attributes that are of type MyObject, are temporarily stored in HttpSession:

```
@SessionAttributes(value = { "x", "y" }, types = { MyObject.class })
```

You can see the order in which listFixedDeposits, getNewFixedDepositDetails and openFixedDeposit methods are invoked by deploying ch11-session-attributes project and perform the actions described in the following table:

Action	Messages printed on the console
Go to http://localhost:8080/ch11-session-attributes/fixedDeposit/list URL	**getNewFixedDepositDetails() method**: Returning a new instance of FixedDepositDetails **listFixedDeposits() method**: Getting list of fixed deposits
Click the 'Create new Fixed Deposit' button	**showOpenFixedDepositForm()** method: Showing form for opening a new fixed deposit
Enter fixed deposit details and click the 'Save' button	**openFixedDeposit()** method: Fixed deposit details successfully saved. Redirecting to show the list of fixed deposits. **getNewFixedDepositDetails()** method: Returning a new instance of FixedDepositDetails **listFixedDeposits()** method: Getting list of fixed deposits

In ch11-bankapp project, we saw that the @ModelAttribute annotated getNewFixedDepositDetails method of FixedDepositController was invoked each time a request was dispatched to FixedDepositController. The above table shows that the getNewFixedDepositDetails method is invoked when request is handled by the FixedDepositController for the first time. As the openFixedDeposit method removes the model attributes stored in the HttpSession, request to listFixedDeposits method results in invocation of getNewFixedDepositDetails method once again.

Now, that we have seen how to use @ModelAttribute and @SessionAttributes annotations, let's look at how *data binding* is performed in Spring Web MVC applications.

11-4 Data binding support in Spring

When a form is submitted in a Spring Web MVC application, request parameters contained in the request are *automatically* set on the *model attribute* that acts as the form backing object. This process of setting request parameters on the form backing object is referred to as *data binding*. In this section, we'll look at Spring's WebDataBinder instance that binds request parameters to form backing objects.

IMPORT **chapter 11/ch11-data-binding** (This project shows a modified version of ch11-session-attributes project that shows how to register PropertyEditor implementations with Spring container. If you deploy the project on Tomcat server and access the URL http://localhost:8080/ch11-data-binding, you'll see the list of fixed deposits in the system.)

The following example listing shows the FixedDepositDetails class of ch11-data-binding project:

Example listing 11-13 – FixedDepositDetails class
Project – ch11-data-binding
Source location - src/main/java/sample/spring/chapter11/web

```
package sample.spring.chapter11.domain;

import java.util.Date;

public class FixedDepositDetails {
  .....
  private long depositAmount;
  private Date maturityDate;
  .....
  public void setDepositAmount(long depositAmount) {
    this.depositAmount = depositAmount;
  }
  public void setMaturityDate(Date maturityDate) {
    this.maturityDate = maturityDate;
  }
  .....
}
```

The above example listing shows that the depositAmount and maturityDate fields are of type long and java.util.Date, respectively. The values of depositAmount and maturityDate fields are set when the 'Open fixed deposit' form of ch11-data-binding project is submitted. The following figure shows the 'Open fixed deposit' form of ch11-data-binding project that is used for opening new fixed deposits:

Open fixed deposit

Amount (in USD):	1200
Maturity date:	01-27-2013
Email:	mail@somedomain.com

Save Go Back

Figure 11-2 'Open fixed deposit' form for opening new fixed deposits

In the above figure, 'Amount(in USD)' and 'Maturity date' form fields correspond to depositAmount and maturityDate fields of FixedDepositDetails class (refer example listing 11-

13). One of the important things to note is that the 'Maturity date' field accepts a date in the format 'MM-dd-yyyy', like 01-27-2013. As depositAmount field is of type long, and maturityDate is of type java.util.Date, Spring's data binding mechanism is responsible for doing the type conversion from String to the type defined by the FixedDepositDetails instance.

The following example listing shows FixedDepositController's openFixedDeposit method that is invoked when a user fills the 'Open fixed deposit' form and clicks the 'Save' button (refer figure 11-2):

Example listing 11-14 – FixedDepositController - Automatic data binding example
Project – ch11-data-binding
Source location - src/main/java/sample/spring/chapter11/web

```
package sample.spring.chapter11.web;

@Controller
.....
public class FixedDepositController {
    .....
    @RequestMapping(params = "fdAction=create", method = RequestMethod.POST)
    public String openFixedDeposit(
        @ModelAttribute(value = "newFixedDepositDetails") FixedDepositDetails fixedDepositDetails,
            BindingResult bindingResult, SessionStatus sessionStatus) {
        ....
    }
    .....
}
```

In the above example listing, the @ModelAttribute annotated FixedDepositDetails argument represents the form backing object on which the request parameters are set when the 'Open fixed deposit' form is submitted. Spring's WebDataBinder instance binds request parameters to the FixedDepositDetails instance.

Let's now look at how WebDataBinder performs data binding.

WebDataBinder – data binder for web request parameters

WebDataBinder uses the request parameter name to find the corresponding JavaBean-style setter method on the form backing object. If a JavaBean-style setter method is found, WebDataBinder invokes the setter method and passes the request parameter value as an argument to the setter method. If the setter method is defined to accept a non-String type argument, WebDataBinder uses an appropriate PropertyEditor to perform the type conversion.

The following example listing shows the MyObject class that acts as a form backing object in an application:

Example listing 11-15 – MyObject class – a form backing object

```
public class MyObject {
   private String x;
   private N y;
   .....
   public void setX(String x) {
      this.x = x;
   }
   public void setY(N y) {
      this.y = y;
   }
}
```

The above example listing shows that the MyObject class defines properties named x and y of type String and N, respectively.

The following figure shows how WebDataBinder binds request parameters named x and y to x and y properties of MyObject instance:

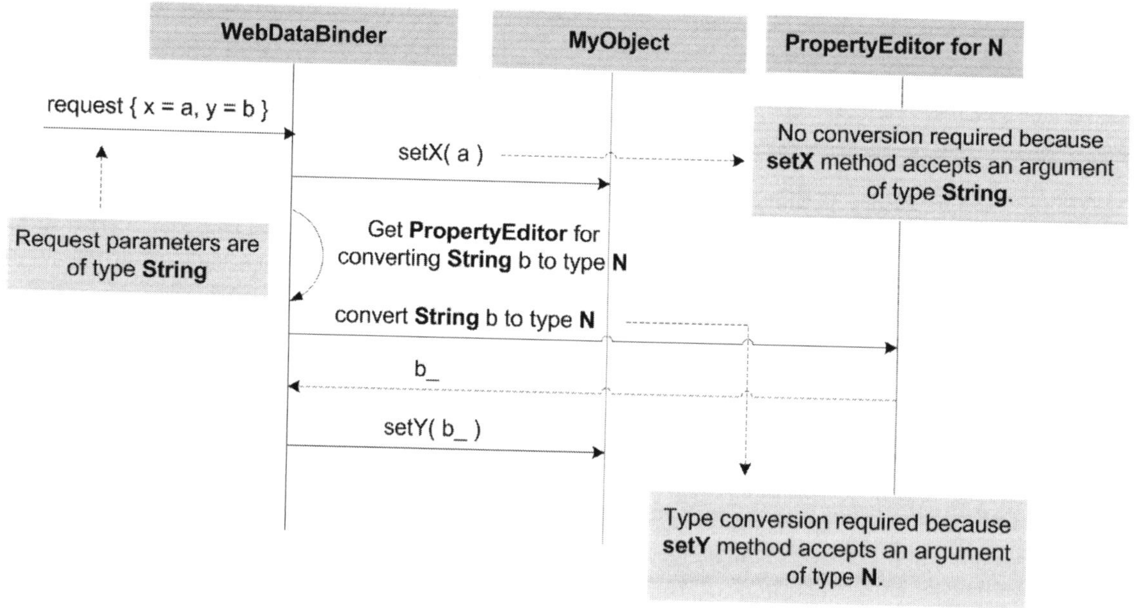

Figure 11-3 WebDataBinder performs data binding by using registered PropertyEditors to perform type conversion

The above figure shows that the WebDataBinder uses a PropertyEditor to convert String value b to type N, before calling the setY method of MyObject instance.

Spring provides a couple of built-in PropertyEditor implementations that are used by WebDataBinder for converting String type request parameter value to the type defined by the form backing object. For instance, CustomNumberEditor, FileEditor, CustomDateEditor are some of the built-in PropertyEditors provided by Spring. For a complete list of built-in PropertyEditors, refer to org.springframework.beans.propertyeditors package.

CustomNumberEditor is used for converting a String value to a java.lang.Number type, like Integer, Long, Double, and so on. CustomDateEditor is used for converting a String value to a java.util.Date type. You can pass a java.text.DateFormat instance to CustomDateEditor to specify the date format to be used for parsing and rendering dates. Both these PropertyEditors are required in ch11-data-binding project because we need to convert request parameter values to depositAmount (which is of type long) and maturityDate (which is of type java.util.Date). CustomNumberEditor is *pre-registered* with the WebDataBinder instance but you need to explicitly register CustomDateEditor.

Let's now look at how you can configure a WebDataBinder instance and register a PropertyEditor implementation with it.

Configuring a WebDataBinder instance

You can configure a WebDataBinder instance by:

- defining an @InitBinder annotated method in the controller class
- configuring a WebBindingInitializer implementation in the web application context XML file
- defining an @InitBinder annotated method in a @ControllerAdvice annotated class

Let's look at each of the above mentioned approach for configuring a WebDataBinder instance and registering a PropertyEditor with it.

Defining an @InitBinder annotated method in the controller class

An @InitBinder annotated method in a controller class specifies that the method initializes an instance of WebDataBinder that will be used by the controller during data binding. The value attribute of @InitBinder annotation specifies the name(s) of the model attribute to which the initialized WebDataBinder instance applies.

The following example listing shows FixedDepositController's initBinder_New method that is annotated with @InitBinder:

Example listing 11-16 – FixedDepositController - @InitBinder annotation usage
Project – ch11-data-binding
Source location - src/main/java/sample/spring/chapter11/web

```
package sample.spring.chapter11.web;

import java.text.SimpleDateFormat;
import org.springframework.beans.propertyeditors.CustomDateEditor;
import org.springframework.web.bind.WebDataBinder;
import org.springframework.web.bind.annotation.InitBinder;

@Controller
.....
public class FixedDepositController {
  .....
  @ModelAttribute(value = "newFixedDepositDetails")
  public FixedDepositDetails getNewFixedDepositDetails() { ..... }

  @InitBinder(value = "newFixedDepositDetails")
  public void initBinder_New(WebDataBinder webDataBinder) {
    webDataBinder.registerCustomEditor(Date.class,
          new CustomDateEditor(new SimpleDateFormat("MM-dd-yyyy"), false));
  }

  .....
}
```

In the above example listing, the @InitBinder annotation's value attribute is set to newFixedDepositDetails, which means that the WebDataBinder initialized by the initBinder_New method applies *only* to the newFixedDepositDetails model attribute. An @InitBinder annotated method can accept same set of arguments (like HttpServletRequest, SessionStatus, and so on) that can be passed to a @RequestMapping annotated method. But, an @InitBinder annotated method can't be defined to accept model attributes and BindingResult (or Errors) objects as arguments. Typically, WebDataBinder instance, along with Spring's WebRequest or java.util.Locale instance, is passed to an @InitBinder method. You should note that the return type of an @InitBinder method must be void.

WebDataBinder's registerCustomEditor method is used for registering a PropertyEditor with the WebDataBinder instance. In example listing 11-16, initBinder_New method registers CustomDateEditor (a PropertyEditor) with the WebDataBinder instance.

You can define an @InitBinder annotated method for each model attribute of a controller, or you can define a single @InitBinder annotated method that applies to all the model attributes of the controller. If you don't specify the value attribute of @InitBinder annotation, the

WebDataBinder instance initialized by the method is applicable to *all* the model attributes of the controller.

Configuring a WebBindingInitializer implementation

A WebDataBinder instance is first initialized by RequestMappingHandlerAdapter, followed by further initialization by WebBindingInitializer and @InitBinder methods.

The <annotation-driven> element of Spring's mvc schema creates an instance of Spring's RequestMappingHandlerAdapter that initializes the WebDataBinder. You can supply an implementation of Spring's WebBindingInitializer interface to RequestMappingHandlerAdapter to further initialize WebDataBinder instances. You can additionally use @InitBinder methods in a controller class to further initialize WebDataBinder instances.

The following figure shows the sequence in which RequestMappingHandlerAdapter, WebBindingInitializer and @InitBinder methods initialize a WebDataBinder instance:

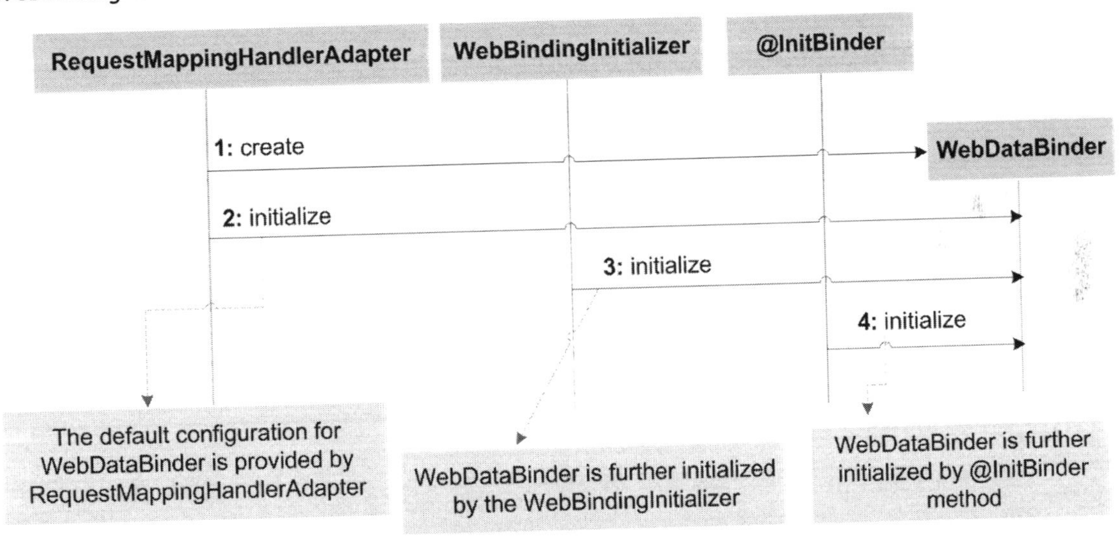

Figure 11-4 The sequence in which a WebDataBinder instance is initialized by RequestMappingHandlerAdapter, WebBindingInitializer and @InitBinder methods of a controller class

WebDataBinder initialization by an @InitBinder method of a controller class is applicable only to that controller's model attributes. For instance, if you use an @InitBinder method in controller X to set the CustomDateEditor property editor on the WebDataBinder instance, then the CustomDateEditor property editor will be available only to the model attributes of controller X during data binding. In MyBank application, the CustomDateEditor was required only by the model attributes of the FixedDepositController; therefore, we used @InitBinder annotated methods in the FixedDepositController class to register CustomDateEditor with WebDataBinder instance.

Spring's WebBindingInitializer is a callback interface whose implementation is responsible for initializing a WebDataBinder with the configuration that applies to *all* the controllers (and thereby to all the model attributes) in the application. Let's look at how to configure a custom WebBindingInitializer when using <annotation-driven> element of Spring's mvc schema.

The <annotation-driven> element of Spring's mvc schema creates and registers RequestMappingHandlerAdapter and RequestMappingHandlerMapping objects with the Spring container. The other objects that are configured by <annotation-driven> element are LocalValidatorFactoryBean (explained in section 11-5) and FormattingConversionServiceFactoryBean (explained in section 13-5). The <annotation-driven> element provides couple of attributes that help you customize RequestMappingHandlerAdapter and RequestMappingHandlerMapping objects. If the customization you want to make to RequestMappingHandlerAdapter or RequestMappingHandlerMapping object is not provided by the <annotation-driven> element, the only option is to remove <annotation-driven> element and explicitly configure RequestMappingHandlerAdapter and RequestMappingHandlerMapping objects in the web application context XML file. As <annotation-driven> element doesn't provide any option to supply a custom WebBindingInitializer instance to the RequestMappingHandlerAdapter object, you'll have to explicitly configure RequestMappingHandlerAdapter and RequestMappingHandlerMapping objects in the web application context XML file.

The following example listing shows how you can use Spring's ConfigurableWebBindingInitializer (an implementation of WebBindingInitializer) to make CustomDateEditor property editor available to all the controllers in the MyBank application:

Example listing 11-17 – WebBindingInitializer configuration

```
<bean id="handlerAdapter"
   class="org.springframework.web.servlet.mvc.method.annotation.RequestMappingHandlerAdapter">
   <property name="webBindingInitializer" ref="myInitializer" />
</bean>

<bean id="handlerMapping"
   class="org.springframework.web.servlet.mvc.method.annotation.RequestMappingHandlerMapping" />

<bean id="myInitializer"
   class="org.springframework.web.bind.support.ConfigurableWebBindingInitializer">
    <property name="propertyEditorRegistrars">
        <list>
            <bean class="mypackage.MyPropertyEditorRegistrar" />
        </list>
```

```
    </property>
</bean>
```

The above example listing shows that RequestMappingHandlerAdapter and RequestMappingHandlerMapping beans are *explicitly* defined in the web application context XML file. The RequestMappingHandlerAdapter's webBindingInitializer property refers to the ConfigurableWebBindingInitializer bean that implements WebBindingInitializer interface. ConfigurableWebBindingInitializer's propertyEditorRegistrars property specifies classes that register one or more PropertyEditors with WebDataBinder. The following example listing shows how MyPropertyEditorRegistrar class registers CustomDateEditor property editor with WebDataBinder:

Example listing 11-18 – MyPropertyEditorRegistrar class

```
import org.springframework.beans.PropertyEditorRegistrar;
import org.springframework.beans.PropertyEditorRegistry;
import org.springframework.beans.propertyeditors.CustomDateEditor;

public class MyPropertyEditorRegistrar implements PropertyEditorRegistrar {

  @Override
  public void registerCustomEditors(PropertyEditorRegistry registry) {
    registry.registerCustomEditor(Date.class, new CustomDateEditor(
          new SimpleDateFormat("MM-dd-yyyy"), false));
  }
}
```

The above example listing shows that the MyPropertyEditorRegistrar class implements Spring's PropertyEditorRegistrar interface, and provides implementation for registerCustomEditors method defined in the PropertyEditorRegistrar interface. The PropertyEditorRegistry instance passed to the registerCustomEditors method is used for registering property editors. PropertyEditorRegistry's registerCustomEditor method is used for registering a PropertyEditor implementation with the WebDataBinder. In the above example listing, PropertyEditorRegistry's registerCustomEditor is used for registering the CustomDateEditor property editor with the WebDataBinder.

As we saw, using WebBindingInitializer for initializing WebDataBinder is quite an involved task. A simpler alternative to using WebBindingInitializer is to define @InitBinder annotated methods in a @ControllerAdvice annotated class.

Defining an @InitBinder method in a @ControllerAdvice annotated class

Like @Service, @Controller and @Repository annotations, @ControllerAdvice annotation is a specialized form of @Component annotation. The @ControllerAdvice annotation on a class indicates that the class provides support to controllers. You can define @InitBinder, @ModelAttribute and @ExceptionHandler annotated methods in the @ControllerAdvice annotated class, and these annotated methods apply to *all* the annotated controllers in the application. As with @Service, @Controller and @Repository annotations, <classpath-scanning> element of Spring's context schema automatically detects and registers @ControllerAdvice annotated classes with the Spring container.

If you notice that you are duplicating @InitBinder, @ModelAttribute and @ExceptionHandler methods in multiple controllers, then consider defining such methods in a @ControllerAdvice annotated class. For instance, if you want to initialize the WebDataBinder with the configuration that applies to multiple controllers in the application, then define an @InitBinder method in a @ControllerAdvice annotated class instead of defining an @InitBinder method in multiple controller classes.

The following table summarizes the three approaches that we discussed for initializing WebDataBinder:

@InitBinder method in controller class	WebBindingInitializer	@InitBinder method in @ControllerAdvice class
Requires defining an @InitBinder method in a controller	Requires explicitly configuring RequestMappingHandlerAdapter in the web application context XML file	Requires defining an @InitBinder method in a @ControllerAdvice annotated class
WebDataBinder initialization applies only to the controller that contains the @InitBinder method	WebDataBinder initialization applies to all the annotated controllers in the application	WebDataBinder initialization applies to all the annotated controllers in the application

Let's now look at how you can allow or disallow fields of a model attribute from participating in the data binding process.

Allowing or disallowing fields from data binding process

WebDataBinder allows you to specify fields of a model attribute that are allowed or disallowed from participating in the data binding process. It is strongly recommended that you specify the fields of a model attribute that are allowed or disallowed from the data binding processes, as failing to do so may compromise the *security* of your application. Let's look at a scenario in which we would like to allow or disallow fields from data binding.

In MyBank application, when a user selects a fixed deposit for editing, the details of the selected fixed deposit are loaded from the data store and temporarily cached in the

HttpSession. The user makes changes to the fixed deposit and saves the changes. The following example listing shows the @RequestMapping methods that are responsible for loading the selected fixed deposit and saving the updated fixed deposit information:

Example listing 11-19 – FixedDepositController
Project – ch11-data-binding
Source location - src/main/java/sample/spring/chapter11/web

```
package sample.spring.chapter11.web;
.....
@SessionAttributes(value = { "newFixedDepositDetails", "editableFixedDepositDetails" })
public class FixedDepositController {
  .....
  @RequestMapping(params = "fdAction=view", method = RequestMethod.GET)
  public ModelAndView viewFixedDepositDetails(
       @RequestParam(value = "fixedDepositId") int fixedDepositId) {
    FixedDepositDetails fixedDepositDetails = fixedDepositService
       .getFixedDeposit(fixedDepositId);
    Map<String, Object> modelMap = new HashMap<String, Object>();
    modelMap.put("editableFixedDepositDetails", fixedDepositDetails);
    .....
    return new ModelAndView("editFixedDepositForm", modelMap);
  }
  .....
  @RequestMapping(params = "fdAction=edit", method = RequestMethod.POST)
  public String editFixedDeposit(
    @ModelAttribute("editableFixedDepositDetails") FixedDepositDetails fixedDepositDetails,) {
    .....
  }
}
```

In MyBank application, a fixed deposit is uniquely identified by the id field of FixedDepositDetails object (refer FixedDepositDetails class of ch11-data-binding project). When a user selects a fixed deposit for editing, the id field value is passed to the viewFixedDepositDetails method via the fixedDepositId request parameter. The viewFixedDepositDetails method uses the value of fixedDepositId request parameter to load fixed deposit details and show them on the 'Edit fixed deposit' form, as shown in the following figure:

Edit fixed deposit

Id: 4 → read-only field

Amount (in USD): 50000

Maturity date: 05-22-2013

Email: a4email@somedomain.co

Save Go Back

Figure 11-5 'Edit fixed deposit' form for editing an existing fixed deposit

As the *id* value (that corresponds to *id* attribute of FixedDepositDetails object) uniquely identifies a fixed deposit in the system, the 'Edit fixed deposit' form doesn't provide any mechanism to change it. When the user clicks the '*Save*' button, the FixedDepositController's editFixedDeposit method is invoked. The editFixedDeposit method saves the changes to the fixed deposit detail.

When FixedDepositController's editFixedDeposit method is invoked, the WebDataBinder instance binds request parameter values to the fields of editableFixedDepositDetails model attribute – the FixedDepositDetails object that was loaded by viewFixedDepositDetails method and temporarily stored in HttpSession (refer @SessionAttributes annotation in example listing 11-19). If a malicious user sends a request parameter named *id* with value 10, then the WebDataBinder will blindly go ahead and set the id attribute of FixedDepositDetails object to 10 during data binding. This is *not* desirable because changing id attribute of a FixedDepositDetails object will compromise application data.

WebDataBinder provides setAllowedFields and setDisallowedFields methods that you can use to set the names of model attribute fields that can and cannot participate in the data binding process. The following example listing shows the FixedDepositController's initBinder_Edit method that specifies that the id field of editableFixedDepositDetails model attribute must *not* participate in the data binding process:

Example listing 11-20 – FixedDepositController – WebDataBinder's setDisallowedFields method
Project – ch11-data-binding
Source location - src/main/java/sample/spring/chapter11/web

```
package sample.spring.chapter11.web;
.....
public class FixedDepositController {
  .....
  @RequestMapping(params = "fdAction=edit", method = RequestMethod.POST)
  public String editFixedDeposit(
   @ModelAttribute("editableFixedDepositDetails") FixedDepositDetails fixedDepositDetails, .....) {
     .....
  }
  .....
  @InitBinder(value = "editableFixedDepositDetails")
  public void initBinder_Edit(WebDataBinder webDataBinder) {
    webDataBinder.registerCustomEditor(Date.class, new CustomDateEditor(
          new SimpleDateFormat("MM-dd-yyyy"), false));
    webDataBinder.setDisallowedFields("id");
  }
}
```

In the above example listing, the initBinder_Edit method initializes WebDataBinder instance for the editableFixedDepositDetails model attribute. As the setDisallowedFields method specifies that the id field of editableFixedDepositDetails model attribute is disallowed to participate in the binding process, the id field is *not* set even if a request parameter named id is contained in the request.

Let's now look at Spring's BindingResult object that exposes errors that occur during data binding and validation.

Inspecting data binding and validation errors using BindingResult object

Spring's BindingResult object provides a controller method with the results of binding request parameters to the model attribute's fields. For instance, if any type conversion error occurs during data binding, they are reported by the BindingResult object.

The following example listing shows FixedDepositController's openFixedDeposit method that creates a fixed deposit only if no errors are reported by the BindingResult object:

Example listing 11-21 – FixedDepositController – checking for binding and validation errors using BindingResult
Project – ch11-data-binding
Source location - src/main/java/sample/spring/chapter11/web

```
package sample.spring.chapter11.web;

import org.springframework.validation.BindingResult;
import org.springframework.web.bind.annotation.ModelAttribute;
.....
public class FixedDepositController {
  .....
  @RequestMapping(params = "fdAction=create", method = RequestMethod.POST)
  public String openFixedDeposit(
    @ModelAttribute(value = "newFixedDepositDetails") FixedDepositDetails fixedDepositDetails,
      BindingResult bindingResult, SessionStatus sessionStatus) {
    .....
    if (bindingResult.hasErrors()) {
      return "createFixedDepositForm";
    } else {
      fixedDepositService.saveFixedDeposit(fixedDepositDetails);
      sessionStatus.setComplete();
      return "redirect:/fixedDeposit/list";
    }
  }
  .....
}
```

In the above example listing, the BindingResult's hasErrors method returns true if the BindingResult object holds one or more data binding or validation errors. In section 11-5, we'll see how validation errors are stored in the BindingResult object. If errors are reported by the BindingResult object, the openFixedDeposit method renders the 'Create fixed deposit' form with appropriate error messages. If no errors are reported, the fixed deposit details are saved in the data store.

You should note that the BindingResult argument must immediately follow the model attribute argument whose BindingResult object you want to access in the controller method. For instance, in example listing 11-21, the BindingResult argument immediately follows the newFixedDepositDetails model attribute. The following example listing shows an incorrect ordering of the model attribute and the BindingResult object for the openFixedDeposit method:

Example listing 11-22 – Incorrect ordering of the model attribute and the BindingResult object

```
.....
public class FixedDepositController {
  .....
  @RequestMapping(params = "fdAction=create", method = RequestMethod.POST)
  public String openFixedDeposit(
    @ModelAttribute(value = "newFixedDepositDetails") FixedDepositDetails fixedDepositDetails,
```

```
        SessionStatus sessionStatus, BindingResult bindingResult) {
      .....
   }
   .....
}
```

In the above example listing, the ordering of the newFixedDepositDetails model attribute and the BindingResult object is incorrect because the SessionStatus argument is defined between them.

If a controller method accepts multiple model attributes, the BindingResult object corresponding to each model attribute is specified immediately after each model attribute argument, as shown in the following example listing:

Example listing 11-23 – Multiple model attributes and their BindingResult objects

```
@RequestMapping
public String doSomething(
   @ModelAttribute(value = "a") AObject aObj,BindingResult bindingResultA,
   @ModelAttribute(value = "b") BObject bObj,BindingResult bindingResultB,) {
   .....
}
```

The above example listing shows that both model attributes a and b are immediately followed by their corresponding BindingResult objects.

Now, that we have seen the data binding process, let's look at how validation is performed in Spring Web MVC applications.

11-5 Validation support in Spring

In the previous section, we saw that the WebDataBinder binds request parameters to model attributes. The next step in request processing is to validate model attributes. In Spring Web MVC applications, you can validate model attributes using Spring Validation API (discussed in section 6-9 of chapter 6) or by specifying JSR 303 (Bean Validation API) constraints (discussed in section 6-10 of chapter 6) on fields of model attributes.

> In this chapter, Spring Validation API and JSR 303 (Bean Validation API) have been used to validate form backing objects (which are model attributes) in the web layer of the application. You should note that both JSR 303 (Bean Validation API) and Spring Validation API can be used to validate objects in *any* application layer.

Let's first look at how to validate model attributes using Spring Validation API's Validator interface.

Validating model attributes using Spring's Validator interface

The following example listing shows the FixedDepositDetailsValidator class of MyBank application that validates FixedDepositDetails object:

Example listing 11-24 – FixedDepositDetailsValidator –Spring's Validator interface usage
Project – ch11-data-binding
Source location - src/main/java/sample/spring/chapter11/web

```
package sample.spring.chapter11.web;

import org.springframework.validation.*;
import sample.spring.chapter11.domain.FixedDepositDetails;

public class FixedDepositDetailsValidator implements Validator {

  public boolean supports(Class<?> clazz) {
    return FixedDepositDetails.class.isAssignableFrom(clazz);
  }

  public void validate(Object target, Errors errors) {
    FixedDepositDetails fixedDepositDetails = (FixedDepositDetails) target;
    long depositAmount = fixedDepositDetails.getDepositAmount();
    .....
    if (depositAmount < 1000) {
      errors.rejectValue("depositAmount", "error.depositAmount.less",
                "must be greater than or equal to 1000");
    }
    if (email == null || "".equalsIgnoreCase(email)) {
      ValidationUtils.rejectIfEmptyOrWhitespace(errors, "email", "error.email.blank",
      "must not be blank");
    }
    .....
  }
}
```

Spring's Validator interface defines supports and validate methods. The supports method checks if the supplied object instance (represented by the clazz attribute) can be validated. If the supports method returns true, the validate method is used to validate the object. In the above example listing, the FixedDepositDetailsValidator's supports method checks if the supplied object instance is of type FixedDepositDetails. If the supports method returns true, the FixedDepositDetailsValidator's validate method validates the object. The validate method accepts the object instance to be validated, and an Errors instance. Errors instance stores and exposes errors that occur during validation. Errors instance provides multiple reject and rejectValue methods to register errors with the Errors instance. The rejectValue methods are used to report field-level errors, and reject methods are used to report errors that apply to the object being validated. Spring's ValidationUtils class is a utility class that provides convenience methods to invoke a Validator, and for rejecting empty fields.

The following figure describes the parameters that were passed to the rejectValue method in example listing 11-24 to report a validation error corresponding to FixedDepositDetails's depositAmount field:

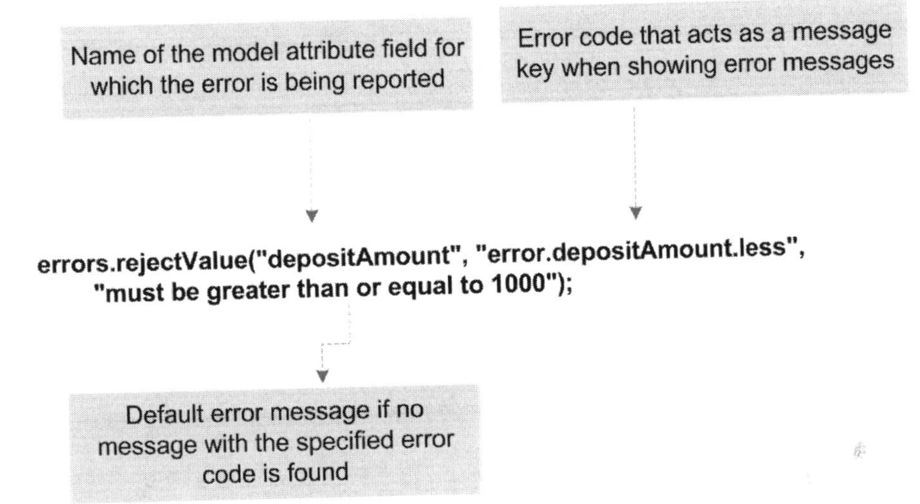

Figure 11-6 Description of parameters that are passed to rejectValue method of Errors instance to report validation error corresponding to depositAmount field of FixedDepositDetails

The above figure shows that field name, error code (which is basically a message key) and a default error message is passed to the rejectValue method. In chapter 13, we'll see how the message keys are used by JSP pages to show messages from resource bundles.

You can validate model attributes by:

- explicitly invoking validate method on Validator implementation
- setting Validator implementation on WebDataBinder, and annotating the model attribute argument in the @RequestMapping method with JSR 303's @Valid annotation

Let's look at each of the above mentioned approaches in detail.

Validating model attributes by explicitly calling validate method

The following example listing shows the FixedDepositController's openFixedDeposit method that uses FixedDepositDetailsValidator (refer example listing 11-24) to validate FixedDepositDetails model attribute:

Example listing 11-25 – FixedDepositController – validation by explicitly invoking FixedDepositDetailsValidator's validate method
Project – ch11-data-binding
Source location - src/main/java/sample/spring/chapter11/web

```
package sample.spring.chapter11.web;
.....
public class FixedDepositController {
  .....
  @RequestMapping(params = "fdAction=create", method = RequestMethod.POST)
  public String openFixedDeposit(
    @ModelAttribute(value = "newFixedDepositDetails") FixedDepositDetails fixedDepositDetails,
    BindingResult bindingResult, SessionStatus sessionStatus) {

    new FixedDepositDetailsValidator().validate(fixedDepositDetails,bindingResult);
    if (bindingResult.hasErrors()) {
       logger.info("openFixedDeposit() method: Validation errors
            - re-displaying form for opening a new fixed deposit");
       return "createFixedDepositForm";
    }
    .....
  }
}
```

The above example listing shows that the openFixedDeposit method creates an instance of FixedDepositDetailsValidator and invokes its validate method. As BindingResult is a sub-interface of Errors, you can pass a BindingResult object where Errors object is expected. The openFixedDeposit method passes the fixedDepositDetails model attribute and the BindingResult object to the validate method. As BindingResult already contains data binding errors, passing BindingResult object to validate method adds validation errors also to the BindingResult object.

Invoking model attributes validation using JSR 303's @Valid annotation

You can instruct Spring to automatically validate a model attribute argument passed to a @RequestMapping method by adding JSR 303's @Valid annotation to the model attribute argument, and setting the validator for the model attribute on the WebDataBinder instance.

The following example listing shows how FixedDepositController's openFixedDeposit method can use @Valid annotation to validate FixedDepositDetails model attribute:

Example listing 11-26 – FixedDepositController – invoking validation using @Valid annotation

```
import javax.validation.Valid;
.....
public class FixedDepositController {
  .....
  @RequestMapping(params = "fdAction=create", method = RequestMethod.POST)
  public String openFixedDeposit(
       @Valid @ModelAttribute(value = "newFixedDepositDetails") FixedDepositDetails
       fixedDepositDetails, BindingResult bindingResult, SessionStatus sessionStatus) {

    if (bindingResult.hasErrors()) {
       logger.info("openFixedDeposit() method:
           Validation errors - re-displaying form for opening a new fixed deposit");
       return "createFixedDepositForm";
    }
    .....
  }
  .....
  @InitBinder(value = "newFixedDepositDetails")
  public void initBinder_New(WebDataBinder webDataBinder) {
    webDataBinder.registerCustomEditor(Date.class, new CustomDateEditor(
          new SimpleDateFormat("MM-dd-yyyy"), false));
    webDataBinder.setValidator(new FixedDepositDetailsValidator());
  }
  .....
}
```

In the above example listing, the initBinder_New method calls WebDataBinder's setValidator method to set FixedDepositDetailsValidator as the validator for newFixedDepositDetails model attribute, and in the openFixedDeposit method the newFixedDepositDetails model attribute is annotated with JSR 303's @Valid annotation. When the openFixedDeposit method is invoked, both data binding *and* validation are performed on the newFixedDepositDetails model attribute, and the results of data binding and validation are made available via the BindingResult argument.

It is important to note that if @InitBinder annotation specifies name of the model attribute, the validator set on the WebDataBinder applies only to that particular model attribute. For instance, in example listing 11-26, the FixedDepositDetailsValidator applies only to the newFixedDepositDetails model attribute. If a validator applies to multiple controllers in the application, consider defining an @InitBinder method inside a @ControllerAdvice annotated class (or use WebBindingInitializer) to set a validator on the WebDataBinder.

Let's now look at how constraints are specified on properties of JavaBeans component using JSR 303 annotations.

Specifying constraints using JSR 303 annotations

JSR 303 (Bean Validation API) defines annotations that you can use to specify constraints on properties of JavaBeans components.

IMPORT chapter 11/ch11-jsr303-validation (This project shows a modified version of ch11-data-binding project that uses JSR 303 annotations to specify constraints on FixedDepositDetails object. If you deploy the project on Tomcat server and access the URL http://localhost:8080/ch11-jsr303-validation, you'll see the list of fixed deposits in the system.)

The following example listing shows the FixedDepositDetails class that uses JSR 303 annotations to specify constraints on its fields:

Example listing 11-27 – FixedDepositDetails – specifying JSR 303 constraints
Project – ch11-jsr303-validation
Source location - src/main/java/sample/spring/chapter11/domain

```
package sample.spring.chapter11.domain;

import javax.validation.constraints.*;

public class FixedDepositDetails {
   private long id;

   @Min(1000)
   @Max(500000)
   private long depositAmount;

   @Email
   @Size(min=10, max=25)
   private String email;

   @NotNull
   private Date maturityDate;
   .....
}
```

@Min, @Max, @Email, @Size, and @NotNull are some of the annotations defined by JSR 303. The above example listing shows that by using JSR 303 annotations FixedDepositDetails class clearly specifies the constraints that apply on its fields. On the other hand, if you are using Spring's Validator implementation to validate an object, constraints are contained in the Validator implementation (refer example listing 11-24).

The following table describes the constraints enforced by JSR 303 annotations on the FixedDepositDetails object shown in example listing 11-27:

JSR 303 annotation	Constraint description
@NotNull	The annotated field must not be null. For instance, maturityDate field must not be null.
@Min	The annotated field's value must be greater than or equal to the specified minimum value. For instance, @Min(1000) annotation on depositAmount field of FixedDepositDetails object means that depositAmount's value must be greater than or equal to 1000.
@Max	The annotated field's value must be less than or equal to the specified value. For instance, @Max(500000) annotation on depositAmount field of FixedDepositDetails object means that the depositAmount's value must be less than or equal to 500000.
@Size	The annotated field's size must be between the specified min and max attributes. For instance, @Size(min=5, max=100) annotation on email field of FixedDepositDetails object means that the size of the email field must be greater than or equal to 5 and less than or equal to 100.
@Email	The annotated field's value must a well-formed email address. For instance, @Email annotation on the email field of FixedDepositDetails object means that the email field's value must be a well-formed email address.

To use JSR 303 annotations, ch11-jsr303-validation project specifies dependency on JSR 303 API JAR file (validation-api-1.0.0.GA) and Hibernate Validator framework (hibernate-validation-4.3.0.Final). The Hibernate Validator framework provides the reference implementation for JSR 303. The Hibernate Validator framework provides additional constraint annotations that you can use along with JSR 303 annotations. For instance, you can use Hibernate Validator's @NotBlank annotation to specify that a field's value must not be null or empty.

It is important to note that JSR 303 also allows you to create custom constraints and use them in your application. For instance, you can create a @MyConstraint custom constraint and a corresponding validator to enforce that constraint on objects.

Now, that we have specified JSR 303 constraints on FixedDepositDetails class, let's look at how to validate FixedDepositDetails object.

Validating objects that use JSR 303 annotations

If a JSR 303 provider (like Hibernate Validator) is found in the application's classpath, and you have specified <annotation-driven> element of Spring's mvc schema in the web application context XML file, then Spring automatically enables support for JSR 303. Behind the scenes, the <annotation-driven> element configures an instance of Spring's LocalValidatorFactoryBean class that is responsible for detecting the presence of a JSR 303 provider (like Hibernate Validator) in the application's classpath and initializing it.

LocalValidatorFactoryBean implements JSR 303's Validator and ValidatorFactory interfaces, and also Spring's Validator interface. For this reason, you can choose to validate an object by calling validate method of Spring's Validator interface or by calling validate method of JSR 303's Validator. As discussed earlier, you can also instruct Spring to automatically validate a model attribute argument passed to a @RequestMapping method by simply adding @Valid annotation on the model attribute argument.

Validating model attributes by explicitly calling validate method

The following example listing shows the FixedDepositController class that uses Spring's Validator to validate the FixedDepositDetails object (refer example listing 11-27) that uses JSR 303's constraints:

Example listing 11-28 – FixedDepositController – validating FixedDepositDetails using Spring Validation API
Project – ch11-jsr303-validation
Source location - src/main/java/sample/spring/chapter11/web

```
package sample.spring.chapter11.web;

import javax.validation.Valid;
.....
public class FixedDepositController {
  .....
```

```
    @Autowired
    private Validator validator;
    .....
    @RequestMapping(params = "fdAction=create", method = RequestMethod.POST)
    public String openFixedDeposit(
            @ModelAttribute(value = "newFixedDepositDetails") FixedDepositDetails fixedDepositDetails,
            BindingResult bindingResult, SessionStatus sessionStatus) {
        validator.validate(fixedDepositDetails, bindingResult);

        if (bindingResult.hasErrors()) { ..... } .....
    }
    .....
}
```

In the above example listing, the LocalValidatorFactoryBean (that implements Spring's Validator interface) is autowired into FixedDepositController's validator instance variable. In the openFixedDeposit method, call to Validator's validate method results in invocation of LocalValidatorFactoryBean's validate(Object, Errors) method to validate the FixedDepositDetails instance. The BindingResult object is passed to the validate method to hold the validation errors. An important point to notice in the above example listing is that the FixedDepositController doesn't directly deal with JSR 303-specific API to validate FixedDepositDetails object. Instead, Spring Validation API is used to validate FixedDepositDetails object.

The following example listing shows an alternate version of FixedDepositController that uses JSR 303-specific API to validate FixedDepositDetails object:

Example listing 11-29 – FixedDepositController – validating FixedDepositDetails using JSR 303-specific API

```
import javax.validation.ConstraintViolation;
import javax.validation.Validator;
import java.util.Set;
.....
public class FixedDepositController {
    .....
    @Autowired
    private Validator validator;
    .....
    @RequestMapping(params = "fdAction=create", method = RequestMethod.POST)
    public String openFixedDeposit(
            @ModelAttribute(value = "newFixedDepositDetails") FixedDepositDetails fixedDepositDetails,
            BindingResult bindingResult, SessionStatus sessionStatus) {
```

```
        Set<ConstraintViolation<FixedDepositDetails>> violations =
                validator.validate(fixedDepositDetails);
        Iterator<ConstraintViolation<FixedDepositDetails>> itr = violations.iterator();

        if(itr.hasNext()) { ..... } .....
    }
    .....
}
```

In the above example listing, the LocalValidatorFactoryBean (that implements JSR 303's Validator interface) is autowired into FixedDepositController's validator instance variable. In the openFixedDeposit method, call to Validator's validate method results in invocation of LocalValidatorFactoryBean's validate(T) method to validate the FixedDepositDetails instance. The validate method returns a java.util.Set object that contains the constraint violations reported by the JSR 303 provider. You can check the java.util.Set object returned by the validate method to find if any constraint violations were reported.

Invoking model attributes validation using JSR 303's @Valid annotation

You can instruct Spring to automatically validate a model attribute argument passed to a @RequestMapping method by adding JSR 303's @Valid annotation to the model attribute argument. The following example listing shows FixedDepositController's editFixedDeposit method that uses @Valid annotation to validate editableFixedDepositDetails model attribute:

Example listing 11-30 – FixedDepositController – invoking validation using @Valid annotation
Project – ch11-jsr303-validation
Source location - src/main/java/sample/spring/chapter11/web

```
package sample.spring.chapter11.web;

import javax.validation.Valid;
.....
public class FixedDepositController {
    .....
    @RequestMapping(params = "fdAction=edit", method = RequestMethod.POST)
    public String editFixedDeposit(
    @Valid @ModelAttribute("editableFixedDepositDetails") FixedDepositDetails fixedDepositDetails,
            BindingResult bindingResult, SessionStatus sessionStatus) {

        if (bindingResult.hasErrors()) { ..... } .....
    }
    .....
}
```

In the above example listing, @Valid annotation on editableFixedDepositDetails model attribute results in its automatic validation by Spring. The constraint violations reported during validation are added to the BindingResult object along with any data binding errors.

Let's now look at how Spring's form tag library simplifies writing forms in JSP pages.

11-6 Spring's form tag library

Spring's form tag library provides tags that simplify creating JSP pages for Spring Web MVC applications. The Spring's form tag library provides tags to render various input form elements and for binding form data to form backing objects.

The following example listing shows the createFixedDepositForm.jsp JSP page of ch11-jsr303-validation project that uses Spring's form tag library tags:

Example listing 11-31 – createFixedDepositForm.jsp – Spring's form tag library usage
Project – ch11-jsr303-validation
Source location - src/main/webapp/WEB-INF/jsp

```
<%@taglib uri="http://java.sun.com/jsp/jstl/core" prefix="c"%>
<%@taglib prefix="form" uri="http://www.springframework.org/tags/form"%>

<html>
.....
  <form:form commandName="newFixedDepositDetails"
    name="createFixedDepositForm" method="POST"
    action="${pageContext.request.contextPath}/fixedDeposit?fdAction=create">
    .....
    <tr>
      <td class="td"><b>Amount (in USD):</b></td>
      <td class="td"><form:input path="depositAmount" />
        <font style="color: #C11B17;"><form:errors path="depositAmount"/></font>
      </td>
    </tr>
    <tr>
      <td class="td"><b>Maturity date:</b></td>
      <td class="td"><form:input path="maturityDate" />
      <font style="color: #C11B17;"><form:errors path="maturityDate"/></font></td>
    </tr>
    .....
      <td class="td"><input type="submit" value="Save" />
    .....
  </form:form>
</html>
```

In the above example listing, the following taglib directive makes the Spring's form tag library tags accessible to the JSP page:

```
<%@taglib prefix="form" uri="http://www.springframework.org/tags/form"%>
```

Spring's form tag library's <form> tag renders an HTML form that binds form fields to the properties of model attribute identified by the commandName attribute. The <form> tag contains <input> tags that correspond to the properties of the model attribute specified by the commandName attribute. When the form is rendered, properties are read from the model attribute and displayed by <input> tags. And, when the form is submitted, the field values in the form are bound to the corresponding properties of the model attribute.

In example listing 11-31, the <form> tag renders an HTML form for opening a fixed deposit. The commandName attribute's value is newFixedDepositDetails, which means that the form fields are mapped to the properties of the newFixedDepositDetails model attribute. The name attribute specifies the name of the HTML form rendered by the <form> tag. The method attribute specifies the HTTP method to use for sending form data when the form is submitted. The action attribute specifies the URL to which the form data is sent when the form is submitted. The URL specified by the action attribute must map to a unique @RequestMapping annotated method in your Spring Web MVC application. In example listing 11-31, the URL ${pageContext.request.contextPath}/fixedDeposit?fdAction=create maps to FixedDepositController's openFixedDeposit method (refer FixedDepositController.java file of ch11-jsr303-validation project). You should note that the expression ${pageContext.request.contextPath} returns the *context path* of the web application.

The <input> tag of Spring's form tag library renders an HTML <input> element with type attribute set to text. The path attribute specifies the property of the model attribute to which the field is mapped. When the form is rendered, the value of the property is displayed by the input field. And, when the form is submitted, the value of the property is set to the value entered by the user in the input field.

The <errors> tag of Spring's form tag library shows data binding and validation error messages that were added to the BindingResult during data binding and validation. If you want to display error messages corresponding to a particular property, specify the name of the property as the value of the path attribute. If you want to display all the error messages stored in the BindingResult object, specify value of path attribute as *.

The createFixedDepositForm.jsp page uses only a subset of Spring's form tag library tags. The following table shows the other tags that Spring's form tag library offers:

Tag	Description
<checkbox>	Renders an HTML checkbox (that is, <input type="checkbox" />) As the value of an HTML checkbox is *not* sent to the server if the checkbox is unchecked, the <checkbox> tag additionally renders a hidden field corresponding to each checkbox to allow sending the state of the checkbox to the server. Example: <form:checkbox path="myProperty" /> The path attribute specifies the name of the property to which the checkbox value is bound.
<checkboxes>	Renders multiple HTML checkboxes. Example: <form:checkboxes path="myPropertyList" items="${someList}"/> The path attribute specifies the name of the property to which the selected checkboxes values are bound. The items attribute specifies the name of the model attribute that contains the list of options to show as checkboxes.
<radiobutton>	Renders an HTML radio button (that is, <input type="radio" />) Example: <form:radiobutton path="myProperty" value="myValue"/> The path attribute specifies the name of the property to which the radio button is bound, and the value attribute specifies the value assigned to the radio button.
<radiobuttons>	Renders multiple HTML radio buttons. Example: <form:radiobuttons path="myProperty" items="${myValues}"/> The items attribute specifies the list of options to show as radio buttons, and the path attribute specifies the property to which the selected radio buttons values are bound.
<password>	Renders an HTML password field (that is, <input type="password"/>)
<select>	Renders an HTML <select> element. Example: <form:select path="book" items="${books}"/> The items attribute specifies the model attribute property that contains the list of options to display in the HTML <select> element. The path attribute specifies the property to which the selected option is bound.

<option>	Renders an HTML <option> element. Example: <form:select path="book"> **<form:option value="Getting started with Spring Framework"/>** **<form:option value="Getting started with Spring Web MVC"/>** </form:select>
<options>	Renders multiple HTML <option> elements.
<textarea>	Renders an HTML <textarea> element.
<hidden>	Renders an HTML hidden input field (that is, <input type="hidden" />)

Let's now look at HTML5 support in Spring's form tag library.

HTML5 support in Spring's form tag library

Starting with Spring 3.0, the form tag library allows you to use HTML5-specific attributes in the tags. For instance, the following <textarea> tag uses HTML5's required attribute:

```
<form:textarea path="myProperty" required="required"/>
```

The required="required" attribute specifies that it is mandatory for the user to enter information in the textarea. The use of required attribute saves the effort to write the JavaScript code to perform client-side validation for mandatory fields. If the user doesn't enter any information in the textarea and attempts to submit the form, the web browser shows a message saying that the textarea is required and must not be left blank.

In HTML5 you can specify type attribute's value as email, datetime, date, month, week, time, range, color, reset, and so on. Starting with Spring 3.1, <input> tag supports specifying type attribute value other than text. For instance, the following <input> tag specifies type attribute's value as email:

```
<form:input path="myProperty" type="email"/>
```

When a user attempts to submit the form containing a field of type email, the web browser checks that the email type field contains a valid email address. If the email type field doesn't contain a valid email address, the web browser shows a message indicating that the field doesn't contain a valid email address. As the web browser performs the validation, you don't need to write the JavaScript code to validate the email address.

11-7 Summary

We looked at many core features of Spring Web MVC in this chapter. We looked at @ModelAttribute and @SessionAttributes annotations which are most commonly used in developing annotated controllers. We also took an in-depth look at how Spring performs data binding and validation. In the next chapter, we'll look at how to develop RESTful web services using Spring Web MVC.

Chapter 12 –*Developing RESTful web services using Spring Web MVC*

12-1 Introduction

Representational State Transfer (also referred to as *REST*) is an architectural-style in which an application defines *resources* that are *uniquely* identified by URIs (*Uniform Resource Identifier*). The clients of a REST-style application interact with a resource by sending HTTP GET, POST, PUT and DELETE method requests to the URI to which the resource is mapped. The following figure shows a REST-style application that is accessed by its clients:

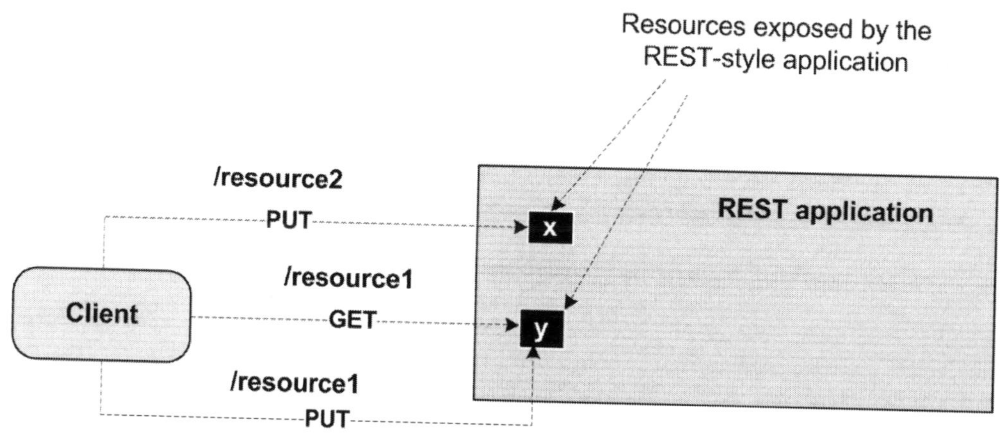

Figure 12-1 REST-style application defines x and y resources that are uniquely identified by /resource2 and /resource1 URIs, respectively.

The above figure shows a REST-style application that consists of two resources – x and y. The resource x is mapped to /resource2 URI and the y resource is mapped to /resource1 URI. A client can interact with resource x by sending HTTP requests to /resource2 URI, and can interact with resource y by sending HTTP requests to /resource1 URI.

If a web service follows the REST architectural-style, it is referred to as a *RESTful web service*. In the context of RESTful web services, you can think of a resource as the *data* exposed by the web service. The client can perform CRUD (CREATE, READ, UPDATE and DELETE) operations on the exposed data by sending HTTP requests to the RESTful web service. The client and the RESTful web service exchange *representation* of the data, which could be in XML, JSON (JavaScript Object Notation) format, or a simple string, or any other MIME type supported by the HTTP protocol.

RESTful web services are simpler to implement and are more scalable compared to SOAP-based web services. In SOAP-based web services, requests and responses are always in XML format. In RESTful web services, you can use JSON (JavaScript Object Notation), XML, plain text, and so on, for requests and responses. In this chapter, we'll look at how Spring Web MVC simplifies developing and accessing RESTful web services.

Let's begin by looking at the requirements of a RESTful web service that we'll implement using Spring Web MVC.

12-2 Fixed deposit web service

We saw earlier that the MyBank web application provides the functionality to display a list of fixed deposits, and to create, edit and close fixed deposits. As the fixed deposit related functionality may also be accessed by other applications, the fixed deposit related functionality needs to be taken out from the MyBank web application and deployed as a RESTful web service. Let's call this new RESTful web service as FixedDepositWS.

The following figure shows that the FixedDepositWS web service is accessed by MyBank and Settlement applications:

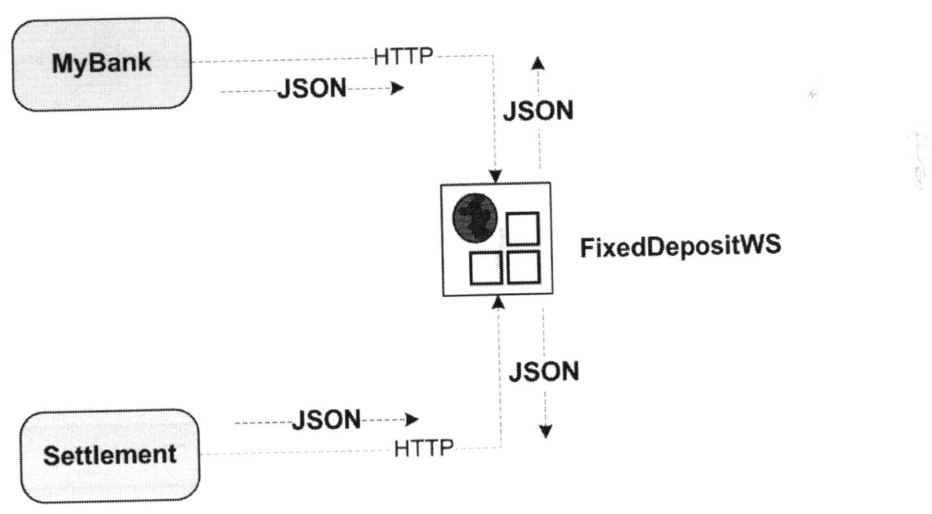

Figure 12-2 MyBank and Settlement applications access FixedDepositWS web service

The above figure shows that MyBank and Settlement web applications interact with FixedDepositWS web service by exchanging data in JSON format. We'll soon see that JSON represents a simpler alternative to XML for exchanging data between applications.

Let's now look at how to implement FixedDepositWS web service as a RESTful web service using Spring Web MVC.

12-3 Implementing a RESTful web service using Spring Web MVC

To develop a RESTful web service, you need to do the following:

- identify resources that are exposed by the web service
- specify URIs corresponding to the identified resources
- identify operations that can be performed on the resources
- map HTTP methods to the identified operations

In case of FixedDepositWS web service, fixed deposit data represents the resource exposed by the web service. If the FixedDepositWS web service maps fixed deposits in the system to /fixedDeposits URI, a FixedDepositWS web service client can perform actions on fixed deposits by sending HTTP requests to /fixedDeposits URI.

In RESTful web service, the HTTP method used by clients for interacting with a resource indicates the operation to be performed on the resource. GET retrieves the resource state, POST creates a new resource, PUT modifies the resource state and DELETE deletes the resource. The following figures shows the actions performed by the FixedDepositWS web service when a client sends GET, POST, PUT and DELETE HTTP requests to the /fixedDeposits URI:

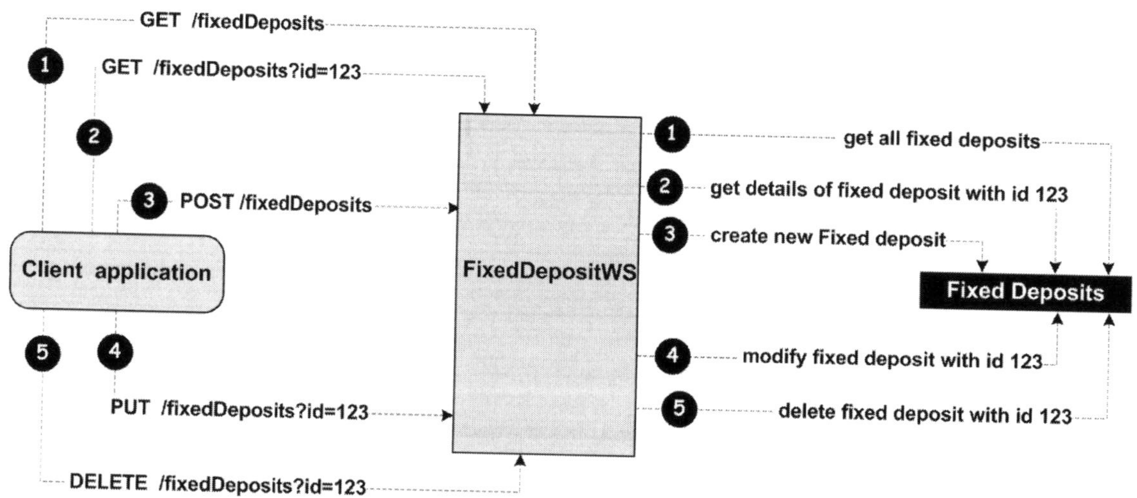

Figure 12-3 HTTP requests are sent by the FixedDepositWS's client to /fixedDeposits URI to interact with fixed deposit data

The above figure shows that the client of FixedDepositWS web service sends GET, POST, PUT and DELETE HTTP requests to /fixedDeposits URI to interact with the fixed deposit data. The id query string parameter uniquely identifies a fixed deposit in the system. The following table defines the purpose of each request shown in the above figure:

HTTP method	URI	Purpose
GET	/fixedDeposits	Retrieve details of all the fixed deposits in the system. The FixedDepositWS web service sends the response in JSON format.
GET	/fixedDeposits?id=123	Retrieve details of the fixed deposit whose id is 123. The FixedDepositWS web service sends the response in JSON format.
POST	/fixedDeposits	Create a new fixed deposit in the system. The web service client sends the details of the fixed deposit to be created in JSON format.
PUT	/fixedDeposits?id=123	Modifies the fixed deposit whose id is 123. The web service client sends the modified details of the fixed deposit in JSON format.
DELETE	/fixedDeposits?id=123	Removes the fixed deposit whose id is 123.

The above table shows that the FixedDepositWS and its clients exchange information in JSON format. Before delving into the details of how to implement FixedDepositWS, let's look at how the data looks like in JSON format.

JSON (JavaScript Object Notation)

JSON is a text-based data format that is used by applications for exchanging *structured* data. As JSON representation of data is more compact compared to XML, JSON serves as a simpler alternative to XML. To simplify conversion of Java objects to JSON and vice versa, you can use JSON libraries like FlexJson (http://flexjson.sourceforge.net/) and Jackson (https://github.com/FasterXML/jackson).

Let's say a Person class defines firstName and lastName attributes. If you create an instance of Person object and set firstName to Myfirstname and lastName to Mylastname, the representation of the Person object in JSON format would look like this:

Example listing 12-1 – Person object representation in JSON format

```
{
  "firstName" : Myfirstname,
  "lastName" : "Mylastname"
}
```

The above example listing shows that each attribute of **Person** object is represented as <attribute-name> : <attribute-value> in JSON format.

You can also represent a collection of Java objects in JSON format. The following example listing shows how you can represent a collection of **Person** objects in JSON format:

Example listing 12-2 – Collection of **Person** objects represented in JSON format

```
[
  {
    "firstName" : Myfirstname,
    "lastName" : "Mylastname"
  },
  {
    "firstName" : Yourfirstname,
    "lastName" : "Yourlastname"
  }
]
```

You don't need to write code to convert an object into JSON representation and vice versa. Instead, the RESTful web service and its clients can make use of FlexJson or Jackson library to perform conversion. As we'll soon see, Spring Web MVC uses Jackson for converting JSON to Java objects and vice versa.

Let's now look at the implementation of FixedDepositWS web service using Spring Web MVC.

IMPORT **chapter 12/ch12-webservice** (This project shows the implementation of FixedDepositWS RESTful web service using Spring Web MVC. Later in this chapter, we'll see how FixedDepositWS web service is accessed by its clients.)

FixedDepositWS web service implementation

Spring Web MVC annotations, like @Controller, @RequestMapping, @RequestParam, @PathVariable @ResponseBody, @RequestBody, and so on, support building RESTful web services. In this section, we'll look at usage of some of these annotations in developing the FixedDepositWS web service.

In FixedDepositWS web service, the FixedDepositController (a Spring Web MVC controller) is responsible for handling web service requests. FixedDepositController is like any other Spring Web MVC controller with the exception that its @RequestMapping methods *don't* render views. The following example listing shows that @Controller and @RequestMapping annotations are used to map web requests to appropriate methods of FixedDepositController class:

Example listing 12-3 – FixedDepositController – web service request handler
Project – ch12-webservice
Source location - src/main/java/sample/spring/chapter12/web

```
package sample.spring.chapter12.web;

import org.springframework.http.ResponseEntity;
.....
@Controller
@RequestMapping(value = "/fixedDeposits")
public class FixedDepositController {
  .....
  @RequestMapping(method = RequestMethod.GET)
  public ResponseEntity<List<FixedDepositDetails>> getFixedDepositList() { ..... }

  @RequestMapping(method = RequestMethod.GET, params = "id")
  public ResponseEntity<FixedDepositDetails> getFixedDeposit(@RequestParam("id") int id) { ..... }
  .....
}
```

The getFixedDepositList method returns the list of fixed deposits in the system, and the getFixedDeposit method returns details of the fixed deposit identified by the id argument. The above example listing shows that the @RequestMapping annotation is used at the class- and method-level to map requests to getFixedDepositList and getFixedDeposit methods. The getFixedDepositList method is invoked when a client application sends an HTTP GET request to /fixedDeposits URI, and the getFixedDeposit method is invoked when a client application sends an HTTP GET request containing id request parameter to /fixedDeposits URI. So, if the request URI is /fixedDeposits?id=123, the getFixedDeposit method is invoked.

The following table summarizes the mapping of request URIs and HTTP methods to the methods defined in the FixedDepositController class:

HTTP method	URI	FixedDepositController method
GET	/fixedDeposits	getFixedDepositList
GET	/fixedDeposits?id=123	getFixedDeposit
POST	/fixedDeposits	openFixedDeposit
PUT	/fixedDeposits?id=123	editFixedDeposit
DELETE	/fixedDeposits?id=123	closeFixedDeposit

We saw in chapter 10 and 11 that @RequestMapping annotated methods return view information that is used by the DispatcherServlet to render a view (like JSP or servlet). In RESTful web services, @RequestMapping methods return data (and *not* the view information) to the client applications. For this reason, the getFixedDepositList and getFixedDeposit methods have been defined to return objects of type ResponseEntity. Let's now look at the usage of ResponseEntity object in the FixedDepositController class.

Specifying HTTP response using ResponseEntity

ResponseEntity represents an HTTP response consisting of headers, body and status code. The object that you set as *body* on the ResponseEntity object is written to the HTTP response body by Spring Web MVC.

The following example listing shows how the ResponseEntity object is created by FixedDepositController's getFixedDepositList method:

Example listing 12-4 – FixedDepositController – creating ResponseEntity instance
Project – ch12-webservice
Source location - src/main/java/sample/spring/chapter12/web

```
package sample.spring.chapter12.web;

import org.springframework.http.HttpStatus;
import org.springframework.http.ResponseEntity;
.....
public class FixedDepositController {
  .....
  @RequestMapping(method = RequestMethod.GET)
  public ResponseEntity<List<FixedDepositDetails>> getFixedDepositList() {
    .....
    return new ResponseEntity<List<FixedDepositDetails>>(
          fixedDepositService.getFixedDeposits(), HttpStatus.OK);
  }
  .....
}
```

In the above example listing, the fixed deposit list passed to the ResponseEntity constructor is written to the HTTP response body. The HttpStatus is an enum type that defines HTTP status codes. The constant OK refers to the HTTP status code 200. Notice that the return type of the getFixedDepositList method is ResponseEntity<List<FixedDepositDetails>>, which means that an object of type List<FixedDepositDetails> is written to the HTTP response body. Spring Web MVC uses an appropriate HttpMessageConverter (explained in section 12-5) to convert the List<FixedDepositDetails> object into the format expected by the client application.

> Later in this chapter, we'll see that client applications can use Spring's RestTemplate to invoke methods defined in the FixedDepositController and to retrieve the objects written to the HTTP response body.

All the @RequestMapping annotated methods of FixedDepositController class define ResponseEntity as their return type. If you *don't* need to send HTTP status code in the response, you can use Spring's HttpEntity class instead of ResponseEntity. HttpEntity represents an HTTP request or response, and ResponseEntity is a subclass of HttpEntity that adds an HTTP status code to the response.

The following example listing shows a modified version of getFixedDepositList method that creates and returns an instance of HttpEntity:

Example listing 12-5 – FixedDepositController – using HttpEntity instead of ResponseEntity

```
import org.springframework.http.HttpStatus;
import org.springframework.http.HttpEntity;
.....
public class FixedDepositController {
  .....
  @RequestMapping(method = RequestMethod.GET)
  public HttpEntity<List<FixedDepositDetails>> getFixedDepositList() {
    .....
    return new HttpEntity<List<FixedDepositDetails>>(fixedDepositService.getFixedDeposits());
  }
  .....
}
```

The above example listing shows that the fixed deposits found in the system are passed to the HttpEntity constructor. As in case of ResponseEntity (refer example listing 12-4), fixed deposits passed to the HttpEntity are written to the HTTP response body.

Both HttpEntity and ResponseEntity objects allow you to set HTTP response headers. The following example listing shows a scenario in which some-header header is set on the HTTP response:

Example listing 12-6 – HttpHeaders usage

```
import org.springframework.http.HttpHeaders;
.....
  @RequestMapping(method = RequestMethod.GET)
  public HttpEntity<String> doSomething() {
```

```
    HttpHeaders responseHeaders = new HttpHeaders();
    responseHeaders.set("some-header", "some-value");

    return new HttpEntity<String>("Hello world !", responseHeaders);
  }
.....
```

Spring's HttpHeaders object contains the headers that are set on the HTTP response. In the above example listing, HttpHeader's set method sets some-header response header (with value some-value). When the doSomething method is invoked, the 'Hello world !' string is written to the response body, and some-header header is written to the HTTP response.

As @RequestMapping methods can be defined to accept HttpServletResponse object as argument, let's look at how you can directly set response body and headers on the HttpServletResponse object.

Specifying HTTP response using HttpServletResponse

The following example listing shows a @RequestMapping method which writes directly to the HttpServletResponse object:

Example listing 12-7 – Setting response on HttpServletResponse

```
import javax.servlet.http.HttpServletResponse;
.....
  @RequestMapping(method = RequestMethod.GET)
  public void doSomething(HttpServletResponse response) throws IOException {
    response.setHeader("some-header", "some-value");
    response.setStatus(200);
    response.getWriter().write("Hello world !");
  }
.....
```

Instead of directly writing response to HttpServletResponse, you should use ResponseEntity (or HttpEntity) object to improve the testability of the controllers.

Let's now look at Spring's @ResponseBody method-level annotation that writes the return value of the method to HTTP response body.

> As of Spring 4.0, @ResponseBody annotation can also be specified at the class level. If @ResponseBody annotation is specified at the class level, it is inherited by the @RequestMapping methods of the controller.

Binding returned value of a method to HTTP response body using @ResponseBody

The following example listing shows usage of @ResponseBody annotation:

Example listing 12-8 – @ResponseBody annotation usage

```
import org.springframework.web.bind.annotation.ResponseBody;
.....
  @RequestMapping(method = RequestMethod.GET)
  @ResponseBody
  public String doSomething() {
    return "Hello world !";
  }
.....
```

In the above example listing, the 'Hello world !' string value returned by the doSomething method is written to the HTTP response body. In section 10-7 of chapter 10, we discussed that if the return type of a @RequestMapping annotated method is String, the returned value is treated as the name of the *view* to render. In the above example listing, the @ResponseBody annotation on the doSomething method instructs Spring Web MVC to write the string value to the HTTP response body instead of treating the string value as the view name. You should note that Spring uses an appropriate HttpMessageConverter (explained in section 12-5) implementation to write the value returned by the @ResponseBody annotated method to the HTTP response body.

Now, that we have seen different ways in which a @RequestMapping method can write to the HTTP response, let's look at how a @RequestMapping method can read information from the HTTP request body using @RequestBody annotation.

Binding HTTP request body to a method parameter using @RequestBody

A @RequestMapping annotated method can use @RequestBody method-parameter level annotation to bind HTTP request body to the method parameter. Spring Web MVC uses an appropriate HttpMessageConverter (explained in section 12-5) implementation to convert the HTTP request body to the method parameter type. The following example listing shows usage of @RequestBody annotation in MyBank application's FixedDepositController:

Example listing 12-9 – @RequestBody annotation usage
Project – ch12-webservice
Source location - src/main/java/sample/spring/chapter12/web

```
package sample.spring.chapter12.web;
.....
import org.springframework.web.bind.annotation.RequestBody;
```

```
.....
@Controller
@RequestMapping(value = "/fixedDeposits")
public class FixedDepositController {
  .....
  @RequestMapping(method = RequestMethod.POST)
  public ResponseEntity<FixedDepositDetails> openFixedDeposit(
        @RequestBody FixedDepositDetails fixedDepositDetails,
        BindingResult bindingResult) {
    new FixedDepositDetailsValidator().validate(fixedDepositDetails, bindingResult);
    .....
  }
  .....
}
```

In the above example listing, the FixedDepositDetails type method argument is annotated with @RequestBody annotation. Spring Web MVC is responsible for converting the HTTP request body to FixedDepositDetails type object. In the above example listing, FixedDepositDetailsValidator class is an implementation of Spring's Validator interface that validates the FixedDepositDetails object before attempting to create the fixed deposit.

An alternative to using @RequestBody annotation is to directly read HTTP request body from the HttpServletRequest object and convert the request body content to the Java type required by the method. Spring's @RequestBody annotation simplifies the conversion because it uses an appropriate HttpMessageConverter implementation to convert HTTP request body to the object type expected by the @RequestMapping method.

Let's now look at the @ResponseStatus annotation that allows you to set HTTP response status.

Setting HTTP response status using @ResponseStatus

You can use the @ResponseStatus annotation to specify the HTTP response status returned by a @RequestMapping method. The following example listing shows usage of @ResponseStatus annotation:

Example listing 12-10 – @ResponseStatus annotation usage

```
import org.springframework.web.bind.annotation.ResponseStatus;

public class SomeController {

  @RequestMapping(method = RequestMethod.GET)
  @ResponseStatus(value = HttpStatus.OK)
  @ResponseBody
```

```
  public SomeObject doSomething() {
    .....
  }
}
```

As the doSomething method is annotated with @ResponseBody annotation, the SomeObject returned by the doSomething method is written to the HTTP response body. And, the @ResponseStatus annotation sets the HTTP response status code to 200 (represented by HttpStatus.OK constant).

Let's now look at how the @ExceptionHandler annotation is used in FixedDepositWS web service to handle exceptions.

Handling exceptions using @ExceptionHandler

In section 10-9 of chapter 10, we saw that the @ExceptionHandler annotation identifies a controller method that is responsible for handling exceptions. Like @RequestMapping methods, @ExceptionHandler methods in RESTful web services are annotated with @ResponseBody annotation or the return type is defined as ResponseEntity (or HttpEntity).

The following example listing shows usage of @ExceptionHandler annotation in FixedDepositController class of ch12-webservice project:

Example listing 12-11 – @ExceptionHandler annotation usage
Project – ch12-webservice
Source location - src/main/java/sample/spring/chapter12/web

```
package sample.spring.chapter12.web;

import sample.spring.chapter12.exception.ValidationException;
.....
public class FixedDepositController {
  .....
  @ExceptionHandler(ValidationException.class)
  @ResponseBody
  @ResponseStatus(value = HttpStatus.BAD_REQUEST)
  public String handleException(Exception ex) {
    logger.info("handling ValidationException " + ex.getMessage());
    return ex.getMessage();
  }
}
```

@ExceptionHandler annotation on handleException method indicates that the handleException method is invoked when ValidationException is thrown by the FixedDepositController during request processing. As the handleException method is also annotated with @ResponseBody annotation, the exception message returned by the handleException method is written to the HTTP response body. @ResponseStatus on the handleException method results in setting the HTTP response status code to 400 (represented by HttpStatus.BAD_REQUEST constant).

In this section, we saw how to implement FixedDepositWS web service using Spring Web MVC. Let's now look at how to access FixedDepositWS web service using Spring's RestTemplate.

12-4 Accessing RESTful web services using RestTemplate

Spring's RestTemplate class simplifies accessing RESTful web services by taking care of managing HTTP connections and handling HTTP errors.

IMPORT **chapter 12/ch12-webservice-client** (This project represents a standalone Java application that accesses FixedDepositWS RESTful web service using Spring's RestTemplate (for *synchronously* accessing the web service) and AsyncRestTemplate (for *asynchronously* accessing the web service) class. The ch12-webservice-client project assumes that the ch12-webservice project representing the FixedDepositWS RESTful web service is deployed at http://localhost:8080/ch12-webservice URL.)

RestTemplate configuration

The following example listing shows how RestTemplate is configured in the application context XML file of ch12-webservice-client project:

Example listing 12-12 – applicationContext.xml - RestTemplate configuration
Project – ch12-webservice-client
Source location - src/main/resources/META-INF/spring

```
<beans .....>
  <bean id="restTemplate" class="org.springframework.web.client.RestTemplate">
    <property name="errorHandler" ref="errorHandler" />
  </bean>

  <bean id="errorHandler" class="sample.spring.chapter12.MyErrorHandler" />
  .....
</beans>
```

RestTemplate's errorHandler property refers to an implementation of Spring's ResponseErrorHandler interface that inspects the HTTP response for errors and handles the response in case of errors. DefaultResponseErrorHandler is the default implementation of ResponseErrorHandler interface that is provided out-of-the-box by Spring. If you don't specify the errorHandler property, Spring uses the DefaultResponseErrorHandler implementation. The above example listing shows that the RestTemplate uses a custom response error handler, MyErrorHandler.

The following example listing shows the implementation of MyErrorHandler class:

Example listing 12-13 – MyErrorHandler class – HTTP response error handler
Project – ch12-webservice-client
Source location - src/main/java/sample/spring/chapter12

```
package sample.spring.chapter12;

import org.apache.commons.io.IOUtils;
import org.springframework.http.client.ClientHttpResponse;
import org.springframework.web.client.DefaultResponseErrorHandler;

public class MyErrorHandler extends DefaultResponseErrorHandler {
   private static Logger logger = Logger.getLogger(MyErrorHandler.class);

   @Override
   public void handleError(ClientHttpResponse response) throws IOException {
      logger.info("Status code received from the web service : " + response.getStatusCode());
      String body = IOUtils.toString(response.getBody());
      logger.info("Response body: " + body);
      super.handleError(response);
   }
}
```

The above example listing shows that the MyErrorHandler class extends DefaultResponseErrorHandler class and overrides the handleError method. If the HTTP response's status code indicates an error, the handleError method is responsible for handling the response. The ClientHttpResponse argument to the handleError method represents the HTTP response received from calling the RESTful web service. The call to ClientHttpResponse's getBody method returns the body of HTTP response as an InputStream object. MyErrorHandler's handleError method logs information about the status code and the body of the HTTP response, and delegates handling of the error to DefaultResponseErrorHandler's handleError method. The above example listing shows that the MyErrorHandler class uses Apache Commons IO's IOUtils class to get the content of the HTTP response body as a String.

Now, that we have seen how a RestTemplate class is configured, let's look at how RestTemplate is used by client applications to access RESTful web services.

Accessing FixedDepositWS web service using RestTemplate

The following example listing shows the FixedDepositWSClient class that uses RestTemplate to access FixedDepositWS web service:

Example listing 12-14 – FixedDepositWSClient class – RestTemplate usage
Project – ch12-webservice-client
Source location - src/main/java/sample/spring/chapter12

```
package sample.spring.chapter12;
.....
import org.springframework.web.client.RestTemplate;

public class FixedDepositWSClient {
   private static ApplicationContext context;

   public static void main(String args[]) {
      context = new ClassPathXmlApplicationContext(
            "classpath:META-INF/spring/applicationContext.xml");
      getFixedDepositList(context.getBean(RestTemplate.class));
      getFixedDeposit(context.getBean(RestTemplate.class));
      .....
   }

   private static void getFixedDepositList(RestTemplate restTemplate) { ..... }
   .....
}
```

The above example listing shows that the FixedDepositWSClient's main method performs the following actions:

- bootstraps the Spring container (represented by the ApplicationContext object)
- calls getFixedDepositList, getFixedDeposit, and so on, methods. These methods accept an instance of RestTemplate, and are responsible for calling the FixedDepositWS web service.

The following example listing shows the implementation of FixedDepositWSClient's getFixedDepositList method that calls the FixedDepositWS web service deployed at http://localhost:8080/ch12-webservice to obtain the list of fixed deposits in the system:

Example listing 12-15 – FixedDepositWSClient's getFixedDepositList method
Project – ch12-webservice-client
Source location - src/main/java/sample/spring/chapter12

```
package sample.spring.chapter12;
.....
import org.springframework.core.ParameterizedTypeReference;
import org.springframework.http.*;
import org.springframework.web.client.RestTemplate;

public class FixedDepositWSClient {
  .....
  private static void getFixedDepositList(RestTemplate restTemplate) {
    HttpHeaders headers = new HttpHeaders();
    headers.add("Accept", "application/json");

    HttpEntity<String> requestEntity = new HttpEntity<String>(headers);

    ParameterizedTypeReference<List<FixedDepositDetails>> typeRef =
        new ParameterizedTypeReference<List<FixedDepositDetails>>() {
    };

    ResponseEntity<List<FixedDepositDetails>> responseEntity = restTemplate
        .exchange("http://localhost:8080/ch12-webservice/fixedDeposits",
            HttpMethod.GET, requestEntity, typeRef);

    List<FixedDepositDetails> fixedDepositDetails = responseEntity.getBody();
    logger.info("List of fixed deposit details: \n" + fixedDepositDetails);
  }
  .....
}
```

In the above example listing, RestTemplate's exchange method has been used to send HTTP GET request to http://localhost:8080/ch12-webservice/fixedDeposits URL. As the FixedDepositWS web service is deployed at http://localhost:8080/ch12-webservice URL, sending HTTP GET request to http://localhost:8080/ch12-webservice/fixedDeposits URL results in invocation of FixedDepositController's getFixedDepositList method. This is because the FixedDepositController's getFixedDepositList method is mapped to /fixedDeposits URI (refer example listing 12-3 or FixedDepositController class of ch12-webservice project).

In example listing 12-15, the HttpEntity object represents the request sent to the web service, the HttpHeaders object represents the request headers in the request, and the ParameterizedTypeReference object represents the *generic* type of the response received from the web service. The Accept request header's value has been set to application/json to specify that the response from the FixedDepositWS web service is expected in JSON format. On the web service-side, the value of Accept header is used by Spring Web MVC to choose an appropriate HttpMessageConverter to convert the value returned by the @ResponseBody annotated method into the format specified by the Accept header. For instance, if the Accept header value is application/json, Spring Web MVC uses MappingJackson2HttpMessageConverter (an implementation of HttpMessageConverter) to convert the value returned by the @ResponseBody annotated method into JSON format. The FixedDepositWSClient specifies the value of Accept header as application/json; therefore, the value returned by FixedDepositController's getFixedDepositList method is converted to JSON format.

The RestTemplate's exchange method returns an instance of ResponseEntity which represents the response returned by the web service. As the generic type of the response received from invocation of FixedDepositController's getFixedDepositList is List<FixedDepositDetails>, an instance of ParameterizedTypeReference<List<FixedDepositDetails>> is created and passed to the exchange method. You can call ResponseEntity's getBody method to retrieve the response returned by the web service. In example listing 12-15, ResponseEntity's getBody method returns an object of type List<FixedDepositDetails> that represents the list of fixed deposits returned by the FixedDepositWS web service.

The following figure shows the role played by MappingJackson2HttpMessageConverter when FixedDepositWSClient invokes FixedDepositController's getFixedDepositList method:

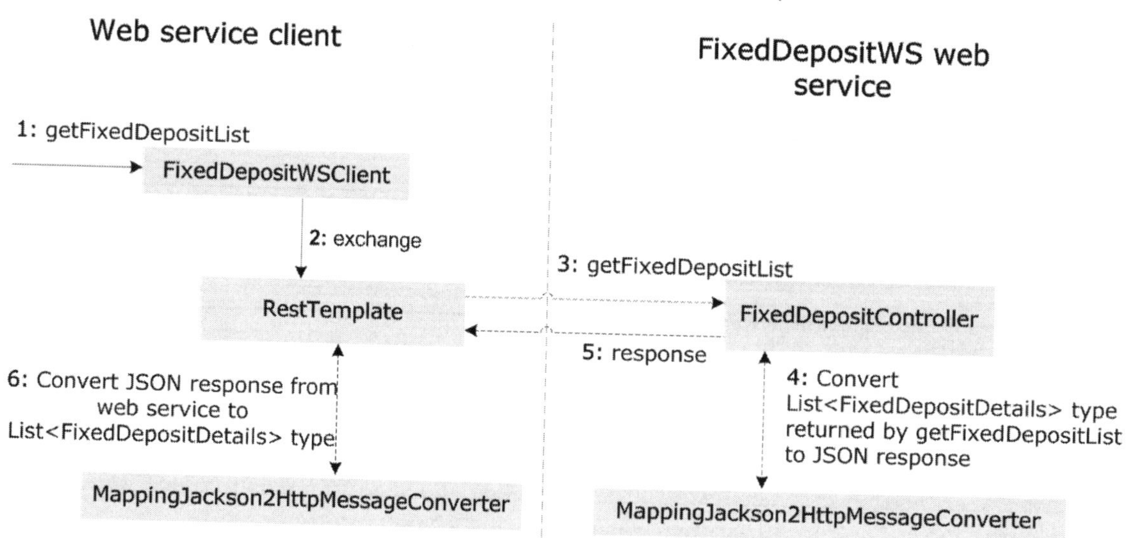

Figure 12-4 FixedDepositWSClient's getFixedDepositList method uses RestTemplate to send a web request to FixedDepositWS web service

The above figure shows that MappingJackson2HttpMessageConverter is used to convert the return value of FixedDepositController's getFixedDepositList method into JSON format. Also, MappingJackson2HttpMessageConverter is used by the RestTemplate to convert the JSON response received from the FixedDepositController to a Java object of type List<FixedDepositDetails>.

In example listing 12-15, RestTemplate's exchange method was used to send an HTTP GET request to FixedDepositWS web service. The exchange method is typically used if the HTTP response from the web service needs to be converted to a Java generic type, and to send HTTP request headers. RestTemplate also defines HTTP method-specific methods that simplify writing RESTful clients. For instance, you can use getForEntity method to send HTTP GET request, postForEntity to send HTTP POST request, delete to send HTTP DELETE request, and so on.

The following example listing shows FixedDepositWSClient's openFixedDeposit method that sends an HTTP POST request to FixedDepositWS web service to create a new fixed deposit:

Example listing 12-16 – FixedDepositWSClient's openFixedDeposit method
Project – ch12-webservice-client
Source location - src/main/java/sample/spring/chapter12

```
package sample.spring.chapter12;

import org.springframework.http.ResponseEntity;
import org.springframework.web.client.RestTemplate;
.....
public class FixedDepositWSClient {
  .....
  private static void openFixedDeposit(RestTemplate restTemplate) {
    FixedDepositDetails fdd = new FixedDepositDetails();
    fdd.setDepositAmount("9999");
    .....
    ResponseEntity<FixedDepositDetails> responseEntity = restTemplate
        .postForEntity("http://localhost:8080/ch12-webservice/fixedDeposits",
            fdd, FixedDepositDetails.class);

    FixedDepositDetails fixedDepositDetails = responseEntity.getBody();
    .....
  }
}
```

FixedDepositWSClient's openFixedDeposit method sends details of the fixed deposit to be created to the FixedDepositWS web service. If the fixed deposit is created successfully, FixedDepositWS returns the newly created FixedDepositDetails object containing the unique identifier assigned to it. The above example listing shows that RestTemplate's postForEntity method accepts web service URL, object to be POSTed (which is FixedDepositDetails object), and the HTTP response type (which is FixedDepositDetails.class). Sending HTTP POST request to http://localhost:8080/ch12-webservice/fixedDeposits URL results in invocation of FixedDepositController's openFixedDeposit method (refer example listing 12-9 or FixedDepositController class of ch12-webservice project).

FixedDepositController's openFixedDeposit method validates details of the fixed deposit before attempting to create the fixed deposit. FixedDepositDetailsValidator is responsible for validating the fixed deposit details. If the fixed deposit amount is less than 1000 or tenure is less than 12 months or if the email id specified is not well-formed, an exception is thrown by the openFixedDeposit method. The following example listing shows openFixedDeposit and handleException methods of FixedDepositController:

Example listing 12-17 – openFixedDeposit and handleException methods of FixedDepositController
Project – ch12-webservice
Source location - src/main/java/sample/spring/chapter12/web

```
package sample.spring.chapter12.web;

import org.springframework.validation.BindingResult;
import org.springframework.web.bind.annotation.ExceptionHandler;
import sample.spring.chapter12.exception.ValidationException;
.....
@Controller
@RequestMapping(value = "/fixedDeposits")
public class FixedDepositController {
  .....
  @RequestMapping(method = RequestMethod.POST)
  public ResponseEntity<FixedDepositDetails> openFixedDeposit(
       @RequestBody FixedDepositDetails fixedDepositDetails, BindingResult bindingResult) {

    new FixedDepositDetailsValidator().validate(fixedDepositDetails, bindingResult);

    if (bindingResult.hasErrors()) {
       throw new ValidationException("Validation errors occurred");
    } else {
       fixedDepositService.saveFixedDeposit(fixedDepositDetails);
       .....
    }
```

```
    @ExceptionHandler(ValidationException.class)
    @ResponseBody
    @ResponseStatus(value = HttpStatus.BAD_REQUEST)
    public String handleException(Exception ex) {
      return ex.getMessage();
    }
  }
  .....
}
```

The above example listing shows that the openFixedDeposit method throws ValidationException if fixed deposit fails validation. As the handleException method is annotated with @ExceptionHandler(ValidationException.class), the ValidationException thrown by the openFixedDeposit method is handled by the handleException method. @ResponseBody and @ResponseStatus(value=HttpStatus.BAD_REQUEST) annotations specify that the exception message returned by the handleException method is written to the response body and the status code is set to HttpStatus.BAD_REQUEST constant (which corresponds to HTTP status code 400).

FixedDepositWSClient's openInvalidFixedDeposit method attempts to create a fixed deposit with deposit amount 100, as shown here:

Example listing 12-18 – FixedDepositWSClient - openInvalidFixedDeposit method
Project – ch12-webservice-client
Source location - src/main/java/sample/spring/chapter12

```
private static void openInvalidFixedDeposit(RestTemplate restTemplate) {
   FixedDepositDetails fdd = new FixedDepositDetails();
   fdd.setDepositAmount("100");
   fdd.setEmail("99@somedomain.com");
   fdd.setTenure("12");

   ResponseEntity<FixedDepositDetails> responseEntity = restTemplate
        .postForEntity( "http://localhost:8080/ch12-webservice/fixedDeposits",
              fdd, FixedDepositDetails.class);

   FixedDepositDetails fixedDepositDetails = responseEntity.getBody();
   logger.info("Details of the newly created fixed deposit: "
        + fixedDepositDetails);
}
```

The openInvalidFixedDeposit method uses RestTemplate to send request to FixedDepositController's openFixedDeposit method. As the fixed deposit amount is specified as 100, FixedDepositController's openFixedDeposit method throws ValidationException (refer example listing 12-17). FixedDepositController's handleException method (refer example listing 12-17) handles the ValidationException and sets the HTTP response status to 400. As the response status code received by RestTemplate is 400, the handling of response is delegated to the MyErrorHandler implementation (refer example listing 12-12 and 12-13) that we configured for the RestTemplate.

RestTemplate allows clients to synchronously access RESTful web services. Let's now look at how to asynchronously access RESTful web services using Spring's AsyncRestTemplate.

Asynchronously accessing RESTful web services using AsyncRestTemplate

To allow clients to asynchronously access RESTful web services, Spring provides AsyncRestTemplate. The following example listing shows how AsyncRestTemplate is configured in the application context XML file of ch12-webservice-client project:

Example listing 12-19 – applicationContext.xml - AsyncRestTemplate configuration
Project – ch12-webservice-client
Source location - src/main/resources/META-INF/spring

```
<beans .....>
  .....
  <bean id="errorHandler" class="sample.spring.chapter12.MyErrorHandler" />

  <bean id="asyncRestTemplate" class="org.springframework.web.client.AsyncRestTemplate">
     <property name="errorHandler" ref="errorHandler" />
  </bean>
</beans>
```

If you compare the above example listing with the example listing 12-12, you'll notice that both AsyncRestTemplate and RestTemplate classes are configured in the same way; they use the same MyErrorHandler instance for handling HTTP errors.

AsyncRestTemplate class defines methods that are similar to the methods defined by the RestTemplate class. The following example listing shows the FixedDepositWSAsyncClient class that uses AsyncRestTemplate to access FixedDepositWS web service:

Example listing 12-20 – FixedDepositWSAsyncClient - openFixedDeposit method
Project – ch12-webservice-client
Source location - src/main/java/sample/spring/chapter12

```
package sample.spring.chapter12;
```

```
import org.springframework.http.HttpEntity;
import org.springframework.util.concurrent.ListenableFuture;
import org.springframework.util.concurrent.ListenableFutureCallback;
import org.springframework.web.client.AsyncRestTemplate;

public class FixedDepositWSAsyncClient {
   private static ApplicationContext context;

   public static void main(String args[]) {
      context = new ClassPathXmlApplicationContext(
            "classpath:META-INF/spring/applicationContext.xml");
      .....
      openFixedDeposit(context.getBean(AsyncRestTemplate.class));
   }

   private static void openFixedDeposit(AsyncRestTemplate restTemplate) {
      FixedDepositDetails fdd = new FixedDepositDetails();
      fdd.setDepositAmount("9999");
      .....
      HttpEntity<FixedDepositDetails> requestEntity = new HttpEntity<FixedDepositDetails>(fdd);

      ListenableFuture<ResponseEntity<FixedDepositDetails>> futureResponseEntity =
            restTemplate.postForEntity("http://localhost:8080/ch12-webservice/fixedDeposits",
                requestEntity, FixedDepositDetails.class);

      futureResponseEntity
            .addCallback(new ListenableFutureCallback<ResponseEntity<FixedDepositDetails>>() {
               @Override
               public void onSuccess(ResponseEntity<FixedDepositDetails> entity) {
                  FixedDepositDetails fixedDepositDetails = entity.getBody();
               }

               @Override
               public void onFailure(Throwable t) { }
            });
   }
}
```

The above example listing shows that the openFixedDeposit method uses AsyncRestTemplate to send a request to FixedDepositWS web service. AsyncRestTemplate's postForEntity method sends an HTTP POST request to FixedDepositWS web service that invokes FixedDepositController's openFixedDeposit method. If you compare the AsyncRestTemplate's postForEntity method shown above with that of RestTemplate's postForEntity method (refer example listing 12-16), you'll notice that the AsyncRestTemplate's postForEntity returns an object of type ListenableFuture (that extends java.util.concurrent.Future interface). ListenableFuture's addCallback method is used to register a callback that is triggered when the ListenableFuture task completes. ListenableFuture's addCallback method accepts an argument of type ListenableFutureCallback that defines onSuccess and onFailure methods. The onSuccess method is called when the ListenableFuture task completes successfully, and the onFailure method is called when the ListenableFuture task fails to complete.

You should note that by default AsyncRestTemplate uses a SimpleAsyncTaskExecutor to asynchronously execute *each* request in a new thread. You can pass a ThreadPoolTaskExecutor to AsyncRestTemplate's constructor to asynchronously execute tasks using a thread from a *thread pool*. Refer to section 8-6 of chapter 8 to learn more about SimpleAsyncTaskExecutor and ThreadPoolTaskExecutor.

Let's now look at the purpose served by HttpMessageConverters in Spring Web MVC.

12-5 Converting Java objects to HTTP requests and responses and vice versa using HttpMessageConverter

HttpMessageConverters are used by Spring in the following scenarios to perform conversion:

- if a method argument is annotated with @RequestBody annotation, Spring converts HTTP request body to the Java type of the method argument
- if a method is annotated with @ResponseBody annotation, Spring converts the returned Java object from the method to HTTP response body
- if the return type of a method is HttpEntity or ResponseEntity, Spring converts the object returned by the method to the HTTP response body
- objects passed to and returned from the methods of RestTemplate and AsyncRestTemplate classes like getForEntity, postForEntity, exchange, and so on, are converted to HTTP requests and from HTTP responses by Spring

The following table describes some of the HttpMessageConverter implementations that are provided out-of-the-box by Spring Web MVC:

HttpMessageConverter implementation	Description
StringHttpMessageConverter	converts to/from strings
FormHttpMessageConverter	converts form data to/from MultiValueMap<String, String> type. This HttpMessageConverter is used by

	Spring when dealing with form data and file uploads.
MappingJackson2HttpMessageConverter	converts to/from JSON
MarshallingHttpMessageConverter	converts to/from XML

HttpMessageConverters mentioned in the above table are automatically registered with the Spring container by the <annotation-driven> element of Spring's mvc schema. To view the complete list of HttpMessageConverters that are registered by default by <annotation-driven> element, refer to the Spring Framework reference documentation.

Let's now look at @PathVariable and @MatrixVariable annotations that further simplify developing RESTful web services using Spring Web MVC.

12-6 @PathVariable and @MatrixVariable annotations

Instead of specifying the actual URI, a @RequestMapping annotation may specify a *URI template* to access specific parts of the request URI. A URI template contains *variable names* (specified within braces) whose values are derived from the actual request URI. For example, the URI template http://www.somebank.com/fd/{fixeddeposit} contains the variable name fixeddeposit. If the request actual request URI is http://www.somebank.com/fd/123, the value of {fixeddeposit} URI template variable becomes 123.

@PathVariable is a method argument level annotation that is used by @RequestMapping methods to assign value of a *URI template variable* to the method argument.

IMPORT **chapter 12/ch12-webservice-uritemplates** and **chapter 12/ch12-webservice-client-uritemplates** (ch12-webservice-uritemplates project is a variant of ch12-webservice project that shows the implementation of FixedDepositWS RESTful web service using @PathVariable annotation. ch12-webservice-client-uritemplates is a variant of ch12-webservice-client that accesses the FixedDepositWS web service represented by ch12-webservice-uritemplates project.)

The following example listing shows usage of @PathVariable annotation in FixedDepositController of ch12-webservice-uritemplates project:

Example listing 12-21 – FixedDepositController - @PathVariable usage
Project – ch12-webservice-uritemplates
Source location - src/main/java/sample/spring/chapter12/web

```
package sample.spring.chapter12.web;
```

```
import org.springframework.web.bind.annotation.PathVariable;
.....
@Controller
public class FixedDepositController {
  .....
  @RequestMapping(value="/fixedDeposits/{fixedDepositId}", method = RequestMethod.GET)
  public ResponseEntity<FixedDepositDetails> getFixedDeposit(
       @PathVariable("fixedDepositId") int id) {
    return new ResponseEntity<FixedDepositDetails>(
          fixedDepositService.getFixedDeposit(id), HttpStatus.OK);
  }
  .....
}
```

Instead of specifying the actual URI, @RequestMapping annotation in the above example listing specifies /fixedDeposits/{fixedDepositId} URI template. Now, if the incoming request URI is /fixedDeposits/1, the value of fixedDepositId URI template variable is set to 1. As the @PathVariable annotation specifies fixedDepositId as the name of the URI template variable, value 1 is assigned to the id argument of the getFixedDeposit method.

If a URI template defines multiple variables, the @RequestMapping method can define multiple @PathVariable annotated arguments, as shown in the following example listing:

Example listing 12-22 – Multiple URI template variables

```
@Controller
public class SomeController {
  .....
  @RequestMapping(value="/users/{userId}/bankstatements/{statementId}", .....)
  public void getBankStatementForUser(
       @PathVariable("userId") String user,
       @PathVariable("statementId") String statement) {
    .....
  }
}
```

In the above example listing, the URI template defines userId and statementId variables. If the incoming request URI is /users/me/bankstatements/123, value me is assigned to the user argument and value 123 is assigned to the statement argument.

If you want to assign all the URI template variables and their values to a method argument, you can use @PathVariable annotation on a Map<String, String> argument type, as shown in the following example listing:

Example listing 12-23 – Accessing all URI template variables and their values

```
@Controller
public class SomeController {
  .....
  @RequestMapping(value="/users/{userId}/bankstatements/{statementId}", .....)
  public void getBankStatementForUser(
      @PathVariable Map<String, String> allVariables) {
    .....
  }
}
```

In the above example listing, URI template variables (userId and statementId) and their values (me and 123) are assigned to the allVariables method argument.

You should note that URI template can also be specified by class level @RequestMapping annotation, as shown here:

Example listing 12-24 – URI template specified at both class and method level @RequestMapping annotations

```
@Controller
@RequestMapping(value="/service/{serviceId}", .....)
public class SomeController {
  .....
  @RequestMapping(value="/users/{userId}/bankstatements/{statementId}", .....)
  public void getBankStatementForUser(@PathVariable Map<String, String> allVariables) {
    .....
  }
}
```

In the above example listing, URI template /service/{serviceId} is specified by the class level @RequestMapping annotation, and /users/{userId}/bankstatements/{statementId} is specified by the method level @RequestMapping annotation. If the request URI is /service/bankingService/users/me/bankstatements/123, the allVariables argument contains details of serviceId, userId and statementId URI template variables.

The scenarios in which you may want to have fine-grained control over what to extract from the request URI, you can use regular expressions in URI templates. The following example listing shows usage of regular expressions to extract 123.json value from /statements/123.json request URI:

Example listing 12-25 – URI templates – regular expressions usage

```
@Controller
public class SomeController {
  .....
  @RequestMapping(value="/bankestatement/{statementId:[\\d\\d\\d]}.{responseType:[a-z]}", ..)
  public void getBankStatementForUser(@PathVariable ("statementId") String statement,
        @PathVariable("responseType") String responseTypeExtension) {
    .....
  }
}
```

Regular expressions in URI templates are specified in the following format: {variable-name:regular-expression}. If the request URI is /statements/123.json, statementId variable is assigned the value 123 and responseType is assigned the value json.

> You can also use Ant-style patterns in URI templates. For instance, you can specify patterns, like /myUrl/*/{myId} and /myUrl/**/{myId} as URI templates.

So far in this section we have seen examples of how to use @PathVariable to selectively extract information from the request URI path. Let's now look at @MatrixVariable annotation that is used to extract *name-value pairs* from path segments.

Matrix variables appear as name-value pairs in the request URI, and you can assign value of these variables to method arguments. For instance, in the request URI /bankstatement/123;responseType=json, the responseType variable represents a matrix variable whose value is json.

> You should note that by default Spring *removes* matrix variables from the URL. To ensure that matrix variables are not removed, set the enable-matrix-variables attribute of <annotation-driven> element of Spring mvc schema to true. When using matrix variables, the path segments that contain matrix variables must be represented by URI template variables.

The following example listing shows usage of @MatrixVariable annotation:

Example listing 12-26 – @MatrixVariable annotation

```
@Controller
public class SomeController {
  .....
  @RequestMapping(value="/bankestatement/{statementId}", ..)
  public void getBankStatementForUser(@PathVariable("statementId") String statement,
        @MatrixVariable("responseType") String responseTypeExtension) {
```

```
    .....
  }
}
```

In the above example listing, if the request URI is /bankstatement/123;responseType=json, the value json is assigned to responseTypeExtension argument. The above example listing also shows a scenario in which both @PathVariable and @MatrixVariable annotations are used to retrieve information from the request URI.

As matrix variables can appear in any path segment of the request URI, you should specify the path segment from which the matrix variable should be retrieved. The following example listing shows a scenario in which two matrix variables with the same name are present in different path segments:

Example listing 12-27 – @MatrixVariable annotation – multiple matrix variables with the same name

```
@Controller
public class SomeController {
  .....
  @RequestMapping(value="/bankestatement/{statementId}/user/{userId}", ..)
  public void getBankStatementForUser(
    @MatrixVariable(value = "id", pathVar = "statementId") int someId,
    @MatrixVariable(value = "id", pathVar = "userId") int someOtherId) {
    .....
  }
}
```

The pathVar attribute of @MatrixVariable annotation specifies the name of the URI template variable that contains the matrix variable. So, if the request URI is /bankstatement/123;**id=555**/user/me;**id=777**, the value 555 is assigned to someId, and the value 777 is assigned to someOtherId argument.

As in case of @PathVariable annotation, you can annotate a method argument type of Map<String, String> with @MatrixVariable to assign all the matrix variables to the method argument. Unlike @PathVariable annotation, @MatrixVariable annotation allows you to specify a default value for the matrix variable using defaultValue attribute. Also, you can set required attribute of @MatrixVariable annotation to false to indicate that the matrix variable is *optional*. By default, the value of required attribute is set to true. If the required attribute is set to true, and the matrix variable is not found in the request, then an exception is thrown.

12-7 Summary

In this chapter, we looked at how to develop RESTful web services and access them. We looked at how to use URI templates along with @PathVariable and @MatrixVariable annotations to access information from the request URI. We also looked at how to access RESTful web services synchronously using RestTemplate and asynchronously using AsyncRestTemplate.

Chapter 13 – *More Spring Web MVC – internationalization, file upload and asynchronous request processing*

13-1 Introduction

In earlier chapters, we saw that Spring Web MVC simplifies creating web applications and RESTful web services. In this chapter, we'll look at some more features offered by Spring Web MVC framework that you may require in your web applications. We'll particularly look at:

- pre- and post-processing requests using *handler interceptors*
- internationalizing Spring Web MVC applications
- *asynchronously* processing requests
- performing type conversion and formatting, and
- uploading files

IMPORT **chapter 13/ch13-bankapp** (This project is a variant of ch10-bankapp project that demonstrates how to incorporate internationalization in MyBank web application, and how to use handler interceptors.)

Let's begin by looking at how to pre- and post-process requests using handler interceptors.

13-2 Pre- and post-processing requests using handler interceptors

Handler interceptors allow you to pre- and post-process requests. The concept of handler interceptors is similar to that of servlet filters. Handler interceptors implement Spring's HandlerInterceptor interface. A handler interceptor contains the pre- and post-processing logic that is required by multiple controllers. For instance, you can use handler interceptors for logging, security checks, changing locale, and so on.

Let's now look at how to implement and configure handler interceptors.

Implementing and configuring a handler interceptor

You can create handler interceptors by implementing HandlerInterceptor interface. HandlerInterceptor interface defines the following methods:

- preHandle – this method is executed *before* the controller processes the request. If the preHandle method returns true, the controller is invoked by Spring to process the request. If the preHandle method returns false, the controller is *not* invoked.
- postHandle – this method is executed *after* the controller processes the request, but *before* the view is rendered by the DispatcherServlet.
- afterCompletion – this method is invoked *after* the completion of request processing (that is, after the view is rendered by the DispatcherServlet) to do any cleanup, if required.

The following example listing shows MyRequestHandlerInterceptor class of ch13-bankapp that implements HandlerInterceptor interface:

Example listing 13-1 – MyRequestHandlerInterceptor
Project – ch13-bankapp
Source location - src/main/java/sample/spring/chapter13/web

```
package sample.spring.chapter13.web;

import org.springframework.web.servlet.HandlerInterceptor;
.....
public class MyRequestHandlerInterceptor implements HandlerInterceptor {
  .....
  public boolean preHandle(HttpServletRequest request, HttpServletResponse response,
        Object handler) throws Exception {
    logger.info("HTTP method --> " + request.getMethod());
    Enumeration<String> requestNames = request.getParameterNames();
    .....
    return true;
  }

  public void postHandle(HttpServletRequest request, HttpServletResponse response,
        Object handler, ModelAndView modelAndView) throws Exception {
    logger.info("Status code --> " + response.getStatus());
  }

  public void afterCompletion(HttpServletRequest request, HttpServletResponse response,
        Object handler, Exception ex) throws Exception {
    logger.info("Request processing complete");
  }
}
```

In the above example listing, the preHandle method inspects each incoming request and logs the HTTP method associated with the request and the request parameters contained in the request. The preHandle method returns true, which means that the request will be processed by the controller. The postHandle method logs the HTTP response status code. The afterCompletion method logs the message that the request was successfully processed.

> Instead of directly implementing the HandlerInterceptor interface, you can extend the *abstract* HandlerInterceptorAdapter class that provides empty implementations for postHandle and afterCompletion methods, and the preHandle method is defined to simply return true.

The following example listing shows how handler interceptors are configured in the web application context XML file:

Example listing 13-2 – MyRequestHandlerInterceptor
Project – ch13-bankapp
Source location - src/main/webapp/WEB-INF/spring/bankapp-config.xml

```
<beans .....xmlns:mvc="http://www.springframework.org/schema/mvc".....>

  <mvc:annotation-driven />
  <mvc:interceptors>
    .....
    <bean class="sample.spring.chapter13.web.MyRequestHandlerInterceptor" />
  </mvc:interceptors>
</beans>
```

The above example listing shows that the <interceptors> element of Spring's mvc schema is used for configuring handler interceptors. The <interceptors> element can have the following sub-elements:

- <bean> element of Spring's beans schema - specifies a Spring bean that implements the HandlerInterceptor interface. A handler interceptor defined using <bean> element applies to all requests.
- <ref> element of Spring's beans schema - refers to a Spring bean that implements the HandlerInterceptor interface. A handler interceptor defined using <ref> element applies to all requests.
- <interceptor> element of Spring's mvc schema – specifies a Spring bean that implements the HandlerInterceptor interface, and the request URIs to which the HandlerInterceptor applies.

The following example listing shows a scenario in which MyRequestHandlerInterceptor is mapped to /audit/** request URI:

Example listing 13-3 – <mvc:interceptor> usage

```
<beans .....xmlns:mvc="http://www.springframework.org/schema/mvc".....>

  <mvc:annotation-driven />
  <mvc:interceptors>
    <mvc:interceptor>
      <mvc:mapping path="/audit/**"/>
      <bean class="sample.spring.chapter13.web.MyRequestHandlerInterceptor" />
    </mvc:interceptor>
  </mvc:interceptors>
</beans>
```

In the above example listing, <interceptor> element of Spring's mvc schema is used for mapping MyRequestHandlerInterceptor to /audit/** URI pattern. The <mapping> element of Spring's mvc schema specifies the request URI pattern to which the handler interceptor specified by the <bean> element applies.

Let's now look at how to internationalize a Spring Web MVC application.

13-3 Internationalizing using resource bundles

Before delving into the details of how to internationalize Spring Web MVC applications, let's look at the internationalization and localization requirements of the MyBank web application.

MyBank web application's requirements

It is required that the MyBank web application supports English (en_US locale) and German (de_DE locale) languages. The following figure shows one of the web pages of MyBank web application in de_DE locale:

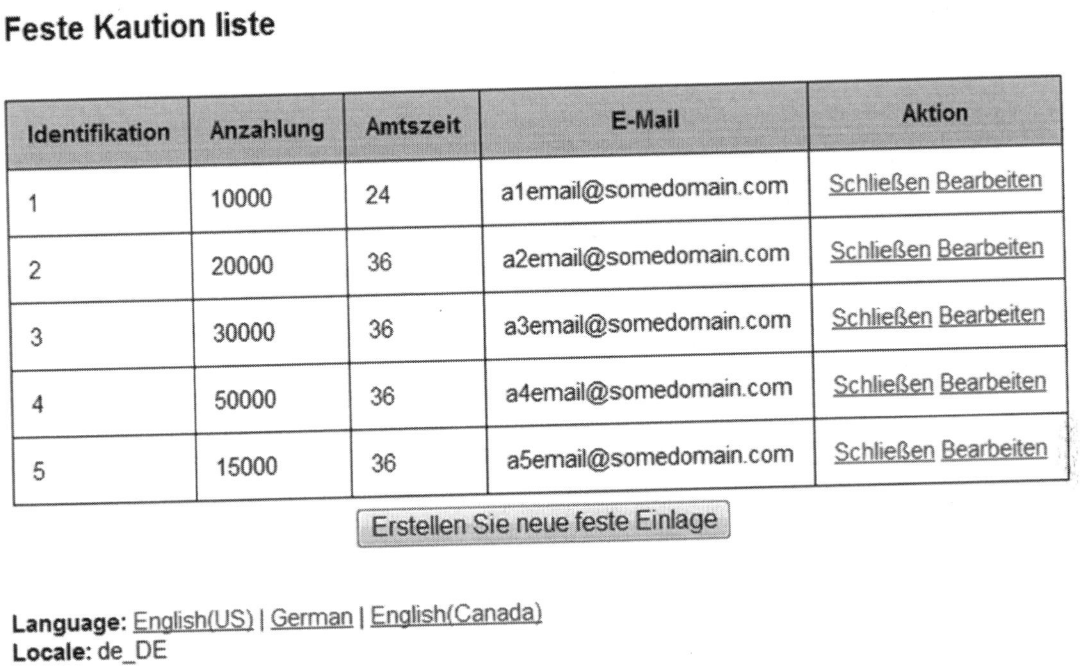

Feste Kaution liste

Identifikation	Anzahlung	Amtszeit	E-Mail	Aktion
1	10000	24	a1email@somedomain.com	Schließen Bearbeiten
2	20000	36	a2email@somedomain.com	Schließen Bearbeiten
3	30000	36	a3email@somedomain.com	Schließen Bearbeiten
4	50000	36	a4email@somedomain.com	Schließen Bearbeiten
5	15000	36	a5email@somedomain.com	Schließen Bearbeiten

Erstellen Sie neue feste Einlage

Language: English(US) | German | English(Canada)
Locale: de_DE

Figure 13-1 Web page that shows the list of fixed deposits in de_DE locale. A user can select a locale from the given options.

The above figure shows that a user can choose one of the following languages: English(US), German, or English(Canada). If a user chooses German language option, the web pages are displayed in de_DE locale. If a user chooses English(US) language option, the web pages are displayed in en_US locale. If a user chooses English(Canada) language option, the web pages are displayed in en_CA locale.

Let's now look at how to address internationalization and localization requirements of MyBank web application.

Internationalizing and localizing MyBank web application

In Spring Web MVC, the DispatcherServlet uses a LocaleResolver for automatically resolving messages based on the user's locale. To support internationalization, you need to configure the following beans in your web application context XML file:

- LocaleResolver – resolves the current locale of the user
- MessageSource – resolves messages from resource bundles based on the current locale of the user

- LocaleChangeInterceptor – allows changing current locale on every request based on a configurable request parameter

The following example listing shows configuration of LocaleResolver, LocaleChangeInterceptor and MessageSource beans in the web application context XML file of ch13-bankapp project:

Example listing 13-4 – bankapp-config.xml
Project – ch13-bankapp
Source location - src/main/webapp/WEB-INF/spring

```
<beans .....>
  <bean class="org.springframework.web.servlet.i18n.CookieLocaleResolver" id="localeResolver">
    <property name="cookieName" value="mylocale" />
  </bean>

  <bean
    class="org.springframework.context.support.ReloadableResourceBundleMessageSource"
    id="messageSource">
    <property name="basenames" value="WEB-INF/i18n/messages" />
  </bean>

  <mvc:interceptors>
    .....
    <bean class="org.springframework.web.servlet.i18n.LocaleChangeInterceptor">
      <property name="paramName" value="lang" />
    </bean>
  </mvc:interceptors>
  .....
</beans>
```

In the above example listing, CookieLocaleResolver (an implementation of LocaleResolver interface) has been configured for locale resolution. If the locale information is stored in a cookie by the web application, CookieLocaleResolver is used for locale resolution. CookieLocaleResolver's cookieName property specifies the name of the cookie that contains the locale information. If the cookie is not found in the request, CookieLocaleResolver determines the locale either by looking at the default locale (configured using defaultLocale property of CookieLocaleResolver) or by inspecting the Accept-Language request header. Spring additionally provides the following built-in LocaleResolver implementations that you can use: AcceptHeaderLocaleResolver (returns the locale specified by the Accept-Language request header), SessionLocaleResolver (returns the locale information stored in the HttpSession of the user) and FixedLocaleResolver (always returns a fixed default locale).

In addition to knowing user's locale, you may also want to know user's time zone to convert date and time in user's time zone. LocaleContextResolver (introduced in Spring 4.0) not only provides the locale information but also the time zone information of the user. CookieLocaleResolver, SessionLocaleResolver and FixedLocaleResolver implement the LocaleContextResolver interface; therefore, if you are using any of these resolvers you can obtain user's time zone in your controllers using getTimeZone method of LocaleContextHolder (or RequestContextUtils) class. If you only want to obtain the locale information in your controllers, you can use getLocale method of LocaleContextHolder (or RequestContextUtils) class.

Spring provides a LocaleChangeInterceptor (a HandlerInterceptor) that uses a configurable request parameter (specified by paramName property) to change the current locale on every request. In example listing 13-4, the paramName property is set to lang. LocaleResolver defines a setLocale method that is used by the LocaleChangeInterceptor to change the current locale. If you don't want to use LocaleChangeInterceptor, then you can change the user's locale in your controller by calling setLocale method of LocaleContextHolder (or RequestContextUtils) class.

Once the user's locale is resolved, Spring uses the configured MessageSource implementation to resolve messages. Spring provides the following built-in implementations of MessageSource interface:

- ResourceBundleMessageSource – a MessageSource implementation that accesses resource bundles using the specified *basenames*
- ReloadableResourceBundleMessageSource – similar to ResourceBundleMessageSource implementation. This implementation supports *reloading* of resource bundles.

Example listing 13-4 shows that the MyBank web application uses ReloadableResourceBundleMessageSource. The basenames property is set to WEB-INF/i18n/messages, which means that the ReloadableResourceBundleMessageSource looks for resource bundles named messages inside WEB-INF/i18n folder. So, if the user's locale is resolved to en_US, the ReloadableResourceBundleMessageSource will resolve messages from the messages_en_US.properties file.

If you look at /src/main/webapp/WEB-INF/i18n folder of ch13-bankapp project, you'll find the following properties files: messages.properties, messages_en_US.properties and messages_de_DE.properties. The messages_de_DE.properties file contains messages and labels for de_DE locale, messages_en_US.properties contains messages and labels for en_US locale, and messages.properties contains messages and labels that are shown when *no* locale-specific resource bundles are found. As there is no messages_en_CA.properties file corresponding to en_CA locale, selecting the English(Canada) option (refer figure 13-1) shows messages from the messages.properties file.

In figure 13-1, we saw that we can change the language of the MyBank web application by selecting English(US), English(Canada) and German language options. We saw earlier that the

LocaleChangeInterceptor can change the locale of the MyBank web application if the locale information is contained in a request parameter named lang. To simplify changing the locale, lang request parameter is appended to the hyperlinks shown by English(US), English(Canada) and German language options, as shown here:

Example listing 13-5 – fixedDepositList.jsp
Project – ch13-bankapp
Source location - src/main/webapp/WEB-INF/jsp

```
<b>Language:</b>

<a href="${pageContext.request.contextPath}/fixedDeposit/list?lang=en_US">English(US)</a> |
<a href="${pageContext.request.contextPath}/fixedDeposit/list?lang=de_DE">German</a> |
<a href="${pageContext.request.contextPath}/fixedDeposit/list?lang=en_CA">English(Canada)</a>
```

Let's now look at how you can asynchronously process requests in Spring Web MVC applications.

13-4 Asynchronously processing requests

A @RequestMapping annotated method that returns a java.util.concurrent.Callable or Spring's DeferredResult object processes web requests *asynchronously*. If a @RequestMapping method returns Callable, Spring Web MVC takes care of processing the Callable in an application thread (and *not* the Servlet container thread) to produce the result. If a @RequestMapping method returns DeferredResult, it is application's responsibility to process the DeferredResult in an application thread (and *not* the Servlet container thread) to produce the result. Before delving into the detail of how Callable and DeferredResult return values are processed, let's look at how to configure a Spring Web MVC application to support asynchronous request processing.

IMPORT chapter 13/ch13-async-bankapp (This project is a variant of ch10-bankapp project that asynchronously processes requests. @RequestMapping methods defined in the FixedDepositController of this project return Callable. You should deploy and run the ch13-async-bankapp project to see asynchronous request processing in action.)

Asynchronous request processing configuration

As asynchronous request processing in Spring Web MVC is based on Servlet 3, web.xml must refer to Servlet 3 XML schema. Also, <async-supported> element must be added to the DispatcherServlet definition in web.xml file to indicate that it supports asynchronous request processing. The following example listing shows the web.xml file of ch13-async-bankapp project:

Example listing 13-6 – web.xml – asynchronous request processing configuration
Project – ch13-async-bankapp
Source location - src/main/webapp/WEB-INF

```
<web-app .....
  xsi:schemaLocation="java.sun.com/xml/ns/javaee java.sun.com/xml/ns/javaee/web-app_3_0.xsd"
  version="3.0">
  .....
  <servlet>
    <servlet-name>bankapp</servlet-name>
    <servlet-class>org.springframework.web.servlet.DispatcherServlet</servlet-class>
    .....
    <async-supported>true</async-supported>
  </servlet>
  .....
</web-app>
```

The above example listing shows that the bankapp servlet is configured to support asynchronous request processing. Now, the bankapp servlet can asynchronously process web requests.

Returning Callable from @RequestMapping methods

The following example listing shows the FixedDepositController whose @RequestMapping methods return Callable:

Example listing 13-7 – FixedDepositController – returning Callable from @RequestMapping methods
Project – ch13-async-bankapp
Source location - src/main/java/sample/spring/chapter13/web

```
package sample.spring.chapter13.web;

import java.util.concurrent.Callable;
.....
public class FixedDepositController {
  .....
  @RequestMapping(value = "/list", method = RequestMethod.GET)
  public Callable<ModelAndView> listFixedDeposits() {
    return new Callable<ModelAndView>() {

      @Override
      public ModelAndView call() throws Exception {
        Thread.sleep(5000);
        Map<String, List<FixedDepositDetails>> modelData =
```

```
            new HashMap<String, List<FixedDepositDetails>>();
        modelData.put("fdList", fixedDepositService.getFixedDeposits());
        return new ModelAndView("fixedDepositList", modelData);
      }
    };
  }
  .....
}
```

The above example listing shows that the listFixedDeposits method returns a Callable<T> object, where T is the type of the result that is asynchronously computed. The Callable's call method contains the logic that needs to be executed asynchronously to produce the result. The call method shown in the above example listing invokes FixedDepositService's getFixedDeposits method, and returns a ModelAndView object containing the model and view information. The Thread.sleep method is invoked in the beginning of call method to simulate a scenario in which the request processing takes time.

If an exception is thrown during the execution of the Callable returned from the controller, the @ExceptionHandler method (or the configured HandlerExceptionResolver bean) of the controller is responsible for handling the exception. For more information on @ExceptionHandler annotation, refer to section 10-9 of chapter 10.

Example listing 13-7 shows that if you want to switch from synchronous request processing approach to asynchronous request processing, you need to move the logic from the @RequestMapping method to the call method of Callable, and change the return type of the @RequestMapping method to Callable<T>.

Let's now look at how requests are asynchronously processed when a @RequestMapping method returns a DeferredResult object.

IMPORT **chapter 13/ch13-async-webservice** and **ch13-async-webservice-client** (The ch13-async-webservice project is a variant of FixedDepositWS web service (refer ch12-webservice project of chapter 12) that asynchronously processes web service requests. @RequestMapping methods defined in the FixedDepositController of this project return an instance of DeferredResult object. The ch13-async-webservice-client project is same as the FixedDepositWS web service client (refer ch12-webservice-client project of chapter 12) that assumes that the web service is deployed at http://localhost:8080/ch13-async-webservice.)

Returning DeferredResult from @RequestMapping methods

A DeferredResult instance represents a result that is asynchronously computed. You set the result on the DeferredResult instance by calling its setResult method. Typically, a @RequestMapping method stores a DeferredResult instance in a Queue or a Map or any other data structure, and a separate thread is responsible for computing the result and setting the result on the DeferredResult instance.

Let's first look at @RequestMapping methods that return DeferredResult type.

@RequestMapping method implementation

The following example listing shows the FixedDepositController whose @RequestMapping methods return DeferredResult objects:

Example listing 13-8 – FixedDepositController – returning DeferredResult from @RequestMapping methods
Project – ch13-async-webservice
Source location - src/main/java/sample/spring/chapter13/web

```
package sample.spring.chapter13.web;

import java.util.Queue;
import java.util.concurrent.ConcurrentLinkedQueue;
import org.springframework.web.context.request.async.DeferredResult;
.....
@Controller
@RequestMapping(value = "/fixedDeposits")
public class FixedDepositController {
  private static final String LIST_METHOD = "getFixedDepositList";
  private static final String GET_FD_METHOD = "getFixedDeposit";
  .....
  private final Queue<ResultContext> deferredResultQueue =
        new ConcurrentLinkedQueue<ResultContext>();
  .....
  @RequestMapping(method = RequestMethod.GET)
  public DeferredResult<ResponseEntity<List<FixedDepositDetails>>> getFixedDepositList() {
    DeferredResult<ResponseEntity<List<FixedDepositDetails>>> dr =
                new DeferredResult<ResponseEntity<List<FixedDepositDetails>>>();

    ResultContext<ResponseEntity<List<FixedDepositDetails>>> resultContext =
          new ResultContext<ResponseEntity<List<FixedDepositDetails>>>();
    resultContext.setDeferredResult(dr);
    resultContext.setMethodToInvoke(LIST_METHOD);
    resultContext.setArgs(new HashMap<String, Object>());

    deferredResultQueue.add(resultContext);
    return dr;
  }
```

```
    .....
}
```

Each @RequestMapping method of FixedDepositController performs these steps:

Step 1 - creates an instance of DeferredResult<T> object, where T represents the *type* of the result that is asynchronously computed. As the type of the result computed for the getFixedDepositList method is ResponseEntity<List<FixedDepositDetails>>, an instance of DeferredResult<ResponseEntity<List<FixedDepositDetails>>> is created.

Step 2 - creates an instance of ResultContext object. ResultContext object holds DeferredResult instance that we created in Step 1, and other details that are required to asynchronously compute the result for the DeferredResult object. In case of FixedDepositController's getFixedDepositList method, result is represented by the list of fixed deposits obtained by invoking FixedDepositService's getFixedDeposits method.

The following example listing shows the ResultContext class:

Example listing 13-9 – ResultContext class for storing DeferredResult and other information
Project – ch13-async-webservice
Source location - src/main/java/sample/spring/chapter13/web

```
package sample.spring.chapter13.web;

import java.util.Map;
import org.springframework.web.context.request.async.DeferredResult;

public class ResultContext<T> {
   private String methodToInvoke;
   private DeferredResult<T> deferredResult;
   private Map<String, Object> args;

   public void setDeferredResult(DeferredResult<T> deferredResult) {
      this. deferredResult = deferredResult;
   }
   .....
}
```

The deferredResult property refers to an instance of DeferredResult, the methodToInvoke property specifies the name of the FixedDepositService method that is invoked to compute the result for the DeferredResult object, and args property (of type java.util.Map) specifies the arguments to be passed to the FixedDepositService method. A separate thread (as explained later in this section) uses the methodToInvoke and args properties to invoke the specified FixedDepositService method, and sets the returned result on the DeferredResult instance.

As the LIST_METHOD, GET_FD_METHOD, and so on, constants in the FixedDepositController class refer to the names of the FixedDepositService methods (refer example listing 13-8), the methodToInvoke property is set to the one of these constants. In example listing 13-8, FixedDepositController's getFixedDepositList method sets the methodToInvoke property to LIST_METHOD constant (whose value is getFixedDeposits) because FixedDepositService's getFixedDeposits method needs to be invoked to obtain the result for the DeferredResult object returned by FixedDepositController's getFixedDepositList method.

Step 3 - stores the ResultContext instance created in Step 2 into a Queue (refer to deferredResultQueue instance variable in example listing 13-8)

Step 4 - returns the DeferredResult object created in Step 1

The above sequence of steps suggests that for each web request an instance of ResultContext is stored in the deferredResultQueue. The following figure summarizes the actions that are performed by FixedDepositController's getFixedDepositList method.

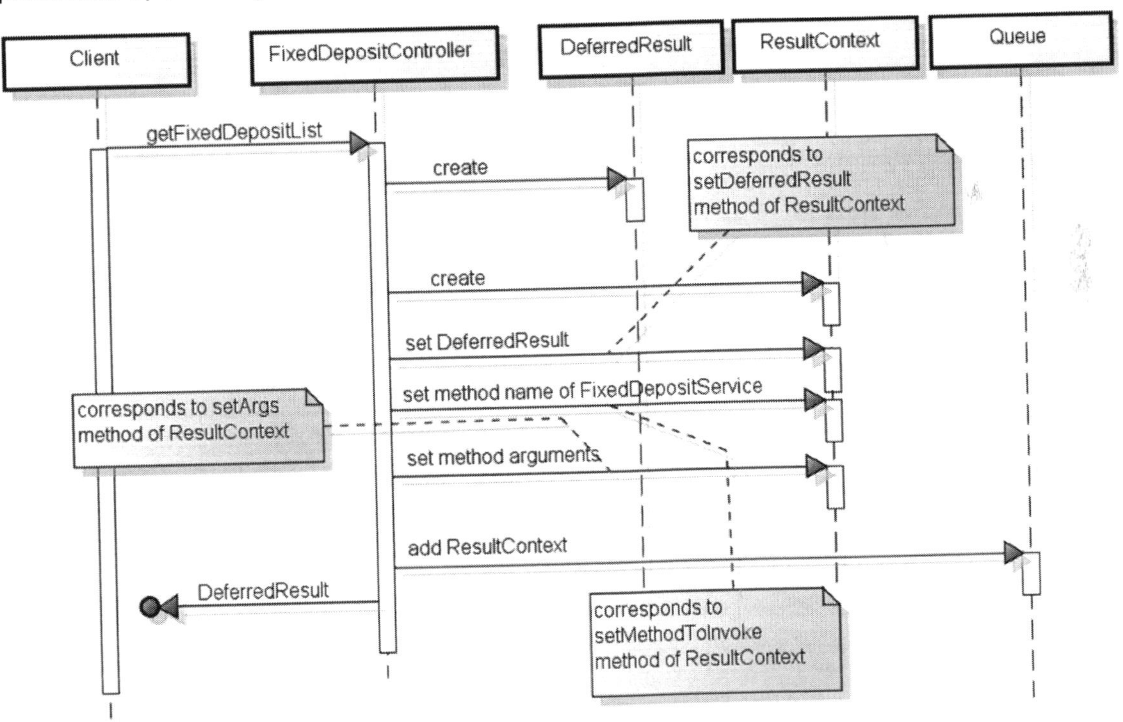

Figure 13-2 FixedDepositController's getFixedDepositList method adds a ResultContext object to the queue and returns a DeferredResult object

Let's now look at how the result is computed for the DeferredResult instance contained inside the ResultContext object.

Computing result for a DeferredResult instance

FixedDepositController's processResults method is responsible for iterating over the ResultContext objects stored in the deferredResultQueue (refer example listing 13-8), computing the result for each DeferredResult object, and setting the result on the DeferredResult object. The following example listing shows the processResults method:

Example listing 13-10 – processResults method – computing and setting results on DeferredResult objects
Project – ch13-async-webservice
Source location - src/main/java/sample/spring/chapter13/web

```
package sample.spring.chapter13.web;

import org.springframework.scheduling.annotation.Scheduled;
import org.springframework.web.context.request.async.DeferredResult;

@Controller
@RequestMapping(value = "/fixedDeposits")
public class FixedDepositController {
  private static final String LIST_METHOD = "getFixedDepositList";
  .....
  private final Queue<ResultContext> deferredResultQueue =
      new ConcurrentLinkedQueue<ResultContext>();
 @Autowired
 private FixedDepositService fixedDepositService;
 .....
 @Scheduled(fixedRate = 10000)
 public void processResults() {
    for (ResultContext resultContext : deferredResultQueue) {
       if (resultContext.getMethodToInvoke() == LIST_METHOD) {
          resultContext.getDeferredResult().setResult(
                new ResponseEntity<List<FixedDepositDetails>>(
                      fixedDepositService.getFixedDeposits(), HttpStatus.OK));
       }
       .....
       deferredResultQueue.remove(resultContext);
    }
  }
}
```

@Scheduled annotation (refer section 8-6 of chapter 8 for more details) on processResults method specifies that every 10 seconds an application thread is responsible for executing the processResults method. The processResults method uses the method name and argument information stored in the ResultContext instance to invoke the appropriate FixedDepositService's method. The processResults method then sets the result on the DeferredResult instance by calling its setResult method. In the end, the processResults method removes the ResultContext instance from the Queue. After processing a ResultContext instance, the processResults method removes the ResultContext instance from the Queue so that it is not re-processed by the processResults method when it executes again after 10 seconds.

Figure 13-3 summarizes the actions performed by FixedDepositController's processResults method to compute the result and set it on the DeferredResult instance.

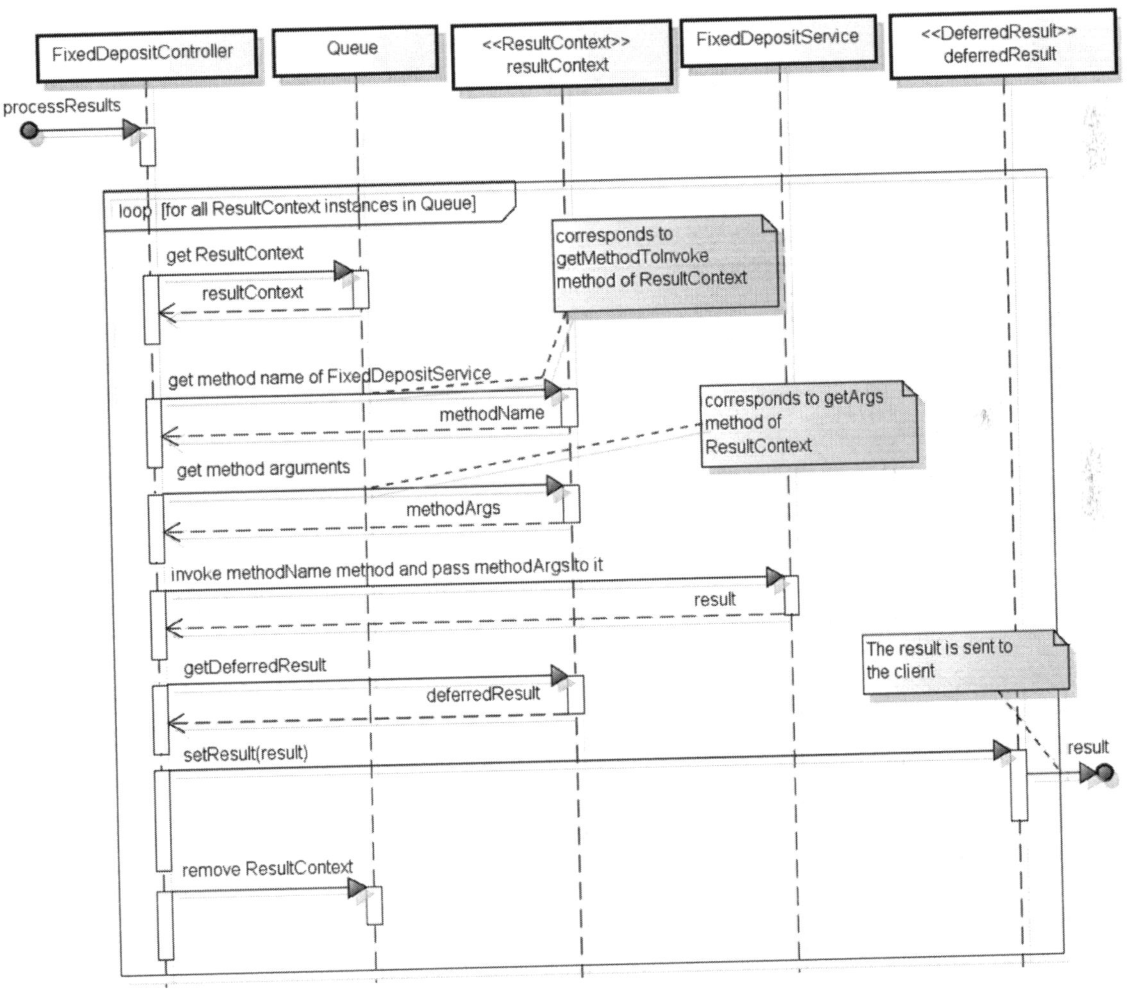

Figure 13-3 The processResults method reads method name and argument information from the ResultContext object to compute the result for the DeferredResult instance

Let's now look at how exceptions are handled when a @RequestMapping method returns a DeferredResult instance.

Exception Handling

If you set an object of type java.lang.Exception using DeferredResult's setErrorResult method, the result is handled by @ExceptionHandler annotated method of the controller (or by the configured HandlerExceptionResolver bean). For more information on @ExceptionHandler annotation, refer to section 10-9 of chapter 10.

The following example listing shows FixedDepositController's openFixedDeposit method that opens a new fixed deposit:

Example listing 13-11 – FixedDepositController's openFixedDeposit method
Project – ch13-async-webservice
Source location - src/main/java/sample/spring/chapter13/web

```
package sample.spring.chapter13.web;

@Controller
@RequestMapping(value = "/fixedDeposits")
public class FixedDepositController {
  private static final String OPEN_FD_METHOD = "openFixedDeposit";
  .....
  private final Queue<ResultContext> deferredResultQueue =
    new ConcurrentLinkedQueue<ResultContext>();

  @RequestMapping(method = RequestMethod.POST)
  public DeferredResult<ResponseEntity<FixedDepositDetails>> openFixedDeposit(
       @RequestBody FixedDepositDetails fixedDepositDetails, BindingResult bindingResult) {

    DeferredResult<ResponseEntity<FixedDepositDetails>> dr =
       new DeferredResult<ResponseEntity<FixedDepositDetails>>();

    ResultContext<ResponseEntity<FixedDepositDetails>> resultContext =
       new ResultContext<ResponseEntity<FixedDepositDetails>>();
    resultContext.setDeferredResult(dr);
    resultContext.setMethodToInvoke(OPEN_FD_METHOD);

    Map<String, Object> args = new HashMap<String, Object>();
    args.put("fixedDepositDetails", fixedDepositDetails);
    args.put("bindingResult", bindingResult);
    resultContext.setArgs(args);
```

```
    deferredResultQueue.add(resultContext);
    return dr;
  }
  .....
}
```

The above example listing shows that the arguments (fixedDepositDetails and bindingResult) passed to the openFixedDeposit method are set on the ResultContext instance so that these arguments are available when the processResults method executes the logic for opening a new fixed deposit. The fixedDepositDetails argument contains the details of the fixed deposit to be opened and the bindingResult argument contains the results of data binding.

The following example listing shows how the processResults method executes the logic for opening a new fixed deposit:

Example listing 13-12 – FixedDepositController's processResults method
Project – ch13-async-webservice
Source location - src/main/java/sample/spring/chapter13/web

```
package sample.spring.chapter13.web;

@Controller
@RequestMapping(value = "/fixedDeposits")
public class FixedDepositController {
  private static final String OPEN_FD_METHOD = "openFixedDeposit";
  .....
  private final Queue<ResultContext> deferredResultQueue =
       new ConcurrentLinkedQueue<ResultContext>();

  @Autowired
  private FixedDepositService fixedDepositService;
  .....
  @ExceptionHandler(ValidationException.class)
  @ResponseBody
  @ResponseStatus(value = HttpStatus.BAD_REQUEST)
  public String handleException(Exception ex) {
    logger.info("handling ValidationException " + ex.getMessage());
    return ex.getMessage();
  }

  @Scheduled(fixedRate = 10000)
  public void processResults() {
    for (ResultContext resultContext : deferredResultQueue) {
      .....
```

```
        if (resultContext.getMethodToInvoke() == OPEN_FD_METHOD) {
          FixedDepositDetails fixedDepositDetails = (FixedDepositDetails) resultContext
               .getArgs().get("fixedDepositDetails");
          BindingResult bindingResult = (BindingResult) resultContext.getArgs().get("bindingResult");

          new FixedDepositDetailsValidator().validate(fixedDepositDetails, bindingResult);

          if (bindingResult.hasErrors()) {
            logger.info("openFixedDeposit() method: Validation errors occurred");
            resultContext.getDeferredResult().setErrorResult(new ValidationException(
                   "Validation errors occurred"));
          } else {
            fixedDepositService.saveFixedDeposit(fixedDepositDetails);
            resultContext.getDeferredResult().setResult(new ResponseEntity<FixedDepositDetails>(
                    fixedDepositDetails, HttpStatus.CREATED));
          }
        }
        .....
      }
    }
}
```

The above example listing shows the @ExceptionHandler annotated handleException method that handles exceptions of type ValidationException. The handleException method logs that a validation exception has occurred and returns the exception message.

To open a new fixed deposit, the processResults method retrieves the fixedDepositDetails (of type FixedDepositDetails) and bindingResult (of type BindingResult) arguments from the ResultContext and validates the fixedDepositDetails object by calling FixedDepositValidator's validate method. If validation errors are reported, the processResults method invokes DeferredResult's setErrorResult method to set ValidationException (of type java.lang.Exception) as the result. Setting the ValidationException using DeferredResult's setErrorResult method will cause handling of the result by FixedDepositController's handleException method.

It is recommended that you deploy the ch13-async-webservice project (which represents the FixedDepositWS RESTful web service) and access it by running the main method of FixedDepositWSClient of ch13-async-webservice-client project (which represents a client of FixedDepositWS RESTful web service). The FixedDepositWSClient's openInvalidFixedDeposit method invokes FixedDepositController's openFixedDeposit web service method such that it results in ValidationException. You can check the logs to verify that the FixedDepositController's handleException method handles the result when processResults method sets ValidationException on the DeferredResult object by calling DeferredResult's setErrorResult method.

Let's now look at how to set default timeout value for asynchronous requests.

Setting default timeout value

You can set the default timeout value of asynchronous requests by using default-timeout attribute of <async-support> element, as shown here:

Example listing 13-13 – Setting default timeout for asynchronous requests
Project – ch13-async-webservice
Source location – src/main/webapp/WEB-INF/spring/webservice-config.xml

```
<mvc:annotation-driven>
   <mvc:async-support default-timeout="10000" >
     .....
   </mvc:async-support>
</mvc:annotation-driven>
```

In the above example listing, default timeout for asynchronous requests is set to 10 seconds. If you don't specify the default timeout, the timeout for asynchronous requests depends on the Servlet container on which you deployed your web application.

Let's now look at how you can intercept asynchronous requests using CallableProcessingInterceptor and DeferredResultProcessingInterceptor.

Intercepting asynchronous requests

If you are using Callable to asynchronously process requests, you can use CallableProcessingInterceptor callback interface to intercept requests before and after the Callable task is executed. For instance, the postProcess method is executed after the Callable has produced the result, and the preProcess method is called before the Callable task is executed. Similarly, if you are using DeferredResult, you can use DeferredResultProcessingInterceptor callback interface to intercept processing of asynchronous requests.

You can configure a CallableProcessingInterceptor using <callable-interceptors> element of Spring's mvc schema. And, you can configure a DeferredResultProcessingInterceptor using <deferred-result-interceptors> element of Spring's mvc schema. The following example listing shows configuration of MyDeferredResultInterceptor (a DeferredResultProcessingInterceptor implementation):

Example listing 13-14 – Configuring a DeferredResultProcessingInterceptor implementation
Project – ch13-async-webservice
Source location – src/main/webapp/WEB-INF/spring/webservice-config.xml

```
<mvc:annotation-driven>
   <mvc:async-support default-timeout="30000">
      <mvc:deferred-result-interceptors>
```

```
        <bean class="sample.spring.chapter13.web.MyDeferredResultInterceptor"/>
      </mvc:deferred-result-interceptors>
    </mvc:async-support>
  </mvc:annotation-driven>
```

Let's now look at Spring's support for type conversion and formatting.

13-5 Type conversion and formatting support in Spring

Spring's Converter interface simplifies converting an object type to another object type. And, Spring's Formatter interface is useful when converting an object type to its *localized* String representation, and vice versa. You can find a number of built-in Converter implementations in the org.springframework.core.convert.support package of spring-core JAR file. Spring also provides built-in Formatters for java.lang.Number and java.util.Date types that you can find in org.springframework.format.number and org.springframework.format.datetime packages, respectively.

IMPORT **chapter 13/ch13-converter-formatter-bankapp** (This project is a variant of ch13-bankapp project that shows how to create custom Converters and Formatters)

Let's first look at how to create a custom Converter.

Creating a custom Converter

A converter implements Spring's Converter<S, T> interface, where S (referred to as the *source* type) is the type of the object given to the converter, and T (referred to as the *target* type) is the type of the object to which S is converted by the converter. Converter interface defines a convert method that provides the conversion logic.

The following example listing shows the IdToFixedDepositDetailsConverter that converts an object of type String (representing the fixed deposit ID) to an object of type FixedDepositDetails (representing the fixed deposit corresponding to the fixed deposit ID):

Example listing 13-15 – Converter implementation
Project – ch13-converter-formatter-bankapp
Source location – src/main/java/sample/spring/chapter13/converter

```
package sample.spring.chapter13.converter;

import org.springframework.core.convert.converter.Converter;
.....
public class IdToFixedDepositDetailsConverter implements Converter<String, FixedDepositDetails> {

  @Autowired
  private FixedDepositService fixedDepositService;
```

```
    @Override
    public FixedDepositDetails convert(String source) {
        return fixedDepositService.getFixedDeposit(Integer.parseInt(source));
    }
}
```

IdToFixedDepositDetailsConverter implements Converter<String, FixedDepositDetails> interface, where String is the source type and FixedDepositDetails is the target type. IdToFixedDepositDetailsConverter's convert method uses FixedDepositService's getFixedDeposit method to retrieve the FixedDepositDetails object corresponding to the fixed deposit ID.

Let's now look at how to configure and use a custom converter.

Configuring and using a custom Converter

To use a custom converter, you need to register the custom converter with Spring's ConversionService. A ConversionService acts as a registry of Converters and Formatters, and Spring delegates type conversion responsibility to the registered ConversionService. By default, the <annotation-driven> element of Spring's mvc schema automatically registers Spring's FormattingConversionService (an implementation of ConversionService) with the Spring container. Spring comes with a couple of built-in converters and formatters that are automatically registered with the FormattingConversionService. If you want to substitute a different implementation of ConversionService, you can do so by using conversion-service attribute of <annotation-driven> element.

To register custom converters with the FormattingConversionService instance, configure Spring's FormattingConversionServiceFactoryBean (a FactoryBean implementation that creates and configures a FormattingConversionService instance) and specify custom converters as part of the configuration, as shown in the following example listing:

Example listing 13-16 – Registering a custom Converter with FormattingConversionService
Project – ch13-converter-formatter-bankapp
Source location – src/main/webapp/WEB-INF/spring

```
<mvc:annotation-driven conversion-service="myConversionService" />

<bean id="myConversionService"
    class="org.springframework.format.support.FormattingConversionServiceFactoryBean">
    <property name="converters">
        <set>
            <bean class="sample.spring.chapter13.converter.IdToFixedDepositDetailsConverter" />
        </set>
    </property>
```

```
  .....
</bean>
```

By default, FormattingConversionServiceFactoryBean registers only the built-in converters and formatters with the FormattingConversionService instance. You register custom converters and formatters using FormattingConversionServiceFactoryBean's converters and formatters properties. As we want our Spring application to use FormattingConversionService instance created by the FormattingConversionServiceFactoryBean, the conversion-service attribute of <annotation-driven> element refers to the FormattingConversionServiceFactoryBean.

The converters and formatters registered with the FormattingConversionService are used by the Spring container to perform type conversion during *data binding*. In the following example listing, FixedDepositController's viewFixedDepositDetails method shows a scenario in which the Spring container uses IdToFixedDepositDetailsConverter<String, FixedDepositDetails> to convert fixed deposit ID (of type String) to FixedDepositDetails instance:

Example listing 13-17 – FixedDepositController's viewFixedDepositDetails method
Project – ch13-converter-formatter-bankapp
Source location – src/main/java/sample/spring/chapter13/web

```
package sample.spring.chapter13.web;
.....
public class FixedDepositController {
  .....
  @RequestMapping(params = "fdAction=view", method = RequestMethod.GET)
  public ModelAndView viewFixedDepositDetails(
        @RequestParam(value = "fixedDepositId") FixedDepositDetails fixedDepositDetails) {
    .....
  }
}
```

@RequestParam annotation specifies that the value of fixedDepositId request parameter is assigned to the fixedDepositDetails method argument. The fixedDepositId request parameter uniquely identifies a fixed deposit. As the fixedDepositId request parameter is of type String and method argument type is FixedDepositDetails, Spring uses IdToFixedDepositDetailsConverter<String, FixedDepositDetails> to perform the type conversion.

The use of ConversionService is not limited to the web layer. You can use ConversionService to programmatically perform type conversion in any layer of your application. The following example listing shows a variant of FixedDepositController's viewFixedDepositDetails method that uses ConversionService directly for performing type conversion:

Example listing 13-18 – Performing type conversion programmatically

```
import org.springframework.core.convert.ConversionService;
.....
public class FixedDepositController {
   @Autowired
   private ConversionService conversionService;
   .....
   @RequestMapping(params = "fdAction=view", method = RequestMethod.GET)
   public ModelAndView viewFixedDepositDetails(HttpServletRequest request) {
      String fixedDepositId = request.getParameter("fixedDepositId");
      FixedDepositDetails fixedDepositDetails =
            conversionService.convert(fixedDepositId, FixedDepositDetails.class);
      .....
   }
}
```

In the above example listing, ConversionService instance that is registered with the Spring container is autowired into the FixedDepositController. The viewFixedDepositDetails method uses ConversionService's convert method to convert fixedDepositId (of type String) to FixedDepositDetails. Behind the scenes, ConversionService makes use of the IdToFixedDepositDetailsConverter<String, FixedDepositDetails> converter registered with it to perform the type conversion.

Now that we have seen how to create and use a custom Converter, let's now look at how to create and use a custom Formatter.

Creating a custom Formatter

A formatter converts an object of type T to a String value for display purposes, and parses a String value to the object type T. A formatter implements Spring's Formatter<T > interface, where T is the type of the object that the formatter formats. This may sound similar to what PropertyEditors do in web applications. As we'll see in this chapter, Formatters offer a more robust alternative to PropertyEditors.

> Spring's tag library tags use the formatters registered with the FormattingConversionService to perform type conversion during data binding and rendering.

The following example listing shows the AmountFormatter that is used by the MyBank application to display fixed deposit amount in the currency that applies to the user's locale, and to parse the fixed deposit amount entered by the user. For simplicity, currency conversion is not applied on the fixed deposit amount; the currency symbol that applies to the user's locale is simply appended to the fixed deposit amount.

Example listing 13-19 – AmountFormatter - a Formatter implementation
Project – ch13-converter-formatter-bankapp
Source location – src/main/java/sample/spring/chapter13/formatter

```
package sample.spring.chapter13.formatter;

import java.text.ParseException;
import java.util.Locale;
import org.springframework.format.Formatter;

public class AmountFormatter implements Formatter<Long>{

  @Override
  public String print(Long object, Locale locale) {
    String returnStr = object.toString() + " USD";
    if(locale.getLanguage().equals(new Locale("de").getLanguage())) {
      returnStr = object.toString() + " EURO";
    }
    return returnStr;
  }

  @Override
  public Long parse(String text, Locale locale) throws ParseException {
    String str[] = text.split(" ");
    return Long.parseLong(str[0]);
  }
}
```

AmountFormatter implements Formatter<Long> interface, which means that the AmountFormatter applies to Long type objects. The print method converts the Long type object (representing the fixed deposit amount) to a String value that is displayed to the user. Based on the language code obtained from the locale, the print method simply appends USD (for en language code) or EURO (for de language code) to the fixed deposit amount. For instance, if the fixed deposit amount is 1000 and the language code is de, the print method returns '1000 EURO'. The parse method takes the fixed deposit amount entered by the user (like, '1000 EURO') and converts it into a Long type object by simply extracting the fixed deposit amount from the user entered value.

Let's now look at how to configure a custom formatter.

Configuring a custom Formatter

You can register custom formatters with the FormattingConversionService using the formatters property of FormattingConversionServiceFactoryBean, as shown here:

Example listing 13-20 – Registering a custom Formatter with FormattingConversionService

```
<beans .....>
  .....
  <mvc:annotation-driven conversion-service="myConversionService" />
  .....
  <bean id="myConversionService"
    class="org.springframework.format.support.FormattingConversionServiceFactoryBean">
    <property name="formatters">
      <set>
        <bean class="sample.spring.chapter13.formatter.AmountFormatter" />
      </set>
    </property>
  </bean>
</beans>
```

AmountFormatter registered with the FormattingConversionService is applied to *all* the Long type fields during data binding and rendering.

You can control the fields on which a Formatter applies by using Spring's AnnotationFormatterFactory. An AnnotationFormatterFactory implementation creates formatters for fields that are annotated with a particular *annotation*. Let's see how we can use AnnotationFormatterFactory to format only the Long type fields annotated with @AmountFormat annotation.

Creating AnnotationFormatterFactory to format only @AmountFormat annotated fields

The following example listing shows the definition of @AmountFormat annotation:

Example listing 13-21 – AmountFormat annotation
Project – ch13-converter-formatter-bankapp
Source location – src/main/java/sample/spring/chapter13/formatter

```
package sample.spring.chapter13.formatter;
.....
@Target(value={ElementType.FIELD})
@Retention(RetentionPolicy.RUNTIME)
@Documented
public @interface AmountFormat { }
```

In the above example listing, the @Target annotation specifies that the @AmountFormat annotation can only appear on fields.

The following example listing shows the implementation of AnnotationFormatterFactory that creates formatters for fields annotated with @AmountFormat annotation:

Example listing 13-22 – AmountFormatAnnotationFormatterFactory class
Project – ch13-converter-formatter-bankapp
Source location – src/main/java/sample/spring/chapter13/formatter

```
package sample.spring.chapter13.formatter;

import org.springframework.format.AnnotationFormatterFactory;
import org.springframework.format.Parser;
import org.springframework.format.Printer;

public class AmountFormatAnnotationFormatterFactory implements
      AnnotationFormatterFactory<AmountFormat> {

   public Set<Class<?>> getFieldTypes() {
      Set<Class<?>> fieldTypes = new HashSet<Class<?>>(1, 1);
      fieldTypes.add(Long.class);
      return fieldTypes;
   }

   public Parser<?> getParser(AmountFormat annotation, Class<?> fieldType) {
      return new AmountFormatter();
   }

   public Printer<?> getPrinter(AmountFormat annotation, Class<?> fieldType) {
      return new AmountFormatter();
   }
}
```

In the above example listing, AmountFormatAnnotationFormatterFactory implements AnnotationFormatterFactory<AmountFormat> interface, which means that the AmountFormatAnnotationFormatterFactory creates formatters for fields annotated with @AmountFormat annotation.

The getFieldTypes method returns the field types that may be annotated with @AmountFormat annotation. The getFieldTypes method in the above example listing returns a single type, Long type, which means that only a Long type field that is annotated with @AmountFormat annotation is considered for formatting by the formatters created by the AmountFormatAnnotationFormatterFactory. The getParser and getPrinter methods return formatters for fields that are annotated with @AmountFormat annotation. You should note that the Formatter interface is a sub-interface of Parser and Printer interfaces.

Configuring AnnotationFormatterFactory implementation

As in case of Formatters configuration, an AnnotationFormatterFactory implementation is registered with FormattingConversionService via formatters property of FormattingConversionServiceFactoryBean:

Example listing 13-23 – AmountFormatAnnotationFormatterFactory configuration
Project – ch13-converter-formatter-bankapp
Source location – src/main/webapp/WEB-INF/spring

```
<beans .....>
  .....
  <mvc:annotation-driven conversion-service="myConversionService" />
  .....
  <bean id="myConversionService"
    class="org.springframework.format.support.FormattingConversionServiceFactoryBean">
    <property name="formatters">
      <set>
        <bean
          class="sample.spring.chapter13.formatter.AmountFormatAnnotationFormatterFactory" />
      </set>
    </property>
  </bean>
</beans>
```

Now that we have seen how to use AnnotationFormatterFactory to enable formatting of fields that are annotated with a specific annotation, let's look at how it is used in ch13-converter-formatter-bankapp project.

The following figure shows the web page of ch13-converter-formatter-bankapp project that shows the lists of fixed deposits:

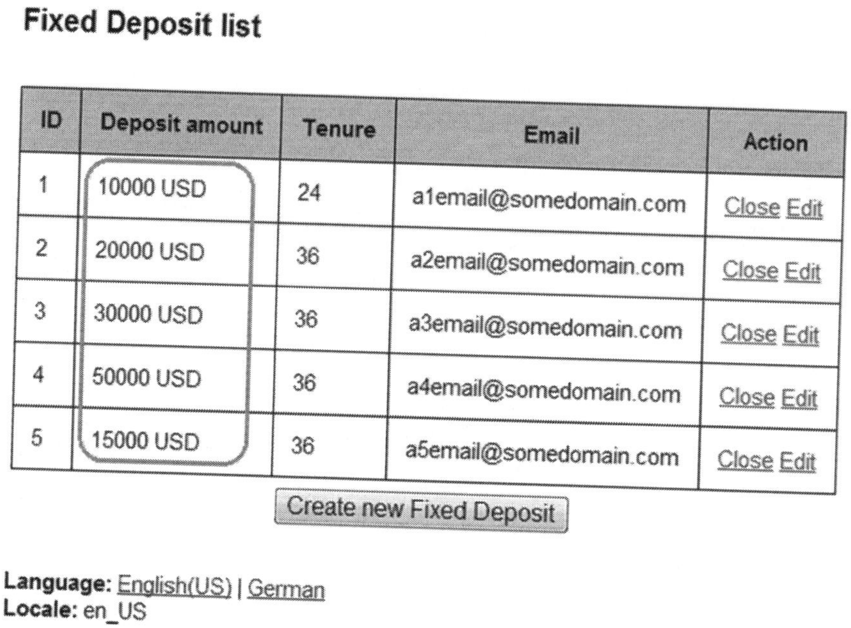

Fixed Deposit list

ID	Deposit amount	Tenure	Email	Action
1	10000 USD	24	a1email@somedomain.com	Close Edit
2	20000 USD	36	a2email@somedomain.com	Close Edit
3	30000 USD	36	a3email@somedomain.com	Close Edit
4	50000 USD	36	a4email@somedomain.com	Close Edit
5	15000 USD	36	a5email@somedomain.com	Close Edit

Create new Fixed Deposit

Language: English(US) | German
Locale: en_US

Figure 13-4 - The 'Deposit amount' column shows USD or EURO depending upon the language code obtained from the user's current locale

The above figure shows that USD is appended to the fixed deposit amount if the language chosen by the user is English. If you switch the language to German, the USD will be replaced by EURO. In example listing 13-19, we saw that the AmountFormatter contained the logic to show USD or EURO depending upon the language code obtained from the user's current locale.

To ensure that the formatters configured with the FormattingConversionService are invoked during page rendering and form submission, Spring's tag library tags (like, <eval> and <input>) have been used in the JSP pages of ch13-converter-formatter-bankapp project.

Let's now look at how Spring Web MVC simplifies uploading files.

13-6 File upload support in Spring Web MVC

You can handle multipart requests in your Spring Web MVC applications by configuring a MultipartResolver. Spring provides the following out-of-the-box implementations of MultipartResolver interface that you can use in your web applications:

- CommonsMultipartResolver – based on Apache Commons FileUpload library
- StandardServletMultipartResolver – based on Servlet 3.0 Part API

When a multipart request is received, DispatcherServlet uses the configured MultipartResolver to wrap the HttpServletRequest into a MultipartHttpServletRequest instance. In Spring Web MVC, an uploaded file is represented by the MultipartFile object. The controller responsible for handling file uploads accesses the uploaded file using methods defined by the MultipartHttpServletRequest or by directly accessing the MultipartFile object.

Let's first look at a sample web application that uses CommonsMultipartResolver for uploading files.

IMPORT **chapter 13/ch13-commons-file-upload** (This project shows how to use CommonsMultipartResolver to upload files. As CommonsMultipartResolver uses Apache Commons FileUpload library, the project is dependent on commons-fileupload JAR file.)

Uploading files using CommonsMultipartResolver

The following example listing shows the file upload form that is displayed by ch13-commons-file-upload project:

Example listing 13-24 – uploadForm.jsp – shows the upload form
Project – ch13-commons-file-upload
Source location – src/main/webapp/WEB-INF/jsp

```
.....
  <form method="post" action="/ch13-commons-file-upload/uploadFile"
        enctype="multipart/form-data">
     <table style="padding-left: 200px;">
        <tr>
           <td colspan="2"><c:out value="${uploadMessage}" /></td>
        </tr>
        <tr>
           <td><b>Select the file to be uploaded:  </b></td>
           <td><input type="file" name="myFileField" /></td>
        </tr>
        <tr>
           <td colspan="2" align="center"><input type="button"
              value="Upload file" onclick="document.forms[0].submit();" /></td>
        </tr>
     </table>
  </form>
.....
```

The above example listing shows that the enctype attribute of <form> element is set to multipart/form-data, which means that the form submission results in sending multipart request to the server. The uploadMessage request attribute shows the success or failure message after the user selects a file and clicks the 'Upload file' button.

The following example listing shows the configuration of CommonsMultipartResolver that resolves multipart requests:

Example listing 13-25 – fileupload-config.xml – CommonsMultipartResolver configuration
Project – ch13-commons-file-upload
Source location – src/main/webapp/WEB-INF/spring

```
<bean id="multipartResolver"
    class="org.springframework.web.multipart.commons.CommonsMultipartResolver">
    <property name="maxUploadSize" value="100000" />
    <property name="resolveLazily" value="true" />
</bean>
```

It is important to note that the MultipartResolver implementation must be configured with id as multipartResolver in the web application context XML file. The maxUploadSize property specifies the maximum size (in bytes) of the file that can be uploaded. If you attempt to upload a file whose size is greater than 100 KB, the CommonsMultipartResolver shown in the above example listing will throw an exception. If an exception is thrown by the CommonsMultipartResolver instance, the controller responsible for handling the file upload doesn't get the opportunity to handle the exception. For this reason, the resolveLazily property is set to true. If the resolveLazily property is set to true, the multipart request is resolved only when the uploaded file is accessed by the controller. This gives the opportunity to the controller to handle exceptions that occur during multipart request resolution.

The following example listing shows the FileUploadController that handles file uploads:

Example listing 13-26 – FileUploadController
Project – ch13-commons-file-upload
Source location – src/main/java/sample/spring/chapter13/web

```
package sample.spring.chapter13.web;

import org.springframework.web.multipart.MultipartFile;
.....
public class FileUploadController {
   .....
   @RequestMapping(value = "/uploadFile", method = RequestMethod.POST)
   public ModelAndView handleFileUpload(
         @RequestParam("myFileField") MultipartFile file) throws IOException {
     ModelMap modelData = new ModelMap();
```

```
    if (!file.isEmpty()) {
      // -- save the uploaded file on the filesystem
      String successMessage = "File successfully uploaded";
      modelData.put("uploadMessage", successMessage);
      return new ModelAndView("uploadForm", modelData);
    }
    .....
  }

  @ExceptionHandler(value = Exception.class)
  public ModelAndView handleException() {
    .....
  }
}
```

FileUploadController's handleFileUpload method accepts an argument of type MultipartFile which identifies the uploaded file. Notice that the @RequestParam annotation specifies name of the <input type="file" .....> field in the uploadForm.jsp page (refer example listing 13-24). If the file is successfully uploaded, the handleFileUpload method sets a success message which is shown to the user. @ExceptionHandler method shows an error message in case an exception occurs during file upload process. For instance, if the file size is greater than 100 KB, an error message is shown to the user.

Now that we have seen how to use CommonsMultipartResolver to upload files, let's look at how to upload files using StandardServletMultipartResolver.

IMPORT **chapter 13/ch13-servlet3-file-upload** (This project shows how to use StandardServletMultipartResolver to upload files.)

Uploading files using StandardServletMultipartResolver

The support for handling multipart request is provided out-of-the-box in Servlet 3. If you want to use the multipart support provided by Servlet 3, enable multipart request handling by specifying <multipart-config> element in the DispatcherServlet configuration, and configure StandardServletMultipartResolver in the web application context XML file. Unlike, CommonsMultipartResolver, StandardMultipartResolver doesn't define any properties.

The following example listing shows the DispatcherServlet configuration in web.xml file:

Example listing 13-27 – web.xml
Project – ch13-servlet3-file-upload
Source location – src/main/webapp

```
<servlet>
  <servlet-name>fileupload</servlet-name>
```

```
    <servlet-class>org.springframework.web.servlet.DispatcherServlet</servlet-class>
    .....
    <multipart-config>
      <max-file-size>10000</max-file-size>
    </multipart-config>
</servlet>
```

As the <multipart-config> element is specified, the fileupload servlet can handle multipart requests. The <max-file-size> element specifies the maximum file size that can be uploaded. Notice that the maximum file size is now specified as part of <multipart-config> element.

13-7 Summary

In this chapter, we looked at some of the important features of Spring Web MVC framework that simplify developing web applications. In the next chapter, we'll look at how to secure Spring applications using Spring Security framework.

Chapter 14 – *Securing applications using Spring Security*

14-1 Introduction

Security is an important aspect of any application. Spring Security is built on top of Spring Framework, and provides a comprehensive framework for securing Spring-based applications. In this chapter, we'll look at how to use Spring Security framework to:

- authenticate users
- implement web request security,
- implement method-level security
- secure domain objects using ACL (Access Control List) based security

Let's begin by looking at the MyBank web application's security requirements that we'll address using Spring Security.

14-2 Security requirements of the MyBank web application

The users of the MyBank web application are *customers* and *administrators* that manage fixed deposits in the system. A customer can open and edit fixed deposits but *can't* close them. An administrator *can't* create or edit fixed deposits but can close fixed deposits of customers.

As only authenticated users can access the MyBank web application, a login form is displayed to unauthenticated users:

Login with Username and Password

User: cust1
Password: •••••
Remember me on this computer.
Login

Figure 14-1 - Login form that is displayed to unauthenticated users

The above figure shows the login form that is displayed to unauthenticated users. If the user selects the 'Remember me on this computer' checkbox, the MyBank web application remembers the credentials entered by the user and uses it for automatic authentication of the user in future visits.

When a *customer* logs in, details of the fixed deposits associated with the customer are displayed, as shown here:

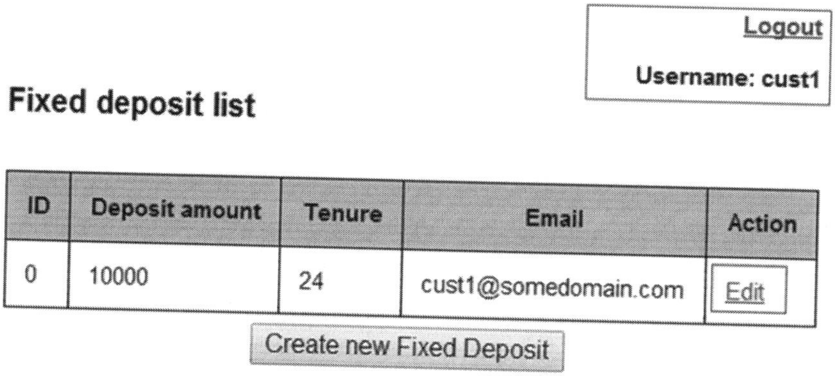

Logout

Username: cust1

Fixed deposit list

ID	Deposit amount	Tenure	Email	Action
0	10000	24	cust1@somedomain.com	Edit

Create new Fixed Deposit

Figure 14-2 - Fixed deposits of the customer are displayed after authentication

The above figure shows a **Logout** hyperlink that the customer can click to logout from the MyBank web application. A customer can edit details of a fixed deposit by clicking the **Edit** hyperlink corresponding to that fixed deposit. A customer can view the form for opening a new fixed deposit by clicking the **Create new Fixed Deposit** button. Notice that the username of the authenticated user is displayed below the **Logout** hyperlink.

When an administrator logs in, details of *all* the fixed deposits in the system are displayed by the MyBank web application, as shown here:

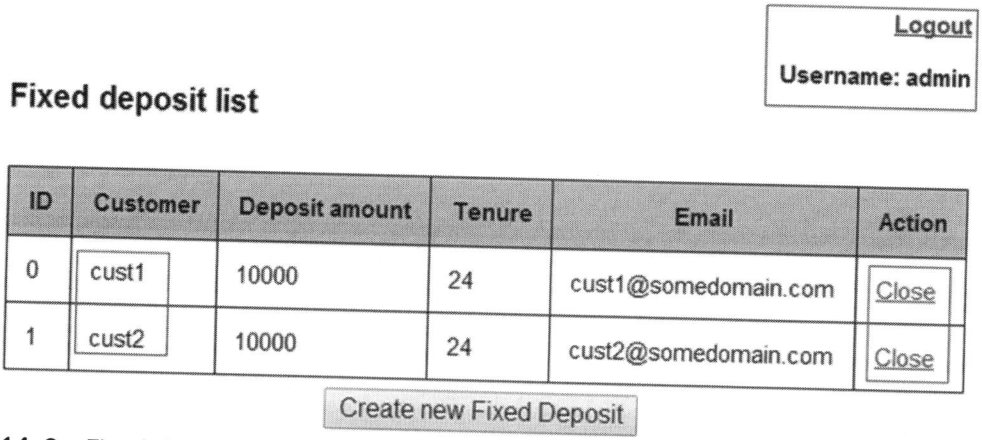

Logout

Username: admin

Fixed deposit list

ID	Customer	Deposit amount	Tenure	Email	Action
0	cust1	10000	24	cust1@somedomain.com	Close
1	cust2	10000	24	cust2@somedomain.com	Close

Create new Fixed Deposit

Figure 14-3 - Fixed deposits of *all* the customer are displayed to an administrator

In the above figure, an administrator can choose to close a fixed deposit by clicking the **Close** hyperlink corresponding to that fixed deposit. As in case of customers, the **Create new Fixed Deposit** button is visible to an administrator also, but an attempt to save details of the new fixed deposit will result in a security exception thrown by the application.

Let's now look at how to address the security requirements of MyBank web application using Spring Security.

IMPORT **chapter 14/ch14-bankapp-simple-security** (This project represents the MyBank web application that uses Spring Security framework for addressing security requirements described in section 14-2.)

14-3 Securing MyBank web application using Spring Security

Spring Security framework consists of multiple modules that address various security aspects of applications. The following table describes some of the important modules of Spring Security:

Module	Description
spring-security-core	Defines the core classes and interfaces of Spring Security framework. This module is required by any application that uses Spring Security.
spring-security-web	Provides support for securing web applications
spring-security-config	Like Spring's tx and mvc schemas, Spring Security defines a security schema that simplifies configuring Spring Security features. The spring-security-config module is responsible for parsing the elements of the security namespace.
spring-security-taglibs	Defines tags that you can use to access security information and to secure the content displayed by JSP pages
spring-security-acl	Enables use of ACLs (Access Control List) to secure instances of domain objects in applications

In this section, we'll look at usage of spring-security-core, spring-security-web, spring-security-config and spring-security-taglibs modules to secure the MyBank web application. Later in this chapter, we'll look at how to use spring-security-acl module to secure domain object instances.

Let's begin by looking at how web request security is configured.

Web request security configuration

You can add web request security to an application by:

- configuring Spring's DelegatingFilterProxy filter in the web.xml file, and
- enabling web request security provided by the Spring Security framework

Let's first look at how to configure DelegatingFilterProxy filter.

DelegatingFilterProxy filter configuration

Spring Framework's *web* module (represented by spring-web-4.0.0.RELEASE.jar file) defines the DelegatingFilterProxy class that implements Servlet API's Filter interface. The following example listing shows the configuration of DelegatingFilterProxy filter in the web.xml file:

Example listing 14-1 – web.xml - DelegatingFilterProxy filter configuration
Project – ch14-bankapp-simple-security
Source location - src/main/webapp/WEB-INF

```
<filter>
   <filter-name>springSecurityFilterChain</filter-name>
   <filter-class>org.springframework.web.filter.DelegatingFilterProxy</filter-class>
</filter>

<filter-mapping>
   <filter-name>springSecurityFilterChain</filter-name>
   <url-pattern>/*</url-pattern>
</filter-mapping>
```

The <filter-mapping> element specifies that the DelegatingFilterProxy filter is mapped to all incoming web requests. The filter name specified by the <filter-name> element carries a special significance in the context of DelegatingFilterProxy filter. DelegatingFilterProxy filter delegates request processing to the Spring bean whose name matches the value of <filter-name> element. In the above example listing, web requests received by the DelegatingFilterProxy filter are delegated to the Spring bean named springSecurityFilterChain in the *root* application context. We'll soon see that the springSecurityFilterChain bean is created by the Spring Security framework.

Now, that we have configured the DelegatingFilterProxy filter, let's look at how to configure web request security.

Configuring web request security

The following example listing shows the application context file that uses <http> element of security schema to configure web request security:

Example listing 14-2 – applicationContext-security.xml – web security configuration
Project – ch14-bankapp-simple-security
Source location - src/main/resources/META-INF/spring

```
<beans:beans xmlns="http://www.springframework.org/schema/security"
  xmlns:beans="http://www.springframework.org/schema/beans"
  xsi:schemaLocation=".....
      http://www.springframework.org/schema/security
      http://www.springframework.org/schema/security/spring-security-3.2.xsd">

  <http use-expressions="true">
    <intercept-url pattern="/**" access="hasAnyRole('ROLE_CUSTOMER', 'ROLE_ADMIN')" />
    <form-login />
    <logout />
    <remember-me />
    <headers>
      <cache-control/>
      <xss-protection/>
    </headers>
  </http>
  .....
</beans:beans>
```

The above example listing shows that the spring-security-3.2.xsd schema is referenced by the application context XML file. The spring-security-3.2.xsd schema is contained in the org.springframework.security.config package of spring-security-config-3.2.0.RELEASE.jar file.

The <http> element contains the web request security configuration for the application. Spring Security framework parses the <http> element and registers a bean named springSecurityFilterChain with the Spring container. The springSecurityFilterChain bean is responsible for handling web request security. The DelegatingFilterProxy filter that we configured earlier (refer example listing 14-1) delegates web request handling to the springSecurityFilterChain bean. The springSecurityFilterChain bean represents an instance of FilterChainProxy bean (refer Spring Security docs for more information) that contains a chain of Servlet filters that are added to the chain by the sub-elements of <http> element.

The <intercept-url> element's access attribute specifies a Spring EL expression that evaluates to a boolean value. If the Spring EL expression returns true, the URLs matched by the pattern attribute are accessible to the user. If the Spring EL expression returns false, access is denied to the URLs matched by the pattern attribute. Spring Security framework provides a couple of built-in expressions, like hasRole, hasAnyRole, isAnonymous, and so on.

In example listing 14-2, the hasAnyRole('ROLE_CUSTOMER', 'ROLE_ADMIN') expression returns true if the authenticated user has ROLE_CUSTOMER or ROLE_ADMIN role. In MyBank web application, the ROLE_CUSTOMER role is assigned to a customer and the ROLE_ADMIN role is assigned to an administrator. As the pattern /* matches all URLs, the <intercept-url> element in example listing 14-2 specifies that only a user with role ROLE_CUSTOMER or ROLE_ADMIN can access the MyBank web application. You should note that the use of Spring EL expression in the access attribute is allowed only if you set the value of use-expressions attribute of <http> element to true.

The <form-login> element configures a login page that is used to authenticate users. You can use various attributes of <form-login> element, like login-page, default-target-url, and so on, to customize the login page. The login-page attribute specifies the URL that is used to render the login page. If the login-page attribute is not specified, a login page is automatically rendered at the /spring_security_login URL.

The <logout> element configures the logout processing feature of Spring Security framework. You can use various attributes of <logout> element, like logout-url, delete-cookies, invalidate-session, and so on, to configure the logout functionality. For instance, you can use the delete-cookies attribute to specify comma-separated names of cookies that should be deleted when the user logs out of the application. The logout-url attribute allows you to configure the URL that performs the logout processing. If you don't specify the logout-url attribute, the logout-url attribute value is set to /j_spring_security_logout by default.

The <remember-me> element configures the 'remember-me' authentication in which the web application remembers the identity of the authenticated user between sessions. When a user is successfully authenticated, Spring Security framework generates a unique token that can either be stored in a persistent store or sent to the user in a cookie. In example listing 14-2, <remember-me> element configures a cookie-based remember-me authentication service. When the user revisits the web application, the token is retrieved from the cookie and is automatically authenticated.

The <headers> element specifies the security headers that are added to the HTTP response by the Spring Security framework. For instance, in example listing 14-2, the <cache-control> element adds Cache-Control, Pragma and Expires response headers, and the <xss-protection> element adds X-XSS-Protection header.

When an unauthenticated user accesses the MyBank web application, Spring Security displays the login page (refer figure 14-1) configured by the <form-login> element to the user. Let's now look at how authentication is performed when the user enters his credentials and clicks the Login button.

Authentication configuration

When a user enters his credentials and submits the login page, Spring Security's AuthenticationManager is responsible for processing the authentication request. An AuthenticationManager is configured with one or more AuthenticationProviders against which the AuthenticationManager attempts to authenticate users. For instance, if you want to authenticate users against an LDAP server, you can configure an LdapAuthenticationProvider (an implementation of AuthenticationProvider) that authenticates users against an LDAP server.

The security schema simplifies configuration of AuthenticationManager and AuthenticationProvider objects, as shown in the following example listing:

Example listing 14-3 – applicationContext-security.xml
Project – ch14-bankapp-simple-security
Source location - src/main/resources/META-INF/spring

```
<authentication-manager>
  <authentication-provider>
    <user-service>
      <user name="admin" password="admin" authorities="ROLE_ADMIN" />
      <user name="cust1" password="cust1" authorities="ROLE_CUSTOMER" />
      <user name="cust2" password="cust2" authorities="ROLE_CUSTOMER" />
    </user-service>
  </authentication-provider>
</authentication-manager>
```

The <authentication-manager> element configures an AuthenticationManager instance. The <authentication-provider> element configures an AuthenticationProvider instance. By default, the <authentication-provider> element configures a DaoAuthenticationProvider (an implementation of AuthenticationProvider) that uses Spring's UserDetailsService as a DAO to load user details.

DaoAuthenticationProvider uses the configured UserDetailsService to load user details from the user repository based on the supplied username. DaoAuthenticationProvider performs authentication by comparing the login credentials supplied by the user with the user details loaded by the configured UserDetailsService. You should note that a UserDetailsService may load user details from a data source, a flat file or any other user repository.

The <user-service> sub-element of <authentication-provider> configures an *in-memory* UserDetailsService that loads users defined by the <user> elements. In example listing 14-3, the <user-service> element defines that the application has three users: admin (ROLE_ADMIN role), cust1 (ROLE_CUSTOMER role) and cust2 (ROLE_CUSTOMER role). The name attribute specifies the username assigned to the user, the password attribute specifies the password assigned to the user, and authorities attribute specifies the role(s) assigned to the user.

Now, if you deploy the ch14-bankapp-simple-security project and access it by going to the http://localhost:8080/ch14-bankapp-simple-security URL, the login page (refer figure 14-1) of the web application is displayed. If you authenticate by entering username as cust1 and password as cust1, the web application will display fixed deposits associated with cust1 (refer figure 14-2) user. Similarly, if you login with username as cust2 and password as cust2, the web application will display fixed deposits associated with cust2 user. If you login with username as admin and password as admin, the web application will display fixed deposits of both cust1 and cust2 users.

Let's now look at how to use Spring Security's JSP tag library to access security information and to apply security constraints on the content displayed by JSP pages.

Securing JSP content using Spring Security's JSP tab library

One of the requirements of MyBank web application is that the option to edit a fixed deposit (refer figure 14-2) is available only to users with role ROLE_CUSTOMER. And, the option to close a fixed deposit (refer figure 14-3) is available only to user with role ROLE_ADMIN. As we need to secure Edit and Close hyperlinks based on the authenticated user's role, the MyBank web application uses Spring Security's JSP tag library to secure JSP content.

The following example listing shows usage of Spring Security's JSP tag library to access authenticated user's username, and to secure JSP content based on the role of the logged in user:

Example listing 14-4 – fixedDepositList.jsp
Project – ch14-bankapp-simple-security
Source location - src/main/webapp/WEB-INF/jsp

```
<%@ taglib uri="http://www.springframework.org/security/tags" prefix="security"%>
.....
<body>
  .....
  <td style="font-family: 'arial'; font-size: 12px; font-weight: bold" align="right">
    <a href="${pageContext.request.contextPath}/j_spring_security_logout">Logout</a>
    <p>
      Username: <security:authentication property="principal.username" />
    </p>
  </td>
  .....
  <td class="td">
    <security:authorize access="hasRole('ROLE_CUSTOMER')">
      <a href="${pageContext.request.contextPath}/fixedDeposit?....." >Edit</a>
    </security:authorize>
    <security:authorize access="hasRole('ROLE_ADMIN')">
```

```
        <a href="${pageContext.request.contextPath}/fixedDeposit.....">Close</a>
    </security:authorize>
  </td>
</body>
</html>
```

The above example listing shows that the Logout hyperlink refers to ${pageContext.request.contextPath}/**j_spring_security_logout** URL. As mentioned earlier, if you don't specify the logout-url attribute of <logout> element, the logout-url value is set to /j_spring_security_logout. So, when a user clicks the Logout hyperlink, the user is logged out of the MyBank web application.

The above example listing also shows that the JSP page includes Spring Security's JSP tag library using the taglib directive. Spring Security's Authentication object contains information about the authenticated user. For instance, it contains information about authenticated user's role(s) and username that the user used for authentication. The <authentication> element prints the specified property of the Authentication object. In the above example, the principal.username property refers to the username property of the authenticated user.

The <authorize> element secures the enclosed JSP content based on the result of evaluation of the security expression specified by the access attribute. If the security expression evaluates to true, the enclosed content is rendered, otherwise the enclosed content is not rendered. In the above example listing, the hasRole('ROLE_CUSTOMER') expression returns true if the authenticated user has ROLE_CUSTOMER role, and the hasRole('ROLE_ADMIN') expression returns true if the authenticated user has ROLE_ADMIN role. In the above example listing, the hasRole expression has been used such that the Edit option is displayed only to a user with ROLE_CUSTOMER role and the Close option is displayed only to a user with ROLE_ADMIN role.

Let's now look at how to incorporate method-level security using Spring Security.

Securing methods

One of the requirements of MyBank application is that a user with ROLE_ADMIN role can view the 'Create new Fixed Deposit' button (refer figure 14-3) but an attempt to save details of the new fixed deposit will result in a security exception. This is an example in which we want to secure the FixedDepositService's saveFixedDeposit method such that only a user with ROLE_CUSTOMER role can invoke it.

We also want to secure other methods of the FixedDepositService so that it is not invoked by unauthorized users. For instance, cust1 user logged in with ROLE_CUSTOMER can invoke the FixedDepositService's closeFixedDeposit method to close an existing fixed deposit by entering the following URL in the browser:

```
http://localhost:8080/ch14-bankapp-simple-
```

```
security/fixedDeposit?fdAction=close&fixedDepositId=<fixed-fixed-id>
```

The <fixed-deposit-id> in the above URL is the fixed deposit id that you want to remove, as highlighted in the following figure:

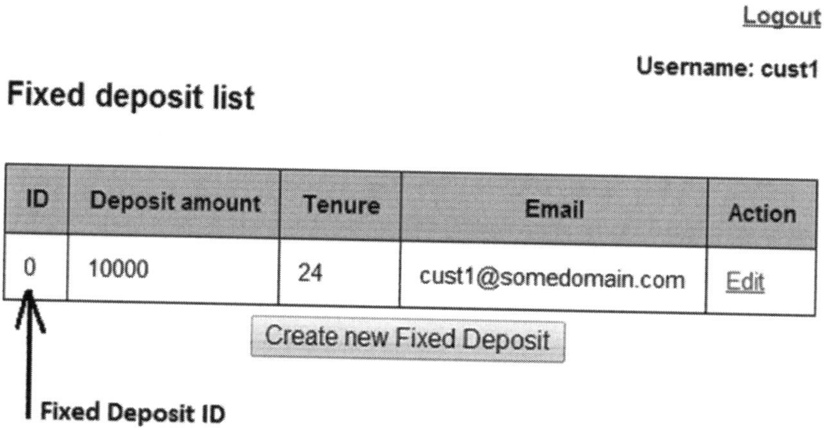

ID	Deposit amount	Tenure	Email	Action
0	10000	24	cust1@somedomain.com	Edit

Figure 14-4 – Fixed deposit ID of a fixed deposit is displayed in the ID column

To add method-level security to your application, you need to do the following:

- configure method-level security for your application by using <global-method-security> element of security schema
- add @Secured annotations to the methods that you want to secure against unauthorized access

Let's first look at the <global-method-security> element.

Configuring method-level security using <global-method-security> element

The following example listing shows usage of <global-method-security> element:

Example listing 14-5 – applicationContext-security.xml
Project – ch14-bankapp-simple-security
Source location - src/main/resources/META-INF/spring

```
<beans:beans xmlns="http://www.springframework.org/schema/security"
   .....>
   <global-method-security secured-annotations="enabled" />
</beans:beans>
```

The <global-method-security> element configures method-level security. The <global-method-security> element is applicable only to the application context in which it is defined. For instance, if the <global-method-security> element is defined in the *root* web application context XML file, then it is applicable only to the beans registered with the root WebApplicationContext instance. In ch14-bankapp-simple-security project, the applicationContext-security.xml (shown in the above example listing) and the applicationContext.xml (that defines services and DAOs) files constitute the root web application context XML files (refer web.xml file of ch14-bankapp-simple-security project); therefore, the <global-method-security> element applies only to the beans defined in these application context XML files.

The <global-method-security> element's secured-annotations attribute specifies whether the use of Spring's @Secured annotation should be enabled or disabled for the beans registered with the Spring container. As the value is set to enabled, you can use Spring's @Secured annotation to specify the bean methods that are secured.

> If you want to secure controller methods, then define the <global-method-security> element in the web application context XML file instead of the root web application context XML file.

Let's now look at how to secure methods using Spring's @Secured annotation.

Specifying security constraints on bean methods using @Secured annotation

The following example listing shows usage of Spring's @Secured annotation to define security constraints on methods:

Example listing 14-6 – FixedDepositService interface
Project – ch14-bankapp-simple-security
Source location - src/main/java/sample/spring/chapter14/service

```
package sample.spring.chapter14.service;

import org.springframework.security.access.annotation.Secured;
.....
public interface FixedDepositService {
    .....
    @Secured("ROLE_CUSTOMER")
    void saveFixedDeposit(FixedDepositDetails fixedDepositDetails);
    .....
    @Secured("ROLE_ADMIN")
    void closeFixedDeposit(int fixedDepositId);

    @Secured("ROLE_CUSTOMER")
    void editFixedDeposit(FixedDepositDetails fixedDepositDetails);
```

```
}
```

The above example listing shows the FixedDepositService interface that defines methods that operate on fixed deposits. @Secured("ROLE_CUSTOMER") annotation on the saveFixedDeposit and editFixedDeposit methods specifies that these methods can only be invoked by a user whose role is ROLE_CUSTOMER. @Secured("ROLE_ADMIN") annotation on the closeFixedDeposit method specifies that the method can only be invoked by a user whose role is ROLE_ADMIN.

> By default, method-level security is based on Spring AOP. If you want to use AspectJ instead of Spring AOP, set mode attribute of <global-method-security> element to aspectj. Also, add spring-security-aspects module to your project, and specify @Secured annotations on the class instead of the interface.

Instead of using @Secured annotation, you can use Spring's @PreAuthorize annotation to apply security constraints on methods. Unlike @Secured annotation, @PreAuthorize annotation accepts security expressions, like hasRole, hasAnyRole, and so on. To enable use of @PreAuthorize annotation, set pre-post-annotations attribute of <global-method-security> element to enabled. The following example listing shows usage of @PreAuthorize annotation:

Example listing 14-6 – @PreAuthorize annotation

```
import org.springframework.security.access.prepost.PreAuthorize;
.....
public interface SomeService {
   .....
  @PreAuthorize("hasRole('ROLE_XYZ')")
   void doSomething(.....);
   .....
}
```

In the above example listing, @PreAuthorize annotation specifies that the doSomething method is accessible only to users with role ROLE_XYZ.

Spring Security also supports security annotations, like @RolesAllowed, @DenyAll, @PermitAll, and so on, defined by JSR-250 - Common Annotations. To enable use of JSR-250 security annotations, set jsr250-annotations attribute of <global-method-security> to enabled. The following example listing shows usage of @RolesAllowed annotation:

Example listing 14-7 – @RolesAllowed annotation

```
import javax.annotation.security.RolesAllowed;
.....
public interface SomeService {
   .....
```

```
  @RolesAllowed("ROLE_XYZ")
  void doSomething(.....);
  .....
}
```

In the above example listing, @RolesAllowed annotation specifies that the doSomething method is accessible only to users with role ROLE_XYZ.

> We saw earlier in this book that JSR 250 annotations, like @PreDestroy, @PostConstruct, and so on, are part of Java SE 6 or later. As security related annotations of JSR 250 are not part of Java SE, you need to add jsr250-api JAR file to your project to use @RolesAllowed, @PermitAll, and so on, annotations.

In this section, we looked at how to use Spring Security to authenticate users, secure web requests and implement method-level security. Let's now look at Spring Security's ACL module for securing domain object instances.

IMPORT **chapter 14/ch14-bankapp-db-security** (This project represents the MyBank web application that uses Spring Security's ACL module for securing FixedDepositDetails instances.)

14-4 MyBank web application - securing FixedDepositDetails instances using Spring Security's ACL module

The ch14-bankapp-db-security project represents a variant of MyBank web application that uses Spring Security's ACL module to secure FixedDepositDetails instances.

Let's look at how to deploy and use ch14-bankapp-db-security project.

Deploying and using ch14-bankapp-db-security project

The ch14-bankapp-db-security project uses MySQL database to store application users, fixed deposit details and ACL information. Before deploying the ch14-bankapp-db-security project, create a database named securitydb in MySQL and execute the bankapp.sql script located in scripts folder of ch14-bankapp-db-security project.

The execution of bankapp.sql script creates the following tables: ACL_CLASS, ACL_ENTRY, ACL_OBJECT_IDENTITY, ACL_SID, FIXED_DEPOSIT_DETAILS, AUTHORITIES, and USERS. Tables whose names begin with ACL_ store ACL related information (more on these tables later in this chapter). FIXED_DEPOSIT_DETAILS table contains fixed deposit details. USERS and AUTHORITIES tables contain user and role information, respectively. The bankapp.sql script also inserts setup data into USERS, AUTHORITIES, ACL_CLASS and ACL_SID tables.

Now, that you have setup the database for ch14-bankapp-db-security project, deploy the project on embedded Tomcat 7 server by executing the tomcat7:run goal from the project's directory (refer appendix A for more information on how to deploy web projects on embedded Tomcat 7 server). Once the project is successfully deployed, go to http://localhost:8080/ch14-bankapp-db-security URL. You should see the login page, as shown below:

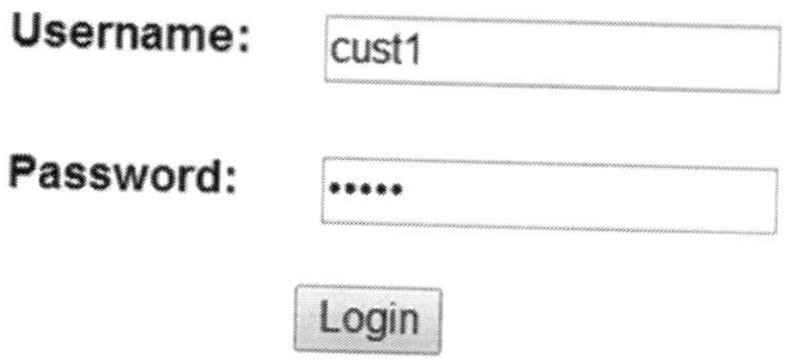

Figure 14-5 – Login page of MyBank web application

By default, the following three users are configured for the MyBank web application: cust1 (ROLE_CUSTOMER role), cust2 (ROLE_CUSTOMER role), and admin (ROLE_ADMIN role). When you login with username cust1 and password as cust1, you'll see the fixed deposits associated with cust1 customer, as shown in the following figure:

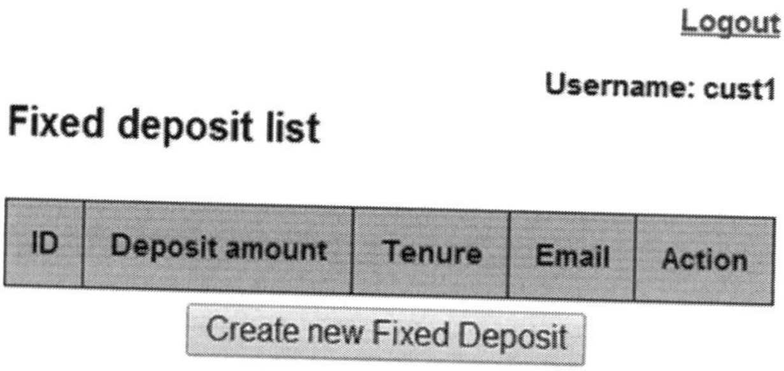

Figure 14-6 – List of fixed deposits associated with customer cust1

As no fixed deposits are currently associated with cust1, the above figure shows an empty list of fixed deposits. Clicking the *'Create new Fixed Deposit'* button opens the form for creating a new fixed deposit. If you create a new fixed deposit, it'll appear in the list of fixed deposits, as shown here:

Logout

Username: cust1

Fixed deposit list

ID	Deposit amount	Tenure	Email	Action	
14	1200	12	cust1@somedomain.com	Edit	Provide access to admin

Create new Fixed Deposit

Figure 14-7 – A customer can edit fixed deposits or make them accessible to the admin user.

In the above figure, the 'Edit' option allows the customer to edit fixed deposit details, and the 'Provide access to admin' option makes the fixed deposit accessible to the admin user. The admin user can only view fixed deposits that are made accessible by customers. Click the 'Provide access to admin' hyperlink to make the fixed deposit accessible to the admin user.

Now, logout from the MyBank web application, and login using admin username and admin as password. The admin user can view all the fixed deposits that were made accessible by customers, as shown here:

Logout

Username: admin

Fixed deposit list

ID	Customer	Deposit amount	Tenure	Email	Action
14	cust1	1200	12	cust1@somedomain.com	Close

Create new Fixed Deposit

Figure 14-8 – The admin user can close a fixed deposit by selecting the 'Close' option

The above figure shows that the admin user can choose the 'Close' option to close the fixed deposit. Closing a fixed deposit deletes the fixed deposit from the FIXED_DEPOSIT_DETAILS table.

To summarize, you can login using cust1/cust1, cust2/cust2 and admin/admin credentials to see the following features of the MyBank web application:

- only cust1 (ROLE_CUSTOMER role) and cust2 (ROLE_CUSTOMER role) users can create fixed deposits
- cust1 and cust2 can only edit fixed deposits that they own. For instance, cust1 can't edit a fixed deposit created by cust2.
- cust1 and cust2 can only make the fixed deposits that they own accessible to the admin user. For instance, cust1 can't make a fixed deposit created by cust2 accessible to the admin user.
- admin user (ROLE_ADMIN role) can only view fixed deposits that are made accessible by cust1 and cust2 users
- only the admin user can close fixed deposits

Before delving into the implementation details of MyBank web application, let's look at the standard database tables required by Spring Security to store ACL and user information.

Database tables to store ACL and user information

Spring Security's ACL module provides domain object instance security. MyBank web application uses Spring Security's ACL module to secure instances of FixedDepositDetails. Spring Security tables (ACL_CLASS, ACL_ENTRY, ACL_OBJECT_IDENTITY and ACL_SID) contain permissions that apply to fixed deposits stored in the FIXED_DEPOSIT_DETAILS table. When a FixedDepositDetails instance is accessed, Spring Security's ACL module verifies that the authenticated user has the necessary permissions to operate on the FixedDepositDetails instance.

Let's look at each of the Spring Security tables that are used to store ACL information.

ACL_CLASS table

ACL_CLASS table contains the fully-qualified name of domain classes whose instances we want to secure in our application. In case of MyBank web application, the ACL_CLASS table contains the fully-qualified name of the FixedDepositDetails class, as shown here:

id	class
1	sample.spring.chapter14.domain.FixedDepositDetails

Figure 14-9 ACL_CLASS table

Table column description

id – contains the primary key

class – fully-qualified name of the domain class whose instances we want to secure

ACL_SID table

ACL_SID table (SID means 'security identity') contains the principals (that is, usernames) or authorities (that is, roles) in the system. In case of MyBank web application, ACL_SID table contains admin, cust1 and cust2 usernames, as shown here:

id	principal	sid
1	true	cust1
2	true	cust2
3	true	admin

Figure 14-10 ACL_SID table

Table column description

id – contains the primary key

principal – specifies whether the sid column stores role or username. The value true specifies that the sid column stores username. The value false specifies that the sid column stores role.

sid – contains username or role

ACL_OBJECT_IDENTITY table

ACL_OBJECT_IDENTITY table contains identities of domain objects that we want to secure. In case of MyBank web application, the ACL_OBJECT_IDENTITY table contains identities of fixed deposits stored in FIXED_DEPOSIT_DETAILS table, as shown here:

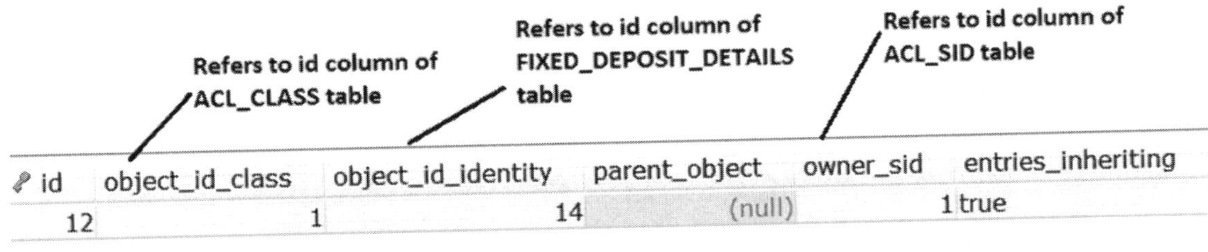

id	object_id_class	object_id_identity	parent_object	owner_sid	entries_inheriting
12	1	14	(null)	1	true

Figure 14-11 ACL_OBJECT_IDENTITY table

In the above figure, the object_id_identity column contains identities of fixed deposits stored in the FIXED_DEPOSIT_DETAILS table.

Table column description

id – contains the primary key

object_id_class – refers to the domain class defined in the *ACL_CLASS* table

object_id_identity – refers to the domain object instance in the FIXED_DEPOSIT_DETAILS table

parent_object – if a parent object exists for the domain object referenced by the object_id_identity column, this column refers to the identity of the parent object

owner_sid – refers to the user or role that owns the domain object instance

entries_inheriting – flag that indicates whether the object inherits ACL entries from any parent ACL entry or not

ACL_ENTRY table

ACL_ENTRY table contains permissions (read, write, create, and so on) assigned to users on domain objects. In case of MyBank web application, the *ACL_ENTRY* table contains permissions assigned to users on fixed deposits stored in FIXED_DEPOSIT_DETAILS table, as shown here:

id	acl_object_identity	ace_order	sid	mask	granting	audit_success	audit_failure
768	12	0	1	1	true	false	false
769	12	1	1	2	true	false	false
770	12	2	3	1	true	false	false
771	12	3	3	16	true	false	false
772	12	4	3	8	true	false	false

Figure 14-12 ACL_ENTRY table

In the above figure, the *acl_object_identity*, *mask* and *sid* columns determine the permissions assigned to a user (or role) on a domain object instance. You should note that an entry in the *ACL_ENTRY* table is commonly referred to as ACE (Access Control Entry).

Table column description

id – contains the primary key

acl_object_identity – refers to the id column of the *ACL_OBJECT_IDENTITY* table, which in turn identifies the domain object instance

ace_order – specifies the ordering of the access control entries

sid – refers to the id column of ACL_SID table, which in turn identifies the user (or role)

mask – specifies the permissions (read, write, create, and so on) assigned to the user (or role). 1 means read, 2 means write, 8 means delete and 16 means administration permission.

granting – flag that indicates whether the entry in the mask column identifies as granting access or denying access. For instance, if the value in the mask column is 1 and granting column is true, it means that the corresponding SID has read access. But, if the value in the mask column is 1 and granting column is false, it means that the corresponding SID *doesn't* have read access.

audit_success – flag that indicates whether to audit successful permissions or not. Later in this chapter, we'll see that Spring Security's ConsoleAuditLogger can be used to log successful permissions.

audit_failure - flag that indicates whether to audit failed permissions or not. Later in this chapter, we'll see that Spring Security's ConsoleAuditLogger can be used to log failed permissions.

As explained so far, the diagram 14-13 depicts relationship between ACL tables. The arrows in the figure represent foreign key references from a table. For instance, the ACL_OBJECT_IDENTITY table contains foreign keys that refer to ACL_CLASS, ACL_SID and FIXED_DEPOSIT_DETAILS tables.

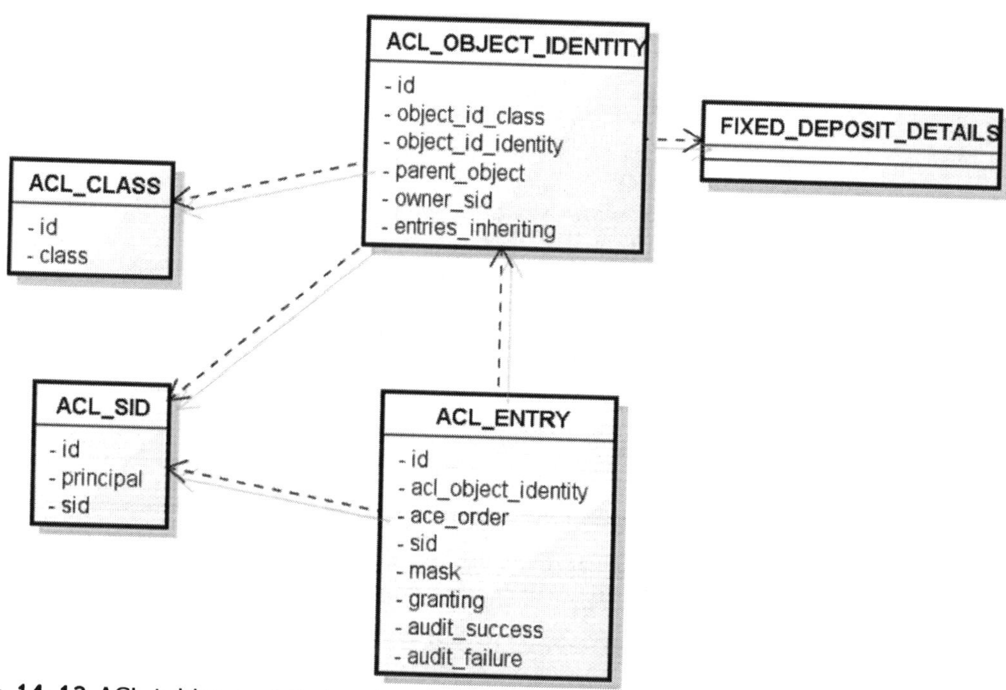

Figure 14-13 ACL tables and their relationships. The arrows represent foreign key references from a table.

Now, that we have seen the ACL tables required to store ACL information, let's now look at the Spring Security tables that store users and their roles information.

USERS table

USERS table stores credentials of users, as shown here:

username	password	enabled
admin	admin	true
cust1	cust1	true
cust2	cust2	true

Figure 14-14 USERS table

Table column description

username – username of the user

password – password of the user

enabled – flag that indicates whether the user is enabled or disabled

AUTHORITIES table

AUTHORITIES table contains the role assigned to each user defined in the USERS table

Table column description

username – username of the user

authority – role assigned to the user

username	authority
admin	ROLE_ADMIN
cust1	ROLE_CUSTOMER
cust2	ROLE_CUSTOMER

Figure 14-15 AUTHORITIES table

Let's now look at how the users are authenticated in MyBank web application.

User authentication

MyBank web application explicitly configures the UserDetailsService to load user details from the USERS and AUTHORITIES database tables, as shown in the following example listing:

Example listing 14-8 – applicationContext-security.xml
Project – ch14-bankapp-db-security
Source location - src/main/resources/META-INF/spring

```
<authentication-manager>
   <authentication-provider user-service-ref="userDetailsService" />
</authentication-manager>

<beans:bean id="userDetailsService"
   class="org.springframework.security.core.userdetails.jdbc.JdbcDaoImpl">
   <beans:property name="dataSource" ref="dataSource" />
</beans:bean>
```

In the above example listing, the user-service-ref attribute of <authentication-provider> element refers to an implementation of UserDetailsService that is responsible for loading user (and their authorities) details based on the supplied username. JdbcDaoImpl is an implementation of UserDetailsService that loads user (and their authorities) details from the data source (specified by the dataSource property) using JDBC queries. Refer to the applicationContext.xml file of ch14-bankapp-db-security project to view the dataSource bean definition. By default, JdbcDaoImpl loads user details from the USERS (refer figure 14-14) table and authorities information from the AUTHORITIES (refer figure 14-15) table. If you already have custom database tables that contain user and authorities details, then set the usersByUsernameQuery and authoritiesByUsernameQuery properties of JdbcDaoImpl to retrieve user details and their authorities from these custom tables.

The usersByUsernameQuery property specifies the SQL query to retrieve user details based on the given username. If user details are stored in a table named MY_USERS that contains USERNAME and PASSWORD columns, you can set the following SQL query as the value of usersByUsernameQuery property to retrieve user details:

```
select USERNAME, PASSWORD, 'true' as ENABLED from MY_USERS where USERNAME = ?
```

You should note that the columns returned by the SQL query must be USERNAME, PASSWORD and ENABLED. If a particular column (like, ENABLED) doesn't exist in your database table, then return a default value (like, 'true') for that column.

The authoritiesByUsernameQuery property specifies the SQL query to retrieve authorities based on the given username. If authority details are stored in a table named MY_ AUTHORITIES that contains USER and ROLE columns, you can set the following SQL query as the value of authoritiesByUsernameQuery property to retrieve authorities:

```
select USER AS USERNAME, ROLE AS AUTHORITY from MY_AUTHORITIES where USER = ?
```

You should note that the columns returned by the SQL query must be USERNAME and AUTHORITY.

If your application stores encoded passwords in the database, you can use the <password-encoder> sub-element of <authentication-provider> element to specify the password encoder (an implementation of Spring's PasswordEncoder interface) to be used to convert the submitted passwords into their encoded form. BCryptPasswordEncoder is a concrete implementation of PasswordEncoder that uses BCrypt hashing algorithm (http://en.wikipedia.org/wiki/Bcrypt). The DaoAuthenticationProvider uses the configured password encoder to encode the submitted password and compare it with the password loaded by the UserDetailsService.

Let's now look at the web request security configuration in the MyBank web application.

Web request security

The following example listing shows how web request security is configured for the MyBank web application:

Example listing 14-9 – applicationContext-security.xml – web security configuration
Project – ch14-bankapp-db-security
Source location - src/main/resources/META-INF/spring

```
<http use-expressions="true">
   <access-denied-handler error-page="/access-denied" />
   <intercept-url pattern="/fixedDeposit/*"
      access="hasAnyRole('ROLE_CUSTOMER', 'ROLE_ADMIN')" />
   <form-login login-page="/login" authentication-failure-handler-ref="authFailureHandler" />
   <logout />
   ....
</http>

<beans:bean id="authFailureHandler"
   class="sample.spring.chapter14.security.MyAuthFailureHandler" />
```

If you compare the web request security configuration shown above with the one we saw in ch14-bankapp-simple-security project (refer example listing 14-2), you'll notice that we have added some additional configuration information.

The <access-denied-handler> element's error-page attribute specifies the error page (refer to scr/main/webapp/WEB-INF/jsp/access-denied.jsp page) to which an authenticated user is redirected in case the user attempts to access an unauthorized web page. The <form-login> element's login-page attribute specifies the URL that renders the login page. The value /login URL is mapped to LoginController (refer to LoginController class of ch14-bankapp-db-security project) that renders the login page (refer to scr/main/webapp/WEB-INF/jsp/login.jsp page). The authentication-failure-handler-ref attribute refers to an AuthenticationFailureHandler bean that handles authentication failures. As the above example listing shows, MyAuthFailureHandler (an implementation of AuthenticationFailureHandler) is responsible for handling authentication failures in MyBank web application. The following example listing shows the implementation of MyAuthFailureHandler class:

Example listing 14-10 – MyAuthFailureHandler class
Project – ch14-bankapp-db-security
Source location - src/main/java/sample/spring/chatper14/security

```
package sample.spring.chapter14.security;
.....
import org.springframework.security.core.AuthenticationException;
import org.springframework.security.web.authentication.AuthenticationFailureHandler;

public class MyAuthFailureHandler implements AuthenticationFailureHandler {
```

```
  @Override
  public void onAuthenticationFailure(HttpServletRequest request,
       HttpServletResponse response, AuthenticationException exception)
       throws IOException, ServletException {
    request.setAttribute("exceptionMsg", exception.getMessage());
    response.sendRedirect(request.getContextPath() + "/login?exceptionMsg=" +
       exception.getMessage());
  }
}
```

AuthenticationFailureHandler interface defines an onAuthenticationFailure method which is invoked when authentication fails. The onAuthenticationFailure method accepts an instance of AuthenticationException that represents an authentication failure. In the above example listing, the onAuthenticationFailure method redirects the user to the login page and passes the exception message as a query string parameter. If you enter wrong credentials (or enter credentials of a user who is disabled in the system) on the login page of MyBank web application, you'll notice that the MyAuthFailureHandler's onAuthenticationFailure method is invoked. For instance, if you enter wrong credentials, you'll see the message 'Bad credentials'.

Let's now look at ACL-specific configuration in MyBank web application.

JdbcMutableAclService configuration

As ACL permissions are stored in database tables, the MyBank web application uses Spring's JdbcMutableAclService to perform CRUD (**C**reate **R**ead **U**pdate **D**elete) operations on ACLs in the tables. The following example listing shows the configuration of JdbcMutableAclService:

Example listing 14-11 – applicationContext-security.xml - JdbcMutableAclService configuration
Project – ch14-bankapp-db-security
Source location - src/main/resources/META-INF/spring

```
<beans:bean id="aclService" class="org.springframework.security.acls.jdbc.JdbcMutableAclService">
  <beans:constructor-arg ref="dataSource" />
  <beans:constructor-arg ref="lookupStrategy" />
  <beans:constructor-arg ref="aclCache" />
</beans:bean>
```

The above example listing shows references to dataSource, lookupStrategy and aclCache beans are passed to the JdbcMutableAclService's constructor. Let's now look at how dependencies (dataSource, lookupStrategy and aclCache) of JdbcMutableAclService are configured.

The dataSource bean identifies the javax.sql.DataSource that holds the ACL tables (refer to the dataSource bean definition in the applicationContext.xml file for more details).

The lookupStrategy bean represents an implementation of Spring's LookupStrategy interface that is responsible for looking up ACL information. The following example listing shows the lookupStrategy bean definition:

Example listing 14-12 – applicationContext-security.xml - LookupStrategy configuration
Project – ch14-bankapp-db-security
Source location - src/main/resources/META-INF/spring

```
<beans:bean id="lookupStrategy"
  class="org.springframework.security.acls.jdbc.BasicLookupStrategy">

  <beans:constructor-arg ref="dataSource" />
  <beans:constructor-arg ref="aclCache" />

  <beans:constructor-arg>
    <beans:bean class="org.springframework.security.acls.domain.AclAuthorizationStrategyImpl">
      <beans:constructor-arg>
        <beans:bean
          class="org.springframework.security.core.authority.SimpleGrantedAuthority">
          <beans:constructor-arg value="ROLE_ADMIN" />
        </beans:bean>
      </beans:constructor-arg>
    </beans:bean>
  </beans:constructor-arg>

  <beans:constructor-arg>
    <beans:bean
      class="org.springframework.security.acls.domain.DefaultPermissionGrantingStrategy">
      <beans:constructor-arg>
        <beans:bean class="org.springframework.security.acls.domain.ConsoleAuditLogger" />
      </beans:constructor-arg>
    </beans:bean>
  </beans:constructor-arg>
</beans:bean>
```

In the above example listing, Spring's BasicLookupStrategy (an implementation of LookupStrategy interface) uses JDBC queries to fetch ACL details from standard ACL tables (ACL_CLASS, ACL_ENTRY, ACL_SID and ACL_OBJECT_IDENTITY). If the ACL information is stored in custom database tables, then you can customize the JDBC queries by setting selectClause, lookupPrimaryKeysWhereClause, lookupObjectIdentitiesWhereClause and orderByClause properties of BasicLookupStrategy. For more details on these properties, please refer to the API documentation of Spring Security.

BasicLookupStrategy's constructor accepts arguments of type DataSource (represents the database that contains the ACL tables), AclCache (represents the ACL caching layer), AclAuthorizationStrategy (represents the strategy to determine if a SID has the permissions to perform administrative actions on the ACL entries of a domain object instance), and PermissionGrantingStrategy (strategy to grant or deny access to secured objects depending on the permissions assigned to SIDs).

In the above example listing, the AclAuthorizationStrategyImpl class implements AclAuthorizationStrategy. The AclAuthorizationStrategyImpl's constructor accepts an instance of GrantedAuthority that specifies the role that can perform administrative actions (like, changing ownership of an ACL entry) on the ACL entries (represented by an object of type MutableAcl) of a domain object instance. In the above example listing, ROLE_ADMIN role is passed to the AclAuthorizationStrategyImpl, which means that a user with ROLE_ADMIN role can perform administrative actions on ACL entries. Later in this chapter, we'll see that the AclAuthorizationStrategy secures the MutableAcl instance from unauthorized modification.

In the above example listing, the DefaultPermissionGrantingStrategy implements PermissionGrantingStrategy. The DefaultPermissionGrantingStrategy's constructor accepts an instance of AuditLogger that logs success and/or failure in granting permissions for an ACL entry in the ACL_ENTRY table. In the above example listing, the ConsoleAuditLogger (an implementation of AuditLogger that writes on the console) logs successful permissions if audit_success column's value is set to true (that is, 1), and logs failed permissions if audit_failure column's value is set to true (that is, 1). For instance, the following message shows output from the ConsoleAuditLogger on successful permission to an ACL entry:

```
GRANTED due to ACE: AccessControlEntryImpl[id: 1037; granting: true; sid: PrincipalSid[cust1];
permission: BasePermission[..............................R=1]; auditSuccess: true; auditFailure: true]
```

BasicLookupStrategy accepts an instance of AclCache object (represented by the aclCache bean in example listing 14-12) that represents a cache for ACLs. The following example listing shows the aclCache bean definition that is used by BasicLookupStrategy to cache ACLs:

Example listing 14-13 – applicationContext-security.xml - Cache configuration
Project – ch14-bankapp-db-security
Source location - src/main/resources/META-INF/spring

```
<beans:bean id="aclCache" class="org.springframework.security.acls.domain.EhCacheBasedAclCache">
  <beans:constructor-arg>
    <beans:bean class="org.springframework.cache.ehcache.EhCacheFactoryBean">
      <beans:property name="cacheManager">
          <beans:bean class="org.springframework.cache.ehcache.EhCacheManagerFactoryBean" />
      </beans:property>
      <beans:property name="cacheName" value="aclCache" />
    </beans:bean>
```

```
  </beans:constructor-arg>
</beans:bean>
```

EhCacheBasedAclCache is an implementation of AclCache that uses EhCache (http://ehcache.org/) for caching ACLs. EhCacheFactoryBean is Spring FactoryBean that creates an instance of net.sf.ehcache.EhCache. The cacheManager property of EhCacheFactoryBean specifies the net.sf.ehcache.CacheManager instance that is responsible for managing the cache. In the above example listing, EhCacheManagerFactoryBean is a Spring FactoryBean that creates an instance of net.sf.ehcache.CacheManager. The EhCacheFactoryBean's cacheName property refers to the cache region to be created in EhCache for storing ACLs.

Now, that we have configured JdbcMutableAclService to perform CRUD operations on ACLs, let's look at the method-level security configuration that uses ACLs loaded by JdbcMutableAclService for authorization purposes.

Method-level security configuration

The following example listing shows method-level security configuration in the MyBank web application:

Example listing 14-14 – applicationContext-security.xml - Method-level security configuration
Project – ch14-bankapp-db-security
Source location - src/main/resources/META-INF/spring

```
<global-method-security pre-post-annotations="enabled">
   <expression-handler ref="expressionHandler" />
</global-method-security>
```

The <global-method-security> element's pre-post-annotations attribute value is set to enabled, which enables use of @PreAuthorize (explained earlier in this chapter), @PostAuthorize, @PostFilter and @PostAuthorize annotations. In the above example listing, the <expression-handler> element refers to the expressionHandler bean that configures a SecurityExpressionHandler instance.

A SecurityExpressionHandler is used by Spring Security to evaluate security expressions, like hasRole, hasAnyRole, hasPermission, and so on. The following example listing shows the expressionHandler bean definition that configures a DefaultMethodSecurityExpressionHandler (a SecurityExpressionHandler implementation) instance:

Example listing 14-15 – applicationContext-security.xml - SecurityExpressionHandler configuration
Project – ch14-bankapp-db-security
Source location - src/main/resources/META-INF/spring

```
<beans:bean id="expressionHandler" class="org.springframework.security.access.expression.method.
          DefaultMethodSecurityExpressionHandler">
```

```
  <beans:property name="permissionEvaluator" ref="permissionEvaluator" />
  <beans:property name="permissionCacheOptimizer">
    <beans:bean class="org.springframework.security.acls.AclPermissionCacheOptimizer">
      <beans:constructor-arg ref="aclService" />
    </beans:bean>
  </beans:property>
</beans:bean>

<beans:bean id="permissionEvaluator"
      class="org.springframework.security.acls.AclPermissionEvaluator">
  <beans:constructor-arg ref="aclService" />
</beans:bean>
```

In the above example listing, the permissionEvaluator property refers to an instance of AclPermissionEvaluator instance that uses ACLs to evaluate security expressions. The permissionCacheOptimzer property refers to an instance of AclPermissionCacheOptimizer that loads ACLs in batches to optimize performance.

Let's now look at how domain object instance security is achieved in the MyBank web application.

Domain object instance security

We saw earlier that the @PreAuthorize annotation specifies role-based security constraints on the methods. If a @PreAuthorize annotated method accepts a domain object instance as an argument, the @PreAuthorize annotation can specify the ACL permissions that the authenticated user must have on the domain object instance to invoke the method. The following example listing shows the @PreAuthorize annotation that specifies ACL permissions:

Example listing 14-16 – FixedDepositService interface – @PreAuthorize annotation with ACL permissions
Project – ch14-bankapp-db-security
Source location - src/main/java/sample/spring/chatper14/service

```
package sample.spring.chapter14.service;

import org.springframework.security.access.prepost.PreAuthorize;
import sample.spring.chapter14.domain.FixedDepositDetails;
.....
public interface FixedDepositService {
  .....
  @PreAuthorize("hasPermission(#fixedDepositDetails, write)")
  void editFixedDeposit(FixedDepositDetails fixedDepositDetails);
}
```

In the above example listing, the FixedDepositService's editFixedDeposit method accepts an instance of FixedDepositDetails. In the hasPermission expression, #fixedDepositDetails represents an expression variable that refers to the FixedDepositDetails instance passed to the editFixedDeposit method. The hasPermission expression evaluates to true if the authenticated user has write permission on the FixedDepositDetails instance passed to the editFixedDeposit method. At runtime, the hasPermission expression is evaluated by the configured AclPermissionEvaluator (refer example listing 14-15). If the hasPermission evaluates to true, the editFixedDeposit method is invoked.

If a method accepts a domain object *identifier* (instead of the actual domain object instance) as an argument, you can still specify ACL permissions that apply to the domain object instance referred by the identifier. The following example listing shows the provideAccessToAdmin method that accepts fixedDepositId (which uniquely identifies a FixedDepositDetails instance) as argument:

Example listing 14-17 – FixedDepositService interface – @PreAuthorize annotation usage
Project – ch14-bankapp-db-security
Source location - src/main/java/sample/spring/chatper14/service

```
package sample.spring.chapter14.service;

import org.springframework.security.access.prepost.PreAuthorize;
.....
public interface FixedDepositService {
    .....
    @PreAuthorize("hasPermission(#fixedDepositId,
            'sample.spring.chapter14.domain.FixedDepositDetails', write)")
    void provideAccessToAdmin(int fixedDepositId);
}
```

In the above example listing, #fixedDepositId expression variable refers to the fixedDepositId argument passed to the provideAccessToAdmin method. As the fixedDepositId argument identifies an instance of FixedDepositDetails object, the fully-qualified name of the FixedDepositDetails class is specified as the second argument of hasPermission expression. The hasPermission(#fixedDepositId, 'sample.spring.chapter14.domain.FixedDepositDetails', write) evaluates to true if the authenticated user has write permission on the FixedDepositDetails instance identified by the fixedDepositId argument passed to the provideAccessToAdmin method.

It is also possible to combine multiple security expressions to form a more complex security expression, as shown in the following example listing:

Example listing 14-18 – FixedDepositService interface – @PreAuthorize annotation usage
Project – ch14-bankapp-db-security
Source location - src/main/java/sample/spring/chatper14/service

```
package sample.spring.chapter14.service;

import org.springframework.security.access.prepost.PreAuthorize;
.....
public interface FixedDepositService {
   .....
   @PreAuthorize("hasPermission(#fixedDepositId,
        'sample.spring.chapter14.domain.FixedDepositDetails', read) or "
        + "hasPermission(#fixedDepositId,
        'sample.spring.chapter14.domain.FixedDepositDetails', admin)")
   FixedDepositDetails getFixedDeposit(int fixedDepositId);
   .....
}
```

In the above example listing, the two hasPermission expressions have been combined using or operator to form a more sophisticated security expression. The getFixedDeposit method will be invoked only if the authenticated user has read or admin permission on the FixedDepositDetails instance identified by the fixedDepositId argument.

If a method returns a list of domain object instances, you can filter the results by using @PostFilter annotation. The following example listing shows usage of @PostFilter annotation:

Example listing 14-19 – FixedDepositService interface – @PostFilter annotation usage
Project – ch14-bankapp-db-security
Source location - src/main/java/sample/spring/chatper14/service

```
package sample.spring.chapter14.service;

import org.springframework.security.access.prepost.PostFilter;
.....
public interface FixedDepositService {
   .....
   @PreAuthorize("hasRole('ROLE_ADMIN')")
   @PostFilter("hasPermission(filterObject, read) or hasPermission(filterObject, admin)")
   List<FixedDepositDetails> getAllFixedDeposits();
   .....
}
```

Like @PreAuthorize annotation, @PostFilter specifies a security expression. If a method is annotated with @PostFilter annotation, Spring Security iterates over the collection returned by the method and removes the elements for which the specified security expression returns false. In the above example listing, Spring Security iterates over the collection of FixedDepositDetails instances returned by the getAllFixedDeposits method and removes the instances for which the authenticated user doesn't have read or admin permission. The term filterObject in the hasPermission expression of @PostFilter annotation refers to the current object in the collection. Notice that the getAllFixedDeposits method is also annotated with @PreAuthorize annotation, which indicates that the getAllFixedDeposits method is only invoked if the authenticated user has ROLE_ADMIN role.

We saw earlier that a customer (ROLE_CUSTOMER role) makes a fixed deposit available to the admin user (ROLE_ADMIN role) by clicking the 'Provide access to admin' hyperlink (refer figure 14-7). When the customer clicks the 'Provide access to admin', application grants read, admin and delete permissions on the fixed deposit to the admin user. We'll see later in this chapter how this is done programmatically. The FixedDepositService's getAllFixedDeposits method is invoked when a user with ROLE_ADMIN role visits the web page that shows lists of fixed deposits (refer figure 14-8). As the admin user should only be able to see fixed deposits for which customers have granted permissions, the getAllFixedDeposits method is annotated with @PostFilter annotation to remove fixed deposits on which the admin user doesn't have read or admin permission.

Let's now look at how to programmatically manage ACL entries.

Managing ACL entries programmatically

You can manage ACL entries programmatically by using the JdbcMutableAclService that was configured in the application context XML file (refer example listing 14-11).

When a customer creates a new fixed deposit, read and write permissions on the newly created fixed deposit are granted to the customer. When a customer clicks the 'Provide access to admin' hyperlink corresponding to a fixed deposit, the MyBank web application grants read, admin and delete permissions on the fixed deposit to the admin user.

The following example listing shows the FixedDepositServiceImpl's provideAccessToAdmin method that is invoked when the 'Provide access to admin' hyperlink is clicked:

Example listing 14-20 – FixedDepositServiceImpl class – adding ACL permissions
Project – ch14-bankapp-db-security
Source location - src/main/java/sample/spring/chatper14/service

```
package sample.spring.chapter14.service;

import org.springframework.security.acls.domain.*;
import org.springframework.security.acls.model.*;
.....
@Service
```

```
public class FixedDepositServiceImpl implements FixedDepositService {
  .....
  @Autowired
  private MutableAclService mutableAclService;

  @Override
  public void provideAccessToAdmin(int fixedDepositId) {
    addPermission(fixedDepositId, new PrincipalSid("admin"), BasePermission.READ);
    addPermission(fixedDepositId, new PrincipalSid("admin"), BasePermission.ADMINISTRATION);
    addPermission(fixedDepositId, new PrincipalSid("admin"), BasePermission.DELETE);
  }

  private void addPermission(long fixedDepositId, Sid recipient, Permission permission) { ..... }
}
```

In the above example listing, the provideAccessToAdmin method uses the addPermission method to grant read, admin and delete permissions to the admin user. The following arguments are passed to the addPermission method:

- fixedDepositId – uniquely identifies the FixedDepositDetails instance on whom we want to grant permissions
- PrincipalSid object - represents the SID (that is, the user or role) whom we want to grant permissions. The PrincipalSid class implements Spring Security's Sid interface.
- permission to grant – The BasePermission class defines constants, like READ, ADMINISTRATION, DELETE, and so on, representing standard permissions that we can grant to PrincipalSid. The BasePermission class implements Spring Security's Permission interface.

The following example listing shows the implementation of addPermission method:

Example listing 14-21 – FixedDepositServiceImpl class – adding ACL permissions
Project – ch14-bankapp-db-security
Source location - src/main/java/sample/spring/chatper14/service

```
package sample.spring.chapter14.service;

import org.springframework.security.acls.domain.*;
import org.springframework.security.acls.model.*;
.....
@Service
public class FixedDepositServiceImpl implements FixedDepositService {
  .....
```

```
@Autowired
private MutableAclService mutableAclService;
.....
private void addPermission(long fixedDepositId, Sid recipient, Permission permission) {
    MutableAcl acl;
    ObjectIdentity oid = new ObjectIdentityImpl(FixedDepositDetails.class, fixedDepositId);

    try {
        acl = (MutableAcl) mutableAclService.readAclById(oid);
    } catch (NotFoundException nfe) {
        acl = mutableAclService.createAcl(oid);
    }
    acl.insertAce(acl.getEntries().size(), permission, recipient, true);
    mutableAclService.updateAcl(acl);
  }
  .....
}
```

As JdbcMutableAclService class implements MutableAclService interface, JdbcMutableAclService instance is autowired into the FixedDepositServiceImpl class.

To grant permissions, the addPermission method follows these steps:

1) declares an object of type MutableAcl. A MutableAcl object represents ACL entries of a domain object instance. MutableAcl defines methods that you can use to modify ACL entries.

2) creates an instance of ObjectIdentityImpl by passing domain object type (which is FixedDepositDetails.class) and identity (which is fixedDepositId) as arguments to the constructor

3) retrieves the ACL entries for the domain object instance by calling MutableAclService's readAclById method. If no ACL entries are found, the readAclById method throws NotFoundException.

    - If NotFoundException is thrown, MutableAclService's createAcl method is used to create an empty instance of MutableAcl that doesn't contain any ACL entries. This is equivalent to creating an entry in the ACL_OBJECT_IDENTITY table (refer figure 14-11).

4) adds ACL entries to the MutableAcl instance using insertAce method. The ACL entries added to MutableAcl are eventually persisted into the ACL_ENTRY table (refer figure 14-12). The arguments passed to the insertAce method are - the index location where the ACL entry is to be added (corresponds to the ACE_ORDER column), the permission to be

added (corresponds to the MASK column), the SID for whom the permission is to be added (corresponds to the SID column), and the flag indicating that the ACL entry is for granting or denying permission (corresponds to the GRANTING column).

5) persists changes made to the MutableAcl instance using MutableAclService's updateAcl method.

The following example listing shows FixedDepositServiceImpl's closeFixedDeposit method that is invoked when the admin user clicks the 'Close' hyperlink to close a fixed deposit (refer figure 14-8):

Example listing 14-22 – FixedDepositServiceImpl class – removing ACLs
Project – ch14-bankapp-db-security
Source location - src/main/java/sample/spring/chatper14/service

```
package sample.spring.chapter14.service;

import org.springframework.security.acls.domain.ObjectIdentityImpl;
import org.springframework.security.acls.model.MutableAclService;
import org.springframework.security.acls.model.ObjectIdentity;
.....
@Service
public class FixedDepositServiceImpl implements FixedDepositService {
  .....
  @Autowired
  private MutableAclService mutableAclService;
  .....
  @Override
  public void closeFixedDeposit(int fixedDepositId) {
    fixedDepositDao.closeFixedDeposit(fixedDepositId);
    ObjectIdentity oid = new ObjectIdentityImpl(FixedDepositDetails.class, fixedDepositId);
    mutableAclService.deleteAcl(oid, false);
  }
  .....
}
```

In the above example listing, MutableAclService's deleteAcl method is used to delete ACL entries of the fixed deposit identified by the ObjectIdentity instance. For instance, if the fixedDepositId is 101, deleteAcl method deletes all ACL entries of fixed deposit 101 from ACL_ENTRY (refer figure 14-12) and ACL_OBJECT_IDENTITY (refer figure 14-11) tables.

Let's now look at how MutableAcl instance is secured from unauthorized modifications.

MutableAcl and security

Spring Security's MutableAcl interface defines methods for modifying ACL entries of a domain object instance. We saw that the MyBank web application uses MutableAcl's insertAce method to add an ACL entry for a domain object instance (refer example listing 14-21). The AclAuthorizationStrategyImpl instance that we supplied to the BasicLookupStrategy (refer example listing 14-12) is used behind the scenes to ensure that the authenticated user has appropriate permissions to modify ACL entries.

An authenticated user can modify ACL entries of a domain object instance if at least one of the following conditions is true:

- if the authenticated user owns the domain object instance, the user can modify the ACL entries of that domain object instance
- if the authenticated user holds the authority that was passed to AclAuthorizationStrategyImpl's constructor. In example listing 14-12, the ROLE_ADMIN role was passed to AclAuthorizationStrategyImpl's constructor; therefore, a user with ROLE_ADMIN role can make changes to ACL entries of any domain object instance.
- if the authenticated user has BasePermission's ADMINISTRATION permission on the domain object instance.

14-5 Summary

In this chapter, we looked at how to use Spring Security framework to secure Spring applications. We looked at how to incorporate web request security, method-level security, and domain object instance security.

Appendix A – *Importing and deploying sample projects in Eclipse IDE (or IntelliJ IDEA)*

In this appendix, we'll look at how to setup the development environment, import a sample project into Eclipse IDE (or IntelliJ IDEA), and run it as a standalone application (if the sample project represents a standalone Java application) or deploy it on Tomcat 7 server (if the sample project represents a web application).

A-1 Setting up the development environment

Before setting up the development environment, you need to do the following:

- **Download and install Eclipse IDE** (or **IntelliJ IDEA**) – You can download the Eclipse IDE for Java EE Developers from http://www.eclipse.org/downloads. To install Eclipse IDE, all you need to do is to unzip the downloaded ZIP file into a directory.
- **Download and install Tomcat 7 server** – You can download the Tomcat 7 server from http://tomcat.apache.org/download-70.cgi. It is recommended that you download the Tomcat 7 bundled as ZIP file, and unzip the bundle into your local file system.
- **Download and install Maven 3 build tool** – You can download Maven 3 from http://maven.apache.org/download.cgi. To install Maven, all you need to do is to unzip the downloaded ZIP file into a directory. Maven is used for converting the sample web projects that accompany this book into Eclipse IDE or IntelliJ IDEA projects.

Let's look at how to import a sample project into Eclipse IDE.

A-2 Importing a sample project into Eclipse IDE (or IntelliJ IDEA)

It is recommended that you download the sample projects that accompany this book from the following Google code project:

https://code.google.com/p/getting-started-with-spring-framework-2edition/

The rest of this section assumes that you have created a spring-samples directory in your local file system that contains all the sample projects that accompany this book.

To successfully import a sample project, you need to do the following:

- Convert the project into an Eclipse IDE or IntelliJ IDEA project
- Configure an M2_REPO classpath variable in the Eclipse IDE (or IntelliJ IDEA). M2_REPO variable points to the local *maven repository* that contains the JAR files on which the project depends.

Let's now look at the above mentioned steps in detail.

Importing a sample project

Each sample project contains a pom.xml file that contains configuration of Eclipse, IntelliJ IDEA and Tomcat maven plugins. These plugins are used by maven for converting a sample project into Eclipse IDE or IntelliJ IDEA project, and for deploying the project on an *embedded* Tomcat 7 instance. You should note that the Tomcat Maven plugin (http://tomcat.apache.org/maven-plugin.html) is configured only for sample projects that represent *web applications*. The pom.xml file also specifies the JAR files (like spring-core, spring-beans, and so on) on which the project depends.

To create Eclipse IDE or IntelliJ IDEA specific configuration files for the sample project, follow these steps:

- Open the command prompt and set JAVA_HOME environment variable to point to Java SDK installation directory:

  ```
  C:\> set JAVA_HOME=C:\Program Files\Java\jdk1.7.0_25
  ```

- Go to the directory containing the sample project:

  ```
  C:\> cd spring-samples
  C:\spring-samples> cd ch01-bankapp-xml
  C:\spring-samples\ch01-bankapp-xml>
  ```

- Add path of the bin directory of your maven installation to the PATH environment variable:

  ```
  C:\spring-samples\ch01-bankapp-xml> set path=%path%; C:\apache-maven-3.0.4\bin
  ```

- If you want to import the sample project into Eclipse IDE, execute the eclipse:eclipse goal of Maven Eclipse Plugin (http://maven.apache.org/plugins/maven-eclipse-plugin/):

  ```
  C:\spring-samples\ch01-bankapp-xml>mvn eclipse:eclipse
  ```

  Executing the eclipse:eclipse goal downloads dependencies of the sample project and creates configuration files (like .classpath and .project) for Eclipse IDE.

  OR

- If you want to import the sample project into IntelliJ IDEA, execute the idea:idea goal of Maven IDEA Plugin (http://maven.apache.org/plugins/maven-idea-plugin/):

  ```
  C:\spring-web-mvc-samples\ch01-xml-config>mvn idea:idea
  ```

Executing the idea:idea goal downloads dependencies of the sample project and creates configuration files (like .ipr, .iml and .iws) for IntelliJ IDEA.

> A pom.xml file is also provided at the root of the source code distribution, which builds all the projects. You can go to spring-samples directory and execute the mvn eclipse:eclipse (or mvn idea:idea) command to convert all the projects into Eclipse IDE (or IntelliJ IDEA) projects.

Now, import the sample project into Eclipse IDE by following these steps:

- Go to File → Import option.
- Select the General → Existing Projects into Workspace option from the dialog box, and click Next.
- Select the sample project (ex. ch01-bankapp-xml) directory from the file system, and click Finish.

Configuring the M2_REPO classpath variable in the Eclipse IDE

When you execute the eclipse:eclipse or idea:idea goal, dependencies of the project are downloaded into the <home-directory>/.m2/repository directory. Here, <home-directory> is the home directory of the user. On Windows, this refers to C:\Documents and Settings\myusername\.m2\repository directory. By default, .classpath file created by execution of eclipse:eclipse goal refers to the JAR dependencies of the project using M2_REPO classpath variable. For this reason, you need to configure a new M2_REPO classpath variable in Eclipse IDE that refers to <home-directory>/.m2/repository directory.

To configure a new M2_REPO variable, follow these steps:

- Go to Windows → Preferences option. This will show the Preferences dialog box.
- Select the Java → Build Path → Classpath Variables option in the dialog box to view the configured classpath variables.
- Now, click New button to configure a new M2_REPO classpath variable. It is important to note that you set the M2_REPO classpath variable to <home-directory>/.m2/repository directory.

We have now successfully imported the sample project into the Eclipse IDE and set the M2_REPO classpath variable. If the project represents a standalone application, you can run the application by following these steps:

- In Eclipse IDE's Project Explorer tab, right-click on the Java class that contains the main method of the application. You'll now see the list of actions that can be performed on the selected Java class.

- Select Run As → Java Application option. This will execute the main method of the Java class.

Let's now look at how Eclipse IDE is configured to work with Tomcat 7 server.

A-3 Configuring Eclipse IDE with Tomcat 7 server

You need to open Eclipse IDE's Servers view to configure Eclipse IDE with Tomat 7 server. To open the Servers view, select Window → Show View → Servers option from the Eclipse IDE's menu bar. To configure a server with Eclipse IDE, first go to the Servers view, right-click in the Servers views, and select New → Server option. You'll now see a New Server wizard which allows you to configure a server with Eclipse IDE in a step-by-step fashion. The first step is 'Define a New Server', wherein you need to choose the *type* and *version* of the server with which you want to configure your Eclipse IDE. The following figure shows the 'Define a New Server' step:

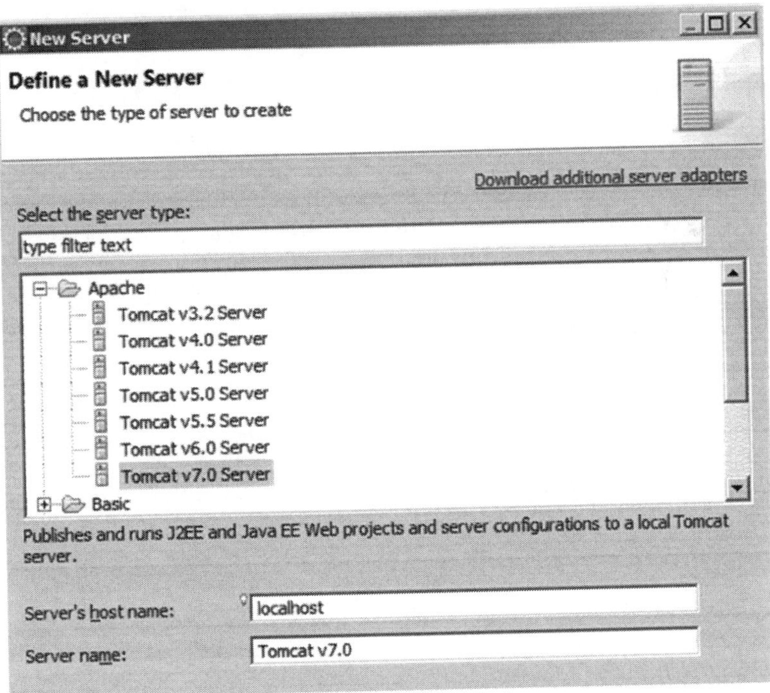

Figure A-1 Select the Tomcat server version that you want to use with Eclipse IDE

Select Apache → Tomcat v7.0 Server as the server, and set 'Tomcat v7.0' as the server name. Click the Next button to go to the next step of configuring Tomcat 7 server with Eclipse IDE. The next step is to specify installation directory of Tomcat 7 server, as shown in figure A-2.

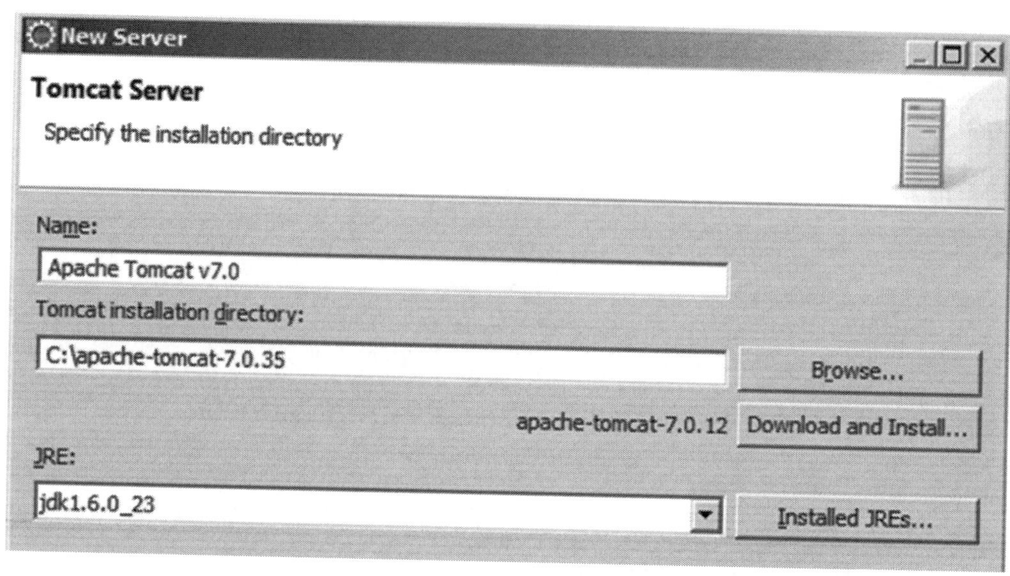

Figure A-2 Specify Tomcat server installation directory and set the Java SDK to be used by the server.

To set the Tomcat installation directory, click the **Browse** button (refer figure A-2) and select the directory in which you unzipped the Tomcat ZIP file. Also, click the **Installed JREs** button and configure the Java SDK to be used by Eclipse IDE for running the Tomcat server. Click the **Finish** button to complete configuration of Tomcat 7 server with Eclipse IDE. You'll now be able to see the newly configured Tomcat 7 server in the *Servers* view, as shown in the following figure:

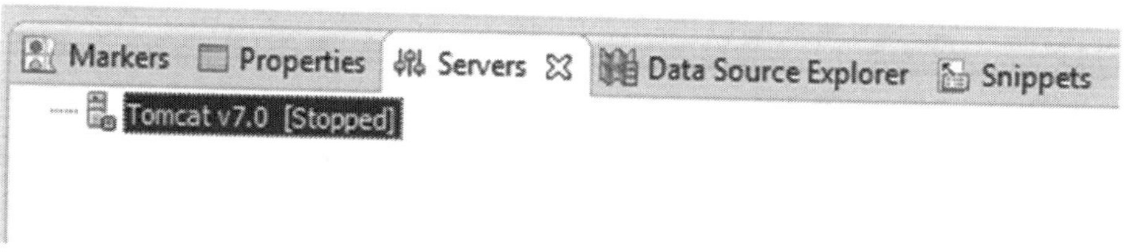

Figure A-3 The *Servers* view shows the newly configured Tomcat 7 server

Now, that we have configured Tomcat 7 server, let's look at how to deploy a sample web project to the configured Tomcat 7 server.

A-4 Deploying a web project on Tomcat 7 server

To deploy a web project (ex. ch10-helloworld) on Tomcat 7 server, follow these steps:

- Right-click on the sample web project in Eclipse IDE's **Project Explorer** tab. You'll now see the list of actions that can be performed on the selected web project.
- If you want to simply deploy the web project, select **Run As → Run on Server** option. This will deploy the web project on the Tomcat 7 server that we configured in section A-3.

  OR

- If you want to deploy and *debug* the web project, then select **Debug As → Debug on Server** option. This will deploy the web project on the Tomcat 7 that we configured in section A-3, and allow you to debug the web project by setting breakpoints in the Eclipse IDE.

If Tomcat 7 server is configured correctly with Eclipse IDE, you'll notice that Tomcat 7 server is started and the web project is deployed on it. If you now open a web browser and go to `http://localhost:8080/<sample-project-folder-name>`, you'll see the home page of the web project. Here, `<sample-project-folder-name>` refers to the name of the folder of the sample project.

Running the Tomcat 7 server in embedded mode

A simpler way to deploy and run a sample web project is to use an *embedded* Tomcat 7 server. In all the sample web projects, Maven Tomcat plugin (`http://tomcat.apache.org/maven-plugin-2.0/`) is configured in the `pom.xml` file. If you execute `tomcat7:run` goal of Maven Tomcat plugin by going to sample project's directory, the plugin takes care of downloading and starting Tomcat 7 in embedded mode and automatically deploying the sample web project on the embedded Tomcat 7 instance. To stop the server, all you need to do is to press Ctrl-C.

Index

B

C

D

M

N

O

P

R

S

T

U

V

W

X